THE PHANTOM STORY

Treble One Squadron's 'M-Mike' in 'Delta' fit (three fuel tanks) plus a full complement of live AIM-9G and Sky Flash missiles. Of note are the skin strengtheners on the outer wing panels, part of a continuing 'beef up' that all Phantoms have been subjected to since leaving the factory in order to extend their useful lives. (RAF via Richard L. Ward)

THE PHANTOM STORY

ANTHONY M. THORNBOROUGH AND PETER E. DAVIES

CASSELL&CO

CASSELL&CO

Wellington House, 125 Strand, London WC2R 0BB

Copyright © Anthony M. Thornborough & Peter E. Davies, 1994, 2000

First published by Arms and Armour 1994
This revised and extended edition 2000

British Library Cataloguing in Publication data:
A catalogue record for this book is available from the British Library

ISBN 0-304-35712-X

Distributed in the USA by Sterling Publishing Co. Inc.,
387 Park Avenue South, New York, NY 10016-8810

Edited and designed by Roger Chesneau

Printed and bound in Great Britain by Bath Press

CONTENTS

INTRODUCTION

Even today, thirty-five years after the breed made its maiden flight, stepping up to a Phantom for the first time—as flight crew, ground crew, engineer or just plain enthusiast—usually elicits wonder. Its size in comparison to most international fighters, its aggressive yet unequivocally sumptuous lines defining its powerful, purposeful shape, evoke feelings which range across the emotional spectrum from fear to awe. And, during those past three and half decades since the Phantom first took to the air, it has grown into a cult—'a legend in its own time', as McAir described its remarkable machine during the latter days of its production run. It is a brute through and through, and one which exudes subliminal appeal, what native Hawaiians, with their inimitable, complex phonetics, might describe as *mamane*—not beautiful, but innately attractive. Incidentally, the capital of this mid-Pacific volcanic shield archipelago was to play host to no fewer than four long-term F-4 Phantom squadrons, as well as serve as a *de luxe* R&R stop for many war-weary crews, rendering the aircraft a regular sight across the islands for much of its career.

To the Israelis on the other side of the globe, who took the F-4 aboard during a particularly turbulent episode in their history, the machine was nothing more nor less than an high-performance tool able to fulfil all of what was required of it. They nicknamed it *Kurnass*, in deference to its ability to penetrate deeply through heavy defences and deposit large payloads. The accolade 'Sledgehammer' refers to its ability to drop tons of metal-encased tritonol on hardened targets, fire radar-homing missiles with a supersonic kinetic punch and poke big holes through even thick-skinned MiGs. No other fighter of that era was of such a good pedigree, and the Israelis were quick to laud its virtues in combat.

To other operators, McAir's Phantom will, inevitably, be associated only with its unique sucking whistle, growl and smoke trails. Even as this is being written, the raunchy blast of some one thousand F-4s' J79 turbojets continue to rattle window panes and kick up the dust at the leading edge of air power across the globe, in locations stretching from Egypt's Nile Delta to the fringes of Europe's troubled southern flank, east to the deserts of the Persian Gulf, and beyond, to the steamy, cragged landscape of the Republic of Korea and the snowy mountains of the Japanese highlands. And, in their country of origin, Phantoms continue to fly daily, performing conversion training, reconnaissance or defence-suppression, albeit in massively reduced numbers—or terminate their careers abruptly by disintegrating into a myriad fragments as hapless target drones, as a new generation of fighter pilots hones its skills with the latest array of hardware, using tired, old, remote-controlled Phantoms for target practice.

Whatever its appeal, the Phantom first took to the air at a time when McDonnell foresaw a requirement for 376 US Navy fighters warranted for a mere 1,000 hours apiece! Only the very far-sighted could possibly have envis-

Right: James S. McDonnell, who founded the McDonnell Aircraft Company on 6 July 1939, stands proudly in front of McAir's 'Five Grand' Phantom, a *Turk Hava Kuvvetleri* example, in May 1978. Production of the Phantom at St Louis eventually totalled 5,057 complete machines, the last of which was flown away on Friday 26 October 1979. This figure excludes eleven F-4EJs provided as knock-down kits to Mitsubishi Industries in Japan, for a total of 5,068 complete airframes. Japan brought the eventual total up to 5,195 when the last F-4EJ was rolled out in May 1981. (McAir)

Left: The Alabama Guard celebrated the Phantom's thirty-fifth birthday in May 1993 by decorating RF-4C-22-MC 64-1041 in this garish scheme. Along its flanks can be seen the flags of the Phantoms' numerous operators over the years: the United States, Britain, Iran, Israel, South Korea, Australia, Germany, Japan, Spain, Greece, and Turkey—an impressive tally for a machine whose original production run was estimated at 376 copies for use exclusively by the US Navy! (McAir)

aged that when production was finally terminated in May 1981, McAir and licensed manufacturer Mitsubishi would have churned out more than 'five grand' examples, of which a substantial portion would amass a similar numerical value in individual flight hours! There are hundreds of F-4s still flying with between 4,000 and 5,000 hours on their clocks, and hundreds more which will likely accrue yet more without any portions of structure snapping off— with or without the benefit of McAir's continuing, safety-conscious, individual aircraft monitoring. To ensure that these, too, are not soon to be consigned to some lesser-known 'boneyard' or missile range, most serving examples groan under an extra ton of high-tensile steel straps screwed into their airframes in judicious places. Other *ad hoc* modifications will ensure that some go on for longer—even if 'Double-Ugly' ends up as 'Triple-Ugly'. To most, that devout, devilish piece of engineering will conjure up many special memories—some good, some bad, but all memorable.

Sorting out the Phantom's structure, plumbing and electrical gizzards, and writing about the type's inordinately more complex operational history, has been a rewarding but, at times, painful process. Much was learnt. The narrative, split into chronological appraisals of the pioneering naval and derivative land-based variants, contains both old and new information: where previously well-trodden ground is covered, every effort has been made to solve old riddles or provide a different perspective on widely held assumptions. Not all of these latter still hold, now that the subject can be examined in a near-definitive historical context and with the benefit of hindsight. Some of the more controversial issues hang in the air: the need for 'two heads' in the cockpit; the use of a multi-role aircraft adapted at some expense to specific tasks such as reconnaissance and defence-suppression (an argument that is still raging, despite this age of microprocessors where new 'strap-ons' can speedily upgrade capabilities 'in a can' but cannot make decisions); and nuclear

readiness and its relative importance in the 'new world order'. And there still exist whole new topics of debate, as fresh material becomes declassified. With 'a grand' of Phantoms still flying, the story is far from over.

In an attempt to get the story right, the authors have pieced together a diverse selection of reminiscences, photographs and data kindly provided by literally hundreds of people over the past decade: for each of those mentioned below, there were at least ten others who kindly provided 'bits and pieces' and to whom the authors gratefully extend their heartfelt thanks. Capt Bruce 'Spike' Benyshek USAF, Maj James R. Chamberlain USAF Ret, Flt Lt David Cutler RAF, Christian Gerard, Paul Guse, Lt-Col John ('Mr Maintenance') Harty USAF Ret, Malcolm Hester, Alan Howarth, Tim Laming, Lois Lovisolo, Flt Lt Mark 'Manners' Manwaring, Lt-Col Ross A. Moon USAF Ret, Sqn Ldr Dominic Riley RAF, Lt-Col John Roberts USAF Ret, Maj James M. Shaw USAF Ret, Lt-Col Terry Simpson USAF, Wg Cdr Nick Spiller RAF, Bettie E. Sprigg, Maj Gerald ('Jerry') Stiles USAF Ret, Lt-Col Jim ('Uke') Uken USAF and Richard L. Ward—we extend thanks to all concerned for their considerable time and energy, and to the key organizations behind several of these names, including the Air National Guard Bureau, the Grumman Corporation, McDonnell Douglas, the Retired Officers' Association, the Royal Air Force, the United States Air Force, the US Navy Archive Office and the US Office of the Assistant Secretary of Defense.

TONY THORNBOROUGH
PETER DAVIES

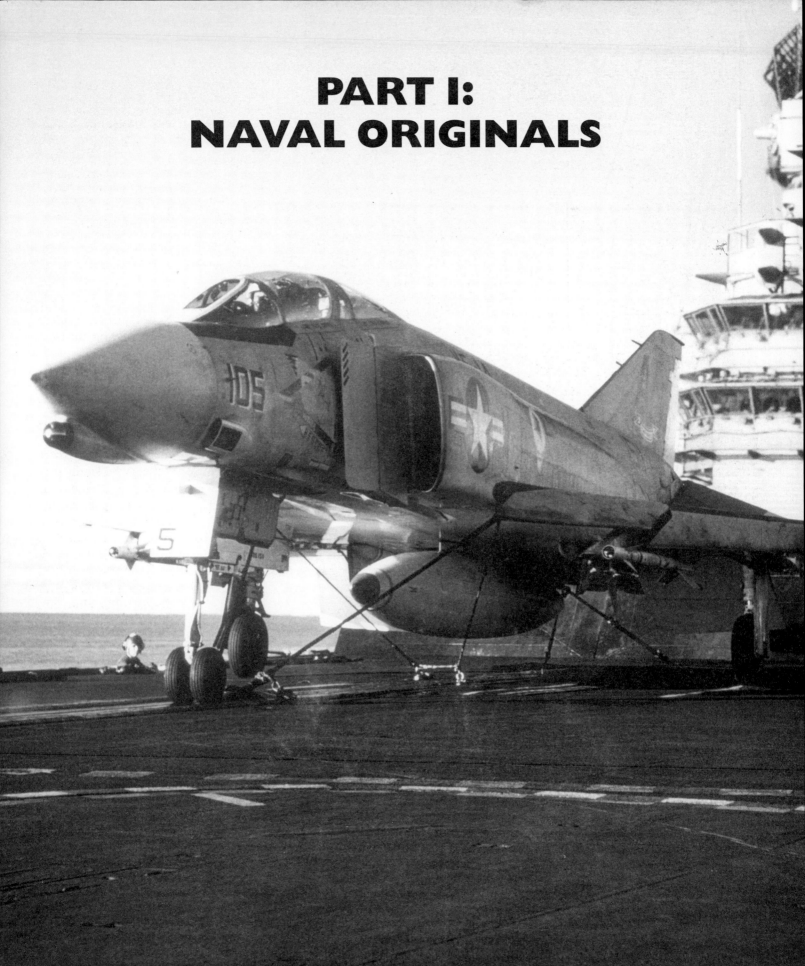

PART I: NAVAL ORIGINALS

I. McDONNELL'S MASTERPIECE

In May 1990 a visitor to the vast AMARC 'Boneyard' at Davis-Monthan might have noticed among the gate-guard aircraft an F-4 in USAF Vietnam camouflage bearing the 'FG' tail code and serial of one of Col Robin Olds' MiG-killers. In fact, beneath the paint sat an ex-US Navy F-4N, and behind the battle-weary Phantom sat over 200 others, cooking in the Arizona heat. Row upon row of dusty grey F-4Ns, F-4Js, F-4Ss and RF-4Bs stretched into the distance, unlikely ever again to experience the rigours of service with the Navy or Marines.

A little over twelve months later VMFA-321 *Black Barons* retired its tri-dent-and-star-spangled Phantoms at a ceremony at Andrews AFB, Maryland. Among those present was another museum piece, the Project 'Sageburner' F4H-1 (BuNo 145307) in which Lt Huntingdon Hardisty won the hazardous World Low Level Speed Record in

1961, a reminder of the Phantom's glorious genesis. The 'Barons' Phantoms had one more tour of duty before they too could rest. Six of them flew to NAS Dallas, Texas, to join VMFA-112 in 'MA' codes.

At the beginning of 1992, when AMARC was close to processing its one-thousandth surplus Phantom, VMFA-112 in turn marked the end of USN/MC F-4 operations. In dreadful weather which hid some of the secretly sobbing cheeks of those present, their last four aircraft were put on show, the other eight having already departed to MCAS Cherry Point, North Carolina, for conversion into target drones. One of those to avoid this ignominious end was also a reminder of past glories. In previous service it was the VF-31 *Tomcatters* F-4J in which 'Top Gun' architect Cdr Sam Flynn scored his MiG kill in 1972.

Thirty years of Phantom flying were at an end. The very last Navy Phantom,

YF-4J BuNo 151473, was retained in flyable storage at NAS China Lake, California, for possible use as an ejection seat trials platform. The rest were mostly to become drones for trainee prospective fighter 'aces' to send flaming into the ocean.

Among the rows of cocooned F-4S models were several bearing the colours of VF-151 and VF-161. Cdr 'Thunder Bud' Taylor was skipper of VF-151 *Fighting Vigilantes*, the last carrier-borne Phantom squadron. Their last carrier shot from the USS *Midway* was made by F-4S BuNo 153879 on 25 March 1986.[1] Right to the end, Cdr Taylor led his men in the traditions developed since VF-151 traded their F3H-2 Demons for F-4B Phantom IIs at NAS Miramar, California, in 1964. Precipitated straight into the Vietnam conflagration, they flew seven war cruises, spent the 1970s patrolling the Indian Ocean and North Pacific, lent support in the Iran hostage crisis and responded to the shoot-down of Korean Airlines KAL-007, while in 1985 they celebrated five years of accident-free flying—in all, a fairly typical record for a go-getting Navy

Part-title photograph: Atlantic Fleet carriers and squadrons were drawn into the WESTPAC war theatre as the pressure built up in 1966. The USS *Franklin D. Roosevelt* made her only war cruise from 25 July 1966 to 29 January 1967 with VF-14 and VF-32 aboard. Ten Skyhawks and two Phantoms were lost to enemy defences. After five successful bombing sorties (marked on the splitter), '105/AB' of VF-14 launches for a BARCAP on 6 September 1966; note the glistening tip of the AN/AAA-4 infra-red search sensor. (USN)
Left: *Black Barons* F-4S at dispersal at Andrews AFB, Maryland. The unit's disbandment on 31 July 1991 marked the end of US Navy/Marines Phantom operations. (Tim Laming)

F-4 squadron, but longer-lasting than most. In its final months the unit continued to take on and beat the new 'solid state' jets in ACM entanglements. 'Thunder Bud''s motto, 'We fight the pilot, not the aircraft', acknowledged the technical deficiencies of his venerable steed's prowess compared with newer types, forged out of the Phantom's hard-won experience.

The F-4's very existence is a tribute to the persistence of James S. McDonnell and his team of designers, including Herman D. Barkey. His company had supplied the US Navy with its first jet, the FH-1 Phantom I, following through with the F2H Banshee and F3H Demon. 'Mac' was then somewhat sidelined by Vought, who gave the Navy its first supersonic fighter, the F-8 Crusader. This superb dogfighter had none of the

performance handicaps endemic in previous carrier-based designs and it provided a real boost to the Service at a time when speed was deemed paramount in military aviation. McDonnell fought back, canvassing all areas of Navy opinion in an effort to formulate the ideal all-purpose follow-on fighter. The result, created out of pure speculation late in 1953, was known as the F3H-G. In October 1954 it earned a Navy Letter of Intent for two prototypes. At first, the drawings bore a strong family likeness to the Demon but added an attack capability reminiscent of the AD Skyraider—distributed on no fewer than eleven hardpoints! By June 1955 the company had clearer guidelines to help formulate realistic proposals. Navy interest by then concentrated on the idea of a fleet defence fighter able to maintain a three-hour combat air patrol (CAP), holding threats to the carrier force at bay with long-range, radar-guided missiles. McDonnell rapidly set about converting their gun-armed, single-seat fighter-bomber (then known as the AH-1) into a two-seat, all-weather interceptor with semi-recessed Sparrow missiles as its primary armament. The AN/APQ-50 radar remained into the flight-test stage

(for eighteen aircraft) but then gave way to the AN/APQ-72 air intercept/missile control and semi-automatic navigation system, on Bureau of Aeronautics instructions, while the original twin J65 Sapphire engine arrangement was soon supplanted by a brace of much more potent General Electric J79s. Both radar and engines were at early development stages: fortunately, both proved to be excellent choices. A mere two weeks' work produced the basic configuration which was to be designated F4H-1, though the prototype, still bearing some resemblance to the YAH-1 mock-up, did not emerge until 8 May 1958.

Vought re-entered the competition when the Navy requested an upgraded Crusader prototype, the F8U-3, but the 1958 fly-off between the two types left little doubt that McDonnell was about to provide the fleet with its next fighter. On

[1] Also on the 'cat' that day was one of VA-93's A-7E Corsairs, another long-serving type bowing out at the same time. The intended successor in both instances was the F/A-18 Hornet, though at the time of writing VF-151 is the only USN Phantom outfit to have kept with the Hornet, VF-161 having disbanded in the 'cuts' of 1988. The rest have all faded into history, or fly the potent F-14 Tomcat.

Left, top: Bob Little flies the first F4H-1, June 1958. On its first two solo flights BuNo 142259 developed retraction problems with its nose-gear door after a hydraulic line failure. The aircraft lasted until 21 October 1959, when a detached engine access door caused its 295th flight to end in a blazing crash which killed test pilot Zeke Huelsbeck. (McAir)

Left, centre: The ill-fated 'Sageburner' F4H-1, toting a B/Mk 43 special weapon shape (a BDU-12/B simulator) on its centreline. One of a pair of Phantoms marked in this way, BuNo 145316 crashed out of control on 18 May 1961 during a speed record attempt, killing Cdr J. L. Felsman. Lt 'Hunt' Hardisty and Lt 'Duke' DeEsch set a record of 902.769mph in the other aircraft, BuNo 145307. Their average altitude was a meagre 125ft AGL! (McAir)

Left, bottom: Lt-Col Robert B. Robinson's name appears under the beefed-up windshield of F4H-1F BuNo 142260, which he used to achieve a new absolute world speed record during Project 'Skyburner' in November 1961. Although this was only the second Phantom built, the tanks and pylons were already 'fleet standard' and the intakes had been modified to production contours. (McAir)

17 December 1958 the company received the go-ahead for an additional two dozen F4H-1s, bringing orders to 45 aircraft.

Among the reasons for the F4H-1 Phantom II's selection were aspects of its design which remained controversial throughout its career. The two-seat configuration, chosen in preference to the Crusader's single-place cockpit in order to provide full control of the radar, stemmed from the 'night fighter' philosophy which had produced the USAF's radar-guided F-89, F-94 and F-101B, and the Marines' F3D Skyknight. The complex and fragile radars of the time required a second crewman's full attention, especially in poor visibility when the importance of the system became most marked and subtleties in radar interpretation meant winning or losing an engagement. Then, as now, there were plenty of fighter pilots who felt they could handle the intercept role single-handed. Flying their Skyrays and Demons, they were used to taking off from carriers and proceeding in a straightline to a point where they could launch their missiles at high-flying simulated threats—which were also proceed-

ing on straight courses. If any 'old-fashioned', clear-air, mass dogfighting were needed, the F-8 jocks would eagerly see to that aspect. The Phantom was initially regarded only as the natural heir to that intercept role, while the Crusader pilots saw themselves as the real air combat exponents. It was to be some years before Phantom crews realized that they were flying a 'real fighter' too! It took

even longer to prove that the air combat scenario could be mastered more efficiently by a two-man team. Some of the more egocentric ex-single-seat fighter types took some time to accept that the 'talking ballast' in the 'luggage compartment' of their Phantoms could actually enhance their air-to-air prowess. In the earliest Phantoms the RIO (Radar Intercept Officer) was confined in some-

TABLE 1: EARLY PHANTOM DEVELOPMENT MILESTONES

1953

Sept 19	Unsolicited proposal submitted to Bureau of Aeronautics (BuAer) for single-seat all-weather fighter called F3H-G/H (general-purpose VF).

1954

June 15	Need for all-weather aircraft arises (no written agreement). BuAer evaluate McDonnell F3H-G/H, F3H-E2 (single-engine version), Grumman proposal and North American proposal. McDonnell's twin J79-powered proposal selected.
July 23	Chief of Naval Operations (CNO) recommends procurement of two AH-1 aircraft.
Oct 18	Letter contract placed with McDonnell for two AH-1 aircraft.
Dec 1	BuAer-CNO conference reached following agreement: BuAer-CNO jointly to take necessary action to redesignate AH-1 to F4H-1; CNO to write requirement for two-seat aircraft; BuAer to initiate design competition for all-weather attack aircraft following receipt of CNO requirement.

1955

June 7	CNO letter indicates requirement for two-seat version of F4H-1 (AH-1).
June 23	AH-1 officially redesignated F4H-1.
July 19	CNO letter defines configuration of F4H-1.
Sept 2	BuAer authorizes procurement of five F4H-1 aircraft.
November	Mock-up review.

1958

May 27	First flight of F4H-1 from Lambert Field, St Louis (Robert C. Little test pilot).
Dec 17	Navy decision to buy F4H-1.

1959

July 3	F4H-1 christened 'Phantom II' in ceremony on McDonnell ramp during celebration of company's twentieth anniversary.
October	F4H-1 released for carrier suitability trials.

1960

February	Sea trials begin with first carrier catapult take-off and arrested landing aboard USS *Independence*.
July	Board of Inspection & Survey (BIS) trials begin at NAS Patuxent River, Maryland.
Dec 29	First aircraft delivered to training squadron VF-121 at NAS Miramar, California.

1961

March	F4H-1 aircraft below No 48 redesignated F4H-1F; Nos 48 and up retain designation F4H-1.
Mar 25	First flight of production F4H-1.
June	First F4H-1 (No 50) delivered to Fleet.
Sept 14	Last of 47 F4H-1Fs delivered to US Navy.
October	US Navy's first F4H-1 operational squadron, VF-74, qualifies for carrier duty.

1962

January	President's Budget submitted to Congress requesting procurement of RF-110A reconnaissance version and F-110A fighter version for USAF. Two F4H-1 fighters, newly designated F-110A, delivered to USAF at TAC Headquarters, Langley AFB, Virginia.
April	Letter contract for first F-110A aircraft received.
May	Letter contract for two prototype RF-110As received.
June 29	First F4H-1 delivered to USMC squadron, VMF(AW)-314.
August	First two US Navy F4H-1 squadrons (VF-102 and VF-74) deployed at sea under Project 'Short Cruise'.
September	F4H-1, F4H-1F, F-110A and RF-110A redesignated F-4B, F-4A, F-4C and RF-4C respectively.

All data by courtesy of the McDonnell Douglas Corporation.

Left, upper: One of the first batch of 72 F-4Bs (BuNo 148412) carries a centreline tank modified to represent the F-14's recessed housing for an XAIM-54 Phoenix missile. At the time (September 1968) the US Navy was considering the various alternatives to the Phoenix-armed F-111B, cancelled in May of that year. (McAir)
Left, lower: VX-5 *Vampires* operated a number of F-4Bs from the Naval Ordnance Test Center at China Lake in the early 1960s, including BuNo 150440. They 'wrote the book' on weapons delivery techniques for Navy Phantom squadrons. A full load of twenty-four 500lb Mk 82 LDGP bombs was one possibility. (McAir)

J79s gave around two and a half times the power of the F3D Demon for an aircraft weighing one and a half times as much when fully laden. Apart from the resulting Mach 2.5 performance of the early, straight-from-the-factory aircraft, twin engines conferred greater safety over water and improved combat survivability. In time, pilots learned that the Phantom's better thrust-to-weight ratio could give it a sustained turning advantage over the F-8, although at great cost in fuel consumption. The twin-versus-single engine debate continued right up to the choice of the Phantom's successor, the 'twin' F/A-18 rather than a single-engine F-16 derivative. However, there is little doubt that the choice of twin J79s was absolutely correct, despite the increase in fuel burning and the engine's one annoying trait—its smoke-trailing signature, which took a further twenty years to eradicate.

More controversial was the requirement for an all-missile armament. The logic, in 1958, of utilizing the long-range, anti-bomber Raytheon Sparrow III missile for flanking high-altitude interceptions was obvious enough, and it lives on in today's tried-and-trusted fourth-generation fighter concepts. In 1955, when the Sparrow was chosen as the standard USN long-range air combat weapon, guns were for dogfighters like the F-8 Crusader and F4D Skyray. Interceptors like the F-101B Voodoo, CF-105 Arrow and F8U-3 relied on missiles to destroy targets the pilot would never see, let alone engage in air combat. Having designed the guns out of the Phantom at the prototype stage, reintroduc-

thing akin to a 'pit' with an almost flat-canopied skylight above, providing him with little to see apart from his raw radar-scope imagery and hypnotic banks of neatly laid-out circuit-breaker buttons. This situation was somewhat improved by the raised canopy profile of the full production F-4 series, when the RIO's 'second pair of eyes' became a valued adjunct to the steely blue vision of the pilot. 'Checking six' then became a by-word of the back-seater's myriad passive flying tasks, though neck strain combined with a hard, bumpy ride made it anything but easy. It became a tradition, post-mission, for back-seaters or 'scopes' to point out their empty 'barf bags' to the pilots or 'sticks', clenching bared teeth

just to prove their stalwart stomach linings. The lack of duplicate rear-seat controls—an omission common to all USN variants—also meant that back-seaters were less able to anticipate the impending onset of hard manoeuvres. NFO (Naval Flight Officer) schools produced a special breed for the Phantom stream.

The choice of twin engines was also open to debate, though it was one of the reasons for the selection of McAir's design. The F-8 had created something of a precedent by having a single turbojet powerplant, and this was in line with the fighter concept seen in the Fury, Demon and Skyray too. However, despite their extra weight and other constraints, twin

ing them to later versions when Vietnam experience decreed their necessity proved to be a lengthy and traumatic process. However, Navy F-4s would never be fitted with a built-in gun, despite numerous trials with gun pods, and this was a major source of contention throughout much of the aircraft's career.

Another restriction on development imposed by the Fleet Defense idea arose from the aircraft's endurance characteristics. As originally conceived, the Phantom was intended to be launched from a carrier in afterburner, fly to CAP station some 250nm from the 'boat' at optimum fuel economy at 30,000ft, remain on station for around 2½ hours and return at cruise altitude. The twin-spool J79's essentially good fuel-economy characteristics suited the F4H-1 to this mission profile. However, 'Mac' had left in their design much of the ordnance-hauling potential of the AH-1 proposal and it was always apparent that the powerful F4H-1 would have a considerable attack capability too. For most of their USN/MC service life, Phantoms carried bomb loads at medium or low altitudes and found themselves indulging in high-energy manoeuvring with the 'burners blazing: fuel economy profiles went out of the window as a result, and the F-4 consequently gained a fuel-hungry reputation, and with it a massive supply of disposable drop tanks and back-up AAR (air-to-air refuelling) support.

Finally, the Fleet Defense mission profile placed a low priority on ACM manoeuvrability. There was little need for a collison-course interceptor launching missiles to be agile, and few of the Phantom's design contemporaries enjoyed this characteristic. It is doubtful whether the 'Mac' engineers could have envisaged their creation 'turning and burning' subsonically with primitive but nimble MiGs in the skies of South-East Asia.

The F4H-1 prototype (BuNo 142259) was ready for its first flight at Lambert Field, Missouri, by 27 May 1958. It encountered undercarriage hydraulic snags on the first two hops. On the third and fourth flights Chief Test Pilot Robert C. Little, flying solo, took the 'bird' to a

TABLE 2: F-4 RECORDS

Project 'Top Flight' (World Absolute Altitude Record)

Date	Aircraft	Crew	Altitude	Previous record
06/12/59	F4H-1 142260 (2nd prototype)	Cdr Lawrence E. Flint USN	98,557ft	94,658ft (USSR)

World Air Speed Record: 100km and 500km Closed-Circuit

Date	Aircraft	Crew	Speed
05/09/60	145311	Lt-Col Thomas H. Miller USMC	1,216.76mph over 500km (inc. 25.5 minutes in full afterburner).
25/09/60	143389	Cdr John F. Davis USN	1,390.21mph in sustained 3g turn over 100km

Project 'LANA' (Transcontinental Speed Record: Bendix Trophy)[1]

Date	Aircraft	Crews (from VF-121)	Speed
24/05/61	Five F4H-1s from Blocks 4d and 5e	Cdr J. S. Lake/Lt E. A. Cowart; Cdr L. S. Lamoureaux/Lt T. J. Johnson; Lt R. F. Gordon/Lt (JG) B. R. Young, plus back-up crews	Best was 2hr 48min (869mph mean speed) over 2,445.9 miles from Ontario Field, California, to Floyd Bennett Field, New York.

Project 'Sageburner' (Absolute Speed Record Below 100m Altitude)[2]

Date	Aircraft	Crew	Speed
28/08/61	F4H-1 145307	Lt H. Hardisty/Lt E. DeEsch USN	902.769mph at 125ft.

Project 'Skyburner' (Absolute Speed Record)

Date	Aircraft	Crew	Speed
22/11/61	142260	Lt-Col R. B. Robinson USMC	1,606.3mph (reached 1,700mph at end of run)

Sustained Altitude Record

Date	Aircraft	Crew	Altitude
05/12/61	F4H-1	Cdr G. Ellis USN	66,443.6ft over 25km

Project 'High Jump' (Time-to-Climb Records)[3]

Date	Aircraft	Crews	Altitude	Time
From NAS New Brunswick, Maine:				
21/02/62	F4H-1 149449	Lt-Cdr J. Young USN	3,000m	34.52sec
21/02/62	F4H-1 149449	Cdr D. Langton USN	6,000m	48.78sec
01/03/62	F4H-1 149449	Lt-Col W. McGraw USMC	9,000m	1min 1.62sec
01/03/62	F4H-1 149449	Lt-Col W. McGraw USMC	12,000m	1min 17.15sec
01/03/62	F4H-1 149449	Lt-Cdr D. Nordberg USN	15,000m	1min 54.54sec
From NAS Point Mugu, California:				
31/03/62	F4H-1 149449	Lt-Cdr Taylor Brown USN	20,000m	2min 58.5sec
03/04/62	F4H-1 149449	Lt-Cdr J. Young	25,000m	3min 50.44sec
12/04/62	F4H-1 149449	Lt-Cdr D. Nordberg	30,000m	6min 11.43sec

[1] 'LANA' stood for '50th Anniversary of American Naval Aviation'.
[2] Cdr J. Felsman was killed during first attempt in BuNo 145316 on 18/05/61. Record set in F4H-1 No 8 from VF-101, Det 'A'.
[3] All records measured from a 'standing start' on the runway, take-offs being conducted without flaps, and all records attained during separate flights. Nordberg's F4H-1 passed 100,000ft at the top of its climb during its 12 April flight.

maximum speed of Mach 1.68. The test programme moved to Edwards AFB, California, in June 1958 when the newcomer was joined by a second prototype (BuNo 142260). By October 1959 eleven F4H-1s were setting spectacular standards throughout the performance envelope and in June of that year the first Block 2b airframe was rolled out. This featured the Westinghouse AN/APQ-72 radar with a 24in scanner and the distinctive bulge of the glass-tipped AN/AAA-4 cryogenic seeker beneath the radome. This latter unit, produced by ACF Electronics/Texas Instruments, gave passive back-up to the main radar by tracking infra-red emissions from the target. A similar unit was used on later variants of the Crusader (from the F-8D onwards), but it had limited success and was deleted in the majority of production aircraft (although the 'blister' was retained, to house alternate mission avionics). Block 3c airframes had further changes to their forward contours. An increase in radar-range requirements necessitated a bigger, 32in dish. The entire nose was therefore enlarged, and drooped in order to preserve airflow patterns ahead of the intakes. At the same time the rear cockpit was raised and the entire canopy profile altered to improve visibility. The main intake area was enlarged, and the system was improved in order to accommodate uprated J79-GE-8 engines. Each of these offered an increase in dry thrust of 1,300lb over

the 9,600lb s.t. of the development J79-GE-2A, and afterburning thrust was increased by 2,200lb to 17,000lb. The revised, automatic inlet arrangement was one of the keys to the Phantom's sprightly performance, assisting with maximum thrust response across the throttle range. Each inlet, mounted 2in off the fuselage so as to avoid sluggish boundary layer air, comprised a fixed ramp ('splitter plate') and a perforated movable ramp ('vari-ramp') to create the variable throat area. This maintained the shock wave in the inlet to prevent supersonic air from stalling the engines, while also ensuring adequate airflow capacity at all speeds. Once the air had been ingested, a bypass bellmouth system (a perforated moving ring installed at rear of the intake) maintained a stable airflow to the powerplant by venting a portion of cooling air around the engine compartment. This was then vented with the thrust exhaust gases, between the primary and secondary nozzles, cushioning the hot exhaust and adding extra thrust; the opening of the primary nozzle flaps in the 'jet cans', together with this secondary air, formed the J79's distinctive convergent-divergent nozzle to guarantee maximum thrust build-up at the efflux point—within the allowable temperature limits of the powerplants.[2] It was very noisy and simple, yet remarkably efficient. There was no excess air pressure to create drag, nor was the flow insufficient to compromise power. Provided the pilot did not dawdle

with the throttles, the engines would provide full thrust within four seconds of a 'wave off' signal. During carrier suitability trials, these manoeuvres were routinely accomplished on one engine, without using reheat.

In this configuration the F4H-1 approached its definitive production status for the Navy, and earlier Block 2 aircraft were redesignated F4H-1F (a term which covered the first 47 aircraft only). These were known as F-4A variants after the September 1962 reorganization of US military aircraft designations by the Department of Defense, and the F4H-1 became the F-4B—the fully fledged production mark, of which an initial six dozen (out of an eventual total of 667, excluding updated F-4As) were ordered under Contract NOa(s)60-0134 on 23 September 1959.

Throughout the development phase it was clear that both manufacturer and user of the new jet could push their product into the world's consciousness quite rapidly by demonstrating the Phantom's performance competitively. For twenty-eight straight months, from 6 December 1959, test pilots proceeded to rewrite the World Record Book, using the Phantoms to their full effect (see Table 2). With initiatives entitled Project 'Top Flight', 'Sageburner', 'LANA', 'Skyburner', 'High Jump' and others, they marked the climax of a heroic era of flight testing which had begun with the headline-grabbing early supersonic flights following the Second World War. McDonnell's dynamic newcomer could hardly have had a more dramatic introduction.

---

[2] Auxiliary air doors in the aircraft's belly popped open to provide additional cooling air during ground operations and low-speed flying, and to relieve excess engine compartment pressure.

2. FLEET PHANTOMS

Flying the World's hottest new jet was good for the image of Navy fighter pilots in 1959 but there remained the hard task of turning the Phantom into a dependable, carrier-borne aircraft which could be handled by regular service personnel. In fact, most of the world records of 1959–62 were attained by 'ordinary' line pilots flying aircraft from the initial service batches, although the aircraft were somewhat 'stripped for action' and the crews hand-picked (some of them went on to become well-known astronauts).

The job of breaking-in the first class of 46 Navy pilots and back-seaters fell to the East Coast RAG squadron, VF-101 *Grim Reapers*, while its counterpart VF-121 *Pacemakers* prepared crews for West Coast units at NAS Miramar, receiving its first Phantom (BuNo 148256) on 29 December 1960. Lt-Cdr G. G. O'Rourke, a powerful proponent of the Phantom at a time when other voices favoured the single-seat option, formed VF-101 at NAS Key West, Florida, at the end of 1959. He led the unit for two years before moving on to command one of the first Fleet units, VF-102 *Diamondbacks*. VF-101 remained at Key West until 1971, forming Det A at NAS

Oceana, Virginia, in June 1960 to introduce the Phantom while the main squadron at Key West cleared its last F4D 'Ford' and F3D Demon classes through the system. Having moved the Phantom operation back to Key West, the Oceana Det was re-established in May 1966 to train in weapons, Carquals (Carrier Qualifications), in-flight refuelling and radar systems. Training switched between the two bases until 1977 when the role passed to VF-171 *Aces*, though at the samc locations. Transition times varied. VF-154 *Black Knights*, entering VF-121 to transition in November 1965, took four months—a record at the time. Others took longer, particularly if they were 'between cruises', when personnel issues compounded the process. Interestingly enough, VF-154 was the first West Coast F-8 unit to move on to the F-4B.

Initially, O'Rourke drew most of his pilot trainees from Skyray or Demon 'second tourists'. The new trade of RIO

Right, upper: F-4B BuNo 153068 about to take a 'cat' shot from the USS *Forrestal*. VF-11 adopted these revised tail markings in February 1967 while operating with CVW-17. (Authors' collection)
Right, lower: Smoking heavily, this *Tophatters* F-4B (BuNo 152327) displays a RHAW antenna on its fin-cap which differs from the definitive AN/APR-30 set fitted to many F-4B/Ns subsequently. Markings are typical of VF-14 in the mid-1960s; by 1968 the red chevron had been moved to the tail. (Via A. Collishaw)

presented more problems. At first these crewmen were known as Systems Operators (SOs) or just NFOs in the Navy, and Radar Pilots in USAFE in the early Phantom years because most had been pilots. Luckily, O'Rourke had Korean War experience in the Marine Corps' F3D Skyknight, about the only two-seat 'radar night fighter' to wear dark blue.

He was able to assemble a team of ex-USMC 'radar heads', and some of their ancient Skyknights, to teach the black arts of AN/APQ-72 management.[1] At least one old F3D was fitted with a complete Phantom nose and radar. Later, a number of TF-9J Cougars assisted in basic training until the 1970s, when TA-4Fs took over. Building effective two-

man crew teams was an uphill task at first but pilots gradually learned to trust their RIOs rather than rely on their own 20/20 vision—even though some RIOs wore glasses for heaven's sake! One RIO had the confidence to reply that 'Without its back-seater the F-4 is just another piece of aerial transportation'.[2] While the Key West instructors were forging the first Fleet F-4 squadrons, a similar operation was in place at Miramar, where the West Coast RTS (Replacement Training Squadron) VF-121 laid claim to being the first F-4 unit—narrowly. They prepared crews for two decades right up to 30 September 1980, when VF-171 took over all remaining Phantom training for the Navy.

Meanwhile the testing programme had been going ahead. Carquals were undertaken by F4H-1 BuNo 143391 (the sixth aircraft) on the USS *Independence* in February 1960 (eighteen launches) and USS *Intrepid* during April 1960 (twenty launches). Carrier suitability trials on board the USS *Franklin D. Roosevelt* followed in November 1961. These were preceded by 75 company-piloted flights at NATC to achieve NPE (Navy Primary Evaluation). Improvements to the aircraft were steadily evolved. Hydroplaning problems with the narrow tyres of the F-4A/B in carrier trials were taken into account when McAir planned their improved USN Phantom, the F-4J, from 1963 onwards. It had the $30 \times 11\frac{1}{2}$ in main-gear tyres of the USAF versions in

Left, top: A 'plain Jane' Block 25-MC F-4B of VF-21 prior to the Squadron's first deployment on the USS *Midway* in November 1968. (Authors' collection)
Left, centre: VF-74 were the first USN F-4 squadron to reach 'deployable' status. Their first cruise was on the USS *Forrestal* from August 1962 to March 1963—this was the first full carrier assignment for the new fighter. F-4B BuNo 150483 is seen here over Roosevelt Roads carrying a KD2B rocket-powered missile target on an LAU-24 trapeze ejector. VF-74 was conducting a practice missile shoot at the time. (USN)
Left, bottom: One of VF-74's Block 14-MC F-4Bs lets loose an AIM-7D missile. This version of the Sparrow III was produced between 1959 and 1962 and was capable of head-on intercepts. It was replaced in 1963 by the longer-ranged AIM-7E. (Raytheon)

Above: By March 1967, when this deck shot was taken, the US Navy F-4 training programme was running at full tilt. This F-4B (BuNo 153915) was not confined to the training role. By 1972 it was with VF-161, and its occupants, Lt Pat Arwood and Lt 'Taco' Bell, used an AIM-9G Sidewinder to knock down a MiG-19 on 18 May. With them was F-4B BuNo 153068 crewed by Lt Bartholemay and Lt Oran Brown; they also 'bagged' a MiG-19 on the mission, the only occasion on which the Navy destroyed MiGs of this type. VF-161 scored four kills between 18 and 23 May 1972 and also made the last kill of the Vietnam War on 12 January 1973, all in F-4Bs. (McAir)

place of the original 30 × 7.7 in. items. The lower pressure also improved track, avoiding the roll-bounce that could all too easily be induced by a hard landing on one wing, sometimes leading to gear legs, and the related pivot assembly, being punched right through the thick, machined skin. As an interim measure, tweaked hydraulics plus a little bulge to provide some 'give', were added to all Navy Phantoms from the F-4B on. Improvements in ejection systems enabled the McDonnell-designed seat used in

the F-4A to be replaced by Martin-Baker's Mk 5.[3] The replacement of the original 'bang seat' was hastened by the tragic death of McDonnell test pilot Zeke Huelsbeck in a failed low-altitude ejection in October 1959.

As the Phantom built up its hours on carriers, air crews were generally impressed by its low-speed landing behaviour, a feature of the BLC (boundary layer control) flap system. Air was bled from the 17th stage of the J79 compressors and literally blown through slots over the leading- and trailing-edge wing control surface flaps to preserve airflow at decreased airspeeds where the otherwise near-delta format wing would have stalled. 'Bolter' rates were low, the aircraft landed firmly without 'floating' down the deck and the tailhook dumped the pendant (wire) neatly after the execution of a 'trap' (arrestment). Above all, the F-4 was stable and predictable in the approach, thanks partly to its excellent AFCS. The thrust response from the J79 was positive and rapid, unlike earlier jets—a spin-off from the twin-spool sys-

tem which staved off inertia, providing 'reserve' momentum in the blades during all but sustained low-throttle settings.

The F-4B's 142kt carrier approach speed was faster than average but it offered a welcome (albeit modest) reduction on the Crusader's 147kts. A few tricky traits began to make themselves known and they would worry 'Phantom Phlyers' for years to come. The first was a tendency to over-rotate during catapult launches, particularly if full wing drop-tanks were carried. The position of the pilot's hand on the control stick at this stage was crucial: a tiny amount of

[1] The very first RIOs were trained in a B-25. Six at a time huddled round a radar scope trying to identify and plot intercept targets on the screen.
[2] Providing a rather forceful expression of the contrasting USAF attitude, Robin Olds is reputed to have said, 'In my airplane the backseater only does what I tell him to do.'
[3] From Block 40 F-4Bs and up this was superseded by the MB Mk H7, which offered zero–zero capability plus new leg restraint 'garters' designed to overcome the problem of lower leg injuries during ejection.

Right: Two Phantoms from the first F-4B production block and a later aircraft in the centre, in March 1963. VF-101 Det A formed at NAS Oceana in June 1960 and introduced the Phantom to the Fleet. (McAir)

excess back stick when the catapult fired could lead to a nose-high launch and the danger of a stall off the bow. One Phantom crewroom maxim read: 'There are two kinds of Phantoms—those who have over-rotated on a "cat" shot and those who are going to do so'.[4] A good launch was indicated by a dip off the bow of the ship, before the Phantom rose into view once more and zoomed away on its mission.

Another unwelcome tendency was the stall-spin hazard, or 'Phantom Thing'. It was soon recognized that energetic control movements at low speed and low altitude could easily lead to a stall and an unrecoverable spin. If a spin developed below 10,000ft, immediate ejection was advocated. Several hundred Phantoms, in various guises and with different Services, are thought to have been lost because of the difficulty in avoiding this snare. For the Navy, it only became a serious problem when F-4 pilots began to dogfight in Vietnam still with bombs on board. Most knew better and jettisoned the ordnance, which soon restored their 'fighter pilot' confidence in the lighter machine. It was not a function of weight *per se*, but more to do with speed and weight restrictions and the inescapable fact that these affected excess power. The limitations were constantly rebriefed prior to strikes when 'iron' was to be hauled aloft, even if only on a 'remember that she can bite' basis. Those who forgot did so at their peril, especially when they slapped the stick about at low level. Again, when the F-4 Phantom was conceived this was an unlikely potential scenario.

A final alarming habit was the F-4B's honeycomb disintegration problem. Early aircraft which had gone supersonic often returned with large 'bites' out of their control surfaces where debonding of the structure had occurred. Manufacturing processes, brought about

by the US's massive R&D in glues and bonding agents as a result of the moon-shooting Space Program, soon eradicated this at source at McAir.[5]

As would be expected at that stage of the 'learning curve', the early F4H-1s continued to provide useful R&D input long after the type's service introduction. At NATC Patuxent River, Maryland, F-4A BuNo 148254 was decorated with the legend 'Look Ma, No Hands!' and was used to test the ACLS (Automatic Carrier Landing System) for the later F-4J. F-4B BuNo 151463 was equipped as a 'double-sonic tanker' with a tubular fairing to drop the hose and

basket well below the aircraft's thrust line. This experiment did not lead to service adoption, and Navy Phantoms used dedicated KA-6D and KA-3 tankers or Intruder 'Buddies'. Several other F-4s spent years on the 'Shake, Rattle and Roll' routine at NATC, simulating every conceivable carrier stress and mishandling, including the mighty thud of a hook engagement with all wheels off deck, or with only the nosewheel in contact! The Phantom soon proved to be a tough bird.

After the inaugural flight of the definitive F-4B (BuNo 148363) on 25 March 1961, a further 650 production exam-

mar, VF-96 *Fighting Falcons* worked up to operational status by June 1962 and prepared to cruise on the USS *Ranger* the following January. The *Black Aces*, VF-41, became the third Atlantic squadron. They spent the early part of their career with other Phantom units at Key West as part of NORAD during the Cuban Missile Crisis before making four cruises on the USS *Independence*. By 1965 no fewer than twenty-two US Navy squadrons had the F-4B on strength, and this mark was eventually to serve with sixty USN/MC units altogether.

Carriers in the 1950s had a 'day fighter' squadron with FJ Furies or F11F Tigers and an 'interceptor' unit of radar-equipped F3H Demons or F4D Skyrays. Crusaders had already replaced the other 'day fighters' when the F-4B arrived to supplant the interceptors. Naturally this led to plenty of rivalry between the two fighter communities and a great deal was heard of the slogan 'When you're out of F-8s, you're out of fighters'. However, the Phantom's progress was inexorable and by 1971 it had replaced Crusaders on all the carriers which were Phantom-capable. Its trusty performance and overwhelming offensive capability placed it simply eons ahead of its rival.[6]

---

[4] The *g* forces experienced on the 'cat' launch also made instruments appear too blurred to read. Crews had microseconds to judge whether the launch was successful or whether to reach for the ejection handles. If the Phantom did enter the water it would probably cause the engines to explode. F-4s sank immediately and underwater ejection was impossible.

[5] Some of the first sea-going Phantom squadrons also encountered severe galvanic corrosion in the rear fuselage, triggered by salt-water action. Whole sections had to be replaced before a better sealing process was devised.

[6] At the time of writing, *Aéronavale* F-8E(FN)s of *Flotille 12F* continue to 'cat' and 'trap' from the deck of the French aircraft carrier *Clemenceau*. However, these jets have undergone continuous extensive refits and have never been subjected to the rigours imposed on US Navy Phantoms around the globe. Moreover, McAir has never published any kind of fatigue index for the the US Navy's F-4s, which would indicate their prospective lifetime. The original models were, after all, warranted for a mere 1,000 hours!

ples were built. They were issued to Fleet units as fast as training would allow. The *Grim Reapers* trained VF-74 *Be-Devilers* (commanded by Cdr Julian S. Lake, the Bendix Trophy Winner) and his unit was 'First in Phantoms' on the East Coast. They swapped Skyrays for Phantoms officially on 8 July 1961, and then proceeded to 'fly in' the F-4B, establishing many of the SOPs (Standard Operational Procedures) through their experience aboard the USS *Saratoga* and then with CVW-8 on the USS *Forrestal*. Appropriately, they were to be the last Atlantic F-4 unit too, flying their final cruise on *Forrestal* from May to November 1982 with the ultimate Navy Phantom variant, the F-4S.

The first West Coast Fleet squadron was VF-114 *Aardvarks* under Cdr J. J. Konzen. They embarked after Carquals for the first of ten cruises on the USS *Kitty Hawk*, the last of which ended in May 1976, when conversion to the F-14 Tomcat took place. The *Aardvarks* were followed chronologically by G. G. O'Rourke's VF-102 *Diamondbacks* on the East Coast, who set sail on board the USS *Enterprise* in September 1961, beating VF-74 by hours in becoming the first Phantom squadron to enter the Mediterranean on 16 August 1962. At Mira-

3. THE FLEET AT WAR

By August 1964 there were 320 Phantoms in US Navy service, including six Marine squadrons. When the first action of the Vietnam War occurred and North Vietnamese (NVN) patrol boats threatened the USS *Maddox* on 2 August 1964, four Navy Phantom units were on station in the vicinity. VF-142 *Ghost Riders* and VF-143 *Pukin' Dogs* had joined CVW-14 on board the USS *Constellation*, while VF-92 *Silver Kings* and VF-96 *Fighting Falcons* were ready with CVW-9 on the USS *Ranger*. These units established the tradition of 'twin squadrons' which survived in many cases throughout the Phantom's career in the US Navy. VF-96 had already come close to conflict in May 1963 when it was put on alert to respond to the Laotian crisis. On 17 September 1964 the prospect of action came much nearer: the squadron was tasked with a retaliatory strike against the MiG airfield at Phuc Yen. Just prior to launch, orders were received from Washington to 'scrub' the mission. It would be a long time before the Navy had another chance at this tempting target. Instead, the F-4s began their war by providing escort to 'Yankee Team' flights of the newly-introduced RA-5C Vigilante over Laos.

At the conclusion of their first 'West-Pac' cruise in May 1963, VF-96 had returned to NAS Miramar as trials squadron for twelve F-4G Phantoms, later to be used in action by VF-213 *Black Lions*. The F-4G was an F-4B with an Approach Power Compensation System and an RCA AN/ASW-21 two-way data link replacing part of the No1 fuel cell. Both pieces of equipment were destined for the F-4J variant.[1] On 19 February 1964 VF-96 made the first data-link-controlled AIM-7 launch at Point Mugu. Cdr Ken Stecker and Lt (JG) Charles Webster destroyed a Q-2C Firebee merely by pressing the missile select switch and operating the intercept radar.[2] Flight controls, search radar and missile release were all signalled from the ground via the data link's automatic control systems. After this interlude VF-96 made seven further combat cruises and their subsequent air combat score made them one of the Navy's most publicized units.

Below: VF-96 *Fighting Falcons* achieved the first MiG kill of the war and went on to score seven more for the Navy. Here F-4B BuNo 152283 releases its 5in Zuni rockets from LAU-10 pods at suspected Viet Cong positions in May 1966. This was the first war cruise for VF-96 and for the USS *Enterprise*, lasting from 21 November 1965 to 14 June 1966. (USN)

The first missions of the war went to *Constellation*'s Air Group. Immediately after the *Maddox* incident they flew BARCAP (barrier combat air patrol) and escorted 'Yankee Team' RF-8A photo flights over Laos. However, CVW-9 was first into the 'Barrel Roll' sortie roster when Cdr Robert Norman led an unsuccessful attack by A-1H Skyraiders with F-4 support on 17 December 1964. VF-96's first live ordnance was dropped by their CO, Cdr Bill Fraser, and Lt (JG) Chris Billingsley on a 'Flaming Dart' flak-suppression sortie near Dong Hoi on 11 February 1965.

BARCAP involved placing a 'barrier' between the Task Force and likely threats from the air. 'Barrel Roll' meant escort for attack sorties, sometimes with air-to-ground ordnance on the Phantoms too. In the circumstances, neither mission profile gave much likelihood of intercepting the kinds of targets that the F-4's original sponsors had envisaged, but they did constitute most of the USN Phantom activity in South-East Asia (SEA). MiG-hunting, the 'hard-charger' aspect of the carrier pilot's career, was a welcome but rare opportunity. The media understandably used each aerial victory as a morale booster in an unpopular war, but the MiG-kills did mean a great deal to sailors and air crews, who wanted some tangible evidence that they were making an impression on an elusive enemy. There were not nearly so many celebration cakes or Cubi Officers' Club parties for airmen outside the fighter community.

However, the vast majority of the VF fighter squadrons' ('Fitrons'') time was spent on far less glamorous activities. Ironically, the only two successful combat missions that received the official label 'Intercept' resulted in the downing of aircraft rather less potent than the F-4 had been designed to tackle: VF-114 *Fighting Aardvarks* and VF-213 knocked down a pair of vintage An-2 biplanes with top speeds around the same figure as the F-4's landing speed. The weapons used were AIM-7 Sparrows, which were far more costly than their targets!

BARCAP

Perhaps better named 'Bore Cap', this was undoubtedly the most persistent, but least interesting, demand upon Phantom crews' time. At most stages in the conflict the NVAF had up to 100 MiGs available and Task Force commanders had to recognize that threat. While MiGs were unlikely to reach the carrier force itself, the crucial air-strike control ship ('Red Crown'), the search and rescue vessels and the 'Big Look' EC-121 recon aircraft were all vulnerable. In retrospect, the removal of the MiG threat early in the war would have been feasible. It was never a considerable deterrent to US operations but it was always present. Washington allowed the NVAF to operate from ten airfields, with an effective radar warning and GCI (Ground Control Intercept) network, right up to the war's end, and the Navy was therefore stuck with perpetual BARCAP for the best part of eight years.

BARCAP involved pairs of Phantoms giving 24-hour cover, flying racetrack patterns about 25 miles offshore near Haiphong. They cruised at around 300kts at 20,000ft, though some crews bent the rules and went much lower, beneath the enemy's radar coverage, in the hope of 'suckering' MiGs out. The legs of a typical circuit would only be 2–3 minutes' flying time, though crews often made the seaward leg as fast as possible and took their time over the landward side in case they could draw some 'trade' from the shore. The Phantoms would refuel about an hour into the mission and then wait for the relief element to show up. Their 2,000lb combat fuel reserve was usually burned off in a little mutual ACM (air combat manoeuvring) duelling on the way home. It is perhaps symptomatic of the level of tedium that some of the best air-to-air Phantom pictures were snapped by BARCAP flyers.

Occasionally there was action. The first three USN Phantom MiG kills came out of BARCAPs. In the first, on 9 April 1965, Lt (JG) Terry Murphy and Ens Ronald J. Fegan of VF-96 probably destroyed a Chicom MiG-17. Their own aircraft (F-4B BuNo 151403) was then downed, either by a MiG or by a Sparrow (as the Chinese claimed). Four Phantoms had launched for BARCAP, the first pair led by the CO, Cdr Bill Fraser. The second element was to have been led by Lt-Cdr William Greer in BuNo 151425, but his F-4B lost an engine on launch and flopped into the sea, leaving

<hr />

[1] Described in Chapter 4.

[2] The intercept radar system is described in detail in the context of F-4C/D operations—see Chapter 9. The manual crew functions of the B/C/D variants were virtually identical at this stage of Phantom development.

Above: For five war cruises VF-154 joined VF-21 in CVW-2 on board the USS *Ranger*. The Air Wing had entered the war on the USS *Coral Sea* in August 1966, losing nineteen Phantoms without any air victories in return. Nevertheless, '401/NE', an F-4B with the AN/APR-30 RHAW fit, launches with a full MiGCAP missile load on 14 December 1967. F-4s usually occupied the '100' and '200' Modex range in an Air Wing, but on this cruise the '200' codes were already taken by VA-22's A-4C Skyhawks. (USN)

its crew on parachutes. It was the first VF-96 loss. Murphy and Fegan, in 'Showtime 611', replaced them with Lts Howard Watkins and John Mueller on their wing. Watkins, some distance behind '611', heard Murphy radio that he had three Chinese MiGs above him just as Watkins' F-4 came under attack by another MiG-17. Fraser's element returned to enter the fray, firing two AIM-7s and a pair of AIM-9s, all of which misfired or missed. The Phantoms then regrouped to find a tanker, but Murphy's aircraft had vanished. He had signalled 'Out of missiles, returning to base' (he

and Watkins only carried Sparrows) at about the time that Watkins had seen a MiG explode and crash without being able to establish who had hit it. Murphy was tracked briefly on radar but a second 'blip' was seen to follow him before his Phantom vanished.

The uncertainty surrounding this incident meant that the first official 'kill' went to VF-21 *Freelancers*. They arrived on 'Yankee Station' with the USS *Midway*'s CVW-2 in March 1965 for the first of eight combat cruises. Their two MiG kills were both made on a BARCAP of 17 June 1965. Korean War veteran Cdr Lou Page, the XO, and his RIO Lt John C. Smith made a classic head-on closing attack on one of four MiG-17s in 'Sundown 01' (F-4B BuNo 151488). 'J.C.' Smith was one of the first batch of RIOs and an acknowledged master of the trade. The engagement could have come straight from a Raytheon publicity handout. Firing at the same time, wing-man Lt Dave Batson, with Lt-Cdr Robert Doremus, 'splashed' a second MiG with

another Sparrow from the F-4B 'Sundown 02' (BuNo 152219). It is likely that a third member of the NVAF formation was also destroyed by debris! Sadly, Franke and Doremus became victims of one of the first SA-2 'Guideline' SAM launches during an attack on the Thanh Hoa bridge on 24 August 1965. Both went to the 'Hanoi Hilton'.

One more BARCAP success was claimed over a MiG-17, by Lt-Cdr Dan MacIntyre and Lt (JG) Alan Johnson of VF-151 *Vigilantes* in F-4B 'Switch Box 107' (BuNo 150634) on 6 October 1965. After that the MiGs stayed clear until 12 January 1973, when Lt Vic Kovaleski and Lt (JG) James A. Wise took advantage of new BARCAP rules. The DoD had just given permission for MiGs to be chased above the 20th Parallel 'bomb line' as part of a less restrictive policy for attacks on the North. Before 1973 the Rules of Engagement prevented American fighters from engaging MiGs unless the latter made the first move. For six years of BARCAP they did not, although there was an occasional provocative dash towards the Fleet or down the coast of North Vietnam to keep the BARCAP guys awake. Kovaleski's victim assumed he was safe once he had crossed the previously enforced 'no go' line for Phantoms. An AIM-9 from 'Rock River 102' (F-4B BuNo 153045) was his second surprise of the day.

Generally, the 'Fitrons' felt the whole BARCAP exercise to have been a huge waste of time and aviation fuel 'Plenty of air patrol but not much combat' was one RIO's verdict. BARCAP requirements placed such pressure on the mission schedulers that the Task Force commanders often had to draw upon Da Nang and Chu Lai's USMC Phantom squadrons to maintain the barrier. Perhaps even less fortunate than the 'BARCAP-ers' were the F-4 crews on 'Alert Five' or 'Condition One' standby. During the early years of the war they had to sit, strapped into their Phantoms, frequently in unpleasantly hot conditions, just in case they were required to launch at five minutes' notice in order to support the BARCAP. Later they were allowed to man the alert from the 'ready room'.

RECCE: RECONNAISSANCE ESCORT

Every USN strike mission involved a recon flight of carrier-based RF-8A or RA-5C data-gatherers to provide target information and battle damage assessment. They also flew 'Blue Tree' sorties constantly over Laos and North Vietnam after 3 March 1965 and were just as busy during the 'Bombing Pause' periods. Their task was mainly to detect movement on the Ho Chi Minh Trails network or any redisposition of defences. Later in the war their role was undoubtedly more provocative, teasing the enemy's defences into play. Despite the general cessation of bombing of the North between 1968 and 1971, the Air Groups were allowed to make 'Protective Reaction' strikes against enemy defences which threatened recce flights.[3] Recce escort was often increased from the usual single Phantom to a fairly large strike force in the hope of bringing up a few MiGs, or attacking SAM sites.

The single-ship escort was a less than favourite mission to draw but it took a large slice of Phantom flight-time. The F-4 held position above and about a mile to the side of the photo-ship and kept a look-out for anti-aircraft activity. Visibility from the RA-5C was limited and the crew had a full workload with the complex reconnaissance gear. Certainly, the F-4 escort kept the MiGs at bay: only two recon 'birds' were lost to enemy fighters during the entire war.[4] Sadly, though, the F-4 often returned without its charge because of the casualties inflicted by ground-fire. Losses of the big, stately Vigilante were proportionately the highest for any USN type—fifteen to AAA, two to SAMs and a single MiG victim. Their hazardous and predictable low-level daylight flight plans put them at constant risk. Their escorts shared the hazards. Vic Kovaleski, the last USN MiG-killer of the war, was also one of the

Below: With the name of its assigned pilot, Lt Winston 'Mad Dog' Copeland, on its red fin-cap, F-4B BuNo 151398 also bears the name *Ragin Cajun* on its splitter plate. This was the nickname of Lt Ken L. Cannon, who was responsible for the MiG kill flag applied beneath this inscription (visible as a tiny red rectangle with a yellow star). He and Lt Roy 'Bud' Morris splashed a MiG-17 in this weathered VF-51 *Screaming Eagles* Phantom on 10 May 1972, at the height of the 'Linebacker 2' air war. Copeland, in turn, got his MiG on June 11; this kill was one of six victories scored by his unit during the war in South-East Asia. (Via C. Moggeridge)

Bottom: VF-151 *Vigilantes* wore these plain colours for their first combat cruise aboard the USS *Coral Sea* from December 1964 to November 1965. The Squadron was teamed with an F-8D Crusader unit, VF-154, on that occasion and shot down a MiG-17—though this was disallowed for several years as it was a Chinese Communist aircraft. VF-151 were paired with VF-161 for the 1967 cruise and the two remained together until 1986, in much brighter colours. (Via C. Moggeridge)

---

[3] The whole subject of 'Protective Reaction' flights is aired more fully in the Chapter 15 in the context of USAF RF-4C operations.

[4] RA-5Cs were also faster than the F-4 at low level and the Phantom had to conserve fuel carefully in the effort to keep pace.

last men to be downed in a Navy Phantom when his aircraft (BuNo 153068) was hit by an SA-2 SAM during a 'Blue Tree' mission two days after his eventful dogfight. Both he and his RIO, Ens Plautz, were recovered.

Occasionally the Navy took revenge on the SAM system in a big way. VF-96 took part in an attack on a SAM storage depot near Hanoi on 5 June 1967 which left at least nine of the missiles writhing smokily about in a scene worthy of the film *Flight of the Intruder*. Avoiding the missiles in flight was much more of a problem. VF-14 *Top Hatters*, one of the Atlantic Fleet squadrons drawn into the war, first encountered them in August 1966. Lt (JG) Greg Schwalber evaded two by using a high-*g* 'split-S' manoeuvre. The Squadron XO, Cdr John 'Smoke' Wilson, put his F-4B (BuNo 151511) through some highly unorthodox gyrations at around 500ft AGL to dodge a salvo of three SAMs. The F-4 did not take kindly to being hauled around at low altitude. VF-14 pilots found it heavy on the controls and physically demanding. Greg Schwalber found that it could be unexpectedly forgiving too. He and his RIO, Bill Wood, managed to launch '112/AB' with its wings in the folded position! Unusual handling characteristics drew their attention to this discrepancy so they cleaned off all the stores and headed ashore for a surprisingly safe landing!

Phantoms also appeared as escorts to OP-2E 'Igloo White' sensor-droppers in 1967 and to EC-121M intelligence-gathering flights. They were also required to accompany some of the solo A-6A Intruder sorties over the North. These hazardous but effective missions usually involved the F-4 in little other than taking flak and were not greeted with enthusiasm. A former Intruder flyer told the authors how his attack squadron, VA-196 *Main Battery*, once fitted Sidewinders to the little-used launch rails of their A-6s to provide their own MiG defence as the 'Fitrons' did not seem very keen to do so. The USS *Constellation*'s 'Phantom Phlyers' were suitably stung and their availability rates improved rapidly there-

after! A few crews actually got lucky on A-6 escort. Lt-Cdr Robert E. Tucker and Lt (JG) Stan Edens from VF-103 *Sluggers* got a MiG-21J during one such sortie on 10 August 1972. At one stage Phantoms were actually allowed to fly their own night interdiction sorties over Hanoi, but only if they used flares to illuminate and identify their targets. Nobody wanted to be that much of a 'flak magnet', so the idea was unpopular.

STRIKE

Phantoms were used in the attacks on North Vietnam as soon as they arrived in the 'WestPac' zone. The A-4 Skyhawk had been an excellent light attacker, but it carried less than half the warload of a Phantom and it had sustained heavy losses, crews included. Almost a third of the casualties among USN CVWs were in A-4 units—the price of being the Navy's mainstay during the costly 'Rolling Thunder' campaign. Douglas Skyraiders had coped with the early years of the war until 1967, when it was decided that the increasingly savage defences made them too vulnerable. The Navy's most sophisticated striker, the A-6A, had none of these problems but it was in short supply. It was therefore predictable that the F-4's pylons would be loaded with as much ordnance as they could carry in a war where bomb tonnages and sortie rates were the yardsticks of achievement. Naval thinking was in any case very attack-orientated. In Korea Navy jets had flown attack sorties, leaving the MiG-tussling to the Air Force Sabres. Fighters were seen as Fleet Defenders and if they could carry bombs, too, so much the better. Thus both Navy and Air Force commanders were told to launch large formations of supersonic interceptors, flying at around 300kts, at medium altitude and often dropping their ordnance straight-and-level above cloud. With hindsight, it was ill-advised.

In fact, the term 'strike' covered a variety of sins, from large 'Alpha' strikes (beginning on 5 March 1966) when Phantoms flew in formations of up to thirty attack and support aircraft, to attacks by sections of two Phantoms. In an 'Alpha',

the Phantom component would usually be loaded with six Mk 82 LDGP 500lb bombs strapped to TERs mounted on the inner wing pylons, a 600 US gallon centreline tank and two AIM-7 missiles in the aft bays. Occasionally, four Mk 84 bombs would be hung under the wings for use against harder targets. The outboard pylons could carry 370 US gallon drop tanks for some missions, but ordnance was preferred on these stations because of the tanks' effect on the aircraft's centre of gravity during a 'cat' launch.

'Alphas' were 'maximum effort' strikes against large, pre-selected targets, and the massive logistical background involved in mounting them meant that they were usually flown even if the weather got worse or the target conditions changed. If the formation had to resort to level bombing, through the clouds, the losses mounted as AAA gunners found the altitude to aim for. During 'Rolling Thunder', Phantoms flew in 'Alphas' alongside bombed-up Crusaders, Skyhawks and Skyraiders or Intruders. On the USS *Coral Sea*'s first 'WestPac' cruise between February and October 1965, twenty-one of these other types were lost from her Air Wing, all to AAA. The resident F-4B squadron, VF-161 *Chargers*, escaped unscathed. On the ship's second cruise in 1966 the two Phantom squadrons (VF-21 and VF-154) were not so fortunate. Among sixteen combat losses were six F-4Bs, five of the Phantoms being downed by 'triple-A' and one by a SAM. VF-21 suffered even worse luck in July 1967 when the tragic fire on the USS *Forrestal* cost the lives of 44 squadron personnel. It was started by an incorrectly connected Zuni rocket firing from the underwing pod of an F-4 which hit a Skyhawk's centreline fuel tank. Mayhem ensued.

By 1967, when the SAM network had been allowed to expand considerably, VF-151 and VF-161 on *Coral Sea* attributed three of their seven combat losses to SA-2 missiles. Other units had a far worse time: on the USS *Bonne Homme Richard* in 1967 the brave Skyhawk pilots lost the equivalent of a whole squadron

Above: VF-151 CAG's F-4B, BuNo 153059, with multi-coloured fin; the regular squadron colours were black and yellow sunrays on the tail. This was one of 228 F-4Bs which became F-4Ns under Project 'Beeline'. (Via Richard L. Ward)

of twelve A-4s during their 112 days on the line.

In a large strike package the Phantoms would launch at the apex of the force because of their high fuel consumption with 'draggy' external stores. They would then top up from a tanker before heading off to the target in 'combat spread formation' at around 300kts and 15,000–18,000ft. VF-96 devised a good exercise to sharpen up the tank-ing procedure. As the KA-3 'Whale' launched ahead of the Phantoms, it began to extend its drogue as its landing gear came up. The first F-4 off the cata-pult had to try and effect a 'plug' into the drogue of the 'Whale' just before the latter's gear was fully raised!

In conditions of reasonable visibility (rare over North Vietnam) the Phantom elements accelerated to 400kts over the coast, approaching the target at around 11,000ft. Bombs were usually released in a 45–60-degree dive at about 5,000ft to stay clear of small-bore ground defences. Most crews opted for a drop with the armament switches set to 'ripple', so as to cover the target effectively. The re-turn to altitude also meant trying to get the strike formation regrouped quickly so that no one could be picked off by MiGs. Traditionally, pilots tended to exit the target in a left turn before return-ing to height. Ground defences soon learned that fighter pilots always turned to the left, and the AAA was set up ready to greet them. Right turns became more popular thereafter.

On their return to the carrier, Phan-toms had to make a 'fuel economy' set-ting, orbit, and wait for the carrier to begin its recovery cycle. Typically, six 'strike' Phantoms would be scheduled for an 'Alpha', attacking first so that they were not tied to the slower-moving

bomber elements. Even the return to the carrier could be quite exciting. Cdr 'Lefty' Schwartz, who took over VF-96 in July 1966, was a former 'Blue Angel'. His speciality was to form a division of F-4s into a four-ship 'Blue Angels Diamond' and then make a high-speed run over Hanoi on the way back to the ship.

In the early stages of the war it was quickly realized that the F-4B lacked a suitable sight for accurate bombing, and in 1964 CVW-9's maintainers came up with the idea of fitting bomb sights from the A-1 Skyraider to the F-4B's sight location. The A-1 had a purpose-built air-to-ground sight with an adjustable reflection plate, allowing different depression angles to be cranked-in. The F-4's was optimized for air-to-air boresighting and it had a fixed baseplate. Steel collars were specially cast at Subic Bay to hold the A-1 sight heads, which

were then adjusted for each sortie by setting the 'pipper' on the horizon at a fixed speed to provide a zero reference. The amount of 'lead' or depression required for a particular ordnance load could then be calculated and entered-in. The sight could still be used for air-to-air purposes, but it made 'down the chute' attacks more predictable.[5]

After the long bombing pause from March 1968, 'Alphas' were resumed against the North in Operation 'Proud Deep' during December 1971. Once again, straight-and-level bombing above the clouds was repeated, and to prove that lessons had not been learned, the losses multiplied. Twenty-three USAF and USN aircraft were lost in the five-day operation. Pairs of Phantoms and 'SLUFs' (the Navy's new A-7 light attack jet) often 'instrument-bombed' on signals from an A-6A lead-ship using the

latter's DIANE system for precise weapons release data and the A-7s' semi-digital INS for navigation. Elements from *Coral Sea* and *Enterprise* flew this type of sortie on 30 December 1971 with commendable accuracy, but without time to avoid SAMs coming up at them through the clouds. Lt-Cdr D. W. Hoffman and Lt (JG) N. A. Charles went down in a shark-mouthed VF-111 F-4B (BuNo 150418), closely followed by the lead A-6A from VA-165 *Boomers*. Neither crew saw the missiles which sought them out.

If crews were shot at and there seemed to be a chance of recovering them, large sections of the strike package would immediately divert to RESCAP. Any F-4s with ordnance remaining would use it to keep enemy heads down while others returned to the 'boat', hot-refuelled on

---

[5] Refer to 'Down the Chute' in Chapter 9.

Left: A double MiG-killer. F-4J BuNo 155769 disposed of two MiG-17s on 10 May 1972. In the hands of Lt Matt Connelly and Lt Thomas Blonski, 'Showtime 106' used its AIM-9G missiles to good effect on a TARCAP sortie with 'Fitron 96', the 'Fighting Falcons'. Randy Cunningham hoped for the TARCAP slot on this mission but he was listed for flak suppression instead, a sortie which yielded three MiGs for him in any case! Apparently, an A-7 driver, anxious to see a MiG at first hand, turned back into the fight and collected two MiGs on his tail. Connelly shot one off and told the A-7 jock to 'get the hell out'. A minute or so later the Corsair reappeared with another pair of MiGs after him. Connelly shot another down and Cunningham watched it explode. The A-7 pilot finally got the message and headed home. 'Showtime 106' is seen here on 4 June, a few weeks after this incident, about to 'trap' on board Constellation. **(USN/ Michael R. Morris)**

deck and returned with more weapons to try and clear a path for the rescue helicopters. Some heroic recoveries were made, but the stark fact remains that only one-sixth of air crews 'down and alive' were actually picked up. Two Navy SAR aircraft were lost for every three crewmen rescued. Among the successes was the Medal of Honor-winning snatch of VF-33 Tarsiers aviators Lt-Cdrs Holtzclaw and Burns, shot down in F-4J BuNo 155546. Helicopter pilot Lt Clyde E. Lassen guided his Seasprite to a pick-up in total darkness over unfamiliar territory, recovering to the ship with only five minutes' fuel remaining.

In order to reduce the crippling menace of AAA, the larger strike forces included an element of flak-suppressing Phantoms. Armed with Mk 82 bombs, or the new Rockeye CBU (Cluster Bomb Unit), the flak flight of two Phantoms went in ahead of the strike to 'take out' known gun sites around the target or to support the 'Iron Hand' flight of Shrike-launching A-7As in attacking missile sites. It was a dangerous assignment.[6] VF-154 was one of many units to lose people this way, including Lt-Cdr Charles Tanner and his RIO Ross Terry, who took a direct 100mm hit from the AAA sites around the Phu Ly railroad complex. They ejected from their burning Phantom, lucky to survive as POWs.

Mining was another variation on strike missions. Phantoms flew this one infrequently, dropping Mk 36 DST magnetically fused bombs which would react to a passing ship. The main use was in Operation 'Pocket Money', the 1972 mining of Haiphong harbour. Phantoms backed up the A-6A Intruders of CVW-15 in order to get the mines in place as soon as possible. Pairs of F-4Js released their mines on a signal from an Intruder, which had more accurate navigation systems than the 'Eclipse Pioneer' dead-reckoning ground position indicator installed in the Phantom.

The hazards for strike Phantoms were numerous. Bad weather, exhaustion and some questionable target selection by the Pentagon planners all took their toll, but the steadily increasing presence of accurate anti-aircraft defences was the main threat. Guns caused the biggest losses, as already described, particularly after Soviet fire-control radars became common, including odd marks of training radar. One hit could easily finish a complex F-4. Lt (JG) McRae and Ens Rehmann had a complete wing blown off their F-4B by a single shell during a December 1966 CAP sortie. At the other extreme, many Phantoms were downed by a few rifle-shot hits or by shrapnel fragments. The lethal radius of an exploding SAM extended for up to 600ft. That was the estimated distance between an exploding SA-2 and F-4J 'Showtime 100', flown by Aces Lt Randall Cunningham and Lt (JG) Driscoll on 10 May 1972. At the end of a fight which brought them three MiG kills, taking their total to five, their Phantom (F-4J BuNo 155800) absorbed small fragments of the SAM which wrecked the aircraft's hydraulics and obliged the famous duo to bale out. A closer explosion by the 280lb warhead of the SA-2 (or Dvina, as the Russians called it) could take out two adjacent aircraft. Formations were planned with spacings calculated to foil the SA-2's guidance radar into seeing a pair of aircraft as a single target. In theory it would then pass between them without detonating. Of the 80 USN aircraft lost to SAMs, thirteen were F-4s, mostly

during the height of the aerial onslaught against the North in 1967 and 1972. When the missiles first appeared in 1965, pilots immediately adopted much lower target approaches, 'popping up' for a dive-release at the target. This profile required very rapid and accurate target identification and ran the risk of small-arms fire on the way in. Before 1966 DECM (defensive electronic counter-measures) and RHAWS (radar homing and warning systems) equipment was virtually absent from USN aircraft. A few had the primitive 'Little Ear' device attached inside the canopy with suction caps and monitored via a headset. It gave a general warning of hostile radar activity but no indication of its direction or urgency. The much-improved Sanders AN/ALQ-51 track-breaking DECM, and the allied AN/APR-27 launch warning receiver, were fitted to F-4s under Project 'Shoehorn' after 1966 as they returned to Miramar or Oceana between cruises.[7] The ratio of aircraft losses to SAM launches improved thereafter. In 1965 it took an average of seventeen missiles to destroy one aircraft; by 1973 the ratio had risen to 60:1.

Visual avoidance and adept manoeuvring were the best bet if a SAM bore your name. An early sighting of the white smoke trail of burning kerosene and nitric acid enabled a Phantom crew to wait until the last possible moment and then turn into the weapon's track. Pairs of aircraft often attempted to roll together around the SA-2's approach trajectory. This technique was clearly much harder at night, as VF-154 boss William Haff and his radar-man Rudy Rudloff discovered. Mistaking a pair of distant orange lights for flares from a

---

[6] The use of the AGM-45A Shrike missile, and defence-suppression in general, is discussed in depth in Chapter 14.
[7] The AN/APR-30 was added later, providing a similar RHAWS capability to that installed in USAF and FMS Phantoms. Refer to Chapter 14. These systems added new forward- and aft-facing antennae to the fin-cap and nose which were readily identifiable on the F-4B. The follow-on AN/APR-32 RHAWS, applied principally to the F-4J variant, featured, inter alia, an aft-facing fin-cap antenna plus 'box' under the radome.

Skyhawk, and lacking any threat warning on their indicators, they almost fell prey to a pair of oncoming *Dvina*. It seems that the missiles had been launched visually in the hope of establishing a radar lock on to the Phantoms during flight. Fortunately, one homed on to a chaff bundle released from the Phantoms and the other passed close by. Haff and his wing-man Harley Hall (later to become boss of the *Blue Angels* F-4J team) found the SAM site and plastered it with CBUs as a token of gratitude. The 'final solution' for SA-2 suppression arrived near the end of the war in the form of the EA-6B Prowler. VF-92 MiG-killer Curt Dose came close to being trapped by a barrage of two SAMs, both of them seemingly unavoidable. His F-4J escaped and he subsequently discovered that the missiles had been successfully jammed by an off-shore Prowler which neutralized their command and fusing frequencies.

Statistically, ground fire of all types was far more destructive than missiles. It accounted for at least 53 out of the total of 71 USN Phantom combat losses. The logic of using $2.5 million jets against ground targets of highly dubious strategic value has often been debated. Phantom crews initiated that forum early in the war, pointing publicly to the absurdity of using an 'F-4 with a pair of Mk 81s on the wings against an empty hooch', as one pilot put it, just to boost the sortie statistics. The experience of another VF-154 *Black Knights* pilot, Lt Van Pelt, on 4 January 1967, focuses the issue somewhat. Targeted against a crude bridge structure, he rolled his F-4B in to drop its bombs, only to be hit by 37mm AAA. Van Pelt managed to keep his mortally injured fighter on course and put all six Mk 82s on the spot. Both crewmen then took to their parachutes after the pilot had managed to coax the Phantom to the coast, and they were pulled out of the sea safely. Weighing the loss of an F-4 against damaging an easily repaired earth and timber structure surrounded by lethal defences was the kind of anguished mental exercise which increasingly preoccupied the air crews.

In fact, the statistics for missions flown and bomb tonnage dropped by F-4 'Fitrons' were astonishing. VF-14 *Top Hatters* made

only one war cruise. They were among several Atlantic Fleet squadrons which were drawn into the expanding war to support the Pacific units. They flew 967 combat sorties from the USS *Franklin D. Roosevelt* in 1966, dropping 650,000lb of ordnance in three months without losing a plane in combat. Commanded by Cdr Dick Adams, the Squadron regularly launched from the 'Rosie''s short catapults with four Mk 82s and four Mk 83s aboard, plus an empty centreline tank which was filled shortly after launch. Deck landing with the carrier's short-span arresting gear was a constant problem. Phantoms had to recover with absolute minimum fuel to achieve correct landing weights, and a 'bolter' meant immediate contact with a tanker for a second attempt. F-4B BuNo 151018 failed to complete a circuit after a wave-off and

went into the sea when its last drops of JP5 were exhausted.

VF-31 *Tomcatters* also made a single cruise beginning in April 1972. Their orders to join the sudden increase in action during 'Linebacker' operations was so unexpected that crews were called back from leave in a matter of hours, parking their cars all over the docks at Mayport, Virginia, for families to collect. En route to battle, the 'Phelix Phlyers' practised 'Alpha Strikes' and completed two line periods in action before retiring to Cubi Point. There they became one of the first Navy units to evaluate Paveway laser-guided bombs (LGBs) with their F-4Js. It was found that fighter escort would be required for operational LGB sorties because the laser-protective goggles worn by air crew while the RIO was using his hand-held laser designator greatly limited their vision and situation awareness.

In practice, the USAF quickly took the LGB scenario unto itself and the Navy played little part in its operational development during the war.[8] VF-31 did fly a number of level bombing sorties with Ubon-based LORAN F-4Ds acting as lead-ships. Less accurate were the numerous bad-weather TACAN bomb-dumping sorties when the Phantoms dropped ordnance over the Laotian forests using map co-ordinates checked against ground-signal bearing references. During this cruise VF-31 made 2,223 deck landings, 536 of them in what was probably the 'ultimate stress' situation for Phantom flyers—the night deck recovery. They flew 4,216 combat hours and even 'bagged' a MiG into the bargain.[9]

Squadrons flying Phantoms from older carriers like the USS *Coral Sea* often had to launch with restricted ordnance loads because of catapult weight limitations. VF-111 *Sundowners* were in this position for all three of their war cruises. VF-151 on the similarly restrictive USS *Midway* still managed to deliver over three million pounds of ordnance in 2,500 sorties during their April 1972 – February 1973 'WestPac' cruise, the longest of the entire war. On average, *Midway* was launching three major 'Alpha Strikes' a day during this period.

TARCAP

Target combat air patrol was really another variation of 'strike'. The TARCAP Phantoms bombed with the main strike force and then remained in the vicinity to cover the force's exit from the target area. Their task was to deter enemy fighters rather than seek them out, but they usually carried a full missile complement rather than the two Sparrows of the main strike Phantoms. In the event, TARCAP proved to be a frequent source of MiG engagements. Eleven kills, about a quarter of the Navy's total, came from TARCAP sorties, and two-thirds of the aerial victories stemmed from either TARCAP or MiGCAP situations.

On occasion this meant stretching the ROE a little. On 6 May 1972 Lt-Cdr Jerry 'Devil' Houston was flying VF-51's 'Screamin' Eagle 100', a gaudily decorated ex-USMC F-4B (BuNo 150456) with an unreliable radio and other evidence of hard use. On a 'Linebacker' mission he left his TARCAP station to head off a MiG-17 which had inserted itself into a procession of A-6As coming off the target. It opened fire on the A-6 flown by their CAG, Roger 'Blinky' Sheets. Houston slipped in behind the MiG but was unable to contact the CAG and warn him that a Sidewinder launched from the Phantom might find the Intruder rather than the MiG. Fortunately, Sheets was watching the proceedings, waiting for the missile to come off the rail, and yanked his aircraft out of its path. The MiG, with its controls locked solid at 500kts and 100ft AGL, absorbed the full impact and exploded all over a ridge.

Another pair of MiGs fell to a TARCAP mounted by VF-142's F-4Bs on 10 August 1967. Lt Guy Freeborn and Lt-Cdr Robert C. Davis found MiGs descending on their 16,000ft CAP position. Although it took a total of seven missiles between them, the Phantom crews 'flamed' a MiG each.[10] Lt Charles Southwick and Ens Jim Laing of VF-114 scored a MiG-17 kill on TARCAP on 24 April that year. The strike force was making the first eagerly awaited attack on Kep, one of the main MiG airfields. Their F-4B (BuNo 153000, call-sign 'Linfield') had to be abandoned shortly after the combat because of AAA damage to its fuel system. A second MiG, rising to intercept, was knocked out by their wing-man, Lt 'Denny' Wisely and Lt (JG) Gareth Anderson with an AIM-9D (in F-4B 'Double Nuts' 153077). Southwick, an ex-Crusader veteran who had gone through the USAF Fighter Weapons School at Nellis AFB and had far more air combat expertise than most of his colleagues, went down a second time. His Phantom was struck by one of his own Zuni rockets, and he became a POW. Jim Laing, an unusually proficient RIO, suffered another shoot-down too but he was recovered by SAR. VF-114 spent its entire Phantom career aboard the USS *Kitty Hawk* (September 1962 to December 1975), but the 1967 cruise was its most costly. By June of that year it had lost seven aircraft, one of which contained MiG-killer Gareth Anderson.

TARCAP's main function as a MiG deterrent was undoubtedly valuable. Only six USN strike aircraft were lost to MiGs during attacks where F-4s or F-8s provided cover. As the post-war 'Red Baron' analysis of MiG activity showed, the NVAF only engaged in combat when the odds favoured them, and the presence of a CAP flight riding with cocked pistols on the USN formation was clearly off-putting. However, the habit of sending lone MiGs to fly near the strike force as bait must have caused much frustration to the CAP crews, who were supposed to stay with their charges.

MiGCAP

Before 1968, MiGCAP consisted of a pair of Navy fighters in racetrack orbit off the coast near Haiphong or on a lateral transit course across the Route Pack VIB area, waiting to be called upon. Most strike packages were 'MiGCAP-ed' at this stage. Towards the end of the conflict only 'Alpha Strikes' and B-52 'Arc Light' missions had MiGCAPs, consisting of up to four pairs of Phantoms positioned close to known MiG airfields. The Phantom elements were in position to cover for MiG launches as the main strike force arrived. Like the TARCAP, their job was to deter MiGs, not to hunt them down. Undoubtedly it was the most adrenalin-stirring of the Phantom missions and it made up for the bomb-hauling, BARCAP and escort duties which constituted the majority of a crew's tour of duty. MiG-fighting seemed to be

---

[8] Refer to 'Pave Phantom' and 'Bridge Busters' in Chapter 10 for a full account of the Vietnam-era USAF laser-bombing systems.

[9] A MiG-21, shot down on 21 June 1972 by Cdr Samuel ('Sam') C. Flynn Jr, and his RIO, Lt William ('Bill') H. John, in F-4J BuNo 157307, call-sign 'Bandwagon 101'.

[10] With RIOs Lt (JG) Bob Elliot in BuNo 152247 and Lt-Cdr Gayle 'Swede' Elie in 150431 respectively, both with 'Dakota' call-signs and each 'bagging' a MiG-21.

TABLE 3: US NAVY F-4 PHANTOM MiG KILLS IN SOUTH-EAST ASIA, 1965–JANUARY 1973*								
1965	1966	1967	1968	1969	1970	1971	1972	1973
4	3	6	2	–	1	–	24	1

*1973 total to 23 January

more in keeping with the Phantom's true nature.

Inevitably, scores and statistics are the language of air warfare. In simple terms, the USN lost seven F-4s to MiGs, one in a dogfight and the others to unseen interceptors. In reply, the Phantom crews destroyed 41 enemy aircraft, including two by USMC exchange air crews in USAF Phantoms. The majority, 22, were old but agile MiG-17s, two were MiG-19s, fifteen were MiG-21s and two were An-2 biplanes. The most intense air battles were fought in 1972–73 when 25 MiGs fell to Navy Phantoms, sixteen of them in May 1972 alone. For the rest of the war the two fighter forces confronted each other sporadically, with long gaps coinciding with the cessation of bombing in the North. Between September 1968 and January 1972 only one USN combat was credited. On 28 March 1970 VF-142 *Ghost Riders* Lts Jerry Beaulier and Steve Barkley were put on 'Alert Five' on the USS *Constellation* to support her BARCAP. Their flight actually took them some distance inland, at low level, to pursue a pair of MiGs. The NVAF had begun to push further south, safe in the knowledge that US pilots were unlikely to be allowed to attack them. By advancing towards them under the Vietnamese radar screen and crossing the coast beyond the BARCAP parameters, the Navy pilots were undoubtedly pushing the ROE in force at the time to breaking point. However, the result was a classic two-on-two fighter duel which resulted in a MiG-21 kill by F-4J BuNo 155875. It was the first victory for the 'Top Gun' fighter course, from which Beaulier had emerged as one of the first graduates a year previously. The psychological boost to the fighter community, whose success rate against the MiGs was teetering around the 2:1 ratio at that

point, was thought to have been worth the breach of protocol. However, the mission was officially logged as a 'Blue Tree' escort 'protective reaction' affair in order to head off any possible political difficulties.

MiG fighting was a comparative rarity in proportion to the number of sorties flown (57,000 from carriers in 1967 alone), and a response to a relatively minor threat. Out of 85 deployments by Air Groups relying exclusively on the Phantom, two dozen included successful MiG engagements. *Constellation* was the highest-scoring carrier, with fifteen MiGs in seven cruises. However, nine of these came from a single cruise in which the Randall Cunningham / Will Driscoll team scored five. The USS *Midway*'s fighters racked up eight MiGs in three cruises, while *Ranger* had only one MiG kill in seven cruises and *Enterprise* two in six. It depended on the state of the bombing campaign during the time of the cruise and the types of targets under attack, although three of *Ranger*'s cruises did occur during peaks in the attacks on the North. See Table 3.

Inevitably there was rivalry between the Phantom and Crusader 'Fitrons' as MiG activity increased. Initially, the gunfighting F-8 had the edge over the F-4 'Missileer'. By the end of 1967 Phantoms had scored 11 MiGs (including two disputed claims), against 15 for the F-8 'MiG Master'. The disparity lay mainly in the background of training: Crusader pilots were accomplished dogfighters, whereas Phantom jockeys had little training in this arena. When the training programme was revamped as a result of the 'Top Gun' initiative in 1969, the USN kill/loss ratio quickly rose to 12:1. By 1972, when these figures were being achieved, the excellent F-8 had vanished from all but the small *Hancock* class car-

riers. However, many Crusader pilots had passed on their skills to the Phantom community back in the United States at 'Top Gun'. The other factor was better weaponry, which took several years to reach the 'Tonkin Gulf Yacht Club'.

On 7 May 1968 five Phantoms from VF-92 and VF-96 engaged two MiG-21s during a CAP mission. In the subsequent dogfight the Phantoms managed to release only two Sparrow missiles, without effect. Worse, F-4B BuNo 151485 was downed by an 'Atoll' missile, though fortunately its crew, Lt-Cdr E. S. Christiansen and Lt (JG) W. A. Kramer, ejected successfully and were pulled out of the sea. Another Phantom, F-4J BuNo 155548 of VF-102 *Diamondbacks*, was lost in a two-on-two MiG fight in which four Sparrows were launched without a hit. This combat took place on 18 June 1968, and in that and the preceding month over thirty expensive AIM-7Es were fired without hitting a single enemy aircraft. Clearly, there were serious problems for NAVAIR Phantom operations and crews began particularly to distrust the Sparrow missile system. Missile reliability was just one of two hundred and forty F-4 air combat deficiencies identified in the Ault Report submitted on 1 January 1969. Capt 'Whip' Ault, skipper of the USS *Coral Sea* in 1966–67 and an experienced naval aviator, was appalled at the 'Fitrons'' poor showing against MiG opposition, and in particular at the apparently deteriorating kill-to-loss ratio. Famous for his blunt honesty, Ault led a team which investigated every aspect of the production, maintenance, training and operational usage of the Navy's premier airborne weapons system. His report was not the first of its kind: in 1966 the USAF's 'Charging Sparrow' initiative was one of several official responses to its disappointing scores with the AIM-7, a system which, on its introduction to service, had appeared to offer huge advances in airborne interception capability. Some critics pointed to the success of the gun-armed Crusader, which had destroyed twenty MiGs by the end of 1968, compared with the Phantom's fifteen. Further study revealed that only one of the F-8 kills had been achieved solely by 20mm gunfire, although it was a contributory cause in two others. The majority were scored with the Sidewinder. The F-8's Mk 12 Colt guns tended to jam in turning fights. Even so, Navy Phantom crews wanted the option of a gun for close-in fighting, having heard of its success with the Air Force. They had limited access to the Hughes Mk IV gun pod, but it was generally thought that this lacked accuracy and reliability so they were happier to take a fuel tank on the centreline instead. Interestingly, USAF Phantoms used their SUU-16/A gun pods in the destruction of eleven MiGs.[11]

Ault's enquiries dealt with the many disparities in the F-4's weapons performance. Of the two key types of missiles used by the USN, the AIM-9 Sidewinder proved more useful in combat than the 'primary' weapons system, the AIM-7 Sparrow. At the start of the war crews stuck to their interception training manuals and went into battle shooting Sparrows. The first three MiGs were demolished with them. Nine of the first fourteen kills used Sparrow, often in near-textbook head-on engagements. Thereafter, the NVAF evolved tactics which attempted to draw Phantom drivers into close, turning fights where missiles would be of little use. Eventually Sidewinders notched up 31 out of 41 Navy kills. Mainly these were combats where the shorter-ranged, quicker-reacting missile could be launched in visual mode after the target had passed inside the minimum launch radius of the AIM-7—as was often the case because crews had to make a visual identification of a target before engaging it. Sparrow was essentially a beyond-visual-range (BVR) weapon. The AIM-7D/E Sparrow III required the F-4B's AN/APQ-72 to 'paint' its target throughout the missile's flight. If lock was broken, for example by the target manoeuvring tightly, the Sparrow was designed to self-destruct. Missiles fired from a turning, *g*-loaded aircraft were also likely to break lock. Moreover, the Sparrow's semi-active radar

homing seeker also tended to lose contact with the radar-painted target if it exceeded 3*g*. Massive improvements in this area were incorporated into the trials AIM-7XE-2 in 1969, blooded three years later by USAF crews.[12]

Phantom 'Fitrons' relied increasingly on their Sidewinders, though the Sparrow was invariably carried too. In the hectic 'knife fights' of 1972, 23 out of 24 MiG kills were made with the AIM-9D/G Sidewinder and only one with the AIM-7E-2. The expanded-acquisition 'Delta' and 'Golf' models used nitrogen-gas cooling contained in the missile launch rails and proved to be a vast improvement over the original uncooled AIM-9B, which the USAF continued to use throughout the 1960s. In fact, the Navy's 'Delta' had been introduced fairly early on in the war and began to be succeeded by the 'Golf' on the production lines as early as 1967; both of these featured improved low-level target discrimination and a better turning performance, rendering them superior to the old uncooled joint-service model. By 1971 Navy Phantoms were even beginning to use the AIM-9H mark, outwardly identical to the previous two but featuring solid-state electronics for even greater reliability. And the statistics suggest that the missiles' overall record was quite good. In all, 80 successful American engagements were made with the Sidewinder.

Poor reliability stemming from abuse of the weapons certainly played a part, but the problem was more complex. When Ault reported, the record of successful Sparrow launches was only one in twelve. His studies drew attention to the complexity of the launch procedure, requiring a difficult pattern of switch-setting by both crewmen in co-ordination.[13] This was permissible in a long-range, high-altitude BVR intercept, but not in a running fight against a pack of nimble MiGs. As Ault put it, F-4 crews were being asked to 'fight a heads-up fight with a heads-down system. You had to look in the cockpit when you were fighting in the F-4'. Using their APQ-72's narrow boresight mode was likened

to 'keeping a flashlight on a frightened fly in a dark room'. RIOs also had to remember that the Sparrow's effective range and turn parameters varied with altitude, airspeed and temperature—and there were no digital avionics to provide instantly re-computed tracking solutions in 1968. Over half the Sparrows they used were fired short of the missile's effective range, or at targets taking evasive action. Sometimes two or more missiles were ripple-fired in the hope of doubling the chance of a hit. The result often was a baffled guidance system and two misses.

The Ault enquiry also pointed to the maintenance difficulties on carriers. Sparrow missiles which performed well in laboratory conditions or on carefully managed test ranges did not respond so well to the brutal impact and vibration of repeated carrier landings and launches. Engineer Mike Fossier gave Raytheon's perspective, explaining that when Sparrow was designed it was envisaged that the missile would be loaded only when it would be needed for BARCAP against a hostile force. 'The critical period of reliability was therefore thought to be the half-minute of missile flight to which it would be subjected shortly after fighter take-off. Months would go by without air combat, during which time the Spar-

---

[11] Refer to 'Gunfighters' in Chapter 9 for the back-ground to the service introduction of the SUU-16/A gun pod. The whole subject of air-to-air weaponry, from the USAF's perspective, is aired in Chapters 9 and 10, and in Chapter 13. The complete cockpit 'switchology' in employing early-model AIM-9B Sidewinders and AIM-7D/E/E-2 Sparrows is discussed in these chapters in the context of similar USAF F-4C/D operations, which had much in common with those of the Navy F-4B—but not of the F-4J, which introduced pulse-Doppler search technology. The latter is covered in Chapter 4 and in the chapters dealing with the British F-4K/M derivatives, 6, 7 and 8.

[12] Refer to Note 11, above. The AIM-7XE-2 was the trials version of the production AIM-7E-2. All Sparrow III missiles were manufactured by Raytheon, as were the Navy models of Sidewinder.

[13] See Note 11. The manual procedures in the F-4B and the USAF's F-4C/D models differed little, except for the fact that the former's rear-seat radar tracking handle was located in the centre, and not on the right-hand console.

rows would be carried daily in a fully operating state on F-4s conducting ground-attack missions of several hours each.' In theory, the Sparrow should have undergone a complete systems check-out after each sortie. However, in practice, their delicate guidance mechanisms and electronics were invariably down-loaded for inspection only after having remained on the aircraft for up to fifty missions! Not included in the Ault Report on Sparrow reliability and air combat doctrine, but recorded by Capt Ault privately, was the comment of a Chief Ordnanceman on a TF.77 carrier regarding AIM-7 utilization: 'Well, I'll tell you sir, you treat them f—— missiles like bombs and they're gonna act like bombs. We're not maintaining them right.' The Air Force usually put their missiles through bench-tests after about ten sorties and shipped them back to depot if required. Improvements in all these technical matters were advocated, and VX-4 *The Evaluators*, the Navy's Air Development squadron, suggested and then tested various upgrades, including the introduction of improved proximity fuses. However, the biggest stride forward came with the aforementioned AIM-7E2 'dogfight' Sparrow, with twice the manoeuvrability of its predecessor along with shorter minimum-range characteristics, which the USAF and Israelis later learnt to use with devastating effect.

Technical improvements were only part of the cure. Most of Ault's suggestions concerned human factors, both in the maintenance of the weapons system and, more importantly, in the training of air crews. Missile misuse also applied to the Sidewinder series. More than half of those launched by USN F-4s were fired outside effective parameters and failed to guide or explode. Technical enhancements included doubling the 10lb warhead to increase the probability of a kill. The missile was also originally limited to a 2*g* launch and its performance was degraded by rain, cloud and ground-masking, all of which were abundant in Vietnam. At first it could not be attached to the F-4B's inboard pylons if they were also configured with TERs, until the

maintainers of VF-21 jury-rigged extended bolts for the missile launch rails. Sidewinder matured fast as a practicable weapon. VF-96 duo Cunningham and Driscoll were among the crews who used it against ground targets too. On the return from their second MiG kill, in which they had escaped another pair of MiGs via a rivet-popping 12*g* turn, they persuaded a Sidewinder to home on the heat signature of a truck engine!

The major training improvements after Ault centred on 'Top Gun'. Randy Cunningham felt that his own success in downing five MiGs owed much to his 'Top Gun' training. By the time he entered combat he had already flown 200 simulated dogfights against A-4E (MiG-17 surrogate) or F-8/F-106 (MiG-21) opponents back home. There was nothing comparable for the Phantom flyers before 1969. 'Top Gun' originated from initiatives within VF-121 *Pacemakers* at Miramar 'Fightertown' and VX-4, including Project 'Have Doughnut' and Project 'Have Drill'. These gave selected VX-4 instructors the chance to fly in and against the USAF's secret 'Red Hat' squadron of MiG-17s and MiG-21s attached to Nellis Tactical Fighter Weapons Center, north of Las Vegas. A small group of instructors, who were convinced that the Phantom was being severely underestimated as a fighter, set up the 'Top Gun' school in a borrowed trailer at NAS Miramar under the auspices of VF-121. The training syllabus of the Fighter Weapons School (as it was properly known), whose first class commenced on 3 March 1969, was to revive the tradition of air combat which had not been taught since the closure of the Fleet Air Gunnery Unit in 1960. Luckily, the F-8 community had preserved and practised many of those skills in the intervening years and many of the instructors came from that background. In simulated dogfights using the MiGs and F-4s far more realistically than the Air Force had done, Tom Cassidy, 'Mugs' McKeown, 'Tooter' Teague and 'Top Gun' boss Dan Pedersen were among the select team who revolutionized F-4 tactics. At first, Air Wings sent four crews

each to undertake the course and pass on the doctrine to their squadrons. The initial batch came from VF-142 *Ghost Riders* and VF-143 *Pukin' Dogs* with CVW-14. They worked around the basic concept of two-on-one combat, learning the strengths and limits of their own and the NVAF's fighters, and pushing their Phantoms way beyond anything they had experienced before. They learned to tackle the primitive but deadly MiG-17 with vertical scissors attacks or barrel rolls, or by turning into the MiG and then extending away, using the F-4's main asset—brute power. The importance of the second pair of eyes in the rear cockpit was also emphasized. Once again, Cunningham was one of many pilots who insisted that the crew team effort was crucial to their success when the tactics were put into practice.

Among the first 'Top Gun' class was Jerry Beaulier, whose 1970 kill began to prove the new aggressive philosophy. It was not until 1972 that the real chance came. In stark terms, between January and June 1972 USN Phantom crews shot down 21 MiGs. 'Top Gun' trainees or instructors scored 60 per cent of the kills. The 'Top Gun' influence affected all the others too. In general, the weapons worked better. Partly this was because the carrier weapons squads were treating sophisticated missiles less like 'dumb' ordnance; mainly it was because the missiles were being used more effectively in the air.

On 10 May 1972 the 'Top Gun' project was vindicated beyond all doubt. VF-96 scored six MiGs, three of them going to the deadly duo 'Duke' and 'Irish'. Curt Dose and James McDevitt of partner squadron VF-92 *Silver Kings* chased a MiG-21 over Kep airfield, departing slightly from their TARCAP, and shot it down. They fired seven missiles in all (including those from their wing-man) before flaming the MiG. Cunningham's team, on the other hand, fired three and shot a MiG each time. Two other VF-96 kills went to Lt Michael 'Matt' Connelly and Lt Thomas J. Blonski (in 'Showtime 106', F-4J BuNo 155769) and a third to the 'Shoeman'—Lt Steve

Shoemaker and his RIO Lt (JG) Keith Crenshaw (in 'Showtime 111', F-4J BuNo 155749). Ironically, the only score by the official MiGCAP that day was by Lt Ken 'Ragin' Cajun' Cannon and Lt Roy 'Bud' Morris in a VF-51 F-4B. Most of the engagements resulted from 'mark one eye-ball' contact rather than radar 'paints'. Later on 10 May the NVAF tried to even the score by luring the Navy into low-altitude turning fights, but 'Top Gun' had taught the Americans to avoid that scenario at all costs. Down in the weeds, in hot weather, the Phantom could not turn with the MiGs, however adroitly handled, and its AIM-9D/G Sidewinders were more likely to be distracted by heat returns from the ground, or moist thermals hanging over the rain forest. Instead, the Navy fighters used the MiGs' own tactics—making use of

their speed advantage to pick selected targets and then disengage at will. In the air combat atmosphere, where, as legend has it, 'You are so scared that you want to puke and your IQ drops to 14', the Navy was once again proving that first-class training and a great fighter aircraft were unbeatable. Throughout the last year of the war the 'Top Gun' tuition increased the Navy's kill ratio six-fold. There were 'Top Gun' tutors in the arena as well: several had returned to operational squadrons and were keen to put their theory into action. Cdr Sam Flynn, who scored VF-31 *Tomcatters'* only victory (in 'Bandwagon 101', F-4J BuNo 157293), had been one of the first to argue for changed tactics and the foundation of a Fighter Weapons School. Cdr 'Tooter' Teague, architect of Project 'Have Drill', was commanding VF-51

Above: Despite their 'Phamously Phearsome Phantom' markings, VF-111 were only allocated one war cruise, although they were on station for Operation 'Endsweep' in 1973 too. They also took their previous mount, the F-8C Crusader, on a single war cruise in 1968. Both excursions yielded a MiG kill. (Via Richard L. Ward)

when he shot down a MiG-17 (in 'Screaming Eagle 114', F-4B BuNo 149473). Lt-Cdr 'Mugs' McKeown, an expert MiG pilot himself from VX-4 days, knocked down a pair of MiG-17s in a single mission on 23 May in F-4B 'Rock River 100' (BuNo 153020) of VF-161 *Chargers*.

Navy pilots used to claim that there was a large sign at Phuc Yen NVAF base which read: 'Rule One. Don't Eat Yellow Snow. Rule Two. Don't Attack Gray Phantoms'. After May 1972 you could well believe it.

35

4. PEACE AND IMPROVEMENTS

The Vietnam years rapidly transformed the Phantom into the US Navy's most versatile warplane. It entered the conflict as a Fleet interceptor and took on a widening range of missions almost immediately. In 1965, around one-third of the munitions eventually to equip F-4 units were either incompletely trialled or in short supply, but systems and weapons development proceeded rapidly. Line squadrons took their share of this process. In 1966, for example, VF-154 *Black Knights* conducted AIM-7 and AIM-9 reliability tests at the Juliet Missile Range, Cubi Point, and at Luzon between 'line periods' of their war cruise. As back-up, a Weapons Quality Engineering Center was established at Yorktown, Virginia, with the sole responsibility of investigating Sparrow misfires.[1]

Combat revealed some minor but surprisingly important design problems, such as the lack of visibility from the rear seat. This was no real handicap to a radar-watching RIO, until he was expected to 'rubber-neck' for MiGs, targets and SAMs too. Fleet squadrons borrowed the Israeli idea of fitting external canopy mirrors. Low-speed handling was also improved by fitting slotted stabilators and drooped ailerons from Block F-4B-26-MC onwards. A more significant handicap was the smoke-trail-producing habit of the GE J79 engine. It advertised the Phantom's presence for a considerable distance and the problem was not really addressed until the latter stages of Navy service. In Vietnam combat, pilots always tried to stay in minimum afterburner when approaching MiGs so as to cut out the sooty plume. Air brakes ('boards') were used to keep airspeed down despite the considerable drag-induced fuel consumption. Communications were impeded by the fact that US Navy F-4s carried only one radio. This caused difficulty because strike and CAP elements operated on different frequencies and were therefore unable to monitor each other's activities.

The biggest single improvement to the breed was the introduction of the F-4J variant. The systems prototype YF-4J, a converted F-4B (BuNo 151473) flew on 4 June 1965, followed by the true example the next spring, precisely eight years after the first Phantom had thrust skyward with gold-helmeted Bob Little on board. It had the slotted 'stab' and drooped ailerons of late 'Bravo' stock, reducing approach speed to 125kts.[2] It would carry an AN/ASW-25A data link (tested in the USN F-4G) and updated AN/APR-32 RHAWS. But an improved AN/APG-59 incorporating the AN/AWG-10 missile control system became its true hallmark. The system featured a pulse-Doppler look-down capability as well as pulse search-and-track, continuous-wave illumination for the Sparrow missile, plus extensive BIT (built-in test) functions to help air crews and their plane captains isolate faults. In its updated AWG-10A format, introduced from 1973, it also added a new digital computer to provide faster missile-away solutions, along with air-to-ground ranging, ECCM (electronic counter-countermeasures) to see through enemy jamming, and a servoed cross on the gun sight for 'head-up' interception steering.[3] For nuclear attack with B/Mk 57 depth charges or B/Mk 61 bombs, a new AN/AJB-7 bombing system gave a similar capability to that installed in the contemporary USAF F-4D. The uprated J79-GE-10s were similar to those in the Air Force's F-4E, developing 17,900lb s.t. in afterburner. It was a formidable package. The F-4J continued in production until 522 had been built, the last being delivered on 7 January 1972.[4] The first lots were issued to VF-101 at Key West on 21 December 1966.

Right: Prominent among VX-4's colourful test fleet was the ultimate 'Bicentennial Bird', BuNo 153088. An F-4J-27-MC with an F-4N radome, the aircraft had slatted wings but was never fully converted to F-4S standard. (*Flying Colours*)

The F-4J rapidly supplanted the F-4B in WestPac squadrons, beginning with VF-84 *Jolly Rogers* in February 1967. VF-33 *Tarsiers* scored the first F-4J MiG kill on 10 July 1968 and went on to fly the 'Juliet' longer than any other front-line unit. Their distinctive yellow-tailed Phantoms, which were acquired in October 1967, were first to enter the war zone the following year, and they remained in use (though in toned-down livery) until mid-1981. Most other squadrons moved to the F-4J between cruises in the two years up to 1969. By the end of the war the Navy and Marines had 448 Phantoms on strength, including 21 squadrons with the F-4J.

Many other systems were introduced to the USN 'family' between the end of hostilities and the close of F-4 operations over two decades later. Among the first was the Honeywell Visual Target Acquisition System (VTAS), which incorporated a helmet-mounted sight for co-ordinated front-seat missile lock-on. This appeared in the F-4J in limited numbers in the last year of the war. Several units, including VF-154, received VTAS F-4Js direct from St Louis and tested them in combat. Basically, it permitted the pilot to track and command Sparrow missiles by line-of-sight. In its refined 1975 form it was coupled to the USAF's new HGU-33/P lightweight helmet.

The mid-1970s also saw the introduction of IWSR (Integrated Weapons System Review), a method of rationalizing and expediting the whole spares supply and ground crew training network for much improved efficiency. It is worth noting here that the F-4J's radar system alone contained 36,000 electrical components. USN Phantoms also benefited from the Automatic Carrier Landing System (ACLS), which has taken much of the anguish out of deck-landing, particularly at night. An earlier improvement was the Automatic Power Compensation System (APCS), trialled in an NATC F-4G in 1966. This auto-throttle maintained the appropriate engine power settings on approach to the ship but had to be switched off by the crew immediately before the crucial trap. This was necessary because throttles had to be advanced to full power before deck contact in case of a missed wire and 'bolter' wave-off. A microswitch oper-

[1] Refer to the Chapter 4 for more details regarding the Sparrow missile reliability issue.

[2] F-4J production began with Block 26z, Mac Ship No 1488, BuNo 153071. The second one built, BuNo 153072, was actually the first true F-4J to fly, making its maiden flight on 27 May 1966. At this juncture the last sixty F-4Bs and first twenty-six F-4Js were produced concurrently. The last of 637 operational F-4Bs destined for USN/MC use (Mac Ship No 1796, BuNo 153915) was delivered on 27 January 1967.

[3] Radar intercept procedures, and the Navy's servoed cross reticle, are discussed in detail in Chapter 9.

[4] The 522nd was Mac Ship No 4201, BuNo 158379, produced under Block 47au. At this point the US Navy ceased to oversee Phantom production and the suffix Block letters were dropped from reference documents.

TABLE 4: PROJECT 'BEE-LINE' F-4B to F-4N CONVERSIONS

153034	150430	150652	150491	150452	150635	150444	151398	150460
151424	150407	150634	150441	151016	151451	150422	151491	150996
151015	150445	150472	151433	151442	151434	151006	151400	150425
150479	150640	150627	150450	150485	150625	152235	152267	150466
151439	152241	151480	150412	151004	152291	151431	150630	152280
150411	152230	150651	150468	151513	151468	151435	150648	150429
151459	151417	151476	151463	150492	152278	151519	150482	150475
151484	150476	152277	150465	151430	151469	150642	151456	151436
152306	151000	151444	151448	150436	152259	152258	152272	150253
151489	152229	150419	152288	150643	150438	151413	150456	150448
150632	150423	151406	152254	152236	150415	150489	151003	152294
152302	151471	152991	152223	152275	150442	151487	150426	150638
152969	153024	152967	152227	151502	151498	151422	150478	152237
152210	153059	153047	151464	150432	150481	153026	151401	153045
153065	150464	152977	151475	152318	152281	153053	152295	153039
153050	153023	152975	153914	152981	153017	152252	152213	152323
151514	151452	151477	150480	150440	153008	152982	151446	153016
152293	150639	151008	152243	153915	152226	151510	152221	151440
152222	152326	153058	153012	152968	152965	151504	153067	152225
152310	152214	152317	152970	153010	152212	152250	150435	152208
153056	152269	152996	152282	151415	150993	151465	152307	152300
152283	152983	153036	153057	152270	152990	152298	152244	153019
153027	152986	153062	153030	153011	151503	151461	152321	151002
152290	152246	151449	151455	152971	153064	159490	152992	152303
152279	150628	151007	152217	151011	150484	153006	151482	152327
151511	152284	153034						

Production sequence is listed in order of work, from left to right and down. It began with Shop Number FP02 (BuNo 153034), the remaining aircraft carrying the new Shop Numbers P001–P227. Note that BuNo 153034 was again re-issued at the end of the sequence as No 227.

Data by courtesy of BARG

ated by the Phantom's weight settling on the landing gear was supposed to provide disconnection of APCS, but manual operation was advised at all times for safety. The system suited the Phantom well as small alterations in power setting had little effect on the aircraft's pitch angle on approach. One ex-F-8 jockey, Rear-Admiral Paul T. Gillchrist, who commanded CVW-3 in 1970, found the F-4 'a dream to fly in the carrier landing pattern. It came the back end of the carrier "slicker" and easier than any carrier plane I have flown in 28 years.' Praise indeed.

The most significant updates, occasioned partly by the slow and costly introduction of the F-14 Tomcat, extended the Phantom's 'deck life' significantly to cover the gap between the originally scheduled F-4 retirement and its planned replacement by the Tomcat. The F-4N and F-4S were rebuilds of F-4B and F-4J airframes, respectively, under CILOP (Conversion in Lieu of Procurement). A similar scheme had been used to 're-life' Crusaders for combat service, and similar successful measures were already under way to update the attack workhorse, the A-6. The F-4N development aircraft, F-4B BuNo 153034, flew at the Naval Air Rework Facility North Island (NARF Noris) on 14 June 1972, setting the process in motion. NARF's conversion lines at Noris and Norfolk, Virginia, processed 227 airframes in all (see Table 4). A few, designated F-4N(AC) had leading-edge manoeuvring slats fitted and went to the Marines. All were comparatively high-

Left: Keith Ferris's angular camouflage patterns were not confined to the Navy. Here an F-4C (63-7411) is testing a two-tone grey scheme at Luke AFB on 6 April 1977 while assigned to the 58th TFTW. (G. V. Mainert via Tim Laming)
Below: The legendary Cdr James Flatley III led a contingent from his Air Wing to HMS *Ark Royal* in April 1975 for Exercise 'Landtreadex 75-2'. His CAG F-4J, BuNo 155510 from VF-102 *Diamondbacks*, complete with updated Sanders DECM fairings, is seen here under tow on the 'Ark''s deck. (HMS *Ark Royal* via Richard L. Ward)

hours airframes selected from Blocks 12 to 28, and all received new Block numbers, from F-4N-1-MC to -46-MC. They were disassembled, fatigue-tested, re-stressed and re-assembled. Project 'Bee Line' also enabled new equipment to be fitted—including VTAS, Sidewinder Expanded Acquisition Mode (SEAM) and improved IFF—and radar modifications to be made. Visually, the F-4N could be distinguished by the long Sanders AN/ALQ-126 DECM fairings on the intake flanks.

F-4N Phantoms were issued to six US Navy and three US Marine Corps units, including a few which did not expect them. VF-21 *Freelancers* and VF-154 *Black Knights* briefly converted to the F-4S model in 1980 in preparation for a cruise on the USS *Coral Sea*. It was found that the F-4S was a little too fast 'over the ramp' for safe landing on the smaller *Midway* class carriers so the two squadrons actually flew their final Phantom deployments in the slightly more docile

F-4N. These included a 'round-the-world' cruise aboard *Coral Sea* in 1983 during which VF-154 became the first outfit to fire the improved AIM-9M all-aspect Sidewinder at a QF-86 drone, resulting in a 'Boola Boola' (kill). Previously, in 1977, they had given the AIM-7F Sparrow its service initiation, carrying it for both F-4N cruises.[5] Other units 'retro-converted' to earlier models too. VF-41 swapped its F-4Js for B models in 1973 and enlarged to a 'super squadron' of eighteen jets to become the USS *Franklin D. Roosevelt*'s only fighter squadron for the tense Yom Kippur War cruise (sister-unit VF-84 was deep in Tomcat conversion). A final swap, this time to the F-4N, gave VF-41 their equipment for their final Phantom cruise in 1975.

The F-4S was the most capable of all Navy Phantoms. Lt-Cdr Bob Randall,

---

[5] The Raytheon AIM-7F Sparrow and AIM-9L/M Sidewinder are discussed in Chapter 13.

TABLE 5: F-4J to F-4S SLEP CONVERSIONS

153779	153882	155561	155812	155901	153780	153884	155562	155813
157242	153784	153887	155565	155818	157243	153787	153889	155566
155820	157245	153791	153890	155567	155821	157246	153792	153891
155568	155822	157248	153798	153893	155570	155823	157249	153800
153986	155572	155825	155750	153805	153898	155573	155827	157254
153808	153899	155575	155828	157255	153809	153900	155579	155829
157257	153810	153902	155731	155830	157259	153814	153903	155732
155833	157260	153818	153904	155733	155834	157267	153819	153907
155735	155836	157268	153820	153908	155736	155838	157269	153821
153909	155739	155839	157272	153823	153910	155740	155840	157276
153824	153911	155741	155845	157278	153825	154781	155743	155847
157279	153826	154782	155745	155848	157281	153827	154786	155746
155849	157282	153828	154788	155747	155851	157283	153832	155515
155749	155854	157287	153833	155517	155753	155855	157290	153835
155518	155754	155858	157291	153840	155519	155757	155859	157292
153842	155521	155759	155862	157293	153843	155522	155761	155863
157296	153845	155524	155764	155864	157297	153847	155525	155765
155869	157298	153851	155527	155766	155871	157301	153853	155528
155767	155872	157304	153855	155530	155769	155874	157305	153856
155531	155772	155876	157307	153857	155532	155773	155878	157308
153858	155539	155779	155879	157309	153859	155541	155781	155881
158346	153860	155542	155783	155883	158348	153862	155543	155784
155887	158350	153864	155544	155786	155888	158352	153868	155545
155787	155890	158353	153869	155547	155792	155891	158354	153872
155549	155794	155892	158362	153873	155550	155801	155893	158370
153874	155552	155805	155896	158372	153877	155555	155806	155897
158374	153879	155558	155807	155898	158376	153880	155559	155808
155899	153881	155560	155810	155900				

Of the 248 aircraft, all but one received Shop Numbers in the J001–J247 range, the exception being BuNo 155892, assigned the Works Number JX35, which was used by McAir at Lambert Field for structural fatigue tests.

Data by courtesy of BARG

Program Officer for the NATC F-4S development, commented: 'This isn't going to put the F-4 into the same class as the F-14 or F/A-18, which are designed to stand on their tails and fight, but it is going to let the pilot push it a little further.' Manoeuvring slats gave a 50 per cent improved turning performance to the 'short nose' and knocked 12kts off the landing speed. They were fitted to all but the first 47 conversions, then retro-fitted to most of those as well. The slats were similar to those used on the USAF/FMS F-4E but featured a revised, squarer cross-section to the outer wing units and longer wing fences.[6] A minor disadvan-

Below: The strange fan-like device protruding from F-4B BuNo 150435's drag 'chute door is the Sanders AN/ALQ-140 Multibrick infra-red countermeasures system, designed to discharge puffs of energy to distract heat-seeking missiles. (Sanders)
Below right: During eighteen months ashore while *Saratoga* was overhauled, the *Sluggers* converted to F-4Js and took them aboard 'The Boat' in July 1969. They made nine more cruises on 'Sara', including one combat WestPac, before switching to the F-4S in 1981 and a final cruise on board the USS *Forrestal*. BuNo 155516 is seen here. (Richard L. Ward)

tage was that the aircraft became slightly less stable around the pitch axis, with consequent limitations on the positioning of certain underwing ordnance.

The F-4S was powered by J79-GE-10B engines which, at last, incorporated an exhaust smoke modification, burning JP5 at higher exhaust gas temperatures (EGTs). It also had the 'digital' AN/AWG-10B weapons control system radar, which introduced, for the first time, automatically computed conventional weapons delivery to sea-going Phantoms, via radar-ranging. F-4J airframes selected for SLEP (Service Life Extension Program) were stripped, cleaned and disassembled. Rebuilding involved a complete Kapton rewiring, new electro-luminescent formation strips, structural strengthening and some 'personal updating' depending upon the state of each airframe. Individual modification numbers were issued (for exam-

[6] Refer to Chapter 11 for a fuller account of the LES development effort. The slats extended at 11.5 units of AOA (angle of attack), retracting at 10.5 units. Originally, the inboard slat section, adjacent to the wing root, was incorporated (mod AFC 601) but this was deleted in the definitive layout (AFC 636). The slats were tested on F-4J BuNo 153088 by NATC and the first slatted F-4S was BuNo 155899, delivered to VMFA-451 in November 1979.

ple, BuNo 153779 became JO12). Eventually, 248 out of the planned 265 machines were 're-lifed', adding to each tired airframe 96 months of operational service and a significantly enhanced capability (see Table 5). Most went to the US Marine Corps (VMFA-451 *Warlords* being the first recipients), which could make greater use of the new radar modes, but four Navy squadrons also received it. The latter moved to the four USN Reserve squadrons by 1984, with a phase-out originally planned for 1988. However, age had finally begun to catch up, and the long-suffering airframes began to appear at AMARC in significant numbers during 1985.

These updates enabled the Navy's F-4 to remain a viable fighter throughout the 1980s alongside new 'glass cockpit' types. However, increasing maintenance requirements and the need for standardization on carriers meant that the older birds became a burden. Deeper fatigue problems began to show up too: in 1982 one F-4S (BuNo 153835) shed a wing during an arrested landing. On carriers, the Phantom's structural density increased maintenance times unacceptably compared with the newer jets, and made inspections tougher. The fact that several operational airframes had been used by deck handlers (used to genuinely retired examples) to practice their repositioning skills just prior to the cruise may also have contributed to some unintended wear and tear resulting from minor knocks: 'Don't sweat about that; that's going to the dump in six months, and we can patch her up until then' was the prevailing mentality when crews might otherwise have been severely rep-

Below left: Another attractive CAG scheme appeared on this CVW-11 F-4J belonging to VF-114 *Fighting Aardvarks*. Their tail logo was borrowed from the 'BC' comic strip. All ten of the squadron's F-4 cruises were made on board the USS *Kitty Hawk*. On the last, they handed over their final 'F-4J' to VF-111—a five-foot long model with 'kiddy car' undercarriage and full 'Aardvark' decor. Rear-Admiral L. A. Sneed, COMFITAEW WingPAC, made the presentation. (Via Richard L. Ward)
Bottom left: The distinctive triple shamrocks of VMFA-333, proudly displayed on an F-4J which features the Marines' crest as well, aboard the USS *Nimitz* for her maiden cruise in 1975–76. (Richard L. Ward)
Below right: An initial 44 early-production Block F-4Bs which did not make the grade for F-4N 'CILOP-ing' received this flamboyant trim preparatory to be being blown to pieces as QF-4B target drones. BuNo 148365 displays the data-link antenna and a pretty Naval Missile Center tail badge between missions at Point Mugu, California, in April 1972. (Via Tim Laming)

rimanded for 'hurting' a Tomcat, Intruder or Hornet. The abuse the aircraft sometimes suffered in the hands of deck and air crews would have made most of McAir's engineers wince!

In the later 1970s the focus of carrier activity shifted to the Mediterranean where two carriers (Task Forces 60.1 and 60.2) were normally on station. Compared with flying conditions over the Pacific, the 'Med' was positively claustrophobic for supersonic fighters. F-4 squadrons joining a Carrier Air Group normally had a six-week indoctrination period to become familiar with the complexity of the area's airspace and communications rules. Ordnance practice was conducted on the ranges at Pachino, Sicily, or Argo Nisi off Crete. The two carriers often launched 'attack' sorties against each other and strike packages

were organized with NATO forces, using established overland low-level routes. Missile practice was held on the Suda Bay range off Crete. Typically, the drone target would be tracked on an F-4B's radar from about 25–30 miles out, with a Sparrow launch following when this closed to around eight miles. In the United States, BQM-34 drones were launched from gaudily painted DP-2E Neptunes. Regular bombing 'Derby' competitions tested accuracy against a towed spar behind the carrier—not quite like the real thing for F-4 crews, perhaps, but at least there were free drinks and bronze plaques for the winners.

Flying in the 'Med' area also meant regular interception of Russian 'Badgers' deployed from Egypt. US Army 'starscopes' were used by RIOs to read off the bombers' numbers at night. For

VF-14, the prospect of real conflict came much closer in 1973. Libyan MiGs fired on a VQ-2 patrol aircraft and F-4 escorts were provided thereafter. On one occasion VF-14 had a flight of Tripoli-based Mirages locked-on with missiles ready to slip from their mountings, at which point the Mirages wisely turned back. VF-14 knew the Mirage well, having frequently exercised with French units during the 1960s.

There were the usual 'Battle E' for efficiency awards to be competed for. This annual trophy was won by VF-11 in 1975 for three accident-free years (10,000hrs) of Phantom flying. Another veteran Atlantic Phantom 'Fitron', VF-74 *Be-Devilers*, celebrated two decades in Phantoms with a specially painted F-4 in 1981. Sadly, their safety record was less than lucky in 1982 when three F-4Ss

were lost in accidents, one in a crash on to the USS *Forrestal's* deck.

Several peacetime incidents were less destructive. On one 350kt sea-skimming flight over the 'Med' an F-4J crew felt a thump from beneath their aircraft. It was not until their return to the 'boat' that they realized that their centreline tank had been wiped off by the waves! Hairier still was an attempted night 'trap' by a pilot who made too high an approach, overcompensated and came in 'wing-low', missing the pendants. His Phantom thundered off the bow, losing height. Mere feet above the sea, he went full 'burner but was simultaneously 'command ejected' by his RIO who had taken the initiative and punched out a fraction of a second earlier. The vacant F-4 climbed majestically away in a steep turn back towards the carrier and plunged into the ocean alongside the No 3 elevator. Lack of crew communication was even more severe in the case of another Navy F-4 which suffered minor pitot tube icing. The consequent faulty airspeed reading convinced the RIO that his aircraft was losing speed and about to enter an unrecoverable stall at any second. In panic, he immediately ejected. The pilot, assuming that there was a major crisis, did the same. In the original production models of the Phantom, the back-seater had to eject first, or be 'command ejected' by the pilot—a standard procedure for the series. However, in the

F-4B, if the RIO's seat failed the pilot could not eject either!

Phantom squadrons were on site at many of the world's political hot-spots in the 1970s. The USS *Midway's* two 'Fitrons' patrolled the North Korean coast after the murder of two US officers by communist guards in August 1976. Three years later these same two units spent 93 days on 'Gonzo Station', lapping circuits near MiG—and Muslim F-4E Phantom—country during the Iran Crisis.

During most of this time squadrons still wore the bright markings of the 1960s, initially on Light Gull Gray and Gloss White paintwork and then on overall Gloss Gull Gray. A few squadrons were around long enough to wear the dull Tactical Paint Scheme (TPS). VF-21 combined the TPS with stylish swept-back black noses, while VF-194 *Red*

Above: What appears to be an unorthodox landing approach by *Blue Angels* No 5 at the Paris *Salon* in June 1973! Led by Lt-Cdr 'Skip' Umstead, 'The Blues' performed at fifteen shows in seven European countries, and in Iran. It was to be their last year with the Phantom. Three crews ejected from a triple mid-air early in the season but Umstead and Capt Mike Murphy died in a second mid-air over NAS Lakehurst in July. (Richard L. Ward)
Right: This February 1969 photograph shows the *Blue Angels* during their eight-week work-up period on the F-4J at El Centro. The Phantom was selected to replace the team's F11F Tigers after evaluation against the F-8 Crusader and (surprisingly) the A-5 Vigilante. 'The Blues' made the Phantom the most impressive demonstration aircraft they had ever owned. (McAir)
Below: The famous *Black Bunny* F-4S, BuNo 155539, the second VX-4 *The Evaluators* Phantom to wear this startling livery. The original machine, F-4J-29ac-MC BuNo 153783, was further adorned with white stars carried on silver-trimmed blue flashes. (Via Tim Laming)

Above: VF301 and VF-302 painted sample F-4S Phantoms in the second Heater-Ferris scheme, using four shades of grey with the lightest, FS35307, on the nose, through FS36375 and 35237 to the darkest, 35164, on the tail. Originally the colours were reversed. The idea was to make portions of the airframe 'disappear' against the sky in ACM. BuNo 153856 was VF-301's first F-4S to receive this scheme. (Jan Jacobs)

Lightnings had a quartet of F-4Js in the angular 'Ferris Scheme' for their 1977 cruise, reminiscent of Second World War battleship disruptive patterns. VX-4 *The Evaluators* also flew these experimental blue-grey decors alongside their famous *Vandy One* gloss black Phantom. An F-4J (BuNo 153783) and two F-4S aircraft were consecutively finished in the striking *Black Bunny* scheme, originally to test the anti-corrosive properties of the paint. The best known of all the special paint jobs was the *Blue Angels* plumage. 'The Blues' used early-development F-4Js powered by J79-GE-8s and with control modifications in the tail to provide a constant 30lb of pressure on the control column with full nose-down trim.[7] Considerable physical strength was needed

to handle the Phantom in this configuration, which was designed to damp down pilot-induced oscillations in close-formation work. Crews flew without *g*-suit bladders so that they could brace their stick-holding right arm against their leg, unimpeded. The afterburner cut-in point on the throttle quadrant was shifted from 94 to 89 per cent in order to give quicker 'lights', essential in tight formation-keeping, and 'good smoke', when wings were occasionally a mere four feet apart! Fourteen F-4Js with lead in their noses (in lieu of radar) were used by the *Blue Angels* between 1969 and 1973. For the first two years they were commanded by the much-respected Cdr Harley Hall, later to be the last USN aviator killed in Vietnam when he was the boss of VF-143 *Pukin' Dogs*. *Blue Angels* shows were awe-inspiring demonstrations of controlled brute force and supreme grace, but operational costs, together with the loss of seven Phantoms (three in a single mid-air collision), dictated a change to the tamer Skyhawk.

Conversion to the Tomcat proceeded inexorably through the 1970s, nine out

of twenty Fleet fighter squadrons having 'traded up' by the close of 1976. In that year, too, the last two Fleet F-8 squadrons, long-time competitors of the Phantoms, finally received F-4Js, while an additional squadron, VF-171, was established in 1977 to absorb all the Phantom training commitments. Four Reserve units were also equipped with Phantoms between 1973 and 1980. Clearly, the old grey 'wonderbus''s time was limited, but right to the end crews found it a worthy opponent for the best of the rest.

---

[7] Fourteen aircraft were assigned to the 'Blues', embracing BuNos 153072, 153075–153086, and 153839. Lt-Cdr Bill Wheat flew the first of the 'Blues' new F-4Js (BuNo 153079) to Sherman Field on 23 December 1968 and the force was established at NAS Pensacola, Florida, on 3 January 1969, flying to its first show at MCAS Yuma, Arizona, on 15 March. Tragically, two mid-air incidents occurred during 1973 involving five F-4Js which killed two pilots and a Plane Captain. The latter fatal incident involving two jets occurred at NAS Lakehurst, New Jersey, on 26 July and the rest of the season was cancelled. The display team subsequently re-formed with A-4F Skyhawks.

5. SEMPER PHI PHANTOMS

The United States Marine Corps was in on the Phantom project from the earliest days. Marine pilots played a full part in the record-breaking flights of 1959–62 and training for operations began within a few months of the USN 'Phantom Phlyers'. Officially, the F-4B became the Corps' air superiority fighter, tasked with clearing the airspace above and around the battle area. Most of the initial classes to be trained in this craft were 'second-tourists' from Crusader, Skyray or Skyknight outfits. VMF(AW)-513 *Flying Nightmares*, -531 *Gray Ghosts* and -542 *Bengals* had all been F3D Skyknight flyers with experience of radar-equipped two-seat night-fighters extending back to the Korean War when they had been VMF(N) units. They were naturally among the first four to convert to

the F-4B. Joint first, concurrent with VMF(AW)-531 at Beaufort, South Carolina, was West Coast unit VMF(AW)-314 *Black Knights* at MCAS El Toro, California. The debate as to which unit was *actually* first rumbles on to this day! Both units began to receive production F-4Bs during June 1962.[1] Other squadrons followed rapidly: VMFA-323 *Death Rattlers* in August 1964, and -122 *Crusaders* (from the F-8A) the following spring. Eventually 22 front-line, training and Reserve squadrons used fighter variants of the Phantom at one stage or another during the Corps' quarter-century on Phantoms.

In changing aircraft, the squadrons also added an 'A' to their VMF name-plates, beginning on 1 August 1963, indicative of the 'attack' role which the Phantom was actually destined to perform for most of its USMC career. In Vietnam, for example, 98 per cent of Marine F-4 sorties were air-to-ground. Back-seaters were at first trained in the same interception tactics as their Navy

[1] McAir papers suggest that Lt-Col Robert J. Barbour's VMF(AW)-314 *Black Knights* were the first, on 29 June 1962. Interestingly, the CO had been the first Marine to fly the Phantom (BuNo 143388) in October 1959 at NAS Patuxent River, Maryland.

Right, upper: With a hefty load of M117 750lb bombs hanging from its racks, an F-4B waits for a strike sortie. VMFA-542 *Bengals* served initially at Da Nang, then at Chu Lai with MAG-32. They flew interdiction or CAS missions almost exclusively, with some TPQ-10 radar bombing and night quick-reaction CAS thrown in. On the last, the pilot ran to the F-4 and started up while his RIO collected the mission brief, strapping in while the 'Rhino' rolled to the ready. The *Bengals* dropped a million pounds of bombs in twenty-two days during spring 1966. This aircraft's side number, '10', is painted with a yellow drop-shadow outline. (Via Richard L. Ward)

Right, lower: The *Silver Eagles*, VMFA-115, wore some of the prettiest markings but had a gruelling time of it in Vietnam. Arriving at Da Nang in October 1965, they flew the Marines' last 'in-country' strikes in February 1971, by which time they had flown 30,083 combat sorties. Moving to Nam Phong in Thailand, they continued to operate against the Khmer Rouge up to August 1973. (Via Richard L. Ward)

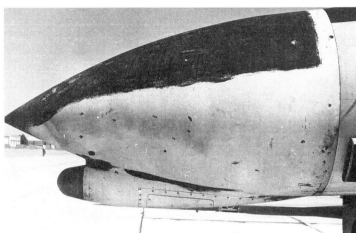

counterparts and probably foresaw a good deal of bomber interception in their futures. 1Lt Raymond Dunlevy, training with VFMA-323 *Death Rattlers* in 1964, saw the F-4B weapons systems as 'an entirely new concept in aerial warfare'. He would have been disappointed to realize how little that 'concept' would be employed in the F-4's 'dumb bombing' role over the following decade. Close air support (CAS) was, and still is, the first priority for Marine Air, and the Phantom's 16,000lb bomb-hauling capacity and high performance were ideal qualifications for that job.

The first Marine Air Group (MAG-11) with the Phantom, including VMFA-314, -531 and -542, regrouped at NAS

Atsugi, Japan, in 1963, conveniently close to the forthcoming battle arena in South-East Asia. VMFA-531 *Gray Ghosts* became the first Marine jet unit to be shore-based in Vietnam. Their fifteen new F-4Bs arrived at Da Nang on 10 May 1965 as part of the 9th Marine Expeditionary Brigade, accompanied by a few EF-10Bs, latter-day trainer versions of the F3D. Lt-Col William C. McGraw, *Gray Ghosts* commander, brought his men to Da Nang to defend the airspace surrounding USMC activity there from enemy air attack. This would certainly have justified the air superiority training, but it was not required and the 'Ghosts'' air combat training was swiftly superseded by a rapid

revision of the Phantom's attack profile diagrams.[2] Their first missions of the war were ground radar-guided bombing, CAS sorties and night attacks using flares. This set the tone for Marine Phantom routines for the rest of the Vietnam War. VMFA-314 *Black Knights* were the first unit to 'Trans Pac' over the Pacific to Atsugi in April 1963, moving to Da Nang shortly after the *Gray Ghosts* with MAG-11. There they were joined by another famous squadron, VMFA-323 *Death Rattlers*, which had traded F-8E Crusaders for F-4Bs in August 1964. They stood 'Alert' at Key West in Florida through the Cuban Missile Crisis and put in some intensive weapons training at Roosevelt Roads, Puerto Rico. In April 1965 they were asked to fly armed reconnaissance (ARREC) over the Dominican Republic to protect US interests following a *coup*. They then jetted to Da Nang in December. VMFA-542 *Bengals*, the fourth Marine Phantom squadron, also joined MAG-11 at Da Nang (at the time, the only jet-capable airfield in South Vietnam) during May 1965. Slightly ahead of the *Bengals* in re-equipping were VMFA-513 *Flying Nightmares*, who conducted their first war tour between June and October 1965 before moving to MCAS Cherry Point in North Carolina.

Left, top, and centre left: Perspectives of a *Gray Ghosts* Phantom and its tail markings. 'Joint First' USMC Phantom unit, VMFA-531 were the first of four F-4B squadrons at Da Nang in 1965 with MAG-11. Lt-Col William McGraw led the first flight of four to the base on 10 April 1965 and CAS sorties were flown three days later by twelve aircraft. By June 1965 they were back home at MCAS Cherry Point, and this very early Block 6f F-4B was still with the unit three years later. The *Gray Ghosts* retained their tail markings in only slightly modified form until the end of the unit's 22-year association with the Phantom. (Via Richard L. Ward)
Left, centre right: A view of the crudely painted 'anti-dazzle' radome hastily applied to 'Victor Whisky Three', BuNo 153416, of VMFA-314. The unit was

nicknamed 'The Volkswagen Squadron' after the'VW' tail code but was more correctly titled the *Black Knights*. Formed under Lt-Col Robert J. Barbour in October 1961, VMFA-314 left for NAS Atsugi in April 1963 and was in battle at Da Nang in early 1965. (Via Richard L. Ward)
Left, bottom: The last USMC Phantom unit to leave South-East Asia, the *Red Devils* (motto: 'First to Fight') spent much of the war at Da Nang and Nam Phong until reassignment to Kaneohe Bay, Hawaii. They suffered the only USMC F-4 loss to MiGs—BuNo 155811, on 26 August 1972. (Via A. Collishaw)
Below: A profusion of interesting markings appear on this blue-nosed F-4J of VMFA-451 *Warlords* during its 1976–77 Bicentennial deployment with CVW-17 on USS *Forrestal*. (*Flying Colours*)

---

[2] Ground-attack systems were strictly manual, as described in 'Down the Chute' in Chapter 9.

Left, upper: A fine study of a pair of VMFA-134 *Smokes* F-4S Phantoms preparing for the unit's penultimate operational mission on 21 December 1988; they flew a test mission from China Lake to provide operational trials for a new bomb fuse. Shortly after this they became the first designated USMC Reserve F/A-18A squadron. (Frank B. Mormillo)
Left, lower: 'Smoke 27', '28' and '29' head for a refuelling rendezvous with a VMGR-352 KC-130R tanker. Phantom '10/MF' demonstrates the weathering properties of the tactical paint scheme's 'rhino hide' appearance. (Frank B. Mormillo)

Operations from Da Nang's increasingly crowded airfield built up rapidly. The Marine F-4Bs carried 500lb bombs, Zuni rockets and napalm, all hand-loaded using a 'hernia bar' for the first few months. In true 'Leatherneck' tradition it was not uncommon for air crews to assist in cranking the heavy weapons up on to the racks. VMFA-323 suffered their first loss a mere seven days after arrival. F-4B BuNo 152261, piloted by the Squadron XO Maj John H. Dunn became the first and only USMC Phantom to be knocked down by a SAM. Dunn was on a night ARREC in RP III over North Vietnam. He survived seven years as a POW but his RIO, John Frederick, died after five years in captivity. The 'Rattlers' launched 407 sorties in their first month over the 'Steel Tiger' area and on 'Firecracker' CAP sorties for Marine RF-4B reconnaissance flights.[3]

Another escort role was to cover for the vulnerable KC-130F tankers, call-sign 'Basketball', which also furnished the Marine Phantoms with fuel. For four straight years refuelling operations went smoothly, until a hideous head-on mid-air collision took place above Phu Bai on the east coast of South Vietnam at around 1322 local time on 18 May 1969. A pair of VMFA-314 birds were blithely taking on fuel from a VMGR-152 KC-130F when a third F-4B, 'Ring Neck 250' from VMFA-542, smacked into the Hercules' right wing. All six in the VMGR-152 KC-130F, call-sign 'Basketball 814', perished, as did 1Lt Charles W. Pigott and his RIO Capt John L. Nalls in 'Ring Neck 250'. Remarkably,

the two refuelling Phantoms' crews evaded death. Maj J. D. Moody and his RIO in 'Thunder Two' ejected over the sea after jettisoning their bombs, while Maj A. Gillespie and his RIO 1Lt Vernon R. Maddox landed their aircraft at Chu Lai. It was a tragic episode, resulting from the dense air traffic that ringed the skies over Da Nang control.[4]

For much of their time in SEA the *Black Knights* were kept particularly busy. Some crews flew up to six missions a day. Mostly these were short-range CAS sorties where the worst hazard was from AAA—especially over Laos. Crews minimized the threat by running in and dropping at very high speeds: 550kts was not unusual, and VMFA-122 were known to go for a 600kt weapons release at 25ft altitude on occasion! This was extremely hazardous, and the tactic relied on the ordnance being 'clawed' back by the trees or terrain after being dropped from the Phantom. Accuracy was respectable, and good pilots could achieve remarkable hits in these conditions.

RIOs, with little call upon their air intercept skills, quickly adapted to the 'navigator' role. There was little hope of meeting MiGs except on the BARCAP sorties which USMC units often had to provide in support of their carrier-based colleagues. These flights involved a half-hour flight from Da Nang to the race-track BARCAP circuit and another 1½ hours on station between Task Force 77 and the likely NVAF threat. In the main, RIOs (or 'scopes') acted as general lookouts for flak, navigation waypoints and the ever-present threat of unexpected high ground. The terrain accounted for an inordinate number of accidents, particularly on night missions when vertigo could so easily tumble the pilot's internal gyros, and the back-seat watch proved valuable as a corrective. RIOs also had access to many of the aircraft's 250 circuit-breakers and the deft tweaking of the correct one in a combat crisis could often save an essential system from failure. Electrical problems were common in the humid, inhospitable climate and delicate systems did not exactly thrive in the ground conditions at Da Nang which

were by turns saturating or penetratingly dusty. After only three months at the base, VMFA-314, known as the 'Volkswagen Squadron' because of their 'VW' tail-code, had only half their eighteen F-4Bs available: the rest had succumbed to enemy ground-fire or were unserviceable.

Damage to an aircraft from its own ordnance was quite common. Debris from an exploding Mk 82 could rise up to 1,000ft, hazarding a wing-man's follow-up attack. Navy F-4B squadron VF-114 *Fighting Aardvarks* lost two aircraft in this way in the spring of 1966 and another to its own Zuni rocket the following year. Normally, the Zuni unguided 5in projectile, carried in four-shot LAU-10 pods made from treated paper, was found to be extremely accurate, and was preferred to the 2.75in FFAR. The favoured bomb was the Mk 82SE Snakeye, which became available after December 1967 when VMFA-122 *Crusaders* introduced it to USMC squadrons. Forward Air Controllers (FACs) would often call for a napalm drop in close-contact situations though crews found it an inaccurate weapon because the unfinned versions tumbled end-over-end in flight after release. The aircraft also had to make a flak-attracting, straight-and-level, shallow-glide attack in order to drop it.

Unlike those in the Navy, most Marine Phantom squadrons favoured the Hughes Mk IV gun pod, which was more suitable for their CAS mission. Normally it was mounted on the centre-line, though VMFA-122 had several of their F-4Bs rewired to carry two more on the outer wing pylons for short-range

---

[3] The RF-4B and its operational history are charted in the last chapter of this book—refer to 'Specters' in Chapter 15.
[4] For the most part, such mid-airs favoured the Phantom. In two separate Air Force collisions between Phantoms and transports, all four F-4 jockeys escaped, whereas only one of the 72 people aboard the other two aircraft escaped. A Marine F-4B RIO similarly turned out to be the sole survivor in a mid-air with a DC-9 over Duarte, California, on 6 June 1971. Obviously, the Martin-Baker ejection seats played a big part, but the robustness of the Phantom soon became legendary with its crews.

Left, upper: In-flight refuelling is not so easy. 'Sierra Hotel 06' was the instructor's F-4 in a flight of three. Here he is seen pulling back from the tanker to observe his two students' first attempt at a 'plug' in their Phantoms. Unfortunately, neither could get his aircraft on to the hose, so the trio had to head home early to Yuma. VMFAT-101 trained the last USN Phantom crews, as well as providing USMC 'Rhino Riders', from 1984 to 1987. (Frank B. Mormillo)
Left, lower: A more successful engagement for this *Gray Ghosts* F-4N as it draws fuel from a VMGR-352 KC-130R near San Clemente Island. The aircraft has the overall FS36440 Light Gull Gray and FS17038 Black fin adopted in the late 1970s. (Frank B. Mormillo)

CAS sorties. The *Crusaders'* 'superstrafer' configuration no doubt resulted in a significant increase on the record 2,100,000 rounds of 20mm fired by USMC fighters during 1968; obviously the 'gunfighter' image died hard. Their aircraft also carried Sparrow and Sidewinder missiles, unlike most Marine Phantoms, indicating an air-to-air tasking. However, the lack of direct contact with MiGs meant that they never had the chance to hose one down with this terrifying arsenal.

Some of the other Da Nang F-4Bs became 'superbombers'. External tank fuel transfer system problems (some of which were 'volunteered' so as to permit this configuration) meant that the jets could not be configured with wing tanks. As there was no time to trace and fix the deficiencies (of course) the aircraft were modified to carry racks on all external pylons. Up to two dozen Mk 82s or a mixture of CBUs and gun pods could be loaded for 'in-country' work, usually on pre-loaded MERs and TERs to save time.[5] These short-range 'iron-haulers' were in big demand when Da Nang came under attack by the Viet Cong. The Phantoms took off repeatedly on ten-minute bomb-dumping sorties around the perimeter of the base. Da Nang maintained two five-minute 'strip alert' sections for urgent CAS requirements, known as 'Hot Pad A' and 'Hot Pad B', rotated among the squadrons. Typically, 'A Pad' jets carried fragmentation bombs and 'B Pad' aircraft a combination of bombs and napalm. A 'normal' day would generate 30–40 sorties from the dozen aircraft and eighteen crews constantly rotating through the day's ceaseless cycle; record days generated double those rates!

Longer sorties meant smaller warloads, partly because a heavily laden Phantom—the 'squirrelly bird', as it was known—was too unstable to take fuel from a KC-130F tanker's basket, owing to abrupt pitch response. Typically, USMC Phantoms carried around 5,000lb of ordnance. This compared favourably with the 3,000lb of the Marines' main striker, the A-4E, but their A-6As usually took aboard seven tons. On a one-hour sortie from Da Nang, Phantoms habitually took six 250lb Mk 81 'Firecrackers' on the centreline MER, a pair of 370 US gallon wing tanks and up to four LAU-10 rocket pods on the inner-pylon TERs. Ordnance statistics were impressive: the *Bengals* released a million pounds of bombs and rockets in 22 days at one stage of their 1966 deployment.

Apart from the visible effects of a good secondary explosion, the BDA results of most attack sorties were hard to assess, or merely disappointing. The *Death Rattlers'* 500 combat sorties in February 1967 officially resulted in the destruction of one AA gun, 179 'structures' (mostly huts), thirteen bunkers, a bridge, a truck (damaged), one confirmed pack elephant and three 'probable' elephant kills—hardly the glamorous fighter pilot's life! Attacks on known troop concentrations made more sense, particularly when the sorties were in support of Marines in contact with the enemy. Troop comm-

---

[5] The various configurations included 24 × Mk 82; 12 × Mk 82 plus seven napalm tanks; 18 × Mk 82 plus sixteen Zunis (four LAU-10s); and ten Cluster Bomb Units and a gun pod.

anders spread an 'air panel' near their position to give pilots a visual reference and then requested ordnance, including napalm, as close as 50yds from their own front line. The F-4B's 45-degree dive-attack 'down the chute' made it more accurate in this context than previous Marine jets, though some crews went for the crazy near-vertical attack to improve accuracy!

The climate presented major difficulties, obscuring ground targets with heavy rain and cloud. Bombing sorties often had to resort to TPQ-10 radar beacons which could be tracked at ranges of up to 50 miles. They provided a fairly accurate ground reference in the absence of visual information. Tropical rainstorms were to be avoided too. Lt-Col Keller, with VMFA-323, suffered a total electrical failure of his Phantom in thunder clouds and hand-signalled his RIO, Capt Hugh Julian, to eject. The unfortunate rear-seater spent nine hours in the sea with a broken arm, no life-raft, no radio and no light and was eventually discovered by a shrimping boat. Keller also escaped, but only after three attempts to fire his ejection seat. The *Death Rattlers* skipper, Lt-Col Harry T. Haga-

man, made an equally hazardous ejection in January 1968 when his F-4B took a clip of .50-calibre fire in the belly during a flak-suppression attack. With his blazing Phantom tumbling end over end at 100ft AGL, he waited until the cockpit was facing skywards before pulling the handle. His 'chute opened seconds before his boots hit the ground and the rescue helicopter snatched him from approaching VC militia.

Even in the early months the increasing congestion at Da Nang made a second airfield vital, so the Marines established an 'instant strip' at Chu Lai in 1965. This enabled six Phantom squadrons to operate from the Republic. Invented at the Marine Corps Development Center, Quantico, SATS (Short Airfield Tactical Support) enabled Marines to put an aircraft carrier deck facility on land, in effect, in around 90 hours. SATS typically embraced 75ft × 2,000ft of interlocking pierced aluminium mats, including mobile catapulting and arresting (MOREST) gear. Chu Lai took slightly longer to establish because it was built on beach sand and plagued by mosquitoes. It hardly had any facilities for aircraft servicing, or

human comfort. Phantoms were maintained in the open by men living in tents and under constant threat of VC mortar attack. MAG-32, consolidating elements of MAG-12 and MAG-13, was established and by 1969 four Marine F-4 units were flying from Chu Lai, leaving only VMCJ-1 with its RF-4Bs at Da Nang where photo-recce back-up facilities could be provided. Chu Lai remained in use until 1970. It was certainly front-line living for those based there. The VC made it a priority target as soon as it was set up, surrounding it with 3,000 regular troops. In repelling the threat, Phantoms barely had time to pull up their landing gear before dumping their warloads on the siege force. After sustaining 600 casualties, the attackers withdrew. Chu Lai was hard on aircraft. Apart from the primitive servicing conditions the aluminium runway quickly wore out the narrow, high-pressure F-

Below: A hefty Mk 77 napalm fire bomb canister is gingerly driven by an MAG-46 ordnanceman on to the VMFA-134 flight-line. The intake grills on the F-4S are FOD screens used during engine ground runs. The aircraft, F-4S BuNo 153856, has it RAT extended. (Frank B. Mormillo)

4B tyres. Phantoms were kept on base when squadrons changed over, and were re-marked for the incoming unit's use. Eventually they were exchanged for specimens fresh from USN overhaul, carried out under contract to Nippi at Atsugi, Japan.

A third base was subsequently established at Nam Phong, Thailand, 300 miles West of Da Nang, during 1972. VMFA-115 *Silver Eagles*, having flown four tours from Da Nang in 1965–66, moved to Chu Lai and thence to Iwakuni. Returning to Da Nang in April 1972 with MAG-15, they flew alongside VMFA-232 *Red Devils* and -212 *Lancers* on many FAC-controlled air strikes in South Vietnam and Laos to help repel the spring invasion. In June 1972 they took up residence at the new facility at Nam Phong with VMFA-232. Like Chu Lai, this was initially a 'bare bones' base, though with permanent runways which were easier on the landing gear and hydraulics. The Seabees gradually set up aircraft shelters, mess halls and even a chapel alongside the 10,000ft runway. Operations there continued after the ceasefire, and Phantom strikes were flown against Khmer Rouge positions in Cambodia up to August 1973.

Although most Marine activity was confined to South Vietnam and the Laotian trails, with some missions in the RP I region of the North there were numerous MiGCAP sorties. Fighter escort was flown for EF-10B or EA-6A radar-jamming missions, and for A-6A interdiction strikes right up to Hanoi and Haiphong in RP VIB. It was on a MiGCAP from the Tonkin Gulf that the Marines scored their first MiG kill since the Korean War. VMFA-333 *Shamrocks* flew alongside VF-74 from the USS *America* from 5 June 1972 to 24 March the following year, the first of several USMC fighter squadrons to operate Phantoms from carriers. Maj Lee 'Bear' Lasseter, the squadron XO, and Capt 'Li'l' John Cummings were well established on a MiG intercept on 10 September when their F-4J's radar went down. Next day they engaged a trio of MiG-21s north of Hanoi (while at the helm of BuNo 155526/'Shamrock 201'). Although it took four Sparrows and a pair of AIM-9Gs from Lasseter and his wingman, one MiG was put down and another scared off. The third returned to the attack and Lasseter managed to damage it with a final Sidewinder shot. Sadly, both Phantoms received mortal harm from an exploding SAM minutes later and all four men went 'feet-wet' to bail out. Lasseter was voted Top USMC Aviator of 1972 and took over command of his unit when the previous CO went down during a recce escort run.

An earlier MiG kill was scored by Capt Doyle D. Baker USMC, but in a USAF Phantom (F-4D 66-8709, call-sign 'Gambit Three') appropriately named *AWOL*. He was on exchange with the 13th TFS *Black Panthers* of the 432nd TRW at Udorn and scored his kill with an AIM-4D Falcon—one of only five with the Hughes missile in Vietnam.[6] Capt Baker elected to stay with the USAF afterwards.

A third kill was shared by Capt Lawrence G. Richard USMC, piloting a 432nd TRW F-4E (67-0239, call-sign 'Dodge One') with a USN back-seater, Lt-Cdr Michael J. Ettel. Their MiG-21 went down during a weather recce flight on 12 August 1972. The Marines' only loss to a MiG came on 26 August that summer when one of VMFA-232's BARCAP F-4Js (BuNo 155811) was jumped by a 'Fishbed' just before the unit's departure from SEA. Their motto was 'First to Fight', and they were the last to leave the war zone too.

The majority of F-4 losses were to groundfire, particularly .50-calibre guns which were sited at innumerable points in the jungle in wait for low-level flyers. It was not unusual for squadrons to lose up to ten aircraft during a tour, mainly from this cause and often from unseen groundfire. According to a October 1973 DoD Comptroller report, the US Navy and Marines lost a gross of F-4B/Js to hostile fire up to January 1973, as shown in Table 6.

Marine Phantoms in Vietnam racked up extraordinary sortie rates. VMFA-314 claimed the record with 28,000 combat sorties. Mostly these were variations on CAS, including cover for the insertion and extraction by helicopter of small recce teams in the jungle. Flying over dense, hostile forest to find and deliver ordnance against elusive ground targets in a heavily laden Phantom (with a stall speed of around 160kts) required considerable skill. The two-man cockpit was a real asset. Often the target was a single hut, or an anonymous map location

Left: Marine Reserve unit VMFA-112 *Cowboys*, from Dallas, Texas, took part in 'Red Flag 81-4' in their F-4Ns. Here they are being prepared for the return trip, the loader being used to raise the wing tanks. This aircraft, BuNo 150643, was passed on to VMFA-321 and then entered AMARC as '8F/121' on 22 September 1983. It was still there seven years later. (Frank B. Mormillo)

marked by 'Willie Peter' rockets from a FAC, and the slow-moving spotter could not locate sources of ground fire until it had opened up on the aircraft. The 'Rattlers' skipper, Lt-Col Miller, was shot down in this way while attacking a tracked vehicle in October 1967, and a second Phantom was lost a few days later on a similar mission. But there were spectacular successes too. Marine Phantoms played a considerable part in saving Khe Sanh and in relieving a beleaguered ARVN Regiment at Ba Gia in 1965.

President Nixon's incremental withdrawal of forces from Vietnam brought about a commensurate reduction in Phantom strength. The first to leave were VMFA-334 *Falcons* in August 1969. VMFA-542 were back at El Toro, base for the West Coast units, early in 1970 and VMFA-513 were reduced to cadre status later that year, before requipping as an AV-8A Harrier unit. While the F-4B remained in front-line use throughout the war, by the autumn of 1972 several squadrons, including those at Nam Phong, had upgraded to the F-4J. Others among the squadrons which survived the 30 per cent cut in post-war Marine strength graduated to the F-4N. In 1976 eleven squadrons still flew Phantoms with 120 'active' aircraft and 27

Reserve units were equipped with them. One of the busiest was VMAT-101 *Sharpshooters*, which trained Marine Phantom crews for a quarter of a century at Yuma, Arizona. Their work on Phantoms ceased in October 1987 when F/A-18 Hornet instruction began. The *Sharpshooters* had merged with the other training squadron, VMAT-102 *Hawks* in 1974 to become the largest USMC Phantom operator, with 36 aircraft on charge. Reserve training became the task of VMFA-321 *Black Barons* at Andrews AFB, Maryland, home of the first Reserve F-4 squadron. Post-Vietnam they set up MAWTS-1 (Marine Aviation, Weapons & Tactics Squadron One) at Yuma to teach CAS. Valuable improvements in air-to-air procedures were also pioneered by this unit at the Yuma ACMI range. Other Reserve units swapped their Crusaders for Phantoms throughout the decade, VMFA-112 *Wolfpack* being the last to re-equip. They also had the distinction of becoming the last USMC Phantom unit, having moved to the F-4S in 1985. Other late converts were VMFA-134 *Smokes*, an El Toro Reserve squadron which changed from Skyhawks to F-4Ns in 1983.

Kanoehe Bay, the first target for the Japanese forces during the infamous attack on Pearl Harbor, was the base for three F-4J/S squadrons, VMFA-212 *Lancers*, -232 *Red Devils* and -235 *Death Angels* throughout the 1970s and 1980s as part of MAG-24. All were ex-F-8 units with Vietnam experience. They were required to 'forward-deploy' one of the squadrons on a six-monthly rota basis to Iwakuni. Regular participation in 'Red Flag' and 'Top Gun' exercises were also part of the syllabus. VMFA-235 *Death Angels* had the last Phantoms in the 'WestPac' area. They re-established at Kanoehe Bay late in 1989 on the F/A-18C Hornet. The final front-line unit to change Phantoms for Hornets was VMFA-312 *Checkerboards*. They had flown highly decorated Phantoms since the

[6] Refer to 'The Falcon Fiasco' in Chapter 9 for a full account of the AIM-4D's strengths and shortcomings, and the other successes achieved with the missile.

TABLE 6: F-4 B/J LOSSES TO HOSTILE FIRE IN SOUTH-EAST ASIA, 1965–JANUARY 1973									
	1965	1966	1967	1968	1969	1970	1971	1972	01/73
South Vietnam	1	8	8	21	10	7	–	2	1
North Vietnam	8	12	25	11	1	–	1	15	1
Laos	2	5	1	–	3	2	–	1	–

Left: Up for maintenance, an F-4S displays its vari-ramp in the seldom-seen, fully jacked-out, supersonic configuration. (Frank B. Mormillo)

the first time too when 'Rattlers' battled it out with several F-100 units. They also held exercises with the illustrious 555th TFS *Triple Nickel* F-15A squadron at Luke AFB, Arizona. In the spring of 1980 they joined VMFA-531 aboard the USS *Coral Sea* in the Gulf of Oman during the Iranian hostage crisis. This was the first time that Marines had occupied both the fighter slots in the Carrier Air Wing (CVW) since the Second World War. Their Phantoms were painted with red and black recognition stripes to prevent confusion with Iranian F-4s had they been required to intervene in the ill-fated rescue attempt, Operation 'Eagle Claw'.

VMFA-333 *Shamrocks* also took to the waves with CVW-8 on the USS *Nimitz*'s maiden cruise in 1976, filling gaps while the regularly assigned Navy units learned to fly their new Tomcats. At the same time VMFA-451 *Warlords* were operating their F-4Js from the deck of the USS *Forrestal*, before going on to become the first F-4S users. VMFA-531 were in fact scheduled to fly the F-14A. In anticipation they deactivated and moved to Beaufort in June 1975 to study the flight manuals, but cancellation of the whole USMC Tomcat plan took the squadron back to El Toro and their F-4Ns for another eight years.[7] When they eventually switched to the F/A-18 Hornet like the other eleven active-duty F-4 squadrons, they took on an aircraft with a greater 'clean' range capable of carrying a similar warload. The Hornet's computers made up for the 50 per cent reduction in crew to some extent, but its radar and CCIP attack modes undoubtedly confer greater and more consistent accuracy with regard to ordnance—a major priority in the CAS scenario.

[7] VMFA-122 were scheduled to become the first USMC F-14 Tomcat unit. They duly laid down their F-4Bs on 14 August 1974, but the plan was scrapped and they returned to the F-4J on 4 December 1975.

early 1960s, progressing through the J and S models as they became available from USN squadrons or the NARF Noris re-work line. By January 1983 all four Beaufort-based East Coast squadrons (VMFA-115, -122, -333 and -451) had the F-4S.

Other war veteran squadrons continued to give valuable post-war service. VMFA-323 *Death Rattlers* became the Marine Corps' most proficient air-to-air exponents, consistently beating Aerospace Defense Command F-106s in 1973 'College Dart' exercises at Tyndall AFB, Florida. It was also the only USMC West Coast unit to be assigned to NORAD (North American Air Defense), completing 26 assignments for the air defence of the USA. Joint exercises were flown with the USAF Air National Guard units for

6. ANGLOPHANTOMS FOR THE ARK

McAir realized the export potential of their Phantom very early in its development. From 1959 onwards their sales teams approached the Canadian and French Governments, but it was the British market which seemed most attractive. The Royal Navy was seeking replacements for its Sea Vixen fleet defender and Scimitar attacker, and the Sandys defence plans of 1957 left no obvious successors. From 1960 tentative approaches were made to Rolls-Royce concerning a possible Spey-powered F-4B. The success of the USN F-4B and the Phantom's adoption by the USAF all helped to focus minds on the obvious advantages of the type. McDonnell's choice of RNAS Yeovilton, Somerset, in south-west England, as a staging point for the F-4B visit to the 1961 Paris *Salon* could hardly have been more pointed. However, Her Majesty's Government opted for the promising, home-produced P.1154 supersonic V/STOL aircraft in 1963 for both Royal Navy and RAF use, with the TSR-2 and the AW.681 transport completing an indigenous defence package. None of these designs reached service use. McAir, noted for their persistence, continued to make increasingly attractive F-4 offers, particularly to the Royal Navy who were never happy with

the P.1154's cost, intended delivery schedule and BS.100 engine. They preferred the Spey, a point not lost upon McAir, who also took the initiative of testing the double-extending nosewheel leg on an F-4B in 1963 to prove the aircraft's compatability with British deck catapults.

The cancellation of the RN P.1154 in 1964 cleared the way for the Phantom. Known originally as F-4B(RN), then F-4J(Spey), the design had been named F-4K when the Navy placed orders for two prototypes on 1 July 1964. With the election of a Labour government in October 1964 came a policy of distrust and cancellation of UK defence projects, leaving the aerospace industry with only the P.1127 as a potential combat aircraft project. Large-scale purchase-on-credit of C-130K, F-111K and F-4 aircraft was advocated as a cost and time-saving

policy. As a palliative, the British manufacturers were offered 50 per cent (later 40 per cent) of the value of each F-4 in manufacturing parts and equipment for the aircraft. In practice, this usually meant the licence-building of US components, which increased costs and stretched delivery timetables. Biting the bullet, BAC Preston agreed to build the aft section of the airframe (normally produced by Fairchild for US Phantoms), while Shorts at Belfast were contracted to make outer wing sections. Ferranti licence-built the AN/AWG-10 radar, and another thirty British companies won contracts for components ranging from the AN/AJB-7 bombing computer to the cockpit instrumentation.

The most important alteration to the F-4J design, which formed the basis for UK models, was, of course, the Rolls-Royce Spey turbofan. On paper, this

Right: 767 Naval Air Squadron's XT863 shakes the windows at RAF Abingdon as it takes off on 18 September 1971. RNAS Yeovilton received this Phantom on 31 July 1968 to commence training of Royal Navy and RAF crews. Later it flew with 892 NAS and was decorated with the logo 'Red Thistle Flight' to mark a visit by Prince Charles. It divided the rest of its career between Nos 43 and 111 Squadrons RAF and was retired in February 1989. (Richard L. Ward)

Left, upper: XT863 at Yeovilton on 14 July 1971 with everything out. (Richard L. Ward)

Left, lower: 700P NAS took delivery of XT859 in May 1968 and in September of that year demonstrated the muscular might of the Phantom to the Farnborough crowds. A year later it set a record for the west–east 'pond' crossing, winning the Transatlantic Air Race. After an extensive RAF career at Leuchars the jet was ingloriously dumped at Adams' scrapyard in Glasgow. *Sic transit gloria mundi!* (Richard L. Ward)

light-up above 45,000ft. Rolls-Royce at Hucknall developed the Spey 202 with many improvements, particularly to the fuel scheduling. However, the diminished performance of the F-4K had to be accepted, including a Mach 1.9 upper speed limit compared to the F-4J's Mach 2.1. Delays in the redevelopment of the powerplant/intake/nozzle combination also added nearly two years to the proposed service entry date.

However, the great advantages of the F-4 outweighed these compromises and the testing programme proceeded at Edwards AFB, California, and NATC Patuxent River, Maryland. YF-4Ks XT595 and XT596 were fitted with instrumented nose probes for airframe and systems tests while carrier trials were effected on board the USS *Saratoga* with XT857 and XT597. The latter was the first Phantom to be delivered to the UK. It reached the A&AEE's Naval Test Squadron in 1967 and remained there for its entire career. On 30 April 1968 700P NAS (Naval Air Squadron) was formed at RNAS Yeovilton to conduct initial Fleet trials while further carrier tests continued at RAE Bedford's dry-land 'deck' and on board HMS *Eagle*. *Saratoga* continued to provide a deck for Carquals, though the ship was somewhat scarred by the experience. The increased downward thrust angle of the Spey and its higher EGT punished the deck more than the F-4J's J79s, and deck plates were buckled and holed by the blast. HMS *Ark Royal* had to be fitted with water-cooled deck plates and blast deflectors.

F-4Ks, known to the RN as Phantom FG.1s, began to emerge from St Louis in

offered a 25 per cent increase in thrust, reducing take-off distances by one-third and at the same time improving fuel consumption by an equal ratio. Set against these obvious attractions was the need to redesign the entire centre-section of the fuselage because the Spey was shorter but fatter than the J79. The fuselage width was increased by six inches, the intake frontal area was enlarged by 20 per cent to increase air-flow and the fuselage beneath the engine bay was deepened. Titanium had to be substituted for other metals in parts of the aft fuselage to allow for higher EGTs. The totally redesigned, wider engine bay interfered with the drag-reducing area-rule contours, while the greater depth caused more base-drag. These factors tended to negate many of the anticipated top-end performance advantages of the Spey.

After the YF-4K's first flight on 27 June 1966 with McAir test pilot Joe Dobronski at the controls, the aircraft (XT595) embarked on trials to test the Spey 201. Few problems had been indicated in bench tests and early test flights reinforced the predictions of improved fuel consumption and better acceleration at low altitude. At higher altitude it was apparent that the performance was inferior to that of the F-4J. Slow throttle response and rapid fluctuation of the flame pattern ('buzz') at 74 per cent reheat were coupled with erratic burner

TABLE 7: F-4J AND PHANTOM FG.1 COMMON DESIGN FEATURES

1. No 7 fuel cell in upper rear fuselage to counterbalance extra weight of AWG-10/Aero-27A weapons system. Cell reduced in size in FGR.2 to house HF transmitter and antenna coupler.
2. Westinghouse AN/AWG-10 pulse-Doppler radar fire control system, licence-built by Ferranti as AWG-11/12.
3. AJB-7 bombing system (similar also to F-4D).
4. Deletion of AAA-4 IR sensor, made possible by improved radar guidance of Sparrow and better internal IR tracking of later Sidewinder missiles.
5. Strengthened main undercarriage and 30 x 11.5in Type VIII tyres in bulged wheel wells.
6. Slotted stabilator, but anhedral angle reduced slightly to enable increased rotation angle with double-extending nosewheel leg.
7. Drooped ailerons (16.5° in neutral droop position).
8. Tail-hook strengthened to 4.8g.
9. Goodyear/Auto Specialties wheels and brakes, but with Hyro-Wire/Dunlop anti-skid system similar to F-4C/D.

Some of the UK specifications fed back into the design of the F-4J. The first two YF-4Ks were built in Block 26 with the first five F-4Js, to use common jigging.

1967–68 at a time when Phantom production was peaking at seventy aircraft a month in response to requirements in Vietnam. They arrived with the same Martin-Baker Mk H5 seats as their USN counterparts (apart from the original six F4H-1s which featured Stanley models). These were subsequently upgraded to zero–zero Mk H7 standard with an under-seat rocket unit. The flight control system was provided by GE, based on their system for the Republic F-105. The armament was standard—the Raytheon AIM-7E-2 Sparrow[1]—and the secondary armament was the AIM-9D Sidewinder, to be superseded by the 'Golf' later in the FG.1's career. FG.1s were not equipped with gun pods in RN service. For ordnance carriage the standard Triple Ejector Rack (MB Metals TER-9a) was replaced by the ML ERU 119 twin-piston Ejector Release Unit which could carry three 1,000lb bombs rather than the TER-9a's trio of 500-pounders. The Royal Navy's FG.1s were expected to deliver the 1,000lb HEMC or BL.755 cluster unit, and the economy-conscious British expected unused ordnance to be brought back aboard the carrier rather than ditched; the ERU

119 fixture was tough enough to cope with landing stresses of that order.

On the cancellation of the P.1154 the Navy was promised 140 F-4Ks. Cost overruns and politics intervened, reducing the total buy to the 50, plus two prototypes, planned before the cancellation of the P.1154. Increasingly, the political climate of the time limited Britain's defence interests to the European context. HMS *Eagle* was to have operated the second sea-going FG.1 squadron. According to her Captain, J. D. Treacher, it would have cost about £5 million to make her fully Phantom-capable. The money was not made available and HMS *Ark Royal*, after an extensive refit, became the only RN Phantom

carrier. Twenty of the Navy's FG.1 order were therefore diverted straight to the RAF.

Yeovilton's 700P NAS, with US-trained instructors heading the roost, received the first seven service FG.1s between June and October 1968. The type's public début was at the Farnborough SBAC in September, when XT859 gave a taste of the brute power of the Spey Phantom. Having completed its acceptance trials programme in January 1969, 700P provided the basis for 767 NAS, which trained air crews for 892 NAS (the front-line unit) and the RAF's first FG.1 squadron, No 43, which was forming at RAF Leuchars in Scotland. Several of 767's Phantoms had RAF green-grey camouflage to remind the Navy that they were on loan, as well as the Squadron's 'Ten Ton Budgie' golden eagle fin decor. 767 taught all-altitude interception, CAP and ACM, and crews also spent range-time on their secondary roles, air-to-ground weaponry and CAS. The Squadron's regime was fairly brief. The comparatively minor requirement for RN training made a separate squadron at Yeovilton too costly, so all FG.1 activity was concentrated at RAF Leuchars from September 1972.

---

[1] Aired in Chapter 10. An extended option on the improved AIM-7F Sparrow was also offered but not taken up.

Right: Hellenic Armed Forces VIPs were no doubt impressed by this deluge of 2in rockets released from an FG.1 in raging reheat. 892 NAS arranged a show of firepower for the Greeks' visit to *Ark Royal* on 26 October 1978. (Via Richard L. Ward)

Left, top: The relatively uncluttered front cockpit of the FG.1. The 'needles and dials' include the standard attitude and horizontal display indicators (at centre, below the radar scope repeater), altimeter and fuel/engine status instruments (at right) plus missile status and radar mode select (at left). Note also the simplified 'dogbone' weapons selection panel behind the stick. (FAA Museum)

Left, centre: The forward left console, dominated by the all-essential throttles, plus canopy jettison and landing gear control 'lollipop' levers. (FAA Museum)

Left, bottom: The back-seater's cockpit in the FG.1 differed little from that of the US Navy variants, and focused on radar management. (FAA Museum)

892 NAS moved there from 19 September, and all 767's jets were transferred to the POCU/PTF (Phantom Operational Conversion Unit/Phantom Training Flight) under RAF control. Royal Air Force air crews progressively filled the slots in the Navy squadron until, at the time of 892 NAS's decommissioning, half its crews were RAF men. Flt Lts Harry Hamilton and Chris Hirst were the first 'crabs' to make 100 deck landings. With such small numbers involved, both 767 and the PTF were able to tailor the syllabuses to suit individuals' experience. In all cases there was a strong emphasis on air-to-air tactics: on virtually all flights to and from attack sorties in Scotland, crews managed around 20 minutes of ACM.

When Lt-Cdr Brian Davies AFC took command of the newly commissioned 892 NAS on 31 March 1969 his squadron adopted a large red fin flash and an omega symbol as their motif on the assumption that they would be the last fixed-wing RN flyers. They flew the FG.1 with distinction for nearly ten years. HMS *Ark Royal*'s refit was not completed until February 1970, so Carquals had to be made aboard the long-suffering *Saratoga*. Once again her deck plates shrivelled and melted under the fiery tongues of Speys at full blast. Four FG.1s embarked, suitably marked 'USS Saratoga' beneath their fins, for a week in October 1969. The brief deployment brought a taste of action when the 'Sara' was put on alert in the Eastern Mediterranean during the Lebanon Crisis. RN Phan-

TABLE 8: ROYAL NAVY PHANTOM FG.1 UNITS

Unit	Established	Disbanded	Comments
700P NAS	30/04/68	00/02/69	Intensive Flying Trials Unit. Based at Yeovilton.
767 NAS	14/01/69	01/08/72	Training unit, based at Yeovilton. Trained over 100 air crew.
POCU/PTF	01/09/72	31/05/78	Post Operational Conversion Unit/Phantom Training Flight.
892 NAS	31/03/69	15/12/78	Only operational RN unit.

toms flew a number of air defence sorties with resident F-4Js of VF-103 *Sluggers*.

The *Saratoga* visit was the start of a long relationship with USN F-4 'Fitrons' during joint NATO and Caribbean area exercises. Cross-decking was arranged with VF-102 *Diamondbacks* on board the USS *Independence* during Exercise 'Landtreadex 75-2'. The legendary Cdr James Flatley III led a contingent of F-4Js, A-6s and A-7s aboard *Ark Royal*. The 'Ark' responded with two FG.1s, a brace of Buccaneers and one of its extraordinary Gannets, which filled in for the E-2B Hawkeye. The British F-4 contingent came away smartly clad in USN leather jackets. Cross-deck activity also involved

RN visits to the USS *Enterprise*, *John F. Kennedy* and *Forrestal* as guests of VF-11 and VMFA-531, one of whose Phantoms received an 'omega' tail job. In September 1975 a trio of 892 NAS aircraft spent four days aboard the USS *Nimitz* with VMFA-333 *Shamrocks*. One FG.1 suffered an undignified engine failure on deck and had to be dropped off at Portsmouth on a lighter when *Nimitz* called in.

USN exchange crews also enjoyed time on *Ark Royal*, including MiG-killer Jerry Beaulier, who was 'borrowed' in 1974. Several very welcome visits were made to NAS Oceana, one by eight FG.1s in April 1976 resulting in 130

ACM sorties against Tomcats from VF-32 and resident T-38s. A March 1976 visit to NAS Cecil Field, Florida, by Cdr H. S. Drake and seven FG.1s was hosted by VA-46 and provided sorties to the Pinecastle range—and Disneyworld. VA-46 personnel apparently discovered that 'trapping' in the RN meant attracting the opposite sex rather than merely heading for the third wire on deck! Another old Navy tradition was gently pointed out in response to the Bicentennial '1776–1976' logos and trim adorning USN jets: one of 892 NAS's Phantoms (XT859) had '876–1976' inscribed on its flank, a reminder of a rather longer naval tradition! The USN had the last 'zap': XV590 was decorated with 1930s-style US insignia and the

Below: Emphasizing the multi-role usage of the Royal Navy's Phantoms, a bomb-laden 892 NAS aircraft is shot from *Ark Royal*'s steam catapult in 1977. The double-extending nose gear made all this possible. (Via Richard L. Ward)

Above: In the air-to-air role the FG.1 carried a complement of AIM-7E-2 SARH Sparrow III missiles plus up to four AIM-9D/G heat-seeking Sidewinders. In this photograph one of the latter zooms away from the magnificent Phantom. (HMS *Ark Royal* via Richard L. Ward)

Below: XV589 blasts the deck plates of HMS *Ark Royal* seconds before launch. In June 1980 this aircraft crashed on approach to RAF Alconbury when its radome opened and folded back. It was one of the first FG.1s to be transferred from the nautical life to Leuchars' *Treble One* Squadron. (Via Richard L. Ward)

legend 'Colonial Navy' during its last visit to Oceana in 1978.

Attack practice sorties were often flown to USN ranges, including SINKEX ordnance attacks on old hulks with 1,000lb bombs. On one of these the FG.1s found only a patch of bubbles for their target: the US Navy Air Wing had got there first. On a previous occasion the reverse situation had occurred. 892's favourite practice range was Vieques Island in the Caribbean, where mock airfields, SAM sites and fuel dumps made excellent targets for their 20-degree dive-bombing and MATRA 68mm rockets.

In July 1973 Exercise 'Sally Forth' yielded a record number of launches from *Ark Royal*'s cramped deck. The Squadron diarist recorded that 'the deck looked as though the FDO had had a brainstorm'. Space was certainly at a premium and pilots from the US 'supercarriers' were impressed by the tight organization of aircraft movements. Exercises such as 'Solid Shield', 'Teamwork' and 'Ocean Safari' put great pressure on 892's limited numbers and kept training at a level which, according to

USN exchange pilot Lt 'Hollywood' Seider, 'would have been the envy of any USN Air Wing Commander'.

'Landtreadex 75-2' occurred during a cruise which got off to a good Leuchars start. Lt Andy Auld, later to command 800 NAS Sea Harriers in the Falklands War, flew a dozen haggis aboard ship when the Squadron first embarked. Sadly, a failed fridge meant that they did not come close to surviving the sixteen days to Burns Night. During the same commission, XV591/'012R' had to be left ashore at Mayport, Virginia, with hydraulic and pneumatic problems. After two unsuccessful attempts to dispatch the Phantom to its waiting carrier, the aircraft developed further time-consuming faults. It then flew 3,500 miles to catch *Ark Royal* at Rio. The unprecedented flight involved two Victor tankers and a stop at Recife, where language problems meant that refuelling took longer than usual.

Long-distance flying of a much more public kind brought 892 NAS into the spotlight much earlier in their career. The *Daily Mail* Transatlantic Air Race

was held between 4 and 11 May 1969 to mark fifty years since the first non-stop crossing by Alcock and Brown. Britain's most recent defence acquisitions, the Phantom and the Harrier, were pitted against each other in the attempt to travel from the top of the Empire State Building to the top of the Post Office Tower in London. The Navy effort, code-named 'Royal Blue', involved three Phantoms with XT864/'004R' as back-up. They flew between NAS Floyd Bennett, New York, and BAC Wisley, with motorcycles and helicopters to cover the additional distances. Lt-Cdr Brian Davies, 892's CO, and his observer Lt-Cdr Peter Goddard knocked nearly 20 minutes off the RAF's best time, despite their lack of VTOL, but they had to exceed service restrictions on the continuous use of afterburner to do so. See Table 9.

The Squadron frequently detached aircraft within Europe too. Luqa in Malta was visited in 1974, and six Phantoms were detached to Ramstein AB, West Germany, in March 1977. In June the same year all twelve aircraft returned briefly to Yeovilton, their base for the

---

TABLE 9: PROJECT 'ROYAL BLUE'

Date	Aircraft	Crew	Time runway-to-runway	Time overall	Remarks
04/05/69	XT860/'002R'	Lt-Cdr Douglas Borrowman/Lt Paul Waterhouse	5hr 3min 18sec	5hr 30min 21sec	Refuelling problem and tail-wind of only 5kts.
07/05/69	XT861/'003R'	Lt Alan Hickling/Lt Hugh Drake	4hr 53min 10sec	5hr 19min 16sec	Radio problem delayed refuelling; burst tyre on landing.
11/05/69	XT858/'001R'	Lt-Cdr Brian Davies/Lt-Cdr Peter Goddard	4hr 46min 57sec	5hr 11min 22sec	Average true air speed to Lundy Island: 1,100mph.

RAF Harrier times (XV741/XV744, St Pancras Station to Manhattan Island): westbound—5hr 57min; eastbound—5hr 31min; overall distance—3,030nm.
Previous record: 5hr 29min 14sec (KC-135 in 1958).

TABLE 10: ROYAL NAVY FG.1 CAT 5 ACCIDENTS

Date	Aircraft	Unit	Details
03/05/70	XV566/'010R'	892 NAS	Crashed into Lyme Bay, Dorset, while under radar control as 'target' for interception practice during initial intensive flying trials from *Ark Royal*; both crew members killed.
19/05/71	XT862/'156VL'	767 NAS	Crashed into sea 25 miles off Newquay, Cornwall; crew ejected.
29/06/71	XV565/'001R'	892 NAS	Crashed into Atlantic off Florida; crew ejected.
10/01/72	XT876/'160VL'	767 NAS	Crashed into sea off Trevose Head, Cornwall; crew ejected.
25/07/73	XT871/'007R'	892 NAS	On return to Rosyth, launched from *Ark Royal* but engine failure caused crash off bow into Firth of Forth; crew rescued by SAR Wessex.
15/10/71	XT869/'002R'	892 NAS	On approach to Leuchars, crashed into Tentsmuir Forest.
18/05/77	XV588/'004R'	892 NAS	Developed engine fire on take-off from Leuchars; take-off aborted and crew ejected (minor injuries) on advice from overflying FG.1; aircraft burnt out.
12/05/78	XT868/'000R'	892 NAS	Wing hit ground during practice display at Abingdon, one crewman ejected, the other killed.

Left: Decorated with an enlarged Prince of Wales crown, FG.1 XV568 leaves RNAS Yeovilton on 28 June 1977 to take part in the Queen's Review of the Fleet at Spithead. In 1978 the '77' Jubilee logo was replaced by the 892 NAS crest, and in December of that year the aircraft was transferred to the RAF. (Via Richard L. Ward)

Below: A line-up of 892 NAS Phantoms during *Ark Royal*'s last year of service. (Richard L. Ward)

Silver Jubilee Review at Spithead. New flashes were added to the radomes, providing a finishing touch to one of the most attractive naval Phantom paint schemes ever. *Ark Royal*'s Air Group was a powerful defence asset and one which was to be greatly missed during the Falklands conflict less than four years after the 'Ark''s last voyage. By 1978 much of her 1940-vintage machinery was beyond economic maintenance, and aircraft carriers were not in favour in Whitehall.

For their final cruise 892 NAS chose to exit with style. A series of farewell 'events' at Leuchars included an advertisement in the local Press for the Station goat at stud and the immersion of two Squadron streakers in a cold Scottish burn as they attempted to avoid arrest. At the official ceremony the Squadron boss, Lt-Cdr John Ellis, received a giant haggis stuffed with rotten meat and old socks. Meanwhile his Phantoms flew a farewell 'Double Diamond' formation over Leuchars. Their departure was a sad moment for the area, but perhaps less so for the proprieters of a Tyndrum hotel whose back yard had recently received a direct hit from a Phantom which accidentally released its drop tanks after an electrical fault. The Squadron returned to St Athan at the end of its commission on 27 November 1978. XT864, the first to touch down, bravely displayed 'Fly Navy' on its rear fuselage. Disbandment occurred on 15 Decem-

ber and 892's jets were issued to the RAF, XV591 (to No 111 Squadron) being the first and XT865 the last (on 6 June 1980).

It was ironic that the Royal Navy, having taken the lead in UK Phantom purchase, received so few of the aircraft it wanted. The Labour administration's cancellation of the proposed CVA-01 aircraft carrier, which could have operated a substantial number, was the largest single factor in the decline of the conventional Air Group concept. The RAF, which had been to some extent railroaded into buying Phantoms when the Navy's cancellation of P.1154 made the project impracticable, did well out of the deal, partly at the Royal Navy's expense.

7. THE ROLLS-ROYCE SPECIAL

While the Royal Navy was delighted with its F-4K purchase, the RAF was initially less than enthusiastic about having Phantoms apparently forced upon it. Cancellation of the RN P.1154 made the project too costly for RAF-only production and an F-4 derivative then became the only realistic alternative. However, the Spey Phantom seemed unnecessarily expensive for a land-based user. The Navy needed the Spey's extra thrust to propel loaded F-4s from *Ark Royal*'s short catapults and they had a legacy of successful Spey experience with the Buccaneer; Royal Air Force mission requirements could have been met easily by an off-the-shelf, J79-powered aircraft, and this would have meant far more Phantoms for their money. In 1964, however, it was not possible to forecast that the RAF's F-4M would cost twice as much as an F-4D, reach approximately the same overall costs as P.1154 and enter service slightly later. The political necessity of the project made the F-4M the most expensive of all production Phantoms, with a £100 million development cost included in the bill—and no one could have predicted that the best-performing RAF air-defence Phantom would eventually prove to be a stock USN F-4J variant!

On 9 February 1965 a credit agreement was signed with the US Government for the supply of sixty C-130Ks (in place of the AW.681) and what would eventually amount to 118 F-4Ms. Actual costs were still uncertain because of development delays, but additional equipment raised the price tag to around £2 million a copy by 1968. In return, the RAF was to get the Phantom FGR.2 which, as its full designation implied, was a tactical, multi-role type (though only one of its intended functions—strike,

Below: The RAF's first front-line 'Phantom Phlyers', No 43 Squadron, in early markings but after the adoption of letter codes in place of the 'last three' numerals on the fin-cap. Fuselage roundels were moved back on some aircraft from the factory positioning (as on XV576/'D') so that the Squadron's chequerboard stripe did not look as if it were being inhaled by the intakes! (RAF via Richard L. Ward)

reconnaissance or air defence—would be required at a time. Such diversity necessitated a more sophisticated equipment fit than the F-4K's. An inertial nav/attack system (INAS) was built by Ferranti, drawing upon their work for TSR-2. An AD470 HF/SSB radio was installed for over-the-horizon communication on low-level sorties and EMI's grandiose reconnaissance pod was designed for carriage on Station 5, along the centreline. After 1971 the original Spey 202 was replaced with the 204, giving a faster afterburner light-up. Altogether the increased proportion of UK-produced components pushed the British share of the FGR.2 to 45 per cent, compared to 40 for the FG1.

The first YF-4M, XT852, flew on 17 February 1967. Apart from the power-plant mis-match difficulties carried over from the F-4K, further delays were experienced while the INAS and AN/AWG-12 radar were successfully interfaced. Development moved to the UK with XV410 as test vehicle for the HF radio and XV406 as trials aircraft for the EMI recce pod.

TABLE 11: DIFFERENCES BETWEEN F-4K AND F-4M

F-4K (FG.1)	F-4M (FGR.2)
Required ground power unit to start engines.	Could use ground power unit or internal 24V battery (the only F-4 with starting battery).
No HF radio fit.	HF shunt antenna in fin for contact with over-the-horizon ground stations.
Not wired for gun pod in RN use (but re-wired on transfer to RAF).	Could carry SUU-16/A with 20mm M61A1 or SUU-23/A (XM-25) gun pod with self-driven GAU-4/A 20mm gun on Station 5.
No Automatic Lead Computing Optical Sight (ALCOS).	ALCOS and gyro fitted.
No reconnaissance fit.	Could carry modified 370-gallon wing tank with 80% fuel and strobe flasher unit for night recon; could carry EMI recon pod. RF-4M variant not developed.
Carrier-capable. Catapult spools under wing root and hold-back bar fitting.	Carrier capability ruled out at planning stage (originally to have reinforced RN carrier air group).
Double-extending leg for nosewheel gear (40in total extension, giving equivalent of 11kts wind-over-deck for shorter RN catapult launch in hot, windless conditions).	Standard F-4C nose gear.
INAS not fitted.	INAS fitted for pin-point overland navigation (also LCOSS).
AN/AWG-11 radar variant of AWG-10; updated 1971.	AN/ASWG-12 variant of AWG-10 (various updates).
Spey 203 with more rapid re-heat light-up for 'bolters' on deck.	Spey 202.
Carrier approach lights in nosegear door.	No carrier approach lights.
'Quick-fold' radome (180° fold).	Standard F-4J radome.
Slotted stabilators.	Standard stabilators.
Strike camera not generally used.	Strike camera fitted in forward missile bay.
No voice recorder in cockpit.	Voice recorder fitted.

TATTERSHALL PHANTOM COLLEGE

RAF experience of the F-4 pre-dated the arrival of the F-4M as several officers had already completed exchange tours with American units, including one posting with VMFA-531 in 1964. Their response was incredibly enthusiastic, despite all the moans and groans of British industry. Their own Phantoms started to arrive at Aldergrove on 20 July 1968, when XT891 passed through in preparation for issue to No 228 Operational Conversion Unit (OCU) on 23 August. It was the first production aircraft and a 'two-sticker' like the remainder of the first two dozen machines built, featuring a detachable control column in the rear cockpit. Incidentally, XT891 was also the first FGR.2 to appear in the toned-down matt camouflage and 'B' type roundels in 1972.

RAF Coningsby in Lincolnshire in eastern England was chosen as No 228 OCU's base and it remained the centre

of Phantom activity until 1987. No 228 was also the longest-serving RAF Phantom organization, training 1,320 crews up to its disbandment on 31 January 1991. Coningsby's training schedule was organized into four sections—ground attack, air defence, ground crew instruction and (from 1970) management of the Redifon F-4 simulator. In its first six years the emphasis was on ground attack and recce, with air defence as a secondary task, but from 1975 Phantoms replaced Lightning F.2As in RAF Germany (RAFG) as air defenders and were in turn replaced by Jaguar GR.1s for the attack mission. No 228 OCU therefore concentrated on developing the versatile Phantom's air-defence capability. Its commanding agency became No 11 Group, Strike Command, rather than No 38 Group, Air Support Command, as in the 'Fighter/Bomber/Strike/Attack' (FBSA) period. Coningsby's syllabuses then moved more into line with the air defence schools man-

aged by Leuchar's POCU/PTF. It therefore made sense to combine the two activities on one base, leaving Coningsby free to commence Tornado F.2 training from 1985. The latter aspect of this plan was frustrated by delays in the Foxhunter radar for Tornado, though concrete ballast-filled aircraft began to arrive at Coningsby in November 1984.

On 22 April 1987, after eighteen years of residency, 228 OCU flew two Phantom four-ship formations over the aero-

Right, upper: The RAF bought Phantoms for the striking power so amply displayed in this view of XV432 on No 6 Squadron, loaded with three AIM-7E-2 Sparrows, an SUU-23/A gun pod, six SNEB rocket pods and a KB-18 strike camera unit. (Via Richard L. Ward)
Right, lower: When No 41 Squadron officially re-formed at RAF Coningsby on 12 July 1972 their Phantom FGR.2s looked ike this. An EMI recce pod hangs beneath XV418/'C'; the code letter is just visible beneath the 'Free French' cross and crown tail marking. Larger code letters were acquired later. (Via Richard L. Ward)

Above: Coningsby's armourers load 20mm shells into an SUU-23/A gun pod before a 1974 sortie. (Richard L. Ward)

drome as a farewell gesture. They carried the markings of No 64 Squadron, the OCU's 'shadow' designation since 1970. Eighteen Phantoms then departed in five waves, the last leaving by 1040Z. The Phantom ASF disbanded on 30 June 1987 and Leuchars' F-4 population rose to fifty-four, including the resident Nos 43 (*Fighting Cocks*) and 111 (*Treble One*) squadrons. Moving to Leuchars took the students closer to their Scottish training areas and reduced the load on the air defence radar network covering the southern and central United Kingdom. A plan to centralize Phantom activity at RAF Wattisham in Suffolk was ruled out, to avoid overcrowding the airspace in that radar area.

Despite the general decline in RAF Phantom activity, No 228 OCU was still flying twenty aircraft as 1990 began, but disbandment was already planned for March 1991 and was actually brought forward two months. All but three of their aircraft had departed by 23 January mostly to Wattisham, and the last, XT906/'CH', left to RAF St Athan on 21 March.

At its inception No 228 OCU had eighteen instructors, trained on USAF F-4Cs. Navigators were given a six-week lead-in course on AWG-12 and INAS before joining their pilots for the main programme. Initially, this covered handling and weapons deliveries, with 'live' and practice weapons sorties, often on the Cowden range. The FGR.2's INAS was fundamentally similar to the Litton package contained in the F-4D, using an analogue inertial platform and navigation computer linked to radar-ranging for semi-automatic or manual 'visual' or 'radar' bombing. In its 'all-up' configuration, the INAS would hold six waypoints fed in either before or shortly after take-off (based on a flight-plan with 'legs' no longer than 500nm each), after which time radar offsets and prominent landmarks would be used to compensate for the inevitable drift in the system. Used for general navigation to assist with complex attack and evasion routes at low altitude, a 'look-up' option furnished precise data on the nav displays pertaining to height, distance to the next waypoint or target, or from an OAP, and wind correction factors. 'Blind' radar bombing employed the customary sector scan sweep, with inertially driven, ground-stabilized cross-hairs superimposed on

the target.[1] Weapons release would follow automatically once the system had been 'committed' and, for safety purposes, a handy read-out furnished data showing the height deviation from ideal parameters, backed up by a warning lamp which lit up on the control panel to inform the crew if they were uncomfortably close to the ground. This helped to guarantee safe clearance from the effects of the ordnance. However, the level of accuracy available during true 'blind' bombing left something to be desired, and it was customary to use the INAS simply to help the crew get to the target area before reverting to trusty drift-assisted visual deliveries using the Automatic Lead-Computing Sight (ALCOS, functionally identical to the American LCOSS) for level and dive manoeuvres—the time-honoured Phantom technique. Ballistics were available for the RAF's full range of bombs, rockets and guns, including the Royal Ordnance 1,000lb 'iron' bomb 'family', Hunting Engineering BL.755 cluster bomb, SNEB/Matra 68mm rockets, the strap-on underbelly GE SUU-23/A 20mm 'Gat' gun and free-fall nuclear weapons, together with the various pre-planned attack modes, by means of 'ballistic plugs' that were inserted into the weapons aiming computer before a mission via a special box. It was considered a more elegant solution than the American 'dial a bomb' approach, and it offered enough flexibility for most air-to-ground solutions on any given mission.

From July 1974 the emphasis shifted to air defence. For this mission pilots learned to fly the Phantom, gained their instrument rating and practised intercepts and visual IDs against both high- and low-level targets, including supersonic 'bogeys'. Some ACM was taught but much of this was picked up on the operational squadron postings. Naviga-

---

[1] A fuller description of radar-bombing techniques is given in Chapter 9, in the context of F-4C/D systems. The description of the INAS is based on a translation of a Ferranti document provided to the authors in German, and thus certain terminology may differ from contemporary RAF usage.

tors also learned why the F-4 had a reputation for making back-seaters airsick.

At any stage in the OCU's history the basic courses led to the CONVEX stage, when crews were prepared in far more depth for specific missions and areas of operation, such as RAFG, UK Air Defence and reconnaissance (when Nos 2 and 41 Squadrons specialized with the EMI pod). With up to 22 Phantoms on strength, No 228 was in a position to 'lend' aircraft and instructors to other squadrons for ACM practice and other specialized tuition. In 1969–72 the pressure was on to generate crews for re-equipment of the FBSA units in the UK and the 2nd Allied Tactical Air Force squadrons in RAFG. The process was retarded in 1970–71 by turbine problems with the Spey. Some of the turbine blades had been built to a lower specification than Rolls-Royce desired as a cost-cutting measure, and blade failures, coupled with a shortage of spare engines, meant delays in starting some of the conversion classes. Crews kept their hands in with the Redifon simulator which arrived in April 1970.

No 6 Squadron, alias the *Flying Can-Openers*, were the first Coningsby graduates. Their course began in January 1969 and they achieved operational status, led by Wg Cdr David Harcourt-Smith DFC, on 6 May. With the kudos of being 'First in Phantoms' came the responsibility of proving the aircraft in service use. Many pilots had Hunter or Lightning experience, while the back-seaters were usually Javelin navigators, used to rather less sophisticated equipment. Having just departed from the Mediterranean area after twelve years in Cyprus, No 6 Squadron soon found themselves demonstrating that overseas deployments in strength could be made by Phantoms to compen-

sate for the rapid shrinkage of Britain's defence establishments. The first Phantom deployment was to their former base at Akrotiri for a three-week APC (Armament Practice Camp) in October 1969. Skip- and retard-bombing, 68mm SNEB rocket firing and gun-pod strafing were all practised. Particularly impressive was the destructive force of the 'Gatling' gun: these tended to remain on the *Can Openers'* aircraft most of the time, re-arming and servicing being carried out *in situ*.

The Squadron was extremely active throughout its four Phantom years. One of its last deployments was also to Akrotiri, a short-notice call on 25 July 1974 to move in a dozen aircraft overnight as airfield protection for a month during the Turkish invasion of Cyprus. In its last year also No 6 Squadron pioneered night attacks illuminated by Lepus flares. A flare-dropping Phantom led a section of bomb-carrying aircraft to the target, releasing its flares in a 'pop-up' manoeuvre to permit co-ordinated attacks on the brightly lit target. The technique was not widely adopted, partly because it led to all the problems of visual disorientation which American pilots had encountered with the method in SEA.[2]

The *Can-Openers* parted company with their Phantoms from 30 September 1974, passing their aircraft to No 29 Squadron and moving to the less spectacular Jaguar. They were preceded in this transition by their No 38 Group base-mates at Coningsby, No 54 Squadron, which in

April 1974 became the first Phantom unit to convert to the 'Jag'. Products of No 228 OCU's second course, No 54 commissioned on 1 September 1969 after fourteen years on Hunters. They shared with No 6 much of the operational work-up of the FGR.2 and the overseas proving flights to Tengah, Singapore and Akrotiri. In May 1970 both squadrons flew non-stop from Coningsby to Tengah in 14hr 8min 19sec., an anatomically challenging experience for their crews. No 54 also ran a flight of aircraft equipped to carry the EMI recce pod and developed tactics with this weighty accessory until No 41 Squadron were commissioned to take over the role full-time.

The commissioning of No 41 Squadron in July 1972 completed the trio of No 38 Group's operational units at Conings-

[2] Refer to 'Pave Phantom' in Chapter 10. The all-up system was fundamentally similar to a marriage between the USAF INS/WRCS and USN/MC Doppler radar but included a larger number of separate 'black boxes' (aiding maintenance, as faults were easier to isolate and fix) together with a significant edge in air combat capability (including that which the USAF had hoped for with CORDS), at the expense of only slightly degraded ground-mapping. However, the INAS was never integrated with advanced air-to-surface 'Pave' devices as were its American and FMS land-based counterparts, although AS.37 anti-radar and AJ.168 TV-guided Martel missile capability was wired in to all F-4Ms produced in Blocks 34–38. A 'Pave' F-4M might truly have been a formidable all-rounder, and McAir studied several Model 98 derivatives (on paper only) with this in mind.

Right: FGR.2 XV492/'Q' of No 6 Squadron takes off from Coningsby in January 1974 with a gun pod and a strike camera. The *Flying Can-Openers* nose patch and gunner's stripe on the fin were retained on the Squadron's transition to the less popular SEPECAT Jaguar in 1974. (Richard L. Ward)

by. The Squadron performed the low-level 'tac-recon' mission for five years and participated in long-haul deployments to the Far East. With attack as a secondary role, they excelled in low-level reconnaissance, coming second in the 1974 'Big Click' Competition and winning the Buchanan Trophy for tactical bombing the following year. Sadly, No 41 Squadron also brought to public notice the risks involved in low-level training when XV493 collided with a crop-spraying PA-25 Pawnee near Downham Market, Norfolk, on 9 August 1974. Coningsby's Station Commander, Gp Capt David Blucke, was unable to avoid the Pawnee at approximately 300ft AGL. He and his navigator, Flt Lt Terry Kirkland, and the Pawnee pilot Paul Hickmott, died in the crash.

Having established Coningsby as the centre of RAF Phantom activity, No 228 OCU began the next phase of its programme—training RAFG crews for the 2nd ATAF commitment. Four more squadrons were therefore prepared, Nos 14, 17 and 31 (all ex-Canberra), to be based at Bruggen, and No 2 as a tactical reconnaissance unit at Laarbruch. Their task was to cover the northern section of NATO's Central Region while 4th ATAF tackled the south. The Phantom's service entry more or less coincided with that of the Buccaneer S.2 and Harrier GR.1, facilitating a vast technological leap from the Canberra/Hunter era. RAFG's first Phantom squadron was No 14, which re-formed at Bruggen on 30 June 1970, followed by No 17 Squadron in September and No 31 at the end of 1971. All three were 'mud moving' outfits like their No 38 Group counterparts, but they were also tasked with a nuclear strike capability. In addition, they were trained to fly all-weather interception and armed reconnaissance. Of all these roles, the nuclear mission was the most demanding in time and effort. As the 'sharp end' of RAFG the Phantoms had to maintain a nuclear QRA (Quick Reaction Alert) in rotation at 24 hours' immediate readiness. Usually one or two aircraft stood ready for the 'worst scenario', with their crews in the cockpits

and with one nuclear store hanging from the centreline station, permitting wing tanks and Sparrows to be carried for a hi-lo-lo-hi sortie. Had they been called to action, the QRA aircraft would have been required to put a decisive, sledgehammer halt to a major Soviet armoured movement against the West.

The RAFG CONVEX also provided training in 'counter-air' airfield attacks, interdiction against logistical and communications choke-points and close air support, under FAC direction. Longer-range interdiction was the job of the Buccaneer flyers. Bruggen's squadrons maintained their multiple FBSA roles until 1976, when the more specialized Jaguar arrived to take over.

One of 2nd ATAF's vital components was No 2 Squadron's reconnaissance capability. At a time when Soviet armoured divisions could cover sixty miles a day, heading your way, rapid intelligence-gathering was crucial. Formed at Bruggen on 7 December 1970, the Squadron moved to Laarbruch and became operational on 1 April 1971. It replaced its namesake, the Gutersloh-based, Hunter FR.10-equipped No 2 which had previously provided the photos. While maintaining their usual strike capability, the FGR.2s carried the £1 million, 2,300lb EMI reconnaissance pod (slung under the belly in lieu of the sheet-metal 600 US gallon fuel tank) as their main occupation. This was interfaced with the INAS to assist with the 'bracketing' of the pod's multitude of sensors. The standard 'kit' fitted to the 24ft-long pod comprised a Texas Instruments RS-700 infra-red linescanner set (IRLS), 15ft-long slotted-waveguide aerials of the MEL/EMI Electronics Type P391 Q-band sideways-looking reconnaissance radar (SLRR) and five optical cameras (one forward-, one vertical- and two oblique-facing F95s with 3in lenses, plus a solitary stereo F135) carried fore and aft, all optimized for two mission profiles, 'low-level at 450–500 kts from the deck up to 6,000ft AGL, or medium, from that up to FL 480'. Night-time work employed a fit of four F135s synchronized with the (Block

Right: The scale of operations in Lincolnshire can be judged from this photograph, in which Phantoms from several different units appear on the flight-line. In the foreground are No 29 Squadron, re-formed in December 1974 and retained at Coningsby as part of the UK/ADR fighter force. (Via Richard L. Ward)

34+ F-4M's) wing flash units, built into modified 'greenhouse' outboard fuel tanks, while the sophisticated F126 was introduced later, this being able to produce pin-sharp pictures by means of motion compensation and autofocus at speeds of up to Mach 1.3 and at altitudes as low as 1,250ft AGL. Needless to say, both squadrons tended to make greater use of the 'fast and lo' profile, in keeping with the NATO philosophy of that era, and of all these advanced devices No 2 Squadron crews tended to regard the IRLS as the primary system, which they found to be incredibly sensitive.[3]

Reconnaissance flying required extremely precise navigation and No 2 Squadron probably gained more experience of INAS/radar integration and operational usage than any other unit at the time. Very accurate definition was also obtainable from the SLRR, although its effective use demanded absolutely straight-and-level flying. In effect a search sensor, it was used over successive missions to build up a radar picture of a specific area so that small changes in the images, such as the movement of large numbers of vehicles, could be detected at night or through cloud. The RS 700 IRLS allowed rather more manoeuvrability as it was roll-stabilized up to ±30°. 'Pod' missions were usually flown at altitudes as low as 250ft AGL, often by crews who knew the German landscape intimately after years of flying Canberra PR.7s. Like their USAFE RF-4C colleagues, they flew basically to the map-and-stopwatch method to ensure that

---

[3] *Luftwaffe* and IDF/AF RF-4Es were retrofitted with provision for ground attack (the former being subsequently deleted, owing to the exigencies of the German defence budget), while most USAFE RF-4Cs were specially outfitted with a working nuclear LABS capability. However, only the RAF's Nos 2 and 41 Squadrons practised the recce-strike mission on a day-to-day basis.

their imagery was recorded on the first pass. Their IRLS and SLRR sensors, together with the less-favoured flash illuminator, gave them the only night reconnaissance capability within 2nd ATAF.

During 1975–76 the Bruggen and Laarbruch squadrons re-equipped with the Jaguar. The process was gradual, with Phantoms and 'Jaguar (Designate)' units operating side by side for up to eight months while the latter progressively replaced the F-4s. While the smaller-winged Jaguar offered a smoother low-level ride, a very accurate NAVWASS weapons delivery system and more precise control response at low altitude, the Phantom's power and the advantages of the two-man crew were sorely missed by the RAFG attack units.

KEEPING THE BEAR AT BAY

The second 'career' for RAFG's Phantoms was air defence. Since 1965 Nos 19 and 92 Squadrons had provided this commitment, initially from Geilenkirchen, then at Gutersloh near the East German border, using Lightning F.2As. Early in 1977 the two units gradually worked up their 'Phantom-Designate' AD squadrons at Wildenrath, a process which was completed by 1 April. No 19 was led by Wg Cdr A. J. 'Bugsy' Bendell, who had been a Flight Commander with No 6 Squadron in the early Phantom days. Wg Cdr D. C. Ferguson took on No 92 Squadron. The FGR.2's pulse-Doppler radar and the immense hitting power of its eight missiles made it the unquestioned 'top dog' in NATO's Central Region. Towards the end of 1977

Bitburg's newly arrived Eagles shifted that balance towards the USAFE contingent, and progressive updates to the F-15C left the Phantom somewhat lagging behind technologically, pending the introduction of Sky Flash and newer Sidewinder missiles, which eventually restored the Phantom's powers to the point where it could more than hold its own with the opposition using hit-and-run tactics.

No 19 Squadron's first Phantom arrived at Wildenrath from Laarbruch on 29 September 1976. It was passed on by No 2 Squadron, like most of No 19's aircraft, and several flew with the distinctive triangular markings of their previous owners for months. On New Year's Day 1977 there was a fête and fireworks in the Squadron's HAS area and even louder pyrotechnics from the back end of an FGR.2 which scrambled to mark the start of the Wildenrath Phantom era. The unit's own markings were dark blue and white chequers, later changed to light blue to avoid confusion with the black and white checks of No 43 Squadron The matt grey and green paint was retained, though the base's first light grey Phantom (XV418) arrived at the end of December 1978. No 92 Squadron also received a complement of ex-recce No 2 birds, the first (XV413/'Z') arriving in November 1976. By 13 January the following year it had ten aircraft on strength. This was the official number each squadron declared to NATO, rather than the 12–15 aircraft of the Lightning years. While this reflected the much greater fighting ability of the F-4, it was also a limiting factor for each squadron's tactical planners: aircraft do not always fly when you want them to! NATO required that 70 per cent of the Wildenrath fleet had to be able to be generated within 6–12 hours. This placed a considerable workload on the base ASF to 'keep 'em flying', but the absence of aircraft for maintenance or detachments elsewhere could make things pretty tight. Later the squadrons each received an eleventh 'in-use reserve' aircraft from the deactivating No 29 Squadron to lend a little more flexibility.

Sharing the German base was No 92 Squadron, which officially re-formed on 1 April 1977, flying a four-ship to commemorate the occasion. In October the Squadron celebrated its sixtieth birthday, attended by Second World War rivals Adolf Galland and Bob Stanford-Tuck. Wildenrath's central position on the NATO front line made it a busy base, with visits and exchanges occurring more often than at most RAF establishments. Exercises and deployments were also a major part of the effort. Exercise 'Central Enterprise' was a periodic test of air defences throughout Europe. The June 1985 event took four Wildenrath aircraft to Coningsby for four days and in 1988 the same exercise saw seven operating from Wattisham. Periodic visits to the United Kingdom

were made to help boost the air defences in several 'Elder Joust' exercises. The point was to demonstrate to any potential adversary that assets could very rapidly be moved to meet the threat wherever it was strongest.

In the 1970s the Tactical Air Meet (TAM) events usually included Wildenrath aircraft, as did the Tactical Fighter Meets (TFM) of the 1980s. The Waddington TFM in August 1986 included a No 19 Squadron pair representing one of the 23 units present. They spent a week on the Otterburn and Spadeadam ranges, alongside 1st TFW F-15Cs and 509th BW FB-111As among others. In the same month Wildenrath hosted eleven F-4Ds from the 170th TFS, Illinois Air National Guard, one of which had to be escorted to base after losing its radio and was found attempting to join the traffic at Düsseldorf Airport.

In September 1986 Wildenrath celebrated ten years of Phantom operations, by which time sixty different FGR.2s had flown with the base's units and only three had been lost. One of these (XV471) crashed in July 1986 after losing power on approach to Runway 27 following a flight test to prepare it for deployment to 'Copper Flag' at Tyndall ADWC, Florida.[4] Four other Phantoms did participate, the first RAF F-4s to do so. This Stateside trip was followed up with a visit by six aircraft to 'Red Flag' at Nellis TFWC, Nevada, in October 1987 where they joined the 'Red' 'Aggressor' force. The Wildenrath squadrons repeated the experience in 1988, taking a No 56 Squadron element too. Training began for a 1990 'Red Flag' session but Middle East tensions intervened, taking No 92 Squadron to Akrotiri as part of Operation 'Granby' and putting No 19 Squadron on standby for the same duty. The chance to use the American training facilities, especially the Nellis ACMI range, was 'like gold dust' to RAF crews.

Akrotiri was also the venue for regular APCs. Up to nine aircraft, effectively the entire Squadron, spent a month each spring refining weapons delivery techniques and then returned to Germany to allow the other squadron to take over.

RAF Valley in Wales was the scene of the annual Missile Practice Camp (MPC), when up to five aircraft were detached to keep air crews current in live launches against flare and Jindivik targets. ACM training took crews to Decimomannu and the ACMI range where they fought it out with other NATO pilots.

The most pressing regular commitment was the TACEVAL, an exercise which, as No 19 Squadron's former boss, Wg Cdr Nick Spiller, explained to the authors, 'dominated our lives in those days'. These regular appraisals of the bases' combat capability generated considerable activity. For example, during the November 1986 TACEVAL Wildenrath's aircraft flew 100 sorties in two days, fitting their take-offs between low-level 'attacks' by USAFE F-111s. The June 1988 MAXEVAL increased this total to 120 take-offs and a TACEVAL the following month generated no fewer than 150 missions in three days. Wildenrath had to train for the real thing, which would have involved every attempt by an adversary to saturate RAFG defences with sheer numbers.

This sort of pressure led to some incidents too. Wg Cdr Spiller recalled that in 1977 No 19 Squadron's first boss, Wg Cdr Bendell, was particularly concerned that his men should be able to meet the TACEVAL Battle Flight requirement to launch two QRA Phantoms in under five minutes. He was apparently Duty Pilot on QRA one Saturday when the hooter went. 'Unbeknown to him it was a false alarm, but as he climbed into his cockpit he smashed his mic/tel lead which gave him all his information, so when he was strapped and plugged in he couldn't talk to anyone. Determined not to let the side down in a TACEVAL he started both engines and began to taxy. His navigator, wondering what the hell was going on, tried to gesticulate to him to stop, but nothing was going to stop the Wing Commander. The aircraft lined up on the runway and the navigator thought: "Well, if I leave my canopy open he won't take off . . .", but then he

---

[4] 'Copper Flag' is discussed in Chapter 13.

TABLE 12: ROYAL AIR FORCE FG.1/FGR.2/F-4J(UK) CAT 5 ACCIDENTS

Date	Mark	Aircraft	Unit	Details
09/07/69	FGR.2	XV395	228 OCU	Horncastle, Lincs.
12/10/71	FGR.2	XV479/'J'	54 Sqn	Near Kamp, Denmark. Engine failure on take-off; both crew members ejected.
15/10/71	FGR.2	XT904	228 OCU	Near Coningsby. Lost control in spin over sea near Cromer; crew ejected.
14/02/72	FGR.2	XT913	228 OCU	Hydraulic failure; crew ejected near Cromer.
20/11/72	FGR.2	XV477/'C'	6 Sqn	Flew into high ground 9 miles E of Penrith.
01/06/73	FGR.2	XV397	17 Sqn	Instrument failure near Kempen, Germany; crew ejected but navigator killed.
25/06/73	FGR.2	XV440	31 Sqn	Crashed into sea off Vlieboss, Holland, at night; crew killed.
22/08/73	FGR.2	XV427	17 Sqn	Hit high ground near Siegen, Germany; crew killed.
09/08/74	FGR.2	XV493	41 Sqn	Mid-air collision with Pawnee near Bexwell, Norfolk; 3 killed.
11/10/74	FGR.2	XV431	31 Sqn	Took off from Bruggen with wings not locked; crew ejected.
21/11/74	FGR.2	XV441	14 Sqn	Engine fire near Lang Hent, Holland, on take-off shortly after delivery to Bruggen; crew ejected.
03/03/75	FGR.2	XV416/'H'	111 Sqn	Crashed near River Witham after engine failure on take-off at Coningsby; crew ejected.
18/09/75	FG.1	XV580/'Q'	43 Sqn	Went out of control during rehearsal of formation 'CanadianBreak' near Kirriemuir, Forfar; crew ejected.
24/11/75	FGR.2	XV405	228 OCU	Crashed into sea off Skegness after loss of control; crew ejected.
17/12/75	FGR.2	XV463/'R'	41 Sqn	Flew into Solway Firth near Mawbury after loss of control; crew killed.
23/07/76	FGR.2	XV417/'I'	29 Sqn	Crashed near Mablethorpe after structural failure of starboard wing; crew ejected.
24/07/78	FGR.2	XV483/'Y'	92 Sqn	Hit ground near Hoxter, Germany, during practice interception; crew killed.
04/08/78	FGR.2	XV403/'M'	111 Sqn	Hit sea 58 miles E of Aberdeen during ACM; crew killed.
23/11/78	FG.1	XT598/'E'	111 Sqn	Crashed into St Andrews Bay on approach to Leuchars; crew killed.
28/02/79	FG.1	XV578/'F'	111 Sqn	Crashed into sea off Montrose after engine failure; crew ejected.
05/03/80	FGR.2	XV463/'E'	29 Sqn	Attempted flapless night landing after hydraulic failure but missed arresting cable and crashed; two fire engines also damaged in rescue attempt, one crashing into a ditch and a second into the rear of that vehicle. Aircraft originally Cat 4 but scrapped at Abingdon 08/87.
03/06/80	FG.1	XV589/'P'	111 Sqn	Radome opened on approach to Alconbury while on ACM detachment; crew ejected. Aircraft placed on Coningsby fire-dump.
11/07/80	FGR.2	XV418	92 Sqn	Hit ground during filming for BBC documentary programme near Diepholz, Germany; crew killed.
12/11/80	FGR.2	XV413/'D'	29 Sqn	Crashed into sea in flames 70 miles E of Grimsby at night. Pilot (Sqn Ldr Stephen Glencorse, CO of 29 Sqn) and navigator never found.
09/12/80	FGR.2	XV414/'R'	23 Sqn	Crashed into sea after engine fire 2 miles NE of Lowestoft; crew ejected.
09/07/81	FG.1	XT866/'O'	43 Sqn	Suffered ADI failure on night finals to Leuchars; crew ejected.
14/04/82	FGR.2	XT912/'F'	228 OCU	Low-level mid-air collision with XT903/'X' as aircraft took off; crew ejected. XT903 landed.
07/07/82	FGR.2	XV491/'F'	29 Sqn	Crashed into sea in fog near Cromer; crew killed.
17/10/83	FGR.2	XV484/'C'	23 Sqn	Hit Mt Usborne, E Falklands, 500ft below summit (possible INS failure); crew killed.
07/01/86	FGR.2	XV434/'J'	29 Sqn	Lost control at low level near West Burton, Yorkshire Dales; crew ejected but injured.
03/07/86	FGR.2	XV471/'G'	19 Sqn	Systems failure on approach to Wildenrath during test flight prior to 'Copper Flag' at Tyndall AFB, USA; crew ejected.
26/08/87	F-4J(UK)	ZE358/'H'	74 Sqn	Low-level collision with peak at Trefenter near Aberystwyth; crew killed.
07/09/87	FG.1	XT861/'AC'	43 Sqn	Crashed into sea off Tay estuary after mid-air collision with XT872/'BT' of 111 Sqn in a five-aircraft formation. XT872 landed.
20/04/88	FG.1	XT860/'AL'	43 Sqn	Crashed into sea 28 miles E of Leuchars during 'Elder Forest' exercise; crew killed.
02/08/88	FGR.2	XV501/'B'	56 Sqn	Crashed at Mayenne, France, after technical failure; crew ejected.
23/09/88	FGR.2	XV428/'CC'	228 OCU	Crashed on to runway at Abingdon after crew became disorientated and attempted pull-out from loop at insufficient altitude; crew killed.
18/10/88	FGR.2	XV437	92 Sqn	Crashed near Holzminden, Germany, following loss of power caused by technical failure during high-level sortie on TLP course at Jever; crew ejected.
09/01/89	FGR.2	XT908/'CW'	228 OCU	Crashed into sea off Dundee; pilot (Sqn Ldr Nelson) killed, navigator ejected.
24/04/89	FGR.2	XT893/'W'	56 Sqn	Crashed into sea 48 miles off Flamborough Head following technical failure; crew ejected.
08/01/91	FGR.2	XV462/'G'	19 Sqn	Crashed into sea 20 miles S of Limassol, Cyprus, during 'Granby' detachment to Akrotiri; crew ejected, rescued by 84 Sqn Wessex.
30/10/91	FGR.2	XV421/'F'	1435 Flt	Crashed into sea N of McBrides Head, E Falkland; crew (inc. 'The Ceej' Weightman) killed.

Total attrition, inc. RN FG.1s: FG.1—15; FGR.2—32; F-4J(UK)—1. Total—48.

heard the 'burners light. The aeroplane was last seen rushing down the runway with the navigator swinging on the canopy trying to close it before it came off. They did get airborne, and had nowhere to go, so they spent an hour orbiting Wildenrath to get down to landing fuel weight. This caused its own merriment as one of the biggest gliding championships of all time was taking place and its route took it virtually over Wildenrath. The navigator was continually ducking as gliders whistled by on either side.'

By no means all QRA launches were false alarms. Between the first Battle Flight scramble, at midnight on 31 December 1976, and the last, on 2 October 1991, some 150 scrambles took place to deter aircraft which were potential intruders into the British Air Defence Sector. Some were misdirected civil pilots, but many were Eastern Bloc fighters making a quick dash at the borderline before turning away. Wildenrath's Battle Flight status was maintained on a 24-hour basis for all but the last year of this period.

Left: RAF Bruggen was home to three Phantom units within 2nd ATAF, including No 17 Squadron. FGR.2 XT905 is seen here after a range sortie using the 'Gatling' gun. (Richard L. Ward)

The Phantom constituted a major element in the NATO air defence plans. As a BVR missile-firing stand-off fighter it had to operate at altitudes below the Nike missile system, to the rear of the 'first-line-of-defence' Hawk missile batteries and ahead of the local defence SHORAD line with its Bloodhound and Rapier launchers. It was theoretically possible to ensure that Phantoms would not become targets for any of these systems in a 'hot' IFF situation. They, in turn, would have used their Doppler radar and BVR missiles to 'take out' low- or medium-altitude strike threats.

In an NATO command situation it was clearly necessary to integrate the RAF fighters with the other available types. The advent of the F-15 Eagle made this possible across the whole NATO front. By 1980 the Mixed Fighter Force (MFF) concept was born out of discussions 'over a few beers' between Wildenrath crews and the Eagle pilots of the 32nd TFS at Soesterberg, Holland. Basically, it involved using the Phantoms or Eagles with their superior radar and missile performance to act as the 'battering rams' against an incoming strike force. Between two and four Phantoms would have led other, less capable fighters which would have followed behind to 'take out' any intruders which slipped through the Phantoms' missile 'screen'—the origins of today's 'Gorilla package' tactics. Initially it was a way of taking WGAF F-104G and F-4F inter-

ceptors into the fight, providing them, it was hoped, with a 'clean tail' in order that they could turn in on any targets approaching them and fire Sidewinders and cannon before moving further downthreat. The introduction of the F-16A in NATO did not invalidate the concept because this aircraft still lacked the long-range, head-down radar capability of the Phantom. Flying at between 2,000 and 3,000ft, RAF crews could use their AWG-12 radar to survey the sky from ground level to 70,000ft and detect targets for themselves and for other fighters.

Wildenrath's constant QRA was a hugely demanding business. For nearly fourteen years it held the highest state of readiness anywhere in NATO, with two aircraft, four air crew and six ground crew at five minutes' alert day and night. In the UK, QRA was normally at ten minutes, in recognition of the slightly longer distances to 'the border', and not always kept for 365 days a year. RAFG aircraft were loaded with live weapons under simulated war conditions for many of the Station exercises too. This led to a potentially tragic situation on 25 May 1982 when Flt Lts Roy Laurence and Alistair Invergarity had the misfortune to shoot down one of Bruggen's Jaguars during a simulated airfield attack. The fact that Laurence's master armament switch had not been taped over in the 'safe' position, plus an unreliable circuit breaker in the missile firing electronics,

coupled with some confusion on board the aircraft about following 'unarmed' intercept routines in an armed Phantom, all led to a Sidewinder impacting Flt Lt Steve Griggs' Jaguar. It was the first incident of its kind in the RAF. Griggs, an ex-Phantom pilot, ejected in good order.

The intensity of operations at Wildenrath resulted in some impressive totals of flying hours for local crews. No 92 Squadron's CO in 1989, Wg Cdr Pollington, was the first RAF Phantom pilot to reach 4,000 hours. A four-ship pass was flown to mark the occasion. The late Mike Mahoney, first and only navigator with 4,000 hours, did not reach his total until 1992 when he was serving with No 74 Squadron (Tigers) at Wattisham. After an introductory 'stint' on Javelins in 1968 in Singapore he spent the remainder of his career on Phantoms. His sad death occurred little more than a year after the loss of No 19 Squadron veteran C.J. Weightman, who was lost while on detachment to No 1435 Flight in the Falklands. 'The Ceej' was a tireless organizer of Phantom Meets and photo sessions. His aircraft, XV421/'F', vanished in the icy South Atlantic.

With the easing of tensions across the German border it was inevitable that Wildenrath's pivotal role would decline. No 92 Squadron was the first to disband, on 5 July 1991. The Squadron flew its final sortie on 27 June and stood down from NATO at the end of that month. Their base-mates, No 19 Squadron, remained a little longer. Having celebrated 25 years in Germany on 1 September 1990, both units ceased Battle Flight duties at the end of the month. The Duty dated back to the 1955 Bonn Convention when the defence of Germany became the responsibility of the tripartite forces rather than the Germans themselves. With German reunification in October 1990, Battle Flight QRA was converted to a 10-minute QRA and it became a NATO commitment rather than a national one. The last true Battle Flight sortie was a 90-minute patrol of the Polish border on 2 October by XV498 and XT909. After that, the duty passed to the F-4Fs of *JaboG 35* and *JaboG 36* and the MiG-29s of *JG 3* (with whom Wildenrath's Phantoms had enjoyed some interesting ACM practice earlier in the year). A twelve-ship formation overflew the so-called 'clutch' airfields used by RAFG, and several German cities, on 10 July 1991 as a farewell gesture. The base's last sortie blasted off on 2 October 1991: specially painted 'blue' Phantoms XT899/'B' (No 19 Squadron) and XV408/'Z' (No 92 Squadron) 'scrambled' from the Q-Shed, waited an untypical ten minutes on the runway for the TV camera cars to catch up, and then roared off for the last official launch.

For Wg Cdr Spiller it was a poignant occasion. He had joined No 19 Squadron as a 'first-tourist' and flew its last mission as Commander. His No 2 on the flight had joined in 1969. Flt Lt Phil Williamson's name was painted beneath the front cockpit of XT899 in recognition of his status as the most experienced No 19 Squadron pilot, with the 'high time' navigator's name to the rear. However, Wildenrath's ASF re-marked the aircraft with the names of the Station Commander, Jeff Brindle, and OC Ops, Al Palfrey, before it was flown to the Czech and Slovak Air Force Museum at Kbely on 16 January 1992 for permanent display. Wg Cdr Spiller, who recalled that XT899 was 'a pig to fly', was rather rueful that it was being displayed bearing the names of two officers who never actually flew with the Squadron!

Right, upper: Seldom seen: the main gear of an FGR.2 retracted into the well with doors and other panels removed. (Authors) Right, lower: A section of the port wing of FGR.2 XV406 with panels off to show the density of its hydraulic and control systems. RAF St Athan in South Wales performed all major overhauls on RAF Phantoms in the latter stage of their careers. The ex-No 228 OCU aircraft was being prepared for display at Carlisle in September 1991. (Authors)

No 19 Squadron stood down from NATO on 31 December 1991 and disbanded nine days later, having made their last deployment to Akrotiri only six weeks previously. The title passed to one of the Hawk squadrons in 2nd TWU and it is hoped that the nameplate will eventually be assigned to an operational EFA unit.

KEEPING PHANTOMS CURRENT

During their fifteen years as air defenders the Phantom force received a number of essential modifications to their airframes and systems. One of the earliest and most visible was the Marconi ARO 18228 RWR (radar warning receiver) system, covering frequencies in the 2–20GHz range (E to J bands). It was mounted in a 'box top' fairing on the fin-cap and displayed a range of threats on a screen which was tucked away rather inconveniently in the bottom left of the rear cockpit. Phantoms were fitted with RWR between 1975 and 1978. RAF F-4Ms also received ILS, with the localizer/glide path vanes fitted each side of the fin. Other 'mods' came late in the FGR.2's service life. The last major update was the Digital Computer Sighting System (DCSS) modification to the

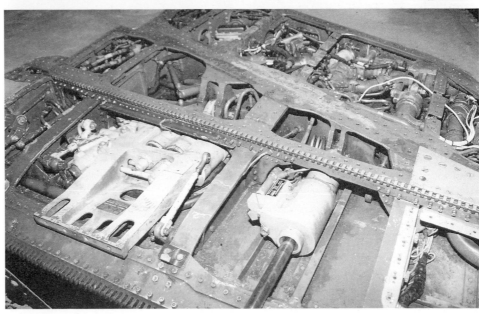

Above: With everything bar the canopies open, No 228 OCU's XT900 blasts through the Mildenhall skies in June 1990. This aircraft was one of 24 'twin-stick' trainers equipped with a removable control column in the rear cockpit to provide basic handling experience for pupils (the instructor in the rear ensuring that the stick was firmly implanted at all times!). (Tim Laming)

radar. This improved definition considerably, particularly at long range, and involved the replacement of all analogue components and substantial modification of the whole AN/AWG-12. Selected Phantoms also received a HOTAS (hands-on-throttle-and-stick) control grip. This enabled the pilot to operate all his weapons switches without moving his left hand from the throttle quadrants. In the late 1980s most aircraft had the Tracor AN/ALE-40 chaff and flare dispensers wired in, with a control panel at the top of the back-seater's instrument panel, and dispensers on the rear of the inner LAU-17 pylons. Although the expending boxes were not always fitted, the systems were regularly wrung out in exercises over water; their use over land tended to result in too many radar-reflective sheep as the creatures devoured the fine metal strips.

Another air defence aid to arrive quite late in the day was the Telescopic Sighting System (TESS). In essence this comprised an Army tank-type spotting sight

fitted to the rear cockpit with its objective lens mounting replacing the port central canopy window. Known as the 'poor man's TISEO', it was useful in situations where a visual target identification at up to five miles was required. It did not appear on 'twin-stickers' as it impeded the already restricted view from the back seat. One major proposal which was not implemented was the removal of the INAS equipment as a weight-saver with the move to air defence. In the end, however, it was thought useful to retain the aircraft's full attack capability, not to mention the autonomous South Atlantic deployment capability it offered, where few landmarks existed between Great Britain and the Falklands.

Among the most significant improvements were those to the weapons system, including the addition of the Sky Flash missile. BAe Dynamics made major improvements to the AIM-7E-2 by fitting a Marconi XJ521 monopulse SARH seeker. Sky Flash tracked more accurately than the earlier Raytheon models and was able to operate effectively in an ECCM mode. Missile warm-up time was reduced from 15 to 2 seconds. Test results at NAS Point Mugu, California, using an USN F-4J as trials platform, proved excellent: sixteen of the 22 pre-production missiles 'killed' their targets, often in very adverse launch and acquisition situations. Sky Flash became avail-

able to Phantom squadrons from 1978, although Tornado units became the main users, with a slightly different variant which was not compatible with the FGR.2. Conversely, Tornado systems were not Sparrow-capable, so Phantom squadrons had an uncharacteristic surplus of E-2s to use up at MPCs in their final years. In 1991–92 No 74 Squadron got through five times as many Sparrows as usual on their missile camps, which made for some enjoyable sorties!

From 1988 onwards the AIM-9G Sidewinder was supplanted by the all-aspect argon gas-cooled 'Nine Lima'. The AIM-9L offered improved seeker sensitivity, and much better tracking stability. The RAF's missiles are licence-produced by Germnany's Bodenseewerk with guidance units supplied by BAe Dynamics. With its updated missiles and DCSS radar fit, the FGR.2 was still one of the best air defence fighters available, and it could easily have flown on into the next century if the need had arisen.

The obvious down-side of such a long and active career was airframe fatigue. Despite their sturdy naval origins, most RAF Phantoms were well into their planned fatigue lives when they switched from the arduous low-level FBSA mud-moving days to air defence. External skin stiffeners began to appear on their wings throughout the late 1970s and most of the fleet was re-sparred in 1989–90.[5] This increased their fatigue life by 200 per cent, permitting at least another ten years of flying, but it added 400lb in extra weight. With progressive airframe reinforcement most RAF Phantoms eventually weighed nearly 1,800lb more than they did when McDonnell built them. At the end of their service lives with the last RAF Phantom unit, No 74 Squadron, the surviving airframes ranged between 5,700 hours at the top and 4,700 hours for the youngest, the average being 5,000 hours—as Sqn Ldr Dominic Riley of the *Tigers* observed, 'not bad value for an aircraft which was originally given a 1,000-hour lifetime!'

---

[5] Many were fitted with new-build BAe outer wing panels too.

8. DEFENDING THE REALM

For the UK Air Defence Region (UK/ADR) the Phantom was seen as an interim replacement for the ageing, short-ranged Lightning, to hold the line until the Tornado became available. The unexpected bonus of twenty FG.1 aircraft from the Royal Navy's original order enabled the RAF to establish No 43 Squadron at Leuchars on 1 September 1969. The availability of ex-FBSA FGR.2s from 1975 onwards enabled the other Air Defence units to re-equip too. The last Lightning squadron wound down in April 1988.

No 43 Squadron (*Fighting Cocks*) assumed responsibility for the northern tier of the UK area, controlled by radar from Buchan Sector Operating Centre. No 43 had been the first RAF Hunter squadron and it led off the Phantom era under Wg Cdr 'Hank' Martin AFC. Operatonal flying began on 1 July 1970 alongside Nos 5 and 11 (Lightning) Squadrons at Leuchars. Much pioneering work was done with the new jet, establishing interception methods which took full advantage of its superior radar and weapons performance. Air crews were delighted, for example, to find that they could make tanker hook-ups using their own radar, virtually without ground radar intervention. The Phantom's increased range enabled No 43 Squadron to intercept Soviet 'Bears' and 'Coots' and shadow Soviet naval exercises while at the same time contributing to the tactical air support of maritime operations (TASMO) for the Royal Navy and NATO. Leu-

chars' 10-minute QRA enabled aircraft to make interceptions up to 700 miles from base.

Until 1975 the *Fighting Cocks* were the only RAF Phantom squadron tasked exclusively with air defence (AD). Their training routine took them to Alconbury to fly against 'Aggressor' F-5Es, to Akrotiri for APCs and to some prestigious assignments as well. For many of their years they provided the RAF's solo

Below: Symbolizing NATO solidarity, No 43 Squadron's 'P-Papa' flies in echelon with a pair of USAFE Bitburg's 525th TFS F-4Es. The latter carry pylon adaptors for the AIM-4D Falcon missile and show off both the original (foreground) and elongated (Midas IV) gun muzzle shrouds. (RAF Leuchars via Richard L. Ward)

aerobatic display Phantom to be hauled thunderously around many air show skies. They also beat the Land's End to John o'Groats air speed record in February 1988. Wg Cdr John Brady and Flt Lt Mike Pugh flew the 590 miles in 46.44 minutes, averaging 757mph. En route their Phantom, XV582/'AF', became the first RAF F-4 to complete 5,000 hours. The Squadron's expertise earned them the Aberporth Trophy (best MPC results), the d'Acre Trophy (most proficient squadron in No 11 Group) and the Seed Trophy (highest air-to-air gunnery scores) in 1982–83.

North Sea CAP missions were lonely and risky, even in the capable Phantom. Crews were always aware that ejection into the freezing and violent sea gave them a minimal chance of survival. Disorientation at night was a constant threat, and loss of control could occur when making low-speed, fuel-heavy, visual identification of 'bogeys' at night. CAPs were usually maintained at around 15,000ft with refuelling at 25–30,000ft.

Below: Following another sortie spent chewing holes in the target banner with 'Gat' gun projectiles, Sqn Ldr George Lee and Flt Lt Pete Gray pose with the *Fighting Cocks* mascot, 'Pilot Officer Alcock'. (RAF via Richard L. Ward)

Tankers could also provide a useful communications link because long-range sorties sometimes took crews beyond their own UHF link with Control.

Leuchars' second Phantom squadron was No 111, which absorbed eight FGR.2s and several crews from No 54 Squadron when that unit disbanded early in 1974. *Treble One* moved to Leuchars on 3 November with nine machines, freeing No 23 (Lightning) Squadron to convert to the Phantom at Coningsby. Although it was attached to Strike Command, No 111 Squadron was a dedicated AD outfit and its presence was urgently required at Leuchars. No 43 was fortunate in having up to eighteen

Above: A brace of *Fighting Cocks* display their August 1981 markings. XV571 awaits the application of chequers to its RWR fairing, and of the code letter 'A'. (RAF Leuchars via Richard L. Ward)

Right: In June 1979 No 56 Squadron had two FGR.2s (XV424 and XV486) specially painted to mark the sixtieth anniversary of Alcock and Brown's transatlantic crossing. Here Sqn Ldr Tony Alcock (nephew of the pioneer) and Flt Lt N. Browne (no relation) pose with XV424. Tony Alcock became a Group Captain and the last RAF base commander of RAF Wattisham. (Via Richard L. Ward)

Below right: Sqn Ldr Alcock (with mascot 'Twinkle Toes') and Flt Lt Browne receive congratulations from Air Chief Marshal Sir Michael Beetham (left) and Sir Douglas Bader (centre) with Air Marshal Sir Dennis Crowley-Milling (far right). (Via Richard L. Ward)

aircraft on strength in the mid-1970s, but they were still kept very busy by the unusually heavy Soviet 'traffic' at the time. *Treble One* alone logged 100 interceptions during one week in April 1980.

As the Royal Navy's Phantom activity closed down in the late 1970s its FG.1 aircraft were passed to the RAF. Clearly, it made sense to standardize Leuchars on the FG.1 model, which offered the same AD capability as the FGR.2 despite the lack of an HF/SSB radio and INAS. No 111 Squadron began to absorb the FG.1s, XV591 being the first, and was all-FG.1 by March 1980. The aircraft were 'de-navalized' by 19 MU at St Athan, which took over the RAF Phantom maintenance jobs from 23 MU (Aldergrove: FG.1) and 60 MU (Leconfield: FGR.2) after 1977. Preparation for RAF service included intensive corro-

sion inspection and the removal of the fast-acting afterburner light-up from the Speys as a standardization measure. In keeping with the fashion of the time, the aircraft began to adopt the three-tone light grey colour scheme, XV589/'P' and XT870/'S' being *Treble One*'s first. Like No 42 Squadron, they usually owned up to eighteen jets, although the official establishment was fifteen like the other UK/ADR units.

The Leuchars Phantom force became a close fighting team, with No 111 Squadron occupying the shelters to the south of the airfield while No 43 Squadron's aircraft took up residence to the north. Training continued to be provided on the FG.1 by the Phantom Training Flight until its disbandment in May 1978. Exchanges were organized with many NATO partners, *331/334 Skv* from the

Left, top: The A&AEE's modified FG.1, XT597, in its IAT/Wilf Hardy decor. The basic 'Raspberry Ripple' Boscombe Down scheme of insignia red, white and blue was sprayed at RAF St Athan during the first two weeks of June 1983 and the '25th Anniversary' (of the Phantom) markings were all applied at RAF Greenham Common on July 20. This Phantom replaced the A&AEE's last Javelin in 1974 and it was used to test radio, navigation and photographic equipment in a modified nose cone. (T. Shia)

Left, centre: AIM-9L all-aspect Sidewinders are loaded on to a Wattisham QRA FGR.2 by NBC-clad ground crews. Note the 'Noddy' caps on the missiles, which are removed just prior to launch, along with the other 'pins'. (RAF)

Left, bottom: A Raytheon AIM-7E-2 Sparrow SARH weapon being eased into its semi-recessed missile well. During the latter years the FGR.2s stopped using Sky Flash and relied exclusively on the American-built rounds (which Tornado could not employ), and crews were treated to numerous live 'shoots' during APCs to make the most of them just prior to the Phantom's phase-out. (RAF)

Royal Norwegian *Kongelige Norske Luftforsvaret* in 1984, the 50th TFW, USAFE, in 1985, 349 Squadron from the Belgian *Force Aérienne Belge/ Belgische Luchtmacht* in 1987 and *51° Stormo* from the *Aeronautica Militare Italiane* in 1988 being some of the most memorable. A swap with *7° AHU* from the *Turk Hava Kuvvetleri* was cancelled in 1989 because of the distances involved, but it demonstrated the Leuchars squadrons' field of interest—from Iceland at one extreme to Turkey at the other flank of NATO.[1]

Despite the hazards of operations in the North Sea area, Leuchars had a good safety record. Each squadron lost four aircraft and two crews in the two decades between 1969 and 1989. All of these losses occurred over land or close to the Scottish coast. However, there were some other near-misses. In August 1985 the navigator in XT870/'S' of No 111 Squadron elected to vacate his cockpit when the Phantom left the runway on take-off and embarked on a bumpy cross-country transit. Declining to eject himself, the pilot managed to haul the jet

[1] 'Fan Angel' exercises with the USAF's 57th FIS in Iceland are discussed in 'Black Knights' in Chapter 13.

aloft and made a successful solo circuit and landing. Nosewheel collapse and other damage resulted in the aircraft becoming a spares source (subsequently redesignated 8913M). No 43 Squadron nearly managed a 'reduced crew' take-off on 21 November 1977, when XV571/ 'A''s lift-off had to be aborted. The crew punched out while their Phantom ran out of steam and came to a rest near the end of the runway.

Heavy utilization began to take its toll on the FG.1 fleet. XV575/'S', with No 43 Squadron in December 1987, was found to have major structural faults and was declared 'Cat 5'. The following year the Squadron's high-time FG.1s were gradually withdrawn and replaced by FGR.2s. It was a short-term measure and the final run-down of Phantom activity began in 1989. *Treble One*'s operations officially ceased on 31 January 1990. 'Black Mike', FG.1 XV582/ 'M' in an all-black colour scheme, made the Squadron's official last flight on 22 September, escorted by some of the unit's new Tornado F.3s at the base's Open Day. By September 1991 virtually all the

Above: FG.1 XT864 developed a fault during No 111 Squadron's November 1988 APC at Akrotiri and remained behind. When No 3 Squadron arrived from Leuchars to take their turn on the ranges they applied this rather large 'zap' to their base mates' unfortunate F-4K. *Treble One*'s boss was unimpressed and the design was quickly removed after the aircraft returned to Scotland. (Richard L. Ward)

unit's aircraft had been scrapped at Wattisham. The *Fighting Cocks* began their run-down in July 1989 and the QRA function passed to No 228 OCU. Their last Phantom flight was booked in for 31 July, and the September 'At Home' featured only the Tornado.

Three other Phantom FGR.2 squadrons emerged from the Coningsby training programme. No 29 Squadron, which became operational in May 1975, remained at the base as part of the UK/ ADR network. Like No 43, it had a SACLANT role as defender of maritime forces, with a secondary AD function. The maritime role was largely a replacement for the AD cover previously furnished by the Fleet's 892 NAS *Omegas*, but obviously over a significantly limited radius. The Squadron had the honour of introducing the Sky Flash missile to UK service in August 1979, having made the first British test firing at Aberporth against a Meteor drone.[2]

After six years at Coningsby, enlivened by regular APCs, 'Priory' exercises and DACT deployments to Alconbury, No 29 Squadron was nominated as defender of the Falklands. Initially the Squadron had detached three aircraft (XV484, XV468 and XV466) to Wideawake airfield, Ascension Island, on 24–26 May 1982 as part of its maritime support role, in this case of Operation 'Corporate'. The Detachment Commander was Sqn Ldr P. R. Morley, who passed the time en route to Wideawake by working through the *Daily Telegraph* crossword book with his navigator Flt Lt Millo. The Squadron took over the QRA

from the Harrier Det based on the island and held it until a month after the Argentine surrender. One intercept was made against a pair of Soviet Tu-20s in the business of shadowing HMS *Hermes*, but greater risks arose from the isolated nature of Wideawake and its lack of ILS or runway arresting gear.

After the recovery of the Falklands, No 29 Squadron moved to Port Stanley. The first aircraft, flown in by ex-No 43 Squadron display pilot Wg Cdr Ian MacFadyen, the Squadron's boss, arrived on 17 October 1982. XV469/'W' had flown 3,750 miles with seven Victor tanker hook-ups. (The aircraft subsequently suffered 'Cat 4' damage after a nasty encounter with Port Stanley's RHAG in October). No 29's 'PhanDet' in the Falklands was maintained until the end of 1982, with crews from all UK Phantom units rotating through the base on four-month tours, later reduced to five weeks to 'avoid degrading training efficiency'. Their resident aircraft had specific radar updates to improve reliability and they carried AN/ALE-40 fittings.

---

[2] Meteor buffs may wish to know that it was a D.16, serial number WH320.

Below: The eagle and buzzard insignia of No 29 Squadron on FGR.2 XV481/'E' in 1975, shortly after it switched from ground-attack to air-defence duties. (RAF Coningsby via Richard L. Ward)

Above: 'Down south' in the Falklands, a No 23 Squadron FGR.2 takes on fuel from a Hercules drogue. A full missile and gun-pod warload confirms that patrolling the Falklands exclusion zone was a deadly serious business. ILS antennae sprout each side of the fin and TESS, the telescopic sight, protrudes from the port side of the canopy. (Flt Lt C. C. M. Lackman via Richard L. Ward)

The drain on UK/ADR of the 'Phan-Det' rotations was considerable and disruptive, so it was decided to designate another squadron for the task—No 23 Squadron, as described later. Coningsby subsequently regained No 29 Squadron, which formed there by the end of February 1983, having left its seven Phantoms in the Falklands. It made one more foreign deployment of note shortly before converting to the Tornado at the end of 1986. Four Phantoms were detached to Gibraltar shortly after the US attack on Libya, as a precautionary air defence force.

No 23 Squadron was one of two units defending the Southern Sector QRA position at RAF Wattisham. It acquired a set of ex-No 14 Squadron Phantoms at Coningsby in November 1975, following *Treble One*'s shift to Leuchars. On a particularly chilly 25 February 1976 the first batches arrived at Wattisham, Suffolk, in the time-honoured manner, comprising two flights of four: the *Red Eagles* had arrived to roost alongside the *Firebirds*, No 56 (Lightning) Squadron. The *Eagles* had a long history in two-seaters— Demon, Venom, Mosquito, Javelin— and their two-man Phantoms greatly enhanced the QRA's effectiveness. Under Neatishead Operations Control Centre, Wattisham protected the southern part of Great Britain and its surrounding sea areas, while the Central Sector, also under Neatishead Control, fell to Coningsby's squadrons. Leuchars guarded the north and generally had the busiest time. Aircraft could be vectored

to any of the three Sectors if trade demanded it.

The *Red Eagles*' stay at Wattisham was comparatively brief. At the end of 1982 they were tasked with defending the Falklands in place of No 29 Squadron. They disbanded at Wattisham on 31 March 1983, re-forming at Port Stanley the following day. With up to eleven aircraft on strength by September 1985, their facilities soon became very limiting. The new £276 million Mount Pleasant base was opened later that year and No 23 moved in to their new home on May Day 1986. Because of the enormous distances involved, changing aircraft was reduced as far as possible, but seven were swapped for freshly serviced UK examples in May and June 1986.

No 23 Squadron surrendered the arduous Falklands duty on 1 November 1987 when it passed to No 1435 Flight. Three of the seven aircraft were returned to the UK. In order to demonstrate that this token remaining force could be expanded if necessary, a series of 'Fire Focus' exercises was arranged, bringing in extra quartets of Phantoms. In practice, this was used as a chance to exchange the aircraft and was carried out flawlessly in March 1988 and February 1990. No 1435 Flight's jets were usually named *Faith*, *Hope*, *Charity* and *Desperation*, in a play on the names of the Maltese Gladiators of the Second World

Left: A study in fire and water as a *Firebirds* FGR.2 burns a hole in a wet April afternoon in 1991. (Richard L. Ward)

War. They maintained the Islands' security until July 1992, when RAF Leeming detached four Tornado F.3s to replace them (these subsequently adopting the same nicknames). Flying them back to the United Kingdom was considered to be an unnecessary task, and by August three of the Phantoms had been ignobly crushed and buried by JCB diggers *in situ* (!), leaving XV409/'H' (*Hope*) as a sole static display example.

The last UK/ADR squadron to train at Coningsby was No 56 from Wattisham, where it had been flying Lightnings. Having followed No 23 through the training programme, the *Firebirds* moved back to their 'home drome' on 8 July 1976 to join the fully operational No 23 on the QRA rota, where they would remain for the next fourteen years. Their arrival completed the Phantom-based No 11 Group AD establishment (though Nos 5 and 11 Squadrons were retained on Lightnings at Binbrook as back-up, right up until 1988). The loss of No 23 Squadron to the South Atlantic in March 1983 left the *Firebirds* as the sole flying tenants at Wattisham, but only for a year: No 74 ('Tiger') Squadron, with an illustrious history on fighters, was resurrected to fill the vacancy.

JULIET JOINS THE RAF

No 74 Squadron was nominated in February 1984 as the recipient of a limited number of ex US Navy F-4J Phantoms. The purchase was an expedient way of filling the gap in the UK/ADR. It also resulted from delays in the availability of

Top: This interesting variation on No 228 OCU's markings was worn by XV428, one of a series of FGR.2s in special colours for the Squadron CO. (Flt Lt C. C. M. Lackman via Richard L. Ward)
Above: A No 23 Squadron trio on guard over the Falklands in May 1986, with XV402 in the lead. (Tristram J. Carter)
Below: XV479/'D' (for *Desperation*), one of 1435 Flight's defenders of the Falklands. The Maltese Cross is a reminder of the unit's extraordinary heroism in defending the island with three Sea Gladiators during the Second World War. This aircraft ended its days with No 74 Squadron and it made the *Tigers'* very last pass over the Suffolk base on 30 October 1992, culminating in a near-sonic zoom climb. (Tim Laming)

sufficient Tornado F.3s. Having recently retired most of its Phantoms, the USN could offer samples of the F-4J for re-work and modification at NARF Noris. The Air Staff wanted a stop-gap fighter with a five-year lifespan and requiring minimal modifications to make them inter-operable with the existing fighter fleet. A team led by the Vice-Chief of Air Staff, Sir Peter Harding, visited the USA to locate suitable airframes from those in storage at AMARC at Davis-Monthan, Arizona. They contracted to buy fifteen refurbished 'J-birds' for a total of £125 million, including all support.

The aircraft were individually transported to North Island for re-work. One of the selected airframes broke loose from its shackles while bring transported by helicopter from AMARC to San Diego and the hapless machine plunged into the sea in full view of the Royal Family on board the Royal Yacht *Britannia*. All other airframes passed through Noris's SLEP line, where they received more or less the same treatment as the F-4Js which NARF had converted into F-4S versions. The main difference was that the leading-edge slats were omitted, mainly as a cost-cutting factor but also because the RAF felt that the agility of the faster 'hard-wing' F-4J would be adequate for its needs. Other modifications to the F-4Js included the fitting of wiring for Sky Flash missiles and the GE SUU-23/A gun pod in lieu of the old Hughes Mk IV system, the installation of TESS and updates to the radar to bring it to AN/AWG-10B digital standard, with RAF special mods following. The aircraft also received 'zero-hour' J79-GE-10B engines with a 1.5sec after-burner response and smokeless exhausts, which gave a better high-altitude per-formance than the Spey. The US Navy MB Mk H7 seats were also later replaced by Mk 7A-4s from surplus Phantom FG.1s to give compatibility with the FGR.2, and in the interim crews flew with USN helmets and harnesses (which they actually preferred!). The AN/ALR-45 RWRs were also re-placed with the ALR-66 model, com-mon to the remainder of the RAF's Phantom force.[3]

84

The F-4Js were all originally built in 1967–68 and had between 2,178 and 4,559 airframe hours apiece. Seven had Vietnam War service behind them. Life-extending fatigue modifications were therefore part of the SLEP process. Ex-tensive anti-corrosion treatment was applied and fatigue meters were installed. Two other features from the aircraft's naval past were retained, and these brought problems. Carrier operations did not require anti-skid brakes; wet British runways did, so the FGR.2 had been suitably equipped. In the absence of an anti-skid system, landing the F-4J on damp strips usually meant taking the cable, or a diversion. More serious was the very cumbersome starting system. US Navy carriers and airfields featured built-in high-pressure air hose systems to start the J79s in motion. The RAF was used to starter trolleys, so the introduc-tion of the F-4J meant that the massive Houchin starter unit had to be in place for each launch. This machine was later supplemented by the smaller, more air-transportable Solar unit. Deployments therefore required these items to be pre-positioned, and diversions to other air-fields were just plain awkward. Ground crews throughout the UK had to be instructed on starting procedures in case the F-4J should drop in. A final, minor problem was the wing-fold mechanism. This was operated from the cockpit of the F-4J rather than manually, as in RAF Phantoms. Because it was little used in RAF service, seals tended to perish, caus-ing hydraulic leaks.

After their extensive refurbishment the fifteen Phantoms were given 'shake-down' flights, which disclosed a few more problems. The new stainless steel hydraulic lines gave trouble and the bleed-air system was prone to leakage. However, preparations generally went well and the initial group of crews con-verted with VMAT-101 *Sharpshooters* at MCAS Yuma, Arizona, flying the near-est thing to their future mounts—the slatted-wing F-4S. Most were second-tour Phantom crews, led by Sqn Ldr Dick Northcote, who already had 2,000 Phantom hours with Nos 54 and 111

Squadrons and an F-4E exchange tour at MacDill AFB to his credit.

The first aircraft, by then named F-4J(UK) rather than Phantom F.3, was rolled out at NARF Noris on 10 August 1984, and it was the first machine of the last of many batches of Phantoms to have passed through the San Diego work-shops. Northcote arranged a series of 'Tiger Trails' to take the aircraft to Wattisham in threes, via Goose Bay, with tanking courtesy of VC-10s from No 101 Squadron. All fifteen were at the Suffolk base by 4 January 1985. Three arrived with inconspicuously painted nicknames, *Mulvaney's Missile*, *Avenida Arrow* and *Brigantine Bomber*, derived from bars in the San Diego area. One aircraft, ZE363, also had a rather crudely painted black fin, acquired at Wright-Patterson AFB, Ohio, during a stop-over for re-pairs. In due course the whole fleet re-ceived this distinctive feature, reviving an old No 74 Squadron tradition.

The F-4J(UK) immediately proved popular with crews. At a time when a fair proportion of the FGR.2 fleet was show-ing its age and was limited to 3g with stores aboard, it was good to have a 're-lifed' airframe which could be turned hard. Flt Lt Mark Manwaring, naviga-tor in the RAF's last solo display Phan-tom, told the authors that the AWG-10B radar was 'absolutely superb'. Its Dop-pler spectrum processor and the fact that all connections were gold-lined gave a 'much cleaner picture' than the FGR.2's AWG-12 set. Other navigators felt it was not quite so useful at close range, lacking the fine-scale tuning for short-range re-turns in order to do visual identifications at around 300yds on CAP duty. Back-seaters needed more F-4J conversion time than pilots. 'In the back cockpit not one switch was in the same position: everything was totally different from the FGR.2,' Mark recalled. One

[3] Much equipment was removed, including underwing catapult hooks (although the recesses were retained), plus the AN/ASW-25 data link, AN/ARA-63 ACLS, AN/AVG-8 VTAS, AN/ALQ-126 DECM, KY-28 secure voice trans-mission system, AN/ASN-54 APCS and AN/APN-154 radar beacon.

advantage was that the RWR receiver was at eye level, not tucked away in the bottom left-hand corner of the cockpit as in the FGR.2. In a more rationally planned back 'office', the navigator's view to each side of the front seat was unimpeded by the British habit of hanging instruments in every available crevice. Another bonus was that both UHF radios could be monitored at once, unlike the FGR.2's pair.

From the pilot's viewpoint the 'J' had superb high-altitude performance. It could easily reach 60,000ft, whereas the FGR.2's turbofans disliked the thinner air at altitude and it 'ran out of steam at about 45,000ft'. Low-level fuel consumption in the 'Juliet' was a little higher than that of the Rolls-Royce Phantom and it lacked ILS and INAS, which can prove useful for the air defence role. The aircraft were normally flown in 'Bravo' fit (high-*g* centreline tank, no wing tanks) or 'Alpha' (no external tanks) and they could pull up in 6*g* straight after take-off. FGR.2s tended to use 'Charlie' fit, with wing tanks only, or 'Delta' with all three tanks, which added weight and created additional drag. The gun pod was seldom carried, though crews were required to fire it once a year at APC in Cyprus. As Sqn Ldr Dominic Riley explained, 'We had no need of it in ACM. The F-4 was a stand-off fighter and there's no need for a gun with the F-15 and F-16 around. If we got into a turning/burning "doggers" we'd blown it.' Former 'Red Arrow' Dom Riley demonstrated to huge crowds that the Phantom could 'turn and burn' pretty well when required. He organized No 74 Squadron's four-ship formation of FGR.2s at IAT 91 and provided some spirited formation aerobatics.

The *Tigers* also did well against other fighters on their first APC in 1985. Having discovered that they lacked the correct software to make their gun pods shoot straight, they turned instead to a little ACM with the fighter elements of

the USS *Nimitz*'s CVW-8 and beat them in a series of encounters. Further success came from the Cambrai Tiger Meet in 1986, at which time the black tails spread through the Squadron. It was also decided to extend the F-4J(UK)'s service life by a further five years in view of continued delays with the Tornado F.3's Foxhunter system; at the time, many aircraft were flying with concrete ballast instead of working AI.24 radars. The F-4J(UK)s were recording very high serviceability rates despite considerable spares shortages and a lack of adequate servicing manuals for the hybrid aircraft. Apparently the Wattisham ASF, which had to handle the 'Juliet' alongside No 56 Squadron's FGR.2 models, adopted the motto: 'When is a Phantom not a Phantom? When it's an F-4J(UK)!'

No 74 ('Tiger') Squadron celebrated its seventieth birthday in 1987 by break-

ing the London to Edinburgh speed record. CO Cliff Spink led the way in ZE361, with ZE360 on his wing. Some protracted afterburning over the North Sea enabled them to complete the course in 27mins 3secs. It was also the year in which the only F-4J(UK) loss occurred. ZE358/'H', with Euan Murdoch and Jerry Ogg aboard, was in a three-ship practising low-level intercepts over the Welsh hills near Aberystwyth. Tragically, the aircraft struck a ridge line, killing both men.

The *Tigers* maintained the QRA at Wattisham until August 1990, when it passed to Leeming's Tornado squadrons. The base operated as a 24-hour Master Diversion airfield until that time and played a major part in air defence exercises such as 'Elder Forest'. The 1988 'Forest' brought attacks by French Jaguars and Mirage IVAs, and another

TABLE 13: F-4J(UK) INDIVIDUAL AIRCRAFT HISTORIES

BuNo	Block No	NARF Conversion no	RAF serial no	Aircraft code	McAir construction no	Date of delivery to RAF	Destination after withdrawal from RAF	'M' no
153768	-28-MC	F909	ZE350	T	1692	04/10/84	Laarbruch BDR	9080M
153773	-28-MC	F907	ZE351	I	1759	04/01/85	Finningley FCT	9058M
153783	-29-MC	F902	ZE352	G	1870	30/08/84	Laarbruch BDR	9086M
153785	-29-MC	F905	ZE353	E	1888	04/10/84	Manston FCT	9083M
153795	-29-MC	F903	ZE354	R	1978	30/08/84	Coningsby FCT	9084M
153803	-30-MC	F904	ZE355	S	2038	04/10/84	Pendine (target)	—
153850	-31-MC	F910	ZE356	Q	2293	26/11/84	Waddington FCT	9060M
153892	-32-MC	F908	ZE357	N	2592	03/11/84	Bruggen BDR	9081M
155510	-33-MC	F915	ZE358	H	2689	13/12/84	W/o 26/08/87	—
155529	-33-MC	F901	ZE359	J	2746	30/08/84	To IWM Duxford	—
155574	-34-MC	F914	ZE360	O	2879	13/12/84	Manston FCT	9059M
155734	-34-MC	F911	ZE361	P	2906	03/11/84	Honington FCT	9057M
155755	-34-MC	F912	ZE362	V	2958	26/11/84	Pendine (target)	—
155868	-37-MC	F906	ZE363	W	3338	03/11/84	Laarbruch BDR	9082M
155894	-39-MC	F913	ZE364	Z	3542	26/11/84	Coltishall FCT	9085 M

regular visitor—a 'chemical attack' by a single A&AEE Hunter, which always cheated, according to No 74 Squadron, and pressed home its attack despite being 'shot down'. ZE355/'S' gave the Wattisham RHAG a bending during the exercise when it made an emergency landing, missed the approach-end cable, attempted a take-off in full 'burner and was dragged to a sudden halt when it caught the central cable.

The year 1988 brought its share of unorthodox tanking incidents too. One F-4J(UK) made an emergency landing at Palermo on return from APC with a Victor's refuelling basket attached. Having failed to pull out after refuelling, the Phantom ripped the entire hose from the tanker. Luckily it sheared off, leaving only the basket stuck on the probe. A second, similar incident occurred when tanking from a KC-135A. The basket snapped off and the F-4's intakes ingested a hose full of raw fuel, converting it into a 100ft torch behind the aircraft but causing the latter no damage.

QRA duty ran from 8 a.m. until the following 8 a.m. and crews had a stand-down day the next day. Eight air crew were involved in the rota, making a big hole in the Squadron's manpower. The two QRA aircraft required six engineers working seven days flat. Southern QRA was not 'scrambled' as often as the Leuchars team but it became more active during Soviet exercises in the North Sea. Mark Manwaring told of one such night when six Wattisham aircraft were scrambled and Q7 was on standby. He

Service history prior to transfer to RAF (where known)	Remarks
NATC Strike Aircraft Test Directorate, Patuxent River.	No DECM fairings.
VF-31 ('110/AC') 00/09/75–00/00/77 → VMFA-251 ('10/DW') 00/00/77 → VMFA-122 ('257/DC') 00/04/80 → VF-33 ('205/AE') 00/08/80 → VF-171 ('203/AD').	Became 'hangar queen' at Wattisham.
VMFA-333 ('101/DN') → VX-4 ('1/XF' *Black Bunny*). Also with VX-4 in grey scheme (replaced as *Black Bunny* by F-4S 155539). To MASDC. Flown out to San Diego 30/11/83 for NARF. First flight 18/03/67.	Became 'hangar queen' 1984–86 and again in 1987.
VF-121 00/05/67–00/02/69 → VMFA-232 ('8/WT') → VMFA-334 (at Chu Lai, Da Nang and Nam Phong with these units 1969–73; reputedly logged 600 combat missions) → VMFAT-101 ('12/SH', '32/SH') 1980–81. Retired 1982; to NARF 1983.	
VF-121 ('100/NJ', 'Commander Fleet Air Miramar') → VMFA-232 (Chu Lai, Da Nang) 00/01–00/03/70 → VF-143 to 00/10/70 (USS *Constellation* 30/04/70–08/05/70; combat cruise) → VF-121 → VF-213 → VX-4 00/06/75 → NATC ('7T/106') early 1981 → VF-121 late 1981. Withdrawn 00/05/82 and stored. To NARF 00/11//83.	First aircraft to be repainted in correct grey scheme at St Athan 1989.
VMFA-232 (Chu Lai, Da Nang) 30/11/69–03/01/69 → VF-121 *Freelancers* (two combat tours, 14/10/69–01/06/70, 27/10/70–17/06/71, both on USS *Ranger*) → VF-121 until c1979 → VF-171.	At St Athan for major service when withdrawal of F-4J(UK)s decided.
VF-33 *Tarsiers* (USS *America*) 00/00/67–c1969 → VF-101 → VF-74 *Be-Devilers* (USS *America* combat cruise 05/06/72–24/03/73; flew 99.4hrs during 'Linebacker II' and subsequently sorties over Laos and Cambodia until 00/03/73) until 00/07/76 → VF-33 *Tarsiers* ('204/AG'), USS *America* → VF-31 ('110/AC') until c1979 → VMFAT-101 ('30/SH'). Storage 00/07/82; to NARF 00/12/83.	
VF-101 → VF-171 ('202/AD', '163/AD') → NATC ('7T/107').	Named *Avenida Arrow* on delivery to 74 Sqn.
VF-103 ('214/AC', USS *Saratoga*) 00/06/76; '204/AC', (Oceana 00/04/79) → VF-102 ('100/AG', CAG aircraft).	
VF-33 ('207/AG', USS *America*) → VF-74, USS *America*, for war cruise 05/06/72–24/03/73 during 'Linebacker II' (flew 88.6hrs in 00/11/72) → VF-31 *Tomcatters* ('106/AC'); USS *Saratoga* 00/00/79 and 00/00/80 ('110/AC', '112 AC'; flown by Capt James H. Flatley III, 08/02.80 → VF-171 ('204/AD', '205/AD'). Storage 00/01/82; to North Island 00/01/83.	
VF-101 → VF-41 *Black Aces*, USS *Independence* → VF-103 ('206/AC') c1976 → VMFAT-101. Storage 00/01/82; to NARF 1984.	
VMFA-235 ('10/DB') → VMFA-334 ('5/WU', '1/WU') → VMFA-101 ('25/SH') until end 1981. History prior to 1976 uncertain.	Named *Mulvaney's Missile* on delivery to 74 Sqn. Resprayed in correct grey scheme.
First flight 00/05/68. VF-154 *Black Knights* (USS *Ranger* combat cruises 28/10/68–17/05/69 (joined ship 00/03/69), 14/10/69–01/06/70, 27/10/70–17/06/71) → VF-92 *Silver Kings* (USS *Constellation* combat cruises 01/10/71–01/07/72, 05/01/73–11/10/73; was '207/NG' flown by Lt Greg Cavin/Ens Ben Arnold; took part in Operation 'Endsweep') → VF-21 00/00/75 → VF-121 ('101/NJ') 00/01/76–00/11/79 → VMFAT-101 ('22/SH'). Storage 00/08/82; to NARF 00/01/84.	
VF-84 *Jolly Rogers* ('206/AE', USS *Roosevelt*) → VF-101 → VF-171, with long periods at North Island for test purposes 1978–80. To NARF 00/01/84.	Named *Brigantine Bomber*, 'Fastest Red Nose' for *Comic Relief*.
VF-121 → VF-154 *Black Knights* (USS *Ranger* from 00/06/70, combat cruise 27/10/70–17/06/71) → VF-142 *Ghost Riders* (USS *Enterprise*, combat cruise 12/09/72–12/06/73 as '201/NK') → VMFA-212 *Lancers* from 00/02/75 → VMFAT-101 ('16/SH') 1980–82. Storage 00/03/82; to NARF 00/01/84.	Resprayed in correct grey scheme.

intercepted two 'Bears' and then had to divert to Keflavik when the standby tanker ran out of gas.

A 'Q' crew coming on duty would do a walk-around check, power-up the aircraft's systems to check instrumentation and then retreat to the 'Wendy House' to await action. If the klaxon went the crew and engineers ran to the QRA Shed, opened the main doors and pulled on helmets and Mae Wests. Having started up (right engine first), the two aircraft taxied out and Q2 stood with engines running until Q1 was safely away to follow its directions from Neatishead Control. Q2 then returned to the Shed. From 1988 the volume of Soviet 'trade' began to slacken and QRA reaction time was extended from 10 to 15 minutes. This meant that normal HAS accommodation could be used to house the QRA despite the slower-opening HAS doors.

By the end of 1990 the increasing cost of keeping the non-standard F-4J(UK)s flying, together with a worsening spares situation, brought about the decision to standardize both Wattisham squadrons on the FGR.2. Twelve 'J-birds' were still in use, with ZE355 and ZE362 in store at St Athan. Mark Manwaring recalled ruefully that the last nine-ship phase-out flypast by the aircraft took place on Day One of the Gulf War! Despite the many flying hours still left in them, the aircraft were rapidly dispatched to other bases or scrapped. No 74 Squadron received a batch of fourteen ex-No 228 OCU Phantom FGR.2s, some of which were later

replaced with 'younger' RAFG examples. After some extensive radar 'tweaking' they were ready for re-declaration to NATO on 1 February 1991, under Wg Cdr Graham Clarke.

The *Tigers'* final boss, Nick Spiller, presided over an interesting close-down year for the Squadron. The *Tigers* provided the RAF's solo aerobatic mount, decorated like the Wing Commander's own aircraft with an outsize tiger's head. The Squadron also provided the head and tail of the sixteen-ship 'Windsor Formation' flypast to celebrate HM The Queen's birthday. Among the crews in the leading diamond formation were the AOC No 11 Group, Air Vice-Marshal John Allison; Wattisham's Station Commander, Gp Capt Tony Alcock; and the Flypast Project Officer, Sqn Ldr Adrian Huggett. The two sides of the diamond were flown by No 56 Squadron.

The end came on 30 October 1992 with a closing ceremony and flypast to mark the cessation of RAF Phantom operations. The crew of XV497/'W' took their Phantom over the assembled crowd at low altitude and near-Mach speed, pulling it up into a thunderous afterburning zoom climb. By the end of the month all that remained of the Phantom era was a bedraggled line of part-dismantled aircraft awaiting the scrap merchant's cutting torch, including the superbly decorated 'tiger scheme' XV404 which the ASF had painted up for The Last Phantom Show.

TABLE 14: F-4K/M TEST AIRCRAFT IN USE AT HSA HOLME AND A&AEE BOSCOMBE DOWN

Holme

XT596	In use for trials installations. To FAA Museum 19/01/88.
XT597	Fitted with navigation, photographic and radio equipment at Holme. Passed to Boscombe Down to replace Javelin XH897. Still in use 1993.
XT598	Used for trials installations. Passed to 111 Sqn and w/o on approach to Leuchars 23/11/78.
XT873	Used for trials installations. Passed to 111 Sqn as 'BA'. Stored and scrapped at Wattisham 1991.
XT875	Used for trials installations. Passed to 111 Sqn as 'BP'. Stored and scrapped at Wattisham 1991.

A&AEE Boscombe Down

FG.1	XT597, XT858, XT865
FGR.2	XT852, XT853, XT893, XT894, XT900, XV406

All the above in use for various trials, mostly short-term.

Left, upper: 'Tigers' to a man, this pair of intrepid jocks are almost as impressive as their specially marked Phantom FGR.2, **XV404.** Unlike them, however, the aircraft had already run out of hours when it was rolled out for No 74 Squadron's photo-call on 23 September 1992. AOC 11 Group was not prepared to have a flying example painted up for the *Tigers'* farewell so this ex No 19 Squadron bird was wheeled over from the 'boneyard' for some paintwork instead. (Richard L. Ward)

Left, lower: A forlorn looking Phantom FGR.2 at the end of its life at Wattisham in August 1992, awaiting the scrap merchant's torch. Blue crosses show reconnaissance satellites that the aircraft is *hors de combat.* (Authors)

PART II: LAND-BASED DERIVATIVES

9. DOUBLE-UGLY

The US Air Force got into the F-4 business when it received the first two of what would eventually total a staggering 2,903 Phantoms to pass through its hands, beginning with a pair of F-110As on 24 January 1962. At the controls of the two glossy grey and white machines (genuine US Navy Block 9i F4H-1s, BuNos 149405 and 149406, McAir Ship Nos 122 and 123) were Cols Gordon A. Graham and George Laven, with Bill Ross and Irv Burrows peering out from the rear. The aircraft braved the poor flying weather to be ceremoniously greeted at Langley AFB, Virginia, by Gen Walter C. Sweeney and Maj-Gen Joseph Moore, to usher in a new era. Over the ensuing eighteen months the USAF would receive 27 further such 'diverts', assigned between Edwards AFFTC, California, for a thorough wringing-out of aerodynamics and systems, and the fledgeling new training base, MacDill in Florida.[1]

When MacDill received its first Navy jet on 4 February 1963, destined for service with the 4453rd Combat Crew Training Wing (CCTW), the base was still brimming with F-84F Thunderstreaks. By the end of spring the following year the concrete paving was groaning under the weight of half a gross of neatly parked chevrons of Phantoms, including a swelling number of the new F-4C mark, the first of which had touched down on 20 November. This new model represented the 'Minimum Change' land-based variant mandated by the DoD

and prescribed by Specific Operational Requirement 200. Apart from its thicker, lower pressure 30 × 7.7in main landing gear (MLG) wheels and new anti-skid system which resulted in a commensurately thicker wing root (all the better to haul up to eight tons of bombs off the tarmac) and its pop-up female dorsal boom refuelling receptacle (which replaced the Navy's retractable probe), it was outwardly identical. The J79-GE-15 engines featured the same convergent/divergent jet cans as the Naval GE-8 models (although, deep in the intakes at the bellmouth, it was possible to see the extended bullet fairings which housed the relocated 20kVA electrical generators, while provisions were also added for sooty cartridge starts). The tail hook was just as chunky, and only the lack of catapult bridle horns built into the wing prevented it from vaulting off the deck of a sea-going vessel.

Two operational F-4C Wings formed in rapid succession, beginning with the 12th TFW, which was declared 'combat ready' in October 1964, and the companion 15th TFW, the nucleus of which had formed that May. Pending the departure of the 4453rd CCTW for drier climes, the base represented a massive Phantom institution which reverberated hourly with the whistle and thunder of the new fighters, launching with afterburners.[2]

Most crews settled into the comparatively roomy supersonic cockpit with remarkable psychological ease but soon found things to complain about once the novelty had worn off and the paint had begun to peel. Many items had been added to the baseline US Navy interceptor layout about which out-and-out

fighter pilots knew or cared little. However, Instructor Pilots (IPs) stuck in the 'pit' acknowledged the improved over-the-shoulder vision facilitated by the lowered rear dashboard instrument panel, together with the all-essential duplicate

Block	McAir Ship No	USN BuNo	USAF serial (all FY62)	Buzz No (all FJ)
9i	122	149405	12168	405[1]
	123	149406	12169	406[2]
14n	267	150480	12170	170
	274	150486	12171	171
	281	150493	12172	172
	288	150630	12173	173
	292	150634	12174	174
	301	150643	12175	175
	307	150649	12176	176
	309	150651	12177	177
15o	312	150652	12178	178
	313	150653	12179	179
	316	150994	12180	180
	317	150995	12181	181
	320	150997	12182	182
	322	150999	12183	183
	323	151000	12184	184
	326	151002	12185	185
	327	151003	12186	186
	329	151004	12187	187
	331	151006	12188	188
	333	151007	12189	189
	336	151009	12190	190
	338	151011	12191	191
	343	151014	12192	192
	345	151016	12193	193
	347	151017	12194	194
	351	151020	12195	195
	353	151021	12196	196

[1]Then 168. [2]Then 169.
Two additional Block 14n F-4Bs (62-12200 and -12201) were reconfigured on the production lines as YRF-4Cs. Serial 62-12199 was assigned to the first true F-4C, Block 15o McAir Ship No 310.

rear stick, pedals, throttles and primary flight instrumentation, all of which were greeted with enthusiasm and represented features which exchange Navy Instructors regarded with some jealousy.

The 'new things', in which some revelled and about which others groaned, were the expanded weapons control panels (WCP) located in the front 'office' and the curious right-hand rear-seat console, packed with all sorts of switches and knobs (including a relocated radar tracking handle), the bulk of which comprised odometer-style lat/long read-outs from the brand new Litton LN-12 (AN/ASN-48) inertial navigation set (INS) and allied AN/ASN-46 navigation computer, and puzzling buttons which obliged pilots to sit patiently in the cockpit for up to a quarter of an hour waiting for the systems to align before taxiing out to the 'hammerhead', piling on the thrust and zooming out from Tampa into the wild blue yonder for some mock combat over the Gulf of Mexico.

To those used to the 'baseline' trainers, many of the new systems and the related cockpit synergistics necessitated going back to the manuals and revising them. Subsequent additions (and there were many) only added to the confusion, with copious new banks of push-button warning lights and switches stuffed into vacant positions in awkward places with every new Block. The urgent needs of the war in Vietnam (in which the F-4C would soon become embroiled), coupled with decrees from higher authority for new weapons systems and associated harnesses and controls, rapidly produced a hodge-podge cockpit layout. Time, rather than ergonomics, was of the essence. McAir engineers seemed to have a monopoly on patience. New requirements were emerging almost weekly, only to be revoked, reinstated, scrapped and substituted. Much of this confusion was rooted in the McNamara-run DoD philosophy of commonality, and the fact that the US Navy, as chief customer, enjoyed principal liaison (and sat in just about every meeting) with McDonnell Aircraft up until the end of 1972, effectively complicating matters.

There existed physiological, aeromedical problems too, resulting from a nation whose people came in all sorts of shapes and sizes and from a multitude of ethnic backgrounds: USAF crews were not subjected to quite the same size-sieving system as Navy aviators. Pilots in the upper and lower percentile height range faced peculiar problems of their own, in spite of the ability to crank the seats up and down six inches. Col Ross A. Moon USAF Ret explained that he used 'multiple seat positions depending on the phase of flight'. He recalled flying as IP with a young lieutenant in the front: 'Charlie was just tall enough to make the height limit for being a USAF pilot. We did the pre-flight and I noticed we had a new set of tyres on the main landing gear. Training sortie over, upon landing I felt the right main gear skid on roll-out and I could feel the tyre bump. I told Charlie to park in "de-arm" and have maintenance check it out before trying to taxi. After checking, the tyre maintenance told us to shut down: the right main tyre had been worn thin. Later, Charlie explained that he was too short to reach the rudder pedals and see to land with the seat in the full-up position. So he lifted his feet to put his heels on the rudder pedal bars. When he put the MLG down on the runway he inadvertently tapped the right brake, and so the tyre was locked when we touched down. I saw Charlie a few years later in Europe. Beaming, he told me that he had actually blown three tyres on landing since we had last seen each other—all for the same reason! The F-4 cockpit was much too awkward for many pilots.' To its credit, it also tended to mirror their flying abilities precisely. Those pilots with innate talent would quickly excel, whereas poor ones had a hard time mastering the complexities of the mass-air manoeuvring required for air-to-air combat or visual ground attack patterns. 'New guy' formation training was reserved for clear blue skies.

However, the rugged aircraft was generally considered a safe one to fly, with few vices.[3] Its safety record was superlative for the era, and ten years later, when the programme had reached full maturity, several Wings were proudly accumulating between fifty and one hun-

---

[1] Gordon A. Graham was later promoted to general rank and became Deputy Chief of the Seventh 7th Air Force at Saigon, South Vietnam, during the 'Rolling Thunder' bombing campaign. He was also a noted RF-4C pilot. See Chapter 15. The two initial F-110As, genuine Navy F4H-1 aircraft wearing USAF logos, were reassigned to Edwards AFFTC shortly after the ceremony, for USAF 'category' tests. Of the other 27 aircraft 'diverted' from US Navy production, eight aircraft came from Block 14n (serialled 62-12170 to -12177), and nineteen from Block 15o (62-12178 to -12196). A further two, Block 14n F-4Bs (serials 62-12200 and -12201), were modified on the production line as YRF-4Cs, as stipulated by Configuration Report No 8995 emanating from SOR 196 (see Chapter 15 for further details). Most of the survivors from the 29 F-4B loans were handed back to the Navy, via the rework depots, as new F-4Cs became available. The Naval Air Rework Facilities—and the USAF AMA depot at Ogden, Utah—performed major maintenance tear-downs on their aircraft every 24 months at that stage of the Phantom's career, equating to once every two cruises or 2½ years' front-line service, respectively. This accounts for the relatively pristine appearance of the non-combat assigned aircraft up till FY72, after which time Depot re-work intervals for the various marks was increased. The first true F-110A-cum-F-4C was McAir Ship No 310, serial 62-12199, bought separately under the unique Contract JO 721-NOw 62-0383i. Subsequent F-4Cs were all acquired under Contract JO-727 NOw(A)63-0032i FY 1963 and JO-732 NOw(A)64-0032i FY 1964 funded specifications, beginning with McAir Ship No 358, serial 63-7421. Interestingly, capable but politically unacceptable Model 98-DA-G1/2 and Model 98-DB proposals of the F4H-1 had been mooted for US Army use during March 1961, combining the basic ground-attack capabilities of what would be the F-4C but lacking its air-to-air combat, aerial-refuelling and high-performance variable-inlet features while incorporating a Vulcan M61A-1 gun and twin 7.7in-wide main landing gear trucks in a much thicker wing root. These were two of hundreds of Model 98 proposals which never got beyond the 'paper' stage.
[2] The 4453rd CCTW shifted home to dry and sunny Davis-Monthan AFB, Arizona, on 1 July 1964, making room for the new combat units. Refer to Appendix V for details of the component squadrons of the 12th, 15th and 4453rd Wings and their numerous TDY deployments to PACAF.
[3] One of the aircraft's few major handling vices was the dreaded flat stall-spin, a subject aired in detail in Chapter 11.

dred thousand hours of accident-free flying, hitherto unheard of during the 'Century Series' era. The 'two of everything' approach embodied in the Phantom's tough design—two rated pilots to occupy the 50ft height/130kt speed minimum ejection parameters of the Martin Baker H Mk 5 'bang seats', two extremely reliable J79-GE-15 engines, re-dundant hydraulics and a pair of complementary missile weapons systems—combined with the machine's peculiar cranked wing and drooping, all-moving tail, necessary for stability in yaw and pitch, quickly gave rise to some affectionate nicknames: 'Double Ugly', 'Buick' and later, based on the type's chunky determined-looking nose-down attitude

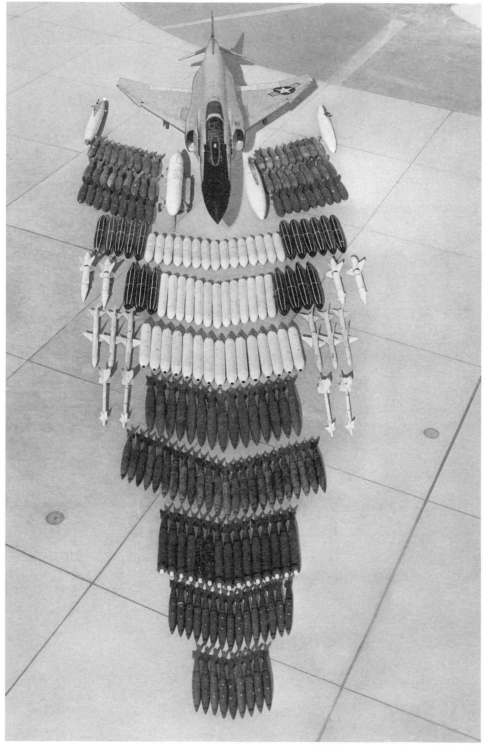

on launch, 'Rhino'. There were other nicknames for pilots who were unable to put a fighter with a solid Navy pedigree down on a long, fixed runway in a no-flare landing, or who appeared unable to do anything but jiggle about in formation, but such people would have had their egos squashed in any aircraft.

The demands of the slowly escalating conflict in South-East Asia meant that MacDill AFB's pioneers pulled out all the stops to feed the growing war machine in the Pacific. The first unit to deploy was the 12th TFW's 555th TFS *Triple Nickel* squadron, which 'TDY-ed' (was assigned on temporary duty) to Naha, Okinawa, between 8 December 1964 and 18 March the following spring, primarily to establish trans-oceanic deployment procedures and test aircraft maintainability away from the luxuries of home. The unit later would become fully committed to the theatre, but beating it into combat was the 45th TFS, detached from the 15th TFW to Ubon RTAFB, Thailand beginning on 4 April 1965. Bearing the new motto 'First to Fight', the 45th TFS not only became the first to fly strike missions but also notched up the first Air Force Phantom MiG kills of the war a month before its return to MacDill on 10 August. By Christmas the F-4C was beginning to become a mainstay fighter in the combat zone, equipping half a dozen squadrons.[4] This force would double over the ensuing eighteen months.

---

[4] Including the 433rd and 497th TFSs at Ubon (the beginnings of a four-squadron establishment) and, in South Vietnam, the 390th TFS at Da Nang (which would soon to swell to three squadrons) and the 'TDY-ing' 43rd plus the semi-permanent 557th and 558th TFSs at Cam Ranh Bay (forming the nucleus of what would also later comprise four squadrons). Refer to the 8th, 12th, 15th, 35th, 366th and 6252nd TFW entries in Appendix V for full details. Additional squadrons would subsequently form at Korat and Udorn, Thailand, and at Phu Cat and Tan Son Nhut, South Vietnam; refer to the aforementioned appendix, plus the entries for the 33rd, 37th and 388th TFWs, and that for the 432nd TRW, for further details. There were many 'chops and changes' over the years, too complex to discuss in the narrative.

Opposite page: A Phantom surveys the awesome ordnance at its disposal, including rockets, 'iron' bombs and Sidewinder, Sparrow and Bullpup missiles, laid out at Edwards, California. This array forms just a tiny part of the jet's extraordinary eventual repertoire, and Edwards was responsible for aerodynamic separation trials for the whole lot. (McAir)

Right: F-4B BuNo 149406, No 123 off the production lines, was one of two F4H-1s ceremoniously inducted into the USAF during January 1962. By April 1964 it was still on the Edwards roster and had received the revised 'buzz' code 'FJ169' (in line with its new serial 62-12169) which replaced the old '406' code. It also received some touch-ups to the gloss white paintwork, and had acquired a test boom as part of its job as a weapons separation platform—in this instance five M117 'iron' bombs and six SUU-7 rearward-ejecting bomblet dispensers. (McAir)

Below: One of the first 'true' USAF Phantoms, F-4C-15-MC 63-7410 was the fifth in the series. It spent most of its life on test duties at Edwards AFFTC, and in this early photograph the production-standard matt Light Gull Gray over Gloss White scheme is shown to good effect, complete with myriad tiny stencils. Category One testing and writing the flight and maintenance manuals for the aircraft overlapped its operational service introduction at MacDill AFB, Florida, by more than a year. Note the redundant radome blister, devoid of an infra-red seeker and not yet adapted to house RHAWS. (USAF via Lucille Zaccardi)

Left: This line-up of J79-GE-15 power-plants shows the extended bullet fairings, housing the electrical generators, to good effect. (Ken Mackintosh)
Right, upper: 63-7407 was the first F-4C Phantom produced under contract JO727-NOw(A) 63-0032i and is often referred to as the first true USAF Phantom; in fact, that honour lay with 62-12199, next to it on the production lines, which was manufactured under contract JO721-NOw 62-0383i and spent most of its time acting as a fatigue test-bed and electronic signals platform. (Frank B. Mormillo)
Right, lower: In 1989 F-4C 63-7654 was fitted with a nose probe once again and made ready for another series of 6512th TS test operations at Edwards AFB. The test force's pristine gloss white and red decor did much to rejuvenate these aged but trusted machines. (Frank B. Mormillo)

DOWN THE CHUTE

The chief bailiwick of the Wings that rapidly settled in the Republic of Vietnam—the 12th TFW, which had transferred to Cam Ranh Bay on 8 November 1965, under the command of Col Levi R. Chase, and the 366th TFW, which was re-established at Da Nang on 10 October 1966 with Col Allan P. Rankin in charge—was close air support (CAS). For convenience, the South was divided into four military regions (MRs, also known as US Marines Corps Tactical Zones or CTZs), ranging from MR I near the demilitarized zone (DMZ) splitting the North and South, to MR IV in the Delta. The new hot-rod Phantom jockeys' job was to ensure that ground forces were provided with air-delivered firepower, at just a radio's call away. To this end, the two Wings each maintained four 'bombed-up' jets each on full-time alert, much like the USMC 'Hot Pad' system, to furnish the TICs (troops in contact) with rapid-response airborne artillery. Payloads for the job typically comprised half a dozen 500lb Mk 82 Snakeye (SE) or low-drag 'slick' fragmentation bombs, or six of the higher-capacity M117 750-pounders, but also unfinned BLU-1/B or -27/B napalm tanks, CBU-24/B CBUs, LAU-3 or -61 2.75in FFAR rocket pods and, on occa-

sion, the AGM-12B Bullpup radio-controlled missile, launched and then steered to the target using its tail flares as a visual reference (though this was more commonly employed on tactical interdiction strikes in Laos). 'Daisy Cutter' adaptations of the 'iron bombs', comprising an M904 fuse stuck on the end of a 3ft-long pipe, used to provide a surface burst, were also a common sight to maximize the area coverage of the fragmentation bombs. A complementary mix-and-match between the two alert jets—typically, aircraft launched in pairs—rapidly gained favour. For example, one would be loaded with 'iron' bombs and the other with napalm, a strike technique that was referred to as 'Snake and Nape', or by the more irreverent nickname 'Shake and Bake'.

Weapons deliveries were usually conducted using dive-bombing techniques at angles of between 15 and 45 degrees. Each of these angles had an optimum weapons release height AGL which the crew would either commit to memory or look up using the charts which accompanied their flight paraphernalia. For example, 15-degree dives with Mk 82 SEs usually called for weapons release at around 800ft; when accuracy was less important and small-arms fire and flak were deemed to be a major hazard,

pilots executed 45-degree dives with weapons release occurring at around 7,000ft AGL. The sequence of events was similar irrespective of the dive angle chosen. First, the front-seater, or AC (Aircraft Commander), selected ordnance, fuses, armed them, then checked that the 'Mils' knob on the fixed gun sight was properly set. This depressed the aiming reticle—the eerie, collimated 'pipper' projected on to the gun-sight glass—for the chosen dive angle and ordnance, to provide the correct aircraft pitch at the moment of weapons release to compensate for the weapon's ballistic fall-off properties. Target run-in was based on an IP (initial point) provided over the radio by the TICs or by an orbiting FAC (forward air controller), who would mark the reference spot with smoke or white phosphorous. Lined up on the chosen heading, the aircraft was then thrown into the roller-coaster dive, and the target or assigned spot of non-descript foliage—at a given distance (usually measured in metres) and bearing from th e marker—was centred in the gun sight. The 'stick' then held the aircraft as precisely as possible at the chosen dive angle and airspeed, while the back-seater continuously called out their descending height over the cockpit intercom. At the predetermined weapons release height AGL, the back-seater called for a 'pickle' (for the pilot to press the bomb release button) and, with the gun sight on target, the ordnance cus-

tomarily fell along the predicted trigono-metric path to smother the target with explosives. This manual bombing tech-nique, known as 'going down the chute' for obvious reasons, was strictly 'canned': any deviancy from the chosen angle and airspeed or delay in 'pickling' the bombs, together with excessive wind factors from higher-altitude drops, would cause the ordnance to go astray—or, as one F-4C aviator described the process, 'Whoops—you bomb the wrong piece of real estate!' By today's standards it was primi-tive, but with practice it could provide very accurate results; and all Phantom crews practised it a lot precisely for that reason. One GIB who spent much of his tour in SEA 'as a talking altimeter on dive-bomb passes repositioning dirt' reck-oned that these strikes were 'very satisfy-ing; that was the mission when the war

really came into focus; we were there to cover our own. Concentration increased greatly and bombing accuracy rose to new levels.' While a number of bombs did go astray, crews prided themselves on 150ft CEPs (circular error probability) in low-threat areas, sufficiently accurate to salvo ordnance right down the throat of the target, even within a few hundred metres of the TICs.

CAS missions over South Vietnam (SVN) were often considered 'milk runs' but possessed their fair share of hazards. Launching fully armed aircraft with tons of tritonol or napalm jelly underwing within gunshot range of guerrilla marksmen squatting in the foliage around Da Nang and Camn Ranh Bay, combined with the occasional barrage of mortar and rocket attacks by dawn and dusk, inevitably took its toll. One attack on 14 July 1967 cost eighteen 390th TFS F-4Cs severely damaged or destroyed. One of them, armed with eight M117 bombs, caught fire and was unloaded by some extremely brave armourers before it too could explode and wreak havoc around it. Another was blown upside down on top of the revetment it was parked in. Life for the maintenance men, who worked in the open under such harassment, around the clock in the steamy, sticky heat or amidst torrential downpours, was particularly exacting. Every jet jockey, down to the last man, heaped praise on his 'Phantom Tweakers'. Very few aircraft were lost to maintenance write-ups simply because the ground crews 'got lazy', and there were remarkably few reported incidents of narcotics abuse, despite the plentiful supply of cheap drugs in Saigon. The Phantoms flew on JP4, and the ground crews drew sustenance from the pallet-loads of beer that were regularly flown in along with the spare tyres and other components to run a successful war machine.

Strikes 'up North' and in the outlying regions in Laos—known as 'tactical interdiction' to the 366th TFW crews—were significantly more dangerous, especially so when flying against point targets in the heavy flak and SAMs that filled the skies around Hanoi. (The North, too,

was divided into various zones known as 'Route Packs', ranging from RP I, just above the DMZ, to RP VIA around Hanoi in the far north. The US Navy usually covered the north-east RP VIB sector around Haiphong, and the RPs below it in the lower threat zones.) The 'canned' dive-bombing methods were frequently used, but the strictly prescribed airspeeds and dive angles put the aircraft into predictable flight paths that were a boon to the enemy gunners. Moderate jinking could be used on the basis that 'variables, once jumbled, tended to compensate for one another'. Depending on the defences, crews generally preferred to enter the target area at low level, then use a 'pop-up' manoeuvre to acquire the target visually by looking up through the inverted Phantom's canopy at the apex of the 'pop', usually at around 6,000ft above the calculated weapons release height (not a profession for the fainthearted), before rolling wings-level and going 'down the chute' at around 350kts, building up momentum to the ideal weapons release speed of 450kts. A rapid climb and egress would be effected in full reheat as soon as the pilot heard the 'clunk' of the bombs being ejected from the racks. Again, weapons typically comprised the conical-finned Mk 82 or M117, or the retarded Mk 82 SE and M117R equivalents which used pop-open cruciform air brakes to prevent the attacker from being punctured by his own ordnance during shallower, low-level drops. The only drawback of the high-drag munitions was that they imposed a 500kt airspeed limitation (above which the bombs' air brakes were liable to fail), providing potential additional hazards during what was already a harrowing procedure.

High-altitude level tactics were also used, especially when there was thick cloud cover which precluded visual bombing. The preferred ordnance for this task was a clutch of M117s, or a pair of Mk 84 2,000lb fragmentation 'hammers' or gargantuan demolition M118 3,000-pounders. Highly inaccurate manual radar 'range line' bombing (discussed later) could be used as a last

resort, but the customary technique employed was code-named 'Combat Skyspot'. This used the SST-181X system (manifested as a single antenna sprouting from behind the canopy fairing) which provided a coded radar blip for the ground radar control to vector the aircraft on to the target and command bomb release at the appropriate time, having due regard for the bombers' altitude, the ordnance carried and other known variables such as wind. The 12th TFW, which focused on CAS in South Vietnam, tended to conduct their target runs one aircraft at a time using USMC TPQ-10, whereas the 366th TFW, striking the North, frequently employed this technique using 'four-ships' with the Air Force's 200-mile range MSQ-77 system. Ordnance could be dropped through thick cloud cover in the knowledge that sprawling targets, such as bivouac or staging areas, had a fair chance of being obliterated.

However, sudden, harrowing losses sometimes happened, when unexpected volleys of SAMs—first encountered on 24 July, when one machine was blown to pieces and two others severely damaged —popped through the clouds to claim their victims. Then there were the defective bombs: in December 1967 the 366th TFW lost two aircraft in a flight of four through premature bomb detonation, and later attributed eight others to the same causes, all previously thought to have been victims of 'Golden BBs' (chance stray shots) by AAA batteries. The Wing adjusted the fuses in their bombs and the losses stopped. The 'Skyspot' technique gradually fell out of favour as newer radio navigation aids became available, but the equipment remained with many of the aircraft right through to their last tours of duty with the Air National Guard and Air Force Reserve, twenty years later. Essentially, the F-4C was not suited to anything other than VFR, clear-weather ground attack using large volumes of airspace in classic dive-bomb patterns. It was, however, a highly capable air-to-air machine compared to its 'Tac-Air' contemporary the Republic F-105, something which the 8th TFW 'Wolfpack' based at Ubon RTAFB, Thailand, knew very well, and exploited.

WOLFPACK

The 8th TFW, organized at Ubon on 8 December 1965 under the command of Col Joseph G. Wilson, was seen by many as the 'glamour Wing' in the theatre. Its missions encompassed 'tac int' over the 'Steel Tiger' panhandle of southern Laos, plus strategic interdiction and MiGCAP over North Vietnam. The latter tasking entailed providing top cover for F-105 'Thud' bombers or RF-101C Voodoo reconnaissance jets winging their way North. In this capacity, they became the first unit fully to wring-out the F-4C's air-to-air systems week by week, and some of its other muddled electronics too. Many reckoned that when the Air Force adopted the Phantom and fitted it with the INS and improved hydraulic systems (adding to the 4,000ft of tubing and 54,197ft of electrical spaghetti comprising 8,856 wires), McAir's ingenious engineers simply stuffed too much into too small a space. This resulted in numerous problems such as varying voltage ground potential, which rendered certain equipment updates such as the installation of RHAWS, which used sensitive signal inputs, a complex task. The actual assembly of the aircraft involved building the forward fuselage in two halves, then splicing these together with most of 'guts' of the equipment already installed before the consoles were capped with switches. (To the end, the F-4's radio was placed under the rear ejection seat, requiring the rear bucket to be painstakingly pulled out and reinstalled every time it required attention.) In jest, some crews reckoned that the only thing that prevented the jam-packed assembly from bursting apart at the seams was the Brunswick nose radome!

The avionics suffered terribly in the water-laden air of SEA. One GIB recalled that 'The potting compound in the electrical plugs, when subjected to hot, humid conditions, would liquify, creating some of the weirdest and most unpredictable manifestations. It was said

Below: By August 1964 MacDill was in business with Phantoms and had begun to deploy to Naha in the Far East to demonstrate the F-4C's wide-ranging firepower. The first jets committed to the combat zone followed soon afterwards. (McAir)

that one pilot, when he keyed his microphone, would experience full rudder deflection! Obviously, that's not a machine one wants to take to war.' The potting compound was subsequently replaced under a programme known as 'Pacer Wave', which also introduced low-capacitance coaxial cables for the new RHAWS and related crystal video displays. The steamy climate and stresses of combat also produced leaking fuel tanks, while of the 454 aircraft delivered between 1965 and 4 May 1966 (when production of this mark closed, at 583 examples), no fewer than 85 were subsequently discovered to have developed cracked ribs and stringers on the folding wing sections.[5] This spurred some impromptu beef-ups—the beginnings of what would eventually amount to 1,800lb of steel

straps and plates by the time the aircraft had received its definitive 're-lifing'—together with a redesigned outer wing, featuring heavier stringers and an extra rib.

That McAir were able to respond to the growing burdens placed on its product was testimony to the dedication of its eager-beaver field engineers (the 'Tech Reps'), along with the service crews who kept the machines flying, day in, day out. With detailed ASIP (Aircraft Structural Integrity Program) monitoring, many of the USAF airframes which survived the war would eventually last five times as long as the manufacturer's orginally warranted fatigue estimate, without the imposition of g-limit constraints that dogged other types such as the 'Thud' in its final months.

The heart of McAir's baseline Model 98 design was its Aero-1A intercept system. Nowhere more than in the air-to-air arena was the 'minimum change' between the F-4B and F-4C more noticeable. Both also went into combat with an identical armament—up to four Philco-Ford uncooled PbS-seeker-equipped infra-red homing AIM-9B Sidewinders and four semi-recessed Raytheon AIM-7D SARH (semi-active

Below: March 1966, and an early 'Wolfpack' F-4C slides in under the boom. The first strikes over North Vietnam employed these M117 'iron' bombs—and documentation camera pods, when striking North Vietnam was still something of a novelty. Note that the aircraft still has not been re-equipped with the curved inner wing pylons which incorporated tougher, USAF-standard MAU-12 racks. (McAir)

radar homing) Sparrow IIIs. The key difference, however, was that the US Navy employed its aircraft primarily as interceptors for barrier protection, and its back-seaters were rapidly moulded into experts with the radar, whereas the USAF typically 'mixed it up' with the enemy MiGs in swirling dogfights at close quarters, partly as a result of the 'Eddie Rickenbacker' tradition (despite the Phantom's initial lack of a gun) and partly because the two rated pilots flying the aircraft were more 'stick' than 'scope' orientated and in the early days seldom developed the type of rapport that was commonplace with the Navy's pilot/RIO teams, with the back-seater vying for AC status. Partly also it was because of the constricting Rules of Engagement (precipitated by the unreliable IFF technology of the era, coupled to one or two 'own goals'), which in all but clear circumstances prescribed positive visual identification before missiles could be let loose for the kill. These factors effectively neutralized the Phantom's one supreme tactical advantage—a front-to-stern quarter attack with a radar-guided Sparrow missile shot at ranges of up to twelve miles. The GE AN/APQ-100 was also designed as a 'do it all' radar with the inherent loss of quality that comes with compromise, and was described as 'Stone Age compared with the Hughes fire control systems' in use aboard NORAD's 'Century Series' interceptors (despite the fact that both 'families' used powerful but primitive thermionic valve technology which was prone to all sorts of breakages). This was relieved only by the Phantom's hydraulically driven antenna control which provided firm, quick action. Even in skilled hands, with no back-up system the radars frequently broke lock amidst the ground clutter. It took several painstaking years to sharpen radar discrimination. The system's intended companion, the ACF Electronic AN/AAA-4 cryogenic receiver, mounted in the chin blister of the F-4B from production Block 6f, was deleted from the F-4C at the outset, and it would be another two decades before an IRSTS (infra-red search and track system) would be seriously reconsidered for the Phantom.[6]

Primary tactics for air combat tended to rely on outside support before the mêlée was joined. This made full use of reporting agencies (such as an offshore airborne early warning EC-121 radar post or Navy radar picket ship), which could detect enemy MiGs taking off and report their position and heading based on the MiGCAP 'bull's-eye' centred over downtown Hanoi. The first of the airborne controllers arrived in April 1965.[7] Vectored straight on to the opposition in flights of four like a sledgehammer, the F-4 crews proceeded to engage in pairs, typically using radar first, with the possibility of a Sparrow shoot, before reverting to stick-and-rudder, manual, tail-chasing engagements with AIM-9Bs. The former required the GIB to employ radar in search mode and lock on to the target using his right-hand radar slew handle. The procedures seemed straightforward but were actually extremely taxing in the rough-and-tumble of a stomach-gyrating, high-g environment.

In theory, as explained by one former 'pitter', 'The GIB would compute the direction of intercept, the track crossing angle (TCA), the collision course and altitude differential [if radically different], while the pilot selected "Missile" and ordnance station number on the WCP. Doctrine called for selecting two AIM-7 missile stations, which would be fired one at a time. The radar was operated in "search mode" until target contact was established, when the GIB manually acquired antenna control by squeezing the trigger on the radar hand control to the first detent. Taking manual control in this manner automatically selected a mode called "supersearch", in which the antenna swept 15° either side of the position commanded by manual control of the antenna and at a scan rate of 30° per second. Fine adjustments of antenna elevation were made with the Vernier control, a wheel on the hand control which was operated using the right thumb. When the target [blip] was centred in the beam, i.e. the brightest possible return as spotlighted in azimuth and elevation, the GIB squeezed the trigger to the second detent. This generated the electronic "gate", which appeared in the vertical strobe and was moved manually by moving the hand control forward to place the "gate" over the target return. The hand control trigger was then released, and—voilà!—lock-on was established. From that point on, intensity of the target and antenna position strobe dimmed and was controlled by the AGC (automatic gain control). While the strobe and target remained

---

[5] F-4C production ended with Block 25y and McAir Ship No 1417 (serial 64-0928). F-4D production had already begun in Block 24x with McAir Ship No 1219 (serial 64-0929), and 35 F-4Ds were produced concurrently with the last 74 F-4Cs according to the McAir Ship Numbers through-flow report, which accounts for the ostensibly identical configuration seen on some hundred newly camouflaged aircraft emerging from the factory during 1966 before two different types of RHAWS—the Applied Technology AN/APR-25 and -26 on the F-4C and the Bendix AN/APS 107 on the F-4D—were applied to the aircraft during field modifications and on the lines at St Louis. Both models thus featured 'clean' radomes and fin-caps at that stage. The reader is referred to Chapter 14 for a fuller account of the varied, externally distinguishing electronic warfare kit.

[6] The renewed IRSTS effort is described in Chapter 13.

[7] The MiGCAP 'bull's-eye' centred in Hanoi was divided into 30-degree (o'clock) radials with coverage of up to approximately 100 nautical miles in five 20nm-range increments. EC-121s were operated by both the US Navy and Air Force, employing teams of up to thirty men per aircraft on airborne missions of up to ten hours' duration. 'Big Eye' referred to the ADC EC-121D model introduced to combat in April 1965. The force later moved from Tan Son Nhut AB, South Vietnam, to Ubon in March 1967, then on to Udorn, adopting the new call-sign 'Disco'. 'College Eye' was the term used by the US Navy's EC-121M variant, introduced to combat in August 1967. 'Red Crown' Navy picket ships also acted as a 'control agency' in concert with the 'Super Connies' and later successfully cleared F-4 crews to shoot at BVR ranges, especially when the latter were fitted with 'Combat Tree' devices (discussed in Chapter 10). It is worth bearing in mind that modern 'netted' AWACS/IFF systems, such as those available to the superlative E-3 series, did not become available until the late 1970s. See Chapter 13.

Left, top: The camouflage respray effort spread throughout the USAF tactical community from 1966, using the same three hues: FS30219 tan, FS34102 medium green and FS34079 forest green. A blanket coat of FS 36622 pale grey similarly replaced the belly's gloss white finish. This example is just about to receive the medium green paint over the still-exposed yellow-green zinc chromate primer. (Ken Mackintosh)

Left, centre: Providing CAS over the Republic meant toting napalm and 'iron' bombs—plus the LAU-3 rocket pods and fat CBU-24s shown here—to do mischief to the enemy. Wing boss Col Al Piccirillo emphasizes the bulk of his jet's surprise package. (Via Richard L. Ward)

Left, bottom: Two 'clips' of Mk 82 LDGP bombs ready-wired on MERs, awaiting loading. Preparation of ordnance in this fashion greatly facilitated turnaround times in the revetments. (Via Richard L. Ward)

visible on the scope, two concentric circles and a dot were generated. The outer circle had a break in it, the trailing edge of which indicated the overtake or combined closing rate, in terms of clock position: for example, if the trailing edge of the break was a nine o' clock, the rate of closure was 900 knots. The dot indicated the direction to steer the airplane. The idea was to put the dot in the centre of the inner circle which began to expand in size at the computed maximum launch range for the Sparrow. It would continue to expand until approximating the missile's mid-range, then shrank until, at minimum missile launch range, the circle changed to an "X", indicating breakaway.[8]

With the radar locked on and glued to the enemy, the front-seat repeater scope furnished a similar 'command course' steering dot and angular steering error (ASE) circle, to assist with maintaining the optimum firing position. However, pilots invariably ignored the repeater and kept their eyes firmly fixed on the MiG through the windshield, using their three-dimensional instinct to position the aircraft correctly in the great slicing chase. One, often two AIM-7D Spar-

[8] Based on an account of the virtually identical procedures used to obtain a lock-on using the F-4D's AN/APQ-109, by courtesy of correspondence with Maj Jim Chamberlain USAF Ret.

rows would then be 'squeezed off' in rapid train (a term alluding to the process of pressing and releasing the red trigger) at what they perceived to be the right moment, at not too high a closure rate, and not too close (the canopy bow-mounted 'shoot lights', designed for LRI, or long-range interception work, came much later, and USAF Phantoms never possessed the servoed cross-reticle of the Navy's F-4J, which was flashed up on the gun sight alongside the 'pipper' to serve as a crude 'head-up' ASE and dot respectively). Usually the GIBs would yell when they were within range—what the manuals described as 'indicating a valid firing opportunity'!—while the pilots attempted to hold the best position relative to the quarry. The high velocity of the Sparrow, which had a burn-out speed of Mach 4, meant that the pilot did not have to maintain his track of the MiG for long, win or miss. If nothing went awry (which all too often it did), the weapon guided to the radar-painted target. The missile had both impact and proximity fusing, either of which would set off a 66lb continous-rod warhead containing two and a half thousand steel fragments —enough to tear a MiG to pieces.

The first of fourteen MiGs to be 'bagged' by F-4Cs volleying Sparrows took place on 23 April 1966 when 555th TFS *Triple Nickel* pilots Capt Robert E. Blake and his GIB 1Lt S. W. George brought down a MiG-17 'Fresco'(one of five MiGs claimed by the squadron that month) while at the helm of 64-0699. The crew were in the 'Number Four' slot in a flight tasked with MiGCAP in support of an F-105 strike against the Bac Giang highway and railway bridge, 25 miles north-east of Hanoi. After an initial head-on encounter, when the MiGs and Phantoms unsuccessfully traded shots with cannon and missiles, the engagement turned into a 'fur ball' at 10–15,000ft. One enemy jet fell to a Sidewinder shot by Capt Max F. Cameron (No 3, in 64-0689, with GIB Lt Robert E. Evans) before he and Blake were given chase by one of the remaining marauding MiGs. Piling on the thrust, the two Phantoms entered into a climb-

ing separation manoeuvre, before they switched to a diving roll and 'came straight down on the MiG', according to Blake's report. The 'Fresco' driver saw them on his tail. 'He applied full power and dove towards the valley. As I came out of the roll I fired one Sparrow. I had a bad angle on him and missed but I realigned and fired again.' This one hit the MiG. 'The smoke looked like taffy streaming from the rear.'

That example would remain the sole USAF Sparrow kill of the war until November, when the newer AIM-7E, featuring a solid rocket motor with massively expanded range characteristics and other refinements, became more widely available. The weapon worked best at its maximum range of up to 28 miles at altitude, but it was never employed in this manner for fear of generating an 'own goal' for the reasons described earlier. In turn, APX IFF fixes were introduced by McAir while Raytheon turned its attention towards improving the minimum range and 'snap-shoot' characteristics of the weapon, which was limited to 3g manoeuvres at that stage in its development—totally unsuited to dogfighting. Moreover, the button-tweaking procedures used to obtain the lock-ons did not gain favour with the pilot-rated GIBs with no background as navigators, who were anxiously awaiting promotion to the front seat and the coveted principal firing trigger.

If 'Fox One', the Sparrow, failed to claim its prize, the pilot would switch over to 'Heat', the serpentine Sidewinder. This really came into play at close quarters, when the engagement had deteriorated (as inevitably it did) into a one-on-one 'knife-fight', described as 'vicious' by veteran ace Col Robin Olds. He assumed command of the 'Wolfpack' on 20 September 1966 and alongside his vice-commander, Col (later Gen) Daniel 'Chappie' James Jr, rapidly became a key exponent of the Phantom/Sidewinder combination. The beauty of this ophidian beast was its simplicity. When NOTS (Naval Ordnance Test Station) engineer William B. McLean conceived the Sidewinder in his spare time in his

garage, the development LP612 round contained a mere nine moving parts and seven radio tubes. By the time the missile had been contracted out for mass production as the AIM-9B to GE and Ford, it still was alleged to contain fewer electrical components than an average domestic radio set. Best of all, it was cheap and reliable. Lock-on was straightforward too: the pilot selected the missile on the WCP and physically pointed it at the target. When the pitch of the weapon 'growled' on the headphones it had locked on to its quarry, and could be fired, leaving the pilot to break off the engagement completely or jiggle into a new position just in case a foe was attempting to blast his rear. Obtaining an ideal lock-on entailed positioning the Phantom in the MiG's six o'clock, at a range of up to about a mile, so that the weapon's passive lead sulphide dome could acquire the enemy aircraft's hot jet exhaust plume. At a push, against a lax opponent, it could claim its prize after ten seconds of flight time at a range of up to 2.6 miles. Pre-flight checks with the original AIM-9B versions were simple: crewmen verified that the rounds were satisfactory during 'last chance', just prior to take-off, by means of ground crews shining bright flashlights to generate the desired aural tone in the headphones! Further checks en route to the target were sometimes conducted using fellow Phantoms' GE-15 engines, when Sparrows, also, received periodic warming, just in case they might be called into action at short notice.

The first ever USAF F-4 Sidewinder kill was accomplished on 10 July 1965, in exacting circumstances. 'TDY-ing' 45th TFS crewmen Capts Kenneth E. Holcombe and Arthur C. Clark dumped F-4C 64-0693's fuel tanks with a MiG in chase and accelerated in full reheat to gain separation, then, using reverse-and-turn tactics, positioned the nose of the Phantom ready for a boresight head-to-head radar lock-on. This was designed to cage the radar in fixed forward alignment through the black radome so that, with the gun-sight 'pipper' on target, the enemy was centred in the radar beam,

making the process of radar lock-on easier—theoretically! 'The target would only appear in the radar trace when the aircraft nose was pointed directly at it. The GIB would then try to get a range lock-on to the target and switch to the "search" mode for tracking. In a dogfight, radar lock-on and tracking was no mean feat. Pulling 6 or 7 Gs while holding the head over the scope trying to get locked on was not a barrel of laughs.'[9] To make matters more complicated, during this particular engagement Clark found the radar to be inoperative, so both fighters swept past one another with the MiG's cannon flickering and Clark repeatedly yelling to his front-seater 'Go heat, go heat!' In the fearful seconds that ensued, Holcombe yanked the machine around the sky, popping a few rivets in the process, and then got on to the MiG's tail before squeezing off all four Sidewinders in under ten seconds. Bits of MiG contained in a large orange fireball fluttered

into a cloud, with the fourth Sidewinder continuing to give chase. Holcombe's wing-man (No 4 in the flight), also fired all four of his Sidewinders, albeit more judiciously in pairs, and added another 'Fresco' to the day's proceedings—the first Air Force kills of the war.

These frenetic engagements against the nimble MiG-17 and the low-wheeling, supersonic newcomer, the MiG-21 'Fishbed', were typical of the close-in tactics espoused early on and are best aired by the crews who felt the emotional and physical strain in their stomachs. 433rd TFS *Satans Angels* AC Maj (shortly afterwards promoted to Lt-Col) Philip P. Combies and his back-seater 1Lt Lee Dutton (flying F-4C 64-0838, call-sign 'Rambler Four') formed one of sixteen Ubon Phantoms that spear-headed a feigned bombing mission up North on 2 January 1967, intended to lure the enemy MiGs up into the air and into battle. It was the famous Operation

'Bolo'. Phil Combies takes up the mission:[10]

'Joining the tankers, we refuel, trying our best to look and act like Thunder-chiefs. Normally, fighter crews don't talk much to each other in transit. But we put out radio chatter to simulate "Thuds" making checks and so forth, as we fly toward North Vietnam. The weather doesn't look good. The cloud tops are at about 6,000ft—a solid undercoat that

---

[9] Based on the AN/APQ-109, as above. Automatic acquisition was later added to lock the 'boresighted' radar on to the target, at a flick of a switch on the throttle (TO 1F-4D-513). The F-4E is believed to have featured this from the outset.
[10] The full-length version of this combat narrative first appeared in Grumman *Horizons* and portions are reproduced here by courtesy of the Grumman Corporation. The attack also included further waves of Phantoms from Da Nang, South Vietnam. The ruse used to lure the enemy MiGs into the air was necessary because bombing or strafing the aircraft on the ground, even if taxying for take-off, was prohibited at that stage of the war!

Left: F-4C-19-MC 63-7552, named *Genie*, belonged to the 558th TFS. The Squadron originally had 'XD' codes but took over the 558th TFS's aircraft after its own transferred to Misawa, Japan, in July 1968. Cam Ranh Bay's jets, which arrived on 8 November 1965 concentrated on the 'in-country' war though did venture north for MiGCAP sorties on occasion. Aircraft '552 saw out its last years with the 199th FIS, Hawaii ANG, and had accumulated 5,066 hours by 1981. (Via Richard L. Ward)
Below: 12th TFW F-4C-21-MC 64-0672 *The Deadly Jester* (with the adverbial portion of its *nomme de guerre* appropriately scrubbed away following its accident!) first flew on 17 March 1965. Assigned to Maj Tom Wallace when it lost its legs, it was subsequently restored to full glory and ended its career with the Arkansas ANG. It was retired to AMARC as article FP135 with over 4,500 hours on the clock. (Jim Chamberlain)

keeps us from seeing the ground and our make-believe targets. This is a problem. We're afraid the MiGs will realize this is no weather for bombing and won't rise to our bait.

'"Bogeys . . . bogeys!" crackles in our headsets from the crews ahead. The MiGs are coming up. "Olds" is mixing it up good and I hear "Chappie" James getting into the middle of things. We start calling "Olds, where are you?" All he answers is "Find your own!" Our flight comes charging down the east side of "Thud Ridge", mountains that aim at us like arrowheads towards Hanoi. We turn over the NVN air base at Phuc Yen, which is below the clouds, and fly up the west side of this 40-mile ridge. Peaks go up to about 6,000ft and the "Thuds" use the side of the ridge to get some masking from the SAMs, but the "Reds" get smart and put some 37mm guns in the area, which makes it a sporty course. But where are the MiGs? We know they're up. We can hear the other two F-4 flights ['Olds' and 'Ford', comprising eight Phantoms ahead of 'Rambler' flight] hassling with them. Finally, I see six MiG-21s pop out of the clouds down at my two o'clock position. They're probably being vectored towards Olds' and James's flights by their NVN P-35 GCI radar. I call out the MiGs to the rest of my flight. They're flying in front of us, from left to right. I don't think they see us, which is beautiful . . . We're high, so we go pouncing down. They seem confused, probably because they're expecting "Thuds" and here comes a bunch of hungry F-4 drivers. The MiG-21 is a good bird, quite comparable to the F-4. The pilots know their airplanes and handle them well. Using their heads, they turn on to us, shooting, but never get to make a pass head-on.

'About 30 secs after sighting, I manoeuvre right onto a guy and work into his 7 o'clock position. He starts working like the devil, turning as hard as he can. We're both pulling about 6 Gs. My GIB is . . . constantly looking behind him to keep MiGs off our tail—keeping me clear. The F-4 is a neck-breaker. I'm able to track this MiG and have a lead on him. I tell Lee I have the MiG where I want him: "Lock-on!" Lee puts his head down in the cockpit, where I sure don't want mine! Once you see the other guy, you never lose sight of him! In a few seconds he has the electronic gear set and says "You're locked on, you're in range". Seconds later . . . I fire the first of my four Sparrows, but I don't pull quite enough lead and the Sparrow goes behind him. We're both in a hard left turn, relatively level at 8–9,000ft. He's pulling a little harder. I don't know what my speed is. I'm in and out of afterburner,

Right: Double MiG-killer 63-7680 *Candy* was the jet in which 8th TFW boss Col Robin Olds scored a MiG kill during Operation 'Bolo', on 2 January 1967. The second was scored by Fred Haeffner and his GIB 1Lt Bever on 13 May that year, call-sign 'Harpoon Three'. Fred Haeffner later rose to become a General and commanded the 58th TFTW at Luke AFB, Arizona, when his Wing introduced garish high-visibility stripes on the Phantoms (and Eagles) there. The aircraft is armed with live AIM-7E Sparrows and AIM-9B Sidewinders at the 497th TFS dispersal. (Frank MacSorley via Richard L. Ward)

trying not to overrun the guy and maintain my advantage by yo-yoing. I want speed, but I also want to conserve fuel. I have the advantage. But one mistake and it's all his. The feeling is almost indescribable. 10–15 secs after the first Sparrow, I fire the second. The '21 blows up—a big orange fireball. I'm startled to see a white 'chute hanging there. How could he get out of the aircraft before the explosion? I suppose he saw the missile coming and ejected. [The AIM-7D/Es then in use produced a conspicuous smoke trail.] Another '21 goes by and I fire my third Sparrow, but the rate of closure is too fast. I don't have a chance. I work behind another '21. "Beautiful; lock-on Lee." "You're set." I fire my fourth Sparrow, but it malfunctions—never leaves. I think one of its electrical pigtails has pulled loose. I think of many other things, none complimentary!

'Over my right wing I notice another of our troops has shot down a MiG. There's a ball of fire over there. Vision and voice blend into a crescendo of activity. Everyone is yelling and cursing. Airplanes are all over the place . . . I continue to climb a bit, and spot two more '21s, low at about my 10 o'clock position. I must be pulling 8 Gs bending around behind them. Another troop over to my right [1Lt Lawrence J. Glynn Jr and his GIB 1Lt Lawrence E. Cary] comes around as tight as he can and slides in beside me. The two '21s start climbing and I yell "I got the guy on my right." Larry calls his OK. The MiGs go into a tactical split, my guy going high and turning, and the other guy going

down, with Larry after him. Larry gets him about four minutes later [with a Sparrow]. The MiGs have cannon and we don't. But I still have four Sidewinders. I'm leading my MiG. But with all the manoeuvring, I'm over-eager and mess up the parameters for firing my Sidewinders. I have to roll my airplane to the right or get more directly behind him. Before completing the roll, while about a mile behind, I fire the first two Sidewinders. They detonate right below his jetpipe, and pieces fly off. I know he can't see me. He's looking for me, but I'm out of sight in his 6 o'clock position —Sweet Six. He's confused. We're up at about 12,000ft, perhaps 6,000ft above the cloud deck. He solves my problems by rolling out and rocking his wings looking for me while still in the climb. I just start pulling the trigger thinking, you idiot, the two Sidewinders, my last weapons, are about half way to the MiG and looking beautiful, really going well. "Bye

Left: The 366th TFW adopted a unique set of individual codes, beginning with 'A' for the 389th TFS *Thunderbolts*, 'B' for the 390th TFS *Blue Boars* and 'C' for the 480th TFW *Warhawks*, with each aircraft adopting an individual second letter. It was the most logical code system for combat use but was unique to the *Gunfighters* and quickly lapsed from use. The Phantom is dwarfed behind this duralumin-coated Stratotanker. (Authors' collection)
Right: An angry SUU-23/A 20mm gun pod ready for action. A 2- or 3-second burst from this weapon created enough lead to show up on the radarscope! (A. Collishaw)

bye," I start to call out. Suddenly one of our F-4 pilots comes on the air yelling, "F-4—I don't know your call-sign—break left, break left!" Cripes, every F-4 up there breaks left . . . I clear myself then roll back to the right where my MiG was. No MiG, just a guy hanging in a chute. His airplane and mine were the only two in that particular piece of the sky that I know about. The MiG probably blew up or fell through the clouds. I put him down as a probable, then come round in a left turn and see two '21s at my 9 o'clock position. Later someone quotes me as saying "We're surrounded!" I start down after these two guys. About half way down I say to myself, "What are you going to do—throw rocks at 'em?". I got out in a hurry.'

Crews often found themselves not only 'Winchester' (out of ammunition and relatively defenceless) after such brief, fierce engagements, but also flying on fumes. Yo-yoing in and out of afterburner after an already long haul to the MiGCAP co-ordinates sometimes pushed them beyond 'bingo' fuel states, and if a tanker were not available to replenish their reserves there was usually only one option—'punch out'. Although ejection was instrinsically hazardous, the thing crews feared most was capture and internment in the infamous Hoa Lo prison—the 'Hanoi Hilton'. Flying on vapours, they devised all sorts of measures to coax their machines away to more suitable ejection co-ordinates to avoid this grim fate, or worse ones in the hands of belligerent natives. On 10 March 1967, while providing MiGCAP for 'Thuds' pounding the Thai Nguyen Iron Works, two F-4C crews from the 433rd TFS *Satan's Angels* found themselves in just such a predicament. 'Cheetah Four' (63-7653), crewed by Capts E. D. Aman and R. W. Houghton, flamed out and was about to go down near the target area. Capt. John R. Pardo, at the helm of 'Cheetah Three' (64-0839), got 'Four' to lower his tail-hook, then tucked in behind him with his windshield against the hook and pushed him out over Laos to a safe recovery area. 'Three' then flamed out too, and both crews leapt overboard, to be plucked out by the 'Jolly Green' rescue helicopters! All went back into new cockpits and two months later, as a Major, Pardo and his still-trusting back-seater 1Lt Stephen A. Wayne 'bagged' a 'Fresco' with a Sidewinder! It was an astonishing episode.

GUNFIGHTERS

All seven 'Bolo' kills were scored by the 'Wolfpack', raising the 8th TFW's tally to thirteen MiGs, while the 366th TFW's credits remained static at just two. In contrast to the Thai-based sanctuary Ubon, operations at Da Nang, in the thick of things near the DMZ, were described as 'a mess': the F-4 community there had 'a little of everything'—night missions over the North, CAS in the South, 'tac int' in Laos—and all the complex paperwork that went with such a multitude of taskings. The standard tour of duty was 100 missions in the North, and missions in South Vietnam *et environs* did not count towards its completion. For Colonels and above the tour was a year regardless of missions flown, hence many did not bother to fly very much. In 1966 the 366th had suffered nine major accidents as a result of monsoon weather operations. Wet runway landings caused considerable problems in the F-4C, despite its anti-skid system. Moreover, the VC were scoring 35–40 hits per month on Phantoms in the landing pattern, Marine jets included. Morale was poor because of non-flying senior officers, poor Wing quarters, the rocketing at night, the lack of transport to the flight-line and the absence of operational directives. The new DO (Deputy Commander for Operations) of the 366th TFW in early 1967 was Col Frederick C. 'Boots' Blesse, who decided to set a good example by flying as much as possible. To turn things around, Blesse had runway barriers installed and established effective wet landing procedures, with the capability to handle up to 260 'BAK-traps' a month without affecting the flow of traffic off and on to the parallel strips. He also scheduled the senior officers to fly more regularly and flew alternate days himself. Above all else, he instigated a new Weapons Section comprising eight hand-picked officers to introduce the brand new GE SUU-16/A gun pod to combat. Strapped on the centreline, the 16ft-long pod housed a RAT-powered M61A1 20mm 'Gatling' capable of spitting out up to 6,000 rounds a minute. A single 2- or 3-second burst launched enough lead to show up on the radarscope!

Although the gun pod was intended primarily as an air-to-surface weapon system, Col Blesse felt that it should be used in air combat over the North as missiles were proving unreliable. He set about establishing its operational effec-

tiveness, placing his F-4Cs in pairs, the lead with the pod and the wing-man without. The logic of this was that the wing-man tended to use more fuel throttling back and forth to maintain formation, giving him less in reserve with which to 'turn and burn' over the target area, while at the same time it was his job to keep an eye on the proceedings and cover his leader's rear in the Richthofen tradition. The lack of a lead-computing gun sight in the F-4C was the first minor problem that had to be resolved for air-to-air combat. As the SUU-16/A was capable of putting a pattern of rounds 8in apart at a range of 2,000ft, the team reckoned that the best approach was to put the fixed 'pipper' on the target then move it forward about twice as far as would be necessary, i.e. to 'over-lead' the target initially. As the amount of lead was gradually decreased, firing could begin, causing the MiG to fly through a concentrated hail of 20mm shells which would slice it apart. (A later feature of the Phantom was to provide a pre-set 1,000ft range lead for the gun-sight 'pipper' at a flick of a switch, using radar caged at boresight for ranging and to servo the later, moving 'pippers', which would compensate automatically for the correct ballistics given the varying parameters of range and aircraft attitude).

The use of the pod was particularly favoured for low-level fights where the missile armament was least predictable owing to the strong RF and 'heat' spectrum reflections from the ground, which provided all manner of spurious distractions that would cause systems to break lock. Tests were conducted with gun pods on both wing stations for attack (and on all three stations for short-range CAS too, described as 'awesome' by all those who witnessed the proceedings or viewed the film which was later shown as part of Da Nang's theatre indoctrination course), while the centreline air-to-air installation was perfected in mock 'shoots' over the Gulf of Tonkin. Having drafted the basics, Blesse then flew to Saigon to brief Gen William Momyer, Commander of 7th AF HQ at Tan Son Nhut, and 'Wolfpack' boss Col Robin Olds, to

seek clearance to use the pods on operations over 'Injun' Country'. After hearing the briefing Olds apparently told Momyer, 'General, I wouldn't touch that with a ten-foot pole'. His concern was that crews would fail to maintain 'guns tight' discipline once the engagement had closed-in to a knife-fight and that the wide dispersion of the 20mm projectiles in all but clear, 'wings-level' engagements (of which there existed few in the 3-D world of fighter engagements) might cause mischief to other swirling Phantoms. However, the gun was aimed at addressing precisely that need—close-in combat—and on one occasion a 'Thud' had returned to Thailand with part of an AIM-9 embedded in its tail, proving that the Sidewinder-shooters did not always display the sharp target discrimination they professed. Momyer, who had heard Blesse's proposals in outline beforehand, allowed the project to continue.

The first missions in May 1967, flown by Blesse and Maj Bob Dilger, drew no MiGs but Col Bolt, Commander of the 366th TFW at Da Nang, allowed them to continue: one was carried by the flight leader, and another on the second element's lead aircraft. Success followed swiftly. On 14 May a mission to RP VIA got three MiGs, two with the 'Gat gun': Capt James A. Hargrove and 1Lt Stephen H. DeMuth (in 'Speedo One', F-4C 64-0660) blasted away a MiG-17, as did Capt James T. Craig and his GIB 1Lt James T. Talley (in 'Speedo Three', F-4C 63-7704). The third 'kill' was also a MiG-17, brought down by a Sparrow missile shot by Maj Sam O. Bakke and Capt Robert W. Lambert. (The previous day Fred Haeffner had got a MiG-17 with an AIM-7 too.) Three of these men were members of the original weapons test team set up by Blesse and his Assistant DO Col Bert Brennan. Blesse had to report back to Momyer with a daily operational summary, and following the events of 14 May he cabled: 'We engaged enemy aircraft in the Hanoi area, shooting down three without loss. One was destroyed with missiles . . . That kill cost the US Govt. $46,000. The other two aircraft were destroyed using 20mm

cannon—226 rounds in one case, 110 in the other, costing $1,130 and $550 respectively. As a result of today's action it is my personal opinion that there will be two pilot's meetings in the theatre tonight: one in Hanoi and the other at the 8th TFW at Ubon.' Col Blesse re-read the report before dispatching it, 'laughing my a— off' in the process', he later wrote. A frank exchange of views took place over the telephone between Cols Blesse and Olds shortly afterwards, but the two patched up their differences at the OC at Ubon a couple of weeks later. Through Blesse's determined efforts the 366th TFW had joined the air-to-air Phantom fraternity and had given it a powerful new weapon to play with—a gun. There was just one more task he wanted to accomplish before departing from the war zone.

When Blesse arrived at Da Nang he was the only pilot in the unit who had ever fought an enemy aircraft. When the Wing was assigned the task of flying escort over the North soon after his arrival, he set about briefing pilots for air combat using the Korean War-era manual *No Guts—No Glory*, of which he was the author. Oddly enough, the Wing was assigned MiGCAP escort for only six weeks before being redirected to 'mud-moving', but it scored eleven kills (of an eventual unit tally of eighteen) during that brief excursion, more than any other Wing in South-East Asia at that time, including Olds'. Four were 20mm kills, the additional gun-pod victories being claimed by Lt-Col Robert F. Titus and his back-seater 1Lt Milan Zimer on 22 May (call-sign 'Wander One' in F-4C 64-0776, which claimed a MiG-21, one of three jets shot down by this duo in the space of two days) and by Maj D. K. Preister and Capt J. E. Pankhurst on 5 June (at the helm of 'Oakland One', F-4C 64-0660, which 'bagged' a MiG-17). Blesse was annoyed that his Wing did not get the Press coverage for their MiG kills that the 'Wolfpack' had received, so he set about making the 366th more catchy for the media. All squadron commanders were locked in a room until they came up with a new insignia and

Above, left and right: A close-up and a line-up of the 'Gunfighters'. F-4D 66-8775 *The Saint* was assigned to 366th TFW CO Col Paul Watson when his alternative steed, *Gunfighter One*, was out for maintenance and wore appropriate tail-codes. In this instance the trim is Kelly green and white and the fuselage bands are (from front to rear) green, red and royal blue again. The darker areas of tan are freshly repainted; the FS30219 paint was prone to weathering and after a year or so degenerated into a lack-lustre sand colour with a pink hue. (Via Richard L. Ward)

name. Eventually somebody chanced upon the winning 'Gunfighters of Da Nang'. Maj Ed Lipsey came up with the 'Spook' insignia carrying a raging gun pod, based on the logo in McAir's manuals, patches were made and the 'Gunfighters' acquired a stage coach which travelled the flight-line twenty-four hours a day, ferrying crews out to their jets and back. It certainly caught the attention of the Press and TV men. After 1 May the unit was always referred to as the 'Gunfighters of Da Nang', or 'Gunfighters' for short. Haeffner's squadron, the 390th TFS *Blue Boars*, even spent a weekend painting a 19ft-diameter version of the new insignia on top of their main hangar—the largest 'patch' then extant in the USAF. Above all else, the groundwork was laid down for a Model 98 featuring an integral nose-embedded 'shooter' with minimum unwanted dispersion characteristics, although this would take another two years to reach the war zone.

Later that spring a 7th AF memo suggested an exchange of information between in-theatre fighter Wings. Each DO had to fly with the other Wings to study their mission, broaden his knowledge and pass that information back to his own unit—the origins of the later Fighter Weapons Instructor Course grapevine. A direct result of this was the introduction of the SUU-16/A gun pod into 8th TFW service.

ENTER THE DELTA

The year 1967 witnessed the introduction of the follow-on USAF variant of the Phantom to combat, the Model 98-EN F-4D, wired up *ab initio* for the SUU-16/A (and the improved gas-driven GE SUU-23/A model). Ostensibly identical to the F-4C which it supplanted—the model rolled off the McAir lines concurrently with its predecessor during Blocks 24x and 25y, both with new 'clean' radomes, without RHAWS, which made them difficult to differentiate at a distance—it was in fact a vastly superior all-rounder, with a lot of new 'black boxes' beneath its skin. It was first flown on 9 December 1965, with test pilot Raymond D. Hunt at the stick, and the initial production examples were handed over to the USAF on 10 March 1966 at Warner-Robins AFB, Georgia, before being hurriedly dispatched ten days later to the 'Thud'-depleted 36th TFW at Bitburg AB, West Germany, for nuclear alert. The 33rd TFW at Eglin AFB, Florida, followed suit in June, creating several combat-ready cadres that re-equipped Ubon's flight lines with the new breed beginning on 28 May the next

year, before going on to furnish new fighters for the expanding units coming under 432nd TRW control at Udorn in the border country in October.[11]

Meanwhile 'Category' tests at Edwards, and FOT&E with the operational Wings, progressed at speed, pending perfection of the 'all-up' systems package. It is worth bearing in mind that, at this stage in the Phantom's production saga, output was gearing up towards a monthly surge of seventy aircraft (peaking at six dozen in June 1967), of five different marks. And, despite the 'through cycle' of eight months between the first parts coming together and the pre-acceptance Functional Check Flight, the pace of the production effort at McAir often precluded all but 'Group A' wiring harnesses and CFE (contractor-furnished equipment) being installed in preparation for planned updates. The finishing touches, comprising 'Group B' GFE (government-furnished equipment), were sometimes left out for reasons of availability or security and were installed only after delivery by teams working at Ogden Air Matériel Area at Salt Lake City, Utah, or at Warner-Robins AMA, Georgia—or, if need be, in the field.

---

[11] Refer to Appendix V for further details. The first to receive F-4Ds in the combat zone was the 555th TFS *Triple Nickel* squadron at Ubon, which was later transferred to the 432nd TRW at Udorn. Udorn's first F-4D unit was the 13th TFS *Black Panthers*, which was re-equipped by Eglin's 16th TFS late in October 1967. In 1972 the 13th and 555th TFSs would operate side-by-side and 'bag' 28 MiGs between them.

The fully operational F-4D avionics suite, introduced on the production lines during Block 26z and retrofitted to earlier examples, consisted of two new core units, the GE AN/ASG-22 servoed Lead Computing Optical Sight Set (LCOSS), which replaced the old fixed, manually depressed gun sight, and the AN/ASQ-91 automatic Weapons Release Computer System (WRCS). Working in concert with the radar, nav systems and a competent crew, these provided the basis for a brand new radar-assisted visual bombing mode known as 'dive–toss', which increased bombing accuracy and crew survivability in one fell swoop. A description of the systems in action best explains why the improvement was eons ahead of the F-4C.

Having rolled down, or 'popped up' on to the target heading at the pre-planned altitude, the pilot selected weapons, stations and fuses (as described previously for 'down the chute' attacks) and then lined up on the target, wings-level, for the dive-bomb run. In the back seat the GIB was presented with a PPI (Plan Position Indicator) radar ground map of the terrain ahead, a 'pie slice' display with a sideways-moving strobe (akin to a windscreen-wiper) flashing up constantly updated radar ground returns with every sweep. Being a visual delivery mode, there was no need for the GIB to identify any specific target from the multitude of blips that degenerated into a solid mass of ground returns at the base of the vertex: all that was required was for him to lock the radar on to the top of the ground return line, which by then would be moving down the vertex as the pilot entered the dive, 'ready for pickle'. Once accomplished, the radar boresight line (RBL) was lined up with the pilot's gunsight LCOSS 'pipper'. Jiggling into position, usually at an altitude where the necessity for jinking was less problematic, the pilot centred the servoed 'pipper' on the target and pressed and held the firing (bomb release) trigger, thereby telling the WRCS to ingest and hold the radar-generated slant-range information to target, which it used automatically to compute the moment for optimum weapons release (also drawing on computed variables derived from the INS and central air data system). Still keeping the button pressed, and with the GIB calling out the descending height over the intercom as 'talking altimeter' for good measure, the pilot pulled back on the stick up out of the dive and the WRCS, sensing when all the release parameters had been met, sent a signal at the speed of light to the bomb ejector racks (which responded lazily by comparison), to deposit the bombs on target. Bombing patterns could be initiated at least 2,000ft higher than when employing manual 'down the chute' procedures, keeping them out of range of small-arms fire—though woe betide any wing-man who pressed home a high-altitude 'dive–toss' when his leader was mixing it up, partial systems out, 'down the chute' below! And, unless excessive jinking was prescribed, owing to such contingencies as an ugly SAM having left its smoky lair on the ground, the radar would hold its lock and the system would provide almost complete freedom in terms of dive angle, airspeed and so on—within the constraints imposed by the ordnance—virtually guaranteeing a 'shack' every time, provided the pilot maintained heading and had not 'goofed' in his placement of the servoed 'pipper'.

Other WRCS-assisted delivery modes were available, including 'dive laydown' and 'laydown' (which never adequately replaced the manual deliveries used previously). In these modes the radar was not locked on to the ground *per se*, and the back-seater would peruse the blotchy PPI sector-scan sweep of the terrain ahead and attempt to pick out navigation features. WRCS-generated cross-hairs appeared on the scope and could be placed over the target either automatically, by calling up stored target co-ordinates in the nav-attack computer, or manually, by the back-seater moving them about with the aid of new right console 'along track' and 'across track' thumbwheels. With the 'freeze' button pressed, the inertial system continued to track the assigned spot and kept the cross-hairs in place, providing radar slant-range data to the WRCS and head-up steering instructions to the pilot via the LCOSS roll index tabs. The pilot simply lined up on the target—using visual cues wherever possible—and pressed and held the 'pickle' button all the way up to automatic weapons release. 'Offset' took the process one stage further and was designed to replace the crude all-weather 'radar range-line' bombing technique introduced by the F-4C (which simply called for the use of radar to line up manually on the target prior to 'pickling' off the bombs when the range strobe intersected the target return), by means of relying on a pre-planned, readily recognizable radar return (such as a bend in a river, or a ground beacon which would generate a bright 'blip') at a known range and bearing to the target, for 'blind' bombing. In this mode, the cross-hairs would be placed over the prominent OAP (offset aimpoint) first, before 'target insert' was pressed. The computers then compared the positions of the two and automatically repositioned the cross-hairs over the (invariably unidentifiable) target on the scope. With all working to order, the INS continued to track the target, while the radar and central air data systems again furnished ballistics information to the WRCS and steering cues to the pilot, all the way up to bomb release. However, all of these deliveries were strictly 'canned' and, owing to the threshold of the cross-hairs and the in-

evitable drift in the INS, produced poor conventional bombing accuracies. Used in this manner, the radar package was better suited to 'special weapons' deliveries when working in concert with the aircraft's AN/AJB-7 all-altitude bombing computer, for the timed release of nuclear weapons over the target from a predetermined offset or initial point. In SEA, radar was employed primarily for navigation to the vicinity of the target prior to resetting the switches for a visual 'dive–toss' strike run—the F-4D's true forte.

The combat Wings soon developed a voracious appetite for the new WRCS-equipped model, and most of the F-4Cs were speedily turfed out of the war zone for peacetime reassignment within PACAF, including the 'G-Gees' of the 347th TFW stationed at Yokota AB, Japan, and the 18th TFW at Kadena AB, Okinawa. Other examples were routed back into the RTU system managed by the 479th TFW at George AFB, California (where, as in the Florida training programmes, uninitiated crews were given the opportunity to fire at least one live practice missile against BQM-34 drones prior to a combat assignment). George performed the lion's share of lead-in combat indoctrination, before 'first-tourists' went on to be subjected to the necessary trauma of jungle survival training in the Philippines.

THE FALCON FIASCO

One controversial aspect of the 'all-up' Block 26z–33ag F-4D was that it abandoned AIM-9Bs in favour of the sophisticated Hughes AIM-4D Falcon, a 134lb sleek, glossy red and white, tail-steered weapon packing a range of six miles and a burn-out speed in excess of Mach 3. It was developed initially as Project 'Dragonfly' under the direction of the eccentric billionaire Howard Hughes, principally for use on board NORAD

Right: Maj Jim Chamberlain, in full flight regalia, prior to a 'Gunfighters' outing. Jim previously flew F-101Bs with ADC and later resumed air-defence duties with the 496th TFS at Hahn, West Germany, where he was an F-4E 'pitter'. (Jim Chamberlain)

interceptors, and the F-4D was rigged to carry four weapons at a time in an unusual inboard-facing slant-two configuration on hefty LAU-42 launchers which housed the plumbing for the gaseous nitrogen cryogenics to cool the Falcon's sensitive infra-red seekers. Systems integration was established at Eglin AFB under Project 'Dancing Falcon' during late 1965, where the programme showed promise.

The AIM-4D's disappointing performance in terms of MiG kills—only five in Vietnam (the first of which, a MiG-17, was claimed on 26 October 1967 by Capts Larry D. Cobb and Alan A. Lavoy flying F-4D 66-7565)—was largely attributed to the missile's inherent design features, which had been chosen with strategic air defence in mind. As Maj James R. Chamberlain USAF Ret, a former Scorpion and Voodoo RO (Radar intercept Officer) with ten years' interception experience behind him before he joined the 'Gunfighters at Da Nang', noted, 'The biggest problem with the AIM-4D was the limited amount of

cooling time available, which meant that the missile could not be pre-cooled for a quicker lock-on. And, once available liquid nitrogen was consumed, the missile was a blind, dead bullet—derisively called the "Hughes Arrow"—which had to be carried home and serviced before it could be used again usefully. Another complaint was that it was not equipped with a proximity fuse, making it a hit-to-kill missile. The forty-pound warhead was twice the size of that of the AIM-9, but Sidewinder's proximity fuse increased the likelihood of target damage.' However, the Falcon's inauspicious combat début had much to do with the general 'lack of trade' provided by the enemy during this stage of the war, compounded by the effective suspension of counter-air operations over North Vietnam the following year—together with not a little misunderstanding regarding the weapon's optimum employment. Statistically, at least, of the remaining 65 kills achieved by USAF F-4s between October 1967 and the last ever shoot-out in January 1973, the Sidewinder accounted for a mere 9.5 during periods of peak activity. Had the Falcon received a more positive reaction from the stick-and-rudder men leading the MiGCAP flights—including Col Robin Olds, who alleged that it cost him his fifth MiG and thus the honour of becoming the first Vietnam ace and who, in disgust, reputedly ordered the Falcons to be removed within twenty-four hours of firing four of them unsuccessfully in combat, thereby signing the missile's death warrant—then things might have been different. Hughes would almost certainly have proceeded with its follow-on AIM-4H version possessing Mach 4 performance and a genuine working range of between

Right, upper and lower: Assigned to the **36th TFS** *Flying Fiends* at Kunsan, South Korea, and on detachment (possibly transferred but not yet re-marked in 432nd TRW decor) to Udorn RTAFB, Thailand, for MiGCAP duties in December 1971, F-4D-29-MC 65-0785 shows off its alert configuration of three 'bags' and four AIM-7E-2 Sparrows and, more unusually, an AN/ALQ-101 ECM pod plus three AIM-4D Falcon missiles on the inner wing pylons. (Larsen/Remington via Richard L. Ward)

half a mile and seven miles, with expanded cooling time. This model was also to feature active optical proximity fusing to 'up' the Pk (probability of a kill), yet it was abandoned during 1971 owing to a lack of interest from the Air Force. Certainly, men who had entered the F-4 RTU pipeline from a background with Aerospace Defense Command saw the weapon in an altogether different light. As ADC and Vietnam veteran Jim Chamberlain went on to point out, 'TAC attitudes were very different from those in air defence. ADC pilots were very much better instrument pilots than the TAC guys who only flew when it was

good enough for bombing patterns of several thousand feet. Also, being day, VFR kinds of guys, TAC people viewed radar, and every other technological improvement, as either an aid to the eye-ball or a threat, but never as a weapon in its own right. I remember flying a mission with an RTU instructor pilot. I was using radar and the heat-seeking head of an AIM-4 missile simulator to track the target. As the missile picked up the target and generated a growl in the headset well before the pilot could see the target visually, he said "Well, I'll be damned." To a TAC pilot, no electro-mechanical device would ever be allowed to beat

him and his Mark X eyeball.' Such BVR lock-ons could be achieved when the radar might be unable to maintain its lock amidst jamming or ground-clutter which would foil a Sparrow shot, thus enabling the crew to destroy its adversary well before the Phantom had strayed within range of the opponent's 'Atoll' missiles or hefty 30mm cannon. However, the desire by the front-seaters to be simply vectored to their targets by the EC-121s and GIBs, preparatory to a hit-or-miss volley outside the weapon's ideal launch parameters (just like Sparrow), followed by a 'turn-and-burn' stick-and-rudder engagement with Sidewinder missiles or guns, ruled the day.[12]

The 793rd F-4D allocated to the USAF was delivered on 28 February 1968.[13] Dual-missile-capable F-4Ds reached operational units in June 1969 following a re-work with new electrical harnesses at Ogden AMA. The Falcon's final use in the war zone was for pure air defence, the first time this job had been given to the Air Force Phantoms in combat on an exclusive basis. However, it was too little, too late. Until January 1969 the task had been undertaken by single-seat 'TDY-ing' F-102s on rotation from Clark Field in the Philippines, and the MiGs had shot one down. Jim Chamberlain again: 'Shortly after my arrival at Da Nang (and totally unrelated to it), the 366th TFW assumed the air defence mission function, maintaining alert with two F-4Ds armed with four AIM-7D Sparrows, four AIM-4Ds and an SUU-23/A gun pod. These two aircraft were in addition to the six other alert aircraft armed for air-to-ground. The air defence role was considered a joke because of the improbability of any kind of offensive air effort by the North Vietnamese [but was put in place because of the base's proximity to the North. However, the 'Buff' crews flying from Andersen in Guam and U-Tapao, Thailand, considered these aircraft integral to their mission]. The air defence aircraft would fly as a "MiG barrier" for the night B-52 "Arc Light" strikes in Laos. The "Buffs" would abort the mission unless there was a protective "MiG bar" which positioned itself between the B-52s and the NVN border. It was never more than an hour and a half of boredom. Apparently, the NVNAF didn't like to fly at night [not at that stage, anyway].'[14] The 366th TFW placidly held down this gradually expanding commitment until October 1972, when the two relevant squadrons (by then upgraded with F-4E models, two examples of which featured trials examples of the Northrop TISEO) were passed over to 432nd TRW control at Udorn, Thailand.[15]

Falcon was hastily relegated to service with USAFE, where it remained active until around April 1973, while forces in South-East Asia were reissued with AIM-9Bs and shortly afterwards upgraded to Ford's new thermoelectric-cooled (TEC), Peltier-effect AIM-9E Sidewinder, some 5,000 of which were built as new or converted from old 'Bravo' stock. This model's wider 'look angle' expanded the lock-on cone emanating from the quarry's hot exhaust and was significantly less prone to distraction by the sun and by water glint than its uncooled forebear. Moreover, as long as electrical power was available and did not burn out the delicate thermocouple, it would not go 'blind' and could be 'locked', disengaged and later instantly pre-cooled again for a new lock-on, at will. However, it would not see action until 1972.

Following President Johnson's pronouncement of 31 March 1968 prohibiting bombing north of the 20th, then 19th, Parallel, US–North Vietnamese negotiations took place in Paris, resulting in what was termed an 'essential understanding . . . to join us in de-escalating the war and moving seriously towards peace'. At 0800hrs Washington time on 31 October all air strike operations over North Vietnam ceased. Just 90 minutes before the President's order was issued, Maj Frank C. Lenahan of the 8th TFW made the last run in an F-4D against a target, near Dong Hoi, ending forty-five months of 'Rolling Thunder' operations. For the next forty months CAS duties would trudge along at their self-rewarding pace while interdiction operations would shift towards night-time work in the 'Steel Tiger' zone in Laos and further south into Cambodia, and also towards armed-reconnaissance sorties, generically code-named 'Commando Hunt', aimed at stemming the flow of enemy troops and *matériel* that supported guerrilla activities in the South. It would be a totally new kind of war for the F-4 Phantom and its hard-pressed crews.

[12] Infra-red-guided models of the Falcon (the AIM-4B to D/G) were employed in 'live shoots' against drones at no fewer than fourteen 'William Tell' ADC competitions held at Tyndall ADWC, Florida, between 1958 and 1986, during which time it consistently established its worth in the face of all manner of countermeasures clutter. While few question that the postwar generations of Sidewinder missiles (the 'Papa' and 'Limas' discussed in Chapters 7, 8, and 13) were vastly superior to even the XAIM-4H, of which only some 25 were fabricated for trials, the point being made here is that, with proper training, the AIM-4D could have been used to much greater effect between June 1967 and October 1968. The USAF F-4D was never a twin-engine, afterburning, supersonic Mustang or Sabre, although it tended to be employed in that manner until the new breed of crewmen with a background in 'systems' entered the fray and honed the team effort in the cockpit. More than one of these confided to the authors that 'the janitor at the Hughes Missile plant probably had a better understanding of AIM-4 employment than did many [of the early pilots in question]'. Block 24–26 F-4Ds in the 64-0929 to -0969 serial range were retrofitted with Falcon capability under TO 1F-4D-508.

[13] The follow-on 32 F-4Ds produced under Blocks 35–37 and 39 of the eventual 825 built were supplied directly to Iran, McAir's second export customer for the Phantom, and delivered in batches of four beginning on 8 September 1968, for issue to 308 Fighter Squadron at Mehrabad AB near Tehran. The F-4Ds were subsequently relocated at Shiraz AB. Rumours of 'F-4Bs' in the region are probably explained by the presence of these aircraft, early examples of which may have been confused with sightings of these jets 'flown by civilians'.

[14] It is contended that the 'Alpha Alert' system at Da Nang deterred at least two North Vietnamese plans, at the paper stage, to conduct hit-and-run strikes on the base. Such attacks against Navy radar picket ships (evoked as a substitute) were thwarted only by Tartar ship-to-air RIM missiles, which downed at least one 'Fishbed' during 1972 during the North's abortive and desperate attempts to pull off some kind of 'scoop'.

[15] The stand-off AN/ASX-1 TISEO (Target Identification System Electro-Optical) is discussed in Chapter 13.

10. HAVE GUN, WILL TRAVEL

Arriving just in time for the revitalized 'Trails Offensive' over Laos, but just four weeks too late to rattle its new internal gun at the enemy MiGs, was the definitive land-based production variant of the Phantom—the F-4E. The USAF would take delivery of no fewer than 865 of this marque exclusively for its own use in the nine years up to 10 December 1976, during which time the type's oustanding performance (and not a little Berlitz-cramming by McDonnell's sales representatives) fostered a hugely successful export business. With only subtle modifications to the 'vanilla' USAF model, it would eventually see service with nine allies, in numbers (including transfers from American stocks) topping 1,100 airframes.[1]

Much of the impetus for the F-4E's success derived from the dramatic, world-touring, peacetime exponents of its dazzling performance potential—the USAF aerial demonstration squadron, the *Thunderbirds*. The Nellis, Nevada-based ADS's F-4Es were the first in the unit's history to wear the patriotic red, white and blue scallops over a complete gloss white airframe (deemed necessary because of the Phantom's complex, multi-hued patchwork of exotic-metal skin panels), receiving their first aircraft on 19 April 1969.[2]

During the course of 518 exciting performances, beginning with their premier show at the Air Force Academy at Colorado Springs on 1 June 1969 and ending with a 10 November 1973 display at NAS New Orleans, Louisiana, the team treated audiences around the world to some hair-raising tight formation work, including high and low 'bomb burst' breaks, 'diamond tactical pitch-ups', 'cross-overs' and precision solo eight-point rolls and inverted, everything-dangling-out, reverberating flypasts. *Happy Hooligans* boss Gen Alexander P. Macdonald, a long-time advocate of the F-4, put it succinctly when he summed up the 'pizzazz' of the displays: 'Who can forget the overwhelming noise, the black smoke from the engines mixed with the white smoke of the show, and the very size of the aircraft as they came over singly and in formation? The . . . sheer sensationalism. It was truly a heart-stopping event that had the children gasping in awe and the adults vowing to return again and again.' It also was good for recruiting, and it 'showed the flag'. During the team's 1971 tour, with Lt-Col Tom S. Swalm presiding as chief of the ADS, European fighter pilots demonstrated a marked tendency to turn green at the sight of the 'T-Birds' hardware!

The operational variant of the F-4E was bulkier, more purposeful and, with its 'lizard' SEA camouflage paint job, more menacing than the pretty test and display aircraft. With an AUW of 58,000lb on take-off (and an eventual 31-ton maximum combat weight), it was the heaviest model to see production. The first example to go into squadron service (F-4E No 3, 66-0286) was flown to Nellis on 3 October 1967 by Col Floyd White, commander of the 4525th FWW,

Below left: The F-4E Phantom was the biggest aircraft to be operated by the *Thunderbirds*. Few can forget the team's dramatic tight formation work on its noisy, glamorous steed. (Frank B. Mormillo)
Right: Five-abreast, the *Thunderbirds* zoom over the Hawaiian *kune hai* during their 1971 season. (McAir)

and MiG-killer Maj Everett Raspberry, Wing Project Officer.[3] However, the type's dazzling service with the *Thunderbirds* and undeniable later export success belie the numerous technical problems which abounded in the early months. Development of the Hughes CORDS (Coherent On Receive Doppler Subsystem), a vital new component of the machine's Airborne Missile Control System (AMCS) created two production

slippages and very nearly curtailed the F-4E TSF programme altogether during the opening phases of Block 31. CORDS was designed to filter out ground clutter at low level so that moving targets, such as a fleeting, low-level MiG, would be picked out and presented as a clear, synthesized target symbol (as opposed to a raw, fuzzy 'blip' competing for prominence with the inevitable returns generated by ground

reflections), to make comparatively light work of target lock-on for the purpose of a missile shot. Hughes flight-tested the system as part of the F-4E's new AMCS package during February 1965 and, with continuing improvements, claimed that it would have the ability to track even subsonic targets flying at around 500ft AGL. However, producing such a complicated package in the pre-microchip age, coupled with the need to contain the

---

[1] Including, at the time of writing, 24 F-4Es loaned to Australia (23 returned in 1973), 35 F-4Es supplied to Egypt, 175 F-4Fs and ten F-4Es procured by Germany, 56 F-4Es bought and 28 acquired by Greece, 185 F-4Es received by Iran (including two long-term and six short-term loans, all of which were subsequently returned), 204 F-4Es sold to Israel, 140 F-4EJs bought or licence-built by Japan, 77 F-4Es acquired by the Republic of Korea and 182 acquired by Turkey, for a total of 1,117 that have operated under 'foreign flags' at various stages of their career. Exact disposition figures have recently become muddled owing to the large number of surplus F-4E airframes, several of which have been acquired simply as 'spare parts lockers', often as sub-assemblies.

[2] *Thunderbirds* ADS's aircraft were drawn from the following eighteen F-4Es: 66-0286, -0289, -0290 (No 8, which crashed on 20 January 1971 and was repaired), -0291, -0294, -0296 (destroyed on 19 March 1973), -0303, -0315 (the No 3

replacement for -0321), -0319 (No 5), -0321 (No 3, destroyed at Andrews AFB, Maryland, on 4 June 1972), -0329 (No 7), -0377 and -0382 ('Lizard' trainer), and 67-0309, -0313, -0327 and -0347 (all 'Lizard' trainers). The 'Lizard' trainers were operational F-4Es which wore standard SEA camouflage and were used when the display aircraft were in the shop or depot for maintenance. Modifications to the aircraft used for display purposes including removing the gun, gun louvres, LCOSS and radar, adding lead ballast and deleting all but the basic rear-cockpit instrumentation. The ejection sequence was altered for single ejection and new VHF radios were installed, linked to the trigger button. Additionally, modifications to the throttles permitted full reheat to be engaged at 89 per cent military power, while Sparrow missile shapes served as oil tanks for smoke (forward) and colour dye (aft), fed into the jet efflux via new, internal plumbing. The eight display survivors, 66-0286, -0289, -0291,

-0294, -0315, -0319, -0329, and -0377, were subsequently assigned to non-operational test duties with the AFFTC at Edwards AFB.

[3] Three prototypes of the F-4E Tactical Strike Fighter (TSF) were authorized on 1 June 1966, based on earlier airframes: F-4C 63-7445 (Model 98-HN), F-4D 65-0713 (Model 89-HO) and the ever-protean YRF-4C 62-12200, equipped with J79-GE-J1Bs (a development model of the long-canned, GE-10/17) and the new M61A-1 20mm gun. The first to fly was the newly redesignated YF-4E 62-12200, on 7 August 1965, with McAir test pilot Joe Dobronski and systems engineer Ed Rosenmeyer in the cockpit. The first 'true' F-4E built (66-0284) was flown for the first time on 30 June 1967, with R. D. Hunt and Wayne Wight at the controls, and was retained for test work at McAir, while No 2 (66-0285), which flew for the first time on 11 September, was delivered to Edwards AFFTC with a massive tail protruberance housing a spin recovery parachute.

guts of the system in a potentially fiercely gyrating environment (above the M61A-1 gun, which, when shot off, subjected the nose to instantaneous vibrations of the order of 100*g*!) eventually proved to be an overwhelming technical challenge, and CORDS was finally abandoned on 3 January 1968. Westinghouse pressed ahead with their 'vanilla' AN/APQ-120(V) fire control system, the heart of the F-4E's transistor radar package which was based on the AN/APQ-109 but designed to fit in the more pointed, 33in-extended nose of the new variant. Yet this, too, was still not ready when the first thirty aircraft were delivered, and the Nellis-based Operational Test & Evalu-

ation unit was obliged to wait until 14 December 1967 before it received its first 'all-up' F-4E (66-0314).[4] A second difficulty was created by the much-welcomed GE Vulcan gun, rated at selectable 4,000 or 6,000spm (shells per minute) rates of fire and fed by a linkless system drawing on up to 639 rounds. Unfortunately, the original gun muzzle shroud configuration (of which there existed two prototype and one production format) created a loud whistling noise and did not dissipate gun gases adequately, frequently resulting in heart-palpitating engine flame-outs. And, without engine power, the sleek F-4 shared the same flying characteristics as a brick.

Above: A perfect display of diamond formation-keeping over Diamond Head, Oahu. The USAF *Thunderbirds* flew stripped-down F-4Es for four years, giving 518 performances before switching to docile T-38As. (McAir)

It took several years of head-scratching by a special 'think tank' of engineers fully to solve the problem, which they eventually did by means of the definitive, elongated Midas IV shroud, first flight-tested in April 1970. This featured additional ventral diffusing louvres so that, during cartridge-popping, the gases tended to pass beneath the nose and under the belly. As a fail-safe precaution, the engines were equipped with a T-4 reset

---

[4] The AN/APQ-120 antenna was 4½in narrower than its Westinghouse predecessors, forming an ellipse in the horizontal to match the F-4E's complex nose contours. Inevitably this configuration resulted in increased noise interference from second-time-around echoes and ground clutter. The solution was to fit a suppressor plate and delete the medium pulse-repetition frequency mode. The radar's ground-mapping and air-to-

air capabilities were gradually sharpened throughout the F-4E's production run, culminating in the LRU-1 modification which gave the F-4E a much improved auto-acquisition capability. In a similar fashion to that used for the transition from the F-4C/D model, there existed a considerable overlap between the F-4D/E production process. The first true F-4E, McAir Ship Number 2234 (serial 66-0284), was assigned its Shop Number in the

factory when a further 264 F-4Ds had yet to be assigned working numbers. Production of the two marks initially hovered around the 6:1 ratio, then wound up at 2:1 when only 127 USAF F-4Ds remained to be completed. McAir Ship Numbers (which do not precisely mirror the manufacturing sequence) indicate that up to 244 F-4Ds and 111 F-4Es flowed through the production line concurrently during 1967–68.

derichment device, electro-mechanically linked to the firing system, which would automatically ditch gas-laden air when the gun was activated. These features were introduced on the production line during 1970 and retrofitted to earlier examples during the course of scheduled depot maintenance cycles, effectively curing the problem. Remarkably, the gun had little adverse effect on the radar's performance, owing to a buffet-proof mounting, and was unequivocally considered a boon by the Phantom jockeys. Other improvements introduced by the chunky F-4E came in the form of the J79-GE-17 engines, each rated at 11,870lb s.t. at full military power (17,900lb s.t. with reheat engaged), providing an extra ton of thrust with the throttles slammed forward. The aircraft was also the only USAF production variant to incorporate the slotted all-moving tail originally developed for the US Navy F-4J. This acted as an inverted aerofoil to provide a more positive pitch response and was especially useful during low-speed manoeuvres in the landing circuit,

and in shortening take-off rolls. An 84 US gallon fuel cell (No7) was also added inside the rear fuselage, counterbalancing the gun and restoring the reduced capacity taken up by some of the additional avionics housed further forward. With everything working as advertised, the E formed a near-perfect equation, and represented what the USAF had been seeking from the outset.

The first operational Wing to receive the aircraft was the 33rd TFW at Eglin AFB, Florida. Ground schools began in November 1967, and by March the following year brand new F-4Es were begining to swell the ranks of the three squadrons operating adjacent to the Armament Proving Grounds and its test fleet—the 4th, the 16th and the 40th TFS *Satans*. New crews and aircraft were moulded into one as Eglin became a 'melting pot' for the new men and machines, working them up to combat-ready status for impending deployment to the war zone. First to be dispatched was the initial cadre of *Satans*, which achieved IOC in July and deployed to the 388th

TFW at Korat RTAFB, Thailand, on 17 November to re-equip the 469th TFS *Fighting Bulls*. The designation change occurred the moment the aircraft put tyres on tarmac. An initial sixteen aircraft were assigned under 'Operation 47, Buck Nine', all with aggressive-looking shark's mouths that would become a long-standing trademark of the new breed, introduced by the new squadron boss Lt-Col Edward Hillding (who even had the design repeated on his flight-line jeep!). The machines went on to fly their first combat missions over Laos on 26 November and quickly attracted a flurry of elaborate artwork and nicknames which extended to successive Wing commanders' jets, including the famous *Arkansas Traveler*, *Betty Lou* and *Spunky VI*. The pace was marred only by the loss of 67-286 and its crew over Laos on New Year's Day 1969 (the first of what would eventually amount to seventy-three F-4E losses by war's end). Close on their heels, the *Satans* trained further batches to re-equip Korat's 34th TFS Rams during May 1969, while Eglin's 4th and

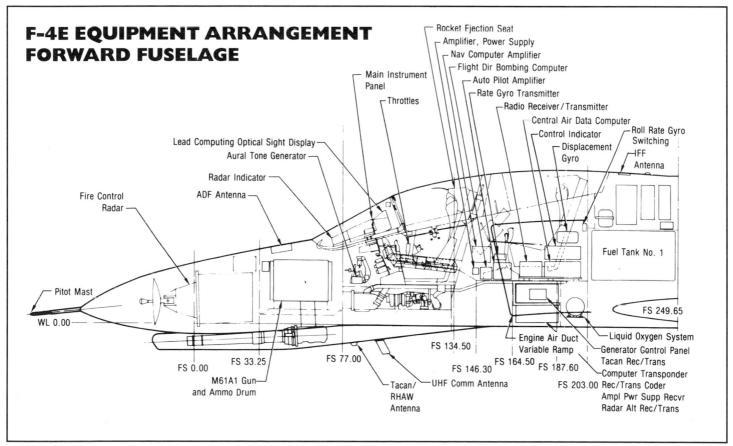

115

16th TFSs similarly provided F-4E men and *matériel* for the 'Gunfighters' at Da Nang during April: the 16th TFS formed the basis for the newly established 421st TFS *Black Widows*, alias 'The Kiss of Death' squadron, while the 4th TFS *Red Devils* moved *en bloc* to its new base. All four squadrons, split between Korat and Da Nang, then proceeded to 'haul iron' to the Trail, provide CAS in the Republic and border regions and furnish MiGCAP barrier protection for the ceaseless B-52D 'Arc Light' bombing effort. Concurrent with the F-4E's combat début, many USAFE units also rapidly leap-frogged from obsolescent types or pre-Block 26 F-4Ds to the new variants, the first of which was the 32nd TFS at Soesterberg AB, Camp New Amsterdam, Holland, which began trading-in aged F-102A 'Deuces' for the swashbuckling new Phantoms during August 1969.

While the gun-toting F-4E was fundamentally similar to the F-4D, and shared its INS, lead-computing LCOSS gun sight, AN/ASQ-91 WRCS 'dive–toss' and AN/AJB-7 nuclear bombing systems and air-to-air prowess, perhaps its greatest innovation was the new breed of fighter crew that accompanied it. Instead of having two rated pilots fly the aircraft, the machines featured a genuine team: better-tempered ACs at the helm had the privilege of a new backseat P-WSOs (Pilot/Weapons Systems Officers), affectionately referred to as 'Wizzos'. Many of the WSOs possessed only rudimentary stick-and-rudder skills (lending the pilot the exclusivity at the helm he had long been seeking) but were extremely adept at navigation, 'weaponeering', electronic warfare and use of the radar. Co-ordinated 'switching' and a new 'systems mentality' were finally beginning to unleash the Phantom's true potential. Crewmen even began talking to one another en route to the target or MiGCAP co-ordinates!

The biggest pay-off from the revised crew division was to maximize the effectiveness of the new electronic 'gizmos' developed from the mid-1960s as part of the burgeoning 'Pave' (Precision Avionics Vectoring Equipment) programmes. Moreover, squadrons began to undertake specialist taskings such as counter-air or deep interdiction, which put significantly less strain on the maintenance system while bolstering availability rates. By keeping the relevant avionics in good working order, it was argued, much better results could be achieved than with the previous practice of attempting ludicrous readiness rates and multi-skilled proficiencies across the board. The first units to make use of this new mentality were the Thai-based Wings, beginning with the 8th TFW 'Wolfpack', which had found a niche as a specialist precision strike unit.[5]

PAVE PHANTOM

One of the chief limitations of the Phantom for the night and bad-weather interdiction role in the 'Steel Tiger' operating zone was its radar and navigation systems. INS drift and the system's alarming 'tendency to dump just when it was needed', combined with the paucity of radar-significant targets and offsets over the endless, jagged, leaf-covered landscape, made accurate 'blind bombing' virtually impossible. Maj Jim Chamberlain, who continued to fly with the F-4D-equipped 480th TFS *Warhawks* after his squadron's reassignment from Da Nang to Phu Cat in April 1969, recalled some of the more 'despised missions' which the mud-movers were tasked with—'Commando Nail'. 'This grew out of the assignment to the Seventh Air Force of some SAC [Strategic Air Command] radar navigators. They reasoned that because the APQ-109 radar had a ground-mapping capability and even a bomb mode, crews should become proficient in radar-bombing. The rub is that any system built to perform a multitude of functions does none of them well. The usual "Commando Nail" mission started as a bombing mission with pre-strike refuelling in Thailand before finding the FAC in Laos, dumping the bombs, then conducting a post-strike refuelling so we could go to some unidentifiable IP to make "dry runs" on bits of indistinguishable karst. The whole thing was recorded on scope film and graded. It was difficult to attain any degree of accuracy because the radar cursor lines positioned on the target or offset aimpoint were, at the lowest threshold of visibility, at least a mile wide! The standard results were usually somewhat lower than WW2 RAF carpet bombing'. Finely tuned accuracies were measured in hundreds of metres.

It was this kind of combat that gave rise to the jokes about 'We scared a lot of parrots, monkeys and snakes and levelled a lot of foliage!'. Only secondary explosions were a positive indication that something had in fact been hit—what Lt-Col Mark Berent described with some optimism at the time as 'great balls of fire which roll and boil upward. A large, rather rectangular fire will let us know we've hit another convoy of supply trucks.' It was hit or miss, and mostly miss, even when working with the more

Right, top: YF-4E 65-0713 actually started life as a Block 28-MC F-4D. It served as an aerodynamic test-bed for the extended nose and gun installation alongside 62-12200; later in its career it tested composite control surfaces. In this view it is performing aerodynamic analysis and separation trials with the Hughes AGM-65A Maverick missile, fitted in clusters on draggy LAU-88 triple launch rails. (USAF via Lucille Zaccardi)
Right, bottom: A menacingly beautiful study of F-4Es taxying in at Nellis after touch-down, with drag 'chutes billowing in their wake. The first operational variants arrived at the base during October 1967. (Frank B. Mormillo)

---

[5] The 8th TFW's aircraft performed both day and night tactical interdiction. The 432nd TRW composite Wing at Udorn began to specialize in counter-air with F-4Ds as an adjunct to its RF-4C reconnaissance operations, the 388th TFW's F-4Es at Korat mainly undertook CAS and tactical interdiction and the 366th TFW's F-4Es at Da Nang specialized in border MiGCAP work, while the sole remaining F-4C unit in the theatre, the CAS-dedicated 12th TFW at Cam Ranh Bay, were wound down between 1968 and 1970. The last F-4Cs to fly combat missions were those assigned to the 559th TFS *Billy Goats*, which ceased operations on 22 March 1970. Shortly afterwards, the 12th TFW took over the 37th TFW's two F-4D CAS squadrons at Phu Cat (until these, too, were disestablished during October and November the following year).

sophisticated 'night eyes' available to the Pave Spectre gunships which sprayed the Trail with fire. Crews provided flak suppression for the latter—the great lumbering AC-119s and AC-130s bristling with computer-controlled Bofors and howitzers—and conducted 'down the chute' or 'dive–toss' attacks against points from which emanated short but dangerous blobs of 37mm and 57mm flak, often putting 'pippers' on the elusive spots dancing in front of their dazzled visors.

To close the gap, the USAF inaugurated project 'Pave Phantom'. This feature was eventually applied to six dozen Block 32–33 F-4Ds assigned to the 8th TFW 'Wolfpack' at Ubon beginning in late 1967 and comprised an ITT AN/ARN-92 LORAN (long-range radio navigation receiver) tied to the INS, and a new Lear-Siegler ballistics computer which held the characteristics of most conventional weapons on the inventory. By comparing the TD (time difference of arrival) of three signal sources, including a 'master' (M) and two of three 'slave' (X,Y and Z) transmitters triggered into action by the 'master', the system could deduce the F-4D's LORAN TD co-ordinates; bomb-

TABLE 16: ARN-92 LORAN-D F-4Ds

Block No	Serial No	Qty
F-4D-32-MC	66-8708 to -8714	8
	66-8719	1
	66-8722	1
	66-8726 to -8728	3
	66-8730 to -8735	6
	66-8737 to -8742	6
	66-8744 to -8745	2
	66-8747 to -8750	4
	66-8755 to -8756	2
	66-8758 to -8759	2
	66-8761 to -8762	2
	66-8765	1
	66-8768 to -8770	2
	66-8772	1
	66-8774	1
	66-8776 to -8777	2
	66-8779	1
	66-8782	1
	66-8784 to -8786	3
F-4D-33-MC	66-8787 to -8799	13
	66-8802 to -8803	2
	66-8805 to -8806	2
	66-8810	1
	66-8812 to -8813	2
	66-8816	1
	66-8818	1
	66-8825	1

Of the 72 aircraft adapted, 23 were stricken during the Vietnam War, owing to hostile fire, operational causes and 'admin' strikes where damaged machines were deemed uneconomic to repair, as follows: 66-8708, -8712, -8730, -8731, -8741, -8742, -8744, -8747, -8749, -8750, -8769, -8770, -8772, -8774, -8777, -8784, -8785, -8791, 8792, -8795, -8796, -8799 and -8818. Thirty-nine survivors were noted in 1985; 37 aircraft were noted in 1987, and all of these were retired during 1988–89.

Top: 'Merry Xmas': 388th TFW F-4Es brandishing suitably decorated Mk 82s with 'Daisy Cutter' fuse-extenders roar to their targets. The aircraft are from the 469th TFS *Bulls*, which began to trade in 'Thuds' for Phantoms during November 1968 and were the first unit in SEA to receive the type. (Via Jim Rotramel)
Above: A pair of 34th TFS *Rams* bulldoze their way on a north-easterly heading from Korat with CBUs and AN/ALQ-87 noise-jamming pods installed. The aircraft off '364''s wing is F-4E-32-MC 66-0313, which 'bagged' a MiG-17 on 6 October 1972 while in the hands of Clouser and Brunson. It was later ferried to Israel as part of the October 1973 'Nickel Grass' emergency resupply effort. (Via Jim Rotramel)

ing could be effected purely on the basis of the TD co-ordinates, or in the customary manner by using a LORAN-inertial combination to keep the INS constantly updated to a much higher degree of accuracy than was hitherto possible. LORAN-D transmitter chains eventually stretched across the entire war zone.

However, the package did not initially prove entirely satisfactory for the precision work required for night-time bombing, and it took three years fully to mature. Part of the problem was that the Pave Phantom originally had its receivers tucked away behind a new dielectric black fin-cap. Reception difficulties,

caused by the recurring electrical anomalies associated with the F-4, prevented the aircraft from picking up the signals under a number of conditions. It would take up to a quarter of an hour for the system to lock-on once the 'Wizzo' had activated the 'M' button, setting the receivers and allied computers in motion, while evasive jinking often caused the system to break lock altogether (as did static 'burst noise' discharges when the F-4Ds connected themselves up for a mid-air top-up from KC-135A tankers), creating the need to start up all over again. The wholesale introduction of static dispenser 'whiskers' glued to the tail and wing-tips helped cure part of the problem, yet the biggest strides came with the retrofitting of the aircraft with a distinctive dorsal Chelton 'towel bar' antenna, introduced in the summer of 1969, shielded by the wing from ground wave reflections. The updated LORAN package was recalibrated shortly afterwards by unarmed 25th TFS F-4Ds flying cross-country sorties under Operation 'Diogenes'. The 'towel bar' soon became a trademark of the Pave Phantoms, along with their gunship grey or semi-gloss black bellies (and the distinctive artwork that flourished on the flanks and avionics cooling scoops). To these crews, all-weather and night-time work were bywords, along with the inevitable jokes—'Daytime fighter jocks are okay, but I wouldn't let my daughter marry one!', and the long-standing remarks by some in the fraternity asking 'Why is a Jewish guy like me bombing Buddhists to make the world safe for Christians?!' It was the kind of humour that fuelled bomber operations in Europe two decades earlier, and it found a new niche at Ubon.

Maj James M Shaw USAF Ret, who joined the 'Wolfpack' after the 'bugs' in the Pave Phantom had largely been cradicated, reflected on the Wing's various taskings. 'Unlike other Wings who rotated day and night duties, we had two dedicated day squadrons (the 25th TFS *Assam Dragons* and 433rd TFS *Satan's Angels*) and two dedicated night squadrons (the 435th TFS *Eagles* and 497th *Nite Owls*). The 25th, my squadron, had the "dawn patrol" and handed the mission off to the 433rd around midday. The 435th picked things up just before dark and handed off to the 497th. There was, of course, some overlap depending on tasking and mission requirements.'

The crews perfected the use of the evolving Pave Phantom in three key roles. The first of these was 'Fast-FAC' pathfinding over Laos with SUU-42/A night flare pods and 'Willie Peter' white phos-

phorous rockets, to highlight targets for US Navy and Air Force strike machines 'fragged' to specific co-ordinates on the off-chance that they could deposit their bomb loads on something vaguely lucrative, using visual delivery techniques. This was particularly hazardous for the pathfinders at night as crews had no automatic terrain-avoidance radar mode, just the 'trusty' old AN/APQ-109 with its PPI sector-scan ground-mapping returns, 'creating thick blobs of green-on-black that thinned out from the bottom of the vertex up, like some kind of shrink's ink-stained blotting paper creation to indicate possible hazardous terrain ahead'. When they reached the correct LORAN co-ordinates, prescribed by intelligence de-

rived from the massively expanding electronic 'Igloo White' network, many crews felt that they were flying into a world of psychedelic metaphyiscal beings, where demons were prepared to devour them. Flying into an 'illuminated sphere' created by the 'Soo 42s' (or 'brick' flares dropped by gunships), outside of which reality seemingly ceased to exist, possessed surreal qualities all of its own, and many losses must be attributed to CFIT (controlled flight into terrain) owing to vertigo. As late as October 1972 unexplained losses continued. Three aircraft went down that month after having checked in with ABCCC (the Airborne Command, Control & Communications Hercules), never to be heard from again.

Right, upper and lower: Artwork was common on 388th TFW F-4Es and *The Wreckin' Crew* (70-279) and *Arizona Chicken* (66-371) from the 34th TFS prove the point. (J. Ward Boyce via Richard L. Ward)

Right: This forlorn battle-damaged F-4E displays the GE M61A1 20mm gun and breech to good effect. The original aerodynamically refined but choking gun fairing was replaced by a long shroud with ventral diffusing louvres during 1970. (J. Ward Boyce via Richard L. Ward)

Then there were the sensor-sowing tasks, conducted in daylight in support of 'Igloo White'. Using 'laydown' techniques at 500ft AGL and 450kts, crews would would deposit strings of ADSIDs (Air Delivered Seismic Intrusion Devices), sensors that would be triggered into action by enemy ground movement (typically trucks) winding their way under the thick foliage, the returns from which would be processed by banks of mainframe computers by Task Force Alpha at Nakhom Phanom, Thailand (known as 'Naked Fanny' or NKP to the crews). Millions of explosive 'pills' which, when trodden on, helped to trigger the 'Igloo White' 'carrots', were also deposited, along with canisters of propaganda leaflets promising pardons to defecting North Vietnamese regulars and Viet Cong. Other loads included what the crews called 'gravel'—anti-personnel explosives resembling 2in square bean bags. These were frozen to an extremely low temperature to keep them stable for delivery and became active once they had tumbled to the ground and had defrosted.

Below: May 3, 1968, and *Nite Owl* F-4D-29-MC 66-7468 trundles along to the active runway with 'wall-to-wall' 'iron' and cluster bombs. (Via Richard L. Ward)

They were capable of removing feet or hands from unwary jungle pedestrians, malevolent or otherwise. The final mission category was all-weather pathfinding at medium to high altitude, when 'friendlies would join up on the Pave Phantom's wing in inclement weather and be instructed to "pickle" their bombs at the appropriate moment'.

'Some LORAN missions were preplanned, others were not. Sensors were always emplaced using LORAN, but most of the actual planning was done by the "Igloo White" staff at NKP from where the sensors were monitored. The frag order to us included little more than the type and number of sensors to be loaded, intervalometer setting to ensure proper spacing, TDs of release point, drop heading, and occasionally a TOT.

For bombing missions you would normally be given target TDs and heading. This could be part of a written frag order or received in-flight from "Hillsborough" or "Moonbeam", the ABCCCs. The WSO had to identify the ordnance to the computer so that it knew the aerodynamic characteristics of the weapon, tune in the LORAN chain covering the target area, and enter the target TDs and release heading. The pilot would then receive steering information on his HSI (horizontal situation indicator) needle. On the run-in to the target the WSO would get a visual count-down in time remaining to release. As long as the "pickle" button was depressed from either cockpit, the weapons would come off automatically at the appropriate release point. The run could be aborted at any time by simply releasing the "pickle" button. After release the release TDs were "frozen" on the WSO's cockpit display so they could be recorded. Up to nine targets or navigation waypoints could be stored at any one time and the computer could translate back and forth between TDs, lat/long and UTM co-ordinates.

'Normally, these "Pathfinder" missions would be fragged as a two-ship with one LORAN and one "dumb" bomber (both loaded with whatever ordnance was called for). We would fly to a pre-planned target, drop on it (the wingman dropping when he saw the bombs come off his leader's aircraft), then the wing-man would go home while the pathfinder would check in with ABCCC for additional instructions. This was usually a poor-weather procedure so that targets not able to be acquired visually could still be "serviced". Other flights of "dumb" bombers would be vectored to rendezvous with the pathfinder, who would then lead them across the target and give them a verbal count-down when to "pickle" their bombs. I flew pathfinder missions approaching six hours' duration when weather was very bad, leading two or three flights over targets, going to a tanker, returning to the target area and doing the same thing multiple times. The bombers included anyone in the theatre who had ordnance and who could talk to us—even F-8 Crusaders. Ordnance involved was anything in the inventory at the time; the computer knew them all.'

Among the mutlifarious munitions employed for Pave Phantom bombing were some very odd-looking devices that would later become known as 'smart' bombs—'smart' because, with a little assistance, they could fly all the way to target instead of tumbling on to approximately the right place as did the unguided 'dumb' or 'iron' bombs and area CBUs hitherto employed for these missions. The 'funny bombs', as they were known

Below: *Ol' Eagle Eye* (F-4D-31-MC 66-7764) boldly displays 8th TFW 'Wolfpack' artwork. The red trim and 'FO' code indicate that it belonged to the 435th TFS *Eagles*. (Via Richard L. Ward)

to those outside the community, used semi-active laser (SAL) guidance—'bang-bang' seeker heads designed to look out for 'sparkled' targets. The gimballed, moving seekers of these bombs were electro-mechanically slaved to their collar fins, thus providing steering all the way to the target. Each would 'ride' up and down within the reflected laser cone (hence 'bang-bang') until they zoomed in on the laser 'spot'. The 'spot' would be marked by Pave Spectres utilizing LLLTV or FLIR imaging sensors slaved to a laser gun for night-time work, or by 'Wolf Buddies' toting the brand-new Martin Marietta AN/AVQ-9 Pave Light. The latter daylight device, unique to the 'Wolfpack', comprised a 75lb pack bolted into the rear cockpit which looked 'left' through the canopy hood once it was clamped shut. Having acquired the target through the telescopic optical viewfinder at slant-ranges of anything up to 20,000ft, the WSO called for the AC to enter a partial pylon turn while he maintained the optic's cross-hairs on the aim-point by means of the unique pistol grip at the base of the 'pack', leaving a companion 'Wolf' to lob its KMU-342 M117-adapted laser-guided bombs (LGBs) into the 'reflected laser basket' (allegedly 6km wide at an altitude of 16,000ft, when using the later KMU-351A/B Mk 84 and KMU-370/B M118 'intellectual' bombs). The Pave Light systems were soon nicknamed 'Zot Boxes' after the BC comic strip, alluding to the 'weird' nature of the combat missions they flew

and enigmatic to all who were not privy to their night-to-night or day-to-day operations. It fuelled the imagination. By the war's end, the fourteen Paveway 'guns' had guided 14,301 LGBs to their targets, with a mission reliability of 99.7 per cent! CEPs were measured in terms of a few feet. Manufacturers Martin Marietta claimed that the AVQ-9 (and postwar AVQ-9A, introduced in 1974, which featured 4× and 10× magnification as used mainly by FMS Phantom operators the Republic of Korea and pre-revolutionary Imperial Iranian Air Forces) could be used in $5.5g$ manoeuvres. Tactics were evolved to reduce vulnerability: 'If the target was easily identifiable, the "Zot" would position himself to one side and not approach it until the "bombers" were stabilized in their dive. The "Zot" would then begin to lase the target and could do so successfully while only going 90 degrees or less around the target, instead of constantly orbiting it. It required co-ordination, but it was not difficult and allowed us to eventually use the "Zot Box" in fairly high-threat areas (even some parts of RP VI).' Medium-high intensity scenarios demanding such g-bladder-inflating designation runs doubtless degraded accuracy. However, in the low-threat areas over Laos and Cambodia, where it was principally employed, it represented a giant leap forward, living up to its designers' claims as being 'the laser system that revolutionized tactical warfare'. Subsequent statistics indicated two orders of magnitude in improved CEPs versus 'iron' bombs (albeit that 'buddy' laser-bombing warranted more obviously lucrative targets, and thus better planning). Security demands stipulated that each and every 'Zot Box' be removed from the cockpit following the strike mission (and prior to ejection!),

[6] Pave Light was reputedly tested on F-4C 63-7407 at Eglin ADTC, Florida, and brackets for the twelve 'Zot Boxes' were installed on the following thirteen F-4Ds selected from Blocks 26–33: 65-0597, -0609, -0612, -0642, -0677, -0705 and -0786 and 66-7505, -8814, -8815, -8817 and -8823. Aircraft 66-8814 was allegedly lost in unrelated circumstances on 28 February 1969.

Above: The fighter ramp at Ubon Ratchitani, Thailand, on 13 November 1972. The top of the photograph is roughly the north-west, and in this view there are some fifty F-4Ds nestling in their revetments. (Jim Shaw)

and luckily no AVQ-9 ships were ever lost to hostile fire.[6] However, the need still existed for something that could deliver even 'smart' bombs under the glimmer of dusk, partial moon or dawn light. Other Pave efforts continued to be funded.

During this time, the requirements for CAS in the southern MRs continued to be provided by F-4Cs assigned to Cam Ranh Bay (until March 1970, when the last of this model bowed out from the combat zone) and subsequently by former 'Gunfighter' F-4Ds at Phu Cat, near Qui Nhon, until the two squadrons also ceased operations there during the autumn of 1971. The process of 'Vietnamization' was in full swing, the

goal of which was to make the Republic responsible for its own air support using F-5 Freedom Fighters and A-37 Dragonflies. Increasing numbers of F-4s were returned home to CONUS for scheduled refits, conducted at that time on all models on a strict 24-month time-compliance basis, ensuring that the 643,000 fasteners used on each and every machine and the parts they held together were still flying in tight formation. Others were reassigned to fledgeling Wings in the more peaceful corners of PACAF, or to USAFE, while the 'Wolfpack' continued to tinker with its weird and wonderful new 'bag of tricks'. Back in Washington, the bean-counters remained busy. They surmised that, in six years of sustained combat through to the end of 1971, USAF F-4 losses to hostile fire had totalled just under 300 strike and MiGCAP Phantoms, as shown in Table 17.[7]

What became of many of the men who were shot down over Laos and

Cambodia—the proverbial 'Heart of Darkness' as echoed in the motion picture *Apocalypse Now*—remains a mystery to this day. While many ejectees, often injured by wind blast or leg or back injuries, were speedily whisked away by 'Super Jolly' ARRS rescue teams who would gladly brave considerable small-arms fire to effect a rescue, an alarming proportion faded into the nothingness and its enemy-held enclaves, never to be heard from again. Many certainly attempted to nurse crippled machines back to sanctuary rather than risk capture, and tumbled into the terrain in the process. The Phantom had 'two of everything' to assist survivability, including redundant hydraulics routed along its

---

[7] Based on the original DoD OASD (Comptroller) Directorate for Information/Operations report, dated 17 October 1973. There have been several revisions since the original report was issued, but portions of the original version have been reproduced here as it is contemporary.

flanks, but there existed certain 'soft' spots which, if punctured, would cause a creeping loss of hydraulic pressure, culminating eventually in its controls 'freezing up'—that is, the flying surfaces would lock solid, with the tail going into full down (nose-up) deflection. The stick-and-rudder controls would became gradually sloppier and more unresponsive. This offered good parameters for a safe ejection with the later zero–zero Mk H7 'bang scats', but nobody really knows precisely what happened to many of the men. Only as this book goes to press, over twenty years later, are a new generation of Washington's officials finally setting forth to seek some unequivocal answers as to the MIA's whereabouts.

TRAINING SHUFFLE

During the so-called 'stand-down', several changes also took place to the domestic RTU pipeline, reflecting the wholesale withdrawal of the 'Century Series' from the Active inventory and the adoption of a second Navy-developed aircraft, the A-7D 'SLUF', for CAS and CSAR (combat search and rescue). During the balmy summer of 1971 the 'basic' and 'conversion' Phantom training function was transferred from the 4453rd CCTW at Davis-Monthan AFB to the 58th TFTW at Luke AFB, just over 100 miles south of Phoenix, Arizona. Jim Shaw was one of the first WSOs to undergo flight training there, and he explains the switch-over (which has caused several historians some angst): 'After seven years' service in the Oklahoma ANG as a C-97G and C-124C navigator I was voluntarily called to active duty on June 1st, 1971, and assigned to the 550th TFTS *Silver Eagles* at Luke as a student WSO in RTU Class 72-A. When we were activated the A-7 RTU programme was in the process of moving from Luke to D-M and the F-4 programme was moving from D-M to Luke. When we arrived at Luke there were a lot of A-7s still on the tarmac, but only four or five F-4Cs. As the class progressed through classroom and simulator phases of training, the F-4 instructors at D-M were graduating their classes,

then flying their F-4s to Luke and trading houses—in some cases literally—with A-7 instructors who were graduating their students and then flying their A-7s south to D-M! For the first couple of months it was a race to see if we could get enough F-4s on the ramp to support the syllabus. This became enough of a problem that the crews in Class 72-B, a couple of months behind us, were split up so as to add the experienced, previously fighter-qualified guys to our class, while those straight from flight training schools were held back to join class 72-C. We ultimately graduated what amounted to a class-and-a-half in February 1972, with Class 72-C doing the same a few months later. Class 72-B never existed except on paper for a few weeks in the fall of 1971.' The 479th TFW at George AFB, in the Mojave Desert in California, changed hands *in situ*, passing to the 35th TFW on 1 October 1971. Within a few years both bases were churning out highly qualified Phantom 'sticks' and 'scopes' on a full-time basis and producing a long overdue 'marriage mentality' between front-seaters and back-seaters, from the outset. Additional RTU functions were provided by elements within the 31st TFW at Homestead AFB, near Miami, Florida (which had absorbed the resources of the former 4531st TFW on 15 October 1970), and by the 1st TFW further north at MacDill AFB (which had similarly taken over the assets of the 15th TFW on 1 October that year). Although RTU graduates might be destined to fly virtually any Phantom fighter variant, the regime rapidly settled into a pattern which witnessed the Arizona Wing specializing in the F-4C, the Florida Wings the F-4D and E and the Californian unit the F-4E. The scale and pace of the RTU schools were staggering, necessary to feed the voracious appetite of the

huge USAF—and burgeoning overseas —Phantom fraternity at its zenith. For example, Luke's 'Phantom College' (memorable for its brightly striped fleet of some 85 F-4Cs while under the command of MiG-killer Brig-Gen Fred Haeffner in the mid-1970s) graduated no fewer than 3,200 pilots and WSOs between February 1972 and September 1982. George AFB, which stayed in the F-4 training business until June 1992, virtually doubled that figure while also expanding its operations to include overseas F-4E/F students and eventually F-4G trainees too. The scale of these training operations surpassed the operational activities of most overseas Phantom customers![8]

CONSTANT GUARD

The superb training programmes and the new systems, together with the matu-

TABLE 17: USAF F-4 LOSSES TO HOSTILE FIRE IN SOUTH-EAST ASIA 1965–71								
	1965	1966	1967	1968	1969	1970	1971	Totals
North Vietnam	10	32	60	34	–	2	–	138
South Vietnam	2	4	15	16	18	4	2	61
Laos	–	6	6	7	39	20	22	100
Totals	12	42	81	57	57	26	24	299

[8] In the mid-1970s Luke's full-length 'new guy' course for prospective ACs lasted 97 working days and encompassed 53 flying sorties, fifteen simulator sorties and some 200 hours of classroom academics. The flying portion was broken down into six phases: thirteen sorties on transition, eight on basic and four on more advanced fighter manoeuvres, five on the use of radar in ground attack, fifteen actually practising ground attack (including at least one night sortie), and a final eight on overall tactical employment (often flying communications-out). Figures provided by the 35th TFW at George AFB, California, which specialized in the slatted-wing F-4E model, indicated that F-4E trainee ACs flew 58 such sorties and WSOs up to 41. Shorter 'Transition' and 'Requal' courses were also run, consuming up to 23 sorties (depending on crew skills and how long they had been out of the cockpit), along with IP and IWSO instructor courses. All of these reflected the various crews' abilities and tended to fluctuate with the constant revisions to training syllabuses and the ever-increasing use made of advanced simulators, in which novices at George AFB spent up to 65 hours' 'flying' time before graduation, thirty calendar weeks after their arrival.

rity of the aircraft were about to pay off. During the night of 29 March 1972 the North Vietnamese began a massive offensive across the DMZ, driving forward at speed with twelve divisions supported by armour, plus flak and SAM batteries which hop-scotched inexorably further south. Additional forces broke in the from the west over the Laotian and Cambodian borders into MRs 2 and 3. The only force which could repel this invasion was US air power, with the Phantom as its vanguard. Caught over a political barrel, the White House gave the go-ahead for full-scale retaliatory action a week later on 6 April, and air strikes against the North—initially codenamed Operation 'Freedom Train'—began within three days of approval. Preliminary reinforcements were provided by the 3rd TFW, which had shifted elements of F-4Ds from Kunsan AB, South Korea, on 31 March. A massive influx followed under Operation 'Constant Guard': in the two months up to the end of May, Phantom strength in Thailand and in the Republic rose by nine squadrons, from 203 to 348 combat-ready aircraft, the entire increase being accounted for by fighter-bomber F-4D/E variants.

Key support from CONUS came from the 4th and 49th TFWs. The concept of

successfully deploying an entire Wing of F-4s across the globe, ready for action after a short interlude, was first successfully demonstrated by the same two Wings several years prior to 'Constant Guard'. The 4th TFW staged *in toto* from Seymour-Johnson AFB, North Carolina, to Kunsan AB, South Korea, between January and July 1968 in response to the 'Pueblo' Crisis', a show of force following the North Korean seizure of a US Navy vessel. The Wing was in place within 72 hours. Testing the concept further, the 334th TFS *Eagles* shifted to Kwang-ju from March, demonstrating the feasibility of conducting operations with minimum facilities such as a 'tent city' and a potable water supply.[9] The commander of the 'Fourth But First' at the time was the famous sound barrier-breaker Col (retiring as Gen) Charles E. ('Chuck') Yeager, who later wrote that his unit made it back 'as neat and clean as a pin. No aborts, no problems.' The following year the 49th TFW received the Mackay Trophy for 'the most meritorious flight of the year' when the unit returned to Holloman AFB, New Mexico, non-stop from Germany in a stream of six dozen jets. The crews performed 504 aerial refuellings, with no aborts. The 'Constant Guard' reinforcements drew on this expertise, flying in cells with a KC-135 tanker constantly replenishing them with fuel and providing navigation; previous tactics used a string of rendezvous points approximately 800 miles apart, by which time even a gaggle of INSs would have gone awry. The rigours of such deployments should not be underestimated. Jim Chamberlain recalled a return ferry trip he made in December

Right: 'New Guy' courses on the F-4C passed from Davis-Monthan to Luke's 58th TFTW in Arizona during 1971, a task for which the Wing was responsible until November 1982. Here one such Phantom heads for the boom of a 22nd AREFS KC-135A over north-east Arizona. (Frank B. Mormillo)

1970: 'Our six airplanes left Camn Ranh . . . and rendezvoused with a tanker over the west coast of Luzon, flying on to Andersen AFB, Guam, where we joined up with another twelve aircraft. For us in the fighters, it was a boring trip. The tanker did all the navigating and all we had to do was fly wing and take fuel. I understand that the flight plans for the tankers were all computer-generated to take advantage of the best possible weather conditions and winds. The tankers kept us filled with enough fuel so that we could make the nearest landing site should an emergency develop. I think we would refuel about two or three times per leg, taking on only 1,500 pounds of fuel per hook-up. We had in-flight box lunches and took turns flying while the other crew member ate lunch. The only relief from the strapped-in position was to raise or lower the seat or massage the legs by means of the g-suit manual inflation valve. Of course, there were no latrine facilities, so breakfast was a high-protein, low residual meal. We were given sponge-filled sealable plastic bags called "piddle packs" which could be used in flight for urination, but that was the extent of the relief facilities. The first two legs, Camn Ranh–Andersen and Andersen–Hickam, were not too bad. The final leg, Hickam to George AFB, California, was seven hours forty-five minutes.' In those days there were no pocket electronic Game Boy machines

Below: A 336th TFS *Rocketeer* from the 4th TFW 'Fourth But First' at dispersal at Seymour-Johnson AFB, North Carolina, during the 'hard wing' era. The Wing provided reinforcements to South-East Asia under Operation 'Constant Guard' in the spring of 1972 and resupplied Israel with Phantoms the following year under Operation 'Nickel Grass'. (Authors' collection)

[9] During the numerous follow-on deployments made by the 4th TFW's squadrons, 'mobility' was further tested. On 1 October 1970 the 336th TFS *Rocketeers* became the first unit to deploy with Modular Bare Base equipment, comprising WRSK (War Readiness Spares Kits) and basic air and ground crew with operations/planning facilities and mess tent, plus the usual Starlifter loads of starters, hydraulic test carts, munitions 'jammers' and ordnance.

(forward operating location) for refuelling and re-arming between dawn and dusk, the crews generated 269 such combat missions over the ensuing nine days. At Ubon and Udorn aircraft were 'pooled'. These employed Bien Hoa for rapid forward turnaround, as well as Da Nang to the north-east to provide support near Hue and Quang Tri. 'We began to fly whichever aircraft were mission-ready in order to simplify the maintenance/operations interface. Initially, the deployed aircraft's "detuned" engines would not allow their Es to keep up with our Ds, but by mid-May they were "tweaked up" to higher EGTs and were okay from then on.'

Within a month the North Vietnamese offensive in the South had been thwarted, and by July the Republic was pushing the last vestiges of the enemy out. Between April and June 1972 USAF Tac-Air alone had notched up 15,858 sorties, many of them by F-4s and crews who had not anticipated a second tour of duty in the theatre. Their experience won the day. For example, of the 25 ACs who deployed ready to fly in the front seats of the 9th TFS *Iron Knights* F-4Ds, twenty had served a previous tour in the theatre and four had seen two. They were skilled in the art of going 'down the chute' to deliver 'shacks', and their knowledge proved invaluable.

BRIDGE BUSTERS

'Freedom Train' interdiction strikes conducted concurrently over North Vietnam—codenamed 'Linebacker I' from 8 May—were similarly fierce and fast-paced. The key objectives were to destroy POL supply depots and to choke the enemy's LOCs—bridges, railyards, anything that helped the North Vietnamese to convey *matériel* south, from the

---

with which to while away the hours, if the inclination struck.

The reinforcements came in three waves: CG I involved 36 F-4Es which departed from North Carolina on 8 April; CG II added another 36 F-4Es from the Florida-based Wings, which departed on 1 May; and CG III comprised the entire 49th TFW, beginning on 7 May. Seventy-one of Holloman's F-4Ds arrived at Takhli on schedule, with the first elements—those from the 417th TFS *Red Rockets*—flying 27 combat missions over An Loc in MR-3 within 24 hours of their arrival, despite the 'bare base' facilities.[10] Using Bien Hoa as a FOL

---

[10] Takhli had been under Thai 'caretaker' status for nearly two years prior to the 49th TFW's arrival, upon which the Wing discovered that the facilities had been stripped, requiring some impromptu restoration work. Apparently there was no lighting, and even the much-needed showers were full of kraits and cobras! In the official words of a contemporary crewman, 'We were greeted at the aircraft in traditional fashion with cold beer and at the same time received a rather sad picture of living conditions. The *Blacksheep* [8th TFS] moved right in, building shelves, tables, benches and a duty desk at Operations out of shipping crates, as well as a bar for the lounge in the living area. We all built our own shelves so that we could unpack. Foot lockers came two weeks later. When we first arrived, using temporary generators, we had been well-stripped after its closure in 1971, including nearly all of the wiring. There was no hot water or air-conditioning on the base, while all water required testing for potability.' Actually, the 'bare base' concept decreed immediate tap-supplied drinking water, and this took two weeks to establish at Takhli. The conditions would be echoed nineteen years later, when crewmen from CONUS and USAFE deployed to South-West Asia in response to Operation 'Desert Shield'.

Right: F-4D-31-MC 66-7693 acted as the test-bed for the Ford AN/AVQ-10 Pave Knife laser pod at Eglin ADTC, Florida, beginning in 1969. This aircraft, assigned to Capt D. E. Wilson and Lt R. K. Potter, features a 'slick' radome and a fin-cap devoid of RHAWS but telemetry antennae sprouting from the nose barrel. Production pods reached the 433rd TFS *Satan's Angels* at Ubon two years later. (Loral)

Chinese buffer zone right down to the DMZ. These witnessed the first use of the 8th TFW's newly perfected, autonomous, precision, 'smart' bombing systems, used with massive effect against the hitherto seemingly indestructible, over-engineered French-colonial Thanh Hoa or 'Dragon's Jaw' Bridge. The structure was given a nasty jolt on 27 April by a force of a dozen Ubon F-4s and the western span was finally knocked off its massive, 40ft-thick, concrete perch on 13 May. By the end of the month the two railway lines running from Hanoi to China had been severed in thirteen key locations and another four bridges linking Hanoi and Haiphong were down. By 30 June over 106 bridges had been felled, lending Col (later Gen) Carl S. Miller's Wing the new nickname 'Bridge Busters'.

The new technology that facilitated this rapid and total severing of the enemy's LOCs comprised two new systems, Pave Knife and better 'smart' bombs, including new TV-guided versions. Twelve 'Zot' ships of the 'Wolfpack''s 433rd TFS *Satan's Angels* were wired up for six production Ford Aeronutronic AN/AVQ-10A Pave Knife pods (of the twelve built, three were held in reserve and three diverted to the US Navy for use on board A-6A Intruders of VA-147 *Swordsmen*), with the equipment and new crews arriving at Ubon in the winter of 1971.[11] The pod was a crooked, banana-shaped device carried on the left inner wing pylon (Station 2), bolted on in an asymmetric configuration which typically included a 370 US gallon drop tank on the starboard wing, plus up to two LGBs (on Stations 1 and 8), along with the regular fit of centreline tank, Sparrows and ECM. The Paveway Is were new too: Texas Instruments had perfected bolt-

on collars and high- and low-speed tail 'groups' for all the key ordnance, although the primary weapons were the KMU-351A/B one-tonner (later designated GBU-10/B) and the KMU-370B/B M118 (GBU-11/B) demolition bomb. Crews would sometimes carry one of each, and merely had to remember to set the release sequence for the 1½-tonner first!

Pave Knife introduced a separate 5in Sony TV display in the rear cockpit,

enabling the WSO to track the target by means of the pod's nose-mounted Dalmo Victor LLLTV (low light-level TV) sensor. This could be slewed about electro-mechanically anywhere below the aircraft, left and right and fore and aft, by

[11] Pave Knife was tested over the Eglin test range on F-4D 66-7693 and wired up into the following dozen F-4Ds (all drawn from Blocks 31) under T.O.1 F-4D-560: 66-7652, -7674, -7675, -7679 to -7681, -7707, -7709, -7743, -7760, -7766 and -7773.

means of the radar tracking handle, to place the target in the cross-hairs prior to target 'illumination' with the laser (which was boresighted with the sensor via a mirror). Initial target acquisition was effected by caging the system at boresight in sympathy with the pilot's gun sight in 'Forward Acquire'; the complex art of tracking through the resultant attack manoeuvre was then in the 'Wizzo''s lap. It was a radical breakthrough, though the system did possess several idio-

syncracies. Capt Harold 'Harry' Edwards was one of the pioneers, either leading or being on the missions which destroyed the Lang Chi hydro-electric plant, plus the tough Thanh Hoa and the Paul Doumer Bridges. He describes the techniques employed in the days before software had improved to provide auto-rotation:[12]

'A design defect caused what we saw in the rear cockpit to appear upside down and backwards! Therefore, when de-

scribing a hard-to-find target to someone looking in the TV, directions such as north, south, east and west could not be used; rather, easily located ground features were used as reference points. In the "Acquire" position, I saw in my TV what the pilot saw in his "pipper". Once I could identify the target I could select

[12] Reproduced by courtesy of author Philip D. Chinnery and publishers Arms & Armour Press from *Life on the Line: Stories of Vietnam Air Combat*, published in 1988.

"Track" on a switch by the radar tracking handle. This handle was utilized to move the picture ['underneath' the fixed cross-hairs] rather than the cross-hairs on the display [as would be the case with radar ground-bombing]. The TV moved via a roll rate gyro, i.e., the longer the tracking handle was held in a certain position the faster the picture moved. This fact, combined with the upside-down and backwards problem, meant that some training was required to become skilled. The training was best accomplished when the pods were off the aircraft and in the shop, connected to a TV there. We could "illuminate" for our own bombs as well as those of others. The "eye" of the bomb would open a

couple of seconds after it left the aircraft and look for the reflected energy from the laser beam. The bomb had to be dropped within a "box" 1,500ft long and 500ft wide, from the point the beam hit the ground, or the eye would not see the energy. This happened only rarely. Once the pilot saw the target he put it in his "pipper", I found it in the TV, went to "Track" and told the pilot I was tracking.' During 'buddy' bombing manoeuvres, always a complex task, the crew informed their companions when to 'pickle' their ordnance.

'On the Thanh Hoa Bridge mission . . . we had the Pave Knife system and one 2,000lb Mk 84 bomb; our wing-man had a Mk 84 and a 3,000lb M118 "Fat

Al". "Fat Al" could not penetrate hard surfaces—it would break up—so it was always set to detonate at ground level or slightly above if the bomb carried a fuse extender.' The latter would customarily be employed with a 'Daisy Cutter' for flak-suppression too. Its huge shockwave would blow out eardrums half a mile away. 'Our bombs scored a direct hit. The western span of the bridge had been completely knocked off its abutment and the bridge superstructure was so critically disfigured and twisted that rail traffic would come to a standstill for at least several months.'

Similar missions were conducted with the 25th TFS *Assam Dragons*, opening up with attacks by 'Biloxi' Flight against the Paul Doumer Bridge on 10 May. Jim Shaw describes the proceedings from the 'Buddy' position: 'The Pave Knife bird would lead a four-ship in [ECM] pod formation at approximately 15,000ft to a "pop up" point where we would climb to the vicinity of 20,000ft while closing in to loose route formation (2–3 ship-widths' separation) for the attack. As we went "down the chute", pilots would concentrate on flying formation while WSOs would clear for threats and, at the last few thousand feet, watch for the bombs to come off "Lead"'s aircraft. We would then call the pickle ("Lead" would too), hit the button ourselves, and immediately "go outside" to clear threats

BRIDGE OFF ABUTMENT

BREAKS IN SPAN

Left, upper: 8th TFW laser-bombers head north, with 'wall-to-wall' one-ton GBU-10 Paveway bombs, on 1 November 1972. The 8th TFW pooled 'smart' bomber designators and all aircraft in this flight were flown by 25th TFS crews (regardless of the 'FG' code of the Pave Light 'Zot Box' lead-ship, F-4D 65-0612, whose tail dominates the camera frame). 'Very early that morning an "Owl" night Fast-FAC had caught a large convoy in Mu Gia Pass and was able to get hits on the lead and trail trucks to block the way in and out. The whole morning schedule was re-fragged to load everyone up with maximum LGBs. The "Wolf Zot" marked target after target, guiding LGBs in on the sitting ducks, until some time around noon.' (Jim Shaw)
Left, lower: The Thanh Hoa Bridge was knocked off its abutment using Pave Knife-guided Paveway I LGBs. This BDA photograph was taken by an RF-4C of the 432nd TRW on 13 May 1972. (USAF via TI)

128

while the pilots moved back out into the protective pod formation. This would require "Lead" to make a partial orbit of the target, but due to the manoeuvrability of the Pave Knife pod it was minimal and the small left turn, required by the pod's position, was immediately followed by various degrees of right turns coming off the target prior to the Flight rejoining in "pod".' Mutually protective 'beacon' jamming from the aircraft's AN/ALQ-87 noise-jammers dictated approximately 2,000ft horizontal spacings stepped up in 500ft increments, though this was 'deliberately varied somewhat in both the vertical and horizontal by ±500ft'.

It was dangerous work. Two Pave Knife machines were lost during July, including 66-7680 on the 5th of the month, shot down by a SAM in the vicinity of RP I while Mike VanWagonen was at the helm, and 66-7707, which burnt out on the runway at Ubon five days later. Jim Shaw was part of the strike force on the latter occasion, led by the 25th TFS commander, Lt-Col Brad Sharp, with 1Lt Mike Pomphrey in the back: 'I was in the second four-ship and was in the arming area watching as they began their take-off. At approx 150 knots (right at the "abort/no-go" decision point), Brad's right main tyre blew. The aircraft settled on to the wheel as Col Sharp dropped the hook and aborted the take-off. At that point pieces from the disintegrating wheel punctured the right drop tank and caused fuel to stream behind the aircraft. Very shortly thereafter they engaged the departure end barrier; it extended to its limits, then retracted, drawing a very hot wheel back into a great pool of leaked JP4! As the aircraft came to a halt it was almost immediately engulfed in flames. Mike got out almost immediately, but Brad got hung up on his straps and when he jumped free of the cockpit he injured his ankle as he hit the runway. Mike, who was now well clear of the fire, saw Brad struggling to gain his feet and ran to his assistance. With Brad leaning on him for support, Mike helped him to a safe distance away from the fire, which ultimately engulfed the aircraft and caused

both the Mk 84 LGBs and both ejection seats to "cook off". The airfield was closed for some hours to fight the fire and clear the debris, and that "Linebacker" mission was cancelled. Mike and two ground personnel, who ran to their assistance, were awarded the Airman's Medal for bravery for rescuing Lt-Col Sharp. He was sent to the USAF hospital at Clark AB in the Philippines, and returned to the States shortly thereafter (his tour was almost over anyway).' He was succeeded by Lt-Col Sid Fulgham.

Philco-Ford addressed Pave Knife's shortcomings and built on its success to produce the superlative Pave Tack, test-flown from 1976, while Westinghouse began packaging a daylight-only system employing a TV boresighted via a mirror with a pulse-coded neodymium YAG laser in a slim pod called Pave Spike, which entered the inventory just as hostilities were drawing to a close. These incorporated many corrective display features and introduced such welcome options as digital alphanumeric data pertaining to distance to target, bombs away, and so forth.[13]

The modular Rockwell International Hobos (Homing Bomb System, otherwise known as the Electro-Optic Guided Bomb, or 'Egob'—the crews concerned found the acronym 'EOGB' a tongue-twister) was a completely autonomous 'smart' bomb which relied on lock-on-and-leave TV guidance. In this respect it was similar to the US Navy/Martin Marietta AGM-62 Walleye which pioneered the technology, but it packed up to three times the punch of the Navy's top-of-the-line 'Fat Albert' (not to be confused with the USAF's M118) by means of kits designed, just like the Paveway LGB series, speedily to transform the Mk 84 and M118 warheads into GBU-8 and GBU-9 'smart' bombs respectively.[14] However, its initiation to combat was not quite as auspicious as that of the relatively inexpensive LGBs. 'Goatee' Flight, led by 8th TFW boss Carl Miller, went into the fray on 10 May at the head of a package designed to knock out the Paul Doumer Bridge, in a separate wave ahead of the laser bomb-

ers. The flight carried eight 'Egobs', two each strapped to four Phantoms' inner wing pylons, and executed a northerly heading designed to provide suitable contrast on the back-seat scopes so as to permit what was hoped would be a firm lock-on-and-leave launch, using a 30-degree dive and 'pickling the weapons' at 12,000ft. Of the seven EOGBs that were kicked free of the MAU-12 ejector racks (one resolutely refused to budge), only three stayed the course and all of those flew through the lattice structure and into the Red River on the other side. The remainder went astray, to serve as unintended flak-suppression in the vicinity of the target. One of the problems was rooted in the use of the F-4D's recently modified Multisensor Display Group (MSDG) radar scope, which had to double as a TV display. Jim Shaw, who qualified on the weapon at Ubon and witnessed its many trials and tribulations, expands:

'There used to be a "smart bombs school" (no official title) at Nellis. Selected crews were sent through a 2–3-week course on the "Egob". It became apparent that this was probably good for a cadre of instructors, but unnecessary for the rank and file users. The vast majority of us became qualified in the field through OJT programmes. (The EOGB programme was a particular example—it taught people how to plan ideal approach angles, based on time of day and sun position for best contact and lock-on conditions, when in the field you

[13] The AN/ASQ-153 Pave Spike is described in the next chapter, 'Silver-Horned Rhinos', and the ultimate AN/AVQ-26 Pave Tack is discussed in Chapters 14 and 15.

[14] The USN/Martin Marietta AGM-62 Walleye was first used by F-4Ds on 24 August 1967. Twenty-two were expended by year's end, and the system became a standard feature from Block 30 up, but with emphasis on the Mk 6 Mod 0 nuclear model which packed a 1kT-yield W72 warhead (added to F-4D 65-0771 onwards, under TO 1F-4D-559). The nuclear models were the only USAF acquisitions to use the AWG-16 ER/DL data-link pod for stand-off lock-on after launch. Interestingly, the later imaging infra-red version of Walleye used the same WGU-10/B seeker as the AGM-65D/G Maverick and GBU-15(V)-2 glide bomb, discussed in Chapter 11.

Left, upper: A one-ton GBU-8 'Egob' on a bomb dolly. The TV-guided bomb came as a kit which was strapped on to a Mk 84 2,000lb 'hammer' warhead or an M118 3,000lb demolition bomb. It was locked on to the target by using the radar scope display as a reference and 'flying' the cross-hairs into position over the desired impact point. Gate mismatch difficulties meant that several months slipped by before the 8th TFW finally sorted out all the 'bugs' in the system. (Rockwell International)
Left, lower: Pave Fire II was an attempt to expand the F-4D's 'dive–toss' precision dumb-bombing capability into night time, by means of a laser-ranging gun slaved to an electro-optic sensor. It was installed on the F-4D's centreline in just the same fashion as a Vulcan gun pod. Ground crews perform the task here at Udorn in September 1971. (USAF)

learned to make do with the weather and light conditions you had for the time of day, and do whatever you had to do to get the job done.) The basic design of the "Egob" was sound, but there were inconsistencies and conflicts in how things would work best. The TV camera in the nose of the weapon looked through a "gate" that was some 2.4 mils wide. When properly boresighted this gate should align with the "pipper" of the pilot's gun sight, which was 1.4 mils wide. There was little that could be done to rectify the difference between pipper/

gate size, but the inadequacy of the radar scope as a TV screen was remedied by installing the ubiquitous Sony 5-inch TV set at the forward end of the WSO's right console (ousting the nuclear consent switch panel in the process), next to the tracking handle. This improved the quality of the available picture immediately, [although] the "Wizzo" was obliged to lean over to the right to peer into the display, while shielding it with his left hand and attempting lock-on with the right! Picture quality was further enhanced by moving the ECM pods from

their normal position in the forward missile wells to a centreline-mounted MER [to keep the ambient light more constant]. We also tried mounting thin wire screen mesh across the "eyeball" of the bombs [to reduce glint]. These two techniques combined resulted in noticeable improvements in picture quality.

The final improvement was one of technique. The "school solution" was to acquire the target in the scope, relate that to where the pilot's sight was, and talk him on to the target so that the gate would be on the target. The difference between the size of the gate as pictured on the WSO's display and the pilot's sight now became apparent—if the WSO said "Right 2" (meaning mils), it was, at best, an approximation. We finally found that the best solution was for the pilot to roll in and position the sight just short of the target. He would then pull the nose up to the target while calling "Approaching, approaching . . ." until the WSO acquired the target at the top-centre of his right-hand TV. At that point he would take control of the aircraft, flying the gate on to the target and squeezing the trigger to effect lock-on. After 2–3 seconds of "good" lock to assure guidance, the bomb was "pickled' off.' As soon as the bomb came off the pylon the TV screen went black and the crew broke off their attack in a bid to put the defences behind them. Alignment checks could be accomplished using aircraft electrical power (the 'Egob''s

Left, upper: F-4D 66-7593 was one of several 8th TFW 'Deltas' outfitted with a new Sony TV designed to facilitate a better 'Egob''s eye-view of its target than the existing dual-mode radar scope (MSDG) tube. The photo was taken in September 1972. 'The centreline station is empty, indicating the ECM pods were still in the forward missile wells, and thus that we had not yet resolved all our picture problems at this time,' recalls Jim Shaw. The ECM was moved back to give the GBU-8 EOGBs a better forward view. (Jim Shaw) Left, lower: The Pave Sword pod featured a passive laser tracker which provided steering cues to a marked target on the pilot's ADI bar and HSI needle. Laser-marking for the LGBs was provided by ground troops, or airborne FACs equipped with laser guns, such as the Pave Nail Bronco and the Pave Spot Cessna 'Push-Me-Pull-You'. (USAF)

battery lasted thirty minutes once activated, so was only ever put into motion near the target) shortly after take-off. Crews would accelerate to 450kts and compare where the gate lay versus the 'pipper' using the aircraft ahead of them as a 'target'. Pre-flight alignment was not reliable because of aerodynamic loading, which often caused an inadequately torqued bomb to 'shift' a little as it settled into airborne flight on the pylon.

With these revisions, the 'Egob' continued in use for many years, until superseded by Rockwell's far superior GBU-15 EOGB-II variant, introduced initially to *Heyl Ha'Avir* service in 1977, five years ahead of the USAF. This new model could be 'tossed' at supersonic speeds and 'flown' all the way to target by means of a brand new toggle switch to adjust lock-on and a two-way Hughes data link which continiously fed the video imagery back on to the radar scope display. This avoided the complexities of having to achieve a satisfactory lock-on smack on the target prior to launch.[15]

Other experiments, with 'Buck Rogers' electro-optical equipment and ray guns, abounded at the start of the 1970s, among them Pave Fire and Pave Sword, which aimed to inject greater precision into CAS and 'tac int' bombing. The LTV Pave Fire II, a one-off programme applied to two F-4Ds (66-7700 and -7701) which were nominally assigned to the 13th TFS at Udorn from April 1971 (they actually belonged to Det 1 of the 414th FWS and were originally coded 'WZ'), represented the first serious attempt to expand the WRCS-equipped Phantom's 'dive–toss' bombing capability into night-time. Pave Fire II comprised a huge centreline pod combining an LLLTV and boresighted laser gun initially caged at the aircraft's velocity vector. Dipping the nose towards the target at altitude, the pilot and his WSO used the image on their cockpit TV to jiggle about and centre the target in the cross-hairs during the dive, then 'squirted' the laser. The reflected laser pulses provided extremely accurate slant-ranging data which was 'fed' into the WRCS in lieu of radar-range returns to compute the automatic release of 'dumb' bombs during the pull-up. Most missions were experimental in nature, designed to evaluate the efficacy of target-acquisition under various conditions, and the aircraft tended to carry only Pave Fire II, Sparrows, fuel and ECM—and, only on occasion, a pair of 'iron' bombs. It was not put into production and, like Pave Knife, its best features were eventually applied to the integrated 'strap-ons'.

The AN/AVQ-11 Pave Sword was by comparison a tiny black pod, fitted to a Sparrow well using a standard ECM

---

[15] The GBU-15 is discussed more fully in Chapter 11.

adaptor pylon, but its size belied its potential. Two aircraft (F-4Ds 66-8738 and -8812) were rigged with the system and assigned to the 497th TFS *Nite Owls* just in time to help repel the North Vietnamese ground offensive. The device passively picked up a reflected laser 'spot' from a target sparkled by ground troops or by one of a few specially modified cloud-wheeling OV-10 'Pave Nail' Broncos (equipped with new inertial-LORAN systems and a laser gun) or simpler O-2A 'Pave Spot' push-me-pull-you's. This in turn generated steering

Below: Eglin's 4485th TS specialized in follow-on operational trials of new weapons systems, including the early AIM-9J Sidewinder missiles (live, but featuring orange bodies for tracking purposes). The latter found their way into the combat zone during 1972, alongside F-4 FWIC graduates, the Sparrow AIM-7E-2 and 'Combat Tree'. (Loral)

instructions to the target. All the WSO had to do was to enter the appropriate 'Mils' depression setting for the stores to be employed (corresponding to those the pilot would normally enter into his gun sight for a 'down the chute' attack), into a special new 'box' in the rear. As soon as Pave Sword acquired the illuminated target, it would furnish steering and dive commands on the pilot's ADI bar and HSI needle which, once centred in the null position on the instruments, meant that his 'pipper' corresponded with the target (whether or not it could be seen through the windshield). The 'Lead' Phantom would line up on the target in this fashion and deposit LGBs (possibly in concert with 'welded-wing' colleagues doing the same on 'Lead''s order for 'pickle'). It put much of the responsibility for getting bombs smack on target in the hands of the FACs and TICs, and was sufficiently successful to be incorporated

wholesale aboard nearly a thousand CAS-dedicated machines later in the decade.[16]

Almost out of the blue, 'smart' technology had come of age. To many in the developing Systems Command, the short and fierce reintroduction of the Phantom to combat in South-East Asia served as a vital melting pot for many new, exciting technological concepts.

'Dumb' bombing also continued throughout 'Linebacker'. Jim Shaw's memorable first trip to Hanoi on 10 May with Maj Charles Pratt tasked the pair against the Yen Vien railway yard just north of the Paul Doumer Bridge as 'Gopher Four', the last to slip into the attack, with the enemy's defences wide awake, carrying 500lb bombs. 'Just as we rolled in over the bridge, which was under attack by four other Flights ('Goatee', 'Napkin', 'Biloxi' and 'Jingle'), I saw what looked like CBUs going off all

around both approaches to the bridge and had the momentary thought "Who's doing flak suppression—I don't remember any flak-suppression being briefed?" before I realized that all those "CBU flashes" were really muzzle-flashes aimed at us!' Crews also did a double-take on 25 June during an attack on the Tri Power Plant, when they encountered 'what could only be called "barrage balloons"'. And, at the height of the monsoons (19 August), 'when we were accused of bombing the dykes—on which they placed AAA sites which we were not allowed to touch—I recall a trip to the ordinarily easily identifiable Bac Giang Thermal Power Plant, which we could not find (although all four INSs in the Flight said we were within half a mile) because flood waters had obliterated all landmarks. We brought our bombs home but were again accused of bombing the dykes.' Interestingly enough, had they chosen to bomb them, the resulting flooding would have crippled the North in one fell swoop. However, contamination of the rice paddies and dispersed 'cottage industries' with salt water was strictly prohibited, on humanitarian grounds.

Each and every mission was a huge tasking effort which embroiled up to forty attacking Phantoms plus up to six MiGCAP flights, two or more escort flights and two to four more providing defence-suppression, involving numerous bases and detailed 'frags' (fragmentary orders). At the head were the 'chaff bombers' which would sow a blanket of radar-reflecting metal strips akin to tinsel to cloak the attackers' precise whereabouts. Initially this conducted using 'chaff bombs' which 'opened one at a time, on a time fuse a certain time and distance after release, making the jets predictably a bit ahead and above the chaff corridor, which took some time to fully blossom and develop. The normal procedure was for "Lead" to call the drops at 10-second intervals,' recollected Jim Shaw, who flew chaff support for the successful Thanh Hoa Bridge strike on 13 May. In late May the 'TDY-ing' 4th TFW's F-4Es took over the job, using new AN/ALE-2 bulk chaff pod dispensers which were simply turned on, to dump chaff out behind. This pod still made these aircraft the most vulnerable portion of the strike package, and created a few poignant episodes. Not long after sun-up on 16 August (local date) Capts Fred W. Sheffler and Mark 'Gunner' A. Massen of the 336th TFS *Rocketeers* (flying F-4E 69-7235) shot down a MiG-21 on the way to a target on the North-East Railroad. 'They were in the second of two chaff flights. Only a week before they had been hit and forced to bail out over the Gulf of Tonkin as they egressed the same area on a similar mission. All four members of "Date" flight got a radar lock on the MiG, and as the leader, Lt-Col Dan Blake, was carefully counting the four seconds "radar settle" time before launching his AIM-7, he was amazed to see his target explode from the Sparrow of his Number Four! Revenge was sweet.'

'Linebacker I' bombing operations ceased north of the 20th Parallel on 31 October, then were resumed on 18 December as the infamous 'Eleven Day War' or 'Christmas Bombing' effort following the collapse of peace negotiations in Paris when, in the words of one irate diplomat, 'the Vietnamese started bitching about trivia such as the shape of the table, and who was sat where'. As an instrument of persuasion, the 8th TFW 'Bridge Busters' were once more thrown into the fray, using their LORAN and 'smart' bombing systems to maximum effect. Among the targets assigned and knocked out was Radio Hanoi, the insidious and insistent propaganda voice of the communists. The transmitter was hit on 27 December and 'Hanoi Hannah' went off the air at precisely the Phantoms' TOT. The 'no holds barred' offensive, which many in the American military establishment viewed as the first time that the kid gloves had been removed, jolted the North Vietnamese severely. Above all else, other technological improvements had ensured that the North Vietnamese MiG pilots had at last come to view the Phantoms painted in tan-and-green as being just as dangerous as the 'gray' ones.

ACES

The Chinese 'Year of the Rat' proved to be the great hunting season for MiG-killers honed with new tactics and weapons designed to ferret out the MiGs and chew them to pieces. No longer were MiGCAP Phantoms crewed by 'day-time jocks' who relied exclusively on visual-engagement tactics which made poor use of the 'all-up' F-4's radar systems. While the blossoming, Nellis-originated Fighter Weapons School did not yet fully espouse the 'loose deuce' MiGCAP concept favoured by the Navy, it did abandon heading into 'Injun' Country' in 'finger four' and provided the leeway for some aggressive (and previously forbidden) low-altitude engagements. Much of this was made possible by reliable airborne early warning and control, which provided unequivocal clearance for BVR 'shoots'. New tactics, training and technology were combined to devastating effect, placing the Phantom back on top of the league tables.

FWS, conducted at Nellis AFB, Nevada, was borne out of the *ad hoc*, Tyndall-managed 'College Dart' effort in Florida which pitted F-4Es and Navy F-4Js against dashing F-106s over the Gulf of Mexico and used a 'building block process' wherein crews climbed the learning curve or were rapidly washed out. A renewed emphasis on instrument flying,

---

[16] Integrated with the HUDs (head-up displays) of some 350 A-7D/K 'SLUFs' and 600 A-10/OA-10A 'Warthogs' as the AN/AAS-38, code-named 'Pave Penny'. The Phantom's passive laser-tracking capability was furnished by the postwar Pave Spike and Pave Tack. In the autumn of 1971 the special Pave systems were redistributed amongst the 8th TFW: the two 'daytime' squadrons, the 25th and 433rd TFSs, began to share LORAN, LGBs and EOGBs and the two night units, the 435th and 497th TFSs, LORAN and Pave Sword. This cross-training meant that aircraft modified for the special systems became pooled, although they retained their original squadron codes. This explains why many Flights, though invariably crewed by members of one particular squadron, were seen with a mix of the four squadron's aircraft ('FA'/25, 'FG'/433, 'FO'/435 and 'FP'/497). Pave Phantom crews were also briefed to drop LGBs 'blind' through the clouds, leaving a hard-pressed 'Pave Nail' OV-10 FAC winging around under the murk to lase the target on their behalf.

brand new Raytheon AIM-7E-2 Sparrow missile, which, despite its potentially annoying 15-second 'warm-up' time and reduced maximum range compared with the basic 7E, offered significantly enhanced reliability and, for the first time ever, a genuine 6g, 'snap shoot', dogfight capability. As a back-up, Ford's new thermo-electrically cooled (TEC) AIM-9E (an AIM-9B with a modified, ogival nose section) was carried in clutches of four under each inner wing pylon. It was no coincidence that most of the initial FWS graduates, and the fresh batches of top-secret AIM-7E-2 and AIM-9E missiles, were earmarked for assignment to the second South-East Asian unit to specialize, the 555th TFS *Triple Nickel*, which since June 1968 had come under the jursidiction of the Composite 432nd TRW based at Udorn RTAFB, Thailand. It was the first Phantom squadron to specialize in 'air superiority'.

As well as the new missiles and training doctrines, there was another ingredient behind the 432nd TRW's becoming an eventual moulding agent for new USAF MiG aces—'Combat Tree'. Fitted in a dozen F-4Ds and integrated with the APQ-109 intercept radar, the system was capable of picking up and plotting hostile IFF 'squawk' signals dispatched from the enemy MiGs, thus permitting positive identification of the 'bogeys' as 'bandits' at BVR ranges, where the AIM-7E-2 could reap maximum rewards.[17] Three 'aces' (two of them P-WSOs and all three FWS graduates) emerged between 16 April and 13 October 1972, Capts Steve Ritchie, Chuck DeBellevue and Jeff Feinstein, along with a host of other triple or double MiG-killers who helped even the score, including Maj Robert A. Lodge (3 victories; sadly, he was killed on 10 May just minutes after 'bagging' his third), Lt-Col Baily (2), Capt Madden (2), Capt Olmstead (2), Capt Pettit WSO (2) and Maj Retterbush (2). Among the survivors of the mêlée who drew return fire was Lodge's triple-MiG-killing 'Wizzo' Capt Roger C. Locher, who evaded capture after being shot down by a gun-blazing quartet of 'Farmers', later took it upon himself to

qualify as a Phantom front-seater and then went on to command one of the first F-117A Stealth squadrons, the 4453rd TES, when the 'Have Blue' 'mirrors' concept was in its infancy. All of the aces' official testimonies have been recounted umpteen times, but lesser-known, barroom anecdotes of their exploits, such as Ritchie having 'just missed smacking into a 200ft tree' during one of his more adventurous low-level engagements, continued to be circulated, adding to the new *esprit de corps*. The new aviators understood implicitly what could be done with radar, Sparrow and Sidewinder and new electronic devices like 'Combat Tree'—and, interestingly enough, not one of the Vietnam 'aces' (Navy men included), 'bagged' any of their MiGs with a gun.

The new 'ace' Captains won their spurs in 1972, as shown in Table 18. A total of fifty MiGs were downed by USAF crew (and one USN/MC exchange team) at a cost of 27 Phantoms to MiGs (most of which were vulnerable chaff bombers) between 1 March and the ceasefire the following January, four of them credited to 'manoeuvring tactics', 6½ to the F-

[17] Fitted initially to a selected number of Block 29 F-4D aircraft, 'Combat Tree' (believed to be designated APX-81) was operated by the 13th and 555th Tactical Fighter Squadrons of the 432nd Tactical Reconnaissance Wing stationed at Udorn RTAFB, Thailand. The system was fitted to eight aircraft which had been transferred from the 3rd TFW in Korea during December 1971 and January 1972. These aircraft can be identified in photographs by a red warning marking stencilled on the port intake splitter vane. This referred to an auto-destruct package triggered by the ejection of the crew which would prevent 'Combat Tree' falling into North Vietnamese (and therefore Soviet) hands. They were also the first aircraft to use the AIM-9J model Sidewinder. Serials were 65-0783, -0784, -0785 and -0801 and 66-0232, -0237, -7463 and -7482. By June three of the original eight aircraft had been lost, and this prompted a second phase of installations which replaced the losses and increased the number of aircraft available. The exact number of aircraft involved in this second batch is unknown but it included aircraft transferred from the United States in addition to machines from other PACAF units. Serials of known 'Combat Tree' F-4Ds delivered between June and September 1972 were 66-0239, -0240, -0267, -0268, -0269, -0271, -7459, -7461, -7468, -7486 and -7501. Data by courtesy of Alan Howarth.

Above and left: F-4D-30-MC 66-7554, McAir Ship No 2091, first flew on 24 February 1967 and is now displayed at Wright-Patterson AFB, Ohio, having last flown with the *Buckeye Phantoms*, AFRES, nicknamed *City of Fairborn*. It is seen here in *Triple Nickel* markings with its two MiG kills on 2 August 1971, a few months before the 'Linebacker' offensives. It 'bagged' its two MiG-17s on 11 November 1967 while flown by Capt Darrell D. Simmonds and 1Lt George H. McKinney, call-sign 'Sapphire One', using the 20mm gun pod. After its transfer to the 432nd TRW is became the personal mount of CO Brig-Gen Darrell S. Cramer (an ace with thirteen kills in the Second World War). Note 'Snoopy''s extended digit! (Larsen/Remington via Richard L. Ward)

the trustworthiness of vectors from a friendly GCI or airborne command post processed by a discriminating backseater, and then learning how to 'turn and burn' an F-4 to its full potential to establish the optimum parameters for a missile shoot, using 'super search' and boresight auto-acquisition, were all part and parcel of the process. Confidence levels rose, and with it respect for the

4E's M61A-1 20mm gun, 9½ to the AIM-9E Sidewinder (one or two of them possibly falling to the more manoeuvrable, cranked-canard 'dash-9J', then just entering service), and no fewer than thirty to the AIM-7E-2 Sparrow. The last kill of the war—in fact, the last combat kill to be achieved by any USAF Phantom to date—took place at 0232 hours on 8 January local time.[18] Vectored on to the target by a Navy 'Red Crown' radar picket ship using the Hanoi 'bull's-eye', 432nd TRW AC Capt Paul D. Howman and his WSO 1Lt Lawrence W. Kullman (behind the controls of F-4D 65-0796, call-sign 'Crafty One') 'bagged' a Phuc Yen-based MiG-21

Below: Jim Shaw was one of the last USAF crewmen to drop bombs over Vietnam, and he is seen here after having been hosed down with bubbly on 6 March 1973. Over his left shoulder is Capt J. D. Allen, who flew with him many times; over his right shoulder, in sunglasses, is Capt Brewster Shaw. Brewster joined NASA in 1978 and has flown as a pilot in the space shuttle *Columbia* and as commander of STS *Atlantis*, retiring as a Colonel in December 1990 before going on to become chief of Shuttle operations at NASA. (Jim Shaw)

'Fishbed' during a night MiGCAP in support of B-52s. Capt Howman later recorded in his official report: 'We picked him up on radar at about sixty miles. We were able to follow him most of the way in as the range decreased.' At about 30 miles Howman and his wing-man punched off their centreline 'bags' and descended to 12,000ft, zooming along at 400kts. At a range of sixteen miles 'Red Crown' gave them permission to fire. 'At ten miles I got a visual on an afterburner plume twenty degrees right and slightly high. I called him out to the back-seater and put the "pipper" on him. At six miles Lt Kullman got a good full-system radar lock-on. Range was about four miles and overtake 900-plus knots when I squeezed the trigger.' The missile rolled a little to the left then guided to its target, but it exploded 50ft short. Capt Howman 'squeezed' off another Sparrow at a range of two miles and 'this one just pulled some lead, then went straight for the MiG. It hit him in the fuselage and the airplane exploded and broke up into three big pieces'. Such a successful engagement owed a great deal to the long overdue 'systems respect' due to the Phantom.

PHANTOM PHADE-OUT

'Linebacker II' missions ceased on 15 January 1973, after the North had shame-facedly returned to Paris to sue for peace, its warmaking capacity all but crippled. In turn, the United States promised to cease all combat operations in exchange for its POWs, 588 of whom were re-patriated under Operation 'Home-coming' by 29 March. However, the blunting of the invasion, the two bomb-ing efforts 'up North' and related activi-ties in Cambodia and Laos had cost many F-4D/E losses to hostile fire, as shown in Table 19.[19]

Maj James M Shaw USAF Ret, who flew on the very first and last missions of the 'Linebacker' campaigns, also lays claim to having flown on the last 8th TFW mission over South Vietnam too. 'On that day [28 January] our Assistant DO, Col Paul Kunichika, and I were flying on the wing of a LORAN Path-

Above: The 13th TFS *Black Panthers* at Udorn were one of two squadrons specializing in 'counter-air' missions, alongside a bit of work over the Trails. This fearsome artwork was seen on the splitter/vari-ramp of F-4D 66-8705 on 23 December 1971. Other similarly marked Phantoms (all coded 'OC', such as 66-7755) also had large shark's-mouths painted behind their radomes by 1973. (Larsen/Remington via Richard L. Ward)

finder in northern MR-1 when, with less than ten minutes to go before the official cessation of hostilities in SVN (when all aircraft had to be out of its airspace), we dropped on a LORAN target in the vicinity of Khe Sanh. Having released our bombs a moment after our leader, I lay claim to the last bombs dropped in MR-1 and probably in SVN.' It was Jim's 199th mission in the theatre, 109 of which had been 'up North'.

With the January 1973 ceasefire, attention shifted towards Cambodia until those missions, too, were halted on 15 August. While in-theatre strike forces drew down for the final time, show-of-force manoeuvres such as Operation 'Commando Scrimmage' continued to demonstrate US potential. However, public demand for an end to the war, coupled with the emerging Watergate scandal, eventually proved to be over-whelming, and the last vestiges of the once-huge F-4 community finally bowed out from Thailand *en masse* beginning in the summer of 1974. The Republic coll-apsed in April 1975 following a second major invasion mounted by the Hanoi regime: on that occasion no US air power was deployed to thwart the attack, and neither were any F-4s made available to the RVNAF in the two years leading up to its collapse. Language problems and the relative sophistication of the Phantom—including the desire not to let it fall into communist hands intact—combined with the post-'Homecoming' return of POWs, effectively precluded transfer under the Vietnamization Program. Instead, surplus F-4Ds trickled into ROKAF service, where the USAF had maintained a strong presence (principally at Kunsan but also Kwang ju, Osan and Taegu Air Bases) since the 'Pueblo' Incident'. Taiwan, too, which had for some time been innovatively and expertly servicing PACAF aircraft at its Tainan facility (possessing E-Systems and CIA 'Air America' connections), was also considered as a serious customer, but US–Chinese relations at the political level, which matured after President Nixon's courtesy visit to Peking, precluded this FMS avenue, and the Republic itself was 'de-recognized' in 1979 in deference to the Carter Administration's consolidation of the United States' new-found friendship with the mainland.

The first 'Peace Pheasant' transfers to the *Hankook Kong Goon*, comprising eighteen F-4Ds, took place on 25 August 1969, making the Republic of Korea McDonnell's fifth overseas Phantom client following purchases of new builds of various marks by the Royal Navy, the RAF, Iran and Israel. A further eighteen 'loans' followed during 1972 (and were formally transferred during 1975), bolstered, *inter alia*, by an additional three dozen F-4Ds over the ensuing sixteen years.[20] With them went batches of the early-model AVQ-9 Pave Light 'Zot Boxes', followed by more advanced Pave electro-optical targeting and weapons systems which still are in use today, all with suitable analogue/digital conversion interfaces. What remained of the dwindling USAF PACAF Phantom assets were gradually updated and re-assigned to bolster the new bastions at Kunsan and Osan, South Korea, Clark

Field in the Philippines, and Kadena, Okinawa.

Whatever the rights and wrongs of the complex politics behind the protracted war in South-East Asia, the Phantom and its brave crews provided the backbone of CAS, MiGCAP and strike assets committed to the theatre. Moreover, they served as technological trail-blazers for many of the integrated weapons systems that reached full maturity two decades later, during the Gulf War. Among the milestones were the perfection of inertial-radar and electro-optical navigation and targeting devices, 'smart' weapons, dogfight-capable air-to-air missiles, electronic countermeasures (discussed elsewhere), and, above all else, a new 'systems mentality' that created a new USAF fighter ethos whereby combat-ready ACs and WSOs could do tours in multiple aircraft types, proficiently. Even in the short term, the exploits of the combat crews would send shock-waves around the world: much-neglected USAFE would be bolstered and provide the impetus for many more significant technology updates, while the F-4 export business was about to flourish, even-

tually expanding from five to a dozen overseas air arms, with Australia, Germany, Japan, Spain, Greece, Turkey and Egypt all following South Korea in rapid succession.

By the close of 1973, fifteen years after the Phantom's maiden flight, its serious rivals could still be counted on only two fingers—and neither of these American products had reached anything like operational maturity. McAir's masterpiece was still a world-beater, and would retain that status for much of the remainder of the decade.

[18] Based on the DoD OASD report dated 17 October 1973. Table 19 excludes one loss over Thailand in July 1972 and three over Cambodia between April and June 1973, for a total of 75 F-4D/Es. Losses to 'operational causes' have not been included; these totalled 62 F-4C/D/Es between 1965 and 1973.

[19] The MiG kill list that appears as Appendix II cites the official dates in Zulu (GMT) time, which in this instance corresponded to 1932Z on 7 January.

[20] 'Peace Pheasant' transfers have also since embraced no fewer than 40 surplus USAF F-4Es and fifteen RF-4Cs, for a total of 127 Phantoms. Factory-fresh examples amount to only 37 Block 64-MC and 67-MC F-4Es.

TABLE 18: F-4 'ACE' CAPTAINS IN SOUTH-EAST ASIA, 1972

Name	Kill	Date	Call-sign	Aircraft	Weapon	Victim
Capt J. S. Feinstein, WSO	1st	16 Apr	'Basco 3'	F-4D 66-7550/'PN'	AIM-7	MiG-21
	2nd	May 31	'Gopher 3'	F-4E 68-0338/'ED'	AIM-9	MiG-21
	3rd	July 18	'Snug 1'	F-4D 66-0271/'OC'	AIM-9	MiG-21
	4th	July 29	'Cadillac 1'	F-4D 66-0271/'OC'	AIM-7	MiG-21
	Ace	Oct 13	'Olds 1'	F-4D 66-7501/'OC'	AIM-7	MiG-21
Capt R. S. Ritchie, AC	1st	May 10	'Oyster 3'	F-4D 66-7463/'OY'	AIM-7	MiG-21
	2nd	May 31	'Icebag 1'	F-4D 65-0801/'OC'	AIM-7	MiG-21
	3rd	July 8	'Paula 1'	F-4E 67-0362/'ED'	AIM-7	MiG-21
	4th	July 8	'Paula 1'	F-4E 67-0362/'ED'	AIM-7	MiG-21
	Ace	Aug 28	'Buick 1'	F-4D 66-7463/'OY'	AIM-7	MiG-21
Capt C. B. DeBellevue, WSO	1st	May 10	With Ritchie, as above			
	2nd/3rd	July 8	With Ritchie, as above			
	4th	Aug 28	With Ritchie, as above			
	Ace	Sept 9	'Olds 1'	F-4D 66-0267/'OY'	AIM-9	MiG-19
	6th	Sept 9	'Olds 1'	F-4D 66-0267/'OY'	AIM-9	MiG-19

TABLE 19: USAF F-4D/E LOSSES TO HOSTILE FIRE IN SOUTH-EAST ASIA 1972–JANUARY 1973

	1972												1973	
	Jan	Feb	Mar	Apr	May	Jun	Jul	Aug	Sep	Oct	Nov	Dec	Jan	Totals
North Vietnam	–	2	–	3	9	11	13	1	4	7	–	2	–	52
South Vietnam	–	–	–	2	4	–	2	2	–	–	–	–	–	10
Laos	1	1	2	2	–	–	–	–	2	–	–	–	1	9
Totals	1	3	2	7	13	11	15	3	6	7	–	2	1	71

11. SILVER-HORNED RHINOS

The USAF Phantoms' prestigious exploits in South-East Asia soon earned it international accolades—and orders, handled by the US Government under the Foreign Military Sales (FMS) programme. As Sanford N. McDonnell later remarked at his keynote speech when the breed was celebrating the thirtieth anniversary of its first flight, 'It is to air combat what the tank is to ground action—brute force, but mobility.' Right from the beginning, it was clear that the Model 98 possessed an enormous potential for growth. It was probably the most versatile fighter aircraft ever manufactured: 'The first Phantom was flying so often that our competition thought we had at least two or three'. James 'Mr Mac' McDonnell, who founded McAir, was so confident about the aircraft that he chose Lambert Field instead of Edwards AFB for the maiden flight. 'The plane has never been withdrawn from

Below: A *Heyl Ha'Avir* **F-4E vaults into the sky with Gabriel III anti-shipping missiles underwing. The poor quality of the photo reveals little else . . . but such is the scarcity value of shots of IDF/AF Phantoms! (IAI)**

combat because it could not handle the mission.' Much of its reputation thus preceded it when McAir's sales team ventured forth.

The launch customer for FMS F-4Es was *La Tsvah Haganah le Israel/ Heyl Ha'Avir* (IDF/AF), in a sale confirmed by President Nixon on 27 December 1968 encompassing an initial fifty Phantoms. Israeli crews began training with the 4452nd TFTS at George AFB, California, during March 1969 and graduated four months later on 25 July, providing the nucleus for the new No 201 *Ahat* Squadron at Hatzor, which received its first quartet of Phantoms on 5 September, with Golda Meir and Air Force Chief Moti Hod in attendance. Led by Maj Shmuel Hetz and senior navigator Menaheim Eini (later to become a Brigadier-General), the force would eventually expand into a five-squadron establishment based at Hatzor (with Nos 105 and 201 Sqns), Hatzerim (No 107 *Zanav Katom*), Ramat-David (No 69 *Ha'patishim*) and Tel Nov (No 119 *Atalev*), with a substantial air defence and quick-strike detachment at Ophir near Sharm-el-Sheikh.

The formation of these units took nearly five years to complete, but the Phantoms were thrown into the thick of it within almost as many weeks, opening up with a strike against SA-2 SAM batteries near Port Said on 22 October and following these up with a series of attacks against Egyptian warehousing, ammunition and POL dumps through February. Supersonic flypasts were also made over Cairo on 5 November (and later Damascus in Syria), laying down concussive sonic booms which shattered the city's window panes and caused a general panic. The War of Attrition gradually escalated from piecemeal strikes and 'booming' to co-ordinated defence-suppression attacks, conducted in response to the Egyptians' moving a line of anti-aircraft defences steadily closer to the Suez Canal. Although there were still only two squadrons (Nos 201 and 69), the strikes graduated into what were known as the *Prikha* or 'Rolling Missile Campaign', the first of which was launched on 16 May 1970 using eight Phantoms equipped with M117s against sites in Ras Banas. Thus began a fierce series of set-piece battles between SAM and flak batteries and groups of six to eight Phantoms, which used a combination of low-level 'pop-up scissors' attacks and 'Indian Circle' tactics with 'iron' bombs and CBUs. Three aircraft were brought down in one week alone: two on 30 June during a strike against three batteries at Rubeiki, with pilot Rami Harpaz uttering the sober words 'I goofed' before following his navigator out of the aircraft in a successful ejection; and another from Col Avihu Bin-Nun's *Ha'patisham* on 5 July, engaged against a battery near the Cairo–Ismailia road.

Right: The front cockpit of an F-4E, similar to but much more cluttered than the F-4C that originated the USAF production line. This photograph depicts a late Turkish example. Atop the coaming, either side of the LCOSS, were added various items relating to Pave Spike and RHAWS. Pilots gradually became more proficient at instrument flying by necessity! (McAir)

All six men escaped their mortally damaged ghostly steeds, but only navigator David Ya'ir was repatriated the same day after being plucked by a Sea Stallion helicopter. This action alone demanded revenge, and new tactics with it, heralding the beginnings of the use of ECM equipment. At 1215 local time on Saturday 18 July the reprisal force took off to engage five SA-2 batteries—plus new AAA and SA-3 defences they did did not anticipate—50km west of Suez. It was a horrific exchange which opened up with one of the SA-3 'Goas' acquiring and exploding near the *Ahat* squadron boss's machine at FL180, despite ECM opposition, showering it with shrapnel. The pilot dumped all ordnance and turned for home, but at 600kts and 100ft from the ground, and still losing height, impact with the desert was imminent. F-4E pioneer Shmuel Hetz went down with the aircraft; his right-hand man Menaheim Eini, the Service's premier 'pitter', ejected and was taken captive, to be released in November 1973 alongside many of his comrades. It was a painful episode for the fledgeling Phantom crews, but they pressed on. Their repertoire expanded the following year to include AGM-45A Shrike anti-radar missiles, brought in alongside a dozen 'Peace Patch' F-4E replacements for those lost in combat or damaged beyond repair, until the War of Attrition finally came to an end with a ceasefire on 7 August 1971. In the space of less than two years the Service had learnt the bitter way how to defeat SAMs.

To the Phantom crews' credit also, their new beast was proving to be a capable air-to-air aircraft. Capt Ahud Hankin and navigator Maj Saul Levy 'bagged' a MiG-21 'Fishbed' on 11 November 1969—the first ever kill with an F-4E—opening up a series of successful engagements which endured in the relative calm that existed right up until 13 September 1973, at which point the IDF/AF had notched up a highly respectable 11:1 MiG-kill ratio. Two of these victories occurred on 30 July 1970, in an action against Soviet-flown MiG-21s, when Cols Avihu Bin-Nun and his wing-man-cum-Deputy Commander Aviem Sella each 'bagged' a 'Fishbed'. It helped to even the score for the Squadron's losses. Interestingly also, as a Major-General, Bin-Nun would later rise to become Chief of *Heyl Ha'Avir*.

Another 'big-league' launch customer for the Phantom, and a source of considerable controversy in the aftermath of the 'Arms for Iran' scandal, was Persia. Under Project 'Peace Roll', the Shah's pro-West regime added no fewer than 177 F-4Es to the 32 factory-fresh F-4Ds it had acquired from September 1968. These were delivered to the *Nirou Hayai Shanashahiye Iran* (IIAF) beginning in April 1971 and formed the basis for a substantial establishment eventually distributed among eight tactical bases dotted around the country, at Bandar Abbas, Bushehr, Chabahar, Dezful, Hamadan, Mehrabad, Shiraz and Tabriz. Eight USAF F-4Es were loaned for in-theatre, 'hands-on' training (including two for use by ground schools), while as part of CENTO they hosted elements from the 401st TFW, USAFE, which deployed from Torrejon, Spain, for 'Shabaz' joint exercises. They would later bear the brunt of Islamic fundamentalism which would tear the units' camaraderie apart, soon afterwards to be exploited by Iran's belligerent neighbour Iraq.

On the other side of the globe, more customers had been getting to grips with the F-4E, notably Japan's *Koku Jie tai*. Under Contract JO782, McAir would build the first two of the new F-4EJ model and provide a further eleven as knock-down kits to be reassembled by Mitsubishi Industries—the beginnings of the only overseas complete Phantom assembly line, which would eventually manufacture 127 additional examples. The first of the St Louis-built pair (Japanese serial 17-8301) flew at Lambert Field on 14 January 1971 and the duo were delivered on 16 July, arriving at Komakai on the 25th.[1] Production would eventually end when 17-8440 was

---

[1] The first Japanese-assembled F-4EJ, serial number 27-8303, flew on 12 May 1972. All fourteen additional RF-4EJ reconnaissance purchases were acquired from the St Louis lines.

handed over to the Air Self-Defence Force on 21 May 1981—Phantom number 5,195, delivered nearly two years after the McAir Phantom assembly line had closed. Early examples were initially assigned to the Air Proving Wing at Gifu, before numbers swelled to permit the formation of the first operational *Hikotai*, No 301 *Frogs*, on 16 October 1973, which later moved to Nyutabaru. Nos 302–306 followed in succession at Chitose (later Naha, Okinawa), Kamatsu, Tsuiki, Hyakuri and Komatsu, respectively, a process completed on 30 June 1981 with *306 Hikotai*, the *Inuwashi* or *Golden Eagles*. Unlike their sun-baked, flak-hammering, Middle-Eastern counterparts, the Japanese aircraft have led a peaceful existence in their snowy mountain bases.

All the F-4EJ aircraft were tasked exclusively with air defence responsibilities, devoid of an air-to-surface weapons capability but retaining the full Falcon/ Sidewinder, Sparrow and M61A-1 gun fit, along with a new GC-1 gun-sight camera and provisions for pressure suits. Japanese F-4EJs were the only variants habitually to employ the plumbing for these, mandated for sustained operations above FL400, and thus theoretically represented the only credible interceptor able to to give a modicum of opposition to the Mach 2.83-capable Soviet MiG-25 'Foxbat'. However, in September 1976 the JASDF failed to do more than light up the radar warning indicator of defecting pilot Michael Belenko's trisonic jet before he 'crash-landed' his 'Foxbat' at Hakodate. The USAF proposed the XAIM-97 Seekbat, an infra-red-guided model of the General Dynamics AGM-78 Standard ARM missile to counter this threat, but it never went into production. Some 117 F-4EJ survivors still fly today, several painted with gaudy 'dayglo' green, orange or blue as Dissimilar Air Combat Training 'Aggressors', updated with new systems.[2]

AGILE EAGLE

Despite its unrivalled success, and its generally forgiving handling qualities, the Phantom did possess one notorious attribute—the flat stall-spin. Drawing sine waves through the air to dodge flak and SAMs and then pulling the jet up again too sharply and slapping the stick

Left: A TISEO-equipped F-4E brandishes a pair of EOGB IIs, known as 'GBU-15s' to the crews. They were a marked improvement on the Vietnam-era 'Egob' and entered service first with the *Heyl Ha'Avir* in 1977, albeit used in a LOBL lock-on-leave mode in those days. (Rockwell International)

Right: An 18th TFW F-4D undergoes an engine change. With only slight modifications the General Electric turbojet stayed the course throughout the Phantom's career and proved to be a reliable asset. The superb intake/engine match was the key to the Phantom's performance. (Ken Mackintosh)

about often caused it to start buffeting, yawing and then to depart from controlled flight into a flat spin, from which there was only one avenue of recovery —ejection! By 1970 it was estimated that the US Air Force had lost well over 100 Phantoms because of this problem; the US Navy figures, which have been released, show the loss of 83 aircraft and 43 crewmen between 1962 and 1980. Navy crews were recommended to abandon ship at or above 10,000ft if they encountered this phenomenon, while the Service attempted to address the issue by embarking on a massive re-education programme. The USAF, by then training many FMS customers, surmised that, as most of their aircraft were engaged in low-level strike (which was gradually working down towards the NATO 250ft AGL minimum in an effort to avoid radar detection, using 'pop up' manoeuvres with weapons deliveries bottoming out at just a few thousand feet), more drastic corrective action was required. Curiously enough, McDonnell Douglas had been exploring improved controllability under its company-funded 'Agile Eagle' effort, designed to fathom out the possibility of incorporating wing-mounted manoeuvring slats for their up-and-coming FX submission, the F-15. In the end, the new Eagle emerged as a supersonic 'hard-wing' aircraft, but the devices, tested on venerable McAir Ship No 266 (62-12200) during the course of a dozen JP4-guzzling flights made between 17 June and 15 August 1969, showed promise.

Fully-fledged field trials were performed in Israel by the IDF/AF. The first such aircraft, adapted by a field team in October 1970, had the extended slats welded in the open position! This machine (F-4E-41-MC 68-0544) bore the Israeli call-number '187' and later

made several appearances at domestic air shows (with a huge set of sharp teeth painted on its nose, the biggest ever to appear on a Phantom), giving 'dirty' flypasts with the hook and wheels down and a stabilizing drag 'chute billowing from its rear.[3] The IDF/AF pushed the test programme wide open and revealed the advantages, in which out-of-control situations beyond even 30 units of angle of attack (AOA) were eliminated, enabling the Phantoms to make hard turns, shaving 2,000ft and 15 seconds off a 180-degree turn at Mach 0.6 at FL100 (although they would run out of sustained energy more quickly if they kept it up for long). Even with the slats in the fixed, open position the aircraft could muster 750kts and pull the aircraft's full positive load factors of +8.6g

The USAF followed this up under Project 'Agile Eagle I', using the No 1 F-4E (66-0284), also with welded, fixed leading-edge slats (LES). Flying in 1971 and drawing on the notes of McAir test pilot 'Bud' Murray and his colleagues, the aircraft was refined through ten configurations which eventually settled on a pivoting outer slat and a fully retractable inner slat which closed up automatically at 10.5 units AOA, or above 600kts. Earlier problems with longitudinal instability were corrected by wing fences,

which also closed the gap between the inner and outer sections in order to maximize efficiency. The fully functioning system was tested on F-4E No 4 (66-0287) between August 1971 and March 1972, resulting in a massive, fleet-wide retrofit programme. McAir received the go-ahead on 25 April 1972 to produce kits for virtually the entire USAF inventory of F-4Es. The Air Force's Ogden Logistics Center in Utah and its subcontractors, such as Getafe in Spain, handled the re-work (TO 1F-4E-566) during routine scheduled PDM overhauls, the first of which was begun by the OOALC on 30 April 1972. Initial examples went to the 'Fourth But First' at Seymour-Johnson AFB, North Carolina, on 22 November that year; the 304th and last Ogden conversion rounded off the programme upon its completion on 4 April 1976, with the 36th TFW F-4Es

---

[2] The force has since been partly superseded by the F-15J Eagle, also licence-produced by Mitsubishi, and 96 of the aged Phantoms are being upgraded with new radar and ground-attack systems, with a secondary air-to-air capability. The Japanese *Kai* effort is discussed in greater detail in 'ICE and Kai Cocktails' in Chapter 13.

[3] The 512th TFS's *Knight Stalker* (F-4E 68-480), specially decorated for the 1983 IAT at RAF Greenham Common, Berkshire, a decade later, ran a close second in the big shark's-mouth contest.

Left, upper: The *Luftwaffe* acquired 175 F-4Fs, the first of which arrived in West Germany on 5 September 1973. The splinter grey/green camouflage had given way to the aesthetically pleasing *Maus* grey scheme by the early 1980s, by which time the aircraft had been updated with AIM-9L Sidewinder and AGM-65B Maverick missile provisions, furnished by the CEI (Combat Efficiency Improvement) effort. A follow-on ICE (Improved Combat Efficiency) drive is adding AMRAAM missile capability and a new AN/APG-65 radar to the breed. (Fritz Becker via Tim Laming)

Left, lower: *JG 74* celebrated 25 years of postwar history in September 1986 by painting up 3756 in this startling blue and golden yellow livery. (Christian Gerard)

from Bitburg AB, West Germany, amongst the last to be processed, handled by CASA Getafe. Several crews who flew with USAFE recalled the days when their squadrons operated a veritable 'mixed bag' of F-4Es, 'including "hard-wing" aircraft, in-theatre modified "slat-wing" and brand new TISEO birds which came to us fresh from the factory with only acceptance and ferry time on them [and] which even smelled new!'[4] Lt-Col MacClean noted that he had seen people perform manoeuvres 'which they would not have dared to do prior to the LES modifications'. Maj Cassidy added that 'You can slap the stick around with no problems; if you did the same in the F-4C/D you could snap it out of control'. Others also viewed the deletion of the BLC as another bonus: if a valve went, bleed air would sometimes cause internal fires, resulting inevitably in the loss of the aircraft. McAir also manufactured LES kits for the IDF/AF and IIAF inventories of 'hard wings', which were retrofitted locally. In fact, the only examples not 're-winged' were the glossy non-operational examples flown by the *Thunderbirds*, which were subsequently assigned for test and chase work at Edwards AFFTC, and the Mitsubishi licence-built F-4EJs of the Japanese *Koku Jiei tai*, which preferred the cleaner, lighter 'hard wing' for its medium- to high-altitude dedicated air defence operations. LES were also introduced on the McAir assembly lines as a standard feature starting with the 756th 'Echo' to

be manufactured (Block 48-MC, 71-0237). This incorporated 'out of station' kits which were applied after assembly had been completed to the original contract specification but prior to delivery. A revised, thicker, lower wing torque box skin was introduced on Block 50 aircraft (beginning with F-4E No 803, 72-0121), this becoming the norm for subsequent FMS F-4E/Fs too, along with the last sixteen RF-4E reconnaissance models completed in Block 66 for Greece and Turkey. The accident rate plummeted, though the programme was not extended to the F-4C/D (nor to any but a few F-4Ns), most of which were already destined for transfer to the reserves to fulfil the Strategic Air Defense mission.

Recipients of brand new LES Phantoms included the customer for the Model 98-KA F-4F, West Germany's *Luftwaffe*. As a spin-off from the sizeable Project 'Peace Lookout' purchase of reconnaissance Phantoms, 'Peace Rhine' added 175 Block 51–59 F-4Fs, the first of which flew on 18 March 1973, resplendent in the service's unique splinter grey-green and aluminium grey paintwork.[5] In fact, aircraft 3701 (USAF/FMS serial 72-1111) was 'officially' rolled out a week later! It contrasted distinctly with the Japanese 98-MJ model in that it featured the original unslotted stabilator but incorporated LES! It also retained full ground-attack provisions, and its Sparrow missile capability was pruned away. It was also short-legged, lacking the No 7 fuel cell and (initially) the plumbing and receptacle for AAR refuelling. For the first few years of its career it would fly with only bombs or improved Sidewinder AIM-9Bs built by Bodenseewerk, and a loaded gun, to be distributed between two intercept *Jagdgeschwader*, *JG 71 'Richthofen'* at Wittmund, which received its first pair of aircraft on 7 March 1974, and *JG 74 'Mölders'* at Neuburg, which began conversion during that July; and two ground-attack *Jagdbomberbeschwader*, *JaboG 35* at Pferdsfeld and *JaboG 36* at Rheine-Hopstein, both of which began operations from April 1975, each comprising two *Staffeln*. The last in the series, 3875 (serial 72-1285), was ceremoni-

ously delivered to *JaboG 35* in April 1976, bearing the name *Spirit of Cooperation*, reflecting the input provided by German industry.[6]

Training was handled at George AFB, California, where the *Luftwaffe* initially retained eight early-production Phantoms to train their novice pilots and navigators (known as *Kampfbeobachter*, or combat observers) using standard American syllabuses modified for the F-4F, under the authority of the 20th TFTS *Silver Lobos*. In the summer of 1977 these were replaced by ten brand new Block 63-MC F-4Es (75-0628 to -0637, without Group B TISEO equipment), freeing the survivors of the F-4F Training Flight for operational use and transferring the final transition process back to Germany and *JaboG 36*'s new third training *Zentrale Ausbildungsstaffel* (ZAS). Pilots would then amass an additional 24 hours before being reassigned to their operational squadrons, where they would climb the proficiency ladder gradually—250 hours to become IMC, and a further 400 to achieve 'Flight Leader' or *Rotteführer* status. Stock American *Silver Lobos* F-4Es were similarly engaged in providing courses for the swelling overseas ranks of newcomers to the Phantom fraternity.

NUCLEAR PHANTOMS

In the post-Vietnam years USAFE held the winning poker hand and could draw upon massive reinforcements in the event of conflict in Europe. This was viewed as more than an academic scenario, especially following heightened tensions in the Middle East, despite the obvious desire for something akin to a 'notional' front line in the absence of a real war, to keep the logistics supply lines and operational units at peak efficiency. Immedi-

[4] Refer to Chapter 13 for a full description of TISEO.
[5] The acquisition of RF-4Es under 'Peace Lookout', which started the *Luftwaffe* Phantom programme off, is aired further in Chapter 15.
[6] Motoren und Turbinen-Union built 448 J79-MTU-17A engines (including spares) for the F-4F; Dornier, Siebel and MBB provided with various offsets. In common with the British Phantoms which featured domestic components, all final assembly was carried out at St Louis.

Above: F-4E 68-0480 from the 512th TFS based at Ramstein featured one the largest shark's-mouths ever to appear on a Phantom, surpassed only by Israeli F-4E tail number 187, which served as test-bed for the LES modification. (Authors)

ately after the cessation of hostilities in South-East Asia, the 4th and 49th TFWs became 'dual-committed' to NATO and began a series of two-week 'Crested Cap' deployments. The first to deploy were the 335th TFS *Chiefs*, who repositioned themselves at Spangdahlem AB, West Germany, for two weeks in July 1975. The process actually began in October 1968 under 'Coronet Finch', when 'Photo-Phantoms' from Mountain Home AFB, Idaho, deployed to Ramstein—the first of 43 different European bases that would play host to CONUS F-4s over the ensuing two decades. The European playground also served as a catalyst for a number of significant post-war weapons systems improvements which built upon Pave experience in SEA. And between 1973 and 1978 two major 'Creek' aligning efforts juggled Phantoms between CONUS and Europe to ensure that all British- and German-based units flew the upgraded F-4D or F-4E with 'smart' potential.

However, the domineering assignment was proficiency in nuclear bombing. The Phantoms' AN/AJB-7 all-altitude refer-

ence bombing system and TD-709 timer helped to compute weapons release using 'loft' or Low Angle Drogue Delivery (LADD). Radar offset or initial points would be employed in the normal manner prior to setting the timer into motion at a set range to the target, using radar as the primary cue to start the 'clock' running. With the system set in motion, a spinning odometer wound down until, at zero, it commanded a 'pull-up' pending the release of the bomb by the analogue sequential timer. These systems were kept in particularly good order.

Nuclear strike, a task for the F-4 which was seldom publicized, remained at the forefront of the Phantom Wings' brief throughout the 1970s. Indeed, most units not only practised for nuclear combat but also maintained fully armed examples on constant call in the 'Victor Alert' 'barns'. Vietnam veteran Lt-Col John Roberts USAF Ret, who was Ops Officer for the 92nd TFS, one of three F-4D squadrons which made up the 81st TFW *Blue Dragons* at RAF Woodbridge in Suffolk, recollected the duty: '2–3 day tours sitting and sleeping in a separate secure area within feet of the aircraft, ready to jump out of bed and go to nuclear war, was a very boring, important job. Targets were primarily the Warsaw Pact fighter and naval bases within

the range of the Phantom. Our Wing also maintained alert birds in northern Italy and the Madrid Wing [the 401st TFW at Torrejon] did the same in Turkey. Last summer [1990] I drove into East Germany and through a small town near a Soviet command centre which had once been my nuclear target. It was a strange feeling to think I could have been sent to destroy this drab, old village and its people—who are now our allies —twenty years ago.[7]

'The alert aircraft carried one B61 thermonuclear weapon on the centreline, two fuel tanks and an ECM pod on the wings and the usual four Sparrow AIM-7 missiles in the recessed fuselage wells. This bomb was only 13.4 inches in diameter and just under 12 feet long, with a parachute-retard capability and selectable yields for various targets. The pilot had to receive a special PAL (Permissive Action Link) code in order to arm the bomb. The handling and delivery of nuclear weapons required heavy standardization and supervision. Each year a crew was required to give a professional certification, briefing a senior officer of the Wing on an entire nuclear mission, including the memorized recitation of the checkpoints on the target run-in. I once got carried away and gave a two-hour presentation while the Wing Commander tried not to fall asleep. No-notice certifications were also conducted on alert. About once a year the Wing was subject to a no-notice ORI by the Team from Headquarters USAFE. A complete war scenario was lived with all possible realism over a period of several days, ranging from early conventional attacks escalating to an all-out simulated launch of the fleet on a nuclear strike. Everything from individual crew performance to weapons loading and maintenance to command and control procedures was thoroughly evaluated. Failure in any area might cause the entire Wing to fail: heads would roll, and a heavy training schedule was undertaken to prepare for the re-test in a few months' time. It was no fun, but it ensured that the mission was performed properly.' Another ingredient was preparation for nuclear support of a ground war—the strategy of limited nuclear counter-force to contain a mass invasion of Soviet armour. 'So we practised and were constantly prepared for a surprise nuclear tasking. A crew would be given a target and be expected to prepare maps, navigation information and target attack tactics for a briefing to Stan/Eval or ORI teams. The crew would then fly an actual mission against a target somewhere in Europe and be expected to arrive over the target within seconds of the designated time.'

The specifics of the mission remain classified to this day. Suffice it to say that the techniques practised on WTDs (Weapons Training Deployments) over Bardenas Reales near Zaragosa, Adana in Turkey, or Nellis, Nevada, were honed for high-speed deliveries using a solitary, 803lb Mk/B61 'Silver Bullet' slung on Station 5. The Douglas BDU-38/B, apart from its concrete ballast and gloss white decor, looked and behaved just like the 'Silver Bullet' and could be 'LADD-ed' using its Kevlar drogue, or 'lofted' in 'slick' format in a half-Cuban-eight 'toss' pull-up manoeuvre. Fusing could be set for a surface or an air burst, depending on the characteristics of the target. The minimum release airspeed to guarantee avoidance of the worst effects of the bomb's thermonuclear shock-wave was 520kts—a mite more sporty than the speeds used for depositing Snakeyes! Navy Phantom crews were also qualified to employ the Mk/B61 (and the older Mk/B57 which was used as a nuclear depth charge to defeat enemy submarines) but, because of the primary BARCAP role, were seldom obliged to maintain the tempo of paranoiac readiness stipulated by USAF 'higher authority'.

As the the Mk/B61's ballistic characteristics were shared by the comparatively innocuous tubby little orange, 10lb Mk 106/BDU-48 'Beer Can' (retarded lay-down) and blue, 25lb Mk 76/BDU-33 'slick' (toss) practice bombs too, there existed little need to 'frighten the natives' with the big white concrete-filled 'training shapes'. To add to the discretion, USAFE (and PACAF) employed SUU-21/A dispensers featuring shutter doors, behind which batches of up to six practice bombs could be installed, allowing for multiple passes on the conventional practice ranges, such as those found on The Wash in England or off Scottish coasts, on a daily basis, without affecting European (or Filipino) sensibilities. The last Phantom unit to maintain the nuclear 'Victor Alert' commitment was the 512th TFS *Pro Pace Vigilare* at Ramstein AB, West Germany. Preliminary arming of the bombs was conducted via a key which was inserted, turned and removed prior to launch from the two relevant Phantoms bunkered down in the extra-hardened 'Zulu' TAB-Vee shelters. In-flight fusing options required the consent of both crewmen to arm and set the weapon for the desired delivery mode. It was until very recently a fail-safe system which, using dual-key procedures, remained in prospective use during emergencies on board many NATO Phantoms.[8]

Alongside the nuclear mission, crews also began to take on board the full array of second-generation Pave technology. Chief amongst these were Maverick and Pave Spike, the electro-optical imagery from which information was flashed up on a brand new radarscope tube driven by a digital scan converter group (DSCG). This converted radar analogue signals to digital while also being able to display the new E-O imagery (but never both at the same time), in a much clearer, sharper format than that previously available from the old combined MSDG. The first aircraft to percolate into operational squadrons following the appropriate re-work reached front-line service shortly after operations were drawing to a close in Thailand.[9]

MISSILEERS

The DSC made the 'Wizzo''s job simpler but more diverse, and featured such boons to 'head-down' scope-monitoring as alphanumeric symbology pertaining to tracking mode, range-to-target and a host of other data previously displayed elsewhere on spinning odometers which necessitated constant and sometimes stomach-wretching cross-scanning. The digital format also facilitated video-taping, and airborne AVTR recorders followed later in the decade, replacing film-based radarscope photography and wing-root-mounted KB-18 strike cameras.

The first of the new weapons systems to arrive was the Hughes AGM-65A Maverick, which represented the earliest operational application of fire-and-forget air-to-surface missile technology to the Phantom. It was allegedly tested in South-East Asia during the 'Linebacker II' offensive, and production models of the tail-steered TV-guided missile reached operational squadrons the following year. The first to begin training on the type were the 334th TFS *Eagles* at Seymour-Johnson, who began to ply this trade on 22 June 1973. Up to six of the missiles could be carried at a time on inboard, pylon-mounted LAU-88 racks, though it was customary to carry four in a slant-two format, or just one pair in conjunction with other ordnance, such

[7] Based on personal correspondence with John Roberts and extracts from his work *The Fighter Pilot's Handbook*, published in 1992 by Arms & Armour Press.
[8] American Chief of Staff Gen Colin Powell's statement following the successful conclusion of Operation 'Desert Storm' that 'We can now do conventionally much more efficiently things we thought we could do only with tactical nuclear weapons' reflected a greater desire by the JCS for the complete removal of both 'dual-key' and 'single-key' weapons from NATO. This is being put into effect. For similar reasons, the Turkish authorities were reluctant to permit more than a token presence at Incirlik during the height of the GulfWar, when nuclear weapons were on standby in case Saddam Hussein's closed circle dared to order rocket launches packing nuclear waste or devastating chemicals. See Chapter 14, in the context of the 3rd TFS's F-4E deployment from Clark Field.
[9] The new DSC fit was introduced on Block 60 F-4E Phantoms (74-0643 and up) and retrofitted to selected F-4D/Es incorporating TOs 1-F-4D-580 and 1-F-4E-582, respectively, along with a new laser code panel for Paveway II bombs. Some of the problems encountered with the original MSDG radar scope display were aired in Chapter 10, in the context of Hobos or 'Egob' lock-ons.

as LGBs, in an asymmetric configuration. Drag, and the often lengthy procedures required for TV lock-on, precluded the 'super Maverick' configuration on all but CAS jets in low-threat areas.[10] Nevertheless, the missile became the chief 'tank-zapper' of TAC, USAFE and the Americans' NATO allies, designed to deter the Red Army's armoured formations from grinding through the Fulda Gap, and went on to become the primary air-to-surface missile of the *Luftwaffe*'s Combat Efficiency Improved (CEI) 'Peace Rhine' F-4Fs too, which were redistributed to the Wings from November 1980.[11] The kinetic energy of the missile combined with its 125lb warhead could do mischief to even the most heavily armoured tank, but most USAF F-4 crews were grateful that they never had to go to war with it in Europe, where lock-on ranges were severely limited by the prevailing cloudy weather. As with so many of the emerging 'smart' missiles and bombs, it was Israel which tended to initiate them into combat, in the clearer skies of the Near East.

By the end of the summer of 1973 the *Heyl Ha'Avir* was operating a veritable electronic circus of F-4Es drawn from eleven different production Blocks, including 29 LES models and 85 surviving 'hard-wings'. The 'old heads', including many Orthodox Jews who flew with *Yarmulke* beneath their helmets, gradually streamlined their protégés into several mission categories for the purpose of drawing up combat and contingency plans, depending on the preliminary proficiency that novices demonstrated in the aircraft's six specific weapons systems—Sparrow, Sidewinder, the M61A-1 gun, gravity bombs, 'smart' weapons and Shrike/Electronic Warfare—and on available aircraft, which were far from standardized even within the squadrons. Only when they had mastered several of these weapons were pilots and navigators permitted gradually to rise above wing-man status, to become what what USAF aviators would describe as 'lead-qualified'. As things turned out, many of those distinctions would prove to be wholly academic.

At 1400hrs on Saturday 6 October 1973 Egypt and Syria launched a simultaneous, ferocious strike against Israel code-named Operation '*Badr*'. The response of the *Heyl Ha'Avir* was swift and dramatic: in the opening minutes of the attack, two alert F-4Es from Ophir flew straight into a formation of 28 enemy aircraft and 'bagged' seven of them in one fell swoop, for which the Flight-Lead Captain concerned was decorated with the *Ot Hamofet*. He had personally 'bagged' four and his wing-man the remaining three.

The next day, with everyone called to duty and the aircraft 'bombed up' for action, whining and screaming J79s poured out soot in seemingly endless trails from the key air bases. Target details were handed up to gloved hands stretching out from open canopies during 'last chance': 'Target co-ordinates? Enemy oppositon? Pile on the thrust . . . and go!' was the prevailing mentality. Great streamers of black smoke twisted together to form an amorphous mass that hung over the nation's troubled skies for days on end. Forces were split into two streams, initially bound west and north, to strike the new mobilc SA-6 SAM and ZSU-23/4 AAA batteries that were already beginning to take a heavy toll of Skyhawks. Six F-4Es were lost during the first day of air strikes, and a seventh, reported to be on fire when it landed at Ramat David AB, was burnt out. This single counter-offensive cost two crewmen killed, nine captured and three injured. The tempo did not cease.

Right, upper: An ADTC F-4E rolls on to an 'Eglin highway' to perform practice lock-ons with the Hughes AGM-65B 'Scene Mag' Maverick. The weapon became the chief tank and truck 'zapper' of the USAF and many FMS customers from 1973, including Greece, Iran, Israel, South Korea and Turkey. (Hughes Missiles)
Right, lower: *Chiefs* taxy out with a full load of Mk 82 bombs for a 'Red Flag 84-4' mission. Some 173 F-4Es received the DMAS digital re-work, which provided the Phantom with a completely 'uncanned' weapons delivery capability. If any part of the system 'went ape', the crews were obliged to revert to 'down the chute' manual bombing methods. (Frank B. Mormillo)

Hundreds of additional *ad hoc* sorties tasked Phantom crews against the enemy airfields, headquarters installations, power stations and port facilities, at a pace that continued right up until 21 October, Day 16 of the Yom Kippur War. At that much-welcomed turning point, Israeli ground forces had finally outflanked the Egyptian opposition in Sinai and had driven the Syrians back to a defensive position on the Mount Hermon line. The United Nations then called for a ceasefire on the 22nd, and all hostilities were finally halted two days later, giving the Israelis time to reflect on the horrific onslaught—and count numbers. Nowhere had the Phantom played such a decisive military role in so short a time, but the cost had been enormous: 37 F-4Es had been lost to hostile fire, six more had been damaged beyond repair and many more were twisted and 'holed' but could be patched up, bringing the total IDF/AF F-4E attrition since 1969

[10] Such as the A-10A 'Warthog'. In the Phantom, lock-on was accomplished by the pilot's entering a gentle dive on to the target, much as with Hobos. The WSO then slewed the target image 'underneath' the fixed cross-hairs by means of the radar tracking handle, before releasing the tracking switch. Following a quick verbal confirmation of target lock-on between the crew, the pilot then 'squeezed it off', after which time he initiated immediate evasive action. AGM-65 capability was retrofitted to F-4Ds from 66-7505 onwards (Block 30-MC and up) and selected F-4Es from 66-0284 to 69-7589 (TO 1F-4E-610), before becoming a production-line feature on USAF F-4E Block 48-MC, starting with 71-0248.
[11] The CEI effort, initiated in 1975 and completed in 1983, resulted in all four Wings possessing a swing-role function, with the *JaboG*s maintaining 40 per cent intercept capability. However, the dual-tasking ended on 1 July 1988, as an economy move. On 1 November 1990 *JaboG 36* was retitled *JG 72 'Westfalen'*, to become the third interceptor Wing, followed by *JaboG 35* which is now *JG 73*. The ZAS Central Training School function, which takes crews fresh from the 9th TFS RTU at Holloman AFB, New Mexico, from the F-4E to the F-4F and provides a 3–4 month 'Europeanization' lead-in, is accordingly now performed by *JG 72*. The current ICE (Improved Combat Effectiveness) programme substantially enhances their air-to-air capability, and will dominate their tasking. The ICE programme is discussed in more detail in the 'ICE and Kai Cocktails' section in Chapter 13.

up to an unpalatable 51 aircraft (with major BDR work salvaging at least a dozen more 'basket cases'). This represented over 40 per cent of the force. However, machines could be replaced. What was more troublesome was the realization that many of the 'old heads' had tumbled, some of whom had been with the programme from its inception.

In an emergency resupply effort codenamed Operation 'Nickel Grass', conducted during the heat of the battle, the US Air Force ferried in three dozen replacements from Seymour-Johnson AFB. These arrived in time to fly 200 combat sorties, during which some of the aircraft were crewed by sympathetic USAF personnel. With them came the AGM-65A Maverick, and tutors to provide a 'cram course' on the weapon, which in the relatively clear skies over the Sinai battlefront attained a success rate of 87 per cent. Suitably impressed by its results at smashing armour and radars alike, the Israelis procured additional lots alongside the F-4 'buy back' deal, including quantities of the AGM-65B 'scene-magnification' model with double the stand-off lock-on range, which became available during 1975. A further

48 new Block 54-62 F-4Es were added to the inventory up to November 1976, including two dozen of the Block 60-62-MC variant featuring TISEO and a 'Purple Fist', long-range AGM-78 anti-radar missile capability—the only F-4Es wired up for this missile. A 'Quick Draw' capability was also provided for the Maverick missile, to speed up the lock-on process in a target-saturated environment, while Israeli Aircraft Industries (IAI) Bedek Division and the domestic weapons manufacturers Rafael embarked on a long-term programme in an attempt to homogenize the fleet.

The 'Fourth But First''s experience with slatted Phantoms and Maverick and its global mobility record put it in good stead. In fact, on 8 December 1974 the 4th TFW became the first unit to mark four years of totally accident-free flying, and improved on that by being accredited with 100,000 accident-free flying hours on 6 March the following year—another first. Despite the F-4's relatively easy handling qualities, losses of all marks exceeded a dozen a year. Some were flown into the ground owing to low 'situational awareness' as a result of the renewed emphasis on low-level

Above: The 347th TFW's flagship salvoes six Mk 82 'slick' bombs. The angle of the terrain relative to the aircraft indicates a 45-degree dive-bomb run, using radar or Pave Spike laser-ranging to help the WRCS compute 'bombs-off' after 'pickle'. The Wing deployed to Cairo West, Egypt, during 1980 for Operation 'Proud Phantom', which helped convert the Egyptian *Al-Quwwat al-Jawwiya Ilmisriya* on to their 35 second-hand F-4Es. (USAF)
Right, upper: A pair of smart 70th TFS F-4Es from the 347th TFW, based at Moody AFB, Georgia, display their svelte lines to the camera off 'Anker 23', a 22nd AREFW Stratotanker. Both jets sport AN/ASQ-153 Pave Spike pods on the port forward Sparrow well adaptors and AN/ALQ-119 ECM pods on the port inner wing pylons. The Wing specialized in Pave Spike laser-bombing and the Maverick missile. (Frank B. Mormillo)
Right, lower: A 70th TFS F-4E slides into position behind 'Anker 23'. Telephoto compression emphasizes the 'area ruled' fuselage of the beast. (Frank B. Mormillo)

training (generally made safer when the slats were introduced), but a few could be attributed to bird-strikes. A 4lb crow hitting the windscreen at a mere 300kts would shatter it, and possibly blind the pilot. At 500kts it would kill him. Over eight 'operational losses' were attributed to bird-strikes by 1976, something the Israelis knew a great deal about owing to

Above: A well-weathered F-4E from Greece's *Elliniki Polemiki Aeroporia* sits dormant between missions. The service acquired 56 F-4Es as new and recently acquired 28 'hand-me-downs' from the USAF. The force is split between two combat wings, *No 110 Pterix Mahis* at Larissa and *No 117* stationed at Andravidha, the latter first receiving Phantoms back in 1974. (Via Tim Laming)

their encounters with the seasonal migration of millions of the creatures.[12] The low-level doctrine presented many other new hazards, notably in navigation. In Europe, for example, the 'million roads and zillion villages' that blossomed as part of the post-Second World War re-construction programme blurred the previously well-defined cities and other, more subtle navigation points. Together with the ever-increasing NOTAMS (Notices to Airmen) that formed a mandatory part of flight-planning, these distracted the crews to ever-increasing degrees. Some USAF crews fresh from combat in SEA and hoping for a 'relaxing' tour were shocked to discover how inhibitive and taxing the USAFE flying environment was becoming. All the same, their ability to cope with it engendered a new professionalism that served well in providing 'ambassadorial' support to fledgeling NATO Phantom operators, particularly in the Southern flank, most of whom were avidly seeking systems expertise.

Seeking to replace obsolescent F-84 Thunderstreaks and F-5A Freedom Fighters, Greece and Turkey joined the Phantom league after signing up for the aircraft beginning in 1971. Under Project 'Peace Icarus', the *Elliniki Polemiki Aeroporia* acquired an initial 36 F-4Es from March

Below: 7-022 looks fresh in its USAF SEA-style camouflage and was photographed during June 1992, illustrating the still widespread use of this paintwork on *Turk Hava Kuvvetleri* Phantoms. (Via Tim Laming)

Above, left and right: Turkish nose and tails. The 'Hill Gray II' aircraft are both ex-USAF ANG machines, and 68-0473 (7-473) still retained its trial one-piece windshield plus Missouri Guard shark's-mouth and crew names when it stopped in for a brief appearance at RAF Boscombe Down in the summer of 1992. (Authors)

1974, these equipping *117 Pterix Mahis* (Combat Wing) at Andravida, divided between two squadrons, *339 Ajax*, specializing in air defence, and *344*, an attack *Bombardismoy* (whose aircraft passed to *338 Ares* during 1977). A follow-on purchase of an additional twenty F-4Es permitted the formation of *337 Fantasma* under *110 Pterix Mahis* at Larissa, also specializing in air defence. The aircraft came from five different production Blocks, the latter two featuring TISEO, and it took some years to standardize the fleet with common avionics, drawing on the Hellenic penchant for US Navy devices (for commonality with its A-7H 'SLUFs'), especially with regard to electronic warfare self-protection items. Greek Phantoms remain the only FMS F-4Es equipped with 'round hole' chaff/ flare dispensers and the intake piping associated with Sanders DECM, previously a feature of the F-4N/S.

The *Turk Hava Kuvvetleri*, on the other hand, opted straight away for the full USAF package; and, owing to Turkey's proximity to the former Soviet Union, the United States was happy to oblige. Under Project 'Peace Diamond III', new F-4E production embraced six dozen aircraft in two separate batches produced under five Blocks, assigned to Eskisehir, Bandirma and Malatya-Erhac. Hand-me-downs from the USAF, totalling some 110 aircraft, have since per-

mitted the force to establish new *Filo* (squadrons) at Konya. At the time of writing, six F-4E *Filo* were operational, plus two RF-4E units with around forty aircraft.[13]

Production of new-build F-4Es continued throughout the 1970s. The process effectively closed with 37 Block 64-MC and 67-MC F-4Es bought by South Korea under 'Peace Pheasant II', to supplement its second-hand F-4Ds. Delivered from September 1977 and assigned to the 17th TFW at Cheong Ju Air Base, these were noteworthy as they included the last McAir delivery, F-4 Ship No 5,057 (FMS serial 78-0744), accepted on 26 October 1979. An additional 47 aircraft had been in the process of manufacture for the IIAF, some seven of which were subsequently reduced to spare parts status following the overthrow of the Shah of Iran, which resulted in a stop-work order on 28 February 1979, 42 days after he fled his country. McAir had already made the decision to cease marketing the Phantom and focus its efforts instead on newer products such as the Eagle and Harrier.

Perhaps the biggest factor in the Phantom's longevity at the 'leading edge' within USAFE and PACAF was its trusty two-man crew, able to provide reliable, all-weather performance—vital to counter the European clouds and fog, and the muggy, seasonal monsoons of the Pacific

region. This, and the new squadron-based maintenance system known as POST/COMO (Production-Oriented Scheduling Technique/Combat-Oriented Maintenance Organization), whereby responsibilities for overseeing aircraft readiness were devolved back to the squadrons as colour-coded AMUs (Aircraft Maintenance Units), also reversed flagging morale in the aftermath of the collapse of Vietnam at a time when spares shortages grew acute owing to changing

[12] Most of the larger birds which migrate to and from Europe and Africa prefer to do so overland using thermals for cruise economy. The result is that they end up 'bottlenecking' over Israel! Extensive IDF/AF-funded studies have ascertained their habits as a means of reducing losses to bird strikes: for example, there are five known days when some 14,000 eagles pass through, and two months when 70,000 pelicans make the journey. Fifteen million birds of 280 species converge over Israel at various stages of the year.

[13] Including Nos 111 and 112 at Eskisehir under the *1ci Ana Jet Us*, Nos 131 and 132 with *3ci Ana Jet Us* at Konya, and Nos 171, 172 and 173 with the *7ci Ana Jet Us* at Malatya-Erhac. The additional unit, 113 *Filo*, was formed using ex-*Luftwaffe* RF-4Es.

procurement priorities. POST/COMO devolved further to individual Dedicated Crew Chiefs and their aides. It significantly enhanced availability rates and turnaround times, and was first put through its paces by the 50th TFW at Hahn AB, West Germany under the new name TAMS (Tactical Aircraft Maintenance System) during Exercise 'Salty Rooster' in January 1977. The base was on a 1,650ft mountain ridge and suffered from some of the worst flying weather in Europe. During the maximum-effort 'sortie surge', the Wing produced 1,060 sorties in the first four days, despite snow. Remarkably, there was only one complaint about the noise! The following year the Wing surpassed itself during another 'Salty Rooster', which began in the early morning hours of 10 April. In spite of the fog and rain, the Wing's AGS and flying squadrons generated their 2,771st F-4E sortie on 22 April, equating to a rate of 2.7 sorties per aircraft per day for the duration of the 'surge'. One F-4E flew seventy consecutive sorties without missing a scheduled take-off, and several managed a straight set of sixty![14]

One of Hahn's specialities was the Westinghouse AN/ASQ-153 Pave Spike, a slim, 12ft long white pod which combined a daytime TV sensor with a YAG laser, installed on the port forward Sparrow well. The system worked much like the Vietnam-era Pave Knife, except in two regards: the imagery was pre-

Left: The F-4E, in both its original analogue and updated ARN-101(V) DMAS configurations, provided the backbone of USAFE, TAC and PACAF striking power throughout the 1970s and early 1980s. This Ramstein-based bird sits under its first-generation shelter between Tactical Air Meet sorties in 1978. (Richard L. Ward)

sented on the DSC radar scope and 'auto-rotated' so that the image was always the right way up, and the resultant data integrated with the Phantoms' ASQ-91 WRCS. In this manner, it could be used to provide much more accurate pulsed-laser slant-range to target in lieu of radar, to compute a 'Spike toss' bomb delivery for 'dumb' or 'smart' bombs. It also featured a new 'release on range' mode as a back-up in case the radar went 'ape', by means of the ROR dial mounted on the pilot's left instrument coaming. Bomb release could be pre-set to coincide with a given laser ROR, and it would come off at the required moment —useful for delivering 'smart' bombs or 'nukes'. A total of 327 F-4D/Es through to Block 45 were wired up for the pod (all received the ROR and pod look-angle indicators, which further inhibited the AC's forward view), and of the 156 Pave Spikes manufactured, around two dozen were supplied overseas, including unknown quantities to Turkey and Israel for use aboard FMS F-4Es. With them came new Paveway II LGB 'groups', still utilizing 'bang-bang' guidance but with the added discretion of laser-coding.

Pave Spike jets eventually adorned the forward-emplaced flight-lines at Bentwaters/Woodbridge, Hahn, Kunsan, Ramstein and Torrejon. However, arguably the most proficient unit with Pave Spike was the 347th TFW, which was established at Moody AFB, Georgia, during September 1975, under its long-standing banner 'Our Might Always'. Assigned to the Rapid Deployment Joint Task Force, the Wing was instrumental in easing the Egyptian *Al-Quwwat al-Jawwiya Ilmisriya* into the 'Phantom Phraternity' at Cairo West too. Egypt was allocated 35 ex-USAF F-4Es as part of the 'Camp David' Middle

East peace accord, with some sixteen jets opening up the 'Peace Pharoah' transfer during September 1979. The balance arrived during January and March the following year, fully equipping No 222 Regiment, which was divided into two components, ground-attack and air defence. Aircraft tasked in the latter were soon resprayed in a two-tone grey scheme known as 'Egyptian One', later frequently to be confused with the USAF 'Hill Gray' scheme despite the different hues, sheen and even patterns of monochromatic paint employed.

The 347th TFW deployed elements to the Nile between June and October 1980 under Operation 'Proud Phantom', teaching tactics and maintenance procedures, and to conduct joint manoeuvres, bedding the place down for possible future RDJTF wartime deployments. It also flew on publicity join-ups over the Pyramids at Giza, in company with its old adversary the MiG-21. However, the Egyptians have always had an inordinately hard time maintaining their aircraft, and the machines were on the point of being phased out, many with defective flight-safety systems which continue to astonish the workers at the American overhaul depots. Further disposals of 'used' but well-looked-after F-4Es overseas during the ensuing decade included gaggles of the jets to South Korea and Turkey: the *Turk Hava Kuvvetleri* currently ranks as the biggest operator—worldwide!

Iran, but for its later anti-US stance and subsequent isolation, might well have laid claim to being the biggest user. In fact, including reconnaissance models, orders and deliveries encompassed 272 aircraft when the stop-work order came into effect. The IIAF got its first taste of action in 1975, supporting the Sultan of Oman against rebels in the Dhofar Region, but it was under the Islamic Republic of Iran banner in the *jihad* against Iraq, which endured from September 1980 to the cease-fire 95 months later, that the aircraft and crews flew their most fierce actions. A US spares embargo had crippled the force, so aircraft were cannibilized pending the cov-

ert 'Irangate' supply of illicit spares (many via Israel and NATO, as ascertained by the examination of an F-4E following a solo defection to Saudi Arabia on 31 August 1984), while morale was initially poor also, owing to the fundamentalist purging of IIAF ranks. It has been estimated that the IRIAF lost over 100 aircraft, including machines bombed on the ground, throughout the drawn-out mêlée. Actions included the infamous 'Tanker War' in the Persian Gulf, where Phantoms employed Maverick missiles (at least one of these aircraft was shot down by an *Al-Quwwat al-Jawwiya Assa'udiya* Eagle on 5 June 1984), and counter-attacks and exchanges of fire during the 'War of the Cities'. The exploits of the service remain largely unreported even within the nation and are impossible to catalogue at the present time, but the machines were reputedly still active over Iraq on 5 April 1992, when eight F-4Es attacked rebel camps opposed to the Tehran regime which were seeking sanctuary over the border. One of the jets succumbed to 'triple-A' near Al Khalis, north of Baghdad, its crew ejecting into hostile hands. An estimated forty or so F-4Es remain operational, excluding a handful of the precious 'Photo-Phantom' variant—a far cry from the Shah's mighty force of yesteryear.

ARNIE

Keeping the Phantom viable within the 'showcase' USAF was a vital task that continued well into the early 1980s, deemed necessary owing to seemingly insoluble problems with LANTIRN (Low-Altitude Navigation/Targeting Infra-Red for Night) pods and with AMRAAM fire-and-forget missiles which had promised to give the F-16 the 'edge' it needed fully to replace the Phantom as an all-weather conventional and nuclear striker. In fact, neither of these

[14] The first in TAC to implement POST/COMO was the 56th TFW at MacDill AFB, Florida, on 15 June 1977. Integrated Combat Turnaround maintenance techniques (simultaneous refuelling, re-arming and so on) cut down 'ground times' from two hours to 30 minutes.

TABLE 20: ARN-101 DMAS MODIFIED USAF F-4Es		
Block No	Serial No	Qty
F-4E-48-MC	71-0237 to -0240	4
	71-0242 to -0243	2
	71-0245	1
	71-0247	1
F-4E-49-MC	71-1072 to -1073	2
	71-1075 to -1077	3
	71-1079	1
	71-1081	1
	71-1083 to -1089	7
	71-1092	1
F-4E-50-MC	71-1391 to -1392	2
	71-1397	1
	72-0122	1
	72-0124	1
	72-0126	1
	72-0128	1
	72-0135 to -0136	2
F-4E-51-MC	72-0139 to -0144	6
	72-0159	1
F-4E-52-MC	72-0160 to -0162	3
	72-0165	1
F-4E-53-MC	72-0166 to -0168	3
	72-1407	1
F-4E-54-MC	72-1477 to -1479	3
	72-1482 to -1485	4
	72-1489	1
F-4E-55-MC	72-1490	1
	72-1492 to -1494	3
F-4E-57-MC	73-1160	1
	73-1163 to -1164	2
F-4E-58-MC	73-1165 to -1168	4
	73-1171 to -1177	7
	73-1180 to -1184	5
F-4E-59-MC	73-1185 to -1189	5
	73-1193 to -1200	8
	73-1203 to -1204	2
F-4E-60-MC	74-0643 to -0650	8
	74-0652 to -0666	15
	74-1038 to -1045	8
	74-1047 to -1049	3
F-4E-61-MC	74-1050	1
	74-1052 to -1056	5
	74-1057	1
	74-1059 to -1061	3
	74-1620 to -1637	18
F-4E-62-MC	74-1638 to -1653	16
	Total*	171

*Some reports suggest that the total is 173 aircraft.

'Lawn Dart Boosters' would achieve IOC before the start of the next decade, obliging the veteran Phantom to trudge on much as it had for the previous twenty years, with updates.

The most extensive update originated from the Aeronautical System Division's Specification ENVG 70-44, which stipulated 'blind and visual delivery modes with an accuracy equal to or greater than Pave Phantom without deleting any F-4D capability'. Between February 1972 and July 1975 Lear-Siegler and ITT Avionics competed for the contract, using a pair of F-4Ds which flew 'head-to-head' (and made extensive LORAN trials against GRM-99 signals simulators) at Eglin AFB, Florida. Although the system was intended at this stage for the F-4D, during April 1972 the bosses at Langley AFB, Virginia, issued TAC ROC-12-72, specifying that the victors of the fly-off develop their systems for installation aboard the F-4E (and RF-4C reconnaissance model) instead. Lear-Siegler won the production contract in August 1975 to equip one trials RF-4C and two F-4Es, and tests began the following March.

Not the least of the accomplishments of what would become known as the AN/ARN-101(V) Digital Modular Avionics System (DMAS), or 'Arnie' to its crews, was the invention of a Kalman filter, permitting constant reliable updating of the system's new inertial measurement unit (IMU). This replaced the old INS and was continuously updated based on LORAN using X,Y and Z receivers tucked discreetly into the Phantom's fin-cap and under a squat 'doghouse' mounted on the spine. An airborne course alignment could be accomplished in less than three minutes (one-fifth of the time previously required for the old 'pulleys, gyros and gears' of the Litton LN-12 class system), while heading accuracy of well within 10 arc/min was possible, with pilot steering instructions presented on both the LCOSS (steering tabs) and HSI (direction needle).[15]

'Arnie''s greatest asset was probably its ability to take the Phantom back towards a tanker at planned ARCP (aerial refuelling co-ordination/control point) references, or to assume track when the system was overridden following a major deviation from the planned course, such as might occur when the crew elected to bypass unexpected defences. WSOs could 'freeze' co-ordinates into the system at a push of a button. Manually programmed with its flight-plan (best accomplished just prior to take-off during 'power on' checks, by entering the legs, one at a time, along with any desired offsets into the 36-button keyer control on the right console) or using the course fed-in via a Data Transfer Module, with the system coupled to the autopilot at cruise height 'Arnie' could provide virtually 'hands-off' point-to-point flight. Moreover, it was not prone to 'dumping'. All the pilot had to do was to watch the throttles and 'pole-push'. 'Arnie' also provided a new 'blind' bombing capability that offered a higher degree of accuracy than the old Pave Phantom, but it worked best with 'smart' weapons and with visual deliveries using CCIP (continuously computed impact point) and the servoed 'pipper'. CCIP relied on ballistic range estimations recomputed every 200 milliseconds and adjusted through sensitivity coefficients every 50 milliseconds. In a nutshell, this fast ballistics processing finally 'uncanned' all the Phantom's ground-attack options (including nuclear strike, not that circular error averages of more than 150–200ft mattered much) by compensating automatically for 'yo-yoing' airspeeds, and jinking, all the way through an attack pass. When the system was 'coming on line', LSI claimed that the 'all-up' DMAS system offered 7 mils visual CEPs as standard, and commensurately better 'blind' conventional CEPs and nuclear CEAs.[16]

Conventional low-level bombing with 'Arnie' was fully exploited using the new range of Goodyear 'ballute' 'iron' bombs (including a brand new BSU-50 adaptation of the Mk 84 'hammer'), which finally unshackled a low-level Phantom from the 500kt limitation previously imposed by the M117R and Mk 82SE bombs. Pilots could manoeuvre furiously all the way through the target run with the throttles slammed forward at all sorts of airspeeds and dive angles, confident that the bombs would hit the target.

Ogden began the 'Class V' DMAS modification (TO 1F-4E-1056) beginning with a 'proof kit' installation conducted in the autumn of 1977. Newly reworked aircraft began to trickle out of

Right, upper: Eglin ADTC F-4E-49-MC 71-1070 served as one of the test-beds for the Lear Siegler ARN-101(V) DMAS and Ford Aeronutronic (later Loral) AN/AVQ-26 Pave Tack updates from the summer of 1976, when the aircraft was transferred from the 57th FWW. Pave Tack was a massive improvement over Pave Spike in terms of capability, but with its sensor head unstowed and looking as depicted it generated about eighteen units more drag than the big centreline fuel tank! The large pod on the starboard inboard station is a telemetry and test data-recording device. (Loral)
Right, lower: A 3rd TFS *Peugeot* drops a deadly one-ton GBU-15 glide bomb. Released at near supersonic speeds, these weapons can be 'tossed' up to eight miles! The 3rd TFS specialized in this weapon, and Pave Tack. (Rockwell International)

the OOALC in September the following year, with many of the first examples being assigned to the 480th TFS *Warhawks* at Spangdahlem AB, West Germany, as the unit began to be upgraded to F-4Es with fresh crews under 'Creek Realign III'.[17] New machines also re-equipped Spangdahlem's other F-4E squadron, the 23rd TFS *Fighting Hawks*, and the 3rd TFS *Peugeots* at Clark Field in the Philippines, while the Wing's-worth of remaining aircraft were reissued to the 'Fourth But First' at Seymour-Johnson, which between April 1982 and September 1985 flew a fourth squadron within its ranks (the 337th TFS *Falcons*) to make the most of the new hardware, partly made possible by the release of 'vanilla' F-4Es elsewhere.

Along with the DMAS came two new devices which only 'Arnie''s integrated avionics suite could handle proficiently—

---

[15] The digital 'guts' of the IMU could 'hold' more than sixty destinations and offset points, and by 1979 Lear-Siegler had perfected an 8K DTM (data transfer module), which could be programmed with the crew's intended flight-plan by means of a Hewlett-Packard computer, available at the units' 'hard' operations rooms. Feeding the data in the days before the microchip truly came of age was a laborious task but, once accomplished, WSOs could carry the battery-powered, pocket-sized DTM out to the flight-line. This would be plugged into the aircraft to 'up-load' the entire flight-plan. The DTMs were later improved and made compatible with the second-generation mission-support systems in time for service during Operation 'Desert Storm', princi-

pally by the F-4G variant, as described in 'Phantomtown, Bahrain' in Chapter 14.
[16] In practice, one 'mil' equates roughly to a one-foot CEP at releases at 1,000ft AGL. Thus an ARN-101 F-4E salvoing its bombs at 10,000ft above the target (though typically these would be straddled via the intervalometer, and not 'salvoed') could expect to deposit the weapons an average of 70ft from the target. With all working to order, 'shacks' became routine. The CCIP bombing accuracy turned out to be double the requirement set down in ROC 12-72. Nuclear deliveries still use the term CEA, or circular error average, although there exists no tangible difference from conventional CEP standards, other than the obvious margin for error!

[17] Operations 'Creek Align' and the subsequent 'Creek Realign' efforts substantially modernized USAFE capability in three waves, as follows with regards Phantoms: 'Creek Align' (published in June and completed in September 1973)—36th TFW to all F-4E, 81st TFW to all F-4D; 'Creek Realign II'—additional F-4 squadrons for 50th TFW, 52nd TFW and 86th TFW, 50th TFW to all F-4E; 'Creek Realign III' (June 1978 to 9 May 1980)—401st TFW to F-4D, 480th TFS to F-4E and 81st TFS to F-4G. The latter two also involved the acquisition of Eagles and 'Warthogs', and CRA-III accounted for the reduction in numbers of 20 RF-4Cs (17th TRS), 80 F-4Cs and 30 F-4Ds, while adding only 40 F-4E/Gs, albeit much improved.

Above: DMAS-mod F-4Es equipped TAC's 4th TFW and 57th FWW, USAFE's 52nd TFW and PACAF's 3rd TFW but the trusty old M61A1 'Gatling' gun still remained a favourite with the pilots! This moody dawn shot shows the 4th TFW 'flagship' popping a few 20mm rounds. Note how the Midas IV gun muzzle shroud louvres vent the cartridge gases beneath the aircraft, to avoid choking the engines. (USAF/4th TFW)

Pave Tack (otherwise known as 'Pave Drag', described later in the book, which achieved IOC with the 4th TFW in April 1983) and the Rockwell International GBU-15 glide bomb.[18] The GBU-15 EOGB-II was a leap ahead of the Vietnam-era 'Egob', primarily because it could be 'flown' all the way to the target by means of a little toggle switch and a two-way Hughes AN/AXQ-14 data link, permitting constant updates right up to impact. The screen in the cockpit went dead when the bomb struck its intended target, not when the bomb came off the rack. In its original lock-on-and-launch format (the weapon uses the same DSU-27/B TV seeker as that perfected for the Maverick missile), the weapon first entered service with the *Kurnass* of the *Heyl Ha'Avir* in 1977 and

was used in anger for the first time in the Syrian Beka'a five years later, the results of which were dramatic.[19] Introduced to USAF service in 1983 after a work-up with the Nellis-based FOT&E force, it became the speciality of three DMAS Phantom squadrons, and some idea of its accuracy can be judged from its performance at 'Red Flag 84-4', when Lt-Col Mike Navarro's 335th TFS *Chiefs* dropped two of them (they were two of 106 live weapons expended by the squadron) during its two-week work-out. The 4th TFW was the 'core' unit for the exercise, and MSgt Fox later told the authors that one GBU-15 smacked right into its target while the other hit the resultant hole and toppled in too—and all that in face of 'Aggressors' which attempted to 'botch' tracking functions by getting the Phantoms to 'dump and turn' or 'screw up their "up a couple of mils, down a couple of mils"' refinement in target acquisition. Best of all, the weapon expanded the F-4's delivery envelop to supersonic. Weapons 'tossed' in this manner could glide a staggering eight to twelve miles (depending on launch speed and altitude). A later

adaptation introduced the WGU-10/B imaging infra-red (IIR) seeker of the AGM-65D/G Maverick, extending the weapon's application in night and limited adverse weather. The bomb remained a 3rd TFS *Peugeots* speciality right to the end of the USAF Phantom story.[20]

In many ways, the venerable 'Rhino' had reached technological perfection as a weapons platform just as its performance was finally beginning to be seriously challenged.

---

[18] Described in Chapter 15. The pod was fitted to the centreline station in lieu of the 600 US gallon tank and was smaller. The derogatory nickname originated in the F-111F community, which also employed Pave Tack but strapped it, semi-recessed, in a low-drag format on a rotating cradle. Eight Pave Tack pods have been acquired by the Republic of Korea for use aboard its F-4E Phantoms, fitted with a one-off analogue-to-digital interface.

[19] The operation is described in the context of SEAD in Chapter 14.

[20] The 52nd TFW transferred their GBU-15s and support equipment to the F-111F-equipped 493rd TFS at RAF Lakenheath, England, during 1985. The 4th and 3rd TFWs retained the capability on their F-4Es until the end of Active Phantom operations in 1990 and 1991 respectively.

12. OLD SMOKY

Brandishing some of the USAF's latest hardware as part of the 'Total Force' concept made the Air National Guard—America's airborne militia—a natural contender for the Phantom. Manned predominantly by part-time ground and air crews, many with past Active duty or current civil flying or engineering experience, and the technical and 'institutional knowledge' that goes with these, meant that the complex F-4 could be gently shoe-horned into service with the prospect of units attaining Code One, combat-ready and 'deployable' status, within eighteen months of their new tasking. The production of F-4Es for the Active forces, which continued until December 1976, and the reduced requirement for combat Wings in South-East Asia, also meant that the process could be initiated when export customers for Phantom could still be counted on only three fingers.

The first of the 'mud-moving' ANG units to convert to Phantoms was the 170th TFS *Vipers*. The 183rd TFG based at Capital Airport, Springfield, Illinois, relinquished the last few examples of the Air Force's obsolete F-84F Thunderstreaks (which the unit had similarly introduced to Guard service) when it signed for its first F-4C on 31 January 1972. Further batches of Phantoms arrived in quartets from April, as the Guardsmen worked up to Code One on the new hot-performers (which included a pair of RF-4Cs used as conversion trainers), while simultaneously establishing logistics requirements that would help 'bed down' further ANG units; among the lessons learnt during the inaugural three years of operations with 'Old Smoky' were the recommendations that, whenever possible, aircraft should receive complete Depot-level refurbishment at Ogden prior to reassignment to the Guard, and that units should be provided with full range and airspace facilities to accommodate their multi-role capability. Most were heeded. The unit eventually reached full combat strength with eighteen jets—the standard Reserve squadron fighter complement—during America's Bicentennial Year, by which time they had settled into a training programme which scheduled the 'Lincolnlanders' on 1½hr-long ground-attack sorties on the Fort Campbell, Kentucky, and Fort McCoy, Wisconsin, ranges, on gunnery practice at Harwood Range, Volk Field, Wisconsin, and on 'turn-and-burn' ACM in a sandwich of sky between FL50 and FL250 over the Mississippi between St Louis, and Quincy, Illinois. Night-navigation and aerial-refuelling practice sorties were also thrown into the Monday-to-Saturday schedule, with two-, three- and four-ship flights launching at 1000hrs, 1430hrs and 1900hrs—not untypical of the schedules adopted by other Guard units that re-equipped with Phantoms close behind them. In all, including the 'dual-committed' Hawaii *HANGmen* and Louisiana's *Coonass Militia*, no fewer than seventeen ANG squadrons would be equipped to fly the 'mud-moving' mission at various stages of their career, representing a force which easily eclipsed overseas F-4 forces in terms of size and, indeed, rivalled that of most international air arms!

Right: A 188th TFG crew salute their maintenance troops before boarding their Phantom for a 'Gunsmoke 85' mission at Nellis TFWC, Nevada. The polished metal and red and white trim of their steed was typical of well-looked-after ANG F-4s. In addition to 'Gunsmoke' shooting matches in Nevada, the unit made one deployment to the Panama Canal Zone and two to Turkey. (Frank B. Mormillo)

Right, upper: Pave Phantoms passed to the AFRES from July 1981, equipping two Texas-based units, the 457th TFS *Spads* at Carswell and the 924th TFS *Texans* at Bergstrom. Both specialized in BAI and were capable of utilizing the AN/ASQ-153 Pave Spike laser marking and ranging pod. This dynamic duo were assigned to the *Spads* and carried the 'TH' codes which alluded to the nickname of their former steed, the 'Texan Humpback', 'Thunderstick II' F-105D, which employed 'blind bombing' systems similar to those on the Pave Phantom. (AFRES)

Right, lower: The 924th TFG at Bergstrom had upgraded to ARN-101 DMAS-modified F-4Es by January 1989 and its aircraft wore a mottled adaptation of the semi-gloss 'Hill Gray II' decor during its three years on the type. This smart example is outbound from Nellis during 'Gunsmoke 89', complete with ACMI pod, BDU-33 practice bombs and a centreline 'bag'.

Many of the Guardsmen's machines possessed an illustrious heritage. The Illinois Guard alone operated no fewer than five MiG-killer F-4Cs at one stage, including 64-0679, one of the first USAF Phantoms to 'bag' a MiG back in July 1965 (also with 4,250 flying hours in its logs by 1977, as the Group's high-timer), and 64-0776, with three kills chalked up, one each with the Sparrow, Sidewinder and SUU-16/A gun pod. Interestingly, one of these would be passed on to the Oregon ANG for a tour as a CONUS aerial defender before being put out to pasture as a BDR (battle-damage repair) article at USAFE bases, still retaining its MiG-kill star and nickname *Red Baron*. It is currently being restored for display at the Coventry Air Museum in England. Other noteworthy aircraft at Capital Airport included 64-0822, a composite aircraft built up by the RAM (Rapid Aircraft Maintenance) teams from two F-4Cs which had plunged into the water off the strip at Cam Ranh Bay, South Vietnam, or had performed wheels-up landings in the theatre—one of around a dozen such hybrids which soldiered on until the early 1980s, seemingly as if nothing untoward had ever happened to them since leaving the factory!

The Illinois Guard officially upgraded to F-4Ds on 1 January 1981 and three years later became the first unit to receive Project 'Seek Smoke' J79-GE-15E powerplants, incorporating a low-smoke combustor and high-energy ignition (TO 2J-J79-1242), which raised EGT but with little effect on the aircraft's infra-red signature or engine wear-and-tear. The twin black smoke trails that had plagued the Phantom for two decades were finally all but eradicated by this modification, making the aircraft an elusive prey for AAA gunners and enemy fighter pilots alike who were previously accustomed to its easy-to-track sooty calling card. Along with the 'low-smoke' modifications came improved afterburner fuel pumps and new seals, plus replacements for 'Pacer Frugal' engine parts which had known characteristics of wearing out quickly, increasing time between major depot overhauls to 1,800 hours— double the previous limit. In August 1985 these improvements were scheduled for application to the entire inventory of (at that time) 3,274 installed and 795 spare GE-15 and GE-17 series engines. While it has always proved reliable, General Electric's wonder engine suffered no subsequent reported cases of any catastrophic failures or shaft-breaking surges for reasons other than FOD ingestion, while maintenance became a more pleasant task. The previously blackened exhaust 'jet cans' and aft empennage steel and titanium plating now maintained their freshly serviced, spotless appearance for months on end with only an occasional bit of polishing from a proud Crew Chief.

Mission assignments for the Guardsmen, who had a Direct Reporting Unit obligation to TAC's Ninth and Twelfth Air Forces and could be mobilized at 48 hours' notice alongside their Active peers, focused on CAS, battle area interdiction (BAI) and sometimes TASMO (maritime support), using the full range of 'iron' bombs and CBUs, including the retarded 'ballute' and new submunitions 'sprinklers' based on the Rockeye and Tactical Munitions Dispenser (TMD) canisters. Specialist capability was wholly dependent on the wiring harnesses fitted, and whether or not the aircraft featured the DSCG modification. For example, whereas Arkansas' *Flying Razorbacks* flew 'vanilla' F-4Cs with no special capability throughout their nine-year tenure on the type, Illinois graduated on to F-4Ds capable of using Maverick missiles, while the District of Columbia's 113rd TFW introduced Pave Spike and Paveway LGBs into the Guard, following their conversion to 'smart' F-4Ds beginning in June 1981.[1]

The 'intellectual bombs' and related pod also were a standard feature on the F-4Es that re-equipped *Lindbergh's Own* at St Louis, along with the *Tigers* at McGuire AFB, New Jersey, and the two squadrons of the Indiana Guard at Hulman and Baer Fields. All four of these squadrons had previously operated F-4C or D models. The 'swap' process began in February 1985, when the Active forces gave up its sixteen-year monopoly on the gun-equipped model. Alongside the trading-in process, the Missouri ANG inaugurated 'Project Hill', the origins of a fleet-wide strip-and-respray programme which replaced 'European One' greens and slate grey camouflage with a smarter, semi-gloss grey paint which made the Phantoms

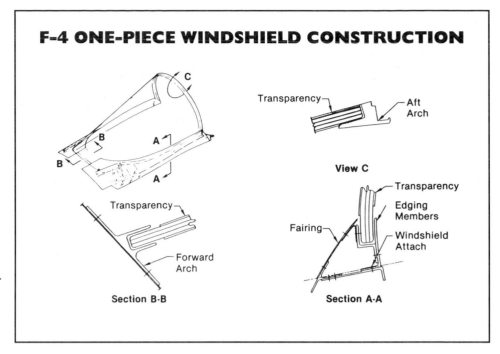

F-4 ONE-PIECE WINDSHIELD CONSTRUCTION

View C

blend into the clouds. The 131st TFW also were the first to test-fly the Goodyear one-piece windshield (applied to F-4Es 68-0345, -0351 and -0448), screwed into a titanium bow frame, which massively improved forward visibility and offered greater resistance to bird strikes, including crow-sized ceatures inadvertently smacking into the glazing at 500kts. Previously, the thin, quarter-view transparencies were liable to implode during collisions at a mere 200kts, and this became an increasing hazard during low-level flights over the instrument- and visual-route (IR/VR) corridors straddling the US, which for the most part double as wildlife sanctuaries.[2] Most significantly of all, on 19 January 1990, with Lt-Col Jerry Shomberg and Maj William Reiter at the controls, Lambert-based double MiG-killer F-4E 68-0338 logged the ten-millionth USAF Phantom flying hour—the equivalent of one jet staying airborne for over 1,140 years! Funnily enough, both crew members were unaware of this feat until McAir's Jack Nelson presented them with a plaque that October. At the ceremony, John 'Mr Maintenance' Harty estimated that the total number of Phantom flight-hours worldwide was around the 17 million mark! It is unlikely that any other fighter will surpass this extraordinary milestone.

MAKOS AND BUCKEYES

Joining the expanding cadres of Guard F-4s were the Air Force Reserve (AFRES), which from 1 May 1983 became a Separate Operating Agency, reporting straight to TAC Headquarters at Langley AFB, Virginia. Only a nation as large and diverse as the United States could afford to operate two separate 'part-time' USAF organizations (in addition to a sizeable Navy and Marines Reserve force) flying supersonic fighters! The first to re-form were the 93rd TFS *Makos* of the 482nd TFW at Homestead AFB, Florida, commanded by Lt-Col D. M. McDowell (who personally flew Robin Olds' veteran double MiG-killer

---

[1] In 1986 the ANG and AFRES operated 213 'smart' Phantoms, including 88 with Pave Spike. [2] The windshields were also test-flown on a pair of F-4Gs of the 561st FS at George AFB, California, where they met with a mixed response; see Chapter 14. Apparently the one-piece windshield's biggest drawback was its wider bow frame, which obscured the pilot's view of tanker lights during delicate aerial refuelling operations. All survivors of the test programme retain the special fit, with at least one of the ex-Missouri aircraft now flying with the *Turk Hava Kuvvetleri*'s *7ci Ana Jet Us*, stationed at Erhac. This aircraft put in an appearance at RAF Boscombe Down in 1991 shortly after delivery, still wearing a Missouri Guard shark's-mouth and crew names but new Muslim star-and-crescent flags (see photos on p.151)

64-0829 and had it daubed with chequered trim on its intakes, tail and stabilator tips, complete with a suitably doctored '482nd TFW' serial). The *Makos* began their surprisingly speedy transition from majestic EC-121 Constellations to F-4Cs on 1 October 1978, eventually working up to a complement of 25 crews and eighteen jets in the standard 1.4:1 manning ratio, using range facili-

ties at Avon Park. They put in their first 'Red Flag' appearance at Nellis in August the next year. Four more squadrons followed suit, all with F-4Ds, including a brand new unit in Ohio, the 89th TFS *Buckeye Phantoms* of the 906th TFG, who achieved mission-ready status with their new mounts at Wright-Patterson AFB, Dayton, Ohio, during the winter of 1982. To complete the initial transition pro-

cess, the *Makos* traded in their F-4Cs for the superior WRCS-equipped D model during the summer of 1983. All five squadrons then possessed Maverick missile-capable aircraft, while the two Texas-based outfits added Pave Spike and some 39 surviving Pave Phantoms to their repertoires (recently pulled from Active service with the 8th TFW at Kunsan, South Korea, and the 52nd

TFW at Spangdahlem, West Germany). The LORAN jets, with their unique rear-cockpit flight instrumentation, provided a long-range precision striking capability unique to the *Spads* and *Texans*, building on experience gained by the latter on the similarly configured saddleback 'Thunderstick II' F-105D.

Just like their counterparts in the ANG, the AFRES focused on CAS and 'tac-

int' BAI during sixty per cent of scheduled sorties, with bouts of ACM (and DACT, where possible) to maintain air combat proficiencies, making up the balance. Also in common with the ANG, several veterans filled the ranks, including a sprinkling of MiG-killing pilots; amongst their personnel the 465th TFS *Sierra Hotels* at Tinker AFB, Oklahoma, counted Lt-Col James P. Feighny and Col Jerry K. Sharpe who, as 1st Lieutenants serving with the 'Wolfpack' in 1967 and 1968, had set up Sparrow missiles in the 'pit' and had 'bagged' a MiG each.

The AFRES also chipped in with the evaluation and introduction of new systems. Most of these comprised subtle improvements ranging from a voice warning system and combined aircraft radar altimeter (installed in most Phantoms under TOs 1F-4-1262 and -1250, respectively, for added low-level safety), to one new major weapons system, fielded by the *Buckeye Phantoms* under Project 'Pave Claw'—the GE GPU-5/A GEPOD. Its pneumatically driven GAU-13 30mm 'Gatling' gun provided devastating firepower against thick-skinned armour at slant ranges of over half a mile, packing 353 rounds contained in a closed-loop feed and storage system housed within the pod's casing (cunningly designed so as to avoid the problem of ejecting 'spent' hot cartridge cases on to friendly TICs below, and that of placing hot spent and live unspent rounds in juxtaposition, which might otherwise result in shells 'cooking off' and the feed-link erupting in flames). Carried on the centreline, the GEPOD offered a rate of fire of 2,400spm, enough for five 1½–2sec bursts using HEI (high-explosive incen-

diary) or AP (armour-piercing) rounds. Ninety Phantoms were wired up for GEPOD by August 1985.

Smoking Phantom gun barrels were a regular sight at Nellis's biennial 'Gunsmoke' air-to-ground shooting matches, reintroduced in the autumn of 1981. In the five meets held up till 1989, F-4 crews wrung out their aircraft during 10-, 20- and 30-degree dives and level 'laydown' deliveries, including carefully calculated ±5sec time gates designed to evaluate navigational accuracy, during which hundreds of holes were made in the desert floor and in gunnery banners. The F-4 teams' analogue hardware tended to push them to the bottom of the league tables when competing alongside the digital navigation and CCIP visual delivery avionics available to the A-7D 'SLUFs' and F-16A/C 'Electric Jets', yet the venue's clear-weather 'OK Corral' atmosphere exuded plenty of bravado, providing side contests for ground crews, including 'Loadeos', while also giving plenty of scope for depositing practice munitions. It was good for morale to loose off a clip or two of 20mm and 30mm cartridges too.[3]

Annual two-week 'Summer Camp' training sessions overseas also were part of the squadrons' regular itinerary. Under the 'Checkered Flag' programme each was required to deploy once every three years. These 'Coronet' excursions took in such far-flung destinations as NAS Keflavik, Iceland, Bodø in Norway, Incirlik and Cigli in Turkey and the Panama Canal Zone as well as regular visits to familiar bases in Britain, Germany, Italy and Spain.[4]

Left: A *Tiger* from the 108th TFW in its lair at McGuire AFB, New Jersey. The unit flew F-4Es until October 1991. Maintenance was carried out on the Phantoms at three key levels: day-to-day flight-line or 'organizational', shop or hangar 'intermediate' level and depot level, the last being performed once every 54 months (or 1,200 hours, whichever came first) on the F-4E. Intermediate work was done on base, at approximately 100-hour intervals, when hydraulics, electrical systems, engines and airframe were given a thorough going-over. (Tim Laming)

[3] It would have been more than interesting to see how the F-4s fared overall had the same event taken place in twilight amidst murky skies reminiscent of a grey, wintry Europe: the superlative F-111 nuclear bomber made a token appearance in 'Gunsmoke 91' and came last! 'Gunsmoke' was simply too tame to show off the Phantom's (or 'Vark''s) true forte. Within USAFE, F-4s (and F-111s) habitually braved all weathers during the autumnal NATO 'Reforger' exercises when F-16s and A-10s remained grounded, firmly secured in their chocks or TAB-Vee HAS shelters.
[4] Refer to Appendix VI for further details of many of the individual deployments.

JAYHAWKS AND JAYHAWKERS

In January 1984 ANG and AFRES Phantom numbers assigned to the strike role—which excluded an additional eight squadrons committed to strategic air defence and a further six units tasked with reconnaissance—reached peak numerical strength, embracing eight squadrons of F-4Cs and a dozen with F-4Ds, for a 'total force' contribution of over 600 jets. Keeping the cockpit vacancies filled was a major undertaking that soon passed to the ANG. This embraced the full spectrum of courses managed by the Active training Wings, including reponsibilities for 'new guy' training previously undertaken at Bergstrom, George, Luke and Homestead AFBs. The Oregon Guardsmen at Kingsley Field assumed responsibilities for air defence, while the Boise, Idaho, Guard

Below: 'Strike School' was handled by the 184th TFG, Kansas ANG, at McConnell AFB, which flew some 57 F-4Ds at its zenith, split between the 127th TFS *Jayhawks* and 177th TFTS *Jayhawkers*, the former holding down an operational commitment in conjunction with managing the F-4 FWIC and the latter performing 'new guy', 'Requal' and 'Refresher' training. Here, in the blur of Flight Lead's exhaust, a quartet of Phantoms amble to the take-off point, ready to head out and pound the 'Smoky Hills' bombing range. (Kansas ANG/TSgt Genelle Clifton)

at Gowen Field prepared fledgeling aviators for the 'Recce Rhino' model. However, the lion's share of the job, training strike crews, fell upon the the Kansas ANG *Jayhawks* at McConnell AFB.

The 184th TFTG had received its first F-4D (65-0590) on 7 August 1979. Four and a half years later, with Col John McMerty in charge, the Group's sole subordinate flying unit, the 127th TFS *Jayhawks*, was brimming with 57 Phantoms, making it the largest fighter squadron in the Free World. Aircraft were painted in a carnival parade of colour schemes, including 'wraparound'

tan and greens, 'European One', the two principal variations on the 'Hill Gray' monochrome finish and glossy ADC 'Aircraft Gray', and there were even a few lingering well-worn machines, about to enter PDM, in the SEA scheme with black serials! Alongside such Vietnam veterans as Air Force Cross recipient Vice-Commander Col Rowland F. Smith, the unit boasted a large pool of full-time flyer-instructors, including 55 of its 63 IPs and 25 out of its 27 IWSOs. IWSO Maj 'Crash' Cassidy pointed out that when he left the Active forces in 1979 the WSO's 'average time on the F-

Right, top to bottom: Many of Kansas' *Jayhawks* carried artwork on their F-4D nosegear doors, including *Dragon Lady* (unidentified), *Naughty Lady* (66-7772, assigned to Capt Ed McIlhenny and Maj 'Crash' Cassidy, with Bill Hayden as Crew Chief), and *Kansas Crop Duster* (65-0798). The Kansas ANG bade farewell to their Phantoms during a ceremony held at McConnell on 31 March 1990. (Kansas ANG/TSgt Genelle Clifton)

4 was about 860 hours, and we considered that quite high'. At McConnell the average was double that. Many IPs and IWSOs had at least '2,000 hours on the F-4 alone'. To meet its new-found training requirements, including the responsibility for FWIC, which devolved from Nellis, the Group's machines were split between the 127th TFS and the newly created 177th TFTS *Jayhawkers*. The brand new unit ('It had no history and we felt it apropos that we create the history ourselves!', recalled 'Crash' Cassidy) provided three separate streams, including F4000BG for 'new guys' and F4000CG 'Requal' refresher training and conversion training, ranging from between 17 and 63 sorties for pilots to between 12 and 57 for WSOs, split down the middle between ACT and air-to-ground using the squadron's mostly 'vanilla' F-4Ds. Ten to fifteen junior officers showed up approximately every six weeks for training, meaning that during the overlap cycle the IPs and IWSOs were catering for four RTU classes simultaneously. They received an unofficial rating as 'best RTU in TAC' during their 1986 ORI, when all the machines flew flawlessly and the novices appeared to know what was going on.

The 127th held down the operational commitment, deploying ten F-4Ds to Oman in 1985 under Operation 'Sentry Tornado' to practice surge operations using 'tent city', 'bare base' facilities. Back at home, it ran the F400FWS FWIC and F4000WT TLP (Tactical Leadership Program) courses. Candidates from the Active and Guard/Reserve forces had to offer a minimum of two years on fighters and 300 hours on the F-4, and be fully IP- or IWSO-rated. Maj Cassidy elaborated at the height of the pro-

gramme: 'The 127th's extremely demanding three-month training programme effectively grants its graduates a PhD in tactically employing the F-4.' It was even recognized in academic circles as providing points towards a Master's Degree. Twenty-seven sorties were devoted to ACM and a further 27 to air-to-surface tactics, with a few extra thrown in at the beginning for pilots unaccustomed to the F-4D's 'hard wing', which would cause problems if stick and rudder were abused at high AOAs. Over the course of 102 days students were permitted to expend 2,000 chaff and 1,120 flare cartridges, 1,200 rounds of 20mm gunpod ammunition, 114 BDU-33 and -48 training bombs, 72 inert Mk 82 'slicks' and Snakeyes, two dozen live Mk 82s, four CBU-58 cluster bombs and two inert and two live GBU-12 500lb LGBs over the Smoky Hills range, not to mention a Sparrow and Sidewinder missile —a staggering amount of pyrotechnics! FWIC undergraduates were continually assessed and graded from 'Dangerous' (!), a fail, to Scale 4, 'reflecting an unusually high degree of ability'. Using the 'building block' process established at Nellis nearly fifteen years previously, crews initially observed briefings and flew the less demanding positions in the flight before rising to lead 'the most demanding of tactical scenarios'. They also were ingrained with a knowledge of such diverse elements as command and

control co-ordination and weapons they might never encounter operationally, such as the AGM-45A Shrike or GBU-15 glide bomb. The FWIC course remained in existence until 20 August 1989.

The training effort placed great burdens on the maintenance teams. By 1986 the F-4Ds averaged 44MMH/FH (maintenance man-hours per flight-hour), with the Litton INS giving the greatest difficulties. Most of these required servicing after every third sortie and drew on the expertise of full-time technicians ('troughers') who worked regular 40-hour weeks as civilians. Committed to the end, the *Jayhawks* stayed in the Phantom business until 31 March 1990. On that date, with due ceremony, the Group bade farewell to their last eight airworthy F-4Ds, which were dispatched directly to the 'Bone Yard', adorned with affectionate *graffiti*. Men with several thousand hours in the aircraft described the F-4D as 'like an old armchair', so accustomed to, and comfortable in, its cockpit had they become. A few grimaced to hide the tears in the corners of their eyes. It was the end of an era.

The last Guard F-4Cs had already bowed out during 1989, and the F-4Es would follow in January 1992, when the 163rd FS *Marksmen* at Fort Wayne MAP relinquished the last few remaining aircraft, including the unit's ceremonial steed 68-0529, whose inscription sadly reflected the fact that it was the 'Last of

Above: A dramatic view of Missouri's double MiG-21-killer, F-4E-37-MC 68-0338, which 'bagged' its first with Capts Leonard and Feinstein on board ('Gopher Three') on 31 May 1972 and its second with Capt Tibbett and 1Lt Hargrove at the controls ('Chevy Three') just a few months later on 16 September. The shark's-mouth design was the unit's trademark, which it wore with pride until the unit converted to Eagles during May 1991. Several of its aircraft, in common with many of the last of the breed flying with the Indiana ANG, were subsequently passed to the *Turk Hava Kuvvetleri*. (McAir)

the ANG Gunfighters'. Most Indiana Guard 'shooters' were reassigned to the Turks at Eskisehir, while the 163rd FS absorbed 'Lawn Darts'. The AFRES, also, was busy staging its 'Phantom Pharewells', the last to go comprising the Texan F-4Es based at Fort Worth and Bergstrom—a mere four years after having upgraded to the marque—and including many pristine ARN-101 DMAS-mod machines with fifteen years' useful life still left on their 'clocks'. It was a sad and shockingly speedy end to an illustrious career that had spanned two decades. At the time of writing, only two dozen strike jets remain with the 124th FG at Boise, all of them F-4G 'Weasels', a more potent breed of Phantom than that to which the part-timers were previously accustomed.[5]

[5] Refer to Chapter 14 for a fuller description of the F-4G 'Weasel Phantom'.

13. POPEYE PHANTOMS

Flying 'counter-air' missions was part and parcel of virtually every Active operational Phantom Wing's jam-packed roster of peacetime duties and, within USAFE's massively expanded cadres (comprising twenty squadrons of the fighter variant at its peak in the early 1970s), it represented a tasking second only to nuclear strike. All but the 32nd TFS *Wolfhounds* based at *Vliegbasis* Soesterberg in Holland remained under direct Third, Sixteenth or Seventeenth

Below: A brace of 32nd TFS *Wolfhounds* F-4Es roar into the sky, outbound with empty Falcon and Sparrow launchers on a 'Tango' training intercept mission. The unit was the first in USAFE to receive the F-4E model, beginning in August 1969. (L. Hansen via Richard L. Ward)

Air Force control during peacetime; in the event of a crisis, depending upon the degree of escalation of any conflict, they were to change operational control ('chop') to the appropriate Allied Tactical Air Force command. The 32nd Fighter (Day) Squadron 'chopped' to NATO in 1954 and remained totally integrated from that time on, flying from the American side of Soesterberg, known as Kamp Nieu Amsterdam, with air defence as an almost exclusive tasking. The *Wolfhounds* received their first F-4E on 1 July 1969 and officially converted to the type on 6 August—the first unit in USAFE to do so.[1]

Maj Jim Chamberlain USAF Ret arrived at Hahn AB, West Germany, on St Valentine's 1970, the same day that

the 496th TFS *World's Finest* received the first of its F-4Es, which would replace F-102As. As soon as the unit had been 'checked out' with 'training shapes' at Torrejon in Spain it was shifted to Ramstein AB to assume 'Zulu Alert' air-defence responsibilities while the 526th TFS *Black Knights* similarly relinquished the last vestiges of the 'Deuce' from

[1] As USAFE's 'front line' unit, the 32nd TFS was constantly kept abreast of the latest F-4E developments, eventually leading to a hodge-podge of Blocks with different capabilities. The first eighteen aircraft were all FY67–68 models. Slatted F-4Es (all FY69) arrived in November 1974, followed by TISEO F-4Es (all FY74) during the spring of 1976. At this point, the aircraft flew a mix of 'hard wings', LES, and LES/TISEO aircraft!

USAFE and Hahn's runway was resurfaced. The Phantom represented a quantum leap in endurance and weapons systems: 'I had pulled my share of five-minute alert over the years, but in Germany, so close to the "bad guys", there was a whole new urgency. In ADC, in the States, any attack would most likely be nuclear, and that was the sort of thing that would take time to develop. [Being] barricaded behind three layers of early-warning radar and two layers of interceptors made the idea of scrambling from five-minute alert, armed with two AIM-4Ds, to intercept the first wave of "Bears" or "Badgers" a rather ludicrous prospect.' The big NORAD chain managed by the Cheyenne Mountain Complex in Wyoming used a Defense Readiness Condition (DEFCON) countdown system, which began at 5 and was cranked down gradually as things hotted up, 'but in Germany, any kind of border incident could quickly become some-

thing greater than local. Our "Zulu" air-defence posture, we were told, was responsible for intercepting any track entering West Germany from Warsaw Pact countries. Although the German Air Force had two F-104 [later F-4F 'Peace Rhine'] squadrons committed to air defence, and kept two aircraft from each of those squadrons on alert, they were not permitted to intercept unknown tracks entering their air space from the East as a provision of the WW2 peace treaty. Nevertheless, in the early '70s,

when a Czechoslovakian airliner was hijacked to the West, it was the Germans that were scrambled for the intercept. Interesting!' In peacetime, GCI controllers provided heading and altitude instructions; provisions for wartime, when communications chatter had to be kept to a minimum, dictated pre-planned patrol orbits.

'Real "active air" [Alpha] scrambles were rather infrequent, triggered more often than not by some exercise. Oftentimes we were alerted with a "Battle

Stations" warning—strap-in and get ready to go. That was much appreciated because the Martin-Baker seat had caused a lot of lower leg injuries in the Cs and Ds; the addition of lower leg constraints solved the problem but made strapping-in much more time-consuming. A scramble was never delayed to fasten those restraints, but we could get them done up while on battle stations.' Maj Jim Shaw USAF Ret recalled that, at Soesterberg, 'We very carefully arranged all our personal gear in the aircraft when going on duty, to include arranging all the various straps exactly to our liking, so that we could get in and cinch-up them up and get off in the most expeditious manner. Our helmet leads and oxygen masks were plugged in and waiting on the canopy rails. Engine start was by cartridge, which was quite fast, but if a "cart" misfired you had to wait five minutes before removing it to try another (this very rarely happened).' Jim Chamberlain was on 'Battle Stations' in the cockpit when he and his pilot set something of a record—'One minute forty-five seconds from "scramble" to wheels in the well in a max afterburner climb!' Jim Shaw remembers getting aloft in under 2mins 45secs from a 'cold' start (when the crew were eating, reading, watching TV or 'shooting pool') when the klaxon rang. Alert forces were typically scrambled in response to contacts picked up by a Dutch or German radar site, which conveyed the message speedily to the Phantom units' Sector Operations Center. 'The klaxon was sounded by whichever controller got to the switch first.' To maintain proficiency, 'Tango' training intercepts were scheduled using German or American GCI vectors too, against squadron mates or other consenting NATO aircraft. Crews used aircraft which were scheduled to be exchanged for freshly serviced examples, so as not to draw on newly preened alert machines.

'One of the most likely avenues of attack was low-level, and in that arena we were severely limited,' recalled Jim Chamberlain. 'Partly due to the smaller antenna, the APQ-120 of the F-4E was a far better set than the APQ-109 of the D, but still not very good close to the ground. Nor did we practice low-level intercepts, partly because the ground radar coverage and open airspace in which to do it, and the combination of good radar coverage and open airspace, [made this] well nigh impossible. Our low-level experience usually came during some big exercise when we floundered around in figure-eight patterns, using half visual scan, half radar scan and missing almost everything passing through our area. Only on rare occasions did we get to work with the MC-130s of the Special Operations Squadron at Ramstein. They provided good low-altitude, ECM and evasive action targets, making far better use of their defences than anything I had ever seen from SAC. The SOS guys were really good. I had some of my best duels with them, and, win, lose or draw, it was always challenging and great fun. By comparison, ADC had been doing low-level intercepts for several years, and had developed radar search techniques which were helpful and which we ROs tried to pass along to those who did not have our experience. Of course, with the F-101B's improved Hughes MG-13 FCS we had the benefit of a superb IRSTS. It made low-level work fun: I would use the radar first, but once locked on, the antenna inevitably broke lock to brighter ground returns and I would end up locking on with the IRSTS with the radar antenna slaved to the seeker head for the simulated shot. None of that, of course, was possible with the F-4; all we could do was use the look-up or look-down methods to detect the target with the radar side-lobes and that resulted in the radar breaking lock to the ground.' Jim Shaw remembers that 'While setting up the intercept, we were usually positioned some 2,000ft below the target so that the radar would have a view uncluttered by ground returns. This required the WSO to constantly adjust the elevation of the radar antenna as you drew nearer the target—not difficult, but requiring constant attention to detail and situation awareness. [This would be especially true at low-level!] On training missions

where we had certain specific training events to accomplish we would tell the GCI controller what sort of set-up we wanted—front, stern, beam, supersonic target, etc. Often the GCI controllers had their own training requirements too and we would let them control the entire intercept, even if we had a "tally-ho" [visual ID] on the target.'

With regard to procedures, Jim Chamberlain recalled that 'Our evaluation exercises always began with a scramble of the alert birds to intercept an exercise target. The lead aircraft would intercept to the identification position, just off the right wing of the target, while the second aircraft dropped back to maintain an optimum firing position should the target take a hostile action. [This was a standard tactic which endured throughout the Phantom's career.] Using standard international intercept procedures, the target aircraft would be led to the nearest NATO base for recovery and detention. In the exercise scenario, that would be the base from which the alert aircraft were scrambled. Once on the ground the target aircraft and crew would become the responsibility of the base security. In one such exercise, the interceptors from Hahn closed on the target, a two-place CF-104, only to find the aircraft on fire. They immediately reported it, watched the crew eject, circled in "RESCAP" until low on fuel and the rescue well underway, then landed at Ramstein. The captain who was the Flight Lead impounded his airplane and had the munitions people inventory his armament and certify that none had been fired from his aircraft.'

'The standard intercept tactic was a front-stern re-attack in which the interceptor was placed on 135-degree TCA from which it could launch a Sparrow [for a maximum radar 'paint', up to the 'breakaway x' point], then turn into the target for displacement, and reverse the turn for a stern re-attack, using either IR missiles or the gun. It was a good, flexible tactic.' In the F-4E, the pilot had a new toggle 'auto acquisition' switch on the outboard side of the left throttle (first trialled in F-4Ds in Vietnam) which he could activate when the radar was in 'boresight' for the stern re-attack; the radar 'gate' would then continuously sweep out to maximum gun range, automatically locking on to anything in the radar trace. It could be used for a short-range AIM-7E-2 'shoot', or guns.

'For about half my four and a half years in Germany, intercept training was the only air-to-air training available, but then [in 1972] we were finally authorized to engage in Air Combat Tactics (ACT) training, but only in very confined airspace. The missions were usually two-on-two, with each flight starting from a diagonal corner of the allotted airspace (marked by TACAN radials and distances). Any means of detection of the other flight was permissible, radar or visual, and once contact was established it became a contest to determine who could attain a gun firing position. These sorties were flown without the external wing tanks to lend reality, and thus ended in about one hour of really good, fun flying. They were unrealistic in that neither flight had the benefit of ground radar, the airspace was restrictive in length, width, floor and ceiling, the violation of any dimension forcing cancellation of the engagement, and all aircraft involved had precisely the same performance. The need to constantly monitor position by navigation instruments really interfered with the training value.' All that changed during Bicentennial year. 'Red Flag' war games were established at Nellis AFB, Nevada, and ACT deployments to Decimomannu in Sardinia, where NATO crews congregated during the winter months, provided a virtually unrestricted combat camp, furnished with dissimilar DACT from the newly established nimble F-5E 'Aggressor' squadrons, opening up an excellent training programme which endured for the remainder of the Phantom's active service.

The ROE remained virtually the same in every theatre of operations. 'There was a list of about nine "hostile" acts, self-evident acts of war, which allowed the combat crew to engage automatically; anything outside those acts required standard international intercept procedures. What this boiled down to in SEA (and in Europe) was the requirement to visually identify the target before engaging. In SEA there was the danger of, one, firing on one of our own aircraft and, two, creating an international incident by firing upon aircraft of a "neutral" nation. Actually, if I had encountered a flight of MiG-21s over Laos, and they were not violating one of those nine hostile acts, I could not engage them. The same was technically true if a flight of MiG-21s overflew Fulda: they would be untouchable. In this regard, the Rules of Engagement and the hostile acts worked to neutralize our advantage in superior radar and missile capability.'

Within USAFE the alert F-4Es were continuing to utilize the AIM-4D Falcon and AIM-7E-2 Sparrow mix, with the nose-mounted 'shooter' as back-up. The new Ford AIM-9J TEC Sidewinder, similar to the E model but with new servo controls linked to revised 130211-model cranked canards, did not arrive until the spring of 1973. However, beginning with F-4E No 756, during the summer of 1972 Phantoms had started to appear fresh from the factory with the Northrop AN/ASX-1 TISEO (Target Identification System, Electro-Optical) installed on the port wing leading edge. This vidicon camera unit could be slaved at the aircraft's velocity vector or to the radar, to present one of two optional TV 'zoom' settings on the MSDG (and later DSCG-driven) radar scope tube, permitting positive target identification when the 'bogey' was otherwise beyond the range of the pilot's naked eye, or was just a nondescript glint in the distance. TISEO had been used on a trials basis in South-East Asia with several 'hard-wing' E models of the 'Gunfighters' at Da Nang after the cessation of 'Linebacker' hostilities and became a standard production feature of all the LES-wing USAF aircraft from Block 48 (71-0237) as well as those of several overseas FMS operators, including the later batches sold to Greece (eighteen produced, in Blocks 65–66), Iran (84, in Blocks 57–63), Israel (24, in Blocks 60–62) and Turkey (five in Block 57 and all thirteen in Block 58, but deleted from subsequent buys)[2]. It was said that, in clear weather, a crew could recognize a 'Bear'-size bomber at ranges of over 40nm and aircraft as small as a swing-wing MiG-23 'Flogger' at around 10nm. Jim Shaw, who encountered TISEO F-4Es fresh from the factory while flying with the 32nd TFS *Wolfhounds* in Holland, recollected that 'In practice, we would search with radar and IFF. When a contact was made, we could get a long-range radar lock, switch to TISEO for an optical lock, then return to radar and break lock. The pilot would have "TV" selected for his repeater scope and would monitor the target for visual ID and to detect evasive action while the WSO continued his radar search for other targets and directed a "no lock-on" interception over the intercom. Meanwhile the target's radar warning gear had only been given a few moments' notice that he was being observed, at the very beginning of the intercept'. The ARN-101(V) DMAS later provided complete integration with TISEO, for co-ordinated cueing (and manual ground target computation too, using known variables such as aircraft position and angular sensor geometry to help check on navigation waypoints or to 'freeze' co-ordinates into the memory for later use). The RAF evolved its own simple optical magnification viewfinder version for the Phantom FGR.2, sprouting from the left cockpit fairing and known as TESS (telescopic sight system). Both devices proved to be particularly useful in the blue skies prevalent over Nevada, the Mediterranean and the Middle East. However, they did little to improve all-weather air defence, where

---

[2] Tracking down TISEO installation details is complicated by the fact that McAir documentation in the public domain does not always differentiate between 'Group A' (structural/wiring) and 'Group B' (system hardware) fits. For example, Block 64-MC Korean F-4Es featured 'Group A' accommodation for TISEO but 'Group B' (the actual capability) was not added, and even 'Group A' was deleted from Block 67. However, the figures quoted in the narrative are believed to be accurate.

circumstances, and not the prevailing meteorological conditions, dictated the schedules.[3]

BLACK KNIGHTS

Despite the aircraft's intrinsic value in this dynamic role, it was not until 1973 that the USAF began to re-equip its dedicated ADC interceptor squadrons with Phantoms. The first unit to receive them was the 57th FIS *Black Knights* at NAS Keflavik, Iceland, which exchanged its 'Deuces' (the last remaining examples still serving with the Active forces) for F-4Cs between April and June that year. Like the remainder of ADC, the crews were provided with a sector of airspace (an air defence identification zone, or ADIZ) which they were obliged to monitor, in this instance the murky North Atlantic, the Danish and Norwegian Seas

Below: Capt Andy Bush congratulates Capt Jim Shaw, WSO, on completion of his 1,000th hour in the Phantom in the spring of 1976. 'Andy arrived at Ubon on the same C-141 that took me home a few minutes later. He then came to the 32nd TFS from there. We were crewed together for almost two years, which just wasn't long enough. [He was] by far the best front-seater I ever had the pleasure to fly with.' Andy Bush retired as a Lieutenant-Colonel and now flies for TWA. (Jim Shaw)

near the Arctic Circle, where the squadron could expect to be scrambled on 'Alpha' intercepts at least 120 times annually.[4] Crews prided themselves on fulfilling the alert roster twenty-four hours a day, all year round, toting live missiles plus hand-held cameras to photograph every subtle nuance of the evolving Soviet 'Bears'.

The dedicated air defence business was very different from the mass clear-air tactics expounded at the RTU bases George, Homestead and Luke, each of which enjoyed around 300 blue-skied flying days annually. As one aviator put it, 'My ADC background placed some premium on the guy who could put you on the target's right wing at 200 yards in the blackest of nights or the dirtiest of weather, or complete a head-on, snap-up attack against a target radiating ECM'. Crews were fully IMC (Instrument-Meteorological Conditions) capable, or rapidly attained that standard, able to press ahead in 'Popeye' weather using all the tools in the cockpit. Despite the hazards of snow and rain below the cloud deck and the dramatic backwash created by the huge counter-rotating propellers of the giant 'Bears' they were sent up to intercept, the *Black Knights* suffered only one major mishap during their twelve

continuous years of Phantom operations: F-4C 63-7475 had to belly-land on a foamy strip after its undercarriage failed to emerge, and was later repaired, ending its days nicknamed *Defender* with the 123rd FIS, Oregon ANG. The Arctic warriors' motto was 'If we didn't get them, they didn't come'. The 57th FIS won the Hughes Trophy for the second time in 1976 and scored an 'Exceptional' 98 per cent rating during an ORI the same year, when EB-57s from the Vermont ANG *Green Mountain Boys* DSES (Defense System Evaluation Squadron) deployed and subjected them to all manner of countermeasures and other tricks, which they did annually. Routine training employed T-33As, which carried pods with aft- and forward-facing reflectors to simulate a realistic-sized target, plus bulk chaff dispensers to attempt to add some confusion. The Icelandic 'Knights' also pioneered the glossy ADC scheme (officially known simply as FS 16473 'Aircraft Gray'), making them some of the smartest in the Air Force, a factor which engendered considerable pride in the maintenance troops. The first such example to wear the new paint scheme was delivered from the Spanish PDM depot CASA Getafe in November 1977.

---

[3] The first reliable IFF fielded comprised the AN/APX-76 retrofitted to F-4Cs 63-7421 to 64-0928 (Blocks 16–25), resulting in a reduced fuel capacity in the No1 fuel cell, and all surviving F-4Ds and previously manufactured F-4Es under TO 1F-4-753. Some of these 'fixes', including 'Combat Tree' (TO 1F-4D-550, described in Chapter 10) were undertaken with extreme urgency. McAir's John 'Mr Maintenance' Harty recalled that 'We did the mods in a couple of weeks, working nights and weekends, and writing the maintenance manuals as the design changes were being made. We went right to combat with them.' Block 57 F-4Es introduced the AN/APX-80 IFF from 73-1165 onwards. Refer also to Note 6.
[4] Although managed separately within NORAD, Aerospace Defense Command did not become a specified Command until 1975, when it was officially termed ADCOM. In June 1979 it became subordinate to TAC as 'Air Defense, TAC', or ADTAC for short, and in December 1985 was realigned under the First Air Force, headquartered at TAC HQ at Langley AFB, Virginia. For clarity, the terms 'ADC' or 'ADTAC' are used throughout the book.

The 57th FIS converted to F-4Es beginning at 1809hrs local time on 21 March 1978, when 66-0328 and -0334 touched down. Jim Shaw, who was Chief of Training and later commanded 'B' Flight at Keflavik shortly after the unit's transition, explained the rigours of flying from this icy outpost—conditions shared by the *Arctic Foxes* flying from Elemendorf in Alaska—and the advantages offered by the E model:

'In general there was little difference between sitting alert at Soesterberg and Keflavik. In both cases we pulled one 24-hour alert shift roughly once a week. We had a two-storey facility with a kitchen and dining area, and ground crew bedroom downstairs (closer to the aircraft—they had to be there first), and the lounge and air-crew sleeping facilities upstairs (complete bathrooms up and down). The Kef "barn" had room for two sets of alert birds, two on either side of the alert facility. During periods of increased activity on their side it was not unusual to cancel part or all of the daily flying schedule and put part or all of the Squadron on alert. The two big differences at Keflavik were that there were no practice scrambles (which would take the

alert force off status for too long), and we were on ten-minute status. The response time was not actually such a big thing there because of the radar coverage provided from Scandinavia, the UK and the North American continent. Also, there were EC-121s when I first arrived, followed by E-3A AWACS three months later in September 1978, plus RAF Shackletons.[5] We generally had lots of warning (a few hours) when something was headed our way. We would generally get a call from the OPCON (Kef was a Naval Air Station and used Navy abbreviations), telling us that "Bears" were headed south or north. These would come out of the Murmansk area and patrol the UK Gap/North Atlantic sea lanes, or proceed on to Cuba. Once in Cuba they would patrol the Eastern and Gulf Coasts of the US (on elint and

Above: 'Kef's *Black Knights* **moved on to the F-4E model from March 1978 and flew the only such examples painted in the glossy ADC Gray livery. They were some of the smartest Phantoms ever to serve. (Via Jim Shaw)**

ASW) for 1–2 weeks, then either return home or fly a resupply mission to the Cuban "advisors" in Angola. From Angola they would generally RTB Murmansk [of which more anon].

'The other part of the ten-minute status involved clothing. Whereas at Soesterberg we dressed "normally" for the time of year, at Kef we wore our personal skivies, then Nomex long-johns. Over that we wore a two-piece set of quilted underwear (which we called "Chinese underwear" because it was so reminiscent of Chinese Army uniforms of the Korean War era). Over that went our

Below: The year 1985 signalled the end for 57th FIS F-4E operations but the unit brought over two of their pristine Phantoms for the static display at IAT-85, held at RAF Greenham Common during that July. (Authors)

immersion "poopy" suits, and finally our Nomex flight suits (2–3 sizes larger than normal). This whole lot was quite cumbersome to wear all day, so we had individual clothing racks where everything was laid out in order that we could spend most of our time in our "Chinese" outfits and bedroom slippers. OPCON tried to time our scrambles very carefully to maximize our time on station, so we would usually get a call some 10–15 minutes before launch to get into our suits, followed by the actual klaxon.

'After launch we were generally directed to contact one of our two GCI sites, Rockville on the west end of the island or Hofn on the east end. They might then hand us off to the EC-121 or AWACS, or we would be sent to pre-planned orbits anticipating the imminent arrival of our Soviet friends. In any event, we were then vectored to a position (usually head-on) from which we could make contact, and would call "Judy" to indicate we were taking control of the intercept ourselves. Head-on, the "Bear"'s huge contra-rotating props made wonderful radar reflectors, and under optimum conditions I have had intermittent contact in excess of 100nm, and good, solid contact at 80nm. The approach was almost always made from an offset head-on making a wide, 180-degree turn to roll out in AIM-7 firing position to the rear of the trailing aircraft (the "Bears" normally flew 2–3nm apart in trail), with overtaking speed. One F-4E would then remain in this "cover" position while the other moved in for identification.'

The 57th FIS always flew with three 'bags' (fuel tanks) and four Sparrows, but seldom with Sidewinders. 'A few years earlier there had been an incident in which an AIM-9 on an alert aircraft in Germany had fired when the safety pins were removed during a practice scramble. It then homed flawlessly on the auxiliary power generator of the mobile control tower at the end of the runway. Since our alert facility faced in the general direction of the international airport terminal, the Icelandic authorities requested that we not load AIM-9s except in times of increased tension or hostilities. [However, the machines were on occasion fitted with six pods full of 2.75in FFAR rockets!] We had a secondary (so secondary it was almost tertiary) mission of anti-shipping aimed at the Soviet "fishing trawlers" that always monitored our operations. We never practised this mission, but the load crews had to be familiar with the ordnance'.

The F-4E's transistor-technology radar was less prone to overheating than the valves used on the earlier models, and 'had a number of features which made it better for the air-to-air role in which I spent the majority of my time.

Above: 'Bear-watching' south-east of Iceland, June 1979. The Tu-95 in the photograph has a stock tail, complete with guns; the Phantom carries AIM-7E-2 Sparrows but no Sidewinders. A few years earlier there had been an incident in which an AIM-9 on a USAFE alert aircraft had shot off when the safety pins were removed, zooming into a power generator near the control tower! 'Kef's alert barns faced towards the International Airport there, so Icelandic authorities requested that AIM-9s not be loaded, except in times of increased tension. (Jim Shaw)

For one thing, the radar had a five-mile range option in addition to the C/D's 10-, 25-, 50-, 100- and 200-nautical mile position settings. This allowed for more precise control of the intercept (or formation join-up, or tanker rendezvous) as the range decreased. It also had a function called "vis-ident" (visual identification) that allowed you to read the range to a locked-on target off a gauge very precisely, down to less than 1,000ft, as well as rate of closure from +300 to −50 knots.[6] The WSO always carried a Nikon camera with a telephoto lens and we did a standard photo series: an overall shot

[5] The Boeing E-3A AWACS airborne warning and control command posts were giant, 100-ton sentinels employing Westinghouse AN/APY-1 rotodomes which would track hostile and friendly aircraft by means of sophisticated IFF interrogation techniques and display the synthesized data on nine situation display consoles so that the operators could provide vectors for hit-and-run LRI work in a dense, RF-spectrum-saturated environment, 'with airplanes all over the place'. The first of what would eventually total 34 USAF Sentries were grouped at Tinker AFB, Oklahoma, during March 1977, shortly afterwards to be committed in two- and three-aircraft TDY detachments around the world, including NAS Kefkavik and the other icy outpost, Alaskan Air Command's Elmendorf Air Base. This other base and its freezing Phantoms provided cover over the Bering Strait as far as the Asian Zone, on 'Bear hunts' lasting up to 2½ hours apiece. The AEW Shackleton is discussed elsewhere in the book, in the context of RAF air defence operations.

[6] The definitive FY74 Block 60–62 aircraft, 72 of which were bought for the USAF by the Israelis as part of the 'buy back' deal, also featured a more advanced IFF interrogator which 'allowed one to not only identify who was the good/bad guy, but also a specific aircraft by call-sign'. These had the APQ-120(V)7 radar (73-1185 onwards) and the new digital-scan converter display (74-0643 onwards) from the beginning. 'In the radar display mode the picture was a computer-generated version of what the radar saw, made up of lots of tiny squares [pixels] of light. It made for a very crisp air-to-air picture.' Actually, Keflavik's machines were more primitive FY66–67 early-build F-4Es updated with various radar and weapons systems enhancements, plus ILS. ILS/VOR was later applied to most aircraft under TO 1F-4-1056.

(to verify type and model), followed by a shot of the door number (they had serials on the nose gear doors instead of the tails), to identify which airframe, followed by an overlapping series of shots along the belly, followed by the same along one side, then the other side, then top views from both sides, finally followed by detail shots of anything which we, as air crews, thought to be of interest. When the intercept was at night we sometimes carried infra-red film, but success with it was so-so. We always recorded the door number of the aircraft so that the "Bear" could be tracked. [On night interceptions the WSO would hold a large-diameter camping torch tightly against the top of the canopy, to avoid a 'milk bowl' effect on the plexiglass, while the pilot 'flew' the beam of light on to the door. The procedures called for the pilot 'never' to come within 250ft of the 'Bear']. After ID and relay of such information as door numbers, heading, altitude and airspeed, we would stay with them until they exited the Icelandic ADIZ.

'I intercepted thirty "Bears" while at Keflavik. My first was on my first alert after being certified MR. We were still doing our crew changeover when we got the "suits" call. Less than ten minutes later were scrambled and thirty minutes after that I was flying in close formation with the big red star. I was immediately impressed with what a beautiful aircraft it was—very sleek, very clean, the sound from its contra-rotating props so very distinct. All the "Bears" I encountered were always very clean and looked to be well maintained, air-show ready. As we moved in from the rear for our ID/ photo passes the tail guns were always at maximum elevation. We were always on the alert for any indication that the gunners might be tracking us on the tail warning radar. Sometimes they waved to us, sometimes not. The cockpit crew never did, and rarely even glanced our way, even when we drew quite near. I always found it fascinating to see them in their leather helmets and earphones. The ones en route to Cuba were invariably at 28–32,000ft in a max cruise mode with

the crews looking happy and waving whilst taking pictures of us taking pictures of them. The ones patrolling the sea lanes were all business, going about their jobs in a professional manner— noting our presence, but getting on with business. The ones returning from Cuba or Angola were again at 28–32,000ft and always looked tired. One memorable intercept was of a 'D' model who was definitely on a tactical ASW/maritime recce mission, whom we first encountered at the customary altitude, but which went into a steep descent to 500ft MSL. We chased him for almost twenty minutes in and out of snow storms, through multiple heading changes (with a lot of help from AWACS), before we were able to get a proper ID on him.' Southbound aircraft were handed over to RAF control at Leuchars, and at this juncture FGR.2s and F-4Es often joined up together on the big silver beast for photo opportunities.

Recovery at Keflavik 'was not necessarily more difficult, but it was distinctly different. The real difference was that instead of your alternate airfields being a relatively short distance away, you had only one alternate, RAF Leuchars in Scotland, and it was 700nm away—so you'd better decide to go there early if it was really needed! In fact, in my whole tour, nobody went there for any reason except for orientation (and to buy good whisky). We had the only USAF F-4s equipped with an ILS then and that helped a lot. We were further aided by the absolutely outstanding service of the Icelandic ground crews who did such a magnificent job under all conditions. I was never aware of the airfield closing even during the most severe blizzard conditions. The alert force was always able to take off, and we could always get down—often into the care of approach-end Icelandic barrier crews the Navy would be envious of. I do not have enough good words for those good folks. (To show our appreciation we used to bring them to our Squadron bar twice a year and get them absolutely stupefied drunk!).

'During the months of relatively good weather at Kef (May–Sept), we invited

our RAF counterparts to participate in our monthly "Fan Angels" exercise. This was an air defence exercise that involved the entire island (Army ADA, USMC perimeter defence, Naval P-3s as targets, AWACS, the whole lot). The RAF would fly in one or more Shackletons on Thursday with support personnel and lots of Green Man or 6X. Two fighters would fly in on Friday and we would spend that night and Saturday abusing our livers. Sunday we would go to bed early awaiting the recall for Monday's STARTEX. Monday and Tuesday were intensive flying days. Wednesdays we would fly against each other, which was a wonderful opportunity to compare techniques. They they would go home on Thursday. I can remember doing this with Nos 43, 56 and 111 Squadrons.'

The combination of the new AWACS and DACT training rendered ADC's Phantoms formidable weapons. Keflavik's F-4Es retained the glossy ADC bluish-grey paintwork they had pioneered on their F-4Cs (they were the only USAF 'Echoes' ever to feature this scheme), and added the flamboyant chequerboards and lances introduced originally for the 1976 'William Tell' competition at Tyndall ADWC, Florida. Air and ground crews alike described the Phantoms as 'beautiful . . . the best maintained F-4s I ever flew'. Seven years later they were just as smart. There was not a single blemish on the spectacular examples making the unit's farewell public appearance at RAF Greenham Common in July 1985.

The shark-mouthed F-4Es assigned to the other icy outpost, Elmendorf in Alaska, held down their mission until 1982. During a sortie on 13 April 1979 Lt-Col Doyle Baker clocked up his 4,000th hour in the Phantom (the first pilot to reach this figure), while his steed, F-4E 67-0208, reached its 5,000th hour minutes later!

Introducing an altogether different paint scheme during 1978—the menacing low-level 'wrap-around' SEA tans and greens combined with low-visibility black codes—was the 'other' *Black Knights* squadron, the 526th TFS at 'Brick City',

USAFE HQ. Ramstein's 'Red Squadron' was one of only two tactical F-4E air combat squadrons extant in the USAF in the post-Vietnam years (the second was the 36th TFS *Flying Fiends*, located at Osan AB in South Korea) which was tasked exclusively with the air superiority mission. For sixteen straight years these aircraft maintained the Phantom at the cutting edge of USAFE while simultaneously providing exchange crews and feedback for the Tyndall-based 'Combat Echo' WSEP (Weapons System Evaluation Program), which wrote the manuals, and ironed out all the

kinks, relating to the continuing systems improvements.

The most significant F-4E update was a fleet-wide upgrade officially termed Modification 2745 but known more commonly as the 'LRU-1 Mod', after the new digital fire-control computer it introduced. Along with this new 'black box' came a digital LRU-20 target detector, 'shoot lights' mounted on the cockpit canopy bow and what was akin to HOTAS (hands-on-throttle-and-stick) weapons and radar selection buttons, all of which was greeted with great enthusiasm (one F-4E pilot on the 1978 Euro-

173

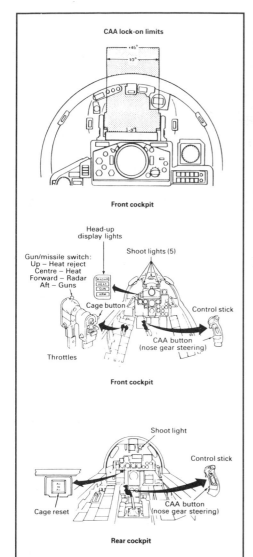

Above: F-4E LRU-1 'Auto-Acquisition' mode. Lock-on limits (top) depict field of auto-acquisition in the 'ACM', close-in, visual mode; front cockpit (centre) shows 'valid firing opportunity' shoot light and radar/weapons systems select modes; and rear cockpit (bottom) depicts shoot light and auto-acquisition select. (Westinghouse via John J. Harty, McDonnell Douglas)

pean air-show circuit describing the refit as producing 'a totally new aircraft').

Previously, the analogue radar system provided target position, range and opening or closing rates. That was all it could usefully manage. By blending the faster processing speed of the digital computer with radar, additional target information such as aspect angle, target velocity, direction and turn rate was obtained, expanding the envelope for LRI with

quicker missile-away solutions while adding a new air combat manoeuvring (ACM) mode to boot. The LRI mode was automatically selected when the target range was greater than 5nm or the altitude greater than 32,000ft, for a blind or 'head-down' missile shot using the ASE circle and steering dot, with initial target tracking being accomplished at ranges of well over 40nm.[7] This package worked best with the Raytheon AIM-7F Sparrow, a brand new solid-state version designed for America's new, third-generation 'Teenage' fighters but remaining compatible with the Phantom. Developed from 1966, introduced to service in 1975 but taking another seven years to reach the Phantom squadrons (which had by then expended their AIM-7E-2s in live shoots over the Gulf of Mexico, or

had consigned them overseas as part of numerous FMS deals), the miniaturized electronics of the new weapon facilitated the installation of a bigger, 88lb blast-fragmentation warhead and a revised, enlarged rocket motor with a genuine sixty-mile range at altitude; yet it expanded upon the AIM-7E-2+ model's dogfight manoeuvrability and minimum range characteristics as well, such that it overlapped Sidewinder and guns! Using the new LRU-1 modification, the steering dot on the radar scope was continuously re-computed to provide a smooth transition between lead-collision (outside maximum missile range, Rmax) and lead-pursuit at the Rmax point, when the parameters opened up for a long-range Sparrow shot. In essence, the combination of the new digital computer and

Left: Standing 'alert' in one of Ellington's barns, an F-4C from the 147th FIS *Ace in the Hole* squadron displays its powerful lines to the camera. (Texas ANG)
Right: 'Flying' between the hangars at RAF Upper Heyford is F-4C-21-MC 63-7699, the *Red Baron*. The aircraft 'bagged' a MiG during April 1966 while coded 'CG' with the 'Gunfighters of Da Nang', later flew with the Illinois and Oregon ANGs and ended its days as a BDR example in England. At the time of writing the aircraft is being restored for display at the Coventry Air Museum. (Tim Laming)

Raytheon AIM-7F expanded both the range and angular parameters (up to a 25° error) for a successful Sparrow volley where the Phantom could inflict maximum damage, before closing into range with the opponent's armament—bearing in mind that Soviet bombers, and even transports and reconnaissance machines too, featured tail cannon as standard armament!

The new ACM mode was automatically selected when the target was within 5nm and fighter altitude below 32,000ft, for a visual sighting and a head-up engagement. The new computer-aided auto-acquisition (CAA) capability was used here, which expanded AA from 'boresight' to 'supersearch'. The radar would scan a box 45° up, 5° left and right and 9° down from the RBL, and all the pilot had to do was to haul his steed around the sky and place the enemy within that scan pattern—in effect, anywhere in the front windshield—for an automatic radar lock-on.[8] Valid firing opportunities for the Sparrow were indicated by a new 'head-up' bank of five 'shoot lights', while the system also assisted with the initial cueing of Side-

winder missiles, prior to receipt of the raised 'chirp' over the headphones which indicated that the 'heat' weapons' seekers had locked on to their quarry.

Sidewinders, too, were gradually enhanced throughout the 1970s, expanding the lock-on parameters for successful intercepts and ACM engagements. The AIM-9J was updated to J-1 status, introducing a new rate bias, a solid-state TEC seeker and a DSU-21/B active optical target detector using GaAs (gallium arsenide) lasers, expanding its usefulness from the rear 'cone' to virtually all aspects. It was redesignated AIM-9P in 1978 (with dash-1–3 models following, including a specialized 9N model for export to FMS F-4E operators), which introduced a revised rocket motor, offering up to forty seconds' flight-time and three times the range of its predecessors. Alongside the Sparrow 7E-2 and 7F, the

AIM-9P-2/3 became a principal weapon for Phantoms assigned to ADC duties throughout the latter half of the 1970s and early 1980s until it was eventually supplanted by the US Navy AIM-9L/M version, which introduced slimmer BSU-32/B canards and argon-gas cooling with broader micron range sensitivity, capable of picking up relatively cool portions of airframe, for genuine all-aspect target acquisition.[9]

The 526th TFS finally left the stage during 1986, their last F-4E departing on 1 July, precisely 217 days after the last of Keflavik's machines had been dispatched home from Iceland in favour of F-15As. Having flown the last of the Active air-superiority US Phantoms, the 36th TFS *Flying Fiends*, at Osan in the Republic of Korea, completed its transition to new 'Teenagers' on 6 January 1989.

---

[7] The basic 'switchology' and related displays were discussed Chapter 9.
[8] The CAA possessed a 'skipover' mode, to cater for two targets lying along the same radar line of sight. The computer automatically selected the nearest, but if this was not the desired target the CAA button on the stick could be pressed and the computer would select the next target in range. This permitted two aircraft selectively to engage their 'own' targets in a two-on-two confrontation and, *in extremis*, a wing-man to shoot down an enemy fighter on the tail of a colleague in a head-on encounter . . . not that this was practised! Additionally, to reduce clutter-related false tar-

gets, the ACM mode automatically became range-limited as the antenna scanned below the RBL, from the full 5nm to approximately 0.5nm at 9° down. (Actual antenna scanning ranged from 57° up to 21° down; the extra 12° was used by the computer to turn the antenna around to perform other clutter-related functions.) *In toto*, Westinghouse produced of 810 LRU-1 modification kits, including batches for selected FMS F-4Es and *Luftwaffe* F-4Fs, the latter of which used the system to provide better Sidewinder missile solutions only, since, although these aircraft retained the Sparrow wells, they lacked the necessary wiring and Aero-7/A 'kick' launchers to use them.

[9] US Navy variants used nitrogen-gas cooling, contained in the launch rails. The USAF argon-cooled versions were fitted to Aero-3A rails which provided electrical power only and were thus 'self-contained'. This important distinction between the two Services' Sidewinders was sustained under separate Sidewinder programmes pursued by the USN/British and USAF/FMS Phantom 'streams'. Beginning with the AIM-9D, the USN/MS and British Phantoms kept with gas while the UDAF/FMS models' AIM-9E introduced TEC. When the two streams finally reconverged after 1981, both insisted in different gas-cryogenics, with the USAF opting for argon!

GUARDIANS OF THE FRONTIERS

Perhaps nowhere throughout the Phantom saga did America's militia shine more illustriously than in the strategic air defence mission. At peak strength the force boasted eight squadrons specializing exclusively in this role, along with two others assigned air defence as a first-equal commitment.

The first unit in the Guard to adopt the 'Navy Bastard' was the 199th TFS at Hickam Field, Hawaii, another long-standing 'Deuce' operator. Flying out of Hickam, Oahu, and using the airspace surrounding such exotic locations as the islands of Maui, Molokai, Lanai and the 'big island', Hawaii itself, as their play-

ground, the unit received their first F-4C on 31 October 1975 and later peaked at 26 aircraft while under the command of Col John Lee. It stayed in the Phantom business for twelve years, practising intercepts and ACM over the wispy Pacific and coastal *hune kai* before trading in its aircraft for F-15A Eagles. It also got out and about on touring exercises two or three times annually, including 'Red Flag' stints at Nellis, 'Cope Thunder' manoeuvres in the Philippines and participation in 'Team Spirit' in the Republic of Korea and even 'Cope North' in Japan. Others assisted with missile re-entry monitoring at the Kwajalein range. Individual aircraft featured names of local avian fauna, or names based on their

individual service antics; instructor aircraft 63-7562 later carried the puzzling name *Olili*, which translates as something like 'joyful shiver'! The 199th also boasted its fair share of MiG-killer jets, for example 63-7647 *Alae'Ula* (which 'bagged' a MiG-17 on 5 June 1967 and which wore two red stars while at Hickam) and 64-0806 *I'iwi* (with an enigmatic four red stars painted up on its vari-ramp, possibly representing the unaccredited April and July 1966 kills, or the past exploits of its veteran crews; its log book was not available for review).

Back in CONUS, the re-equipment programme kicked off with the 119th FIG at Hector Field, Fargo, North Dakota. The *Happy Hooligans* received their first F-4D on 15 March 1977—they were the first ANG unit to re-equip with this model—and were followed in rapid succession at approximately six-month intervals by further units across the United States, ranging from the *Eager Beavers* in Oregon in the north-west, to the *Ace in the Hole Squadron* at Houston, Texas, as 'Guardians of the Gulf Coast', and across to the north-east and the waterfall spectrum-ruddered Phantoms of the New York Guard at Niagara Falls. The process of converting from well-loved but aged 'Century Series' interceptors to the comparatively new Phantoms was completed during the winter of 1983 by the 144th FIW *Bald Eagles* at Fresno Air Terminal, California, which received its first F-4Ds in November 1983.[10] By the following summer ADTAC boasted a complement of 220 F-4C/Ds, most by then resplendent in dazzling 'Aircraft

[10] Those F-4C units which did not subsequently convert directly to F-15A Eagles or F-16ADFs (Michigan, New York and Texas) upgraded to F-4Ds before acquiring F-16ADFs—see the ANG Interceptor Squadrons histories in Appendix VI. Several other ADTAC/ANG units 'skipped' F-4C/Ds altogether and went straight from F-106A/Bs to 'Teenagers', including Florida (to F-16), Massachussetts (to F-15), Montana (to F-16) and New Jersey (to F-16). The F-16 is a fine machine for VFR, clear-weather operations, and it sustains a remarkable operational availability rate, but many question its value in 'Popeye IFR conditions', where weather, enemy countermeasures and other factors would all too likely prove overwhelming to a solo crewman.

Opposite page: Guardsmen 'in the groove' for gas, behind a 22nd AREFW KC-10A Extender. The low-visibility camouflage and miniature stars-and-bars insignia introduced by the 'Hill Gray' scheme are readily apparent here. Within the interceptor community the scheme first appeared on the F-4Cs of Hickam's 199th TFS *HANGmen* during 1987. (Frank B. Mormillo)
Above: A pair of 171st FIS *Michigan Wolves* prepare to pile on the thrust and roll, April 1990. By this time, during the last few months of the F-4's career, the glossy ADC Gray scheme had largely given way to the subdued 'Hill Gray II' finish, and this pair highlights the difference! (Scott Van Aken via Tim Laming)
Right: The 114th TFTS *Black Hawks* provided the 'Interceptor School House' for the ANG community, flying from Kingsley Field, Oregon. This example was photographed while flying over the Mojave Desert during a 'Lobo Flag 88' 'Red Force' mission. (Frank B. Mormillo)

Gray' festooned with bold USAF and stars-and-bars logos and eye-catching unit liveries.

For many, although it was very much in its twilight years, the Phantom had now reached its zenith. However, this lively new assignment was not trouble-free. The *Bald Eagles* received their machines in appalling condition, with most of the missile-related electronics, such as the Sparrow Aero-7/A launchers, requiring a complete rebuild. Many of the aircraft had spent the majority of their recent service lives at Homestead AFB developing novices' air-to-ground tal-

ents, and, pending remanufacture in Fresno's hangars with spares shipped in from Ogden and McAir, the alert commitment had to be held down by the unit's former 'Sixes' for three months. The Texas and Hawaii Guards chipped in with aircraft and crews while the unit got going; it worked up to operational status in autumn 1984 in practice intercepts against SAC bombers during the latter's annual 'Proud Shield' bombing competition.

Once up to strength, each squadron maintained a minimum of two, some-times four, Phantoms on full-time alert

(and occasionally six, when committed to maintaining two detachments away from the home 'fort': Minnesota's *North Star Squadron* held down detachments at both Loring AFB, Maine, and Tucson, Arizona, at one stage). It was a busy schedule which generated up to 3,000 sorties annually per squadron. As well as standing alert duties, many crews were involved in exacting exercises: 'Red Flag'; participation in the biennial 'William Tell' shooting matches held at Tyndall ADWC in which Phantoms made their first appearance in 1976 (when the F-4 'top team' comprised a section from the

177

'Fourth But First'); and, from 1983, newly created 'Copper Flag' USAFIWS interception weapons school manoeuvres. These made increasing use of Tyndall's newly installed Cubic Corp ACMI (air combat manoeuvring instrumented) range, one of many sprouting up across the United States, with two others located overseas in the Mediterranean and Pacific Rim.

Tyndall's ACMI was first put through its full paces during 'Copper Flag 83-3' held between 14 and 26 August that year. Presiding over the manoeuvres was ADWC boss Brig-Gen 'Dusty' Davis, who reckoned that this was the only peacetime way of providing 'an effective means of exercising air defence forces against a variety of realistic threats'. Over fifty aircraft and 500 crewmen participated in the 'test match', including elements of AWACS from the 552nd AW&CW and F-4Cs from New York's 107th FIG. Missions included low-level engagements against fleeting SOS MC-130Es and ADWC jets which did their best to foil radar and 'heat' by pumping out chaff and flares and radiating RF-spectrum and IRCM countermeasures. Each aircraft carried an ACMI pod similar to a Sidewinder body to relay its position, attitude and other data for post-mission analysis on the 'big screen'. RAF exchange pilot Flt Lt Tim Neville, with over 3,000 hours in Lightnings and 'Sixes', claimed at the time that it 'cuts out all the bull. The pilots come in and watch a video replay of the mission

they've just flown, see their mistakes and the things they did right. They see a real-time, true picture of their mission . . . a God's-eye view, high enough to see an area 100 miles wide down to two miles wide, as well as horizontal, vertical, side and cockpit views.' Aircraft entering the ACMI range forty miles apart typically engaged in under two minutes. Most crews could expect to fly fourteen sorties, beginning with one-on-one engagements and culminating in four-on-four DACT entanglements.

However, the really exciting missions were those sponsored by the ADWC's 'William Tell' shooting match, which employed live weapons against BQM-34 Firebee, PQM-102A Pave Deuce and later QF-100 'Hun' unmanned drones. Phantom participants—usually three teams of five aircraft each, including a 'spare'—flew two 'live' profiles, using snap-up and cut-off attacks with Sparrow, stern attacks with Sidewinder and gunnery practice against towed TDU-10 darts reeled out 2,300ft behind the 'towers' (usually provided by 347th TFW F-4Es and crews from Moody AFB, Georgia). To add to the action, one of the profiles typically started with an exhilarating and exhausting 300yd sprint to the cockpit! Winners came away from the meet with trophies after having created much scrap metal over the Gulf of Mexico and runners-up had the benefit of having shot off at least one live missile and seen at first hand what it was capable of doing. There were prizes for timing

and spit-and-polish performance too, and aircraft markings became particularly attractive. Lt-Col Funkhouser's 57th FIS F-4E (66-0382) appeared at WT-82 festooned with badges and red, white and blue splitter plates, while Michigan's 191st FIG introduced the beginnings of immaculate airbrushed artwork that would spread throughout the squadron, each carefully painted on clear decal film then applied to a freshly scrubbed nose barrel. Among the designs was Bare Metal Decals' El Mason's *Garfield* and *This One's for You, Baby*. The loving care lavished on these aircraft was extraordinary, and the high availability rates reflected the 'dressed to kill' cosmetics. It was all good food for morale. The Phantoms appeared at every meet between 1976 and 1988, in which latter year fifteen jets from the New York, Oregon and Texas ANGs made the type's final appearance.

To ensure adequate manning, on 1 April 1983 the *Black Hawks* were formed at Kingsley Field, Oregon, taking over the air defence 'school house' job from the *Jayhawks* in Kansas (although both units constantly liaised with one another, adding to rather than detracting from the exclusivity). By February 1984 the Squadron's designation had been settled as the 114th TFTS, and it would retain this role until a year before its last machines left ADTAC service in December 1989. While many of the Guardsmen were 'old heads', a steady intake of 'new guys' was necessary and demand was such that enthusiastic applicants up to

Right, upper: 57th FIS crews effect a 300yd sprint to their steeds preparatory to taking off for 'Profile 3' of WT-82. At Keflavik crews 'stood by' in the alert barns in their quilted 'Chinese outfits' and slippers, waiting for the klaxon call! (Via Lt-Col Jerry Hicks)
Right, lower: In common with their strike counterparts, the interceptor Guardsmen got out and about a lot on deployments and exercises, including TDY stints at Ramstein AB, West Germany, between April 1986 and April 1987 to provide 'Zulu Alert' while the resident unit re-equipped with F-16s. The project was code-named 'Creek Klaxon' and involved F-4Ds from the California, Minnesota and North Dakota ANGs. (Via Tim Laming)

Above: F-4D-25-MC 64-0945 from Adj-Gen Alexander P. Macdonald's North Dakota ANG 119th FIG *Happy Hooligans* lets loose an AIM-7E-2 Sparrow missile in pursuit of a drone over the Gulf of Mexico. This machine served as test-bed for the Hughes IRSTS . . . (Capt Larry Harrington/North Dakota ANG)

the age of thirty were considered for WSO slots. Kingsley Field's course typically comprised 33 sorties for prospective ACs and 28 for WSOs, spread out over seventeen weeks, covering classical fighter manoeuvres, air combat manoeuvring and point interception. The base boasted 400 full-time personnel, including twelve IPs and ten IWSOs. Six of Col Steven V. 'Slick' Harper's instructors were Vietnam veterans and two were former 'Aggressor' pilots. In all, the unit ran a five-course curriculum to cater for different experience and skill levels, plus an annual Operation 'Sentry Eagle' exercise. Some 105 students passed through the course each year, learning anything from the basics to Advanced Superiority Tactics (AST).

Overseas deployments also tested the force, as part of the 'Checkered Flag' 'Coronet' programme. The 159th TFG

Coonass Militia deployed to Iceland under 'Coronet Rodeo' in the summer of 1982, while for a full year beginning in April 1986 aircraft and crews from the California, North Dakota and Minnesota Guards maintained a rotational TDY presence, code-named 'Creek Klaxon', at Ramstein, near the 'Iron Curtain', as the 526th TFS *Black Knights* and its companion squadron the 512th TFS *Green Dragons* traded in their F-4Es in favour of F-16Cs. The crews found themselves being scrambled 12–15 times a month on 'Alpha' and 'Tango' missions using the eight deployed F-4Ds.[11] 'Creek Klaxon' was performed flawlessly, making many wonder why the Phantom was being relegated to the scrap heap or to the equally ignominious role of BDR trainer (when an unflinching 'RAM-er' would casually puncture the airframes with an ice pick and hammer, ready for the battle damage repair teams to practice their patching-up skills).

By New Year's Day 1990 the once proud force had dwindled to five F-4D units, wearing subdued monochromatic 'Hill Gray II' camouflage, distributed among the Michigan, Minnesota, New York, North Dakota and Texas Guards-

men. All of these would rapidly disband their Phantoms in favour of freshly reworked F-16ADFs over the ensuing ten months, bringing about a sad end to what had been a very colourful and productive era.

ICE AND KAI COCKTAILS

But for the end of the 'Cold War', the Phantoms might well have soldiered on for many more years. Key exponents of the 'Rhino' were Fargo's 119th FIG *Happy Hooligans*, led by its charismatic adjutant-general Maj-Gen Alexander P. Macdonald. He not only lobbied Washington to keep the programme alive but also was instrumental in pursuing an F-4D update effort that very nearly led to some 180 such aircraft being retrofitted with Hughes IRSTS (gutted from retired Voodoos, 'Deuces' and 'Sixes'). According to 'Hooligan' Maj Ronald W. Seager, the proposal was presented to the OOALC by the ANG/AFRES

[11] The aircraft concerned comprised 64-0963, -0968 and -0972 and 65-0585, -0595 and -0648 from the 179th FIS, Minnesota ANG, and 65-0740 and -0747 from the 194th FIS, California ANG. Crews were rotated on a two-week basis, including personnel from CONUS and Hawaii.

Fighter Weapons Office and in 1984 Ogden tasked Hughes to test their improved IRSTS in conjunction with the APQ-109 radar. 'The heart of the IRSTS was a cooled cross-array lead selenide detector. Prior to 1980 the cooling was provided by a bulky, closed-cycle liquid nitrogen system. Beginning that year, Hughes replaced the nitrogen system with a solid-state, four-stage Peltier-effect type of thermocouple, allowing for a large weight and space saving in the aircraft.' The TEC model was also 58 per cent more sensitive than its predecessors. F-4D 64-0945 (tail number '06', a 'vanilla' F-4D lacking the digital scan converter) was jury-rigged for the trials, with the IRSTS mounted ahead of its windshield. Between 29 June and 15 October 1985 the *Happy Hooligans* flew 32 test sorties and looked set to launch a massive upgrade effort.

'The IRSTS was integrated with the APQ-109 radar system in a manner which allowed independent or slaved operation of the radar antenna and the IR seeker head. This meant that for the first time the F-4D could track two targets simultaneously. [IRSTS was passive and stealthy like the F-4E's TISEO, making it immune to jamming by RF-spectrum electronic countermeasures.] The addition of a second system also meant that one could still be used to search for targets while the other was tracking a previously located aircraft.' Total retrofit costs for the envisaged ventral installation, in front of the nose gear, were of the order of $140,000 per aircraft in FY85 dollars (cheaper than an air-to-air missile), and the system would have given the Phantom a capability that engineers were seeking to introduce with the original ACF AN/AAA-4 twenty-five years previously. Options were also explored in integrating newer Hughes AN/APG-63 or -65 planar-array radars used in the higher-performance 'Teenagers'. However, the programme was abandoned when the decision was made to withdraw the F-4D from strategic air defence in favour of the easy-to-maintain ADF-modified 'Lawn Dart', some 270 of which have been fielded since

March 1989, alongside the midcourse-updated 'fire-and-forget' AIM-120A AMRAAM (Advanced Medium-Range Air-to-Air Missile).

Many hundreds of Phantoms still had plenty of hours left on their airframes when they were shipped to the 'boneyard'. Based on an annual utilization rate of 180hrs for the F-4C and 198hrs for the F-4D, McAir estimated that, with ASIP (Aircraft Structural Integrity Program) monitoring, 326 of them (alongside 379 F-4Es) would still be good for unrestricted combat at the start of the new millenium. Astonishingly, most were cleared to fly to their ASIP instrumented limits of $-1.8g$ and $+7.8g$ right through to retirement. The *Green Mountain Boys* at Vermont pointed out that the limits in the technical manuals were more like $-3g$ and $+8.5g$, although they were only in the business for a few years back in the mid-1980s, in between DSES EB-57s and F-16As. The only thing which let the aircraft down was their flagging, antiquated avionics. All ASIP could do was quickly to weed out the bad airframes, and 'cannibalization' of the avionics became prohibitively expensive from a political perspective when set alongside

the 'switch-on and fly' F-16, whatever the latter's obvious operational drawbacks.

Overseas intercept systems improvement programmes, which have risen from strength to strength amidst a declining worldwide inventory of Phantoms, include the *Luftwaffe*'s F-4F *Kampfwertsteigerung* (KWS, also known as the Improved Combat Effectiveness or ICE) and Japanese *Koku Jie tai* F-4EJ *Kai* ('Phantom Plus') efforts. The ambitious German KWS incentive represents the biggest undertaking since the 'Peace Rhine' upgrade which started in 1975 and was completed in 1983 and which revolved around reliability improvements to the Westinghouse APQ-120 radar and the adoption of the Bodenseewerk licence-built AIM-9L Sidewinder (accompanied

Below: . . . seen here installed at Hughes' Van Nuys, California, facility, along with the company's AN/APG-63 pulse-Doppler radar. The combination of these new sensors would have given the F-4D a massive new lease of life, but the programme was terminated because of its cost. A total of 32 test sorties using the IRSTS and vintage AN/APQ-109 radar were flown between June and October 1985. (Hughes via North Dakota ANG)

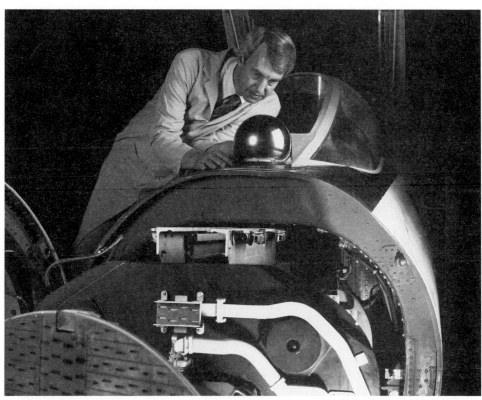

by a Maverick missile-capability and digital air-to-ground enhancements for CCIP attack). The KWS goes a step further as part of the Service's steady effort to transform its 'vanilla' F-4Fs into more capable machines, the crux of which is the Hughes AN/APG-65 (F/A-18 Hornet) radar, providing air-to-ground mapping (including an MTI mode) as well as lookdown, track-while-scan options with the company's AMRAAM, which will be 'plugged' into new Frazer-Nash missile well launchers—representing the first application of medium-range missiles to the *Maus*-camouflaged Phantoms. Additional equipment comprises Mil-Std 1553 databuses, Litef digital fire-control and GEC Avionics CPU-143/A air data computers and a Honeywell inertial H-423 ring-laser-gyro INS platform. These do not break down; they only break when someone hits them with a hammer! A

hundred aircraft are to be reconfigured with KWS, for assignment with *JG 71 'Richthofen'* at Wittmund; *JG 72 'Westfalen'*, currently at Rhein-Hopsten but due to move to Laage near Rostock; the new *JG 73* (due to re-form during 1994 to replace the former *JaboG 35*), which is scheduled to move from Pferdsfeld to Falkenberg and operate alongside MiG-29 'Fulcrums', its former foes from the East; and *JG 74 'Mölders'* at Neuberg/Donan. The first production examples were re-issued fresh from re-work at MBB Manching (home for the test F-4F, 3715, flown by *Wehrtechnische Dienststelle für Luftfahrzeuge*, WTD 61) and the *Luftwaffe*'s general maintenance facility at Jever, in April 1992. The programme will be completed by 1996, providing sufficient overlap until the EFA (European Fighter Aircraft) is ready for operations.

The not dissimilar Japanese *Kai* effort, first test-flown on 17 July 1984 (aboard F-4EJ 07-8431) is also being applied to 96 machines and includes the substitution of the now unreliable APQ-120 with the company's lightweight AN/APG-66J (as originally designed for the F-16), along with the domestically produced APR-4 RWR, INS and HUD and a new central computer, plus the capability to carry Mitsubishi AAM-3 air-to-air and ASM-1C anti-ship missiles. Refurbished to extend their fatigue lives by 2,000 hours to keep them viable for a further fifteen years of front-line duty, the aircraft are in the process of being issued to three *Hikotai*: the 301st *Shirokuno Gama* (*Frogs*) stationed at Hyakuri, the 302nd *Ojiro Washi* (*Mountain Eagles*) at Naha, Okinawa, and the 306th *Inu Washi* (*Golden Eagles*) at Komatsu. The aircraft currently employ AIM-7F Sparrows for air-defence duties in the Western, South-Western and Central sectors, but the adoption of newer American missiles like AMRAAM is likely before the last of this 'hard wing' breed—the only such F-4Es serving worldwide—finally succumb to age and obsolescence, with 5,000 hours on their clocks. In common with the German Phantoms, the fleet has led a relatively tame existence, with none firing a single shot in anger—yet!

Left, upper: A dozen F-4Fs make up this impressive formation to celebrate *Jagdgeschwader 74 'Mölders'* 25th anniversary on 27 September 1986. (Christian Gerard)

Left, lower: F-4EJ 67-8379 from the 306th *Hikotai*, the *Golden Eagles*, based at Komatsu, is one of eighty Japanese Phantoms which had been upgraded under the *Kai* programme at the time of writing, with twenty more aircraft due to follow. The machines have been re-equipped with the AN/APG-66J digital radar, J/APR-4 RWR (note the twin antennae on the trailing edge of the fin-cap) and provision for AIM-9Ls and AIM-7Fs together with the new Mitsubishi AAM-3 air-to-air heat-seeking and ASM-1C anti-ship missiles. Most of the aircraft retained the original US Navy-style colour scheme of 'eggshell' Gull Gray over gloss white when this photograph was taken in May 1990, although recent re-works have been appearing in subdued, darker matt grey finishes. (Via Tim Laming)

PART III:
SPECIAL ASSIGNMENTS

14. SAM-BUSTERS

One of the most dangerous undertakings performed by Phantom crews was what is known today as SEAD (suppression of enemy air defences)—taking the anti-aircraft war about-face and back right down the throat of the opposition. While military aircraft have been engaged in pounding flak batteries for decades, the advent of the tiered, co-ordinated air defence system packing GCI fighter control, command-guided SAMs and computer-directed AAA which derived their target data from a 'netted' multiplex of radars, dictated the development of a specific counter-force. The lesson was brought home during the Vietnam War on 24 July 1965, when the first three of what would eventually total 9,058 SAMs were fired against marauding American jets. The SAM's début was particularly unpleasant: Ubon-based F-4C 63-7599 and its 'TDY-ing' crew from the 47th TFS were blown out the sky by the mortifying orange-brown eruptions of three SA-2 'Guidelines', while two of the hapless victim's wing-men sustained extensive battle damage. By the end of the year 194 SAMs had been fired, claiming ten more US aircraft.

The United States reacted swiftly to the first loss. Strikes were mounted against the offending site two days later, using a package of 46 'Thuds' toting M118s and M117s to obliterate it. However, by that summer there were already thirty such combat-ready installations—'Fan Song' radars ringed by up to six fixed SA-2 launchers apiece—dotted around the inner sanctuaries in Route Pack VI. And a plentiful supply of missiles and radar hardware kept rolling off the Russian ships at Haiphong, out of bounds to USN crews covering that sector (who had the tricky job of interdicting supplies in the barges cruising between ship and shore), to replenish attrition. If American jets spent all their time knocking out these installations, there would be none left to strike the primary targets. Looking at the statistics in a cold-blooded fashion, it was clear that the North Vietnamese could train missile and radar operators in *their* task much more quickly than the Americans could train volunteer air crews for tours of duty. This was exactly what the enemy intended—to keep the US busy knocking out anti-air defences instead of their main targets, and forcing Phantom and 'Thud' drivers to take immediate evasive manoeuvres and jettison their stores at the sight of a smoky acid launch. This trial of nerves was the origins of the so-called 'cat and mouse' game, which in reality bore more resemblance to a 'mongoose and cobra' duel (but for the fact that the aviators, with their ever-jocular perspective, perceived themselves to be in some kind of *Tom and Jerry* scenario!).

Early losses ran as high as 14 per cent on occasion and were clearly unacceptable. One of the immediate knock-on effects was the rapid development of electronic countermeasures pods under various Quick Reaction Capability contracts issued to Hughes-Hallicrafters and General Electric, designed to provide RF-spectrum jamming so that the strike crews could go about their business without 'dumping' ordnance at the first 'puff' of a SAM launch. The companies concerned quickly furnished the first of many QRC-160 AN/ALQ-71 and AN/ALQ-87 SAM radar noise-jammers, and the AN/ALQ-72 designed to disrupt the enemy MiG-21's higher-frequency 'Spin Can' systems, the first of which were taken into combat by Phantoms in early 1967. These dictated formation-pattern spacings to create a 'superblob' on the enemy's radars, so that missiles fired at a Flight passed between the individual aircraft, without (it was hoped) doing any damage. Confusing and confounding the early-warning devices at the beginning, to mask ingress/egress routes, was the job of the EB-66C Destroyers which attempted to keep the NVN operators guessing by means of sector-whiting barrage noise-jamming 'at arm's length'. However, the jammers did not prove wholly satisfactory: MiGs were sometimes vectored towards Flights simply to break them apart, in turn permitting the SAMs to ravage the easily located stragglers (and, on occasion, the MiGs!). The Destroyers, also, had to be progressively withdrawn. One of these 'silver bullets' was shot down by a SAM on 26 February 1966 and a further example succumbed to a squad of MiGs on 14 January 1968, by which time the limited number of aircraft concerned were primarily engaged in stand-off electronic reconnaissance (elint). The Phantom jockeys and their 'Thud' colleagues would very soon be obliged to fight their own electronic warfare battles. But, first and foremost, they needed to be alerted to the threats—something which the vulnerable 'EBs' and 'RBs' had previously done for them over the radio.

Arriving concurrently with the ECM pods were freshly re-serviced F-4Cs featuring the Itek Applied Technology AN/APR-25 RHAWS and allied AN/APR-26 launch warning receiver (LWR), which finally made use of the redundant radome blister and added new antennae

Part-title photograph: Decorative changes ensued when semi-gloss 'Hill Gray II' began to adorn the 'Weasel' fleet in 1987. This beast from the 563rd TFS *Aces* totes a combat armoury of Shrikes and CBUs during 'Green Flag' war games over Tonopah, Nevada. (USAF)
Above: Three dozen F-4Cs were adapted to the 'Wild Weasel IV' configuration between 1966 and 1969, incorporating special ER-142 receivers to back up the standard kit of RHAWS and LWR. The first examples equipped Nellis's 'Willie Weasel College', these grouping under the 66th FWS from September 1971. The unit specialized in training, and the RTU function would pass to George AFB in July 1975. (USAF/MSgt Frank Rolling)

to the trailing edge of the fin-cap for all-round coverage. The RHAWS and LWR became standard items on board the F-4C (being retrofitted to all survivors under TO 1F-4C-548), with the former providing a compass-rose perspective of the threats on a small crystal video screen, presented as green strobe lines whose intensity and direction indicated proximity and azimuth and the latter furnishing a bank of rectangular lamps which lit up to highlight imminent attack by 'Fire Can', 'Fan Song' or MiGs.[1]

Owing to the ferocity of the enveloping SAM and radar network—SAM launches would double to 1,096 in 1966, and exponentially to 3,202 sightings the following year—ever more sophisticated countermeasures were required. While the US aircraft were far from being 'SAM magnets', something was required which could bite back, to take the fight to the enemy and intimidate him into 'shutting up shop', without drawing on massive strike reserves to overwhelm each and every threat. Brig-Gen K. C. Dempster's 'Blue Ribbon' Task Force in Washington, which had instigated the development of RHAWS and QRC ECM work following its initial August 1965 seminar, also recommended the immediate fielding of a vanguard that would plunge headlong into the enemy radar defences and 'take them out'. The codename for the new force was 'Wild Weasel', adopted with some affection from the small mustelid which is so adept at sniffing out and destroying vermin. Crews' initial reaction to this concept was 'You've Gotta Be Sh—— Me!', and the abbreviation 'YGBSM!' became their trademark from then on, worn with pride on shoulder patches and reproduced on other 'Weasel' memorabilia. New, specialist RHAWS would act as 'sniffers' with which to ferret out the sites, which could then be knocked out using a combination of area weapons such as CBUs and the Navy's AGM-45 Shrike radar-homing missile.[2]

A stop-gap force of half a dozen twin-seat F-100F Super Sabres, with a pilot to fly the aircraft and a 'bear' in the back to

---

[1] The F-4D received a similar 'kit' built by Bendix, designated AN/APS-107A. The latter, installed from Block 30 (66-7505) onwards and retrofitted to earlier aircraft under TO 1F-4D-512, offered improved sensitivity but exhibited numerous technical problems which were not fully resolved until the system went digital in its definitive APS-107E configuration. Even the F-4's LWR function all but fell out of favour, despite the fact that the displays were retained pending updates. The Bendix package was eventually superseded by the superior ATI AN/ALR-69(V)-2 from around 1981, which replaced the 'slick' bulge under the radome fairing with a grotesque, functional cluster of spiral 'button' receivers. The first F-4Es also were delivered 'blind' to begin with, and later added ATI AN/APR-36 and -37 systems derived from the -25/26 series, the basics for which were installed on the production line beginning with F-4E No 68 (66-0351), although the full modification was not completed for several years in some instances. This package was upgraded to digital 'Compass Tie' AN/ALR-46 standard in the mid-1970s, linked to the new generation of Westinghouse AN/ALQ-119 and -131 noise/deception devices featuring selective jamming which responded to individual threats via 'power management', and was revisited yet again around 1980 when it was upgraded to AN/ALR-69 'Compass Sail' standard to improve SAM-launch warning. The digital upgrades replaced the old strobe lines on the video display with alphanumeric symbology, such that a '2' represented an SA-2, a '6' an SA-6, an aircraft symbol a radiating MiG, and so on, whose position in the display relative to the centre indicated the threat's azimuth and range.

[2] The US Navy developed the Shrike after encountering SAM threats for the first time over Cuba. The Service similarly created 'Iron Hand' teams equipped with CBUs and Shrike missiles but concentrated on fitting the radar-receiving apparatus on board attack types like the A-4 and A-6 but not the F-4, which was reserved for the customary BARCAP, MiGCAP etc missions as back-up to its fleet defence role. The US Navy and Air Force rarely liaised in any depth, so the 'mandatory' Phantom-related seminars were probably very productive! Follow-on anti-radiation missile (ARM) development, including the AGM-78 STARM and -88 HARM, were also overseen by the USN. The division, with the USAF taking the lead, came after the Gulf War owing to the latter's confidence in TI's ability to produce the AGM-88C-1, discussed later.

monitor the threats, was hurriedly dispatched to the war zone pending perfection of 'Wild Weasel' variants of the mainstay 'twin-tub' strike jets of the era, the F-105F and Phantom. As things turned out, the Phantom's muddled electronics held it back for nearly four years, and it was the venerable 'Thud'—some sixty of which were later brought up to full F-105G SAM-slaying status—which would bear the brunt of USAF SEAD requirements in South-East Asia, equipped with the 35-mile-range Navy/ General Dynamics Pomona AGM-78A/ B Standard ARM radar-hunting missile.

WILD WEASEL IV

Eager to press ahead with the Phantom/ 'Weasel' concept, the USAF tentatively established two successive classes under the 'Willie Weasel' college at Nellis, Nevada, during 1966—WWIV-A and WWIV-B. The original goal was to furnish a dozen F-4Cs with the basic fit of ATI APR-25 RHAWS and -26 LWR and add a new IR-133 receiver in a 'can' to be carried under the port aft Sparrow missile well. The latter would provide a panoramic display representing a glorified version of the RHAWS compass rose, with data to assist with the 'prioritization' of threats before an att-

ack. However, erratic displays, caused by varying ground voltage potential, meant that there were no aircraft available for dedicated 'Weasel' training, so the inductees spent the best part of a year flying ACM in 'vanilla' F-4Cs over sunny Nellis, perfecting their air-to-air skills instead, and devoted little time to resolving the engineering dilemmas. The programme was subsequently put on 'hold' for a further year and the trainees posted to Col Olds' 'Wolfpack' in Thailand, where it was intended that they could help introduce general tactics to defeat the SAM threat. In fact, of the fourteen men who were posted to Ubon, seven became MiG-killers, three of whom got two apiece. These included the deadly duo Capts Dick M. Pascoe and his EWO Norman E. Wells, who blasted a MiG-21 on 6 January 1967 with a Sparrow (in F-4C 64-0839, call-sign 'Crab One') and then downed a nimble MiG-17 with a Sidewinder on 5 June (in F-4C 63-7647, call-sign 'Chicago One'). These exploits were far removed from 'Weaseling', but the Air Force was not about to complain!

Fully fledged examples of the Phantom 'Weasel'—of which 36 were hurriedly converted from F-4C Blocks 16–

24 beginning in June 1968, once the new equipment problems had been resolved —equipped the 'Willie Weasel' college shortly afterwards. Pilots, usually Captains with around 500 hours on the F-4 and demonstrating a leaning towards the team concept, took to the aircraft with relative ease while co-ordinating their talents with the new back-seat Electronic Warfare Officers. These men, known in the community at that time by the more popular trade-name 'bears', were a specialist breed of WSO who had undergone an additional EW course at Mather AFB, California, where they were instructed in the art of sorting out and locating the real threats amidst a multiplex of signals.[3] At Nellis, once checked-out in a 'vanilla' Phantom, crews were introduced to the new equipment on board one of three specially reconfigured T-39F Sabreliners bristling with direction-finding interferometers and signals-deciphering superheterodynes, one of which mirrored the 'Wild Weasel' kit installed in the few precious 'Wild Weasel IV' aircraft available. This comprised the standard F-4C fit of RHAWS and LWR, plus a new long-range ER-142 direction-finding receiver to replace the IR-133. Its associated panoramic signals display on the right-hand dashboard in the 'pit' of the Phantom could provide extremely accurate azimuth data, with the ability to 'correlate' the threats—the origins of later

computer-assisted 'prioritization', when the real dangers had to be isolated quickly in a dense signals environment. Combined with the chirping and warbling noises received over the headphones, these visual and aural inputs helped the EWO (taking turns at the displays and headphones in the T-39F trainers) to gain an edge on enemy tactics and vector his pilot on to the most hazardous emitter preparatory to an attack.

In the 'real Weasel', chewing the radars to pieces was made possible by two primary weapons systems, the AGM-45A Shrike anti-radiation missile (wired in as a standard feature of the F-4D/E models, which seldom used them, and retrofitted to the F-4C under TO 1F-4C-523), and the ubiquitous CBU, of which there existed several types based on the SUU-30/B canister. 'Weasels' were furnished with the latest types of CBU, containing hundreds of 'fruit salad' bomblets (named after the guava, orange and grapefruit which they resembled in size), any one of which could put a radar dish out of action.

When the third 'Weasel' Phantom class, WWIV-C, graduated in October 1968, the bulk of the trainees found themselves posted to Japan. Initially the F-4C conversions had been distributed amongst the squadrons, but by the end of 1969 they were reconsolidated under the 80th TFS *Headhunters* at Yokota AB, Honshu, Japan. The 347th TFW was

also amongst the first to receive freshly re-worked F-4C war veterans refitted with 'Pacer Wave' electrical connectors, coaxial cables and the updated electronic warfare kit, beginning on 6 March 1969. With their new electronic warfare specialists filling the 'lean-to' rear-seat Martin-Baker positions, the unit spent two years working up to a full complement of two dozen F-4Cs, including fourteen of the freshly adapted 'Weasel' model, before the SEAD contingent was reassigned during April 1971 to form the

---

[3] Some claim that the term 'bear' originated during the Vietnam War as an abbreviation of 'back-seat ears', but the explanation which seems to be gaining greater favour alludes to the rear cockpit of the Phantom being a 'pit'—hence 'bear pit' and 'bear'. Back-seat 'wizzos' (Weapons Systems Officers) and EWOs are widely known also as 'pitters'. The term 'bear' lapsed from use after the last of the former 'Thud Weasel' EWOs left the community in about 1984.

nucleus of the 67th TFS *Fighting Cocks* at Kadena AB, Okinawa. The next spring and summer served as a launch pad when two separate deployments were made to troubled South Korea. Nosing out of Kunsan AB permitted the crews to check out their new gear passively against the communists' 'Fan Song' and GCI/EWR training radar arrays dotted north of the 'buffer zone', placing them in reasonably good stead for combat. With the 'Linebacker' offensives over North

Below: Perhaps the best known of all 67th TFS F-4C 'Weasels' was 63-7470, named *Rub-a-Dub-Dub, Two Men in a Tub*. The photo was taken in February 1973, just before the machine returned to Kadena. (Larsen/Remington via Richard L. Ward)

Vietnam gearing up to a crescendo, a half dozen machines were dispatched to Korat RTAFB, Thailand, on 23 September, these staying in place until 18 February 1973.

Routine combat stores included wing drop tanks, a pair of Sparrows, an AN/ALQ-87 noise jamming pod and a pair of Shrikes, plus either a centreline tank or an MER rack toting four CBUs—'not that the aircraft mixed it up much,' according to one former EWO. The big drawback of the 'Wild Weasel IV' package was that the aircraft possessed no ranging capability: the APR-25 and ER-142 provided only target bearing, on to which the EWO would vector the pilot. This meant that if crews did not respond

quickly, they would all too soon find themselves overflying the enemy SAM complex and acting as 'clay pigeons' to lure the SAMs away from the strike package—a definitely suicidal tactic! So instead crews tended to fire off a Shrike at the earliest opportunity, either in level flight, or in a 'loft' manoeuvre to maximize missile range, before breaking off. Israeli 'over-the-shoulder' tactics, when crews fired missiles just prior to rolling out wings-level in 'pretend' dive–toss attacks, were a little too adventurous!

The missile, which possessed a maximum range of around ten miles, would guide only for as long as the enemy radar operators stayed on the air, after which

time it would 'go ballistic'. This resulted in very few kills, but it did oblige the enemy to revert to 'dummy' standby mode for fear of being 'zapped' by a Shrike, often long enough for friendly strike aircraft to get to and from their targets. In all, the 67th TFS flew 460 combat missions and incurred no losses, lobbing their Shrikes against sites dotted around North Vietnam and the treacherous passes straddling Laos.[4] By the time the second deployment had ceased operations on 2 May 1975 the Phantom Weasel concept had been proved and aircraft wore flamboyant red trim on canopy rails, stabilators, fin, pylon and tank tips (including the now famous 'YGBSM!' logos on the nose-gear doors)

plus artwork reflecting the alleged insanity of the mission—being 'first in and last out' over the target and attempting to destroy systems specifically designed to shoot them down! Among the classics were *Brain Damage*; *Rub-a-Dub-Dub, Two Men in a Tub*; *Jail Bait*; and *Squirrelly Bird*. Above all else, the entire 'Weasel' (and Navy 'Iron Hand') programme had been an unequivocal success: initial casualties to SAMs during 1965, which had afflicted a 5.7 per cent loss rate, had fallen to 0.9 per cent during the closing stages of 'Rolling Thunder' and rose only to 1.15 per cent during 'Linebacker', despite the density and sophistication of the new Sino-Soviet-supplied arrays which had had nigh on four years to reconstruct.

The establishment of a 'Wild Weasel' squadron at the new 'cutting edge' of West Germany, to provide first-line SEAD for USAFE, involved an equally convoluted 'bedding down' process. The 81st TFS *Panthers* at Hahn AB converted to F-4Cs from May 1969 and added a dozen 'Weasel' Phantoms to its ranks that December before being subsequently detached and then transferred to 86th TFW control at Zweibrücken and, thence, a further eighteen months later on 15 January 1973 (when the parent Wing shifted to Ramstein as part of Operation 'Battle Creek'), to 52nd TFW control at Spangdahlem. Both the 81st and 67th TFSs would remain in place at 'Spang' and Kadena for a further six and a half years, flying the same odd-job collection of radar-sniffing apparatus that evolved to include the Vietnam-era kit

and newer, digitally enhanced AN/ALR-46 and -53 receivers (replacing the APR-25/26 and ER-142, respectively).[5] These substituted the strobe lines with alphanumeric symbology and expanded frequency-coverage but still offered no ranging capability. Moreover, the primary weapon system still comprised the TI AGM-45A, of which there existed eight prinicipal seeker-head variations to cater for emerging, different threats. An experiment by Project Officer Capt Jack R. Suggs was conducted using ADU-315 dual launchers (comprising two LAU-34 launchers bolted together) to increase the payload to four missiles alongside wing tanks, but problems with stores vibration and drag soon put paid to that idea.[6]

Back in the States, during July 1975 the 'Willie Weasel' college shifted from Nellis TFWC to George AFB in the Mojave Desert, later coalescing under the 39th TFTS *Cobras*. Realistic training in a peacetime Air Force presented several challenges in the years before integrated EW ranges were established at Tonopah, Nevada, and Polygone in Europe. EWO Maj Gerald 'Jerry' Stiles USAF Ret, who converted to the Phantom at George preparatory to a USAFE assignment, explained some of the 'sophisticated' early training 'systems': 'Noise jamming on the radio. Most of our missions out of George AFB were conducted on the Nellis AFB practice ranges which had a lot of fixed, simulated radars and radar signals. Whenever we operated on this range we had to be in radio contact with the ground, and by pre-

---

[4] Detachment One of the 414th FWS had already sent two aircraft from Nellis to Udorn RTAFB, Thailand, in the spring of 1971, for Pave Fire II trials. Two additional aircraft (possibly 65-0657 and -0660), which were fitted with both the Bendix AN/APS-107 RHAWS and ER-142 panoramic receivers, may have also entered the fray interfaced with the stand-off, 35-mile-range AGM-78B Standard ARM missile (unavailable to the F-4Cww), for field trials during the numerous 'Protective Reaction' strikes conducted against North Vietnam during 1971. Unfortunately the relevant reports remain classified, and no photographs—the hard evidence—seem to exist to support this contention.

[5] These updates, performed concurrently with the

mid-1970s F-4E and RF-4C switch to integrated 'Compass Tie' ATI AN/ALR-46 receivers featuring CW radar reception (described in Note 1, above), effectively replaced the terms 'RHAWS' and 'LWR' with the collective acronym 'RWR', standing for radar warning receiver. The latter became a standard term in everyday parlance, although papers and manuals still referred to RHAWS, LWR etc for many years.

[6] F-105G 'Thud Weasels' encountered similar problems in drag and payload 'buzz'. Curiously, the only two aircraft types to use the ADU-315 with any degree of success came from either end of the SEAD spectrum—USN A-4 'Scooters' and giant RAF 'Black Buck' Vulcans. The latter employed the system during the Falklands War.

arranged agreement the ground provided noise-jamming. Well, jamming may hardly be the word, because it consisted of someone holding open a microphone on the frequency we were working and whistling, humming, singing or doing something equally irritating! It was crude, but it worked. We had to learn how to work around or avoid this distraction. In Europe there weren't any good ranges to practise on which contained a good assortment of "enemy" radars. In fact, one of our best ranges was in Merry Olde on the Spadeadam complex on the border of Scotland. It was disadvantageous in that each and every one of these emitted from the same small piece of real estate, much unlike the real world. After about your second or third time on the range you knew exactly where the radars were and the challenge of finding the target diminished rapidly. In the real world, one would hardly expect the foe to concentrate his radar systems at one spot and then put a big white radome on them!'

As for the controls, there was little standardization between the aircraft. 'On some aircraft, for instance, the airspeed indicator would be in one location on the panel and in a different location on others. Many of the switches and controls would be moved about and on some aircraft were missing entirely. Nothing is quite as disconcerting as to reach for a control, especially in a time-compressed environment, only to find that it is not in the expected location.'

The F-4C Weasels soldiered on in this capacity at all three bases until ousted by the vastly superior F-4G 'Advanced Wild Weasel V'. The last unit to relinquish the F-4C was the 81st TFS, whose final example left Spangdahlem on 26 July 1979. Most of the aircraft passed to the Indiana ANG at Hulman and Baer Fields, where they were operated as pure strike machines before being either relegated to the scrap heap or found a temporarily extended lease of life with Flight Systems Inc at Mojave, California, as trials platforms. There was talk of some 'weaseling' in prospect, and 63-7481 flew from Indiana with a shark's-mouth design and aluminium coloured gear legs (unique for the F-4C), plus fully

functioning 'sniffing' apparatus for the mission, but no Shrikes were issued.

ADVANCED WILD WEASEL

Development of the F-4C's successor was initiated as early as 1968, and later was fuelled by the same degree of urgency as that enjoyed by its predecessor. Israel's losses during the Yom Kippur War in the autumn of 1973, which included 33 F-4Es felled by radar-directed SAMs and AAA (excluding four to unknown causes), served as the primary catalyst. The Sinai had effectively served as FOT&E for many new systems after the cessation of hostilties in South-East Asia, and the US defence establishment was shocked to discover that their top-

Right, upper: USAFE got into the F-4C 'Weasel' business in December 1969 when the 81st TFS received its first examples while under the 50th TFW at Hahn. The Squadron was shifted to 86th TFW control at Zweibrücken in July 1971 and thence, on 15 January 1973, to the 52md TFW at Spangdahlem AB, Germany. The *Panthers* would continue to specialize in operating Phantoms in the SEAD mission for a further two decades! (A. Molton via Ben Knowles)

Right, lower: Shark-mouthed F-4C 'Weasel' 63-0481 served out its last few years with the Indiana ANG at Fort Wayne, whose aircraft retained their 'sniffing' apparatus but were not employed in the SEAD role. (Authors' collection)

of-the-line electronic warfare equipment had performed so badly. Many Phantoms tumbled to the SA-6 'Gainful' missile which guided home using CW illumination from the 'Straight Flush' tracking radar, not via 'join-the-dots' command guidance. 'Straight Flush' was effectively invisible to the existing RWR kit and immune to jamming. The mobility of this new SAM battery, carried in threes on tracked armoured vehicles, was particularly irksome, as was the devastating firepower of the completely self-contained caterpillar ZSU-23/4 AAA flak battery. Both these new threats created a need for 'real time' target assessment as well as new countermeasures. Israeli crews had already been

making noises about the more primitive SA-3 system during the War of Attrition three years previously. Obviously, the Soviets and their Arab allies had been keeping these cards close to their chests for well over a year and the US was taken completely by surprise.

The quintessential impetus for the 'Advanced Wild Weasel V' was the rationale that 'If it could happen to them, it could happen to us'. In fact, the programme had already been simmering away on the back boiler for three years, and just needed a push. Two Block 30 F-4Ds (66-7635 and -7647) were converted for trials with the new McDonnell Douglas/IBM AN/APR-38A homing and warning computer (HAWC) and

were test-flown at Edwards AFFTC, California, under the management of former 'Willie Weasel' instructor Lt-Col Frank O'Donnell—the start of what was envisaged to encompass ninety F-4D conversions. Maj 'Jerry' Stiles, who at the time was serving in the Pentagon between flying assignments to help push the project along administratively and politically, described the initial objective: 'To conduct, essentially, a "smoke test" on the newly developed configuration. It was called a "smoke test" because, for all practical purposes, in order to conform to a DoD-mandated schedule, we had to initially test-fly the configuration by a certain date. Our goal was thus to cram the equipment into the F-4D, get it airborne and hope that nothing caught fire —no smoke. We did, and it didn't, so we called the test successful and declared the milestone was met!' Problems abounded with the power systems, while the central computer (then with only a 32K memory) rapidly became filled up and could not digest any more software. A 64K system was substituted, and the far-off war in the Middle East saved the programme. 'The big bosses in charge of the monies decided that the new Weasel was a "must" regardless of cost and schedules. It was concurrent with this new idea that I came up with: as long as we were going to spend time and money, why not put the advanced equipment in a newer airframe, namely the F-4E?'

Left, upper: PDM tear-downs were performed on all Phantoms once every two years during the early part of the programme, with PACAF and AAC (Alaskan Air Command) aircraft routed through Air Asia's facility in Tainan, Taiwan. This 67th TFS F-4C 'Weasel' has had its gizzards inspected and refurbished and awaits its wing assembly prior to the final touch-up top-coat of paint. (Ken Mackintosh)

Left, lower: A handful of ex-'Weasels' spent their last hours with Tracor Flight Systems Inc at Mojave. This example sports the bolt-on AAR probe which enabled it to refuel from hose/drogue baskets too, a feature employed originally by the *Heyl Ha'Avir* and also adopted more recently by nine remaining RF-4Cs flown by the Spanish *Ejercito del Aire Español* at Torrejon, near Madrid. (Frank B. Mormillo)

Right: F-4D-30-MC 66-7635 was one of two 'Deltas' adapted to the 'Advanced Wild Weasel V' standard with the AN/APR-38A HAWC. When the decision was made to adapt the F-4E LES to the task instead, '7635 passed to General Dynamics where it undertook trials with the Westinghouse AN/APG-66 Air Combat Fighter radar—the primary system employed by the F-16 and since adopted by Japan for its F-4EJ *Kai* upgrade. (Westinghouse)

The idea was soon adopted. The F-4D test-beds had been stuffed to the brim with the new equipment, including the almost inaccessible dead space between the engines which would have been a nightmare to service in the field, whereas the F-4E—newer, bigger, and with the safety bonus of LES slats—offered the capacity for the new equipment. By early 1975 the equipment was shaping up also. Maj Stiles recalled the only two remaining obstacles he wished to push aside: the pilots' trauma associated with the removal of the beloved 20mm gun to house the forward receivers, and the aircraft's designation.

'We studied the problem in depth and there was no other viable solution. The sensitive antennas had to be mounted in an assembly on or near the nose. No other place would do. Some suggested the wing-tips, but vibrations there caused inaccuracies; some suggested under the fuselage, but this limited signal reception. We looked into placing the antenna configuration in a bump below the gun lip, but the instantaneous vibrations from firing the guns precluded that. We even looked into placing the antenna complex above the nose radome, but this caused problems for the pilot in seeing ahead. We had to either remove the gun or remove the radar, but no one wanted to do the latter—it would limit the "Weasel" to visual conditions only. The gun had to go.' Apparently, a MiG-killer General at the conference stood up and protested, until he was told to 'sit down and shut up' by a presiding Four-Star! As for the designation, converting the F-4E into the 'Advanced Wild Weasel' configuration was tantamount to a 'sex change', and it needed a new suffix for the separate maintenance and technical paperwork. The USAF 'brass' rejected 'Jerry' Stiles' idea that the new 'Weasel' be designated F-4W, in recognition of its

role, and insisted instead on the designation F-4G. This was coincident with the F-105G 'Weasel Thud' then in service, despite the fact that it had already been used by a dozen US Navy aircraft in 1965–66 engaged in automatic carrier landing trials. 'Although this USN designation was now defunct, I half-jokingly suggested that some day, some giant computer with a long memory would try and land the Wild Weasel on an aircraft carrier. I lost the argument, but still suspect that some day . . . !'

The first (69-7254) of what would eventually amount to 134 F-4G conversions was rigged with the AN/APR-38A at St Louis and test-flown on 6 December 1975. It was an immediate success, and differed little in terms of handling from the well-established F-4E LES except in one minor regard: 'The nose on the F-4G is heavier, so has a tendency to bleed off airspeed faster "uphill" and accelerate faster "downhill".' The newly perfected black boxes and automated processor and interactive alphanumeric displays—including a huge PPI just left of centre on the new expanded wall of rear instruments, plus related panoramic and homing indicators to the right—worked like a dream. The system would 'prioritize' the threats based on the library programmed into the HAWC, and flash up five, ten or fifteen at a time as alphanumeric symbols on the PPI, depending on the intensity of the 'electronic thicket' into which the F-4G was flying and the EWO's preferences in terms of 'task saturation'. One of these would be singled out as the most dangerous by the HAWC and be highlighted by a triangular surround. If the EWO

objected to the computer's automatic choice, based on data he was receiving on the headphones and that flashed up on the panoramic and homing indicators (providing such detailed esoteric information as pulse-repetition rates, frequencies and so on) he could override the choice by inching the diamond cursor on to the preferred threat symbol. Once positoned, all relevant data on the hostile emitter—including precise range and bearing triangulated by the APR-38A's myriad antennae—could be 'handed off' to an AGM-78D Standard ARM missile via a navigational coupler unit interface, ready for launch. This was simply accomplished using a button located on the lower left-hand side of the EWO's main instrument panel. Threat-monitoring on the PPI could be conducted at ranges of up to 200 miles, at various selectable range increments, providing plenty of scope for stand-off or close-in 'weaseling'.

The Standard ARM, which had an effective range of up to 35 miles (even when fired off-axis from the target), still required the hostile emitter to remain on the air to ensure a kill, so typically might be given a different priority as the 'Weasel' closed in and the EWO stumbled across newer, more important threats. 'The F-4G effort was a well thought out modification which resulted in a good cockpit'. The 'prioritized' threat would also be repeated on the pilot's modified LCOSS gun sight, providing what was known during development as a 'pseudo blind bombing capability', but was especially useful for conducting surprise bombing manoeuvres through cloud, or amidst rain and general murk. Once the aircraft was vectored towards the target, the red reticle served to highlight the radar's position and would slide into view. By lining this up with a green cross in the centre of the gun sight (which was slaved to radar for 'dive–toss'), given suitable assistance from the 'rear office', and pickling the bomb load, the 'Weasel' could deposit area weapons like CBUs with a high probability of at least holing the enemy emitter and thus rendering its SAMs impotent. Shrike, Maverick and

the GBU-15 glide bomb were also soon made available, opening up the options, and in service the F-4Gs would frequently be flown with all manner of asymmetric stores configurations. With this potential, it is hardly surprising that even today, eighteen years after the new 'Weasel' first took to the air, it is still widely regarded as the most potent SEAD aircraft in the world.

HIGH DESERT BASE

Product Support Engineer John J. 'Mr Maintenance' Harty, who worked on Phantoms for 28 of his 36 years at McAir ('I was completely fascinated with what McDonnell was doing') and who rose through the ranks from Airman to Lieutenant-Colonel within the 131st TFW, Missouri ANG, just across the ramp at Lambert Field, recalled that, when it came to developing the F-4G, 'We handled the programme just as if it were a new aircraft'. Machines selected for conversion were drawn from production FY69 Blocks 42–45, built during 1970, twenty-one of which had previously been on loan to the Royal Australian Air Force under Project 'Peace Reef' and eight to Iran during the start-up of 'Peace Roll'.[7] McAir built the prototype plus the 'trial installation' aircraft (69-7263) before handing over the process to Ogden Logistics Center at Hill AFB, Utah, which began its production

Left: A captivating study of the F-4G testbed, 69-7254, taken against a snowy backdrop next to Ogden Logistics Center, Utah. The aircraft first flew in this configuration on 6 December 1975, with the No 1 HAWC kit installed by McAir, which served as Program Manager for the trials. The aircraft was taken into Ogden during May 1978 to receive a scheduled refit including the 'all-up' HAWC configuration. Kit No 27 was installed and the aircraft was redelivered to George AFB on 7 January 1979. (Brian C. Rogers)

[7] The RAAF received two dozen F-4Es straight from the McAir lines on loan from the US pending the arrival of its much-delayed F-111Cs. Delivery commenced on 14 September 1970 and aircraft were distributed between Nos 1 and 6 Squadrons at RAAF Amberley, near Brisbane. All but one (69-7203, which was written off at Evans Head Ridge on 16 June 1971) were returned between 25 October 1972 and the following June, ferried home by 388th TFW crews. The serials were 69-304 to -0307, 69-7201 to -7217 and 69-7219, -7220 and -7224. All but the write-off and aircraft 69-0305 and -0307 were converted to F-4G standard under the initial batch in 1976–81; and the latter two were re-worked during the second F-4G conversion run in 1987. Aircraft 69-0246, -0254, -0263, -0265, -0275, -0277, -0283 and -0285 were the eight F-4Es leased to the pre-revolutionary Imperial Iranian Air Force; all of these were subsequently converted to F-4G standard during the first batch.

TABLE 21: 'WILD WEASEL' PHANTOMS

Bk Serial no Remarks

F-4C Block 16–20/22–24-MC Wild Weasel IV (complete F-4Cww batch, 1966–69):

Bk	Serial no	Remarks
16	63-7423	
	-7433	
	-7437	
	-7440	
17	-7443	
	-7447	
	-7452	
	-7459	
	-7462	
	-7467	
18	-7470	
	-7474	
	-7478	
	-7481	W/o 03/03/82; Indiana ANG
	-7508	
	-7512	
	-7513	
19	-7564	N422FS[1]
	-7565	
	-7567	N402FS[1]; pres. Travis AFB
	-7574	
	-7594	
	-7596	
20	-7607	N423FS[1]
	-7615	
22	64-0675	
23	-0741	N403FS[1]
	-0757	
	-0781	
	-0787	
	-0790	
	-0791	
	-0815	
24	-0840	
	-0844	
	-0847	

F-4D Block 30-MC Advanced Wild Weasel V test-beds:

Bk	Serial no	Remarks
30	66-7635	Later a GD radar test-bed

Serial no	Remarks
-7647	Decomm. and re-assigned to 31 TFW

F-4G Block 42–45-MC Advanced Wild Weasel V (initial batch of 116 conversions, 1976–81):

Bk	Serial no	Remarks
42	69-0236[2]	
	-0237	
	-0238	
	-0239	First op del 28/04/78
	-0240	W/o 16/06/82; 'SP'
	-0241	4 kills[3]
	-0242	3 kills[3]
	-0243	
	-0245	3 kills[3]
	-0246[4]	
	-0247	
	-0248	8 kills[3]
	-0250	12 kills[3]
	-0251	
	-0252	W/o 08/11/82; 'SP'
	-0253	6 kills[3]
	-0254[4]	
	-0255	
	-0257	W/o 01/06/81; 'WW'
	-0258	
	-0259	
	-0261	
	-0263[4]	
	-0265[4]	
	-0267	
	-0269	
	-0270	
	-0271	W/o 08/01/81; 'WW'
	-0272	
	-0273	
	-0274	
	-0275[4]	
	-0277[4]	Det 5 TAWC
	-0279	
	-0280	W/o 23/05/84; 'SP'
	-0281	
	-0283[4]	W/o 12/01/81; 'PN'
	-0284	
	-0285[4]	
	-0286	8 kills[3]
	-0292	
	-0293	
	-0297	
43	-0304[5]	
	-0306[5]	
	-7201[5]	
	-7202[5]	2 kills[3]
	-7204[5]	
	-7205[5]	W/o 29/03/80; 'WW'
	-7206[5]	Det 5 TAWC
	-7207[5]	
	-7208[5]	
	-7209[5]	
	-7210[5]	3 kills[3]
	-7211[5]	
	-7212[5]	5 kills[3]
	-7213[5]	First w/o 13/03/80; 'SP'
	-7214[5]	
	-7216[5]	
	-7217[5]	
	-7218[2]	
	-7219[5]	W/o 21/11/86
	-7220[5]	
	-7223	W/o 01/06/84; 'WW'
	-7228	
	-7231	
	-7232	8 kills[3]
	-7233	
	-7234[5]	
	-7235	Det 5 TAWC
	-7236	W/o 21/08/89; 'SP'. To be Spang gate guard.
	-7251	
	-7253	W/o 06/07/81; 'WW'
	-7254	Prototype
	-7256	3 kills[3]
	-7257	
	-7258	
	-7259	W/o 18/03/80; 'WW'
	-7260	
44	-7262	3 kills[3]
	-7263	First production a/c
	-7268	Last prod a/c in first batch; 3 kills[3]
	-7270	
	-7272	
	-7286	6 kills[3]
	-7287	
	-7288	
	-7289	
	-7290	First Ogden a/c
	-7291	
	-7293	6 kills[3]
	-7295	
	-7298	
	-7300	
	-7301	
	-7302	
	-7303	
	-7546	
	-7550	
	-7556	6 kills[3]
	-7558	
	-7560	
	-7561	
	-7566	
	-7571	W/o 90/01/91; 'SP' (Gulf)
	-7572	
	-7574	
45	-7579	4 kills[3]
	-7580	
	-7581	
	-7582	
	-7583[2]	
	-7584	W/o 17/12/80; 'WW'
	-7586	W/o 01/06/82; 'WW'
	-7587	5 kills[3]
	-7588	W/o 06/11/85; 'WW'

F-4G Block 42–45-MC Advanced Wild Weasel V (follow-on batch of 18 conversions, 1987–88):

Bk	Serial no	Remarks
42	69-0244	
	-0249	
	-0260	
	-0264	
	-0278	4 kills[3]
	-0290[2]	
	-0291	
	-0298	
	-0303	
43	-0305[5]	First del 12/06/87; 'WW'
	-0307[5]	
	-7252	
44	-7261	
	-7267	6 kills[3]
	-7294	
	-7297	
	-7551	
	-7557	

NOTES

[1] Civil serials indicate subsequent use by Flight Systems Inc at Mojave, California.

[2] First batch to AMARC 25/02/91, all former 90 TFS aircraft.

[3] 81 TFS aircraft, with 'kills' scored in strikes on Iraqi radar (see Table 22).

[4] Former 'Peace Roll' leases to Iran.

[5] Former 'Peace Reef' leases to Australia.

The first F-4G lost was 69-7213, which crashed on Mt Moncayo, 36 miles west of Zaragosa, en route to the Bardenas Reales weapons range on 13 March 1980. Three F-4G losses—those on 19/03/90 ('PN', near Chongu, South Korea, during a 'Team Spririt 90' exercise), on 21/08/91 ('SP', in the Arabian Peninsula) and on 15/05/93 (a Tracor Flight Systems civilian operated example which crashed 65 miles west of Las Vegas)—were not attributed to specific serials at the time of writing.

linc with the 'kit proof' aircraft (69-7290), under McAir supervision.[8] All three initial aircraft were used for some time in an FOT&E test capacity. John Harty recalled the hectic schedule when he was dashing back and forth between Salt Lake City and St Louis: 'There were over 100 special retrofit drawings and 250-plus pages of data prepared by my group to describe this mod, making it one of the largest ever accomplished on the USAF F-4 series. I personally had three of my retrofit people working two shifts to work out the problems in the drawings and data.' The actual conversion process took an average of 14,420 man-hours per aircraft spread out over 110 days, encapsulating 3,100 line items grouped into 161 assembly packs. In addition to the new 'Weasel' tail 'torpedo' and nasal proboscis, computers, wiring and displays, the aircraft also received provisions for an F-15 fuel tank, expanding centreline 'full bag' limits up to 6g, a feature later applied to all USAF Phantoms (except the C model) and *Luftwaffe* Phantoms under TO 1F-4-1308. It gave the 'Weasel' its much needed 'popping' capability near the lethal target, when heavily laden pairs of the aircraft would porpoise up and down in the vicinity of the emitter, preparing to 'zap' it.

April 28, 1978, marked the beginning of a new era when the first true production F-4G (69-0239) thundered into George AFB, the new 'Home of the Wild Weasels', located fifty miles west of Los Angeles near Victorville, California. At the helm was 35th TFW boss Col Dudley J. Foster, with his 'pitter' Capt Dennis B. Haney. With USAF 'top brass' in attendance, the aircraft was officially handed over to the 39th TFTS *Cobras* for

crew transition training, to be followed by further F-4Gs at a steady flow of about three aircraft a month from Ogden.

United States Air Forces Europe underwent transition to the new 'Weasel' variant soon afterwards. The first to cross the Atlantic was 69-0273, piloted by Lt-Col 'Duke' Green, Commander of the 81st TFS *Panthers*, and EWO Capt Mike Freeman, and it touched down to a welcoming reception on 28 March 1979. In the meantime, the Philippines-based 3rd TFW had also started to equip with a dozen 'Weasels', operated alongside the 'vanilla' F-4Es of the 90th TFS *Pair-O-Dice*, after officially receiving 69-0275 and -0279 at Ogden on 30 July. The first batch of six shark-mouthed F-4Gs to complete the 'TransPac' arrived in late August.

By the time the 116th and last machine from the initial batch was handed over in June the summer of 1981, the crew training programme was nearing its zenith. New arrivals assigned to the 562nd TFTS *Weasels* rigorous syllabus were typically experienced pilots and navigators to begin with, but as the programme matured crews came straight from LIFT (Lead-In Fighter Training) or EWO classes from Mather AFB, California, before going on to be subjected to additional academics and flying split into

two phases, the first introducing them to the 'stock' F-4E Phantoms at the base and the second to the expensive 'Weasel' models. The full 'new guy' course, F4GOOWW, put pilots through ten sorties and EWOs through seven under Phase One, and both through 22 sorties under Phase Two. Conversion training for more experienced flyers took nearly as long, at twenty missions apiece. The syllabus included at least two low-level and one night sortie.

'Jerry' Stiles, three-times recipient of AFA and AOC awards and a Tactical

---

[8] As primary contractors on the programme, McAir received the original prototype (69-7254) in April 1976 and completed the aircraft for test duties by that December, as described in the narrative. Aircraft 69-263 was received on 21 October 1976 and served as a 'trial installation' for TCTO 1F-4E-600, which provided the conversion kits, tools and instructions to do the 'Group A' structural and wiring modifications to the aircraft. Having been 'sex-changed' in this manner, TCTO 1F-4G-501 provided for the installation of 'Group B' AN/APR-38 equipment. It was delivered to Hill AFB in March 1977, to help establish a conversion line there, and thence to Nellis on 28 September for test duties. The first OOALC conversion, 69-7290, was begun on 13 July 1977 and was ferried to Nellis on 30 December 1977. Once the test programme had been completed, prototype 69-7254 was re-inducted to depot on 12 May 1978 and re-delivered to George AFB on 7 January 1979.

Air Warfare Center Project Officer with Detachment 5 at George, who returned to the base in the autumn of 1979, was one of the original inductees: 'I had helped sire the bastard and now I was to participate in its upbringing, which seemed a fairly natural thing to do! The Mojave Desert hadn't changed much since my short visit there a few years prior, and neither had the threats against which we practised our skills. Our typical training profile consisted of taking off from George AFB at any time between 6.00 a.m. (a real grind!) and the early evening hours, head north by north-east for approximately 180 miles to the great Nellis-based exercise range, and then engage the various simulated radar threats which were scattered around Tonopah. The basic idea was for us to 'work' over the sites: to learn how to acquire them, differentiate between dummy emitters and potential threats, and to then engage them using practice bombs and missiles'. The latter comprised captive-carried TGM missiles which the crews 'pretended' to shoot, including Mavericks. Throughout the 1980s the scenario became steadily more challenging as portable training radars, such as the flatbed trailer-mounted MST-T1A and MSQ-T13 systems which simulated numerous Soviet radar types, were introduced. To these were added 'MUTES' (Multiple Threat Emitter Simulators), 'Smoky SAM' fireworks, strobes simulating the worrisome flicker of 'triple-A' and a host of EWEP electronic warfare evaluating systems capable of providing realistic training and of quantifying air-crew performance. Best of all were the SPS-66 'Nitnois', portable, expendable marine radars which could be used for live ordnance practice, introduced by intrepid 'bear' 'Jerry' Stiles. Wargames and practice sorties over Nellis thus became far removed from the 'flying club' it had been only a few years beforehand. In addition, dur-

Left: F-4G 69-7263 displays its lethal armoury of underwing missiles over the China Lake weapons range on 1 August 1981, including the TI AGM-45A Shrike, GD AGM-78D Standard ARM, Hughes AGM-65B Maverick and TI AGM-88A HARM. Three F-4Gs were assigned to USAFTAWC's Detachment 5 (pooled from Wing reserves) to perform QT&E (Qualification Test & Evaluation). The giant Standard ARM, interfaced directly with the HAWC, was phased out of operational service by 1984, having been superseded by the superior HARM (though Israeli Phantoms still have stocks of the weapon to hand, for use on their Block 60-62-MC F-4Es). Other stores include an aft-facing launch documentation camera, a centreline 'bag' and an AN/ALQ-119(V)-17 ECM pod. The 'wraparound' camouflage was introduced to the fleet the same year this photograph was taken. (US Navy via Jerry Stiles)

Right, upper: The photogenic F-4G, in this instance 69-7263 from the pioneering test force (a role shortly afterwards assumed by Detachment 5, USAFTAWC), banks over the Nevada Desert in June 1978. (USAF/SSgt Joe Smith)

Right, lower: The 81st TFS Panthers at Spangdahlem AB, West Germany, upgraded from F-4Cwws to F-4Gs during 1979: its first 'Advanced Weasels' arrived on 28 March and its last F-4Cww departed on 26 July. F-4G-44-MC 69-7556 arrived at 'Spang' in March the following year and was one of the first units to employ the new 'deep' Westinghouse AN/ALQ-131 jamming pod. (Lindsay Peacock)

ing 1982, USAFTAWC boss Maj-Gen Thomas S. Swalm (former *Thunderbirds* F-4E leader and veteran of 220 Phantom combat sorties in South-East Asia), instigated 'Green Flag', a spin-off from 'Red Flag'; this specialized in electronic combat, with the goal of introducing crews to 'ten realistic war scenario missions' to push them over the initial 'shock hurdle', where Vietnam experience had shown crews to be most vulnerable. These two-week 'wars' threw the 'Weasels' and a host of other specialist electronic combat types into an electronic mêlée in which they had to accomplish their jobs amidst such eccentric distractions as 'Comfy Sword' communications jamming and the full spectrum of SAM, MiG and AAA defences. Crews in turn learned how to work around these, and later to evolve mutually protective tactics capable of supporting large strike packages. As 'Jerry' Stiles later reflected, 'SAMs nominally locked on to the other aircraft the "Weasel" was protecting, rather than the "Weasel" *per se*. Thus a SEAD air crew must recognize when other, supported aircraft are jeopardized.' 'Weaseling' was and remains fundamentally a paternalistic mission, designed to 'protect one's own', with the emphasis on intimidation wherever possible, so that armaments can be reserved for those who wish to 'play rough'; the art is subtle and complex. During the early years at 'Green Flag', the 'old heads' in the EWO community (many, such as Lt-Col Sam Peacock, still known as 'papa bears' because of their previous experi-

Right: The EWO's 'office' in the F-4G, complete with panoramic, homing and detail display indicators with which to monitor the threats. The system would search for priority threats at selectable ranges of 10, 25, 50, 100 or 200 miles and could be 'handed off' to a Standard ARM at the flick of a switch at the bottom left of the main instrument panel. The view forward was, and remains, non-existent. The updated AN/APR-47A WASP equivalent is virtually identical, though the computers are more powerful and the buttons have been optimized for the AGM-88 HARM missile. Optical lock-on with Maverick was achieved using the radar-scope display at the bottom, in conjunction with the right-hand radar slew handle. (McAir via John J. Harty)

ence on 'Thuds') would attempt to pass on the 'sixth sense' of flushing out hostile radars to the 'baby bears' using the aural and visual inputs available—never an easy feat. After recovery at George or Nellis crews would spend up to four hours going over what had happened in the air, comparing notes and so on, 'wherein some "lively" conversations could result!' This candour behind closed doors was the only way to get maximum feedback from the training effort.

Tense moments bubbled up during this period of peace. On 26 August 1981 the North Koreans took a pot-shot at an SR-71A flying near the newly activated Choc Ta Rie SA-2 site near the North/South divide. The *Dvina* missile missed the 'Habu' by two miles, and, while the diplomatic rhetoric continued, four further Blackbird sorties were scheduled along similar tracks within strict 30sec TOT gates, confident that their multi-million dollar 'Def' systems would protect them. During each of these, F-4Gs from the *Pair-O-Dice* porpoised up and down from a low-level orbit near the DMZ, 'bombed-up' with CBUs and ARMs and ready to strike the offending SAM site within a minute of any hostile action. The North declined the invitation and the 'Weasels' returned home on all four occasions with ordnance still attached. No subsequent shots were reported, even after the 'Weasels' had departed.

Also during this time a number of improvements were being effected to

keep the F-4G abreast of the threats. From the outset, the 'Advanced Wild Weasel' was being preened for the US Navy's 'third-generation' anti-radar missile, the TI AGM-88A HARM. The 'H' in this weapon's prefix was self-explanatory—high-speed, the idea being that a 'Weasel' (or Navy 'Iron Hand' jet) should be able to knock out a radar before the anti-aircraft system could inflict any injury. With the dish out of action, either the SAMs would have lost their mid-course guidance information or the 'Weasel' and its trustees would no longer be illuminated, so even if a SAM had already been fired it would have difficulty finding its target and 'go ballistic'. The other advantage of HARM was that, although it possessed only a 125lb warhead (barely more than half that of the Standard ARM), it was a 'smart' missile, capable of being pre-programmed prior to take-off for a 'pre-brief' launch at maximum range against anticipated radar sites. Alternatively, it could be integrated with the 'Weasel''s sniffing gear, like the old AGM-78D, for launch in the 'self protection' or 'target of opportunity' modes. In all cases, when interfaced with a sophisticated SEAD jet

like the F-4G, it could 'remember' the target's azimuth after launch and had a fair chance of taking out the emitter even if the threat reverted to 'dummy' stand-by load, thanks to the missile's sensitive but discriminating AN/AWG-25 seeker. Above all else, it could be carried on Teflon-coated universal LAU-118 (Aero-5A) launch rails and was much less cumbersome than the aged GD-Pomona equivalent, permitting up to four to be slid underwing at a time in conjunction with a centreline fuel tank (a configuration known as 'wall-to-wall and one bag'). The weapon entered service during 1984, by which time the AGM-78D had been completely ousted from the inventory. Production also shifted to the AGM-88B model, which could be programmed with 'pre-brief threat data' at the base instead of having to be dispatched to the missile depot for adjustment. As a consequence, most of the Standard ARMs were diverted to the Israeli Air Force, which had recently expended a large quantity over the Beka'a.[9]

Improvements to the actual aircraft were performed concurrently, beginning with Phase One of the F-4G Performance Update Program (PUP). This upgraded the existing APR-38 to APR-47 standard by adding a new Sperry CP-1674 Weasel Attack Signal Processor (WASP) and expanded computer memory threefold, to 250K capacity. Three kits were installed during March and April 1985 in George's Detachment 5 QT&E test aircraft, and these soon proved capable of analysing threats five times as quickly, thereby minimizing exposure during contour-hugging operations to brief 'pops' while expanding frequency coverage to boot. The system became operational on the fleet during the spring of 1987, following re-work under TO 1F-4G-529. The aircraft also received the digital navigation and attack ARN-101(V) update (TO 1F-4G-504) at this time, 'uncanning' the attack options and providing the 'stock DMAS' right console-mounted 36-character keyboard control plus the new LED Detail Display Indicator read-out, which replaced the old spinning counters.[10] Further improvements had already come, including 'low-smoke' J79-GE-17F engines, which incorporated 'Pacer Frugal' components to extend times between engine changes, all originally designed for FMS operators Israel and pre-Revolutionary Iran. Bearing in mind that the Phantom never featured much in the way of LRUs (line replaceable units) and that all maintenance had to be conducted on the aircraft, *in situ*, the improvements were greatly welcomed by ground crews. Crew Chiefs discovered that they could spend less time worrying about avionics and powerplants and focus more time on isolating recurring snags such as hydraulic or fuel leaks, to produce a higher MCR (mission-capable rate). With improved spares, too, these rose to 83.7 per cent at the end of the decade, despite the increased age of the aircraft.

The final change that occurred late in the aircraft's career was its numerical strength and distribution amongst the three Wings. By 1985 peacetime attrition had claimed fifteen aircraft, so replacements were sought. A further eighteen analogue F-4Es from Blocks 42–45 (all of those extant) were stripped of Pave Spike and laser munitions capability under Class V Mod 3177 and re-kitted to the latest radar-killing F-4G standard, with the first new delivery (69-0305) arriving at George AFB on 12 June 1987. With them came the 'slick' new 'Hill Gray' semi-gloss camouflage paint, which Det 5 had established as the 'most survivable'. Numbers were also bolstered in a different manner: as pioneered by the *Pair-O-Dice* at Clark Field, 'hunter-killer' elements were organized at both George and Spangdahlem, mixing F-4Gs with F-4Es (and later F-16Cs) to maximize the 'Weasels'' impact in the event of war. The companion jets would act as nimble 'Serfs' taking extra arms (Shrikes, CBUs, even HARMs) into battle, leaving the F-4G to concentrate on the serious threats. It was a system which worked well for five years in peacetime—until the spectre of combat rose following the Iraqi Republican Guard's invasion of Kuwait on 2 August 1990. As the vanguard force during any aerial operation, it was inevitable that the 'Weasels' would be dispatched to South-West Asia at the earliest opportunity to counter possible further aggression into neighbouring Saudi Arabia. It was a serious errand, so the F-4Gs and crews were rapidly reconsolidated back into their former pure ranks.

PHANTOMTOWN, BAHRAIN

George's 561st TFS were the first to be mobilized, with orders handed down the day after command of the squadron had passed to Lt-Col George ('John Boy') Walton. Two dozen machines were ready to roll within 48 hours, and these departed on 12 August, stopping off at Seymour-Johnson AFB for four days prior to the big leg from the States to the Gulf. This mandated an exacting twenty AAR plugs per aircraft, and when the tired and exhausted crews finally arrived on station—a map reference only, accompanied by a satellite shot of the base—they discovered a brand new facility unspoilt by even the merest tyre skid or oil stain. The first twenty jets had arrived in advance of the Crew Chiefs, so after taxying to the parking spots the EWOs unceremoniously jumped out of the back, legs like jelly after the long haul, and stuffed sandbags either side of the MLG, for chocks. While the higher-ranking officers quickly poached the few dormitories available at what was akin to a 'bare base', later shared with a few eminent Bahraini RF-5E 'Tigereye' and USMC crews, a great 'Tent City' erecting process ensued with the arrival of the ground and support crews. Some 250 such billowing canvas structures blossomed, including a giant, green-striped 'beer tent' which proved appropriate to the 'Weasels'' subsequent mission call-signs—'Michelob' and 'Budweiser' among other frothing proprietary names.

TSgt James R. Clark of the 561st AMU was one the eager 'Weasel' DCCs who arrived on 18 August with the main crowd on commercial transports after a long haul from the US, which flew via Chicago and Brussels, and stopped at Dhahran in Saudi Arabia. He was the Dedicated Crew Chief for what would become the 35th TFW(P)'s overall high-flyer, F-4G 69-7207. 'We disembarked and fell into a line single file with other branches of the Service, numbering 500 or more. We stayed at Dhahran till about 2 a.m. and departed by bus to Sheikh Isa. When we arrived we were briefed about flight-line and base hazards. We slept the first three days in the hangar parking lot under a car port. Because we were so close to the Gulf, the humidity would cause condensation to roll off the roof of the car port, soaking everything and everyone beneath. We spent part of the

---

[9] Described later in some depth, in the context of the build-up to Operation 'Desert Storm'.

[10] The origins of the ARN-101(V) DMAS modification and the related enhancements to attack functions were aired in 'Arnie' in Chapter 11; the advantages it offered in terms of navigation capability are discussed in context of RF-4C operations in Chapter 15. The system was applied to the F-4G fleet under TO 1F-4G-504 and was fundamentally similar to that 'kitted' on selected F-4Es and RF-4Cs except that it lacked the LORAN module used by those aircraft—there simply was no space in which to house the receivers! Phase Two of PUP was to have added a directional receiver group (DRG) under TO 1F-4G-530, but this was subsequently cancelled owing to cost and technical problems.

next day building the first tents of "Tent City" in the 120°-plus heat, working 12-hour shifts. By the end of the first week in-theatre, we had begun to sleep in these.' There was no ice to cool the drinking water, so 'we would use liquid oxygen to cool it to less than bath-water temperature!'

'Tent City' bedded things down in time for the reinforcements. The first of these were dispatched from Spangdahlem and arrived on 5 September, further bolstered during December to bring total F-4G assets up to fifty jets, including two envisaged attrition replacements. 'It was extremely crowded and noisy,' recalled TSgt Clark, '[with] over 150 aircraft on the flight-line. When Spangdahlem's jets arrived we had no place to put their aircraft so we parked them on the taxiway until the steel revetments were built.' 'Red Horse' en-

Desert Storm Combat Veteran

Aircraft 69-7207

This aircraft flew 62 sorties and 223.7 hours over Iraq and Kuwait between 17 January and 3 March 1991. A total of 27 missles were fired from its wings to defend freedom and repel the aggression of the enemy.

DCC: TSgt Clark   AC: SSgt Umstead

Below: 'Desert Shield' and the ensuing 'Desert Storm' witnessed the rapid establishment of the 'Wild Weasel Desert V' force at Sheikh Isa AB, Bahrain, during August 1990. The first unit to deploy was Lt-Col 'John Boy' Walton's 561st TFS on the 16th of the month, followed by the 81st TFS from Spangdahlem on 5 September. Overall boss of the 35th TFW(P) was Col Ron Karp, and he forms the apex of this .38-calibre pistol-brandishing 'V'. (Lt-Col Jim Uken)

gineering teams worked at all hours to build the protective revetments. Some funny things happened to lighten the hard work and stresses of the heat and humidity. 'Myself and a couple of other people had volunteered to work permanent weekend duty. On this particular Saturday, early in the morning, we had been instructed to move all of the 370-

and 600-gallon WRM (War Readiness Materials) tanks out of revetments so that "Red Horse" could cap them off with concrete. All went well apart from one 600-gallon tank rolling off the forks, and, undaunted, we moved to the second revetment, where manoeuvring the MJ4 "jammer" was a little more difficult and required coming at the tanks from a

Right: 'Red Horse' teams construct revetments at Sheikh Isa. The base was brand new but lacked sufficient hangar facilities for the 'Weasels'. Note the 81st TFS F-4Gs parked on the runway apron in the distance. (Lt-Col Jim Uken)

better than 45° angle. We finally manoeuvred the forks under the tank but when it was nearly three feet off the ground it would go no higher. We continued to apply lift unaware that the "jammer" forks had become locked in the corrugated sides of the revetment. By the time we finally realized this the fork popped free, launching the 370 gallon tank 15 feet in the air! We had our MRE lunch and towed 69-7233 up to the main hangar for a wash. This proceeded without incident until my friend Tim Kroger called for some water to be sprayed on the right wing. All I saw was a brush waving back and forth and someone saying "Over here", so I sprayed. When I walked around the back of the aircraft there stood one soaked TSgt Kroger. During this time the Nevada ANG was arriving, all dressed in their new uniforms. We stared at them and awed at how good they looked, and they stared at us and how after 90-plus days TDY our uniforms were kind of haggard. The funny thing is, we thought we looked sharp that day!' [11]

Operations continued at a fair rate as new equipment was unpacked and checked, and the F-4Gs' systems were wrung out on peripheral border flights of 1.34 hours' average duration, to lay the foundations for the main assault during Operation 'Desert Storm'. It was a well-prepared operation orchestrating a thousand aircraft in a massive strike designed to overwhelm Iraqi defences, as sacked Air Force Gen Dugan had briefed the Press several weeks earlier. For some of the more senior commanders, especially at the height of the opening stage of the air war, it was all terribly worrying. Nobody really knew how well the 'Wild Weasels' would measure up in combat, despite the successes of the Israelis in their very similar (but comparatively small-scale) operation over the Beka'a in the spring of 1982.

To digress a little, the Israeli operation had enormous relevance. The catalyst for Operation 'Peace for Galilee' was the incessant shelling of northern Israeli settlements by the PLO from their sanctuary in the Lebanon. A total of 1,548 attacks between October 1973 and 1982 had killed 103 Israeli settlers, and counter-attacks, including the March 1978 Operation 'Litani' campaign which created a 25km buffer zone in southern Lebanon, were failing to deter the shelling. The final straw came on 3 June 1982 when terrorists shot Shlomo Argov, the Israeli Ambassador to Great Britain. 'Peace for Galilee' was then given the go-ahead, set to begin at 1100 local time on 6 June 1982. The goal of the invasion was to create an extended buffer zone stretching north to the Beirut–Damascus highway, which inevitably meant engaging the 30,000 Syrian troops posted in the Beka'a, bisecting the Lebanon north to south. It was clear that the Syrians' air defences needed to be neutralized if the operation were to succeed, with the IDF/AF F-4Es' long-range striking power and diverse weapons capability inevitably placing them at the head of the attack.

Preceding the Phantoms, and operating for several weeks beforehand, were scores of TV-equipped Mastiff and Scout elint UAVs, which relayed data to ground terminals in 'near real time'. The Syrians had committed the error of 'digging in' their SAMs and radars, making pre-strike elint 'fingerprinting' and precise position-plotting possible. Curiously, the Syrians ignored the UAVs for the most part, regarding them as innocuous 'toy aeroplanes'. Phase One of the aerial attack employed the UAVs again, but this time serving as true decoys; they were configured to appear as strike jets on radar, and they flew into the valley with the sun behind them. The Syrians took the bait, firing off most of their missiles that were ready for launch. As soon as back-up Boeing 707 ESM platform had confirmed that the radar sites were active, Phase Two was set in motion. Massive electronic 'smoke-screens' designed to jam Syrian GCI

[11] The 12th TRS *Blackbirds*, equipped with RF-4C reconnaissance Phantoms, deployed from Texas just before Christmas 1990. By the start of hostilities there were 87 Phantoms in the theatre, comprising eight RF-4Cs, four F-4Es and twelve F-4Gs at Incirlik, Turkey, and fifteen RF-4Cs and 48 F-4Gs at Sheikh Isa, Bahrain. See Chapter 15 for a fuller account of RF-4C operations during Operation 'Desert Storm'.

combined with artillery fire opened up, while virtually simultaneously, at 1414 local time, the first wave of two dozen F-4Es entered the fray, lobbing Shrikes and the special AGM-78B/D Standard ARMs, which latter *Heyl Ha'Avir* crews knew by the code-name 'Purple Fist' because of its crimson-red phosphorous smoke marker, used to highlight the impact point for possible mopping-up operations with CBUs and high-speed, straked-fin 'iron' bombs. Astonishingly, seventeen out of nineteen SA-6 'Gainful' batteries were wiped out in under ten minutes, without loss to the Phantoms! The immediate counterforce of around eighty MiGs of all marks, flying 'blind' without GCI support and circling in figure-of-eight patterns exhibiting little situational awareness, were chewed up by marauding F-15 *Baz* fighters vectored by E-2C Hawkeyes, resulting in something akin to a 'turkey shoot'. Twenty-three MiGs were shot out of the sky that day; by the end of the operation 85 had been brought down. The attack was an outstanding example of how the thirty-year-old Phantom could still be used to devastating effect, at the head of the attack force.

A Soviet panic reaction resulted in the deployment of five Syrian SA-8 'Geckos', installed on six-wheeled AFVs and employing monopulse radar at ranges of up to fifteen miles, backed by LLL optical tracking—a potentially fearsome package. To the Soviets' disgust, the IDF/AF sent in its F-4Es and smashed them to pieces, but at a cost: one of the Phantoms was felled on 24 July by a sneaky 'Gecko'. Worst of all, its crew were shot at during their parachute descent, and navigator Maj Aharon Katz, a much-respected veteran who had survived the rigours of the Yom Kippur conflict, was killed. The aircraft was equipped with sensitive avionics, and a follow-up strike was called to pulverize its remains beyond recognition; this killed eleven Soviet engineers who were busily engaged in dismantling the wreckage.

The last and 116th confirmed kill by an Israeli F-4E had taken place over the dizzy Beka'a on 11 June. The pilot concerned attained 'ace' status when he

downed a Syrian 'Fishbed' with a Rafael Python III heat-seeking missile, one of several exclusively Israeli armaments optimized for the desert skies.[12] It was the last reported kill by a pastel blue and sand-brown Phantom—in fact, it was the 280th and last reported Phantom MiG kill worldwide.[13]

A further F-4E loss occurred on 16 October 1986 during strikes against AAA and SAM sites 'managed' by the Hezbollah near Sidon. Both crew members bailed out; the pilot was whisked away hanging precariously on the skids of a Bell 'Huey' (!), but his navigator Ron Arad remains in captivity seven years on, with a glimmer of hope of repatriation in exchange for extremist Sheikh Obeid. This political haggling over prisoners predates the Crusades.

The lessons learned by the Israelis were clear: the use of UAVs and decoys in combination with stand-off SEAD weapons and Army artillery (or rockets . . . and cruise missiles, if one possessed them!) was the best way to defeat enemy air defences. The service proceeded to field Samson TALDs (Tactical Air-Launched Decoys, precursors to the Brunswick ADM-141s later acquired by the US Navy), while the units at Hatzor, Ramat-David and Tel Nov swapped notes with the Americans and replenished their armoury of Standard ARMs.

Against this backdrop, but with no combat experience extant in the 35th TFW(P) (the last of the Vietnam veterans had retired in the mid-1980s), the 'Gulf Weasels' were confronting much more sinister defences, and everyone else counted on them to succeed. Moreover, the air crews were patently aware that the enemy operators would be paying them particularly close attention, with a high price on their heads. The F-4Gs featured no provisions for stealth combat, just 'downright intimidation', and had to live up to their fearsome reputation—'YGBSM!', as some of the pilots reiterated, harking back to the pioneering days in South-East Asia. Apparently, one senior pilot developed the annoying nervous habit of flipping the zippers up and down on his flight-

Right, upper: Weapons loaders express their sentiments as aircraft prepare to taxy out on the morning of 17 January 1991 during the opening phase of the 'SEAD Campaign'. (Lt-Col Jim Uken)
Right, lower: Capt Pat Pence of the 81st TFS sends his love to Saddam. The primary weapon employed for SAM-busting was the AGM-88B HARM, which could be programmed with the latest threat data prior to take-off. Lobbing these weapons to saturate the Iraqi radar defences dominated the first three days of the 'Weasels' air war. (Lt-Col Jim Uken)

suit pockets when addressing his men, making some of them quizzical and jumpy. Certainly, the view from the top was demanding, and orchestrating their part of the preparations for what Lt-Gen 'Chuck' Horner described as the 'aerial ballet' must have produced a modicum of stage fright. But all pressed ahead like 'mission-ready soldiers', mostly bemoaning the closure of the famous striped 'beer tent' (known as the 'Weasel Dome'), which had ceased trading shortly before the outbreak of hostilities.

Opening the air assault on the night of 17 January were ground-launched Northrop BQM-174C 'Scathe Mean' Chukar drones launched by the USAF's 4468th TRS (composed of former GLCM cruise missile personnel), and Navy air-dropped Brunswick free-gliding ADM-141 TALDs, both lobbed against Iraq to emulate manned strike jets and 'wake up' the radar defences. Initially standing back at arm's length with clutches of 'pre-briefed' AGM-88B HARM missiles (a 'shop', as opposed to a depot-level, characteristic of this new model) the F-4Gs and Navy/Marine Hornets volleyed salvoes of them as soon as it was anticipated that the Iraqi radars would come on the air to counter the

---

[12] These include IAI Griffin and Guillotine LGBs, sharing a similar performance with the USAF/TI Paveway II SAL series, and the Elbit Opher, Rafael Pyramid and Popeye EO-guided weapons. The service also uses Gabriel III anti-shipping missiles.

[13] The record still stands as IDF/AF Phantoms have been employed exclusively in ground attack ever since, although IIAF F-4Es may have had the final say during the *jihad* with Iraq. However, none of the latter claims have been substantiated, and they involve helicopters, not jets.

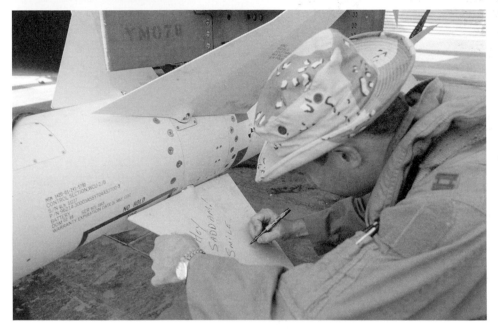

ented when describing training operations back at George in the 1980s, 'The mission briefing would describe each sequence which would occur along each leg, and explain how we would would all interact, and in general cover how the whole operation would be conducted. While it looked good on the board, it rarely happened because of the many, many factors which would change.' During 'Desert Storm', EWOs had access to MSS computers and could plan their flights in soft-copy format, working out routes and fuel requirements, all of the information being kept as up-to-date as possible. Mostly, the DTMs loading flight-plans into the aircraft's ARN-101s 'included a "standard load", including tanker-track IPs and ARCPs, plus common-knowledge "Bull's-Eyes", kept in the aircraft on a day-to-day basis, with any "mission specifics" put in by the EWO prior to the start of the mission'.

Stalwart EWO Lt-Col Jim 'Uke' Uken, Assistant Operations Officer for the 81st TFS, led the first of his squadron's 'four-ships' tasked to Kuwait, covering strikes against Ali Al Salem, Ahmed Al Jaber and Shaibah airfields. Initially, the SEAD forces were 'tiered' so as to open up corridors: on this occasion the F-4Gs were supporting Marine F/A-18s, which in turn penetrated more deeply to cover an 'Alpha Strike' against Al Basra airfield. 'The actual number of HARMs fired in the Kuwaiti Theatre of Operations was approximately 200 in the first 24 hours,' recalled Lt-Col Uken. At this stage of the 'SEAD Campaign', the 81st TFS spent two-thirds of its time over the KTO, flying with a centreline 'bag' and wall-to-wall HARMs underwing. The Baghdad-bound strikers launched with three 'bags' and two HARMs. However, 'Those lines of distinction soon evaporated when we became more "reactive" and scheduled on a daily basis'. While the 81st TFS usually employed 'deep' Westinghouse AN/ALQ-131 ECM pods, the 561st had access to some of the newer Raytheon AN/ALQ-184 models (adapted from the Westinghouse -119 series) which featured Rotman lenses with ten or more times the effective radi-

drones, decoys and sea-launched cruise missiles. This procedure of firing as many missiles as possible against threats previously mapped by elint was to dominate the first three days of the air war, in an effort known as the 'SEAD Campaign'. Literally dozens of SAM complexes were knocked out within minutes of the opening offensive alone, to the war cry of a HARM launch—'Magnum!' HARM flight was so rapid that EWOs would watch the 'threats' disappear from the scope shortly after launch. The shock of seeing it go so fast also produced spots in the crews' eyes: none of them had witnessed a HARM launch by night, and only a few had grown accustomed to 'squinting' with a 'Rifle' (Maverick) shot under similar circumstances.

The 561st *Black Knights* put up the initial dozen F-4Gs tasked to the Baghdad area (with 69-7288 apparently the first in), followed by jets from the 81st *Panthers* which were tasked in support of aircraft 'fragged' to knock out chemical and weapons storage sites in proximity to Salman Pak on the Tigris. It was during that mission that Maj Bart Quinn and Capt Ken Hanson (eventually credited with six radar kills) won their Silver Stars, pressing home their attacks amidst a wall of flak.

Nerves ran high, and planning requirements for all but tanking sorties had to be constantly adjusted to take account of new, emerging threats. As Vietnam 'Thud Weasel' veteran and F-4G proponent Maj 'Jerry' Stiles comm-

ated jamming power. These would be used as a last resort against 'terminal threats' attempting to down the 'Weasels' but were otherwise kept switched off so as not to interfere with APR-47 surveillance: the 'Weasels' were there primarily to cover 'other asses', not their own.

F-4G crews got right into the thick of it, flying initially at around 20,000ft and then stepping up altitudes by 2–3,000ft a day until by the end of the week the aircraft were routinely flying at FLs 280–300, out of range of lighter-calibre AAA. However, they were not immune to the pounding barrels of the heavy flak batteries. Capt Kevin 'Grince' Hale, EWO, was flying in the back seat in a racetrack pattern between the southeast and north-west of Baghdad one night when the enemy gunners 'walked' 100mm fire across his jet's path, severely concussing the Phantom. 'We flipped upside down with about 120 degrees of bank and lost about 8,000 feet of altitude,' he later recorded. His pilot yelled out that they were out of control, instinctively 'blew off' the wing tanks, recovered the beast, and then clawed back up to 32,000ft, to get well out of danger. An AWACS vectored them to a tanker and the crew landed safely at Sheikh Isa, with the aircraft's port lights, part of one of its hydraulic systems and the ALQ-184 ECM pod completely shot up.

Then there were the SAMs. On the third night of the air war Maj Steve Jenny and his EWO Capt Mark ('Bucci') Buccigrossi had six shot at them in less than three minutes. Escorting some 'Buffs' which were just about to drop their bombs on Republican Guard positions dotted along the Iraq/Kuwait border, the APR-47 displays suddenly lit up with some new threats posing a major threat to the bombers. Two missiles started climbing at the 'Weasel''s ten o'clock position, prompting the pilot to shout, 'Get the pod! Get the chaff!' Taking evasive action, two more missiles came up from the same site. Luckily, the

Left: The leading SAM-killer of the 81st TFS was Capt Vinnie Quinn (flying with EWO Maj Ken Spaar), with a dozen radars destroyed. (Lt-Col Jim Uken)

pod and chaff worked as advertised and the SAMs exploded at a safe distance. However, all the jinking and cavorting had lost the F-4G precious speed and altitude, eventually placing it in the midst of the thick 'fireworks'. Pilot Steve Jenny was eventually obliged to dive further to build up enough momentum (one of the F-4G's handling assets) to climb back up, just as a third pair of SAMs were shot at them, which the crew also evaded in good measure, having sweated off another couple of pounds and disposed of the remaining chaff cartridges. It had the desired effect. Distracted by the decoying antics of the scurrying 'Weasel', the enemy radar operators ignored the comparatively vulnerable B-52Gs, none of which received even a scratch. Then, shortly after recovery and de-suiting, the same crew were told to ready themselves for take-off again 35 minutes later, without a formal briefing! They were tasked to provide SEAD for forty F-16Cs striking a nuclear facility on the south-east side of Baghdad. As things turned out, they possessed the only fully functioning APQ-120 radar in their Flight. Already exhausted, they found themselves acting as pathfinders for their colleagues. Both men received the Silver Star for their gruelling night's efforts.

Remarkably, the only loss incurred was that of F-4G 69-7571, which tumbled on the night of 19 January. *Panthers* Capt Tim Burke and his EWO Capt Juan Galindez were 'running on empty' at the close of their mission over H2 airfield near the Jordanian border and attempted an aerial top-up, but dense fog prevented them completing a successful plug and they were vectored instead towards King Khalid Military City by an AWACS command post. The 'Weasel''s approach lights were out, requiring the use of precision radar, and the aircraft may have been suffering other electrical problems. The jet's engines, by then flying on fumes, seized up on the fifth attempt at recovery, forcing the crew to eject. Apparently the weather was fine except for the critical final 400ft which was obscured by fog. Both crewmen ended up 'punching out' on short-

final, with the EWO landing in the middle of a busy runway! Both returned to duty forty-eight hours after arriving back at Sheikh Isa, stirred but not shaken. The loss was originally ascribed to 'mechanical failure', but a subsequent analysis of the wreckage allegedly seemed to show that enemy anti-aircraft fire had holed the jet's fuel tanks, according to the DoD, so Washington officials put it down as 'lost to hostile fire'. The distinction was not wholly academic: the Pentagon wished deliberately to down-play the vital support role offered by the drones and 'Weasels' in order to make the F-117A 'glow', and a 'combat loss' would illustrate just how vulnerable these so-called 'obsolescent F-4Gs' were. However, most of the 'Weasels' reckon the aircraft simply 'ran out of gas', and even F-117A drivers, several of whom boasted previous tours with the F-4G (including at least one former EWO), knew better. None would have wished to go into combat without the radars already largely silenced, with or without a polyhedron-shaped steed covered in 'velvet black', radar-attenuating paint to help mask their rear.

After the first three days of the air war, when the majority of the Iraqi radar sites that were likely to come on the air and be destroyed had already been obliterated, the 'Weasels' flew 'what we called direct support or area-suppression,' recalled Lt-Col Jim Uken. 'Direct-support missions were where we were tied to a strike package. [This usually tasked four F-4Gs, but up to six against targets dotted around Baghdad, providing covering fire for packages of up to sixty jets at a time.] Area-suppression was as it sounds: we got to a particular area and provided support for any given number of flights, firing against targets of opportunity'. Ten or so days into the air campaign, the latter evolved into what the crews called 'Weasel Police' tactics. The 35th TFW(P) tasked two-ship flights to cover all of Kuwait and south-eastern Iraq over a radius of about 100 miles at a time, using AWACS co-ordination to cover a particular sector while strikes were going on, having due regard for their TOTs.

'Any threat that popped up in that area we would neutralize with the HARM missiles. In reality there many different attacks going on, and quite often we would not be in a position to support both packages at the same time. What we would end up doing, if a threat popped up in proximity to a package we were not able to support, was to give them a radio call and tell what the nature of the threat was.' 'Weasel Police' missions typically tasked six F-4Gs, split into sections of two. Each would loiter in the target area for half an hour, with two ships inbound and two outbound for aerial refuelling replenishment. After 4–5 hours, another six-ship would take over. This schedule provided 24-hour coverage over the KTO, with aircraft configured with two HARMs each. The two squadrons continued at this tempo until combat operations ceased at the end of February, by which time the mere mention of a 'Weasel' beer call-sign or a real or feigned HARM launch 'Magnum' over the airwaves often prompted the enemy to shut up shop completely. All the signals would revert to 'dummy' on the APR-47 displays. The 35th TFW(P) launched over 1,100 HARMs in all, mostly AGM-88Bs, accounting for some 54 per cent of the total number of these missiles expended during the Gulf War.

Despite a Vietnam heritage of colour, artwork on the aircraft was prohibited, and even Wing badges and other sundry markings (excluding serials and codes) had been erased. Only one or two 'European One' machines broke up the endless lines of anonymous but formidable 'Hill Gray'. As TSgt James R. Clark recalled, 'We were forbidden to have any nose art, although in early November I did have my picture taken with "Laura L" written in chalk on the nose. She flew the entire war with my wife's name written on top of both intakes. I think the only other people who knew it was there apart from my air crew, assistant and myself were the tanker boom operators.' The machine eventually notched up 62 combat sorties. Aircraft 69-7300 similarly carried the discreet name *Miss Carole*. Other 561st AMU

Above left: TSgt James R. Clark, DCC, poses by his charge, 561st TFS F-4G 69-7207, named *Laura L* after his wife. The 'Weasel' amassed 62 combat sorties (223.7 hours) over Iraq and Kuwait and fired 27 missiles. (TSgt Jim Clark)

Above right: DCC TSgt Alan Martin worked the night shift with 69-7263, nicknamed *#1 SAM-Slammer*. The aircraft launched 37 HARMs, two Mavericks and a Shrike. (Frank B. Mormillo)

aircraft of note included 69-7263 *#1 SAM-Slammer*, which DCC Sgt Alan Martin (who worked the night shift and launched the aircraft as one of the initial Baghdad-bound gaggle) claimed had fired 37 HARMs, two Mavericks and one Shrike during the conflict. This machine was subsequently adopted as the Wing commander's personal Phantom, despite the fact that it was one of the jets which required constant attention from the maintenance troops. Others which played up with endless radar and avionics malfunctions included 69-7216 and 69-7201, each with fifty combat sorties. The 'Wild Weasel Desert V' force's machines averaged 38.5 sorties and 142.8 combat hours a month, with an MCR of 88.7 per cent. In all, the 561st generated 1,176 sorties, with most of its crews logging 100 combat hours.

Spangdahlem's high-flyer was F-4G 69-7212, which amassed 158 sorties between 5 September 1990 and 5 April the following year, when the force finally bid farewell to Sheikh Isa AB and returned to Germany. Sixty of those were in combat, and the machine was subsequently

redecorated as the 81st's squadron ship for the air show circuit showing three HARMs (the machine was actually credited with five radar kills). The *Panthers* accounted for 1,167 combat missions, compiling 4,200 hours, during which time they made 142 radar kills in just forty days of combat. The highest scores went to Capt Vinnie Quinn and his EWO Maj Ken Spaar. They fired just 30 missiles and knocked out a dozen confirmed sites, while AC Lt-Col Ed Ballanco came a close second with eleven sites destroyed. The *Panthers'* high-scoring Phantoms included 69-0250, with twelve sites to its credit, followed by 69-7232 and -0286 with eight apiece. 81st TFS operations officer Lt-Col Daniel 'Gramps' Shelor summed up their effectiveness in the *Spangled Banner*: 'There was never a loss of Coalition aircraft due to SAMs while the Wild Weasels were flying, and that's not a coincidence'.

PEUGEOTS

Covering the northern Iraqi sectors were the 23rd TFS *Fighting Hawks*, deployed as a mixed element—unique to the war—comprising thirteen F-16Cs and a dozen F-4Gs (bringing in-theatre SEAD Phantom assets up to sixty-one jets). The unit moved to Incirlik AB, Turkey, during December 1990 and flew 900 combined sorties as part of the three-waves-a-day 'Proven Force' routine, providing integral SEAD support for the specially formulated 7440th Composite Wing, the first 'Superwing' to be created and tested in

battle. The 'Superwing' concept proved basically sound, but 35th TFW(P) crews flying out of Sheikh Isa, who provided round-the-clock coverage, sometimes discovered to their consternation that they were supporting packages north of Baghdad at the same time that the go-it-alone 7440th were routing their 'Weasels' from the north to the south of the conurbation! The Incirlik 'Weasels' returned home on 15 March, by which time several aircraft and crews had notched up a respectable tally of combat missions: 69-0244 *Night Stalker* carried a winged rhino on its nose, while 69-7582 amassed 42 black individual Phantom 'Spook' mission symbols, the unit's highest, some of which had seen the use of the call-sign 'Shotgun' (signifying a Shrike launch).

Elements from the 'Weasel Wing' at Clark Field also put in a token appearance. Ten 3rd TFS DMAS-mod F-4Es departed from Clark in two waves of five aircraft (call-sign 'Clan') beginning at 0700 on Saturday, 16 February. Staging through Andersen and Hickam in the Pacific, and then across the USA via George and McGuire, where the detach-

Right: Two absorbing studies of F-4Gs at the 'hot pit' at Sheikh Isa. Up to two dozen 'hot pits' were in operation during peak periods of action, refuelling USAF and USMC jets. Fuel was pumped to the aircraft from large bladders, which were in turn replenished by a constant string of trucks which plied back and forth between the port of Manoma and the base. (Lt-Col Jim Uken)

RANGING AN ENEMY EMITTER USING PHASED INTERFEROMETRY

This process was employed by the F-4G Advanced Wild Weasel, permitting target range to be derived for optimum ARM launch. Standard ARM was employed initially, but with the advent of the APR-47 the definitive technique was to launch an AGM-88 HARM in 'Range Known' 'Equations of Motion' mode. Both ARMs could be fired off-axis from the target, but to maximize stand-off range the aircraft would be turned towards the threat before launching the missile. Depending on the strength of the enemy signals, only one or two 'cuts' might need to be made. Further cuts, which were repeated automatically, merely refined accuracy, and changing altitude by ascending or descending in an arc would also provide different declination angles, which would further refine the ranging process. Without 'Range Known', F-4G crews would fire HARMs in Self-Protect mode.

Direction of arrival or first azimuth 'cut'

Declination angle I

Aircraft attitude

Second 'cut'

2

Third 'cut'

3

Aircraft course

Enemy radar

TABLE 22: 81st TFS F-4G 'DESERT STORM' SAM-BUSTERS

Pilot	EWO	Kills
Capt Vinnie Quinn	Maj Ken Spaar	12
Lt-Col Ed Ballanco	(Lt Chris Chelakes 4)	11
	(Lt-Col Don Whittler 3)	
	(Capt Steve Garland 3)	
	(Maj Bob Dorsey 1)	
Capt Mike Deas	Maj Gary Rattray	8
Maj Bart Quinn	Capt Ken Hanson	6
(Capt Lou Shogry 4)	Capt Sean Copelin	6
(Col Neal Patton 2)		
Capt Bruce Benyshek	Capt Larry Allen	5
Capt Mike Gardner	Capt Ed Holland	5
Lt-Col Randy Gelwix	Maj Jim Uken	5
(Lt.Col Ed Ballanco 3)	Capt Steve Garland	5
(Maj Mark Turberville 2)		

Capt Steve Garland is listed twice. Only crews with three or more kills are listed, except where they flew with higher-scorers. The aircraft concerned were as follows:

Aircraft	Kills						
69-7202	2	69-0242	3	69-7262	3	69-7286	6
69-7210	3	69-0245	3	69-7267	6	69-7293	6
69-7212*	5	69-0248	4	69-7268	3	69-7556	6
69-7232	8	69-0250	12	69-7270	5	69-7579	4
69-7234	4	69-0253	6	69-0278	4	69-7587	5
69-0241	4	69-0256	3	69-0286	8	Total	113

*81st TFS 'high-flyer' with 60 combat missions; flew 158 sorties between 05/09/90 and 05/04/91.

ment rendezvoused ready for the long, straight leg from New Jersey to Turkey, the force was gradually whittled down to six. Then, in order to mollify their Islamic brothers, the Turkish government requested further pruning, so only four F-4Es eventually made the whole trip. With WSO Det commander Lt-Col Craig Lightfoot on board, these arrived on 20 February to be personally greeted by 7440th CW commander Brig-Gen Lee A. Downer. Unfortunately, the unit's main equipment, the underbelly AN/AVQ-26 Pave Tack pods, were held up by weather in a cargo aircraft at Hickam, Hawaii. Flak-suppression with pairs of CBU-87/Ds (each packing 214 BLU-97/B combined-effects muntions) thus became the order of the day, using ARN-101(V) CCIP and back-up 'down the chute', manual, visual delivery strikes (call sign 'Bull') to keep the enemy gunners' heads down.

The first of these was flown four days later near Baghdad. Follow-up missions were flown on the 26th and 27th against Mosul, the latter amidst a huge thunderstorm raging over the target. The crews pressed home their attacks and tanker support was on hand there and back over the freezing inhospitable vastness of Lake Van Golu bordering Iran, with 'Arnie' holding the CP and IP co-ordinates for tanking and to avoid the irksome possibility of trespassing into hostile Iranian airspace. The Pave Tack pods finally arrived in time to assist with a planned GBU-10/B 'smart' bombing mission against, *inter alia*, Iraqi Airbus transports to be conducted on the 28th. However, this was put on 'hold' following the formal suspension of hostilities on 3 March. The fervour then dissipated. Following some joint manoeuvres with the Phantoms of the *Turk Hava Kevvetleri*, the Clark contingent departed on 19 March for the US—with the aircraft on a one-way mission to AMARC, and retirement. In

Left: Gulf veteran Capt Bruce 'Spike' Benyshek near his 'office'. He generously gave the authors a guided tour of F-4G 69-0247 and wrote the narrative 'Ride the Rhino' which appears in this chapter. (Authors)

Above: 81st FS F-4Gs at their peacetime roost, Spangdahlem AB, Germany. The Squadron was to have disbanded in the spring of 1993 but it received a reprieve owing to the demands being placed on it as part of its 'Swatch' and 'Provide Comfort' commitments in the Gulf. It will phase out soon, with many of its crews moving to the 561st FS. (Christian Gerard)

all, six of the seven crews at Incirlik flew in combat.

Meanwhile the draw-down in the Pacific continued, with Clark Field relinquishing its last three gun-equipped Phantoms on 3 June. The communist faction the New People's Army of the Philippines were pleased to see them go, but many natives wondered if the wrath of the gods had not been invoked with the departure of the Americans and their 'Rhinos': nine days later Mount Pinatubo erupted after having remained dormant for some 600 years, covering the base in ash and pumice. This unpleasant episode was followed by an onslaught by tropical typhoon 'Yunya'! It was an ironic ending. The aircraft staged through George prior to reassignment to the Idaho ANG or a dustier fate at Davis-Monthan.

A similar end-of-an-era ceremony took place at George the following spring, though amidst much greater pomp and ceremony, marking the end of twenty-seven years of F-4 operations at the base. The 35th FW's 21st FS *Cheetahs* and 561st FS *Black Knights* were deactivated on 30 June 1992; the 20th FS *Silver Lobos* had already gone on the 5th of the month.

Four of the *Luftwaffe*'s 1st GAFTS F-4Es, alongside thirteen 'vanilla' USAF models, were transferred to Holloman AFB, New Mexico, under the jurisdiction of the newly reactivated 9th FS *Iron Knights*, complete with new armoured head insignia on their noses. This left only Spangdahlem's *Panthers* in the game, not just as 'Weasels' but also as the only Active operational Phantom squadron in the USAF.

The 81st FS officially reverted to all-F-4G status during April 1991 and shortly afterwards dropped its 'tactical' prefix in common with the remainder of the Air Force. Elements of the new Fighter Squadron had already transferred to 4404th CW(P) control at Dhahran airport in Saudi Arabia, where they maintained a vigil in the ensuing Operations 'Desert Calm' and 'Southern Watch' ('Swatch', covering the sector up the 32nd parallel) under the guiding hand of squadron boss Dan Shelor and later WSO Det commander Jim 'Uke' Uken, with further forces kept at Incirlik (maintaining a vigil in the northern exclusion zone, above the 36th parallel). The 'Weasels' went into action on several more

occasions, lobbing CBUs and HARM missiles whenever a threatening Iraqi radar dared to flicker its invisible beam across the path of marauding Allied aircraft. The first of these actions comprised President George Bush's farewell present to Saddam Hussein, when six 'Weasels' supported a strike package of 114 aircraft. Only shoulder-launched SAMs were encountered; however, it woke the SAM batteries up. Between 17 and 21 January F-4Gs responded with HARMs and CBUs on three separate occasions, suppressing SAM and AAA sites at Mosul and Bashiquah. Further HARM shoots took place in April and July, to keep Iraq's radar operators and gunners aware of the hazards of 'shooting from the hip'.

For the most part, however, the missions were a 'grind' which kept all at an uncomfortable distance from the German draught beer. Gulf veteran Capt Bruce 'Spike' Benyshek very generously takes up the story, describing a typical 'Swatch' mission conducted during one of what he described as his TDY 'prison terms at Dhahran', from which much can be learned about handling the Phantom from the front seat:

RIDE THE RHINO

'Let's go for a ride—a typical ride in an 81st FS F-4G. The mission starts with the schedule. The "Show Time" will be posted for use the day before our flight. Because of the 24-hour-a-day coverage of "Swatch", our show time may be just about any time of the day or night. It is usually about three hours prior to take-off. When we arrive at the Squadron, our first stop is at the duty desk. This is an area where the day's flying schedule is posted, and acts as a focal point for tracking the flying activities. Here we "sign out" for the aircraft—our signatures attest that the flights will be conducted in accordance with all applicable rules and regulations. We check the weather for the flight and the "NOTAMs" (Notices to Airmen) in regards to airspace restrictions and airfield status. With these preliminaries accomplished, we can begin planning the tactical portion of our flight.

'Our next stop is to pick up a classified document—the "frag" (Fragmentary Order). This document is published every day and contains the directions and mission objectives for every aircraft participating in the day's operation. All aircraft are included—tankers, bombers, fighters of all types, etc. We scan through the many pages of this order to find all the particulars for our flight, such as callsigns, IFF codes, mission objective, tankers and other participating aircraft. Today our callsign is "Bud 6-1", where Bud is short for "Budweiser". The Flight Lead begins writing down the information we will need for our mission and puts it on the "Line-Up Card", a 4 × 7-inch card each crew member will carry with oft-used information for our flight. Shortly thereafter we attend a "mass brief", where

the other fighter crews in our mission will meet. We are briefed on the weather and the overall mission flow in Iraq. The "Intel Officer" briefs us on the latest intelligence and covers the threats in our area of operation. The mission commander co-ordinates altitudes and times so as to "deconflict" our aircraft. The mass brief usually takes about ten minutes. After we adjourn, our Flight spends another 20–30 minutes planning our portion of the mission. Usually, the Lead EWO will work with the other EWO on our flight-plan (the "Form 70", which is a listing of route points, headings, distances, etc), while the Flight Lead and the other pilot work on frag items, the line-up card and co-ordination items with other "players". We then spend about 30 minutes behind closed doors, briefing our flight in detail. We cover all aspects of the flight, to include normal ops and the plan of action for hostilities, and emergency procedures.

'It is now one hour prior to take-off—time to step to the aircraft. We go to Life Support and get our equipment: personal helmet and mask, G-suit, survival vest and parachute harness which connects to the 'chute in the seat. For "Swatch" missions we also carry a .38-calibre pistol, which is holstered in the survival vest. Ground operations typically have us step at one prior to take-off. When we arrive at the aircraft, we look over the "forms"—the maintenance records. We "preflight" the jet, that is, give it a thorough look-over. Strapping-in takes several minutes, as there are quite a few connections to make: two leg straps per leg, one above the ankle, the other above the knee; two seat-kit connections (near each hip); the lap belt (or seat belt); two parachute connections (Koch fittings, pronounced "Coke"); and, finally, the oxygen hose and communications cord. The Crew Chief pulls the last of the seven ejection seat safing pins, and he removes the access ladder.

'Start is normally at 30 minutes prior to take-off, and is accomplished with an external power cart. "Air one", and the right engine begins to turn. At 10 per cent rpm the ignition button is depressed

and the throttle moved forward of cut-off. Light-off occurs at around 15–20 per cent. The engine winds up slowly. At 45 per cent the external air is cut off and the engine winds up to 65 per cent, which is idle rpm. The process is repeated for the left engine. After start, about ten minutes are required to align the INS, "Arnie". During this time the EWO is busy inputting our route of flight into the INS, as well as programming the APR-47 with the pertinent data for our mission. The pilot is busy with flight control checks of various sorts: normal control movements, verification of augmentation systems, normal flap and slat operation, proper trim (controls near the neutral point), and, finally, the Crew Chief ensures there are no hydraulic leaks. It has been said that the only Phantom that does not leak is one that has no hydraulic fluid in it!

'During the last few minutes prior to taxi, the Lead EWO will check-in the flight on the radio. He will verify the operation of our radios in the jam-resistant mode ("Have Quick"), and also in the secure-voice mode (a cipher-scrambler). It is 15 minutes prior to take-off: time to taxi. At taxi time, the INS is placed in the navigation mode (as opposed to the "align" mode), the wheel chocks are removed and we move out. A call to Ground Control gives us permission to taxi and the current altimeter setting. On the way to the runway, we perform checklist items for "before take-off", which ensures the aircraft and crew are ready for flight. But we are not ready to fly yet—our first stop is the quick check or "arming area". The arming area is a wide parking ramp with eight parking slots. We pull in and are facing a large retaining wall. There are two principles for the arming area: (1) It is the "last chance" for ground personnel to look over your aircraft for problems; and (2) the ordnance is armed here, away from other personnel or aircraft. This in theory would minimize any catastrophe should a bomb explode or a missile depart the aircraft prior to being intended to do so! A note here: the arming area is also frequently called the EOR, as it is normally at the end of the runway.

'Our munitions load today is standard: we are carrying two AGM-88C HARMs for our defence-suppression role. We also carry two AIM-7F Sparrow air-to-air missiles. Other expendables include chaff and flares. All US missiles are armed by means of a T-shaped key, which is rotated and then removed. The chaff and flares are armed by removing safing pins from their dispenser modules. The EOR crew looks us over one last time for hydraulic leaks, salutes, and we are ready to go. (Even though we refer to ourselves as "armed", the weapons are not ready to be fired. The EOR arming merely allows us to achieve normal arming in flight). The Flight Lead holds up two fingers as a signal for everyone to go to Channel 2—tower frequency. "Tower, Bud six-

Below: Scourge of the radar: the F-4G 'Weasel' looking proud. This sun-hooded example belonged to Det 5, USAFTAWC, and was one of a trio (69-0277, -7206 and -7235) which from the summer of 1987 became 'permanently' assigned to QT&E work, bearing 'Oscar Tango' codes. Two of these aircraft continue to fly today with the 422nd TES, 57th TEG; tail number '206 had been relegated to the duty of non-flying maintenance trainer. (Frank B. Mormillo)

one, in sequence, three-four left". The reply, "Bud, the wind 3-1-zero at 12 knots, cleared for take-off"; and our response—"Bud". As we line up on the runway, the lead EWO points at his canopy, and, with the wing-man nodding ready, the rear canopies come down when the lead EWO nods his head and lowers his hand. The front-seat canopies follow suit moments later from the signals of the Flight Lead. The line-up checks are quickly accomplished, and Lead looks at his wing-man. "Two" nods his head as being ready for take-off. Lead twirls one hand in the air as a signal for "Run 'em up". Both aircraft advance their throttles to achieve 85 per cent rpm on both engines. (You must be careful not to go higher than this, as the tyres may rotate on the wheel rims! The pilots make a quick scan of all the engine instruments—fuel flow, rpm, EGT, nozzle position, oil pressure and boost pumps. In actual practice, the absolute readings are not examined so much as ensuring that both engines indicate the same. If they are different, then one of them if wrong!

'Today, everything is fine. We look at Two, who nods that all is well. With a

salute, we look forward, engage nose-wheel steering, release brakes, advance power to "mil" (maximum power without reheat), pause, and select afterburner or "AB". Techniques vary slightly, but for us the stick is held full-forward at brake release. This minimizes drag and maximizes the effectiveness of nosewheel steering should a tyre fail. As we accelerate, we watch the airspeed indicator. "Off the peg" is called as it comes to life, somewhere around 50 knots. "80" is called as the needle passes the first incremented mark on the instrument, followed quickly by "100". At this speed we will take off if we blow a tyre, so the nosewheel steering is released and the stick comes full back. (Nosewheel steering is accomplished by engaging or activating the system with the ring finger on your right hand, pushing on a red button on the bottom of the control-stick grip. However, the actual steering is accomplished with the rudder pedals).

'From brake release to 100 knots takes about ten seconds. Even though the stick is full back, it takes another five or six seconds until the nose starts to rotate. In our configuration, this normally happens around 160 knots. As the nose starts

to rise, we adjust the stick to hold the nose at 5–10 degrees nose-high. About five seconds later, at 180–185 knots, the legendary "Wild Weasel" is airborne.

'There is very little trim change upon becoming airborne, although two or three "clicks" nose-down on the stick-mounted trim button will make it perfect. At about 50 feet (200-plus knots) the gear and flaps are retracted, and the focus is again on airspeed, hoping to get them up and locked prior to the gear and flap limit speed of 250 knots. It is usually close, with the red lights going out at about 240 knots. We come out of after-burner at 300–350 knots. In afterburner, our total fuel flow is a whopping 80,000–90,000lb an hour! Considering we burned 1,000–2,000lb prior to take-off, our remaining 18,000lb could be exhausted in less than fifteen minutes!

'We briefed our flight to automatically change to Channel 3 upon becoming airborne, thereby saving extraneous radio chatter. "Director, Bud 6-1, airborne." "Roger, Bud, you are cleared on course, traffic your 11 o'clock, 6 miles, out of 5,000 for 3,500." "Bud, radar contact." We are climbing at 325 knots, with our power about 2–3 per cent less than military. This allows our wing-man a power advantage so he may catch us. At low altitudes (less than 15,000 feet) the rate of climb is 4,000–6,000 feet per minute. The fuel flow is about 7,000lb per hour, per engine. As we wait for Two, we arm our chaff system and check the status of missile, radar and RWR. Today all systems are functioning normally. If we had found a problem, we have various means of trouble-shooting to try and cure the fault. If it is not too serious, and cannot be corrected, we will continue. It must be pointed out that despite being one of the oldest fighters in the USAF inventory (only the EF-111 is older), we have an in-commission rate equal to or better than many of the so-called modern fighters. It is a subject of justified pride for us. We are waiting for Two as standard practice calls for separation of take-offs by 20 seconds. This is mandatory when carrying live ordnance. While on training missions we may make

formation take-offs (or "section", in naval jargon), but you would not want to be ten feet from your wing-man if he loses an engine or a tyre when the possibility exists he could swerve into you with things that go boom!

'Two joins us now, on our left, and about 20 feet out. We roll slightly to the right and our EWO dispenses a single bundle of chaff. As Two sees the silvery wisp peel away in the airstream, he gives us a nod of the head. Then he rolls slightly left, and we seen the thin puff scooting away from the belly of his aircraft. With a nod of the head and a big "thumbs up" from us, Two knows his chaff system is working normally. We wiggle the rudder, and "kick him out" to "route", a fluid position usually defined as up to 500 feet away from Lead. We are now passing 20,000 feet, en route to 24,000 feet. Our climb rate has dropped considerably, to about 1,000–1,500 feet per minute. The airspeed is still 325, but the fuel flow has dropped to about 6,000lb/hr per engine.

'We are approaching the limits of radar coverage for our airfield. "Bud 6-1, no traffic, frequency change to tactical approved, have a nice day." "Bud, push 6." There are two ways of sending our flight to a new frequency. If we had said "Bud, go 6" we would expect the response "Two", and then he would change frequency. The use of "push" means no response is required, again, in keeping with our disdain for unnecessary radio chatter. The EWO announces the new "freq" (pronounced "freak") is set. We pause, giving Two a few moments to change his radio. "Bud." "Two." We are assured he is on the same channel as us. Our next step is to "check in" with AWACS. "Bulldog, Bud 6-1 airborne, as fragged." "Searching." Our statement tells the AWACS that everything in our portion of the mission is as ordered in the "frag". We are now level at 24,000 feet. Indicated airspeed is 330–350 knots, depending on weight. Fuel flow is down to 4,000–5,000lb/hr per engine. The true airspeed is about 480–500 knots.

'The low to mid "twenties" in altitude are the optimum altitudes for the Phan-

tom. There is a marked change in performance when passing 25,000–27,000 feet. The aircraft is much more manoeuvrable and stable in the mid-twenties. Engine performance drops significantly in the upper twenties, and turn performance suffers too. The lower twenties offers the right balance of high true airspeed and low fuel flow (for good range), while providing adequate indicated airspeed for manoeuvring. The Phantom has two characteristics which define its altitude and speed range. The first is it likes to cruise at .83 Mach. When the thrust from the engines is tapering off, and you haven't much to spare, the airplane will usually stop accelerating at .83 Mach. The other axiom is the airplane doesn't like to fly slower than 300 knots. As you may deduce, somewhere around 30,000ft, .83 Mach and 300 knots indicated become one and the same! Obviously, the F-4 can fly much higher and faster than this, but for extended missions this presents a practical limit. Hopefully, this little aerodynamics lesson will shed some light on the flying characteristics of the "Rhino".

'From level-off, we now have about fifteen minutes of cruising flight. We can look around, scan our instruments or even tell a joke or two (in our respective aircraft, of course!). Oftentimes it is spent double-checking all systems and/or our route of flight for the mission. Our next phase of the mission is aerial refuelling. About 100 miles from the refuelling track, the EWOs will begin to search in earnest for the tanker on their radars. From the "frag", each EWO will have the IFF codes for our particular tanker, and he will interrogate the radar returns until he gets one that replies to the mode and code he has set. On the F-4E or G radar, aircraft or other radar returns look like little "blips". If the EWO interrogates and the contact is carrying the right mode and code, it will have two small horizontal lines adjacent, one above and one below. This system allows us to positively identify each aircraft as coded in the "frag". As we approach 50 miles to the refuelling circuit, we adjust our altitude to be at least 1,000 feet above or

Right: A beautiful study of a 3rd TFS *Peugeots* F-4E complete with Pave Tack on its belly. A detachment of *Peugeots* commanded by WSO Lt-Col Craig Lightfoot was assigned to Incirlik AB, Turkey, under Operation 'Proven Force' and flew flak-suppression sorties in support of 7440th CW strike package operations against Iraq in February 1991. (Frank B. Mormillo)

below the tanker. This prevents a mid-air should we botch the rejoin or have a late visual. The tanker will fly a steady altitude, on an oval track, roughly 40 miles long and 10 miles wide. Typical F-4 refuelling altitudes are in the low twenties. Again, this is because our engine performance begins to suffer if we fly much higher. Refuellings have taken place as high as 31,000–32,000ft, but it is extremely difficult. Approaching three miles, we push to the "boom freq", that is, the boom operator's frequency. Slowing through 320, we can open the refuelling door with a switch just behind and outboard of the throttles. As we slide on board to the tanker today, we slow to 310 knots, which is the standard refuelling speed.

'The F-4 is not an easy aircraft to refuel, and because of that there are as many techniques as there are pilots. One of the difficulties lies in the canopy bow: for most pilots, it blocks the view of the "director lights", which are mounted on the forward belly of the tanker and give the pilot an indication of which way to manoeuvre to keep the boom centred in up/down and in/out. Some pilots raise their seat all the way up and look over the canopy bow; others drop their seat and look under it. Our technique is to use a visual reference for up and down: leave the seat in the normal place, and superimpose the canopy bow just below the boomer's position, and use the centre rear-view mirror to watch the boom and boom housing; this gives a very precise indication of in and out. We pull in directly to the boom today and, using the above technique, we are "plugged" in about fifteen seconds. "On the apple," calls the EWO, in reference to the orange ball painted on the boom. When the boom is extended the proper amount

(based on our position relative to the tanker), the "apple" will line up with the edge of the boom housing. As we take fuel, the second difficulty in refuelling this beast is apparent: it is not very stable. The pilot will have to make constant, tiny corrections, lest he get too far out of position and "fall off the boom". When observing an F-4 on the boom, one can note the almost oscillatory movements of the stabilator. Fuel on-load rate is about 2,000–2,500lb/min, so, typically, one must spend four or five minutes on the boom. This can be very tiring, I assure you! If we happen to be on the boom when the tanker is at the end of the track, power may be a problem if we are refuelling high and the tanker uses a steep (20-degree) bank angle. If the tanker uses 30 degrees of bank, we will probably have to go to AB on one engine in order to hold position! You must remember that in "mil" we are essentially only at 65 per cent of our available power, while the tanker has the luxury of being able to go to 100 per cent power without afterburner!

'Having full tanks, we disconnect and let our wing-man get his drink. Checking the current time versus the time we must be at our first route-point, we see we have a few minutes to top-off one more time. Satisfied now that we are as full as we can be, we leave the tanker and proceed to our first point. Our route of flight is determined by several factors. First and foremost, our mission is to protect other Allied aircraft. This means

our route must put us in some proximity to them to ensure a timely response from us, if needed. The types of aircraft we may support could be F-15Cs, F-16Cs or Mirage 2000s performing MiGCAP, or we could be covering F-15Es, F-14s or A-6Es conducting reconnaissance missions. There is a factor of mutual support between us and the "Cappers", as we protect them from surface-to-air threats while they protect us from air-to-air threats. Technically, we and they are both performing an air superiority mission—our actions allow the strikers/recces to move unimpeded with impunity. Today our route has been chosen to protect some F-15Es performing a reconnaissance sweep over most of eastern Iraq. We will "push" (leave the first route point) about the same time as the F-15Cs move north to cover us. We will be several minutes in front of the "strikers". This allows us to loiter near potential trouble spots, receive radar emissions and build an accurate ground "picture". The altitudes and speeds involved here are classified, but we can say the speed is chosen to allow us to remain "in country" for the entire time the strikers could be affected by threats. This window of time is called the "vul time" (vulnerability time), and it is spelled out for us in the "frag". En route to our push point, we switch radio freq to AWACS again. Periodically they will provide us with "picture" calls—a God's-eye view of aircraft activity in our area of concern. Again, the ranges and capabilities of

AWACS are classified, but let it suffice to say they are very good. One may make the analogy that AWACS' radar gives us "the big picture" while a fighter's radar is looking through a section of pipe. If they give us an initial picture, we concentrate our search in that area, and then take the appropriate action.

'Leaving the push point, our wing-man automatically moves out to "tactical", a position abreast of us and 1.5 to 3 miles out. Usually he will also "stack" high or low—that is, he will not be at the same altitude as us. In an aerial engagement, if you see one opponent, it is very easy to find his wing-man if he is level with his leader—that is, the tendency of the visual scan. However, if he stacks, the visual pick-up is much more difficult. The purpose of tac formation is to allow each aircraft to "check six" behind other aircraft for any approaching bandits or missiles, and have sufficient time to transmit a warning to his wing-man. This is necessary as all aircraft have blind zones where they are vulnerable to undetected attack.

'We cruise northward and take note of the geography of south-east Iraq. It is barren wasteland out here. The border between Iraq and Kuwait is actually very easy to see—a small ravine, the wadi at Batin, was the pre-war border. Now it has been bolstered by a paved road, parallel and several miles further west. As we proceed north we encounter the numerous airfields Saddam Hussein built during his regime. Tallil, Jalibah and Al Rumailah all guard the southern edge of the Tigris/Euphrates delta. All of them still bear the scars of war—bomb craters and rubble have not been cleared. There is quite a remarkable change in scenery as we approach the delta: the desert waste gives way to farm land, and there is a verdant belt of green 70 miles wide and 150 miles long. Granted, it is not the productive farmland one might find in the UK or United States, but there is abundant water and vegetation— a striking contrast to the rest of the Saudi peninsula.

'We have arrived at our first turn point. Turning our Phantom is not a simple matter of moving the stick at this point. Our wing-man is in tactical formation, so when we turn we are really turning the formation. One cannot just turn and expect the wing-man, three miles away, to be able to maintain his line-abreast position. Therefore, let's examine the "tac turn". We are heading north and our wing-man is two miles on our right, at 3 o'clock. We want to turn left, so we make an exaggerated bank to the left (about 45–60 degrees), pause and roll out. At this point our heading has changed only slightly. Our wing-man, upon seeing this, goes into a 3g turn to the left. We still continue straight ahead. When he reaches a position of about 4.30 or 5 o'clock, we start our turn to the left. If timed properly, we will roll out abeam him on the desired heading. Much practice has gone into these types of turns, beginning in pilot training, to allow us the ease of consistently achieving the proper formation on roll out. It becomes apparent that the good Flight Lead must plan ahead for his turns, as it takes about two miles to accomplish. In other words, starting your tac turn one mile south of the 32nd parallel would have you roll out on the wrong side of the line!

'The rest of our "vul time" will be spent in a similar manner. We will shadow our strikers, perhaps spending a little time in particular areas if we find anything of interest. All the while, AWACS and the "Cappers" will be watching any activity north of the 32nd parallel. Every few minutes, AWACS will provide "picture calls". Of course, we may look with our own radar when we so desire.

'Let's talk about the heart of our mission—defense suppression. The F-4G is the best aircraft in the world for this job. The reason is a specialized piece of RWR gear that only we have—the APR-47. The 47 is a very sophisticated receiver that determines an emitter's location by determining the "angle of arrival" of a signal, and then triangulating any additional emissions from that site. The triangulation is performed by a powerful computer in the 47 that is tied to the INS. The 47 gives both crew members a 360-degree picture of emitters around the aircraft. While system capability is classified, it is safe to say it is extremely accurate. Should the tactical situation call for us to employ a HARM, the EWO will designate the site and "hand-off" to the missile. "Hand-off" means the 47 will transfer various bits of information about the site to the missile. These parameters will be used by the missile to find the target. Having done this, the missile is ready to shoot. Either the pilot or the EWO can shoot the missile. Actual employment of the weapon is an impressive sight. At "pickle" there is a resounding "clunk!" as the missile comes off the rail. Usually the pilot's first view of the missile is when it is already 1,000ft in front of the aircraft—this is a fast missile! After launch, the system is entirely passive, so we are free to do as we please. There is no "lock on" we must maintain. The actual range and lethality of the HARM are, again, classified, but, let it be said, it is deadly—the 81st Fighter Squadron is credited with 142 radar kills during the Gulf War.

'Our time "in country" will be governed by the strikers' mission and by our fuel state. In American fighter operations, two fuel states will be briefed. The most important is "bingo" fuel. Bingo fuel allows a return to the tanker or home base with an acceptable safety reserve. The other fuel is "joker" fuel. Joker is only slightly more than bingo. If a fighter crew found themselves in an air-air or surface-air engagement upon reaching joker, they should think about disengaging—so that they can be on their way home by bingo fuel. In general, we will reach bingo about one hour after we left the tanker. At this point we will proceed back to the tanker. The second tanker rendezvous wil be similar to the first. Normally our missions only call for us to be refuelled before the initial push and once during the "vul time", but, if need be, we could keep this up as long as the tanker had fuel to give and we had missiles to shoot!

'We now push back in for a second "vul" period. This will often be very similar to the first push. When the "vul time" from the frag is finally completed, we will depart Iraqi airspace. We check out with AWACS, who often will give us an update on the weather at our home base. With our aircraft now much lighter, typical cruising altitudes are a little higher, usually in the upper twenties to low thirties. Cruise airspeed at this lower weight is typically 320–330 knots, and total fuel flow is 8,000lb/hr. If this is a day mission, we will bring our wing-man in close to us by rocking our wings. As he comes on board, we give him a visual signal with thumb and forefinger that looks like a "check" mark. This is the comm-out signal for "battle damage check". During these relatively calm periods, it is not so much a check for damage due to ordnance but rather a chance to ensure no hydraulic leaks or missing panels etc as we prepare to land. He manoeuvres up and down and underneath our aircraft, looking us over. As he does so, we examine him as well. Both satisfied, we give each other a thumbs-up. Still 150 miles away from base, we call the squadron and pass our maintenance codes—the condition of the aircraft which alerts maintenance to any problems they will have to trouble-shoot.

'We switch to Approach Control. "Director, Bud 6-1, 100 miles out, flight-level 2-3-0." "Bud, radar contact, descend pilot's discretion to 2,500 feet, altimeter 30.03." "Bud is out of 2-3-0 for 2,500, 30.03." We will usually begin our descent at 90–100 miles from home and descend at 330–350 knots. Typical arrivals during the day will be to an "overhead pattern" (a visual circuit). If it is night, or the weather is poor, we will remain together until a fifteen-mile final, then the wing-man will "drag" to allow about five miles' separation between aircraft. A word about both types of recovery is in order.

'The overhead pattern is normally entered from about ten miles out. We approach the runway on centreline, at about 1,500ft, 350 knots. About five miles out, we rock the wings—the signal for Two to join to "close", a position about five feet out and three feet lower than us

and, for this runway, on our right (as it is a left-hand pattern). As we fly over the approach end of the runway, we look left to make sure the downwind leg is clear of traffic. We look at Two, twirl a hand and hold up five fingers. This is the signal for the "break": the five fingers means five seconds spacing between aircraft in the break. Looking ahead again, we snap the stick over and roll into 60–70 degrees of bank, and pull. The 2g break is a continuous turn to downwind and slows us from our "initial" speed to one compatible for landing. About half way through the turn we make a slight power reduction, to about 85 per cent. Airspeed is slowing through 275 knots. As we roll out on downwind, the airspeed is below 250—the landing-gear handle is pushed down and the flap switch is pushed down. The gear drops with a clunk; the nose actually locks first, in about 3 seconds, followed by the mains at about 6–7 seconds. The flaps are protected by a speed switch, and they usually do not begin to move until about 220–210 knots (even though they are certified to 250). We call out to the EWO, "Three down, out and down, anti-skid on, light out, good pressure, landing light". We increase the power slightly to hold about 220 knots in this "dirty" configuration. "Out and down" refers to the slats being out, the flaps being down; "anti-skid on, light out" means the switch is on and the associated warning light is not illuminated; "good pressure" means the utility hydraulic pressure is holding steady.

'We are approaching the "perch point", which is the point from which we will start our continuous turn to final. When the runway threshold is 45 degrees behind the wing line, or 135 from the nose, you are at the perch. "Tower, Bud 6-1, base, gear down, stop on the left." "Bud, the wind 330 at 10, cleared to land runway 3-4 left." "Bud 6-1." At the perch, we roll to about 45–60 degrees of bank. Normal airspeed coming off the perch is 180–200 knots. Air Force Phantoms have an aural tone system, which gives the pilot an indication of angle of attack [AOA] through the pitch tone, modulated by pulses. It is an excel-

lent system and allows the pilot to fly the correct airspeed without reference to his airspeed indicator. This allows us to concentrate our view on the runway. About half way through the turn the bank angle starts to decrease, as we see we will be able to roll out on final without going wide ("overshooting", which means something else entirely to an RAF aviator). As the bank angle decreases, power is modulated so we slow to "on-speed". This airspeed will vary according to gross weight, but will always be 19.2 units. The term "units" does not refer to an angle; rather, it is an arbitrary calibration of the AOA indicator. Now on about a half-mile final, we double check the landing gear, and concentrate for the landing. The indicated airspeed will be in the vicinity of 170–180 knots. We concentrate on a spot 500 feet down the runway from the threshold—this is our desired touch-down spot.

'Control of glidepath and airspeed is similar to that in light aircraft: if the touch-down spot is drifting up in our windscreen, we will go long. Glidepath is most easily controlled with power, while refinement of AOA is generally controlled with the stick, although the two are always interdependent. Down now to ten feet above the runway, we "flare", or raise the nose slightly to reduce our sink rate ("round-out" in RAF jargon). There are two techniques for touchdown: some pilots like to slam the airplane on to the runway, as 10–20 knots of airspeed are instantaneously scrubbed away and "it never hurt the Navy airplanes". Our technique, though, is to flare the airplane until we are slightly slow, and let the jet land gently, since runway length is not a problem and unnecessary abuse of the Phantom can't possibly be good for it! For those who use the latter technique, the F-4 is a very easy airplane to land smoothly—in fact, easier than civil aircraft such as Cessnas or Pipers.'

'If we were to have performed a straight-in, we would have maintained 300 knots and called for our wing-man to "drag" at about fifteen miles [from the runway]. He would go to idle and deploy his speed brake. As he slowed through 250, he would have configured with gear and flaps and slowed to 180 knots. We, having maintained 300 knots until ten miles, will end up five miles in front of Two. Now we can perform individual landings in conditions when visual separation is not possible, such as night or poor weather. The rest of the landing is the same as for the overhead pattern.

'Upon touch-down we deploy the drag 'chute via a handle just to the left of the pilot's left hip. A normal landing will use up 7,000 feet of runway if we use minimal braking, although the aircraft can be landed in as little as 3,500–4,000 feet with heavy braking. Today we clear the runway via a high-speed taxiway at the 8,000-feet mark. "Ground, Bud 6-1 is clear of the left, taxi to de-arm." "Cleared." We proceed to de-arm, which is at the departure end of the runway. Here, we reverse the process we went through in the arming area. We will also release our drag 'chute here, and the arming crew will gather it. Now safed, we call Ground for taxi-back to park. After parking the aircraft and shut-down, we proceed to the maintenance facility. Here we discuss any problems with the specialists, and document these problems in the aircraft forms. We now head back to the Squadron, where we record our flying time and log any particular training we accomplished. The last item to cover is a short debrief, where we discuss the flight—what went right, what went wrong and what could have been done better.

'It is now some seven or eight hours after we first entered the Squadron. It has been a long day, and we are physically drained. And our day may not be over yet: every member of the Squadron has an "additional duty", an office job besides our primary duty of flying. We may spend several more hours in the Squadron accomplishing these duties until we finally go back to our quarters. That is a typical "Swatch Weasel" sortie. In two days, we start again.'

The oustanding success of the 'Weasels' has meant that complete dissolution, and the loss of the 'institutional knowledge' that goes with it, was a ludicrous proposition (although it was indeed mooted as part of the latest round of defence cuts). The original plans called for a complete phase-out. The compromise settled on the establishment of two ANG units to operate eighteen F-4Gs each—the 190th FS under the authority of the 'Gem State' at Boise and the 192nd FS at Reno, Nevada (both long-standing reconnaissance Phantom units, the former with RTU abilities)—and for the 81st FS to disband its F-4Gs by the end of April 1993. However, the demands of 'Swatch' meant that only one F-4G (69-7580) was ever painted up in full Nevada Guard *High Rollers* regalia before that plan was revised too, substituting the freshly reactivated 561st FS at Nellis on 1 February, while Spang's *Panthers* were given a reprieve as a mixed 'Lawn Dart' and 'Weasel' squadron again, until the newly formed Idaho Guard and 561st FS were ready fully to assume the 'Det' duties in Saudi. This was a process which endured until the end of year, including support in the form of men and *matériel*. In fact, the vital support role offered by the 81st FS means that it may solider on in this capacity for even another year!

The resurrection of the *Black Knights* was announced on 29 December 1992 and the first of eighteen aircraft subsequently winged their way twelve miles north of Las Vegas on 21 January. Advance elements, making up Detachment 6 of the 79th TEG (activated at Nellis in August 1992 to replace USAFTAWC's 'Det 5'), received their trio of testers. This left just two *de jure* units in place by the following summer, along with their 'TDY-ing' colleagues at Incirlik and Dhahran. Numbers are likely to remain pegged at four dozen jets for the next few years, until specially modified F-15 Eagles enter the stage, equipped with 'Weasel in a can'. For now, the 'Weasels' remain the only 'Phantom Phighters' on the USAF's inventory.

PHANTOM 2000

On Saturday 7 May 1988, when the 131st TFW, Missouri ANG, hosted the Phantom's thirtieth birthday celebrations at Lambert Field, the USAF still boasted a force of 1,192 operational F-4s, with the USMC accounting for 86 more and foreign nations (excluding the enigmatic Iranian element) a further 1,106.[14] The lion's share of these comprised dash-17-powered 'long-horned Rhinos' and, based on an average utilization rate of 243 flying hours annually, McAir projected that 1,000 would remain airworthy when the type is old enough to celebrate its fiftieth birthday. The since radically altered geopolitical world and the knock-on shift towards 'leaner-but-meaner' defence forces have already all but ousted the USAF contingent as already noted, while the overseas representatives will barely amount to more than a few hundred beyond the turn of the century. However, among the nations adamant that their dwindling inventories will at least reach the start of the new millenium is Israel, which was flying 142 Phantoms—including 128 F-4Es, two Block 44 F-4E(S) 'Peace Jack' models and fourteen conventional RF-4E reconnaissance jets) when it embarked on its *Kurnass 2000* initiative.

Building on American weapons technology, together with a host of indigenous developments (Israeli Phantoms can be rigged in over 500 different combat configurations, using any weapon on

---

[14] McAir cited the following 'potentially operationally capable Phantom' figures for overseas operators at its thirtieth birthday party: West Germany—245 (eight F-4Es, 159 F-4Fs and 78 RF-4Es); UK—144 (36 F-4Ks, 94 F-4Ms and fourteen F-4J(UK)s); Egypt—33 (all F-4Es); Turkey—144 (136 F-4Es and eight RF-4Es); Greece—57 (4 9 F-4Es and eight RF-4Es); Japan—135 (125 F-4EJs and ten RF-4EJs); South Korea—81 (36 F-4Ds and 45 F-4Es); Spain—35 (32 F-4Cs and three RF-4Cs); Iran—unknown; and Israel—142, as outlined. Unfortunately, these figures did not reflect many already 'mothballed' aircraft. For example, Britain had two F-4J(UK)s in storage along with numerous grounded FG.1/F-4Ks, while Spain had consigned most of its F-4Cs to the hangar. However, the 'unknown' Iranian element probably made up for these! It is disturbing to reflect also that these figures would shrink dramatically over the ensuing five years, in the aftermath of the collapse of the Soviet Union and a worldwide economic recession.

Right, top and centre: Israeli F-4E No 334 served as initial test-bed for the P&WA 1120 engine, flying first of all with a mix of engines on 31 July 1986 and then with a pair of 1120s the following 27 April. The Phantom's thrust-to-weight ratio was improved from 0.76:1 to 1.04:1, providing much improved sustained turning performance and acceleration. However, the programme was abandoned when the Lavi fighter project was cancelled: producing the engines for the Phantom alone was prohibitively expensive. (IAI). **Right, bottom:** Israeli Aircraft Industries' Bedek Division is remanufacturing most of its surviving Phantoms up to *Kurnass 2000* standard, with new wiring harnesses, digital computers and buses, dual cockpit CRT displays, a HUD and a new Norden multi-mode radar. One conversion, F-4E ('Nickel Grass' 66-0327), was lost during the early operational development phase owing to an electrical fire, but the 'bugs' have since been eradicated and the machines are proving their worth. Eleven aircraft can be seen in this shot of the re-work line, including an RF-4E reconnaissance model. (IAI).

the inventory!), it comes as no surprise that the *Heyl Ha'Avir* was more than eager to see its long-ranged striking assets maintained in indefinite service, especially when there was no prospect of F-15Es to replace them. This capability was brought to the fore following the highly successful Beka'a operation in Syria and the bombing of the PLO HQ in Tunis on 1 October 1985, when the supersonic 'Sledgehammers' ventured an unprecedented 1,200 miles, building upon a 'deep strike' tradition established with Ouragans. The other impetus of the ambitious update—originally known as the 'Super Phantom'—was for Israeli Aircraft Industries to offer an upgrade package on the international market, by modernizing and refurbishing airframes and equipping them with more powerful Pratt & Whitney/United Technologies 1120 augmented turbofans, originally developed for the Lavi.

The performance gains drafted on slide rules and computer—a 21 per cent reduced take-off distance, 595kt speeds 'on the deck' with a 9,000lb payload and an 11 per cent improvement in turning capability in the combat configuration at Mach 0.9 at FL300—were borne out shortly after the test-bed, No 334, made its first flight on 31 July 1986. After-

Above: The first unit to receive the *Kurnass 2000* was the *Ahat* squadron at Hatzor, which has since moved to Ramon AB. This stunning view of No 678 shows the unique Israeli camouflage scheme to good effect, along with the AAR probe plumbed into the spine. The aircraft can refuel using either boom or basket techniques. This aircraft also features TISEO and Pave Spike; for night-time operations, the crews would employ a small FLIR pod. (IAI)

burning thrust was increased by 15 per cent and military thrust by 25, yet the powerplants offered reduced fuel consumption at commensurate throttle settings. However, the Lavi fighter programme, which would have provided a relatively long production run of the afterburning turbofan, resulting in a correspondingly inexpensive Phantom re-engining, floundered and the 'Super Phantom' initiative was abandoned in favour of the more modest 'Phantom 2000' update. The key to this was to give the airframe a thorough overhaul and replace antiquated, unreliable avionics with more modern systems, including a complete rewiring.

The package that evolved includes an Elbit Jason/Singer-Kearfott bomb-nav computer tied to a Litton LW-33 digital IMU for all-weather 'uncanned' weapons deliveries, interfaced with a FLIR pod and wide-angle Kaiser HUD for navigation and target-cueing by night.[15] To complete the suite, the aircraft's AN/APQ-120s would be deleted and replaced wholesale by an Elta/Norden synthetic aperture radar, based on technology evolved for the USN Avenger II. This is designed to offer crisp ground maps by means of clutter-suppression techniques and has an MTI plus 'patch' and 'strip' mapping capability. The radar was beset by numerous technical difficulties, all of which have allegedly since been eradicated, with initial sets delivered during 1992. The avionics package is formidable, managed by a multiplex of Mil Std 1553B databuses which integrate the systems, including weapons and the tiny low-drag FLIR pod, and drive the new dual 5in multi-function CRTs and 30° FOV HUD. It is strike-dominated. Air-to-air features are secondary, despite the fact that the radar has provisions for synthesized 'look-up', 'look-down' and beacon 'B-scan' modes, to be used purely for self-defence. In part this reflects the prevailing philosophy that the Phantom should assiduously avoid becoming entangled in 'turn and burn' engagements, but it is also aimed at helping to preserve the airframes. Aluminium and steel deep in the structure 'has a memory', as the old saying goes, even if 're-lifed' for a further fifteen years' service by new skins and spars. A further measure to increase the jets' useful life-span has been to reduce the force from five squadrons (officially reported to exist in August 1985) to three, permitting the 54-aircraft total converted to spread out the reduced number of flight-hours amongst them.

The first unit to receive the 'Phantom 2000' from IAI's Bedek Division was the *Ahat* at Hatzor in September 1989, with a test-and-evaluation and operational commitment. It has since been relocated to Ramon AB (freeing its former home for conversion to F-16s), to be followed by the *Atalev* at Tel Nov. One further unidentified squadron was also formed after 1992, drawing on the production run of two aircraft a month—probably the *Ha'patisham* at Ramat-David, also with a long-established tradition on Phantoms. As might be expected, these units have been kept busy, and will no doubt continue to be so well into the future.

---

[15] Details of the FLIR are sketchy but it is believed to comprise a small, forward-looking device carried under the port forward Sparrow missile well. It originated in a 1973 specification calling for an EOS/FLIR (electro-optical system/forward-looking infra-red), which entered service later in the decade.

15. RECCE-RHINOS

Manufacturers of jet fighters tend to make proposals for reconnaissance variants of their designs at an early stage in their aircraft's genesis. The Phantom II was no exception: the first version, Model 94-B, was drafted as early as 25 August 1953, the same date as the original fighter variant. By January 1961 the concept had advanced to a much firmer configuration as the USAF Model 98-DF RF-110A. One of the interim models was the 98-AK, sketched out in 1957, designed specifically for the US Navy and referred to as the F4H-1P. The baseline configuration gradually became more elaborate, with sideways-looking radar and an elint pod added, until the Air Force took over and the 98-DF took root, based on SOR 196.

The programme was formalized on 28 May 1962. Two aircraft (bearing the USAF serials 62-12200 and -12201 in compliance with contract JO 722) would be 'pulled' from the F-4B production line and adapted to the reconnaissance configuration. Modifications to the airframe, stipulated by Configuration Report 8995, revolved around a 33in nose extension capable of housing mapping radar and a battery of up to six optical cameras. Behind this, the aircraft's belly was beautifully recontoured, with smooth aerodynamics replacing the gouges normally employed for Sparrow missiles. The remainder of these two prototype YRF-4C airframes were fundamentally similar to stock F-4Bs stripped of operational equipment The aircraft were rolled out during July 1963. The first to fly was 12200, bearing the 'buzz code' FJ-200, which left the ramp at St Louis on 8 August with test pilot Bill Ross at the controls. From the outset this 'slicker' model proved that it was capable of faster top speeds and offered better handling characteristics than the contemporary fighter variants. As all pilots would acknowledge, the dash-15-powered RF-4C could far outstrip the performance of even the J79-GE-17-propelled fighter variants.

Right, upper: 'Father of Phantoms'. 62-12200 (McAir Ship No 266) was adapted on the production lines from an F-4B to become one of two YRF-4C test-beds. It later served as YF-4E test-bed, and ultimately as a fly-by-wire CCV (control-configured vehicle) with canards (as seen here, in August 1974) before being retired to the Air Force Museum. The trim is medium and dark blue on a glossy white airframe. (McAir via John J. Harty)

Right, lower: White and dayglo-red RF-4C-25-MC 65-0850 was one of many 'Photo-Phantoms' consigned to the 6512th TS at Edwards AFFTC, California, for test pilot training, chase and flight systems development. The sleek shape of this variant is readily apparent in these views; even with the J79-GE-15 engines it could outstrip the performance of the 'dash-seventeen'-powered fighter variants. (Frank B. Mormillo)

Left, top: RF-4C-18-MC 63-7743 was the fourth production standard 'Photo-Phantom' for the USAF and spent its entire career flying test duties, ending with a stint working with the Air Force Special Weapons Center at Kirtland AFB, New Mexico. This early photograph shows the original 'Navy' scheme to good effect. (USAF via Lucille Zaccardi)
Left, centre: A fine study of an 18th TRS RF-4C on approach to Shaw AFB during 1971. Shaw operated the primary recce RTU until the summer of 1982, when the duty passed to the 67th TRW at Bergstrom AFB, Texas. (Authors' collection)
Left, bottom: RF-4Cs entered the combat zone in South-East Asia on 30 October 1965. A first batch of nine aircraft from Shaw's 16th TRS arrived at Tan Son Nhut, South Vietnam, on that date and were initially overseen by the 2nd Air Division. They passed to 460th TRW control on 2 February the following year. RF-4Cs were some of the last Phantoms in the combat zone to receive twin-letter tail-codes, applied during 1969. (McAir)

paint) plus a new pair of photo-flash compartments tucked into the rear empennage behind flip-open doors, similar to those hiding the back-up RAT (ram-air turbine generator) propeller further up its curvaceous area-ruled flank.

Operational deliveries to Shaw AFB, South Carolina, began on 24 September 1964, the first jets going to the 4415th CCTS of the base's TARC (Tactical Aerial Reconnaissance Center) and subordinate 363rd TRW, whose motto was, appropriately enough, 'Voir C'est Savoir' ('To See is to Know').[1] Seeing the RF-4C for the first time certainly was knowing, too! It exuded all the qualities of the 'hot' Phantom that newcomers had anticipated, while adding a little mystique. Reconnaissance missions have always conveyed an element of the 'cloak-and-dagger', while the aircraft's pointed, sleeker nose made it distinctly less 'ugly' than the fighter variants. The machine soon earned the sobriquets 'Peepin' Phantom', 'Photo-Phantom' and 'Recce Rhino'.

Crews were taught to fly to pin-point targets for their cameras—bridges, vehicle concentrations, airfields and other tactical sites, snapped as low as 500ft at between 420 and 540kts, working up in 60kt increments (which tied in well with the back-seater's stop-watch). Images

Production of the fully fledged RF-4C mark began with McAir Ship No 412, USAF serial 63-7740, in Block 17q (though McDonnell Douglas insisted that the 'initial starting effectivity of RF-4C production was Block 16p', owing to an lengthy start-up as suitable full-scale production tooling procedures were established). This flew for the first time on 18 May 1964 and was handed over to the Air Force the following month. It represented the 'all-up' aircraft, the first of 503 'Romeo-F-4' models to be produced up to Block 53, to which were added 46 RF-4Bs for the USMC and 152 RF-4E/EJ derivatives for export, for a total, including prototypes, of 703 dedicated reconnaissance Phantoms.

The new RF-4C operational variant looked ostensibly similar to the two prototypes, except that it featured the F-4C's thicker wing roots and larger MLG, a USAF-standard AAR receptacle and landing/taxy lights, a dielectric long-range HF shunt antenna built into the fin (conspicuous by the white neoprene

TABLE 23: PRINCIPAL RF-4 CAMERAS

Designation	Image format (in)	Optical angular coverage	Focal lgth (in)	Remarks
KS-87A/B CAI	4.5 × 4.5	73° 44'	3	Day/night forward, vertical, vertical-split and left or right oblique framing camera. Replaced KS-72A. Stations 1, 2 or 3 (up to six). E-O version available.
		41° 06'	6	
		21° 14'	12	
		14° 14'	18	
KA-1 (Ca13B) Fairchild	9 × 18	41°06' × 73°44'	12	Med/high-altitude mapping camera. Station 2. KC-1B or T-11 6in high-altitude mapping camera also could be fitted to Station 3.
		21°14' × 41°06'	24	
		14°14' × 21°14'	36	
KA-56 Fairchild	4.5 × 9.4	73°44' × 180°	3	Low-altitude day panoramic camera. Station 2.
KA-82A-C Fairchild	4.5 × 29.3	21° × 140°	12	Medium-altitude day panoramic (replaced very similar KA-55 on RF-4Bs). Station 3.
KA-91B CAI	4.5 × 18 or 4.5 × 29.2	14°14' × 60° 14°14' × 93°	18	High-altitude panoramic camera. Station 3.
KS-127A CAI	4.5 × 4.5	3°54'	66	Daytime stand-off LOROP. Occupies Stations 2 and 3.

Note: Several sensors could be installed at various depression angles, thus providing different picture 'footprints' based on look-angle, aircraft altitude and attitude and the optical angular coverage of the lens cone. For example, in the vertical mode at 1,000ft AGL the KS-87B with a 3in lens covers an area 1,500ft square whereas with the 18in lens cone it covers an area 250ft square.

were recorded by their Chicago Aerial Industries (CAI) KS-87 or Hycon KS-72 cameras through the forward oblique/vertical No 1 station at six frames per second. Behind this, the No 2 station held a KA-56 low-altitude panoramic camera producing transverse strips with very fine detail up to 1½ miles each side of the aircraft's track—the most versatile camera on board, given its wide tolerance for banking and navigation-track errors. Navigation and timing were based on dead-reckoning (DR) using the clock and kneeboard maps, with the spinning odometers of the AN/ASN-46 navigation computer and allied INS providing only a 'guesstimate' of position—never wholly adequate for pinpoint recce duties. Some did not even bother to use it, nor its 'two-point' storage capability. Crews spent up to four hours at the map table with pens, geometry instruments of various descriptions and copious spreadsheet maps, planning every detail of the route. At low level, a deviancy of more than a few hundred feet from the planned track might not have produced the right pictures, allowing for the elements of

wide-angle distortion and limited sensor coverage during banking and turning. The plan always assumed a 'first pass–only pass' recce run to avoid ground defences, and the aviators cut out strips from bigger-scale (UK-equivalent Ordnance Survey) maps to follow on the last 10–15 miles of the approach route to the target.

The tip of the slim nose of the beast housed a TI AN/APQ-99 forward-looking radar (FLR) unique to the series, which provided several modes, including terrain-following and ground-mapping. It could do both simultaneously, though one former RF-4C WSO wondered 'how it did that without coming off its gimbals'! In the TF mode, the antenna scanned a 'box' +10°/−15° in the vertical, and 5° horizontally, on the look-out for hazards, raising and dipping its RBL 'ski-toe' during dives and climbs and presenting the terrain data on the radarscope located in the top left of the pilot's instrument panel, known to all concerned as the 'E Scope' or 'E Square'. This presented an eerie, strobe-like profile of the terrain ahead known as

the 'grass' along with a command or 'ride line' template; the idea was to keep the 'ride line' above the terrain or 'grass', 'so as not to fly into "cumulo rocks"'. An additional terrain-avoidance cue was provided by the pitch bar on the ADI (attitude director indicator), but the system was never able to be coupled to the AN/ASA-32 AFCS autopilot (which provided only Mach and altitude hold anyway) and crewmen were thus obliged to skim the terrain manually. This was not much of a problem during daylight, but in the dark, or fog, pilots quite naturally opted to keep well clear of the hard ground. Novices were expected to stay at around 1,000ft AGL, then step down to around 500ft (250ft during daytime), only venturing lower if they felt confident in the aircraft's systems and their abilities. It was always a trade-off between the desire to sneak beneath a potential enemy's radar defences and the intrinsic dangers of the ground below and ahead.

In the ground-mapping mode, used chiefly by the back-seater while the pilot monitored his 'E Square', the radar provided a PPI sector-scan to help plot potentially hazardous terrain ahead which would create tell-tale radar shadows. Recce-WSO Lt-Col Terry Simpson, waggling his hands to explain the process, recalled that 'while the pilot was watching the up-and-down radar, I was looking at the side-scanning sweep. I could tell if there was a hill out there. If there was a big shadow and I'm not "painting" over the top of it, that was bad joo-joo.' In addition to his terrain-monitoring job, the back-seater also used the PPI 'jizzle band' as the principal means of navigating to the target by night or in the weather, especially in the absence of a reliable INS. The system featured an offset cross-hair capability to ease the complexities of target interpre-

[1] The aircraft initially fell under 4411st CCTG control, TARC. The Squadron—which became the 33rd TRS on 15 October 1969—passed to 4402nd CCTG/TARC control on 1 July 1966 and began to report directly to the 363rd TRW from 1 February 1967. However, for clarity, it has often been stated that the initial deliveries went to the 33rd TRTS of the 363rd TRW!

tation, which, once entered, could be refined using cog thumbwheels on the left console (which would help establish the all-important initial point on the scope). Once the aircraft was lined up and the crew ready to go, and having selected camera stations (including compensation for cloud cover, altitude, and day or night filming), 'master operation' of the devices was always activated manually using a single push-button on the right console. Back-seaters ensured that the sensor coverage was 'bracketed', straddling the target with a series of exposures, with 'film remaining' counters indicating available frames for each camera, punching the master button on and off at the appropriate time. For a target line-up from a higher altitude (around 20–25,000ft), the pilot would utilize his

Below: Additional 'School House' duties were performed by the 67th TRW at Mountain AFB, Idaho, which was organized there on 1 January 1966, and by the 75th TRW at Bergstrom AFB, Texas, which followed suit on 17 May the same year. The two Wings were consolidated under the 67th TRW banner at Bergstrom on 15 July 1971. One of its squadrons was the 45th TRS *Polka Dots*, a former Voodoo unit which took over Bergstrom's 4th TRS assets during October 1971; two of the unit's aircraft are illustrated here while staging through snowy McChord AFB, Washington, on 2 February 1972. Four months later these aircraft would adopt the standard 67th TRW 'BA' code. (Larsen/ Remington via Richard L. Ward)

right-hand instrument panel LA-313A viewfinder. This was linked directly with the 12in focal length optics of the KA-55 vertical panoramic camera which could be housed in station No 3, and with a grid superimposed on the display to help compensate for drift. The hardware was introduced on Block 20 machines and retrofitted to earlier examples under TO 1F-4(R)C-501. This gave the pilot a bug-eyed perspective, the left scope providing 'E Square' and the right a vertical drift-sight view. Forward vision through the windshield was uninhibited by the myriad gun-sight and control indicators that crowded the fighter variants' coamings.

Mastering all this technology took some time, but flying was unrestricted. Below FL 180, outside the civil airspace sectors covering the big towns, crews had a free hand—it was their sky. At Shaw, pilots could expect to fly 48 sorties and back-seaters about 30 before graduating on to operations. Building on massive institutional knowledge in the skilled art of reconnaissance, in August 1965 TARC's first operational RF-4C squadron was declared ready; the 16th TRS had barely formed as a cohesive unit when the pressing demands of the war in Vietnam decreed its reassignment to the theatre. An initial nine machines deployed to 2nd Air Division control at Tan Son Nhut AB, South Vietnam, on

27 October 1965, arriving three days later. They flew their first missions the following day!

ALONE, UNARMED AND UNAFRAID

Three additional squadrons swelled the combat ranks of 7 AF in the war zone over the ensuing two years, supplementing and later supplanting the venerable RF-101C Voodoo, to become a permanent fixture for the duration of the decade. Tan Son Nhut's establishment, by then under 460th TRW parentage with Col Edward H. Taylor in command, was doubled on 2 September 1966 with the arrival of an additional Photo (Jet) unit, the 12th TRS *Blackbirds*, which was reassigned from Mountain Home AFB, Idaho.[2] To the west, two new squadrons formed at Udorn RTAFB, Thailand, near the Laotian border country south of Vientiane. The first of these left Shaw as Detachment One of the 9th TRS on 26 July 1966 and metamorphosed into the 6461st TRS when it touched down at its new home three days later. It was redesignated the 11th TRS in October, shortly after control of the Squadron had passed to the newly created 432nd TRW, under the command of Col Robert W. Shick. The fourth and last to enter the fray, the 14th TRS, was attached to Udorn from Bergstrom AFB, Texas, on 28 October 1967. Intended

Above: The front instrument panel of the RF-4C was simple in format and was dominated by two CRT displays: the drift-sight tube on the right and the radar 'E Square' on the left (removed from this particular machine, though outwardly similar to the display at right). The angled square at bottom left featuring only a multi-pin plug normally housed the RIIAWS indicator. (Richard L. Ward)

Left: Both flanks of the RF-4C's empennage contained photo-flash ejector compartments, capable of generating billions of candlepower for night photography. They were later turned over to chaff, for self-protection. (Richard L. Ward)

only as a stop-gap force, this new Phantom unit was formally reassigned on 6 November and went on to become the longest-lived tac-recon squadron committed to the theatre.

By the end of 1967 these four squadrons had created a force of just over sixty standby 'Photo-Phantoms', the precise numbers fluctuating with losses, new arrivals and aircraft coming in and out of deep maintenance at Ogden, Utah, and later Air Asia at Tainan, Taiwan. Indeed, while AUE was nominally eighteen aircraft per unit, actual strengths waxed and waned between twelve and twenty apiece, with at least two machines 'in the shop' for major repairs, RAM BDR or modification at any given time,

and crews rotating in and out on an almost constant basis, adding to the difficulties of tracking physical strength. What mattered most was sorties per squadron, to fulfil the seemingly insatiable appetite of 'higher authority': target assignments were drawn up at Tan Son Nhut at 7 AF headquarters, and by Det 1, 7 AF, at Udorn (with the 432nd TRW reporting to 13 AF headquarters at Clark Field in the Philippines for logistical support), which 'fragged' missions over the Laotian panhandle in the 'Steel Tiger' operating zone in addition to 'Rolling Thunder' excursions over North Vietnam. Patrolling for enemy enclaves in the Republic of Vietnam was ceaseless, especially along the border infiltration

areas. Troop movements, MiG and SAM installations and the whole gamut of intelligence necessary to keep an eye on proceedings, were garnered by the 'Photo-Phantom' crews. Consequently, it was not unusual for each squadron to generate two or three two-ship missions a day, compared to the on-and-off cycle experienced by the strike units they were supporting. And as 'mission-ready' soldiers they obliged. Sometimes these were even scheduled on a 'no-notice' basis, though no 'alert' system was maintained as such. Usually crews would review the roster the previous day, this indicating whether they would be scheduled to fly in a 'high threat' area or on a 'milk run', permitting some time for adequate 'psyching'. During the height of RF-4C operations in 1967 and 1972, crews could clock up 100 missions over the North in just over three months, not counting assignments in 'lower threat' areas!

RF-4C operations in SEA followed close on the heels of the Voodoo (several of whose pilots converted to the sophisticated new model after brief transition courses at Shaw and, occasionally, Mountain Home AFB in Idaho). The 'pole-pushers' very quickly adjusted to the initially undervalued luxury of having an extra pair of eyes in the back with an innate ability to do quick maths, while the dual-qualified GIBs in turn tinkered with new technology, much of it 'cosmic' in comparison to the Voodoo's, including elint receivers such as the AN/ALR-17 ELRAC.[3] Other devices included a novel AN/AVD-2 laser-mapping radar (applied to eight aircraft's high-altitude station, under TO 1F-4(R)C-603, on an experimental basis), together with other systems de-

---

[2] Two RF-4C Wings followed close behind the 363rd TRW at TARC, the 75th TRW at Bergstrom AFB, Texas, and the 67th TRW at Mountain Home AFB, Idaho, which had a major RTU function. In July 1971 the 67th TRW designation passed to Bergstrom and the two Wings' aircraft were consolidated there.
[3] And later AN/ALR-31, applied to 177 aircraft under TO 1F-4(R)C-625 (selected from serials 63-7740 to 69-0366), capable of annotating film with basic information pertaining to the whereabouts of selected enemy radars.

Above left: Navigator Capt J. Ward Boyce poses next to his sleek steed, RF-4C-32-MC 66-0459. *Night Owl* was assigned to the 11th TRS at Udorn RTAFB. Note the lack of built-in pilot steps, the installation of which was precluded because of the SLR radar fit in the cheeks of the nose. (J. W. Boyce via Richard L. Ward)

Above right: 'War's hell'. *Snoopy* (an unidentified Block 26-MC RF-4C) was assigned to the 432nd TRW at Udorn RTAFB, Thailand, where artwork flourished. The Wing operated two 'Photo-Phantom' squadrons, the 11th TRS *Inferne Ibimus* (formerly the 6461st TRS, which had deployed as Detachment One of the 9th TRS from Shaw AFB in July 1966) and the LORAN-equipped 14th TRS (assigned to, and subsequently transferred from, the 75th TRW at Bergstrom in October 1967). RF-4C operations continued at the base right through to June 1975. (J. W. Boyce via Richard L. Ward)

scribed later, aimed exclusively at expanding the 'Photo-Phantoms'' reconnaissance repertoire into night and inclement weather. Many of the hard-learned lessons passed quickly down to the combat school at Shaw and rapidly expanding cadres at Bergstrom AFB, Texas, and Mountain Home AFB, Idaho, where instructors would indulge their novices in improvised tactics to improve survivability further and to address new technological requirements, which they had to learn 'off the bat', alongside mission-planning. Typical training flights embraced only two aircraft, so the ACs and their back-seaters had to get to grips with mission specifics and fuel management right from the beginning, without the benefit of slowly working up to 'Lead Qualified' status (jokingly referred to as 'lean qualified', alluding to the practice of novices peering over the shoulders of more experienced flyers), along with coffee-making, answering the phone and other duties assigned to 'first-tourists' in the fighter Wings' map-laden ops rooms.

Many of the more mundane technical issues also were addressed directly to St Louis via the Field Reps to help refine further production Blocks of McAir's new pedigree, these feeding back in the form of subtle modifications such as the 'tweaking' of bobweight-related 'stick feel', changes to instrumentation and minor alterations deep in the structure. The most innovative of these was the adoption of a re-faired nose from Block 44 onwards. This new configuration, which changed the 'chisel' angled off the radome from 33° to 23°, virtually eliminated aerodynamic boundary layer separation over the Station 1 vertical window, thus improving camera resolution by ridding the pane of wisps of soggy air. The deeper format would also prove useful in helping to accommodate additional electronic 'black boxes' later in the jet's career.

Much classified work was also accomplished in improving the security of live communications, so that recce crewmen did not have to resort to inventive 'bull's-eyes' to relay their position relative to lucrative and well-defended targets. Security speech units such as the KY-28 UHF, along with long-range high-frequency communications broadcast through the jet's massive built-in fin shunt antenna, were installed first in the 'Recce Rhinos'. These 'real time' verbal reports, including weather reconnaissance, often proved to be just as important as the images captured on celluloid.

For the most part, missions involved pushing the throttles to the firewall, jinking through the flak and SAMs and getting the pictures, much as the Voodoo had done before. Lt-Col John Taylor, who flew 48 'Recce Rhino' combat missions from Udorn at the height of the 'Rolling Thunder' campaign in 1967–68, recollected the ferocity of the enemy's defences, and the tactics used to avoid them: 'Our prime duties consisted of BDA (bomb damage assessment), exploratory recce, or just trolling—you know, randomly seeking out targets. A good way of doing this was just to find out where any shooting was coming from. Like Yen Bai, about 30–40 miles northeast of Hanoi and right on the Red River, or Banana Valley, just south of Hanoi. Plus anything east of 'Thud Ridge', anything in town itself, of course, and anything south of the Haiphong Ridge.' All missions were two-ship. On his second excursion Lt-Col Taylor recalled that 'We were two RF-4Cs, up near the Chinese buffer zone at about 22,000 feet—as high as I've ever been over there. We were coming back and got some "bandit" calls just as we were finishing up our targets. It was obvious that they were coming in on us. We were staying high like that to conserve fuel but then we picked up some weak strobes on the RHAWS and went down, got right down "to the weeds". I kept an eye on my six o'clock, making weaving turns to check from time to time.' By unloading the airframe in a zero g descent and piling on the thrust, the Phantoms would accelerate rapidly, leaving most opponents way behind them. Having dropped the tanks, and being unhindered by bombs or guns, the 'Photo-Phantoms' had an impressive transonic dash capability at low level. 'The best tactics you could use were to go low, because the MiGs were limited to 560 knots, maybe 570 knots, below 10,000 feet. We were always low: I used to fly 500–1,000 feet AGL and there were a lot of guys who used to go even lower—100–500 feet kind of thing. But that can be damned dangerous! I would keep to 500 minimum.' These altitudes enabled detailed photographs of gun emplacements and a host of other targets to be obtained.

Fuel was eaten up voraciously on such high-speed, low-level runs, but it gave the crews that 'edge', and these tactics were also espoused by their combat peers flying the 1950s-vintage Voodoo. 'We would hit 420 to 480 knots at the pre-IP and at the IP (the co-ordinates at which the recce-run begins) we'd be at 550–580 knots. Over Hanoi, of course, you couldn't go low because of the intense gunfire. So we would pop up to medium altitude just before running in. Over town they would throw up a real barrage, and if the wing-man was following behind he could get in real trouble. The safest place to work was 8,000 feet—at the most, 14,000 feet—to avoid the SAM-2s and triple-A. You could spot the SAMs by the smoke and flame when they left the ground, but the big problem for the pilot was that he'd be so busy looking at the target that there was no time to look for stuff like that. My 'gator would call the flak too: 37 and 57mm, and some 85mm stuff as well. Very black puffs, that 85. It was all radar-controlled and they knew just when to stop firing if the MiGs were coming in. Those gunners on the 85s, if they hit your altitude and got you once ahead and once behind, they'd just walk the stuff up to you and you were finished. They were really great gunners. The best way, though, to beat the enemy threats was to g-load the aircraft, positive and negative, while you were popping up to locate the target (which had to be done visually from the IP onwards). [This threat-reaction manoeuvre drew a sine wave through the air which Col Taylor scratched out on paper like the Swiss Alps.] Downtown we'd probably be picking the target at 10,000 feet or so. Standard targets included POL, the MiG fields or the Paul Doumer Bridge just north of town.

Once the photos had been taken, a quick egress was in order: 'A kid named John Ward came up with something we termed "The Slice". This was the fastest way to get out of this high-threat area, into the 'weeds' and home. It was just to pull 135 degrees right or left, nose down and split for home at full power.' During his second encounter with MiGs on 13

January 1968, while at the 'stick' of RF-4C 65-0847, Col Taylor returned home with half flaps, only 600lb of fuel remaining and a 3ft hole in the left inboard trailing-edge flap.

However, many RF-4Cs succumbed to enemy fire, and this was where the new Martin-Baker Mk H7 seat came good. It was fitted as standard equipment to the 'Photo-Phantoms' first, and the seat's extra rocket pack helped the crew to place themselves farther from a flaming aircraft ripped apart by a SAM, as happened on four occasions in 1967 and on three during 1972. Wing-men occasionally captured the horrific proceedings on their oblique KS-87s. One harrowing sequence shot on 12 August 1967 showed 432nd TRW RF-4C 65-0882 being blown to pieces by a *Dvina* near the Red River area of Hanoi. Remarkably, Lt-Col Edwin L. Atterberry and Maj Thomas V. Parrott ejected from the inferno of their gyrating jet, to become POWs (though, sadly, Lt-Col Atterberry died in captivity).

FLASHBULB PHANTOMS

One facet of the RF-4C's operations which differed substantially from those of its predecessor the 'One-O-Wonder' was its night-time image-gathering capability, hitherto available to only a few specially adapted 'Toy Tiger' Voodoos toting centreline flash pods and a bank of KA-45 and -47 cameras. Flash photography was built into the RF-4C from the outset, using cartridges ejected from LA-307 and -308 units located in the Phantom's empennage (the same compartments that were turned over to chaff 'tinsel' for daytime flights).[4] Ejected *en masse*, their one billion candlepower was enough to light up the entire vista below—not a particularly desirable feat, given that it would light up the Phantom

---

[4] Fitted on all aircraft up to RF-4C-49-MC (71-0259), comprising four ejectors mounted in pairs on each side, each capable of holding 27 M112 (260 million candlepower peak) photo-flash cartridges. Block 51 RF-4Cs (72-0145 and up) introduced one LA-429A ejector battery on each side, each with 20 M185 (1 billion candlepower peak) cartridges.

too! A better option was the AN/AAS-18 infra-red linescanner set tucked under the navigator's seat, capable of producing swathes of imagery based on the infra-red electromagnetic energy emanating from the terrain, and things on it, below. In this manner, the aircraft could track vehicles, POL dumps, troop bivouacs and arms caches under cover of canvas or netting. It was especially effective over areas which had been subjected to defoliants. Anything that moved or had moved recently was 'warm' enough for the IR to pick up and record on film. Often the back-seat navigator would use his set of throttles to keep the aircraft at around 540kts true airspeed during the 'lo' part of the mission profile while watching the radar and constantly mentally computing position and time and heading to the next destination point, freeing the pilot to concentrate on terrain-avoiding steering and observation, bearing in mind that the AN/APQ-99 FLR radar provided no form of 'hands-off'

Below: MiG sanctuary Yen Bai airfield in North Vietnam (in the centre of the photograph, visible beneath the spotty clouds); the view is to the south-east, down the Red River valley towards Hanoi, 50 miles distant. There was no ramp area at Yen Bai: the aircraft were dispersed in caves hewn into the rocks surrounding the airfield. (Jim Shaw)

automatic flight. Over Laos and stretches of North Vietnam there existed too many nasty karst rock outcrops cloaked by vegetation to trust the radar implicitly, and then there were the tropical rainstorms to contend with, which could adversely influence the radar, requiring intense concentration and situational awareness. Crews often relied on their battle adrenalin-boosted 'sixth sense' and flew just below the height at which they felt 'comfortable', as related earlier.

Combat over the open areas of Route Pack VIA would also be especially scary because enemy missiles were abundant and more sinister at night: there were no puffs of smoke on the ground to look out for, and, if there was cloud, no tell-tale rocket plumes either—until the nearby vapour-laden air began to glow menacingly, signifying a potential brush with death. Crews became increasingly reliant on ECM as the war progressed, initially using only carefully timed noise-jamming designed to pre-empt the SA-2 'Guideline''s command detonation signal but graduating on to more sophisticated techniques designed to override the enemy's automatic range-gate systems at the tracking phase. Crews from the 11th TRS were the first to introduce the Westinghouse multiple-band 'stretched' QRC-335 AN/ALQ-101(V)-

3/4 deception jammer to combat, which effectively drew away the SAMs, short or long of their intended prey, by means of amplitude-modulated output matched to the threat emitter's signals, to fool its AGC. These generated 'ghost targets' at a distance designed to do no harm to the 'Recce Rhinos', and avoided the problem of having to define the precise command detonation frequencies used by the SAMs.

Deception jamming of this sort was necessary also because of the tactics indulged in during reconnaissance—one- or two- versus four-ship flights—which obviated the possibility of mutual protection. It took enormous discipline and courage to sit through a barrage of missiles with the knowledge that the SAMs should theoretically erupt beyond harm's reach but somewhere nearby. Indeed, one McAir tech-rep recollected a novice crew ready to throw in their wings after drawing no fewer than sixteen SAMs on their first combat mission in the 'slot' position over North Vietnam! The fact that they had returned without a scratch on the matt green and tan paint coating their metal steed seemed to have eluded them for several hours. However, it was not until 1969 that RF-4Cs began using these systems in quantity. In the interim, Itek ATI AN/APR-25 RHAWS and the APR-26 LWR became standard features from Block 34 (67-0443) and were retrofitted to all survivors from previous production, alerting the crew in time for evasive action.[5] Provisions for ECM came with them, including multi-station wiring for the carriage of two pods, one on each inner wing pylon.

In the pioneering days, jammers were confined to obsolescent AN/ALQ-71 and -72 noise-jamming pods designed to 'white out' the 'Fan Song' SAM and 'Fire Can' flak radars or a dashing MiG-21's radar scope with a snowstorm's worth of electronic noise, so it paid to have one of each. Two of the later AN/

[5] Under TO 1F-4(R)C-551. These were later updated to APR-36 and -37 format similar to those used in the F-4E, under TO 1F-4(R)C-589, and subsequently to digital AN/ALR-46, and then -69, RWR standard. Refer to Chapter 14.

Right: A pair of LORAN-equipped RF-4Cs thunder into the sky, with distinctive dorsal 'towel rack' antennae. These machines first saw action with the 14th TRS at Udorn, Thailand; in the postwar period they were operated by the 26th TRW at Zweibrücken, Germany, and the 67th TRW at Bergstrom, Texas. Here two *Texicans* tuck up their wheels during a formation take-off from runway 21L at Nellis, outbound for 'Red Flag 80-1'. (Frank B. Mormillo)

ALQ-101s could be carried with only minimum drag penalties. However, in the crews' minds, their best friends were the night, weather and speed—and stand-off sensors capable of operating in these demanding circumstances.

True all-weather reconnaissance was made available by the Goodyear AN/APQ-102A sideways-looking radar (SLR), an area surveillance sensor packaged into the Phantom's cheeks (thus serving unintentionally as additional armour-plating). As explained by 'Recce-Rhino' boss Maj-Gen Gordon Graham in his 1966 official report to 7 AF shortly after the 'Photo-Phantom''s initial combat assessment, 'SLR can detect a variety of targets under day or night conditions and can penetrate haze, smoke and most clouds. It is claimed that it can record targets such as convoys on open sections of road, trains, airstrips and support facilities, parked aircraft, bridges, boats and missile sites. Its high-resolution mapping mode can be used in conjunction with its moving-target indicator (MTI) mode to clearly show moving vehicles against a high-resolution background. The minimum speed at which moving vehicles can be detected and recorded is a direct function of the altitude, speed and angle between the aircraft and vehicle movement, with targets moving at 90 degrees to the aircraft's flight-path giving the best returns. The SLR offset capability allows it to cover targets as much as 30 miles to one side of the flight-path, providing the aircraft safe separation from defended target areas. Optimum altitude for SLR flights is 30,000 to 35,000 feet, although lower altitudes at times provide better shadows on some targets to improve interpretation potential. Unfortunately,

SLR has many limitations, chief of which is its fixed scale of 1:400,000. This is far too small a scale to provide good interpretation, and special skills and techniques must be developed in order properly to exploit the product. SLR cannot separate targets closer together than 50 feet, penetrate foliage or water, or detect targets under trees or similar cover.' The problems related to 'spot size' and took several years to resolve. In the meantime the actual 'Group B' installation was deleted from the production line, to be replaced by lead ballast, although all machines featured the 'Group A' wiring to employ it, and it still offered virtually all-weather reconnaissance, around the clock.

The 14th TRS, which was re-equipped with the lion's share of twenty brand new Block 40 and 41 RF-4Cs kitted with the AN/ARN-92 LORAN, which provided precise all-weather navigation and accurate sensor cueing, were best able to provide the smooth coverage required for optimum SLR operation. Arriving in late 1969, these aircraft were easily distinguished by the subsequent installation of the Pave Phantom-type Chelton 'towel rail' antenna, which became their trademark. They also were the first to sprout static-discharging 'whiskers' on their tips, plus electro-luminescent night situation strips.[6] Because of the fundamentally different operating procedures of these new sensors, two extra sensor control panels were fitted for SLR and IR, permitting activation independent-

ly of the 'master operate' button. This allowed for greater mission flexibility.[7]

On completion of a mission the aircraft's cameras were rapidly unloaded for the Photo Processing and Interpretation Facility (PPIF) to analyze their contents. These were handled by specialists in what evolved into portable trailers—Goodyear WS-420A/B PPIFs for black-and-white film and the ES-75 on the few occasions colour film was used. Every negative was marked with a coded rectangle giving full details of time, speed, date, compass heading, altitude and aircraft attitude in digits. The crew's debrief resulted in a mission report for planners and commanders to act upon, in which valuable first-hand feedback on defences and fortifications, perhaps difficult to ascertain speedily from the celluloid imagery, might prove invaluable to an Army or intelligence commander. Lt-Col Terry Simpson emphasized the crew's involvement: 'I knew where I

---

[6] The LORAN package was applied under TO 1F-4(R)C-622. The basics of the system, and some of its technical limitations, were aired in Chapter 10. Along with LORAN came a new AN/ASQ-134 data set, for the accurate annotation of film with aircraft position, attitude and height, to assist with interpretation. The luminescent strips were applied to all USAF Phantoms following TO 1F-4-776 and were introduced on the production line beginning with Block 48-MC RF-4C 71-0248.

[7] Applied under TO 1F-4(R)C-632 to all survivors in Blocks 17 to 44. Later FY71-72 aircraft produced under Blocks 48 to 53 featured this from the outset.

went, when I turned the cameras on, and what I saw, especially the target I was "fragged" against, which I could pick out quickly. I could save the Photo Interpreter (PI) an immense amount of time by reviewing the film with him prior to him completing his report.' About two hours after touch-down this would be supported by the finished photo prints from the PPIF, though negatives might well be conveyed 'wet' within an hour of touch-down in an emergency. Infra-red S02498 film from the AN/AAS-18 set and data film used in the AN/APQ-102 SLR would also pass through the PPIF. Early Phantoms were able to eject exposed film cassettes by parachute, a system activated by the bomb button in the front cockpit. The idea of dropping urgent data for immediate processing en route might have been sound, but it was impractical in the operational environment and was seldom used, and the capability was eventually deleted from production RF-4Cs beginning with 69-0376 in Block 44.

Senior theatre commanders, Maj-Gen Gordon Graham among them, demonstrated a penchant for the RF-4C, and flew combat missions to 'show the troops' that they were not desk-bound. One such senior officer lost his life in the process: on 23 July 1968 Maj-Gen Robert F. Worley, Vice-Commander of the Seventh Air Force, was hit by gunfire northwest of Saigon. He went down with the Phantom but his navigator, Maj Bob Brodman, ejected from the burning jet in textbook fashion. The loss of a 'hard hat' sent shockwaves through the system, and 'supreme boss' Gen William W. Momyer put an end to the practice of 'brass' flying combat ops on the grounds that leading had as much to with inspiration as flying. Whatever the prevailing philosophy of leadership, RF-4Cs continued to pour out of St Louis to make good losses and replace the venerable Voodoo, still very much active. A further by-product of Bob Worley's unfortunate demise—which served as catalyst for a thoroughgoing inquiry—was a speedy modification programme, which Dynalectron completed by 24 January

the following year. The pressure exerted on Worley's hood, resulting from the customary departure of the back-seater first, was subsequently demonstrated, under certain conditions, to preclude a successful departure for the pilot. Three other failed front-seat ejections were attributed to this too, so extra gas-operated pistons were installed in all Phantoms' canopy rails to ensure reliable ejection for both crew members. Many have since benefited from this modification. It is important to reflect here that the Martin-Baker 'bang seat' was and has always remained an asset. Recent fatalities amongst FMS operators have been attributed to maintenance malpractice, or plain and simple neglect.

COMMANDO HUNT

The conclusion of Operation 'Rolling Thunder' on 30 November 1968 brought no respite for the reconnaissance crews: if anything, the RF-4C's war was just beginning. As the intractable conflict trudged on, attention broadened further towards Laos in a series of 'Commando Hunt' operations in an effort to monitor and provide the co-ordinates of the endless convoys of trucks bringing thousands of tons of supplies through the arteries of the Ho Chi Minh Trail. Sadly, most crews' visual sightings tended to be ignored, while huge volumes of exposed celluloid ran past their 'sell-by date' unexamined as 7 AF preferred, instead, to place greater emphasis on the 'Igloo White' 'Mussel Shoals' electronic network being sown across the DMZ and along the Republic's western borders. It was a technological reaction to the shock of the Tet Offensive in the Chinese New Year of 1968. With hindsight, it is clear that those in command committed a *faux pas* by ignoring the 'Photo-Phantom' crews' increasingly alarming reports about possible imminent invasion. At the time it was discarded as bad news-mongering, and all privy to the data were told to 'go away and shut up'.

Meanwhile the crews pressed ahead with their duties. Laos was particularly hard on the AN/APQ-99 'Forward Looker', and the limited numbers of IR

and SLR were further fine-tuned too. A good proportion of the crews' tasks were spent providing weather reconnaissance —tops and bottoms of clouds, winds, and so on—along with communications reports for the 'Fast-FAC' and laser bombers of the 8th TFW 'Wolfpack'. Although the idea was discussed, RF-4C crews knew better than to loiter in the target area with a Pave Light 'zot' gun and preferred to concentrate on cameras and on plotting co-ordinates in high-speed, swooping passes. Day and night recce in this zone was the speciality of the 432nd TRW operating from Udorn in Thailand. To the east, the 460th TRW continued its arduous task of updating outrageously inaccurate French-colonial maps of the entire region with the aid of high-altitude T-11 mapping cameras, capable of producing nine-inch-square negatives offering fine resolution. They also continued to provide recce over the troubled Republic of South Vietnam, plotting the habitat of the elusive and increasingly subterranean Viet Cong, often using the (then less than secure) security communications radio and 'fuzzy' AAS-18 IR sensor. However, both Wings were engaged in occasional overflights of North Vietnam—the really dangerous missions. The directive which had brought an abrupt end to 'Rolling Thunder' operations did not extend to the 'Photo-Phantoms' and, after President Nixon's inauguration in January 1969, authority was given for retaliatory air strikes to be conducted whenever recce jets drew hostile fire in breach of the tacit 'Open Skies' agreement.

In February 1970, after RF-4Cs had been shot at for the second time that month, 'protective reaction' sorties were launched against specific SAM and AAA batteries, accounting for sixty separate operations during the ensuing two years. Some of these intensified into what were known as 'reinforced protective reaction' strikes, which commenced during the opening four days of May when some 500 Phantom and 'Thud Weasel' sorties were launched against air defence and logistics sites near the Ban

Above: An RF-4C 'gases up' en route to the target area, with the WSO keeping a watchful eye on the boom. (Tim Laming)

Karai and Barthelamy Passes straddling North Vietnam and Laos, all with pre- and post-strike RF-4C support of course. However, an increasing burden was placed on the LORAN-equipped 14th TRS as a spin-off from the 'Vietnamization Program' and increased reliance on 'Igloo White'. The 14th TRS's sister-squadron in Thailand, the 11th, had already been deactivated on 10 November 1970, while reconnaissance assets in the Republic of Vietnam had all but sublimated, the 16th TRS having transferred to Misawa AB, Japan, on 3 March that year (although it continued to maintain a small detachment of four jets at Nakhon Phanom, Thailand, until February 1971). The only other squadron in the theatre (apart from the Marines' limited RF-4B presence at Da Nang, described later), was the 12th TRS *Blackbirds*; this was destined to relocate to Bergstrom AFB, Texas, during August 1971 and in the meantime fo-

cused its energies on the Republic and the flak-filled valleys gouged into the inhospitable Laotian border.

Yet another RF-4C loss, that of 68-0601 on 21 November 1970, prompted a second major strike against Ban Karai and Mu Gia, with additional strike and reconnaissance resources being committed along the DMZ to monitor the sinister new establishment of enemy SAM sites that were creeping further and further south. This on-and-off tempo continued into the following year, 'fragging' RF-4Cs into 'Injun' Country' until aircraft drew fire for the 'Weasels' to act upon: in February 1971 Operation 'Louisville Slugger' committed 67 aircraft back to Ban Karai, accounting for the destruction of five SAM batteries, fifteen SA-2 missile transporters and related radar and support facilities, without loss to any of the attackers, including the four RF-4Cs that braved the flak to get the pictures 'before and after'. A similar successful operation, code-named 'Fracture Cross Alpha', was executed on 21 and 22 March. Meanwhile reconnaissance continued unabated throughout the entire war zone, including Cambodia (when many USAF crews carried no ID and, if shot down, were under an obligation to deny any involvement with any US military operation of any kind!). Increasingly hazardous sorties began to be flown as part of the renewed 'MiG watch', conducted by crews of the truly 'alone, unarmed and [debatably] unafraid' 14th TRS. The only other 'game in town' which flew low enough to draw flak as well as the customary pattern of SAM-launches was SAC's unmanned AQM-34 drones. Meanwhile, space-suited crewmen at the helms of U-2Rs and SR-71As wheeled their recce 'loops' way above the defences or shot across in an east–west pattern like lightning bolts. Interestingly, the first pilot to command an SR-71A combat sortie was Jerome F. O'Malley. He later assumed command of the 460th TRW at Tan Son Nhut for its final month of operations in August 1971 and eventually attained the rank of General, in command of TAC (until he and his wife tragically perished in a freak

take-off accident in a commuter jet on 20 April 1985).

When 7 AF finally caught up with the backlog of unprocessed imagery, the results proved alarming. By the autumn of 1971, after a respite of three years, the communists had built up a force of 250 MiGs, some of which—such as those at Yen Bai near the Red River—were embedded into shelters hewn into sheer rock faces adjacent to their easily repaired parallel runway strips. Yet encounters with these MiGs were extremely rare, indicating that something was awry. Washington finally relented in the face of this growing threat and authorized a massive series of raids for 7 and 8 November 1971, striking Dong Hoi, Quan Lang and Vinh, and these were followed by 1,025 sorties against a variety of lucrative targets south of the 20th parallel between 26 and 30 December, conducted entirely on instruments by means of 'Combat Skyspot' techniques and LORAN. During this so-called 'slack' 37 months of action since November 1968, the RF-4C community suffered some twenty-six 'Photo-Phantom' casualties, bringing total losses in the theatre up to 72 (excluding non-combat related crashes and 'admin strikes'). Yet more sinister was the evidence being garnered by the Recon Wings of a massive North Vietnamese build-up of forces, including a quarter of a million troops plus brand new Soviet armour, prompting Gen John Lavelle (7 AF commander from August 1971) to issue a report warning of an 'imminent large-scale invasion'. He requested a massive reinforcement of air power, which in effect meant turning the 'Vietnamization' MAP programme right round. His deep concerns were to prove correct. However, Washington was reluctant to bolster in-theatre forces and felt that Lavelle's recent 'protective reaction' strikes had overstepped the ROE. He was soon succeeded by Gen John W. Vogt, who took up his post a matter of days after the enemy began its sweeping attack south on 29–30 March 1972. The incisive data-collection capabilities of Col Charles A. Gabriel's 14th TRS were once more

RF-4E EQUIPMENT ARRANGEMENT FORWARD FUSELAGE

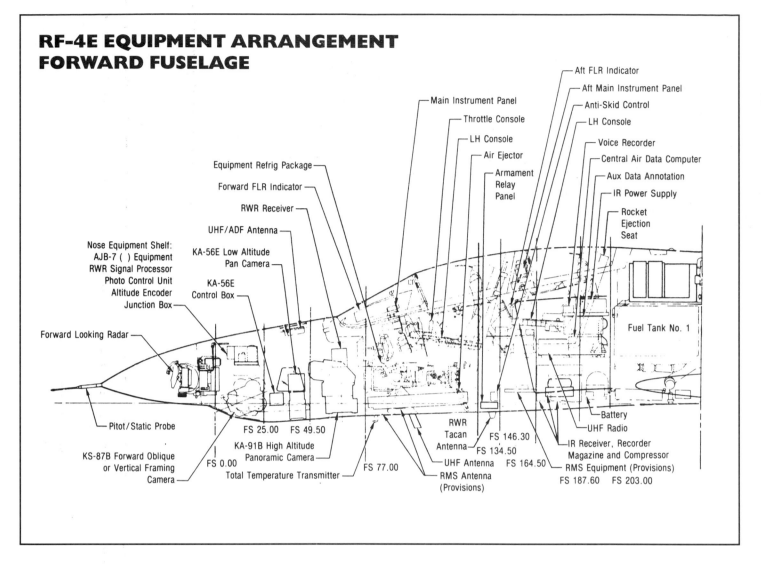

thrown into the fray, tracking enemy movements and staging areas for the artillery, bombers and gunships which over the course of the next two months blunted the enemy's advance, then pushed them back, with professional ferocity. Udorn's 'Peepin' Phantoms' also began to roam further north with increasing regularity, shifting attention away from Laos and the DMZ to note targets of interest in preparation for round two—Operations 'Freedom Train' and 'Linebacker'.

The 1972 bombing campaign, as already described in this book, opened up with interdiction strikes aimed at cutting off the enemy's LOC and supply depots, namely the railways that ran from Dong Hoi right up to Hanoi then split into a trident leading east to the port of Haiphong and north and west to China,

over the innumerable bridges that connected these. Other targets embraced POLs and warehouses, marshalling yards and the power stations which provided the energy for the key command and control networks and dispersed 'by-lightbulb' war-manufacturing industry. During the ensuing five months the 'Recce Rhinos' of the long-suffering 14th TRS bore the brunt of reconnaissance in the theatre, unassisted by 'Constant Guard' which brought in only airlift, strike Phantom and electronic warfare reinforcements. Proud of their job, they muscled into the thick of it again, providing pre-strike weather and post-strike damage assessment, with the photos to compare 'before and after'. On 20 April Maj Ed Elias and his back-seater Capt Ernest Clark (flying in 68-598) were brought down by flak near Vinh. 'Woody'

Clark managed to evade capture, his squadron mates Capts Don Pickard and Greg Bailey eventually establishing a 'fix' from the downed flyer's survival radio which permitted ARRS HH-53C 'Super Jolly' rescue forces to pluck him away from danger, fifty hours after he and his pilot had ejected. Don Pickard found himself in a tricky predicament too during the opening phase of 'Linebacker I' on 10 May. After providing recce coverage of the Paul Doumer Bridge strike, he and back-seater (flying 68-606, call-sign 'Cousin Two') came under pursuit by both MiGs and SAMs, so he jettisoned the wing tanks to assist a rapid egress. Unfortunately one of the 'bags' (probably half full; the manuals stipulate that tanks must be more than 75 per cent full or else not contain more than 10 per cent fuel when dumped) struck the wing, creating a leak. Pickard eventually recovered at Udorn on one engine with a 'fogged' windshield and with less than 200lb of fuel remaining! Only cool nerves prevented a complete disaster. The veteran later went on to command the 'First Tac' at RAF Alconbury.

A further six RF-4Cs were brought down during 1972, and by August the following year, when hostilities finally ceased, the community had suffered 84 losses, seven of the tally being attributed to 'operational' causes. (Four had been demolished on the ground in their revetments during the 1968 Tet Offensive.) Yet, all things considered, these losses remained satisfying low in the crews' minds, given their record of eight years of sustained combat operations comprising 70,000 missions!

Below: The export launch customer for the 'dash-seventeen'-powered RF-4E export derivative of the 'Photo-Phantom' was West Germany's *Luftwaffe*, which acquired a massive 88 of them under Project 'Peace Lookout'. Initial examples went to *AG 51 'Immelman'* at Bremgarten, beginning on 20 January 1971. The unit continued to fly the type for nearly 22 years, until its formal disbandment on 17 September 1992. This gaudy beast was photographed during July 1984, when the Wing celebrated its 25th anniversary. (M. D. Tabak via F. Visser)

Operations by the 14th TRS eventually drew to a close during June 1975, two years after the cessation of hostilities, leaving the 15th TRS *Cotton Pickers* at Kadena AB, Okinawa, as the only USAF 'Photo-Phantom' outfit in the Pacific. Within TAC, two Active Wings continued to fly the type—the 363rd TRW at Shaw, still the bastion of 'Photo-Phantom' operations, including the type's RTU, and the consolidated 67th TRW at Bergstrom AFB, Texas. In common with the 'Phantom Phighter Phraternity', in the aftermath of the Vietnam War the RF-4C force would shift its attention more towards Europe, the Middle East and Korea. The 503rd and last of the line (72-0156, McAir Ship No 4396) was delivered on 15 January 1974, at which point over 360 aircraft remained operational, leaving plenty to go around.

EUROPEAN CHISEL-NOSES

While the early 1970s and 'Linebacker' remains at the forefront of many 'Photo-Phantom' jockeys' memories, the decade also ushered in the beginnings of a huge McAir FMS programme mirroring the F-4E export business. Berlitz manuals to hand, McAir's sales team rushed to and from the war zone, St Louis and numerous foreign destina-

tions with their hungry sales pitch, suitably harnessed to lingaphone courses. One of the first customers (and certainly the biggest) for the 'Photo-Phantom', was West Germany's *Luftwaffe*. 'Peace Lookout' offered an advanced military capability from across the Atlantic when fellow Europeans tended still to mistrust them. And, as LRI and sophisticated attack options were not available, reconnaissance seemed a good way to make a real splash of it. The *Luftwaffe* would take well to the Phantom, eventually absorbing 88 Block 43-47-MC RF-4Es under contract JO787 and a further 185 gun-equipped models.[8]

The first to receive their splinter grey-green RF-4Es, advanced models equipped with the more powerful J79-MTU-17 engine, were *Aufsklärungsgeschwader (AG) 51 'Immelmann'* at Bremgarten on 20 January 1971. Four machines (including cell leader 3501, USAF/FMS serial 69-7448, nicknamed *Spirit of St Louis*) made the Atlantic crossing and were ceremoniously accepted with Air Force Chief of Staff Lt-Gen Gunther Rall, a Second World War 'ace' with 275 victories to his credit, in attendance.

[8] See Chapters 11 and 13 for further details of the *Luftwaffe*'s activities with the F-4E/F models.

Left, top: A second *Luftwaffe* RF-4E Wing, *AG 52*, stationed at Leck, formed close on the heels of *AG 51*; during the summer of 1984 one of its jets wore the most impressive 'tiger' scheme ever contrived for the Phantom. MTU licence-built the J79s for the series, while numerous other components (mostly avionics) were also fabricated by German industry. Many of the aircraft have since been handed down to Turkey. (Kai Anders via Tim Laming)
Left, centre: Japan's *Koku Jie tai* received fourteen RF-4EJs built at St Louis. These exports, in common with all but Germany's variant, featured the deeper, rounded nose profile. The thirteen survivors are flown by the 501st *Hikotai* (*Woodpeckers*) at Hyakuri and, as the sole *Teisatsu Kokutai* (reconnaissance Wing) in the game, it is receiving supplementary F-4EJs equipped with French Thompson-CSF Raphael SLR and ASTAC elint pods to bolster the force. (Via Tim Laming)
Left, bottom: Spain's *Ejercito del Aire* acquired an initial four second-hand RF-4Cs (re-coded 'CR12-41' and upwards) from 363rd TRW stocks during October 1978. These were supplemented with eight more jets during January 1989, drawn from the Kentucky ANG. Nine remain operational with *123 Escuadron* at Torrejon, fitted with J79-GE-15E smokeless engines, updated RHAWS and UHF radio, APQ-172 FLR and a laser-gyro INS, with the option of bolt-on AAR probes. Of the forty F-4C fighter models acquired from USAF stocks between March 1971 and October 1978, most were retired during April 1989 in favour of Hornets and only a handful remain in service as 'hacks', performing target-towing duties. (Tabak/Vandeberg via F. Visser)

Aircraft 3501 had first flown on 15 September the previous year, during which time an initial cadre of *Luftwaffe* crews had been undergoing training at St Louis and at George and Shaw AFBs. Deliveries of aircraft up to 3588 (69-7525) proceeded at a steady rate of eight a month, permitting *AG52* at Leck to undergo re-equipment from 17 September 1971. Four were retained for test and ground instruction duties with *Eprobungsstelle* (*ESt*) *61* at Manching and *Technischeschule 1* at Kaufbeuren. The aircraft carried a full suite of KS-87B and KA-56D cameras, IR and SLR and were outwardly identical to pre-Block 44 USAF RF-4Cs (equipped with the original nose fairing), except for the bigger 'cans' associated with their more powerful engines. The aircraft integrated well within NATO, and 82 survivors were equipped for ground attack between November 1979 and 1983. MBB's Manching and Ottobrunn facilities added a gun sight and weapons computer, provision for AN/ALE-40 chaff/flares and the necessary wiring and MAU-12 racks to permit the aircraft to tote up to 5,000lb of ordnance. Concurrent with this update, the aircraft were repainted in the new *Zitronenfalter* two-tone green and dark grey 'brimstone and butterfly' camouflage. The aircraft flew in the 'swing' role until 1988, when the secondary ground-attack tasking was dropped for reasons of economy.

The other launch customer for the high-performance RF-4E—the hottest of all Phantoms built—was Israel, which acquired three batches of six aircraft produced in Blocks 45, 63 and 64, the last with a data-link capability and 'Compass Ghost Gray' camouflage. These began to be delivered in March 1971, when the two loaned Project 'Peace Night Lite' RF-4Cs (flying out of Israel since August 1969) were returned to the United States. Their distribution within the *Heyl Ha'Avir* remains a closely guarded secret, but they were believed to have been headquartered at Tel Nov. The addition of a limited ground-attack capability subsequently knitted them into the strike squadrons. Fourteen remain operational at the time of writing, bearing plenty of battle scars. Perhaps their most noted exploits have been the occasions when they have served as 'bait'. One such notable operation took place on 13 February 1981. A pair of 'Photo-Phantoms' entered Lebanese airspace at FL400 at 1319Z, drawing Syrian MiG-25P 'Foxbats' up into the air. When the enemy fighters established radar contact at a range of 60 miles, the Phantoms broke formation and dumped clouds of chaff behind them, with the 'Foxbats' giving chase. Seemingly out of nowhere, an F-15A *Baz* zoomed up to greet the MiGs and 'bagged' one of them in a head-on Sparrow attack. The remaining MiG fled. It was the first time that this threat had been engaged and defeated.

Following Germany and Israel was Japan, which acquired fourteen Block 56-MC examples between 26 November 1974 and 8 June the following year (bearing the *Koku Jie tai* serials 47-6901 to -6905 and 57-6906 to -6914). These were assigned to the 501st *Hikotai* at Iruma, which shortly afterwards was re-located to Hyakuri. Iran's *Nirou Hayai Shahanshahiya* acquired sixteen Block 48-MC and 61-62-MC examples concurrent with its 'Peace Roll' purchase of fighters, for service at No 1 Tactical Air Base, Mehrabad, while Greece and Turkey closed the production line in April 1979 when they each acquired eight Block 66-MC RF-4Es, for service with *348 Mira Taktikis Anagnoriseos Matla* at Larissa and *113 Filo* at Eskisehir respectively. All of these featured the re-faired nose, while Greece's aircraft have been configured with US Navy-standard DECM and RWRs and, in common with the machines of the *Turk Hava Kuvvetleri*, feature LES—the only 'Photo-Phantoms' ever built with slats.

It was during this period that the inevitable 'hand-me-down' process began, percolating older aircraft through to the USAF ANG and later to Spain's *Ejercito del Aire* and Korea's *Hankook Kong Goon*. The Guard beat the foreigners to it by seven years; in fact, the RF-4C was the first variant of 'Double-Ugly' to enter service with the Reserves.[9] The first unit to receive it was the 106th TRS *Recce Rebels* at Smith ANGB, Birmingham, Alabama, on 25 February 1971, drawing aircraft returning from the war zone in South-East Asia. The unit achieved Code One status in the early months of 1973 under the command of Col (later

[9] Spain acquired an initial four RF-4Cs from the USAF's 363rd TRW during October 1978, followed by eight reinforcements in January 1989; nine of these aircraft currently equip *123 Escuadron* (*Titans*) under *Ala 12* at Torrejon AB near Madrid. *Ala 12* initially received three dozen ex-81st TFW F-4Cs on 31 May 1972, following re-work at CASA Getafe. Seven were lost in accidents before their retirement from front-line operations in 1989. The F-4Cs, all drawn from Block 25-MC, were coded C12-02 to -36. The RF-4Cs wear the CR serials 12-41 to -52, these now featuring the fixed, exterior hose-compatible AAR probe originally introduced to service on Israeli Phantoms.

Above left: RF-4E-61-MC 01728 (74-1728) of the *Nirou Haya Shahanshahiye Iran* executes a dramatic zoom climb during its pre-acceptance FCF (Functional Check-Flight), its clean lines interrupted only by its EROS collision-avoidance pod. Iran took delivery of sixteen 'Photo-Phantoms' (with serial numbers 2-433 and upwards) to add to its impressive purchase of 209 factory-fresh F-4D/E models, and was in the throes of acquiring sixteen more when the Shah was overthrown and a 'stop-work' order came into effect at St Louis on 28 February 1979. The five part-built airframes already in progress were reduced to spares and taken by truck to Ogden Logistics Center, Utah, to help refurbish USAF Phantoms undergoing overhaul. Three of the original batch were written off prior to the bloody Iran–Iraq conflict, and it is doubtful whether more than four or five remain operational today. (McAir)

Top right: The US Air National Guard got into the 'Recce Rhino' business during 1971 and remains in the job over two decades later. At peak strength, the force included eight squadrons (nine have flown it), including the 123rd TRW based at Standiford Field, Louisville, Kentucky. The unit had authority over the RF-4C squadrons of the Nebraska, Idaho and Nevada reconnaissance Groups and first deployed to Europe with Phantoms in the winter of 1978 under 'Coronet Snipe'. Two of its aircraft are seen here formating with a *Luftwaffe* RF-4E from *AG 51*. (Via P. E. D.)

Above right: The 165th TRS, 123rd TRW, Kentucky ANG was awarded its third Spaatz Outstanding Unit Trophy following its faultless deployment to Karup, Denmark, for the NATO-sponsored 'Best Focus 82' competition, in which in participated with these colourful tail markings. Seven years later it transferred eight of its aircraft to the Spanish Air Force and switched to C-130s and the cargo mission. (M-Slides)

Brig-Gen) Addison O. Logan and by the following year had accumulated 10,000 hours on the aircraft. A total of nine ANG squadrons would eventually operate the type—ten if one includes the 124th TRG Idaho Guard's 189th Tactical Reconnaissance Training Flight, which was established in September 1984 to provide a 'Recce Rhino School House'. Crews would specialize in dead-reckoning navigation and optical day-time photography yet picked up many cups and trophies at competitions around the United States and Europe.[10]

CEASELESS WATCH

USAFE had got into the RF-4C business during 1965 close on the heels of the home-based Wings and, for the next twenty-six years, would become the launch pad for many exciting new technologies. The first to form were the 1st TRS *First Tac* at RAF Alconbury near Cambridge, which on 1 May 1965 began to replace their stately RB-66Cs with elegant light grey and white supersonic Phantoms. Tail numbers 64-1019 and -1025 came direct from the 4415th CCTS at Shaw AFB, which had begun training a batch of crews bound for Europe the previous January. These initial arrivals, with the 10th TRW commander Col Dewitt S. Spain and his backseater Capt J. W. Combs leading and Maj L. E. Alumbaugh and Capt E. R. Goodrich tucked in on their wing, opened up a force which would eventually total 90 machines split between RAF Alconbury and the 26th TRW which would later settle down at Zweibrücken in West Germany.[11]

The RF-4C was originally designed to take many of its intelligence images from high-speed passes at around 40,000ft. Although high-altitude KA-55A cameras were routinely fitted to his steeds, linked to the viewfinder, Col Spain emphasized that the RF-4C 'had no place as an area surveillance aircraft' and the 10th TRW trained from the outset as low-level, 'in the weeds', missile and radar-avoiding tacticians, snapping exposures at up to 1/3,000th of a second with their KS-72 and -87 cameras which each held up to 1,000ft of 2.5-mil film. Along with the usual gamut of framing and panoramic cameras, the unit pioneered the AN/AAS-18 IR and AN/APQ-102 SLR in the European environment. Training schedules progressed well, and within a year of their establishment the 10th TRW declared themselves able to respond to most ground commanders' requests for reconnaissance coverage within an hour. By 1970 crews were operating intensively over routes in Germany, France (despite large 'entry fees' to her airspace) and the United Kingdom. British residents in the more rugged, rural areas soon became used to fleeting, smoking Phantoms winding in pairs through valleys and around mountains, searching out the landmarks ringed in grease pencil on the crews' 1:50,000 scale maps.

Sixteen peaceful years on, the basic mission remained very similar and the jets looked much the same but for their 'wrap-around' camouflage finishes.[12] In fact, considerable internal modification behind the paintwork had taken place to accommodate new systems, these coming 'on line' following numerous 'swaps' for freshly re-worked aircraft. The most important of these were the Lear Siegler DMAS, compatible with the Ford Aeronutronic (later Loral) Pave Tack pod, plus Goodyear (also later Loral) AN/UPD-4 SLR, and the Litton-Amecon TEREC. These boosted the reconnaissance capability to enable the aircraft to undertake true all-weather, around-the-clock operations, with the added bonus of a new digital navigation capability which finally offered an alternative to dead-reckoning. They also ushered in two new concepts, area surveillance and 'near real time' reconnaissance, which put a premium on the data retrieved with or without the crews returning as planned!

The Lear-Siegler AN/ARN-101(V) DMAS was applied to sixty Block 37 to 53 RF-4Cs following test flights at Eglin and validation of the 'Group' fit on board 65-0905 flown by Air Force Logistics Command at Ogden. The package was fundamentally similar to that incorporated on the F-4E model except that it was interfaced with the 'Recce Rhino''s TI AN/APQ-99 radar cursors and AN/ASQ-154 data display (annotation) set

Below: A flight-line of RF-4C-30/31-MC tails in Cambridgeshire. Only CONUS-based aircraft are still parked in strings in this fashion: USAFE and PACAF aircraft began to be dispersed and sheltered under giant TAB-Vee reinforced-concrete monoliths during the latter half of the 1970s. (Via Richard L. Ward)
Bottom: The 26th TRW was one of four USAFE Wings that operated RF-4Cs at one time or another between 1965 and 1992.

Between January 1966 and January 1973 its subordinate 38th TRS was located at Ramstein AB, West Germany, and several of its aircraft featured this dramatic finish complete with shark's-mouths and green diamonds on white fin-caps. This example also sports 'Royal Flush' 'zaps'. The '38th Tac' subsequently moved to Zweibrücken AB and stayed in the business until its disbandment in early April 1991. (APN via P. E. D.)

---

[10] Refer to Appendix VI for full details of the units' formation, 'Coronet' deployments overseas and achievements at exercises and competitions.
[11] See the 10th, 26th and 66th TRW entries in Appendix V for full details of the initial formation of squadrons at Alconbury, Toul-Rosières, Upper Heyford and Ramstein. The eventual split between Alconbury and Zweibrücken did not fully mature until January 1973, when the 26th TRW assumed control of two squadrons at the latter location under Operation 'Battle Creek'.
[12] The first USAFE jet to appear in this new scheme was 65-0708, delivered from CASA Getafe in June 1978. The even darker 'European One' camouflage first appeared on 69-0383 at the end of March 1984.

TABLE 24: RF-4Cs WITH UP-DATED NAVIGATION SYSTEMS

Block No	Serial No	Qty
ARN-92 LORAN-D		
RF-4C-40-MC	68-0594 to -0611	18
RF-4C-41-MC	69-0349 to -0350	2
	Total operational	20
ARN-101 DMAS-modified		
RF-4C-27-MC	65-0905*	1
RF-4C-37-MC	68-0548	1
	68-0550 to -0557	8
	68-0561	1
RF-4C-38-MC	68-0562 to -0565	4
	68-0567 to -0568	2
	68-0570 to -0572	3
	68-0574	1
RF-4C-39-MC	68-0580 to -0583	4
	68-0585	1
	68-0589	1
	68-0592	1
RF-4C-41-MC	69-0357	1
RF-4C-42-MC	69-0359	1
	69-0362	1
RF-4C-43-MC	69-0369 to -0370	2
	69-0373	1
RF-4C-44-MC	69-0376 to -0378	3
	69-0380 to -0384	5
RF-4C-48-MC	71-0248 to -0249	2
	71-0251 to -0252	2
RF-4C-49-MC	71-0254 to -0255	2
	71-0258 to -0259	2
RF-4C-51-MC	72-0145 to -0147	3
RF-4C-52-MC	72-0149 to -0152	4
RF-4C-53-MC	72-0153 to -0156	4
	Total operational	60

* Logistics Command verification platform.

and provided digital position with a navigational margin of error of less than 1nm/hr—negligible given that the system could be constantly updated using radar waypoints or a Kalman-filtered LORAN C/D (if a chain were available) or be corrected by means of a visual identification of prominent landmarks along the planned flight-path, providing a precision capability that was not available to the strictly map-and-grease-pencil analogue variant. The system could, moreover, be 'programmed' with up to around 100 'destinations' for various recce modes, out to the RF-4C's maximum range (allowing for any required time on station). Alconbury, Zwei-brücken and the solitary PACAF squadron received the bulk of the modified aircraft, with most of the balance being retained at Bergstrom AFB, Texas. Shaw received none. In fact, Shaw's days as the 'Home of Reconnaissance' were numbered: between March and September 1982 the nucleus of the RF-4C RTU 'School House' would shift from there to Texas, leaving only the 16th TRS still in place in South Carolina with analogue models before it, too, finally disbanded on 30 September 1989. Its last aircraft departed on 16 December, bringing to an end a career on the 'Photo-Phantom' which had spanned just over twenty-five years. Shaw's distinctive 'JO'

code, named after Jo Stopanian, the wife of a former 363rd TRW pilot, had also long since gone. The jets spent their last six years daubed with the 'SW' DUIs.

Among the big updates performed concurrently with the ARN-101 DMAS was the installation of the AN/AVQ-26 Pave Tack, a laser targeting pod which was fully interactive with the DMAS, that is, it could be cued to stored target co-ordinates and feed in new ones of opportunity via the 'freeze' system. Its resolution was unmatched at the time, thanks to the pod's huge FLIR 'window', which offered two FOVs (wide-angle and zoom) and which proved effective at ranges of up to twelve miles, weather permitting. FLIR images could be recorded on AVTR video to assist with debrief as well as garnering reconnaissance products. Following some 200 flights in the USA aboard RF-4C 69-0378, the system was tested during the 1977 'Autumn Forge' exercises in USAFE, when the 'Arnie' was also trialled. Initially, it was intended that the bulk of the sixty DMAS 'Photo-Phantoms' receive both systems as part of the SCAR (Strike Control & Reconnaissance) 'Fast-FAC' mission. However, at the conclusion of the test effort, it became the speciality of just a handful of recce crews flying with the 12th TRS at

Right: A close-up view of one of the develpment Pave Tack pods, which clearly shows the huge zinc sulphide FLIR window and gallium arsenide laser transmitter/receiver 'peep-holes'. The parent aircraft here, 69-0378, performed the lion's share of the recce-Tack and SCAR (strike control and reconnaissance) integration trials from 1976. The package entered service with the 12th TRS at Bergstrom three years later. (Loral)

Left: On 1 October 1982 Shaw's 363rd TRW became a fighter Wing and began conversion to F-16s, leaving only the 16th TRS still in place as the last bastion of the once huge 'Recce Rhino' establishment there. The codes were changed from 'JO' to 'SW' at the same time. These two 16th TRS steeds were photographed on the March AFB ramp in California during their participation in exercise 'Gallant Eagle 88', a year before the Squadron disbanded. (Frank B. Mormillo)

Once we put the Pave Tack on we had 10–15 minutes max. [Crews quickly began to refer to it as 'Pave Drag', and so it was used judiciously.] I could look at either Pave Tack or radar, but not both at the same time. At low level, when I was getting close to the target, I would flip the switch and start looking. I would then track it all the way through the pass with the handle, and then off into the distance too, getting good imagery. [Target-tracking was supposed to be fully trim-stabilized but typically the WSO had to use the new right console multi-function slew stick to keep the cross-hairs on the target.] The only place where it was hard to see was off each wing-tip. What we liked to do was to turn off, belly-up in an arc and hold the pod on the target for 15–20 seconds.

'Its real advantage was at night: it gave you another sensor instead of just the IR, and it gave you a stand-off capability which was especially good compared to the two IR systems I had used, the AAS-18 and later AAD-5 [either of which occupied the space under the navigator's seat]. The original AAS-18 was

Bergstrom and the 1st TRS at Alconbury.[13] WSO Lt-Col Terry Simpson, who conducted FOT&E at the former base and fully fledged operations at the latter with the 'First Tac', elaborates:

'The ARN-101 digital-inertial was a very good system, enabling an interface with Pave Tack. We carried this on the centreline, and it took a fuel tank away from us. It was very draggy. Once you unstowed the head of the pod, the drag just went up exponentially: the drag index for a "three-bag" RF-4 was something like 21 units; the drag index of a Pave Tack pod alone was about 39 units. I used to take new guys out on a demo and show them how much drag it had. I'd say, "Okay, stabilize the airplane, set the throttles and don't touch them." I'd then unstow the head of the pod, and when it came down it was like opening a barn door. It took ten knots off in less than ten seconds. This cut down on the range. From Alconbury with just two tanks, no centreline, we could go to Leuchars in Scotland and fly for over 25 minutes low-level before heading back.

Below: During its final year of operations, Alconbury's 1st TRS gave RF-4C-38-MC 68-0567 this racy nose trim and the nickname *Starize*. (Christian Gerard)

[13] A similar tasking was earmarked for the 183 DMAS-mod F-4Es, but Pave Tack ended up being employed only by a select number of aircraft at Seymour-Johnson, North Carolina, and Clark Field, in the Philippines, owing to cost and other factors. Refer to Chapters 11 and 14.

very grainy and not the world's greatest. The AAD-5 was a quantum leap, but you still had to overfly the target. The margin of error was pretty slim too; it was easy to overbank. [The Honeywell AN/AAD-5 featured variable-swath, 60° or 120° coverage and compensated for a bank angle of up to 30°.] The lateral coverage of the thing was three times your height. So, if you're at 500 feet, you've only got 1,500 feet of coverage. You've got to be within 750 feet of the target when you're clipping along at a few hundred feet at night, otherwise you could easily miss it. Now the Pave Tack could compensate for navigation error as you could cue it, for one, and the FOV was wider. Also, the resolution was better: you could see through haze; and real thin stuff like fog and condensation didn't bother it. It had good resolution, with magnifying power: cows showed up really well, farmers on tractors could blind you! You could see ships in the North Sea and tell by the heat contrast how much fuel they had; you could see airplanes on runways, on the tarmac, could tell if their motors had been running to tell you how many had been flying, and you could even see the heated concrete behind them. [Such imagery also revealed recent surface movements of vehicles by day when their former locations were shielded from sunlight—such as under camouflage netting or the cloak of a wood—as after moving out into the open the 'targets' were cooler than their surroundings. The other great advantage was that it could be used with its back to the sun, and this was especially useful at dawn and dusk when IR was singularly useless owing to low solar grazing angles. The imagery would all be taped on AVTR, while the co-ordinates of points of interest could be frozen into the ARN-101 system for later use too.] We did have a lasing capability for other aircraft carrying LGBs too, as a spin-off from the SCAR concept, where we could conduct "buddy lasing" using a stand-off orbit. Tactics were flexible and varied with aspect angles, the threats, and so on. Timing was important there: you didn't want the beam on for any

longer than you needed to. Generally speaking, Pave Tack was about as "real time" as getting the tape back and re-playing it—there wasn't any playback editing capability in the aircraft. Its supreme advantage was that it gave us a stand-off night-time sensor.'

Lt-Col Simpson rated the ARN-101 DMAS as being eons ahead of the navigation systems available to the 'vanilla' model:. 'The INS in the old analogue RF-4 was archaic at best, and you could find things like . . . Dallas! It was good at finding Dallas, Waco or Fort Worth, anything like that! I never even set the counters. Everything was done DR. Even sensor operation was manual, and as a general rule you would select every camera and sensor you had on board, because somebody was shooting at you and you had to catch it quick.

'The hybrid inertial-LORAN ARN-101 was very accurate. [It replaced the antiquated Litton AN/ASN-46A navigation computer and AN/ASN-56 INS with a new NC and inertial measurement unit (IMU), respectively.[14]] It was linked into LORAN-C and performed system updates automatically. Even if it didn't lock on to the LORAN it was still accurate: you could store offsets and update the system using radar (or Pave Tack). Another great thing was that it was impossible to miss the time-on-target because it had an ETA read-out. If you wanted to be somewhere at 12 o'clock, you pushed the throttles until it

Above: Alconbury's famous *Triple Nickel* (RF-4C-37-MC 68-0555), safely tucked away in its giant TAB-Vee shelter between sorties. The aircraft carries three 'bags' (including a centreline Eagle tank) and an ALQ-131(V) jammer on the port inboard pylon. (Tim Laming)

read "12 o'clock". It was idiot-proof. [This employed a simple arithmetical computation based on speed and time and was one of those 'nice-to-have' features which made the WSO's life easier in the hustle and bustle of high-speed, low-level operations.]

'The ARN-101 could handle sensor operation—cameras, IR, SLR and TEREC—automatically over the target area. You could manually programme the ARN-101 or do it totally automatically, using a series of points: either a "D" point [destination waypoint] or a "T" point. The cameras were activated using the "T" point—simply a matter of typing "T" instead of "D" on the keyer control when entering the specifics. Then you could get the cameras to run, say, a mile before and a mile after. [Program-

---

[14] Collectively forming the new hybrid LORAN-INS. The basic iteration period of INS equation was 50 milliseconds. Error estimates were added to the INS navigation solutions to obtain corrected solutions for position, velocity and heading every 400 milliseconds. If the LORAN were lost, the INS would continue unabated in this manner; it would usually draw on fresh LORAN inputs automatically as the signals became available, 'looking' at 5- to 10-minute intervals.

ming could be done before take-off or in flight, punching in the data using the new 36-button keyboard on the right console.[15]] Also, this thing would do "area coverage", which was a fun trip. It would turn on the sensors for you too. You would load in the "start point" or first corner of the area to undergo surveillance and tell it the desired path-width and dimensions [of the rectangle: Col Simpson sketched out a square before going on]. You could then engage the autopilot at 15,000 feet and just sit back. The airplane then flew along and activated the cameras, did a 90-degree then 270-degree turn, then another 90 and 270, and so on. It was *insane!* The only thing you had to watch was the throttles: when it reached the turn point—*whooops!* It would fall out of the sky if you were not careful.'

It could also be programmed to avoid certain 'hot spots' or 'no-go' areas. If circular avoidance area locations were identified and programmed-in, 'Arnie' automatically interrupted the path coverage, or turned the aircraft at the appropriate time, to steer the machine around the avoidance area periphery. This 'hands-off' feature could be used for up to twenty consecutive 'adjacent parallel coverage' sensor runs for such systems as a mapping camera or SLR; or for 'racetrack' for TEREC, SLR or other sensors. Full 'point-to-point' navigation was also possible, including tanker rendezvous co-ordinates, multiple targets and so on—very useful features, it was discovered, in the Gulf War, where rendezvous with tanker air refuelling control points (ARCPs) under radio silence, with minimum 'deconfliction' assistance from AWACS, demanded careful navigation. 'You could programme it in and put it in auto-sequence,' continued Col Simpson, 'and it would take you anywhere you wanted to go. All you had to

do was monitor the throttles and move the stick.'

Cameras were still widely employed at Alconbury, Bergstrom and Kadena for low-level work, including KS-87s, the versatile low-altitude panoramic KA-56 and the higher-altitude panoramic KA-91 'with 60° or 90° selectable scan—very good close up, and personal, with a big 18-inch lens'. Support was pre-positioned at forward operating locations such as Gutersloh in Germany so that sensors could be down-loaded, the film reviewed and the aircraft 'gassed-up' again for another mission.

At Zweibrücken, 'tac recon' had another meaning which had more in common with Israeli operations: the '38th Tac' tended to specialize in medium-altitude operations using the new UPD-4 SLR and AN/ALQ-125 TEREC sensors, which put the machine on a par with the 'hot-and-high' SR-71A 'Blackbird' in terms of intelligence-garnering capability.

The AN/UPD-4 sideways-looking synthetic aperture radar (SAR-SLR) was probably the most revolutionary advance. As related earlier, the original APQ-102 system suffered from limited resolution owing to 'spot size', a problem rectified by Goodyear engineer Carl Wiley. The technology was explained to the authors by one of the company's other engineers, Brian Lynch: '"Spot size" or a "resolution cell" is the area covered on the imagery by a single point target. This area is determined by multiplying the across-track by the along-track resolution of the radar. As range

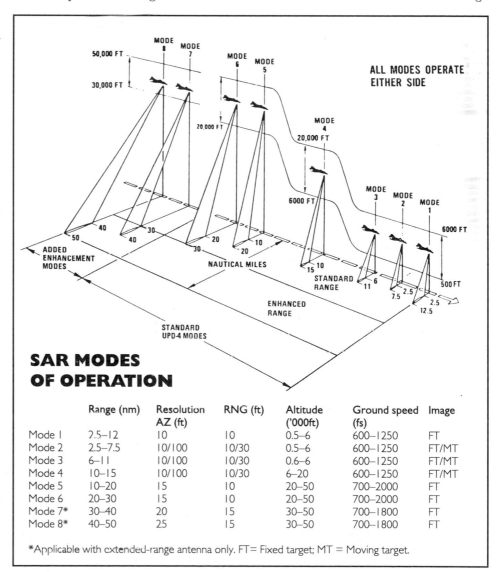

SAR MODES OF OPERATION

	Range (nm)	Resolution AZ (ft)	RNG (ft)	Altitude ('000ft)	Ground speed (fs)	Image
Mode 1	2.5–12	10	10	0.5–6	600–1250	FT
Mode 2	2.5–7.5	10/100	10/30	0.5–6	600–1250	FT/MT
Mode 3	6–11	10/100	10/30	0.6–6	600–1250	FT/MT
Mode 4	10–15	10/100	10/30	6–20	600–1250	FT/MT
Mode 5	10–20	15	10	20–50	700–2000	FT
Mode 6	20–30	15	10	20–50	700–2000	FT
Mode 7*	30–40	20	15	30–50	700–1800	FT
Mode 8*	40–50	25	15	30–50	700–1800	FT

*Applicable with extended-range antenna only. FT= Fixed target; MT = Moving target.

---

[15] Data entry was customarily performed prior to take-off using the new keyboard on the right console. The DTM capability, added from late 1979, proved to be unreliable, was seldom used (especially as it allegedly had to be plugged into the sensor compartment and not the cockpit) and thus did not gain much favour.

Above left: USAF and derivative Phantoms could be started up using cartridges but more commonly employed compressed air furnished by a hose, generated by an A/AM32A-60A trolley. (Tim Laming)
Above right: ER/DL (extended-range data link) was furnished by this 50nm-range SAR/SLR installation, which employed the standard centreline 'bag' design and even held fuel in the nose and tail compartments! The 38th TRS acquired nine of these pods, while the capability was also fitted to selected *Luftwaffe* RF-4Es and to the last batch of six RF-4Es procured by the *Heyl Ha'Avir*. It freed the nose cheeks for use by TEREC and other elint equipment. (McAir via John J. Harty)

lected target radar imagery by means of a laser correlator-processor. Back at base, the resultant imagery was decoded back into images by a companion correlator-processor to produce photo-quality pictures. Tested in Europe during the 1974 annual 'Reforger' (Return of Forces to Germany) exercise, the system furnished imagery with a constant scale of 1:100,000 across and along the film. This permitted the imagery to be magnified to scales as high as 1:2,000, which not only showed up individual parked aircraft, tanks or even oil barrels but also

permitted PIs to classify the hardware by model! It was a remarkable breakthrough. Such recce products had previously only been possible by means of daring low-level flights over the target using cameras, and then tended to be

Below: To provide a 'near real time' reconnaissance facility, Zweibrücken's SAR/SLR radar-mapping jets were retrofitted with the rounder, deeper nose able to accommodate the data-link black boxes and associated 'top hat' antenna door. The latter was interchangeable with a standard No 2 Station camera hatch, so was seldom seen. (McAir via John J. Harty)

increases, real aperture radar cell size expands disproportionately in the along-track mode, creating an asymmetric, distorted view which consequently suffers from a loss of detail. [The resolution cell size for the UPD-4 SAR at a range of 25nm was something like 100 sq ft, with cell ratio of 1:1.] This constant scale across and along track is what made it so superior.' There was no perspective. Moreover, it would be magnified in 'hard copy' on the printers and the tape loads later could be manipulated in all sorts of ways in 'soft copy' form on a TV screen to produce the fine detail required for target recognition.

The UPD-4, part of the 'all-up' AN/APD-10 RMS (reconnaissance mapping set), proved capable of building up a radar image covering a swath ten miles wide at stand-off distances of around thirty miles, by recording a series of neat synthetic portions of the returning ref-

patchy in coverage owing to sensor limits and cloud. The RF-4C could now cover several thousand square miles of territory at a time in one sortie, and do it in virtually all weathers!

Concurrent with the USAFE trials which began in late 1973, climaxed with 'Reforger 74' and culminated in the modification by McAir of an entire squadron's worth of eighteen jets specially for use by the 38th TRS, the system entered operational service with numbers of the *Luftwaffe*'s 'Peace Lookout', and the final batch of Israeli 'Peace Echo', RF-4Es. These two Services' machines employed an extended-range antenna system, effective at up to 50nm from altitudes of up to 50,000ft, offering a resolution of around 20ft. This was made possible by means of a podded installation, based on a standard centreline fuel tank (and actually featuring sealed com-

Below: A spick-and-span area-surveillance 'Photo-Phantom' being preened by its Crew Chief between missions. The 38th TRS specialized in the Loral AN/UPD-8 SAR-SLR and the Litton-Amecom AN/ALQ-125 TEREC using medium-altitude 'race-track' and 'parallel-coverage' sensor runs. (Robert Marx via Tim Laming)

partments fore and aft housing 214 US gallons of fuel), with the SLR housed in a reinforced centre section. A recorder was added to the nose compartment (Stations 2/3) and the 'chisels' were refaired in the ECP 3126 format introduced as standard from Block 44. The deeper ventral format of the rounded fairing permitted the incorporation of the recorder and, when required, the substitution of the Station 2 door with a new one sporting a 'top hat' data-link antenna, to convey the SLR's signals back to ground in a timely manner for processing, while the RF-4E remained in flight. Israeli aircraft incorporated an F-15 central computer and INS for improved radar-mapping cueing, while the German model's GA-3214 extended-range/data-link (ER/DL) package made do with the existing navigation equipment.

In turn, during 1976 USAFE's 38th TRS had begun to incorporate data link, broadcasting its findings over a secure radio link, for 'near real time' radar reconnaissance, which could be made available within a quarter of an hour of receipt by the ground-based TIPI (Tactical Information Processing & Interpre-

tation) cabin. Moreover, automated target-recognition functions were steadily improved. The system would compare old and new imagery of the same terrain to pinpoint fresh targets or point out movements of forces. Following the successful QRC76-01 demonstration, all eighteen AN/APD-10 RF-4Cs were re-equipped with the 'near real time' AN/UPD-8 model. In 1979 these were also earmarked for upgrade to the ER/DL podded system. Nine pods were produced and Zweibrücken's aircraft received the relevant Mod 3011 update during re-work at Messerschmitt-Bölkow-Blohm at Manching (under TO 1F-4(R)C-671), conducted through 1985. These worked with the ARN-101(V) DMAS to provide quality 'hands-off' parallel coverage of the assigned target area and reliable annotation of the sensor imagery. The use of the new pods permitted significantly greater flexibility in aircraft scheduling as well as the improved ER/DL collection modes, while allowing the now redundant 'SLR cheeks' to be turned over to a new sensor, TEREC.

The AN/ALQ-125 Tactical Electromagnetic Reconnaissance sensor, first

assigned to Zweibrücken in experimental form from 27 August 1975, was added *en bloc* from 1978 after a five-year gestative period borne out of Project 'Pave Onyx', originally spawned during the Vietnam War to plot the North Vietnamese SA-2 SAM network. TEREC could be fused with the AN/APD-10 and was capable of working in real time too, conveying its findings direct to ground-based TEREC remote terminals (TRTs) and TEREC portable exploitation processors (T-PEPs). In flight, the 'tactical ferreting' mission could employ the ALQ-125 in all-round or left- or right-only modes, programmed to pick up as many as ten different emitter types and, by means of DOA (direction of arrival) triangulation techniques, plot their position. During the 'auto search', five priority radar types could be singled out for 'real time' coverage and, when any one came on the air, it could be singled out for individual scrutiny using the WSO's 'location' display. This would in turn provide an LED read-out pertaining to target bearing, estimated range in miles and coordinates, all of which could be conveyed over secure radio for dispatch to friendly fighter-bombers. Data link covered all ten emitter types programmed into the system, and post-mission analysis, where the magnetic tape would be scrutinized, could encompass a 'full spectrum search' to help plot a complete enemy EOB (electronic order of battle).

TEREC was a remarkable elint tool which proved a boon to the EF-111A radar-jammers' and F-4G SEAD missions. An eventual total of 23 systems were fielded, distributed mostly between the 15th TRS at Kadena and the 38th TRS at Zweibrücken, where they remained operational right to the end, fused with SAR-SLR to help plot the whereabouts of mobile anti-aircraft systems and even maritime traffic: tests had wrung-out both systems over the Mediterranean as well as over Central Europe, proving the concept of overland and overwater reconnaissance in exacting circumstances.

Along with these improvements came a steady flow of communications up-

dates, including an AN/ARC-190 HF long-range radio scrambled by a Parkhill KY-75 secure speech system, plus Vinson Have Quick anti-jam, secure UHF radio. These offered obvious tactical advantages but had the additional benefit of providing crews with long-range radio entertainment too. Equally significant was the new TI AN/APQ-172 radar, an APQ-99 with new digital line replaceable units, the signals from which were fed through a digital scan converter on to new cockpit radar tubes for improved resolution and reliability. A voice warning system linked to a combined radar altimeter also was installed. Together, these proved to be a considerable asset to crews in terms of low-level safety.[16]

Between them, these numerous initiatives had the desired 'force multiplier' effect. 'Near real time' reconnaissance meant that products could be disseminated to field commanders within as little as twelve minutes of their collection, and half an hour at the outside. This more than compensated for the shrinking numbers of RF-4Cs committed to USAFE, which had dwindled to forty between January 1976 and December 1978, as a result of the 'Creek Realign' and 'Ready Team' initiatives.[17] Reinforcements were always to hand during a potential crisis by means of deployments from CONUS under the 'Salty Bee' programme. Alconbury hosted the first such deployment in March 1976, when Shaw's 62nd TRS brought across eighteen jets as 'Coronet Rally'. Subsequent annual 363rd TRW deployments tended to find accommodation elsewhere. In June 1978 eighteen 'Coronet Heron' RF-4Cs dropped into RAF Coltishall, while Aviano in Italy took an equal number for the 1980 visit. The other Tac Wing, the 67th TRW at Bergstrom AFB, Texas, made a series of similar excursions to Zweibrücken.

By the mid-1980s, greater emphasis was placed on night flying. The populations of Huntingdon and Saarland were already used to the ghostly moan of the RF-4C's BLC system as aircraft returned to 'homeplate' through the hours of darkness. Training of this kind was on the

syllabus from 1966 onwards but two decades later a good percentage of missions were conducted after sunset, and flown only just above the peacetime 250ft AGL daylight limit. The operational scenario was simulated regularly. 'Tactical Air Meet', 'Best Focus' and 'Royal Flush' were all chances to swap skills with NATO partners and to compete directly for the 'cup'. The professional exuberance exhibited by USAFE, 'Coronet' deploying Guardsmen and their German NATO partners was reflected in the glowing reports that flooded into the commanders' offices following the major autumnal 'Reforger' manoeuvres. However, their days were numbered. The revitalized U-2R (known by the misleading interim designation TR-1A) was entering the fray with all manner of new stand-off 'Senior' 'near real time' sensors, including second-generation synthetic aperture radar. On 6 February 1986 the DoD announced that the 1st TRS would be disbanded and some 1,000 personnel withdrawn from the United Kingdom the following year. Eighteen aircraft returned to CONUS, leaving the unit with only a pair of 'spares' which were eventually to be passed to the 26th TRW at Zweibrücken. Cynics observed that the huge expenditure on TAB-Vee construction at the base immediately prior to this decision was a little excessive for two Phantoms! Nevertheless, the shelters were used once again in July 1986 when the 16th TRS from Shaw brought eighteen RF-4Cs for one of their customary 'Salty Bee' deployments.

The remainder of the 1st TRS's final year was eventful. Phantoms took part in the large-scale 'Hammer' exercises in which over 300 aircraft were involved in 'attacking' or 'defending' targets in eastern England over a two-hour period. The year was marred by the loss of 72-

---

[16] Applied to RF-4Cs under TOs 1F-4(R)C-693 (Parkhill HF) and -704 (ARC-190); and to RF-4C and F-4D/E/G aircraft under TOs 1F-4-1241 (UHF antenna mod), -1252 (CARA), -1262 (VWS), -1315 (UHF battery bus) and -1320 (Vinson UHF).

[17] Refer to the 10th and 26th TRW entries in Appendix V.

0146 and its crew. After a slow flypast at RAF Brawdy's Open Day on 24 July, the RF-4C failed to accelerate and flopped down into shallow sea just off Newgale Beach. Flying in the murky Northern European or North Pacific weather provided particularly realistic training, and the terrain was just as hard as that below the flak-filled skies of Vietnam and Laos: USAFE exponents the 10th and 26th TRWs lost nineteen other aircraft between 2 June 1965 and 6 November 1985.[18] This was a sobering end to an incredible era. The 1st TRS, the last Phantom squadron based in England, was deactivated on 29 May 1987, leaving just the 38th TRS in place under 17 AF control in Germany, where it would remain for a further four years, providing the only realistic photo-reconnaissance capability in NATO alongside the *Luftwaffe*'s two *Aufklärungsgeschwader*—plus, of course, the nominal Greek, Spanish and Turkish contributions, which totalled only eighteen RF-4C/Es on the Southern Flank.

During all this time the 15th TRS and their detachment at Osan, South Korea, continued to thunder around the Pacific. A quantity of DMAS machines were made available to the 'Nogun Shoguns' for accurate photo-reconnaissance, but perhaps their greatest accomplishment—and most enigmatic—was their continuing surveillance of the North Korean border country, always a source of anguish to the United States and its allies. Fulfilling this task meant flying with a 22ft-long, two-ton centreline pod known as the 'Box Bird', a remarkable piece of kit which cleared the ground by barely more than a foot. Known originally as the General Dynamics G-139, the pod had been developed during 1970 under Project 'Peace Eagle'. Test-flown at Shaw from October the following year aboard RF-4C 66-0419, it housed the enormous 66in focal length HIAC-1 LOROP (long-range oblique optical camera system), plus unspecified sigint (signals intelligence) gathering sensors. The HIAC-1 offered 1m resolution in left or right oblique seventy miles deep into enemy territory, producing crisp

Above: On its formation in July 1975 VMFP-3 continued to operate RF-4Bs in VMCJ-2 markings. After a period with plain 'RF' codes they adopted this slinky scheme. BuNo 151980 was retired to AMARC in October 1989. It is seen here en route from MCAS El Toro, California, to a 'Gallant Eagle 84' sortie at the USMC Combat Center. (Frank B. Mormillo)

images by means of image compensation, autofocus and autoexposure at rates of up to 1/3,000th of a second, with a half f-stop error margin. 'Box' missions continued unabated right up until the 460th TRG assumed control of the former 15th TRS Osan detachment at Taegu, South Korea, in October 1989. The Squadron was deactivated in December 1990 and its aircraft passed to the *Hankook Kong Goon*, which also received eight brand new 'Pave Drag' pods for its Phantoms. The whereabouts of the 'Box Bird' pod remains unclear.

Interestingly, the HIAC-1 also formed the basis for three very unusual Israeli Phantoms (69-7567, -7570 and -7576) modified to the F-4E 'Special' configuration during 1975–76 by General Dynamics Fort Worth under Project 'Peace Jack'. Two of these F-4E(S) aircraft remain operational today, integrated with the IAF/DF's F-4E force. Originally, it was intended that the aircraft receive revised vari-ramp inlets and PCC (pre-compressor-cooled) water-injection saddleback tanks, plus beefed-up titanium canopy bow frames to cope with the heat and stress of high-speed flight, to offer Mach 2.4 cruise and a dash speed of Mach 3.2! This exploratory component of the programme was dropped, but all three F-4Es, beginning with the test-bed -7576, received a brand new nose extended by a further foot. A HIAC-1 magazine holding 1,000ft of film was included, along with provision for a vertical/oblique KA-90 panoramic camera. As with PACAF's 'Box Bird', very little is known about these machines'

operational service, save that one was allegedly lost on 24 July 1982 during Operation 'Peace for Galilee'.[19]

SPECTERS

Eleven months before the RF-4C made its maiden flight the US Navy had received definitive proposals for a carrier-based version known as the Model 98-DH or RF-4B. This was a response to the Service's agreement to join the 'Photo-Phantom' programme in May 1962, as the overseer of procurement on behalf of the US Marine Corps.

The first RF-4B was also a production line F-4B conversion with the recce nose. BuNo 151975 first flew on 12 March 1965, almost two years after the contract was finalized. Initially the USN wanted the new aircraft too, but the Fleet still operated a high proportion of the 144 RF-8A Crusaders which had been built between 1956 and 1958, and was about to acquire the first of what would eventually amount to 140 'hot and high' RA-

---

[18] Of 713 Phantoms written off from the USAF inventory by August 1988, 131 were 'Photo-Phantoms'; a further 25 of the latter were struck off for other reasons.

[19] Refer to Chapter 14 for a fuller description of operations in the Beka'a.

Left, upper: The Sierra Nevada makes an attractive back-drop for this VMFP-3 RF-4B in its three-tone grey scheme: FS36375 and the lighter FS36495 on top, and FS26633 below. Carrier deployments on the USS *Midway* were part of the Squadron's duties from 1975 to 1984. (Frank B. Mormillo)
Left, lower: A quartet of USS *Midway* birds, their probes eagerly extended for a top-up, slide into position behind a VMGR-352 Hercules tanker. Four RF-4Bs was the usual quota for a *Midway* detachment. (Frank B. Mormillo)

1965, VMCJ-2 at MCAS Cherry Point, North Carolina, and VMCJ-3 at El Toro, California, beginning with the latter at the same time that the Phantom II was awarded the Glenn H. Curtiss Memorial Award as 'Outstanding Aircraft of the Year'. By this stage it was clear that there would be an increase in the operational demands for theatre reconnaissance in South-East Asia, so aircraft from both units were also passed to the Iwakuni-based VMCJ-1 in 1966. At the same time the RF-8A Crusaders attached to those units were transferred back to the Navy as attrition replacements, to be re-worked for another twenty years of service.

VMCJ-1 remained in Vietnam longer than any other unit on consistent deployment, operating from Da Nang from 3 November 1966 until mid-1970. Much of the groundwork had been done for them by the RF-8A pilots, flying from carriers on 'Yankee Team' sorties over Laos from May 1964. The Phantom brought many improvements to the mission since it added SLR and IR imagery to the basic photographic data previously available. Night infra-red recce soon achieved considerable importance as a means of monitoring enemy troop movements. Like their RF-8A forebears, the RF-4B pilots relied on speed and guile to elude the formidable defences, though twenty Crusaders were lost to flak. Phantoms were targeted against three or four separate sites on a typical

5C Vigilantes, 79 of which would be built to this standard as new, with sideways-looking radar and infra-red as integral sensors. The USMC therefore became the sole operators of the RF-4B. The first order was for twelve, increased to 36, all of which were produced under Blocks 20–27.

Essentially similar to the RF-4C from which it grew, the Marines' model in fact embodied most of the features of the F-4B, including the lack of duplicate flight controls in the rear 'office' and the slotted stabilator and fixed inboard leading-edge flaps introduced during Block 26 production.[20] The other key differences from the USAF stock variant included in-flight rotatable camera mounts, an emphasis on the KS-87 framing and KA-55/56 panoramic cameras only and, unique to this model, a set of telescopic steps built into the fuselage above the

port APQ-102 SLR bay—all Navy models had to be self-contained in this regard, to reduce clutter on crowded flight decks. Also unique was the AS/ASN-74 INS. The RF-4B was the only carrier-compatible model to employ an inertial navigation set, allied to the improved ASN-46A nav computer installed from aircraft No 10 (BuNo 153089). Later, a second batch of RF-4Bs was ordered to meet the Marines' increased workload during the Vietnam period. The last five of these ten aircraft, produced under Blocks 41 and 43, had the 'thick' wing, drooped ailerons and main gear of the F-4J together with the aft fuselage, fin and rounded nose sections standardized with late RF-4C production. The final example, BuNo 157351, was handed over on Christmas Eve 1970.

The first deliveries were made to the two home-based Marine recce units in

---

[20] Other naval features included probe/drogue refuelling; catapult provisions; the F-4B's 'thin' wing with 30 × 7.7in MLG wheels; J79-GE-8 engines; and carrier approach lights and a single taxy light in the nose gear door.

sortie, maintaining high altitude for the transit portion of the mission and then dropping to around 3,500ft for a 600kt-plus run over the 'target'. The requirement to maintain straight and level flight for the photo-run exposed the aircraft to inevitable risks from groundfire, but pilots made sure they jinked energetically on the exit route.

In November 1968 VMCJ-1, under the command of Lt-Col E. B. Parker, flew 188 photo sorties out of Da Nang for a total of 241.2 hours. In that year the squadron was averaging 200 missions a month and this figure remained fairly constant over the following two years. In October 1969 RF-4Bs were sent against 174 photo 'targets', failing to reach another 77 because of cloud cover or storms and 51 on account of camera

Below: Two Guard squadrons that have just recently bowed out of the 'Recce Rhino' league, or are about to do so, are represented here: Mississippi's 153rd RS based at Key Field, Meridian, which received its first RF-4Cs in September 1978 and switched to KC-135Rs in April 1992; and the Californian 196th RS, which converted from F-4Es during July 1990 and is scheduled also to switch to KC-135Rs during FY94. The immaculately maintained 'Hill Gray II' camouflage finish was typical of Guard Phantoms. (Scott Van Aken via Tim Laming)

malfunctions. The Squadron's nine available Phantoms covered 738 miles with IR imagery and 174 with SLR, but the statistics for the consumption of film make more impressive reading: in the same month the Phantoms' three camera types ran through 108,983 negatives on 92,000ft of film. However, all these figures were exceeded in June 1970, which became a record month for the unit. A total of 751 'targets' were successfully photographed on 235 sorties, while IR coverage rose to 6,735nm. The unit's photo laboratory processed no less than 310,245ft of film for the PIs to peer at. Darkroom enthusiasts may wish to know that a total of 81,300 gallons of water were needed just to wash the photos!

On 29 June 1970, VMCJ-1's CO, Lt-Col P. A. Manning, flew the unit's 25,000th combat sortie. Throughout the month his squadron averaged eight available RF-4Bs, with four being ready on the ramp most days. Most of their 186 sorties had been by day, but 49 of them occurred in darkness. Forty-one were flown on 7 AF-generated missions and the remainder provided a wide range of data for the US Army, ARVN and Marines in MR-1. Despite such a high utilization, the recce Phantoms managed to avoid serious mishap. The only

flak damage was to BuNo 153101, which took a 14.5mm round in its APQ-102 SLR installation.

Apart from regular Progressive Aircraft Rework (PAR) at NAS Atsugi, the Phantoms received few equipment updates during their war service. The main, and most welcome, innovation was the 'Shoehorn' modification which was also applied to F-4Bs. This took individual aircraft to Cubi Point in the Philippines for about a week at a stretch to have the AN/APR-25 RHAWS and -27 LWR added, along with an internal AN/ALQ-51 DECM fit.[21] However, by 1975 it was obvious that the sensor fit was in need of a general upgrade. Many airframes were also showing high hours and major refurbishment was clearly in order if the small RF-4B force was to continue as a valuable asset. The answer was Project 'SURE' (Sensor Update and Refurbishment Effort), and the improved RF-4B was designated Model 98-MA. Organized jointly by McDonnell Douglas and NARF, the project produced a development aircraft in the spring of 1978 and 28 kits to update other surviving aircraft

---

[21] Additional equipment which crept aboard included an AN/ALE-29 countermeasures dispenser and AN/ALA-31 countermeasures control.

deemed worthy of the refit. The SURE package included the AN/ASN-92 carrier-aligned inertial navigation set (CAINS, provided with present position up to launch by the ship's SINS, or manually by the back-seater in the customary manner), the AN/ASW-25B ACLS 'Look Ma, No Hands!' data link, AN/ALR-45 RWR and the Magnavox -50 SAM launch alert system, plus new Sanders AN/ALQ-127 DECM break-lock deception jammers contained in fairings on the intake trunks. Sensor updates matched those introduced by the USAF and revolved around the variable-swath Honeywell AN/AAD-5

Below: RF-4C dispersal at Sheikh Isa, with suitable runway warnings to denote possible jay-walking ruminants! The machines are from Bergstrom's 12th TRS, which arrived just before the festive season in December 1990. At this juncture 'TDY-ing' aviators from the Nevada 192nd TRS *High Rollers* took over the Alabama Guard's force, with RF-4C strength teetering around the seventeen mark. They performed the chief role of BDR and LOROPS data-gathering in the absence of the SR-71A, retired only a year beforehand! (Lt-Col Jim Uken)

IR linescanner, plus the Goodyear AN/UPD-10 SAR-SLR derived from the UPD-8. At a cost of $4.5 million per aircraft, the programme was completed by 1981 and brought all RF-4Bs to a consistent standard which gave them nearly ten more years of useful service. Externally, only minor variations in the nose shape and wing root/undercarriage differentiated the three surviving definitive Block 43 models from those of an earlier lineage.

Preservation of the small force was in the interests of the US Navy too. The retirement of the 'Vigi' in 1979, followed shortly afterwards by the withdrawal of the variable-incidence-wing RF-8G Crusader left carriers with a gap in their reconnaissance capability that 'recce in a can' F-14A TARPS 'Peeping Toms' were not yet able to fill in quantity. Plans were hurriedly laid for a number of RF-4B carrier deployments. In all, seventeen RF-4Bs had been lost by the time SURE was completed, (four in SEA, two to hostile fire and the balance to 'operational causes'), so it obviously made sense to both the USN and USMC to maxi-

mize the effectiveness of the surviving aircraft. This had the incidental result of making them the longest-serving of all Phantom variants in Navy hands.

In 1975 the operational framework of RF-4B activity was changed. The experience of Exercise 'Solid Shield', which drew upon combinations of USMC squadrons, convinced 'The Corps' that a centralized base for its reconnaissance activities was more cost-effective. VMFP-3 *Specters* was therefore established at MCAS El Toro, combining the assets of the three Composite Recon (VMCJ) units on one base but with the responsibility of providing recce products for all three Active Air Wings. It was also tasked with detaching aircraft to Iwakuni on rotation, and with providing carrier-based 'dets' when necessary. For this reason RF-4B crews were required to perform annual 'Carquals'. Some of the carrier deployments lasted for the duration of a cruise, such as those performed on the USS *Kitty Hawk*. The commitment to the USS *Midway* was much longer. From August 1975 to 1984 VMFP-3 kept a continuous 'det' of four aircraft and five

Right: Operation 'Desert Shield' brought the 106th TRS Alabama Guard *Recce Rebels* from Birmingham MAP to Sheikh Isa AB, Bahrain, during August 1990. Several of their jets were equipped with the CAI KS-127 LOROPS. RF-4C-22-MC 64-1044 shown here was lost on 8 September 1990 along with its crew—the only Phantom fatalities during the entire Gulf conflict. (David Robinson)

crews aboard the ship to furnish the Seventh Fleet with radar reconnaissance. This included cover for *Midway*'s three Indian Ocean cruises during the Iran Crisis.

Other detachments were made on a regular basis, with up to six RF-4Bs at East Coast air stations or in Puerto Rico, or, on one occasion, in Denmark for NATO manoeuvres. In August 1990, after fifteen years of valuable service, it was decided to retire the 'Eyes of the Corps'. The alternative scheme of maintaining a handful of aircraft until July 1991 was ruled out and Lt-Col M. S. Fagan, the last commanding officer, had the sad task of presiding over the deactivation of the longest-serving collection of Phantoms to wear the proud, bold logo 'Marines' on their flanks.

HIGH ROLLERS

By the time the Iraqi invasion of Kuwait had hit the headlines, many of the old analogue RF-4Cs had been retrofitted with a more accurate inertial reference system by means of RLG (ring laser gyros). These added a precision navigation capability to the previously 'dead-reckoning' photo-ships in service with the ANG—and just in time. When the mobilization orders came, half a dozen RF-4Cs from the Alabama ANG and a commensurate number of crews dropped pens and other normal professional paraphernalia and headed out to Birmingham MAP, for briefing and redeployment to Sheikh Isa AB, Bahrain.

The Alabama Guard RF-4Cs which deployed to 'Phantomtown' were capable of being fitted out with the CAI KS-127A LOROP. These were restricted to the Guard and a few Greek machines, offering 1–2ft resolution from stand-off ranges of up to 25 miles—perfect in

the clear skies over the Persian Gulf. Oblique sighting relied on rear cockpit sill-mounted sights as opposed to the downward-looking drift-sight, with a temperature gauge added to the navigator's main instrument panel to ensure that the system did not overheat. Amongst the 'tails' configured for this task, which took up the entire aft two Stations, was the 106th TRS 'flagship' 65-0853, crewed by detachment commander Lt-Col Ben Robinson, WSO. All combat jets received 'mini shark's-mouths' devised for the Gulf War by Maj Barry K. Henderson and Lt-Col Stephen G. Schramm. Ironically, in May 1988, at the Phantom's 30th birthday party, Steve Schramm described his charge as 'a good, strong meat-and-potatoes airplane. There's nothing fancy about it.' Tragically, on 8

October 1990, while flying a 'Desert Shield' 'Eager Light' sortie in 64-1044, he and Barry Henderson tumbled into the ground 100nm west-south-west of Al Dhafra, Abu Dhabi, during a misjudged simulated AAA threat-reaction manoeuvre. They were the only tac-recon casualties during the entire conflict, and they were missed by all.

The Sheikh Isa Guard recce force was handed over to crews from the 'TDY-

Below: 'Phantom Bosses' at Sheikh Isa: from left to right are Lt-Col Chuck Chinnock, 192nd TRS Ops Officer; Lt-Col Mills, 12th TRS Commander (CC); Col Neal Patton, 35th TFW(P) Deputy Commander for Operations; Col Woody Clark, 192nd TRS CC; Lt-Col George 'John Boy' Walton, 561st TFS CC; and Lt-Col Randy Gelwix, 81st TFS CC. (Lt-Col Jim Uken)

TABLE 25: USAF F-4 ASIP AIRCRAFT DAMAGE INDEX*								
	0–0.2	0.2–0.4	0.4–0.6	0.6–0.8	0.8–1.0	1.0–1.2	1.2–1.4	1.4–1.6	1.6–1.8
F-4C	1	6	6	40	108	99	24	2	1
RF-4C	121	163	41	8					
F-4D	3	13	38	159	151	75	5	2	
F-4E	40	303	164	9	4	1	2		
F-4G		52	56						

*Aircraft Structural Integrity Program data compiled during inspections up to March 1982, under TO 1F-4-101. The index, synthesized using several variables such as airframe hours, peculiar damage and readings from VGH recorders (applied in the cockpit and behind access panel 121R on 13 per cent of the force), and on statistical counting accelerometers (located on the centre wing keel of all aircraft, accessed through the right wheel well via door 89R), was used to monitor load stress factors of between −1.8g and +7.8g. Individual aircraft could then be selected for early retirement or systems improvements. The low wear-and-tear on the veteran RF-4Cs was particularly noteworthy.

ing' 192nd TRS *High Rollers* from Nevada during December. With them came attrition replacement jets, drawn from the Nevada and Mississippi ANGs. Crews left Reno on 3 December with Col 'Woody' Clark and his Ops Officer Lt-Col 'Chuck' Chinnock in charge. Another six aircraft from Bergstrom's 12th TRS, commanded by Lt-Col John Mills, brought a night-time recce capability from Texas on 20 December. All were embroiled during the subsequent mêlée, flying relentless 'Scud' missile-hunting sorties and providing general pre-strike reconnaissance and BDA. They offered a deep-strike, stand-off, low- to medium-altitude capability which the U-2R was unable to handle, especially when the weather closed in. For example, when the Iraqis starting disgorging oil into the Gulf from the Almadi pumping station, it was a LOROP RF-4C that was sent in to get the intelligence required to help plan the subsequent smart-bomb attack which successfully stemmed the flow, not the high-flying 'Dragon Lady'. Crews used 'tree' callsigns ('Redwood', 'Oak' etc) and planned their intelligence-gathering missions to coincide with the presence of F-4G 'Weasels' in the vicinity, which provided a SEAD umbrella. The ANG aircraft alone accounted for 412 sorties, with 64-1047 suitably inscribed and bearing the apt nickname *Scud Seeker*. The commander's LOROP machine flew a respectable 90 sorties. One further machine, 64-1056, was lost on 31 March while performing mop-up reconnaissance in the aftermath of the campaign; both crewmen ejected successfully and returned home in one piece. Regular and Reserve forces redeployed to the United States between 9 and 16 April 1991.

To the north, Brig-Gen Lee Downer's largely autonomous 7440th CW had found itself 'naked' without a recce detachment. Target images from satellites and other sources took an alarming 24 hours to reach combat crews, so the Wing pressed for 'tac recon' to be deployed at the earliest opportunity. Zweibrücken's '38th Tac' filled the void, arriving with six jets in the evening of 3

Below: Alabama Guard 'flagships' and their entourage, ready to roll. The *Recce Rebels* were the first in the Guard to take Phantoms, in February 1971, and were still operational at the time of writing 22 years later! Plans exist to keep them flying for several more years, in company with the RF-4Cs of the Reno-based *High Rollers*. (Scott Van Aken via Tim Laming)

Right: Based at Cannon IAP at Reno, Nevada, the 192nd RS *High Rollers* flew Gulf combat missions using mostly 106th TRS jets, though one of its aircraft, 65-0886, was represented. This flight was captured at altitude by ace photographer Frank B. Mormillo from the No 4 position while en route to the NAS Fallon Military Operating Area for a recce-sweep. The unit, to be upgraded with the new Loral 66in focal length EO-LOROPS camera system, remains operational as one of two surviving RF-4C squadrons. (Frank B. Mormillo)

February 1991, seventeen days into the air war. Using 'comm-out' techniques and launching in the early hours with F-16 CAP to catch up with the Wing's BDA requirements, the 'det' was later integrated into the three strike waves put up daily by the 7440th. Between 5 February and the successful completion of the campaign late in the month, the detachment flew 103 'Proven Force' sorties, with Maj Chuck Lavelle's aircraft (68-0570) clocking up 21; aircraft were decorated with 'Kodak' symbols, each denoting five missions. The aircraft returned to Zweibrücken in March and the unit was disbanded on 4 April, the official ceremony taking place the following day when Squadron boss Lt-Col Rowland's jet (69-0383) was placed in a hangar and inscribed with signatures from the crews prior to dispatch to AMARC. USAFE 'Photo-Phantom' operations had come to an end. The following year the last remaining regular squadron, Bergstrom's 12th TRS *Blackbirds*, was decommissioned. On 28 August they bade farewell to their Phantoms, marking the finale to twenty-eight years of continuous Active RF-4C operations.

The *Luftwaffe*'s two RF-4E Wings also bowed out during 1993, the duty passing to Tornado units. Forty-five of the surviving 73 RF-4E airframes were passed to Turkey, fifteen of them knocked-down to 'spare parts locker' sub-assemblies, while a further 27 of the aircraft passed to Greece (seven of them as 'spares'), bolstering Hellenic Air Force assets from

a surviving five LES airframes to a composite squadron of 25 jets, all flown by the Larissa-based *348 Mira*. This shift of forces has effectively quadrupled Mediterranean 'Photo-Phantom' assets split between Greece, Spain and Turkey to over seventy machines, but has left a ghost in the north.

On 28 May 1993, when the Phantom community was commemorating its thirty-fifth birthday, the 117th TRW *Recce Rebels* celebrated the occasion with a suitably marked aircraft: 64-1041 was festooned with the flags of the dozen nations that had flown the F-4 and roared over St Louis' famous gateway. That summer the ANG RF-4C establishment was about to undergo a serious contraction, leaving only Alabama and Nevada

still in the game. The once massive USAF Phantom fleet was in the throes of being reduced to just four operational squadrons, three of them reservists, with the complete phase-out on the horizon.[22]

---

[22] Since this book was first published the Phantom has bowed out from USAF service. The 561st FS *Black Knights* flew their last 'Southern Watch' mission on 9 January 1996, led by Col Uken. On that occasion he flew 69-7232, which was the first Coalition fixed-wing aircraft to enter Kuwaiti airspace during 'Desert Storm'. Col Uken led the last eight F-4Gs to AMARC on 26 March 1996. The Boise Idaho Guard deactivated their last F-4G on 20 April 1996. RF-4Cs from the Nevada Guard *High Rollers* were deactivated on 27 September 1995 and RF-4C 65-0886, a Vietnam veteran which had also flown the first tac recce sortie of 'Desert Storm', assumed new duties as Reno gate guardian.

Right: RF-4C 69-0362, in use with the 4485th Test Squadron at Eglin's Tactical Air Warfare Center. (Authors' Collection)

16. WILD WEASEL IV EXTRA

Since the first edition of this book was published, more has emerged about the activities of the small pioneer cadre of F-4 crews who flew the F-4C Wild Weasel IV during Operation 'Linebacker', the final air onslaught of the Vietnam War. Operating with the 67th TFS, they were known as . . .

DON'S DIRTY DOZEN AND CREW CHIEFS

In mid-September 1972 half a dozen F-4C Wild Weasel IV and nine crews from Lt-Col Donald J Parkhurst's 67th TFS *Fighting Cocks*, on a TDY to Kunsan, South Korea, were ordered to redeploy to Korat to bolster the USAF's combat-committed defence suppression forces. Squadron mobility officer and Weasel pilot Lt-Col William C. McLeod II recalled:

'Lt-Col Parkhurst and Maj Belles determined which aircrew members would be going. The aircraft flew down on 23 September. This bunch was highly experienced. All the pilots had previous combat tours and over 1,000 hours in the F-4. Pilots Capt Bremer and Capt Myers were both Fighter Weapons School graduates. Our old, beat-up, worn-out F-4Cs were the oldest F-4s in-theatre and the fact that we flew them at a sortie rate of almost 1.0 was unbelievable. I beat the hell out of '423, pulling scab patches off the wings almost every night I flew it, and my crew chief kept putting it back together until finally an inspection team caught up with it and grounded it, sending it back to Kadena for repair.

'When we got to Korat we were given a room in the 17 WWS Ops, but we operated as an independent squadron. Aircraft configuration for all early missions was two outboard fuel tanks, an AGM-45 Shrike (either -3, -3A or -3B) on an LAU-34 launcher mounted on each inboard station, an ECM pod in the starboard front Sparrow well, two AIM-7E-2 missiles, plus chaff in the speed brakes. [A centreline fuel tank, which was jettisoned as soon as it was empty, was subsequently added for "Linebacker II" missions.] As soon as we completed Theater Indoctrination we started flying B-52 escort missions in the lower Route Packs and over MR.1.[This gave time to modify established F-105G Wild Weasel tactics for the F-4C WW.] The first mission was on 25 September by Floyd and Palmer. Initial missions were flown as wingman with an F-105G "Thud Weasel" as lead. We didn't do this very long because the F-105Gs operated at lower altitude than the F-4 was optimized for and they ran us out of gas. We then flew a few missions as a separate element

Below: F-4C WW 64-0840, armed and ready with a pair of Shrikes, 28 December 1972.

Above, left: Lt-Col Parkhurst and Maj Dick Taylor with 64-0791 *Squirrely Bird*. (Maj Al Palmer)
Above, right: *Jail Bait* (63-7423) and its occupants, Capt William McLeod and Maj Don Lavigne. (Maj Al Palmer)

with an F-105G two-ship as lead [about 5,000ft below us] before we began to operate independently.

'We flew missions both day and night and quickly determined that operating single-ship with altitude separation in the target area was far better than trying to stay in formation. We also determined that we could provide adequate coverage by remaining in orbits at key points and thus did not copy the tactic used by some F-105G crews of flying a parallel course to the B-52s. As far as I know, no one had a SAM shot at them during this period. Many of these missions lasted three to four hours and covered more than one B-52 mission.

'It was during November that the 67th TFS Weasel aircraft acquired some very flamboyant markings: "DDD & CC's" was painted on the vari-ramps (standing for "Don's Dirty Dozen and Crew Chiefs"), red flashing (the 67th squadron colour) was added to the canopy rails, drop tank, stabilator and fin tips and also on the nosegear doors which carried the legendary Wild Weasel exclamation "YGBSM!—You Gotta Be Sh***in' Me!" '

Individual artwork also flourished on the nose barrels, all with a story behind them. EWO Capt Al Palmer's machine was christened *Brain Damage*, 'for an accident in which I was seriously injured by a hit-and-run bicycle in early November. Ironically, I was hit by a drunk driver on the flight line after a night combat mission over North Vietnam!

When I returned from hospitalization in Okinawa I discovered that my Crew Chief had painted the name on the nose for my arrival.' *Squirrely Bird*, the Det Commander's aircraft, got its nomme de guerre 'because Don kept writing it up as feeling "squirrely" in flight, much to the dismay of the maintenance troops who couldn't figure out why.' Bill McLeod's *Jail Bait* originated with his EWO Don Lavigne: 'Don clearly intended for us to go into harm's way, and therefore messing with this "female" (i.e. the aircraft) had the potential for getting us both into a lot of trouble.

'When "Linebacker II" kicked off on 18 December, Night 1 was just like flying on the Nellis EW Range. There were signals everywhere and you could pick and choose what you shot at. The North Vietnamese completely lost signal discipline that night and we must have seriously hurt them as a result. They re-learned rapidly, however, and from Night 2 they didn't have many signals up. They clearly had their radar systems hooked together and apparently used a surveillance radar or a gunlaying radar to provide the picture for the entire system. Some of their missiles were launched without guidance; others were launched with only the guidance active ("Fan Song" TTR not operating) and were clearly being command-guided off another radar's picture.

'Our standard mission scenario was to brief, take off and refuel as a flight, then split up as we headed inbound and

proceed to individual orbit areas on the western side of Hanoi (when the B-52 target was Hanoi) from which we could engage any radars that came up. We usually arrived in the orbit areas just in advance of the B-52s and normally were fragged to operate at 18,000ft. We operated without lights (kept the AAA from shooting at us) and stayed until our gas ran out or the B-52s were clear of the target area. Then we returned to the post-strike tanker, single-ship, refuelled and returned to Korat by ourselves. Each of us had our own procedures for doing this. In my case I not only blacked out the aircraft, but my cockpit as well. I had all the switches set well before I entered the target area and once there my attention was 100 per cent outside the aircraft. I taped over all the warning and other lights in the front cockpit so that they would not "blind" or distract me if they illuminated and I hooked the map light up in a way that would allow me to use it to dimly illuminate the Attitude Indicator if it didn't fall off during the manoeuvres. Any navigation I did was done visually, and when I used a map (not often) I read it by moonlight.

'On Night 3 one of our aircraft (Floyd and Palmer) was attacked by a MiG-21 while proceeding into the target area.

The North Vietnamese vectored the "Fishbed" into their classic head-on pass from above (with a slight offset) followed by a stern conversion to employ an Atoll. Tom picked up the MiG visually, outmanoeuvred it and ended up behind it. He fired an AIM-7 but it didn't guide. Night 3 was rough: six B-52s were shot down.'

Bill McLeod considers that the toughest mission he flew during his two tours was a night mission on Night 4, flying as 'Suntan 01': 'On Night 4 Seventh Air Force decided they had to do something about the B-52 losses and they fragged a night hunter/killer mission against the Hanoi air defence system during the B-52 strike. The mission was made up of five F-4Cs and five F-4Es with CBUs. I planned and led the mission. Someone showed up at my room late on the morning of Day 4 and told me I was needed at the squadron (this was early as I normally slept until early afternoon during LB II). When I arrived at the squadron Maj Belles filled me in on the "frag" change to add the night mission and told me to go over to Intel and find my EWO. When I got there Don already had the night's targets plotted (all in the Hanoi area) and had pretty well analyzed the mission. We discussed it for a few minutes and decided on a plan: we divided the aircraft up into three two-ship flights (one F-4C and two F-4Es), one two-ship (one F-4C and one F-4E) and two single F-4Cs. We assigned one three-ship to

the Bac Mai Complex and the other to an area north-west of the city. Both these flights were backed up by a single F-4C in an orbit ten miles or so to the rear. The two-ship was assigned to another SAM complex which was somewhere along Thud Ridge. We also determined that we would be unable to protect the E-models adequately without carrying Dive-modified Shrikes on three of our aircraft. Col Jack Chain [388th TFW Director of Operations and later CINC-SAC] approved their use.

'I briefed the five F-4C crews before the mass briefing and then we went to a briefing room at the squadron that was providing the F-4Es, the 34th TFS. I told them how we had arranged the "frag" and gave them an overview of the mission. When I got to the part about splitting up while heading inbound a young Captain in the back of the room spoke up and said, "I am not going single-ship to Hanoi." [Two ship was standard.] I didn't have time to argue with him, so I told him he could get on my wing and I would take him. With the two crews who would be going with me we briefed for operations against the Bac Mai Complex. I would be in an orbit just to the west of the complex, with the Major in an orbit just to the North and the Captain orbiting just to the south. Whenever one of the SAM sites in the complex launched they were to roll in and drop CBU on it. I would roll in also and point

my nose at the complex so I could fire a Shrike "down the throat" if one of the sites fired at one of the F-4Es.

'We were the first flight off the tanker and everything went according to plan until we had crossed into North Vietnam. Both E-models were flying route formation on me and I had my strip lights on to allow them to stay with me. Then "Red Crown" called and told us they had a MiG-21 in front of us, several thousand feet high, head-on. He said there were no friendly aircraft in front of me, meaning "shoot the guy head-on". I immediately told the two F-4Es to break off while Don locked the MiG up on the radar. The offset was just starting to develop so I needed to manoeuvre slightly to engage him, but when I looked outside to make sure my wingmen were gone one of them was still hanging on, so I turned out my lights in the hope that he would get the hint. He didn't, and he still tried to fly formation on me in the moonlight. At this point I decided that the biggest threat was a mid-air with my wingman, so I turned slightly into the MiG to take away his offset, lowered the nose and blew through directly under him. The three of us then pressed on and set up in our briefed orbits.

'The B-52s came into range of the SAMs about a minute or so after we reached our orbits and the sites to the north and east of us opened up, firing some seventy missiles in the following

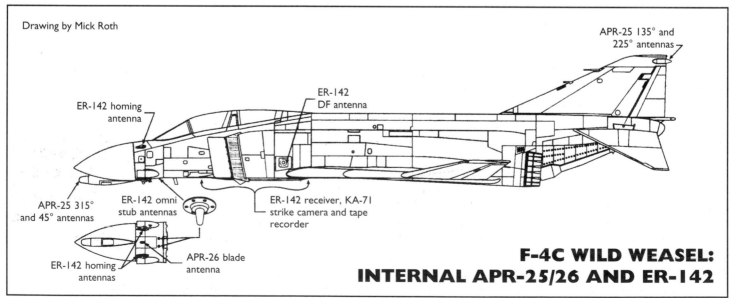

Drawing by Mick Roth

APR-25 135° and 225° antennas

ER-142 DF antenna

ER-142 homing antenna

APR-25 315° and 45° antennas

ER-142 omni stub antennas

ER-142 receiver, KA-71 strike camera and tape recorder

ER-142 homing antennas

APR-26 blade antenna

F-4C WILD WEASEL: INTERNAL APR-25/26 AND ER-142

TABLE 26: 67th TFS F-4C WILD WEASEL IV TDY TO KORAT, 23 OCTOBER 1972–18 FEBRUARY 1973: AIRCRAFT AND CREWS

Tail no	Aircraft name	Pilot/EWO
37 423	*Jail Bait*	Capt William C. McLeod II, Maj Donald J. Lavigne
37 433	*Dick's Peace Machine*	Capt Richard H. Graham, Capt John O. S. Williams
37 470	*Rub a dub dub, two men in a tub*	Maj Robert G. Belles, Maj. Palmas S. Kelly III
37 474	*Brain Damage*	Capt Thomas W. Floyd, Capt Burdette A. Palmer
40 791	*Squirrely Bird*	Lt-Col Donald J. Parkhurst, Maj Richard D. Taylor
40 840	*Super Cocks Swiss Samlar*	Capt Stuart Stegenga, Capt Hanspeter Zimmerman

Additional crews with 'unassigned' aircraft included: Capt John R. Bremer/Capt Harold W. Bergmann; Capt Richard B. Myers (at the time of writing a Four Star General and Vice-Chairman of the Joint Chiefs of Staff)/Capt Don M. Triplett; and Capt Robert L. Tidwell/ Capt Dennis B. Haney.

RADAR SITE KILLS

Date	Call-sign	Crew	Site claimed
18 December	'Hammer 01'	Belles/Kelly	VN266
18 December	'Hammer 02'	Bremer/Bergmann	VN119 (probable)
18 December	'Hammer 03'	Floyd/Palmer	VN255
18 December	'Hammer 04'	Tidwell/Haney	VN159
22 December	'Paste 03'	Floyd/Palmer	VN086 (probable)
24 December	'Bertha 01'	Belles/Kelly	VN119 (probable)

This list is incomplete owing to the difficulty of assessing night-time radar kills. For example, on Night 6 of 'Linebacker II' McLeod /Lavigne almost certainly wiped out a 'Fire Can' radar.

ten minutes. Two B-52s were hit, one going down into the city while the other made a sweeping right turn, streaming flames but still flying. Unfortunately the turn took him over Than Hoa and a site there shot him down. Then the Bac Mai Complex fired a couple of SAMs and my E-models rolled in with their CBUs. I rolled in to protect them, only to have one of the sites fire at me instead of the F-4Es. The missile lifted off in my windscreen at very close range. I had just enough time to slam the stick and rudder pedals into the front right corner and move the aircraft before the missile went down my left side and exploded in my rear-view mirror. The missile was obviously being command-guided off another radar's picture because no "Fan Song" TTRs were up in the complex, but the guidance light on the APR-25 was illuminated. Not long after this occurred both E-models called "Winchester" and left the target area.

'Once the F-4Es had left, Don told me that one site on the east side of Hanoi was responsible for the hits on both B-52s (despite the fact that numerous sites were firing missiles) and that the site in question had an "India Band" radar co-located with it. It was apparent to both of us that this was a new site and that under the plan we had put together no one was operating against it, so it was up to us to do something about it. The site was several miles further to the east, however, and was separated from us by several B-52 Target Boxes. I asked Don if he could get us there without getting us blown away by a bomb from a B-52. He told me that he could and we ended up in an orbit between the site and the B-52 ingress and egress routes. We stayed in a figure-of-eight orbit at about 18,000ft at this location until the last B-52 had cleared the threat ring to the east. The EC-121 called us about a minute before the last B-52 was clear and told us that we were the last aircraft in the target area. He made it plain that he thought we should get out of there. As soon as I answered the EC-121, "Red Crown" came up on Guard frequency and announced "SAM, SAM, SAM!", which was followed by Don's calm voice from the rear cockpit saying, "We're the target." My APR-25/26 lit up with a classic full-system launch and a strobe that went clear to the edge of the scope and partway back to the centre. The launch audio started screaming and two SAMs lifted off at my 11 o'clock. I kicked my left rudder to put the strobe and the missiles at 12 o'clock and fired both Shrikes at the guy. Then I rolled into an inverted slice and pulled the aircraft towards the ground with at least 4 to 5g. As soon as the nose was well down I rolled out part of the bank and reacquired the two SAMs over the canopy rail. Just as the SAMs reached a point where I expected them to start back down towards us, and I was preparing to use all the energy I had just acquired to pull over them, Don said, "He's down." This meant the site had shut down because of our Shrikes, and he then calmly gave me instructions on how to get out of the manoeuvre we were in without hitting the ground or heading the wrong way. We split out of the bottom on a westerly heading very close to supersonic and blew across the city while using our excess energy to pop back up to our fragged altitude. The North Vietnamese then brought up various "Fire Can" radars to check our progress and shot at us with several batteries of 85mm AAA. They were very careful, however, and would shut down the "Fire Cans" as soon as we started to point our nose at them—they clearly knew they were dealing with a Weasel. I could also see the muzzle flashes of the 85mm guns, so as soon as I saw a battery fire I would just move the aircraft to a different place and then watch as the place we had just vacated exploded with ten or twelve bursts.

'On the way back to Korat after refuelling Don went "cold mike" and wrote a message about the use of the "India Band" radar which he sent immediately after we landed. My comments in my log were, "A very busy, but not successful night. Don't fly Night Hunter/Killer unless the ground is visible and there is a good moon." '

The Phantom Weasel crewmen all earned two DFCs or a Silver Star and DFC for their involvement in 'Linebacker II', which has remained a little-known aspect of the war since they flew mostly at night and solo.

What EWO Don Lavigne had witnessed on Night 4 was the T-8209 TTR, based on a modified AAA fire control radar piece. The Vietnamese were using the range data to bring their SAMs to bear, and then using track-on-jam azimuth information, available from 'Fan Song' working in a passive mode, to obtain a straight point-to-point firing solution by lining up the missile's beacon with the jamming strobe from the B-52s and relying on the missiles' proximity fuses inflicting damage. For the F-4C Weasels the only effective counter was the AGM-45A-6 tuned to I-band, and further examples were supplied to Korat in an emergency airlift operation.

Bill McLeod picks up the story from the 67th TFS perspective again: 'Starting on Night 5 the B-52 targets were moved out of the downtown area for a couple of days and thus away from the heavy defences located there. One of these missions on Night 6 went well north of the city and resulted in at least two of our F-4C crews (including Don and I) flying orbits in the Chinese Buffer Zone. On this particular mission, which was pretty much outside the SAM threat, a "Fire Can" was being used to gather the radar picture for the North Vietnamese. The operator was very careful and would shut down whenever anyone pointed his nose in his direction. Don and I played with this guy for quite a while and were eventually able to get a missile above him and turn away before he came up again. He didn't know we had fired a missile and there was a reasonable chance that we killed him because he went down at missile impact. If we didn't hit him we sure scared him because he never came back up again. Other Weasels fired at "Fire Can" radars that night also, which led to an interesting development a few days later when the Wing received a high-level classified message which claimed that the Chinese were complaining that someone had shot at a "Fire Can" radar located in China and had missed the radar but had (of course) killed or injured some civilians.

'After the short Christmas break the B-52s were back over Hanoi and we continued to fly the same sort of missions until "Linebacker II" ended. While this was going on at night the squadron was

also flying B-52 escort in the lower Route Packs during the day. Once "Linebacker" ended we continued to escort missions into Route Packs 1–4 until the ceasefire. We stood down on 28 January 1973 and then flew combat missions again between 3 and 13 February: all appear to have been over Laos. The aircraft redeployed to Kadena on 16 February.'

There was one last shot for the F-4C Weasels. In April 1975, as the North Vietnamese were grinding their way south, President Gerald Ford ordered the evacuation of all US citizens under Operation 'Frequent Wind'. Nine F-4C WWIVs from the 67th TFS were detached from Kadena to Korat once more between 20 April and 7 May to provide defence-suppression support, flying a protective orbit adjacent to Saigon. 'Once at Korat the Weasel crews were "married up" with crews from the 34th TFS to form two-ship hunter/killer packages—the F-4C WW with two AGM-45s and two external tanks, the F-4D with two external tanks and four CBUs on the centreline. The crews worked out their tactics and then were put on standby. The missions were launched on 29 April and covered the evacuation of Saigon throughout the day. The airspace over Saigon was divided up into several areas of responsibility with two

hunter/killer teams assigned to each area so there would be continuous coverage. "Miller" Flight [its F-4C WWIV lead component crewed by Captains Jack R. "Jay" Suggs and John Dewey] launched, refuelled and worked in their area of responsibility, which was north-east of Saigon in the vicinity of Bien Hoa. They alternated between the area and their tanker throughout the day, logging over five hours with four periods on station in their area. During their fourth period on station the F-4D crew told "Miller" Lead that he was receiving AAA fire and suggested he start moving his aircraft around a bit more. Shortly thereafter Jay Suggs spotted the muzzle flashes of the battery that was shooting at them, obtained permission from "Cricket" (the controlling ABCCC) for a defensive reaction strike, and then cleared the F-4D to attack the gun battery with CBUs, knocking out one of the guns and getting a good secondary explosion from within the battery area.' 'Miller' Flight's action was the last ordnance expended by USAF fighters during the Vietnam conflict and apparently put a stop to the AAA fire from the North Vietnamese Army which was rolling towards Saigon.

Below: F-4C WWIV rear cockpit instrumentation. (Mick Roth)

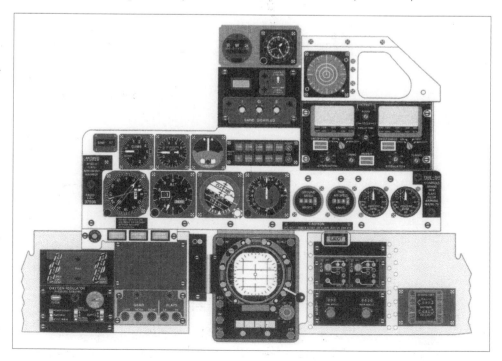

17. PHANTOM 2020

As the twenty-first century got under way over a thousand Phantoms remained in service with all but one of the nations which originally ordered it. The United Kingdom, its first overseas purchaser, was alone in phasing it out completely. Several of the other users intend to retain the type in front-line units for at least another decade, extending its overall service life beyond a half-century since the first F4H-1 flight.

ISRAEL
Israel, as initial customer for FMS F-4Es, upgraded 54 F-4Es (a 55th crashed pre-delivery) to *Kurnass 2000* standard, terminating the programme only when purchase of the F-15I Eagle was assured under 'Peace Fox V' with deliveries beginning in January 1998. Unmodified F-4Es have been stored. The very capable Kurnass 2000 continues in use with 119 'Bat' Squadron and 201 'The One' Squadron at Tel Nov air base alongside two F-15 units and with 142 (Reserve) Squadron at Hatzerim, sharing the base with 69 Squadron ('The Hammers') and their F-15Is. Among the Tel Nov F-4s there are also ten surviving RF-4E *Orefs* and the two Block 44 F-4E(S) 'Peace Jack' aircraft with HIAC-1 cameras and additional electronic reconnaissance equipment. Although the *Kurnass* won the last of its many air-to-air kills in June 1982, its air-to-ground mission is still a valued part of the IDF/AF's renowned hitting power and it is likely to serve as an F-15I trainer and Reserve unit type for up to a decade.

Israeli Aircraft Industries continue to offer an upgrade package based on the Elbit ACE-3 computer with a 1750 avionics interface, APG-76 multi-mode radar, El-Op (Kaiser) HUD, HOTAS and multi-function cockpit displays. In the *Kurnass 2000* the avionics suite includes a digital weapons delivery and navigation system and improved ECM protection. Variations on this package have been offered to other Phantom users, including the Turkish Air Force.

EGYPT
Egypt's air force, one of Israel's primary adversaries in the 1973 Yom Kippur War, received its 35 'Peace Pharaoh' F-4Es in 1979 through a new relationship with the United States. A further seven attrition replacements arrived later. About thirty remain active in the two squadrons of the 222nd Tactical Fighter Brigade, the 76th and 88th Squadrons. Throughout many of their thirty years of service they suffered from maintenance problems which severely reduced their availability rates. Egypt's technicians, used to two generations of Russian fighters, found difficulty in transitioning to the more complex F-4E's idiosyncrasies. The task was taken on by new teams led by McDonnell Douglas and USAF personnel, considerably improving the situation though aircrew still preferred their previous, more nimble, single-seat MiGs and Mirages. Despite its discontent with the F-4, the EAF agreed to have successive batches of five F-4Es fully overhauled at Cherry Point. Various upgrade packages have been evaluated, including one with the Raytheon AN/APG-65 radar as used in the German F-4F ICE.

TURKEY
As one of the biggest Phantom operators, Turkey continued to receive large batches of ex-USAF and ex-*Luftwaffe* aircraft up to 1994, when the balance of 32 RF-4Es were received from Germany. By the end of 1999 over 250 F-4Es and RF-4Es had been delivered and around 180 remained in use with the *Turk Hava Kuvvetleri*, which plans to keep its Phantom force operational until 2020, sharing fighter/strike duties with the F-16.

Upgrades have therefore been vital, and in the early 1980s Turkey elected to improve the EW suite with ALR-46 RWR, ALE-40 chaff and flare dispensers and AN/ALQ-119 jamming pods. A second upgrade phase, beginning in 1996, has involved the IAI Phantom 2000 package for 54 'F-4E 2020 Terminators' in a programme which yielded its first two aircraft in January 2000. Twenty-six airframes will go through the IAI modification line, and the remaining twenty-eight will be fitted with components from IAI-supplied kits at the THK's Eskisehir base. Structural strengthening, GPS/INS and Rafael Popeye 1 capability are also included, plus a new dark grey colour scheme. Terminators will equip two squadrons, *111 Filo* 'Panther' and *171 Filo* 'Buccaner', both specialist attack units.

GREECE
On the opposite shores of the Aegean Sea, the Greek Air Force also retains most of its F-4E/RF-4E element. Its original eight RF-4Es were supplemented in 1993 by 29 ex-*Luftwaffe* airframes (including nine airframes for cannibalization), and they equip a single Larissa-based unit (348 MTA), while the F-4Es are with three interception/multi-role squadrons at Larissa and Andravida. Seeking an appropriate modernization programme, Greece also opted for the

IAI Phantom 2000 fit, but Israel's commitment to the Turkish F-4E upgrade programme made this politically awkward. Greece therefore settled for the equally potent DASA proposal, similar to the ICE update it devised for German F-4Fs. In collaboration with Hellenic Aerospace Industries (HAI), DASA is installing the Hughes AN/APG-65Y radar, GPS, GEC CPU-143/A digital air data computer and a new Elbit Systems fire control unit. Under the 'Peace Icarus' programme, this will enable 39 F-4Es to handle AIM-120 AMRAAM and AGM-130 missiles. Cockpit revisions include a HUD, HOTAS and multi-function displays, while a Litton ALR-68(V)-2 RWR completes a very 'twenty-first century' re-fit. The first 'Peace Icarus' F-4E flew in Germany on 28 April 1999. At the same time HAI is undertaking a structural life extension programme (SLEP) for the entire F-4 fleet, including those aircraft which do not benefit from 'Peace Icarus'.

IRAN

Iran, the second overseas F-4 purchaser, has operated around 240 F-4D/E/RF-4E aircraft, including loaned USAF F-4Es, since 1968. They were the IRIAF's principal multi-role type during the bitter Iraq–Iran War (1980–88), when over sixty were lost in the first year of conflict. Spares shortages after the cessation of US support in 1979 were apparently remedied by clandestine supplies from Israel and the West, while many Phantoms were modified to carry the AS-11 'Kilter' anti-radiation weapon, the Chinese C802 anti-shipping missile and an air-to-ground modification of the Raytheon Standard missile. Locally manufactured update components for the APQ-120 radar, providing limited moving target indication, and an indigenous chaff and flare installation have helped to keep the reduced F-4 fleet viable in the new century.

GERMANY

In Western Europe, the main F-4 owner, Germany, uses its four F-4F Wings as its primary air defence following the withdrawal of the type from the ground-attack role in the mid-1990s as the Tornado took over. A comprehensive SLEP and the ICE (Improved Combat Efficiency, or, as one of its designers dubbed it, 'In-Cockpit Entertainment') initiative were fortunate choices in view of the delays in service entry of the Eurofighter. ICE Phantoms will now hold the fort until around 2012, whereas their RF-4E counterparts have been replaced by reconnaissance variants of the Tornado since 1994. By 1999 twenty-five F-4Fs had been lost in accidents, but 113 had received the full, three-stage ICE upgrade and another 43 (distinguishable by black radomes rather than the new grey AN/APG-65Y versions) retained the original downgraded APQ-120 radar and therefore lack AIM-120 capability. The other non-ICE survivors (around 37) received the SLEP and Honeywell laser INS. Some of these equip the *Taktisches Ausbildungskommando* at Holloman AFB, which has replaced the F-4E–equipped 9th FS as the *Luftwaffe*'s US training unit. Others fly with JG 73 *Steinhoff* alongside MiG-29s. F-4Fs are frequently detached to Goose Bay, Canada, for low-altitude training, and ACM is practised over the North Sea ACMI range. Since 1996 F-4F crews have also taken part in 'Red Flag' biennially. JG 73 flew to Nellis for the 1999 event with a mixture of F-4Fs and MiG-29s. All F-4Fs are still heavy smokers as the smoke abatement kit became an economy cut. A final upgrade to the F-4F could include a new radio, improved IFF and a VCR to record cockpit voices plus radar and HUD imagery.

SPAIN

After the withdrawal of Spain's F-4C fleet in 1990 the *Ejercito del Aire* (EdA) kept its fourteen RF-4Cs with their CASA/IAI-designed fixed refuelling probes. The eight ex-Kentucky ANG machines, received in 1989, had smokeless engines and VOR-ILS navigation systems, and the whole fleet has received the new INS, a revised ECM system, a real-time data link and digital solid state AN/APQ-172 terrain-following radar. Having failed to acquire ex-*Luftwaffe* RF-4Es, the EdA took on a further six ex-USAF RF-4Cs from the Nevada ANG in 1995. This batch had AN/ALE-40 chaff/flare dispensers, 'Have Quick' digital radios, AN/ALR-46 RWR and an AIM-9L Sidewinder capability, all of which have been retro-installed across the rest of the fleet. The planned phase-out year for Spain's reconnaissance Phantoms is 2010, when recce-pod-equipped EF-18 Hornets are scheduled to absorb the task.

SOUTH KOREA

In the Far East, South Korea reached a peak Phantom roster of around 145 F-

Below: One of the ex-Indiana F-4Es operated by *338 Mira* of the Greek Air Force during a visit to the United Kingdom. (Authors)

4D/E/RF-4Cs in the 1980s, of which roughly 130 continue in use with five tactical fighter squadrons and the 131st Tactical Reconnaissance Squadron. Economic constraints have ruled out the proposed Boeing upgrade package for these aircraft though the Pave Tack, AGM-78 Standard ARM and 'Popeye' capability conferred on the fleet in the 1990s is still a useful asset.

JAPAN

About ninety F-4EJ *Kai* Phantoms equip three of Japan's fighter squadrons, while a fourth unit, the 501st *Hikotai*, flies the remaining RF-4E/RF-4E *Kai* variants. Each squadron also contains a number of unmodified (non-*Kai*) aircraft for training and second-line duties. Now in the last stages of its service career, the F-4EJ awaits a successor, which could be the indigenous Mitsubishi F-2 or an import such as the F/A-18E/F or JAS Gripen. To supplement the surviving RF-4Es, nineteen F-4EJs were dedicated to the reconnaissance role, using a variety of centreline pods. These include the LOROP pod, a tactical recce pod with three cameras or a tactical electronic reconnaissance version holding the Thomson CSF Astace elint system. The original weapons and radar capability are retained. Clearly, until a decision is made concerning a successor, the Mitsubishi-built F-4s are due for several more years' life alongside the more recent but far more costly F-15J Eagles.

UNITED STATES

Since its withdrawal from the USAF, USN and USMC the F-4 has found a second career as a research and airborne target vehicle in its various 'QF' guises. An initial batch of forty-four QF-4Bs were the first to be converted to drones, beginning in 1972. These lasted until 1987, the final specimens being used as targets for the AIM-120 and Patriot missile prototypes. Next through the modification line were 78 QF-4Ns, fitted with AN/ASA-32 analogue autopilots to allow manned flight (which occupies over ninety per cent of their flight time) or NOLO (no live operator onboard) op-

eration in which they are directed by a ground operator 'pilot' flying the aircraft via a TV screen and a small cockpit stick. On many 'unmanned' flights a safety pilot is actually carried in case of in-flight emergencies, and the NOLO configuration is employed mainly for destructive missile testing, which is the final flight of many for a QF-4N.

In its research role the QF-4N has been a test-bed for a variety of systems, including the Airborne Turret Infrared Measurement System (ATIMS) and various decoy flare and countermeasures systems such as the GE Warfare Platform. QF-4N operators the Naval Weapons Test Squadron (the *Bloodhounds*) at Point Mugu needed a follow-up aircraft and the F-4S was a logical choice as it passed out of USMC service. A single development QF-4S (BuNo 158358) was converted by NARF in 1995 using an automatic flight control system which gives fifteen 'command words' for a variety of unmanned flight manoeuvres and a pair of colour video cameras to provide imagery for the ground operator to steer the Phantom. Radar and most of the weapons control system are deleted, all circuit breakers are moved to the front cockpit (this is a single-seat Phantom) and a Trimble GPS set is fitted together with a new EW suite. After the initial batch of ten QF-4S conversions a further twenty are planned through 2000–2001, depending on need.

Former USAF RF-4C, F-4E and F-4G airframes have passed through the Tracor/Flight Systems Inc conversion line at Mojave since February 1992. Having run out of QF-106 drones to

Above: Before conversion to a drone, QF-4S 155542 belonged to VMFA-112 Cowboys, who flew the last tactical Phantoms in USN and USMC service. (API)

provide realistic missile-shooting practice, Tyndall AFB-based fighter trainees required a new live target to blast into the sea on Weapons Training Detachments. Three lots of F-4s totalling 108 aircraft were converted by May 1999 for Tyndall's 475th WEG, with follow-on contracts which could result in more than 200 further F-4G/E Phantoms becoming Full Scale Aerial Targets by 2006. Conversion is expensive and time-consuming (4.5 months each) so the drones are expected to provide a number of near-misses before final destruction at the end of their lengthy working lives. For this reason the Interim Vector Scoring System is carried (with six sensors at the aircraft's extremities) to record missiles passing close by. Lower-time airframes also get offensive or defensive EW equipment to prolong their lives in the 'dangerous' skies off the Florida coast. Offensive formations of up to four QF-4s can be flown in NOLO configuration to provide realistic multiple targets. Tracor also operate four F-4Ds for trials work, including the aerial launching of AQM-37C rocket-powered target drones. Phantoms for drone conversion are still in plentiful supply in the AMARC desert store, and many more of these former hunters will become prey for a new generation of fighter pilots for whom the F-4 is still the aircraft which set the parameters for supersonic, missile-shooting air combat.

GLOSSARY

AA	Auto-Acquisition	**APC**	Armament Practice Camp
AAA	Anti-Aircraft Artillery	**APCS**	Automatic Power
AAR	Air-to-Air Refuelling		Compensation System
AB	Air Base	**AREFW**	Aerial Refuelling Wing
ABCCC	Airborne Command &	**ARM**	Anti-radiation (radar) missile
	Control Center	**ARN**	Airborne Radio Navigation
AC	Aircraft Commander (USAF		(aid)
	front-seater)	**ARREC**	Armed reconnaissance
Ace	Aviator with 5 or more	**ARRS**	Aerospace Recovery &
	aircraft kills		Rescue Squadron (now
ACC	USAF Air Combat		SOS)
	Command, combining the	**ARVN**	Army of the Republic of
	former SAC and TAC since		Vietnam
	June 1992	**ASE**	Angular steering error
ACLS	Automatic Carrier Landing		(circle)
	System	**ASIP**	Aircraft Structural Integrity
ACM(I)	Air Combat Manoeuvring		Program
	(Instrumented range)	**ASW**	Anti-Submarine Warfare
AD	Air Defence (RAF); Air	**ATI**	Applied Technology
	Division (USAF)		Industries
ADC	Aerospace Defense	**AUE**	Authorized Unit
	Command		Establishment
ADI	Attitude Director Indicator	**AVTR**	Airborne video tape
ADIZ	Aircraft Identification Zone		recorder
ADR	Air Defence Region	**AWACS**	Airborne Warning &
ADTAC	Air Defence TAC; 1st AF		Control System
ADWC	USAF Air Defense Weapons	**AW&CS/W**	Airborne Warning &
	Center, Tyndall, Florida		Control Squadron/Wing
AF	Air Force	**BAI**	Battle Area Interdiction
AFB	Air Force Base (USAF)	**Bandit**	Aircraft identified as hostile;
AFCS	Automatic Flight Control		cf *Bogey*
	System	**BARCAP**	Barrier combat air patrol
AFRES	Air Force Reserve (US)	**BDR**	Battle Damage Repair
AFV	Armoured fighting vehicle	**BDU**	Bomb, Dummy Unit
AG	*Aufklärungsgeschwader*	**BLC**	Boundary-layer control
	(Luftwaffe)		(wing)
AGC	Automatic Gain Control	**BDR(T)**	Battle damage repair
AGL	Above ground level		(trainer)
AGM	Air-to-ground missile	**Bogey**	Unidentified aircraft; cf
AGS	Aircraft Generation		*Bandit*
	Squadron (USAF)	**'Buff'**	Big Ugly Fat Fella—the
AIM	Air Intercept Missile		B-52
ALC	Air Logistics Center	**BuNo**	Bureau of Aeronautics serial
AMA	Air Matériel Area (now		number
	ALC)	**BVR**	Beyond visual range
AMARC	Aircraft Matériel &	**CAA**	Computer-aided Auto
	Reclamation Center		Acquisition
AMCS	Airborne Missile Control	**CAG**	Carrier Air Group
	System		(commander)
AMRAAM	Advanced Medium-Range	**CAI**	Chicago Aerial Industries
	Air-to-Air Missile (AIM-120)	**CAP**	Combat air patrol
AMU	Aircraft Maintenance Unit	**CARA**	Combined Aircraft Radar
ANG	Air National Guard (USAF)		Altimeter

Carqual	Carrier Qualification
CAS	Close air support
CBU	Cluster Bomb Unit
CCIP	Continuously computed
	impact point
CCTS/W	Combat Crew Training
	Squadron/Wing (USAF)
CEA	Circular error average (of
	nuclear weapons strikes)
CEM	Combined Effects Munitions
CENTO	Central Nations Treaty
	Organization
'Century Series'	USAF F-100 to YF-107
	series fighters; sometimes
	said to include the F-110
	Phantom II
CEP	Circular error probability (of
	conventional weapons); cf
	CEA
CIA	Central Intelligence Agency
CILOP	Conversion In Lieu Of
	Procurement
CNI	Communications, Navi-
	gation, Integrated (or
	Interrogated)
Comm-Out	Communications Out (radio
	silence)
CONUS	Continental United States
CP	Control (or Contact) Point
CRT	Cathode ray tube
CSAR	Combat Search & Rescue
CVW	Carrier Air Wing
CW	Combat Wing; continuous-
	wave
DACT	Dissimilar Air Combat
	Training
DCC	Dedicated Crew Chief
DECM	Defensive Electronic
	Countermeasures
DMAS	Digital Modular Avionics
	System
DMZ	Demilitarized Zone
DO	Deputy Commander for
	Operations (of USAF
	Wing)
DoD	Department of Defense
DR	Dead Reckoning
DSC(G)	Digital Scan Converter
	(Group)
DSES	Defense System Evaluation
	Squadron
DST	Destructor
DTM	Data Transfer Module

'Dumb'	Free-falling or non-stabilized gravity bomb or missile
DUI	Distinctive Unit Identity (tail-code)
ECM	Electronic countermeasures
EFA	European Fighter Aircraft
'Egob'	See EOGB
EGT	Exhaust gas temperature
Elint	Electronic intelligence
ELRAC	Elint receiver and recorder
EOB	Electronic order of battle
EOGB	Electro-optically guided bomb
ER/DL	Extended-range data link
ETA	Estimated time of arrival
EW	Electronic warfare
EWO	Electronic Warfare Officer
FAC	Forward Air Controller
'Fat Al'	'Fat Albert'. A generic term for large 'smart' bombs, including the AGM-62 Walleye ER/DL, and the GBU-9 and -11 weapons based on the M118 3,000lb demolition device
FBSA	Fighter/Bomber/Strike/Attack
FCT	Fire Crew Training
FFAR	Folding-fin aerial rocket
FG	Fighter Group; Fighter/Ground Attack
FGR	Fighter/Ground Attack/Reconnaissance
FIS/W	Fighter Interception Squadron/Wing
Fitron	Fighter squadron (USN)
FL	Flight level (in hundreds of feet)
FLIR	Forward-looking infra-red
FLR	Forward-looking radar
FMS	Foreign Military Sales
FOD	Foreign object damage
FOT&E	Follow-On Test & Evaluation; cf QT&E
FOV	Field of view
'Frag'	Fragmentary order, part of a large, integrated plan
FS	Fighter Squadron
FWIC	Fighter Weapons Instructor Course
FWS/W	Fighter Weapons Squadron/Wing; Fighter Weapons School
GE	General Electric (USA)
GIB	Guy in the back (seat)
GBU	Guided Bomb Unit
GCI	Ground Control Intercept
'Hard wing'	Wing with BLC instead of LES (q.v.)
HARM	High-speed ARM (the AGM-88)
HAS	Hardened Aircraft Shelter
HAWC	Homing & Warning Computer (the APR-38A)
HSD/I	Horizontal Situation Display/Indicator
HUD	Head-up display
IAI	Israeli Aircraft Industries
ID	Identification
IDF/AF	Israeli Defence Force/Air Force (*Heyl Ha'Avir*)
IFF	Identification Friend or Foe
IFR	Instrument Flight Rules
IIAF	Imperial Iranian Air Force (*Nirou Hayai Shanashahiya Iran*)
IIR	Imaging infra-red
IMC	Instrument Meteorological Conditions; Instrument Mission-Capable
IMU	Inertial Measurement Unit
INAS	Inertial Navigation and Attack Set
INS	Inertial Navigation Set
ILS	Instrument Landing System
IOC	Initial Operational Capability
IOT&E	Initial Operational Test & Evaluation; cf QT&E
IP	Initial Point; Instructor Pilot
IRCM	Infra-red countermeasures
IR(LS)	Infra-red (linescanner)
IRIAF	Islamic Republic of Iran Air Force
IRSTS	Infra-Red Search & Track System
IWSO	Instructor WSO
JaboG	*Jagdbombergeschwader* (Luftwaffe)
JASDF	Japanese Air Self Defense Force (*Koku Jie tai*)
JBG	See *JaboG*
JG	*Jagdgeschwader* (Luftwaffe)
Jihad	Muslim Holy War
KTO	Kuwaiti Theatre of Operations
LADD	Low-Angle Drogue Delivery
LANTIRN	Low-Altitude Navigation/Targeting Infra-Red for Night
'Lawn Dart'	Derogatory term for F-16
LCOSS	Lead-Computing Optical Sight System
LGB	Laser-guided bomb
Lead	Flight leader
LED	Light-emitting diode
LES	Leading-edge slats
LLL(TV)	Low-Light-Level (Television)
LOC	Lines of communication
LOROPS	Long-Range Oblique Optical System
LORAN	Long-range radio aid to navigation
LRI	Long-range intercept
LRU	Line replaceable unit
LSI	Lear-Siegler Incorporated
LWR	Launch warning receiver
MAP	Military Assistance Program; Military Airport
MBB	Messerschmitt-Bölkow-Blohm
MER	Multiple Ejection Rack
McAir	McDonnell Aircraft
MiGCAP	MiG combat air patrol; applies to CAP against fighters of Soviet or Chinese origin
MLG	Main landing gear
MMH/FH	Maintenance man-hours per flight-hour
MOREST	Mobile arresting gear
MR	Military Region (in South Vietnam); mission-ready
MRE	Meals, ready-to-eat
MSDG	Multi-Sensor Display Group
MSL	(Height above) mean sea level
MSS	Mission Support System
MTI	Moving Target Indicator
MU	Maintenance Unit (RAF)
NARF	Naval Air Rework Facility
NAS	Naval Air Station; Naval Air Squadron
NATC	Naval Air Test Center
NATO	North Atlantic Treaty Organization
NFO	Naval Flight Officer
NORAD	North American Air Defense
NVAF	North Vietnamese Air Force
NVN	North Vietnam(ese)
OC	Officers' Club
OCU	Operational Conversion Unit
OOALC	Ogden Air Logistics Center (Hill, Utah)
OPCON	Operational control
ORI	Operational Readiness Inspection
PACAF	Pacific Air Forces (USAF)
Pave	Precision Avionics Vectoring Equipment
PDM	Programmed Depot-level Maintenance
PGM	Precision-guided munition; cf 'dumb' ordnance
PI	Photo Interpreter
Pilot	Usually the front-seater or AC; originally the USAF term for a back-seater (also known as GIB, q.v., and later P-WSO or WSO, q.v.)
Pitter	GIB or WSO
PLO	Palestine Liberation Organization
POCU	Phantom Operational Conversion Unit
POL	Petroleum, oil, lubricants (storage facility)
Popeye	See IFR, IMC
POST/COMO	Production Orientated Scheduling Technique/Combat Orientated Maintenance Organization
PPI	Plan Position Indicator
PPIF	Photo Processing and Interpretation Facility
PTF	Phantom Training Flight
P-WSO	See Pilot
QRA	Quick Reaction Alert
QRC	Quick Reaction Capability
QT&E	Qualification Test &

	Evaluation (the current embracing term for IOT&E and FOT&E, q.v.)
RAAF	Royal Australian Air Force
RAF	Royal Air Force
RAFG	Royal Air Force, Germany
RAM	Rapid Aircraft Maintenance (BDR)
RBL	Radar boresight line
RDJTF	Rapid Deployment Joint Task Force
RESCAP	Rescue combat air patrol
RG	Reconnaissance Group
RHAWS	Radar homing and warning system
RIO	Radar Intercept Officer
RN	Royal Navy
RNAS	Royal Naval Air Station
ROE	Rules of Engagement
ROK	Republic of Korea
ROR	Release on range
RP	Route Pack (in Vietnam)
RS	Reconnaissance Squadron
RTB	Return to base
RTU	Replacement Training Unit
RVANF	Republic of Vietnam Air Force
RWR	Radar warning receiver
SAC	Strategic Air Command
SAL	Semi-active laser
SAM	Surface-to-air missile
SAR	Search and Rescue; synthetic aperture radar
SATS	Short Airfield Tactical Support
SCAR	Strike Control and Reconnaissance
SEA	South-East Asia
SEAD	Suppression of enemy air defences
SL(A)R	Sideways-looking (airborne) radar
SLEP	Service Life Extension Program
SLUF	Short Little Ugly Fella—the A-7
'Smart'	See PGM

SOR	Specific Operational Requirement
SOS	Special Operations Squadron
Stan/Eval	Standardization and Evaluation (inspections)
STARTEX	Start of exercise
SURE	Sensor Update and Refurbishment Effort
SUU	Suspension Underwing Unit
SVN	South Vietnam
TAB-Vee	Theatre Air Base Vulnerability (HAS)
TAC	Tactical Air Command (USAF)
TALD	Tactical Air-Launched Decoy
TARC	Tactical Air Reconnaissance Center (Shaw, South Carolina)
TARCAP	Target combat air patrol
TARPS	Tactical Airborne Reconnaissance Pod
TASMO	Tactical Air Support for Maritime Operations
TAWC	Tactical Air Warfare Center (HQ Eglin, Florida)
TCA	Track crossing angle
TD	(Hyperbolic radio wave) time difference co-ordinate (LORAN)
TDY	Temporary duty
TEC	Thermo-electric cooled
'Teenager'	American fighter bearing a numerical suffix in the 13 to 19 range, e.g. the F-15 Eagle
TER	Triple Ejection Rack
TEREC	Tactical Electromagnetic Reconnaissance system
TESS	Telescopic Sight System
TF(T)G	Tactical Fighter (Training) Group
TF(T)S	Tactical Fighter (Training) Squadron
TFRS	Tactical Fighter Replacement Squadron

TF(T)W	Tactical Fighter (Training) Wing
TFWC	Tactical Fighter Weapons Center (Nellis, Nevada)
TFW(P)	Tactical Fighter Wing (Provisional)
TGM	Training air-to-ground missile
TI	Texas Instruments
TIC	Troops in contact (with the enemy)
TISEO	Target Identification System, Electro-Optical
TR(T)S	Tactical Reconnaissance (Training) Squadron
TO	Technical Order
TOT	Time over target
TPS	Tactical paint scheme
TSF	Tactical Strike Fighter—the F-4E
TWU	Tactical Weapons Unit
UAV	Unmanned Air Vehicle
UK/ADR	United Kingdom Air Defence Region
USAF	United States Air Force
USAFE	United States Air Force Europe
USAFIWS	USAF Fighter Interception Weapons School
USAFTAWC	See TAWC
USMC	United States Marine Corps
USN	United States Navy
UTM	Universal Transverse Mercator
VC	(Communist) Viet Cong
VFR	Visual Flight Rules
'Victor Alert'	Nuclear standby
VMCJ	(USMC) Composite Squadron
VMFA	(USMC) Fighter/Attack Squadron
VMF(AW)	(USMC) All-Weather Fighter Squadron
VMFP	(USMC) Reconnaissance Squadron
VF	(USN) Fighter squadron
WASP	Weasel Attack Signal Processor (the APR-47)
WestPac	West Pacific (cruise)
'Wizzo'	See WSO
WOPE	Without personnel or equipment
WRCS	Weapons Release Computer System
WSO	Weapons Systems Officer
WWIV/V	'Wild Weasel IV/V'
XO	Executive Officer (USN)
Z/Zulu	Greenwich Mean Time
'Zulu Alert'	Air defence standby

Left: An RF-4E makes a 'dirty' flypast with gear, hook and flaps down and the photoflash/chaff ejector ports popped open. The 'hard-wing' RF-4E was the fastest production Model 98 Phantom of all. (Tim Laming)

APPENDICES

APPENDIX I: F-4 PHANTOM SERIAL NUMBERS

USN/MC PHANTOMS

Model	Block	Serials	Nos
XF4H-1F	1a	142259 to 142260	2
		Subtotal	**2**
F4H-1F/ F-4A		143388 to 143392	5
	2b	145307 to 145317	11
	3c	146817 to 146821	5
	4d	148252 to 148261	10
	5e	148262 to 148275	14
		Subtotal	**45**
F4H-1/ F-4B	6f	148363 to 148386	24
	7g	148387 to 148410	24
	8h	148411 to 148434	24
	9i	149403 to 149426	24
	10j	149427 to 149450	24
	11k	149451 to 149474	24
	12l	150406 to 150435	30
	13m	150436 to 150479	44
	14n	150480 to 150493	14
		150624 to 150651	28
	15o	150652 to 150653	2
		150993 to 151021	29
		151397 to 151398	2
	16p	151399 to 151426	28
	17q	151427 to 151447	21
	18r	151448 to 151472	25
	19s	151473 to 151497	25
	20t	151498 to 151519	22
		152207 to 152215	9
	21u	152216 to 152243	28
	22v	152244 to 152272	29
	23w	152273 to 152304	32
	24x	152305 to 152331	27
	25y	152965 to 152994	30
	26z	152995 to 153029	35
	27aa	153030 to 153056	27
	28ab	153057 to 153070	14
		153912 to 153915	4
		Subtotal	**649**
F-4J	26z	153071 to 153075	5
	27aa	153076 to 153088	13
	28ab	153768 to 153779	12
	29ac	153780 to 153799	20
	30ad	153800 to 153839	40
	31ae	153840 to 153876	37
	32af	153877 to 153911	35
		154781 to 154785	5
	33ag	154786 to 154788	3
		155504 to 155569	66
	34ah	155570 to 155580	11
		155731 to 155784	54
	35ai	155785 to 155843	59
	36aj	155844 to 155866	23
	37ak	155867 to 155874	8
	38al	155875 to 155889	15
	39am	155890 to 155902	13
	40an	157242 to 157260	19
	41ao	157261 to 157273	13
	42ap	155903	1
		157274 to 157285	12
	43aq	157286 to 157297	12
	44ar	157298 to 157309	12
	45as	158346 to 158354	9
	46at	158355 to 158365	11
	47au	158366 to 158379	14
		Subtotal	**522**

The following twelve F-4Bs from Block 14n were produced as F-4Gs: 150481, 150484, 150487, 150489, 150492, 150625, 150629, 150633, 150636, 150639, 150642 and 150645.

USAF PHANTOMS

Model	Block	Serials	Nos
F-4C	15	62 -12199	1
		63 -7407 to -7420	14
	16	-7421 to -7442	22
	17	-7443 to -7468	26
	18	-7469 to -7525	58
	19	-7527 to -7597	71
	20	-7598 to -7662	65
	21	-7663 to -7713	51
		64-0654 to -0672	19
	22	-0673 to -0737	65
	23	-0738 to -0817	80
	24	-0818 to -0881	64
	25	-0882 to -0928	47
		Subtotal	**583**
F-4D	24	64-0929 to -0937	9
	25	-0938 to -0963	26
	26	-0964 to -0980	17
		65-0580 to -0611	32
	27	-0612 to -0665	54
	28	-0666 to -0770	105
	29	-0771 to -0801	31
		66-0226 to -0283	58
		-7455 to -7504	50
	30	-7505 to -7650	146
	31	-7651 to -7774	125
		-8686 to -8698	13
	32	-8699 to -8786	88
	33	-8787 to -8825	23
		Subtotal	**793**
F-4E	31	66-0284 to -0297	14
	32	-0298 to -0338	41
	33	-0339 to -0382	44
		67-0208 to -0219	12
	34	-0220 to -0282	63
	35	-0283 to -0341	59
	36	-0342 to -0398	57
	37	68-0303 to -0365	63
	38	-0366 to -0409	44
	39	-0410 to -0451	42
	40	-0452 to -0494	43
	41	-0495 to -0547	53
	42	69-0236 to -0303	68
	43	-0304 to -0307	4
		-7201 to -7260	60
	44	-7261 to -7273	13
		-7286 to -7303	18
		-7546 to -7578	33
	45	-7579 to -7589	11
	48	71-0224 to -0247	24
	49	-1070 to -1093	24
	50	-1391 to -1402	12
		72-0121 to -0138	18
	51	-0139 to -0144	6
		-0157 to -0159	3
	52	-0160 to -0165	6
	53	-0166 to -0168	3
		-1407	1
	54	-1476 to -1489	14
	55	-1490 to -1497	8
	56	-1498 to -1499	2
	57	73-1157 to -1164	8
	58	-1165 to -1184	20
	59	-1185 to -1204	20
	60	74-0643 to -0660	18
		-1038 to -1049	12
	61	-0661 to -0666	6
		-1050 to -1061	12

	-1620 to -1637	18	
62	-1638 to -1653	16	
Subtotal		**993**	

Forty-four diverted aircraft from FY68 Blocks 38–41-MC (4 from Block 38, 8 from 39, 12 from 40 and 20 from 41) comprised the first batch of F-4Es for Israel, sanctioned by the Nixon Administration on 27 December 1968, while a further 24 from FY69 Block 43-MC were delivered directly to the Royal Australian Air Force, on loan, of which 23 were later returned. USAF F-4B loans and RF-4C production are detailed separately below.

EXPORT PHANTOMS

RN/RAF F-4K/M acquisitions

YF-4K	26	XT595 to XT596	2
	Subtotal		**2**
F-4K	27	XT597 to XT598	2
	30	XT857 to XT858	2
	31	XT859 to XT862	4

32	XT863 to XT870	8	
33	XT871 to XT876	6	
34	XV565 to XV571	7	
35	XV572 to XV578	7	
36	XV579 to XV585	7	
37	XV586 to XV592	7	
Subtotal		**50**	

YF-4M	29	XT852 to XT853	2
	Subtotal		**2**
F-4M	31	XT891 to XT895	5
	32	XT896 to XT906	11
	33	XT907 to XT914	8
		XV393 to XV398	6
	34	XV399 to XV405	7
	35	XV406 to XV435	30
	36	XV436 to XV442	7
		XV460 to XV476	17
	37	XV477 to XV499	23
	38	XV500 to XV501	2
	Subtotal		**116**

Originally 50 F-4Ks were ordered for the Royal Navy, increased to 140 on the cancellation of the P.1154, then reduced to 120, then 80, then 60 and finally 48 (plus four development aircraft). Twenty of these went directly to the RAF and the remainder were transferred to that Service in December 1978 after receiving avionics updates (including ILS). The original F-4M order totalled 160; this was reduced to 118 but the number of deliveries was boosted when 20 aircraft from the original RN order were transferred. The can-cellations were as follows:

F-4K-?-MC XV604 to XV610 (7 aircraft)
F-4M-33-MC XT915 to XT919 (5 aircraft)
F-4M-?-MC XT920 to XT928 (9 aircraft)
F-4M-?-MC XV520 to XV551 (32 aircraft)

Totals constructed, by year: 1966—3 F-4K; 1967—2 F-4K, 2 F-4M; 1968—24 F-4K, 62 F-4M; 1969—23 F-4K, 54 F-4M; grand total—170.

Sample contruction nos: XV393 to XV442 were c/n 9223 to 9272; XV460 to XV501 were c/n 9273 to 9314.

Below: F-4As on the line at St Louis, October 1960. The aircraft visible were all Block 5e, comprising fourteen airframes with BuNos 148262 to 148275; nearest the camera is 148266. The next batch, Block 6f, were the first F-4Bs. (McAir)

F-4E direct deliveries to the *Heyl Ha'Avir*:

'Peace Echo I'

38	68-0396 to -0399	4
39	-0414 to -0417	4
	-0434 to -0437	4
40	-0454 to -0457	4
	-0469 to -0472	4
41	-0499 to -0502	4
	-0519 to -0525	7
	-0539 to -0547	9
	Subtotal	**44**

'Peace Echo II'

42	69-0294 to -0296	3
	-0299 to -0301	3
	Subtotal	**6**

'Peace Echo III'

43	69-7224 to -7227	4
	-7237 to -7250	14
	Subtotal	**18**

'Peace Patch'

	44-7547	1
	-7549	1
	-7553 to -7554	2
	-7567 to -7570	4
	-7575 to -7578	4
	Subtotal	**12**

'Peace Echo IV'

48	71-0224 to -0236	13
49	-1071	1
	-1080	1
	-1082	1
	-1090	1
	-1093	1
50	-1393	1
	-1396	1
	-1399 to -1402	4
51	-1779 to -1796	18
	Subtotal	**42**

'Peace Echo V'

54	72-1480 to -1481	2
	-1487 to -1488	2
55	-1491 to -1492	2
	-1495 to -1496	2
	-1497	1
56	-1498	1
	-1499	1
57	73-1157 to -1159	3
	-1161 to -1162	2
58	-1169 to -1170	2
	-1178 to -1179	2
59	-1190 to -1191	2
	-1201 to -1202	2
60	74-1014 to -1015	2
61	-1016 to -1021	6
62	-1022 to -1037	16
	Subtotal	**48**

'Nickel Grass' transfers from USAF stocks

66-0313	1
-0327	1
-0352	1
67-0326	1
-0340	1
-0346	1
-0362	1
-0368	1
-0383	1
68-0331	1
-0333	1
-0380	1
69-7229	1
-7255	1
71-0246	1
-1074	1
-1078	1
-1394 to -1395	2
-1398	1
72-0121	1
-0123	1
-0127	1
-0129 to -0133	5
-0137 to -0138	2
-0157 to -0158	2
-0163 to -0164	2
Subtotal	**34**

Deliveries included 24 in 1969, 44 in 1970, 12 in 1971 (all 'Peace Patch'), 24 in 1972, 52 (including all 34 'Nickel Grass' transfers) in 1973, 10 in 1974, 10 in 1975 and a final 28 in 1976.

New-build F-4D/E acquisitions by the *Nirou Hayai Shanashahiye Iran*:

'Peace Roll'

F-4D	35–36	67-14869 to -14884	16
	37–38	68-6904 to -6919	16
		Subtotal	**32**
F-4E	46–47	69-7711 to -7742	32
	51–56	71-1094 to -1166	73
	57–59	73-1519 to -1554	36
	63	75-0222 to -0257	36
		Subtotal	**177**

Originally bearing the IIAF serials 3-601 to 3-632, the F-4Ds were officially delivered between 8 September 1968 and 27 October 1969, though not in precise serial sequence. Thirty of these aircraft were later renumbered 3-663 to 3-691 in sequence (two having been written off beforehand, including 3-603/67-14871 on 1 November 1968 and 3-605/67-14872 on 9 February 1972), to conform with the F-4E numbers. The latter deliveries took place between 30 April 1971 and 2 September 1977, bearing the IIAF serial range 3-692 and upwards. The following USAF F-4Es were also leased from the 401st TFW at Torrejon AB, Spain, as an offshoot from the CENTO Shabaz manoeuvres, to help introduce the F-4E to IIAF service: 69-0246, -0254, -0263, -0265, -0275, -0277, -0283 and -0285.

New-build F-4EJ acquisitions by, and Mitsubishi licensed production for, the *Koku Jie tai*:

F-4EJ	45	17-8301 to -8302	2
		27-8303 to -8306	4
		37-8307 to -8310	4
	47	-8311 to -8313	3
		-8314 to -8315	2
		-8314 to -8323	10
		47-8324 to -8352	29
		57-8353 to -8376	24
		67-8377 to -8391	15
		77-8392 to -8403	12
		87-8404 to -8415	12
		97-8416 to -8427	12
		07-8428 to -8436	9
		17-8437 to -8440	4
		Subtotal	**140**

Aircraft 27-8303 to 37-8313 were delivered as knock-down kits to Mitsiubishi, with the forward fuselages for -8311 and -8312 released concurrently with Block 46. Aircraft 37-8314 and -8315 comprised forward-fuselage trial-fit kits only and had no McAir number assigned. All aircraft and components produced by McAir were originally serialled with the 17- prefix. The JASDF later renumbered aircraft 47-8324 to 47-8331 with the '37-' prefix.

New-build F-4E/F acquisitions by the *Luftwaffe*:

'Peace Rhine'

F-4E	63	75-0628 to -0637	10
		Subtotal	**10**
F-4F[17]	51	3701 to 3714	14
	52	3715 to 3727	13
	53	3728 to 3740	13
	54	3741 to 3754	14
	55	3755 to 3772	18
	56	3773 to 3796	24
	57	3797 to 3820	24
	58	3821 to 3864	44
	59	3865 to 3875	11
		Subtotal	**175**

Luftwaffe F-4Fs bore the USAF serials 72-1111 to -1285.

F-4Es transferred to *Al Quwwat al-Jawwiya Ilmisriya*:

'Peace Pharaoh'

32	66-0337	1
33	-0340 to -0341	2
	-0343	1
	-0349	1
	-0353	1
	-0358	1
	-0360	1

	-0362	1
	-0364	1
	-0366	1
	-0375	1
	67-0211 to -0213	3
34	-0220	1
	-0231	1
	-0236	1
	-0238 to -0239	2
	-0264	1
	-0278	1
35	-0289	1
	-0305	1
	-0307	1
	-0309	1
	-0313	1
	-0317	1
	-0322	1
	-0332	1
	-0341	1
36	-0355	1
	-0366	1
	-0371	1
	-0373	1
	Subtotal	**35**

A first batch of aircraft were delivered from 16 to 18 September 1979, with the balance being transferred during January and March 1980. All came from the 31st TFW at Homestead AFB, Florida, or fresh from re-work at Ogden Logistics Center, Utah.

F-4s transferred to the *Hankook Kong Goon* (ROKAF) from USAF stocks:

'Peace Pheasant'

First batch: 18 F-4Ds, 1969

64-0931	64-0950 to -0951
-0933 to -0935	-0955
-0941	-0957 to -0958
-0943 to -0944	-0961 to -0962
-0946 to -0948	-0966

Aircraft on short-term loan between 1968 and 1975 included 64-0938, -0940 (delivered in 1968 for initial familiarization) and -0954 and 66-7548, all of which were written off or returned.

Second batch: 18 F-4Ds, 1972

64-0978	65-0630
65-0582	-0640
-0589	-0650
-0591 to -0592	-0678
-0605	-0691
-0610	-0715
-0620	-0732
-0622 to -0623	-0762

These aircraft were loaned during late 1972 and formally transferred during 1975. Two additional aircraft, 65-0663 and -0709, were provided in 1973 and 1970 respectively. 64-0978 was an

attrition replacement delivered in 1975, when the formal handover was made.

Third batch: 8 F-4Ds, 1983–84

65-0679	65-0797
-0689 to -0690	66-7476
-0755	-7479
-0786	
-0797	

Fourth batch: 4 F-4Ds, 1986–87

65-0778	66-0239
-0795	-0274

These attrition replacement aircraft were delivered between 3 November 1986 and 28 January 1987.

Fifth batch: 24 F-4Ds, 1987–88

66-7507	66-7753
-7555	-7758
-7577	-7762
-7608	-8701
-7673	-8734
-7690	-8737
-7709	-8756
-7715	-8758 to -8759
-7732	-8765
-7737	-8806
-7747	-8810
-7750	

Deliveries comprised four aircraft on 14 December 1987 and, during 1988, one on 11 January, one on 1 February, one on 10 February, three on 22 February, two on 4 March, two on 17 March, two on 21 March and a final eight on 1 April.

40 F-4E transfers, 1985–91

66-0382	68-0353
67-0224	-0355
-0228	-0360
-0283	-0365
68-0309	-0376
-0312	-0406 to -0407
-0347	-0421
-0351	-0431
-0369	-0439
-0322 to -0323	-0441
-0325	-0453
-0329 to -0330	-0458
-0336	-0468
-0339	-0483
-0341	-0493
-0344	-0513
-0349	-0530

This list includes four aircraft delivered during 1985, eighteen transferred 'across the apron' from 51st TFW stocks at Osan and Taegu, South Korea, during 1989 and a final fifteen from 3rd TFW stocks previously based at Clark Field in the Philippines during 1990. Three 'tails' are unidentified.

15 RF-4C transfers, 1990

64-1001	66-0440
-1009	-0446

65-0940	68-0549
66-0438	69-0366

Seven aircraft not identified. All came from the 460th TRG located at Taegu, South Korea.

New-build F-4Es acquired under Project 'Peace Pheasant II'

Delivered 1978:	76-0493 to -0511	19
Delivered 1980:		
	78-0727 to -0744	18
	Total	**37**

The second batch of new-builds terminated with the last McAir delivery, Ship No 5057 (FMS serial 78-0744), accepted on 26 October 1979. Including static fatigue examples and part-built aircraft 'kits', this machine was actually number 5068, bringing total Phantom production (including wholly Mitsubishi licence-built F-4EJs) up to 5,201 aircraft.

F-4Es transferred to the *Elliniki Polemiki Aeroporia*:

67-0345	68-0424
-0350	-0426
-0377	-0432
-0381	-0438
68-0318	-0440
-0361	-0442
-0363	-0444 to -0445
-0381	-0480 to -0481
-0393 to -0394	-0496
-0402	-0506
-0405	-0515
-0408	-0517
-0412	

In July 1991 President Bush announced that two dozen F-4Es would be donated to the Hellenic Air Force. In fact, 28 aircraft were transferred, beginning with two cells comprising ten aircraft which were delivered via Spangdahlem AB, Germany, during August that year. Cell-leaders in the initial batch of ten, 67-0381 and 68-0318, bore large Greek Flags on their fins. The follow-on batch of 18 included eight aircraft ferried-in in mid-October and the final ten in November. All came from ex-Indiana ANG stocks. These supplemented the survivors of 56 new F-4Es acquired under FMS Project 'Peace Icarus', as follows.

'Peace Icarus' new-build F-4Es

	72-1500 to -1535	36
	74-1618 to -1619	2
	77-1743 to -1760	18
	Total	**56**

The first batch were delivered from March 1974 onwards, the second in June 1976 and the third in December 1978.

F-4Es transferred to the *Turk Hava Kuvvetleri*:

'Peace Diamond'

First batch of 15, 1981:

66-0293	67-0251
-0312	-0259
-0373 to -0374	-0262
67-0215	-0304
-0222	-0336
-0227	-0338
-0242	68-0307

Second batch of 15, 1984–85:

66-0305	67-0248
-0307	-0258
-0318	-0273
67-0208	-0290
-0216 to -0217	-0316
-0221	-0342
-0233	-0387

Third batch of 40, 1987:

66-0297	67-0210
-0300 to -0301	-0226
-0303 to -0304	-0230
-0309	-0232
-0314	-0268 to -0269
-0317	-0272
-0320	-0274
-0323	-0280
-0333	-0285
-0336	-0298
-0339	-0302
-0344 to -0345	-0334
-0347	-0344
-0351	-0354
-0354 to -0355	68-0313
-0361	-0319
-0370	-0350
-0379	-0448

Aircraft officially delivered between 18 June and 23 November 1987 in batches of four on 18 June, 9 and 27 July, 10 and 25 August, 14 and 22 September, 13 October and 23 November (with one on 28 October and three on 3 November).

Fourth batch of 40, 1991–92

66-0292	67-0398
-0328	68-0308
-0334	-0342
-0359	-0346
67-0298	-0383
-0265	-0400
-0301	-0403
-0319	-0409
-0331	-0427
-0360	-0474
-0372	-0498
-0376	-0528
-0391	69-7585
-0395	

Thirteen aircraft not identified at the time of writing. The first four—67-0398 and 68-0403, -0409 and -0498—were handed over at Eskishehir on 25 March , 1991. All 27 F-4s identified above were handed over by 29 April 1992.

F-4E New-build acquisitions:

73-1016 to -1055	40
77-0277 to -0308	32
Total	**72**

These aircraft bring total THK F-4E deliveries—new builds and USAF transfers—to 182 aircraft. The survivors of eight new RF-4Es are being supplemented by 45 ex-*Luftwaffe* machines, up to thirty of which will be assigned to operations with the balance consigned for spare parts, bringing total THK operationally capable receipts by the end of 1993 to 220 aircraft and making it the third largest operator ever outside the US forces. F-4E 77-0290 was McAir Ship No 5,000 and wore a flamboyant scheme appropriate to the occasion on its delivery on 27 May 1978.

RF-4 'PHOTO-PHANTOMS'

US Air Force:

RF-4C	Block	Serials	No
RF-4C	15	6212200 to 6212201	2
	16	63-7740	1
	17	-7741 to -7742	2
	18	-7743 to -7749	7
	19	-7750 to -7763	14
	20	64-0997 to -1017	21
	21	-1018 to -1037	20
	22	-1038 to -1061	24
	23	-1062 to -1077	16
	24	-1078 to -1085	8
		65-0818 to -0838	21
	25	-0839 to -0864	26
	26	-0865 to -0901	37
	27	-0902 to -0932	31
	28	-0933 to -0945	13
		66-0383 to -0386	4
		-0388	1
	29	-0387	1
		-0389 to -0406	18
	30	-0407 to -0428	22
	31	-0429 to -0450	22
	32	-0451 to -0472	22
	33	-0473 to -0478	6
		67-0428 to -0442	15
	34	-0443 to -0453	11
	35	-0454 to -0461	8
	36	-0462 to -0469	8
	37	68-0548 to -0561	14
	38	-0562 to -0576	15
	39	-0577 to -0593	17
	40	-0594 to -0611	18
	41	69-0349 to -0357	9
	42	-0358 to -0366	9
	43	-0367 to -0375	9
	44	-0376 to -0384	9
	48	71-0248 to -0252	5
	49	-0253 to -0259	7
	51	72-0145 to -0148	4
	52	-0149 to -0152	4
	53	-0153 to -0156	4
		Subtotal	**505**

US Marine Corps:

RF-4B	Block	Serials	No
RF-4B	20	151975 to 151977	3
	21	151978 to 151979	2
	22	151980 to 151981	2
	23	151982 to 151983	2
	24	153089 to 153094	6
	25	153095 to 153100	6
	26	153101 to 153107	7
	27	153108 to 153115	8
	41	157342 to 157346	5
	43	157347 to 15735	5
		Subtotal	**46**

Luftwaffe:

RF-4E	Block	Serials	No
RF-4E	43	69-7448 to -7455	8
	44	-7456 to -7462	7
	45	-7463 to -7481	19
	46	-7482 to -7510	29
	47	-7511 to -7535	25
		Subtotal	**88**

Heyl Ha'Avir:

	Block	Serials	No
	44	69-7567	1
		-7570	1
		-7576	1
	45	69-7590 to -7595	6
	63	75-0418 to -0423	6
	64	-0656 to -0661	6
		Subtotal	**21**

Nirou Hayai Shanashahiye Iran:

	Block	Serials	No
	48	72-0266 to -0269	4
	61	74-1725 to -1728	4
	62	-1729 to -1736	8
	68	78-0751 to -0754	4
		-0788 to -0854	2
	69	-0855 to -0864	10
		Subtotal	**32**

Turk Hava Kuvvetleri:

	Block	Serials	No
	66	77-0309 to -0316	8
		Subtotal	**8**

Elliniki Aeroporia:

	Block	Serials	No
	66	77-0357 to -0358	2
		-1761 to -1766	6
		Subtotal	**8**

Koku Jiei tai:

RF-4EJ	Block	Serials	No
RF-4EJ	56	47-6901 to -6905	5
		57-6906 to -6914	9
		Subtotal	**14**

The two Block 15 RF-4Cs were prototypes converted on the McAir lines from F-4Bs, the three Block 44 Israeli aircraft were F-4E(S)s converted from F-4E fighter-bombers and the sixteen Blocks 68 and 69 Iranian aircraft were part-built but not delivered. USAF RF-4C disposals to the *Hankook Kong Goon* (15) and *Ejercito del Aire Español* (12) are not included here, nor are the ex-*Luftwaffe* RF-4Es which went to Turkey (45, of which fifteen were provided as spares) and the Mitsubishi licence-manufactured F-4EJs subsequently converted for reconnaissance duties (17) with the addition of Thomson-CSF Raphael SLAR or ASTAC elint pods.

APPENDIX II: F-4 PHANTOM AERIAL VICTORIES IN SOUTH-EAST ASIA

US AIR FORCE

Date	Victim	A/c	Serial no	Code	Sqn	Parent unit	Pilot	Back-seater	Call-sign	Weapon
10/07/65	MiG-17	F-4C	64-0693	–	45TFS	2 AD	Holcombe, Capt K. E.	Clark, Capt A. C.		AIM-9
10/07/65	MiG-17	F-4C	64-0679	–	45TFS	2 AD	Roberts, Capt T. S.	Anderson, Capt R. C.		AIM-9
23/04/66	MiG-17	F-4C	64-0699	–	555TFS	8TFW	Blake, Capt R. E.	George, 1Lt S. W.	? 04	AIM-7
23/04/66	MiG-17	F-4C	64-0689	–	555TFS	8TFW	Cameron, Capt M. F.	Evans, 1Lt R. E.	? 04	AIM-9
26/04/66	MiG-21	F-4C	64-0752	–	480TFS	35TFW	Gilmore, Maj P. J.	Smith, 1Lt W. T.	? 01	AIM-9
29/04/66	MiG-17	F-4C	?	–	555TFS	8TFW	Dowell, Capt W. B. D.	Gossard, 1Lt. H. E.	? 03	AIM-9
29/04/66	MiG-17	F-4C	?	–	555TFS	8TFW	Keith, Capt L. R.	Bleaky, 1Lt R. A.	? 01	Manoeuvring
30/04/66	MiG-17	F-4C	?	–	555TFS	8TFW	Golberg, Capt L. H.	Hardgrave, 1Lt G. D.	? 04	AIM-9
12/05/66	MiG-17	F-4C	64-0660	–	390TFS	35TFW	Dudley, Maj W. R.	Kreingelis, 1Lt I.	? 03	AIM-9
14/07/66	MiG-21	F-4C	?	–	480TFS	35TFW	Martin, 1LT R. G.	Kreips, 1Lt R. N.	? 02	AIM-9
16/06/66	MiG-17	F-4C	63-7650	–	555TFS	8TFW	Jameson, 1Lt J. W.	Rose, 1Lt D. B.	? 04	AIM-9
14/07/66	MiG-21	F-4C	63-7489	–	480TFS	35TFW	Swender, Capt W. J.	Buttel Jr, 1Lt D. A.	? 01	AIM-9
05/11/66	MiG-21	F-4C	63-7541	–	480TFS	366TFW	Tuck, Maj R. E.	Rabeni Jr, 1Lt J. J.	Opal 01	AIM-7
05/11/66	MiG-21	F-4C	63-7535	–	480TFS	366TFW	Latham, 1Lt W. J.	Klause, 1Lt K. J.	Opal 02	AIM-9
02/01/67	MiG-21	F-4C	64-0838	FG	433TFS	8TFW	Combies, Maj P. P.	Dutton, 1Lt L. R.	Rambler 04	AIM-7
02/01/67	MiG-21	F-4C	64-0720	FG	433TFS	8TFW	Stone, Capt J. B.	Dunnegan Jr, 1Lt C. P.	Rambler 01	AIM-7
02/01/67	MiG-21	F-4C	64-0692	FG	433TFS	8TFW	Glynn Jr, 1Lt L. J.	Cary, 1Lt L. E.	Rambler 02	AIM-7
02/01/67	MiG-21	F-4C	63-7680	FP	555TFS	8TFW	Olds, Col R.	Clifton, 1Lt C.	Olds 01	AIM-9
02/01/67	MiG-21	F-4C	63-7683	FY	555TFS	8TFW	Radeker III, Capt W. S.	Murray III, 1Lt J. E.	Olds 04	AIM-9
02/01/67	MiG-21	F-4C	63-7710	FY	555TFS	8TFW	Raspberry Jr, Capt E. T.	Western, 1Lt R. W.	Ford 02	AIM-9
02/01/67	MiG-21	F-4C	63-7589	FY	555TFS	8TFW	Wetterhahn, 1Lt R. F.	Sharp, 1Lt J. K.	Olds 02	AIM-7
06/01/67	MiG-21	F-4C	64-0849		555TFS	8TFW	Hirsch, Maj T. M.	Strasswimmer, 1Lt R. J.	Crab 02	AIM-7
06/01/67	MiG-21	F-4C	64-0839	FP	555TFS	8TFW	Pascoe, Capt R. M.	Wells, 1Lt N. E.	Crab 01	AIM-7
23/04/67	MiG-21	F-4C	64-0776	AK	389TFS	366TFW	Anderson, Maj R. D.	Kjer, Capt F. D.	Chicago 03	AIM-7
26/04/67	MiG-21	F-4C	64-0797		389TFS	366TFW	Moore, Maj R. W.	Sears, 1Lt J. F.	Cactus 01	AIM-7
01/05/67	MiG-17	F-4C	63-7577		390TFS	366TFW	Dilger, Maj R. G.	Thies, 1Lt M.	Stinger 01	Manoeuvring
04/05/67	MiG-21	F-4C	63-7668	FP	555TFS	8TFW	Olds, Col R.	Lafever, 1Lt W. D.	Flamingo 01	AIM-9
13/05/67	MiG-17	F-4C	64-0739	FG	433TFS	8TFW	Kirk, Maj W. L.	Wayne, 1Lt S. A.	Harpoon 01	AIM-9
13/05/67	MiG-17	F-4C	63-7680	FG	433TFS	8TFW	Haeffner, Lt-Col F. A.	Bever, 1Lt M. R.	Harpoon 03	AIM-7
14/05/67	MiG-17	F-4C	63-7699	CG	480TFS	366TFW	Bakke, Maj S. O.	Lambert, Capt R. W.	Elgin 01	AIM-7
14/05/67	MiG-17	F-4C	64-0660		480TFS	366TFW	Hargrove, Maj J. A.	Demuth, 1Lt S. H.	Speedo 01	20mm
14/05/67	MiG-17	F-4C	63-7704		480TFS	366TFW	Craig, Capt J. T.	Talley, 1Lt J. T.	Speedo 03	20mm
20/05/67	MiG-21	F-4C	64-0748		389TFS	366TFW	Janca, Maj R. D.	Roberts Jr, 1Lt W. E.	Elgin 01	AIM-9
20/05/67	MiG-21	F-4C	64-0777		389TFS	366TFW	Titus, Lt-Col R. F.	Zimer, 1Lt M.	Elgin 03	AIM-7
20/05/67	MiG-17	F-4C	63-7623	FG	433TFS	8TFW	Pardo, Maj J. R.	Wayne, 1Lt S. A.	Tampa 03	AIM-9
20/05/67	MiG-17	F-4C	64-0829	FG	433TFS	8TFW	Olds, Col R.	Croker, 1Lt S. B.	Tampa 01	AIM-7
20/05/67	MiG-17	F-4C	64-0829	FG	433TFS	8TFW	Olds, Col R.	Croker, 1Lt S. B.	Tampa 01	AIM-9
20/05/67	MiG-17	F-4C	64-0673	FG	433TFS	8TFW	Combies, Maj P. P.	Lafferty, 1Lt D. L.	Ballot 01	AIM-9
22/05/67	MiG-21	F-4C	64-0776	AK	389TFS	366TFW	Titus, Lt-Col R. F.	Zimer, 1Lt M.	Wander 01	AIM-9
22/05/67	MiG-21	F-4C	64-0776	AK	389TFS	366TFW	Titus, Lt-Col R. F.	Zimer, 1Lt M.	Wander 01	20mm
05/06/67	MiG-17	F-4C	64-0660		480TFS	366TFW	Preister, Maj D. K.	Pankhurst, Capt J. E.	Oakland 01	20mm
05/06/67	MiG-17	F-4C	63-7647	FP	555TFS	8TFW	Pascoe, Maj R. M.	Wells, Capt N. E.	Chicago 01	AIM-9
05/06/67	MiG-17	F-4D	66-0249	FY	555TFS	8TFW	Raspberry Jr, Maj E. T.	Gullick, Capt F. M.	Drill 01	AIM-7
24/10/67	MiG-21	F-4D	66-7750	FG	433TFS	8TFW	Kirk, Maj W. L.	Bongartz, 1Lt T. R.	Buick 01	20mm
26/10/67	MiG-17	F-4D	66-7565		555TFS	8TFW	Cobb, Capt L. D.	Lavoy, Capt A. A.	Ford 04	AIM-4
26/10/67	MiG-17	F-4D	66-7546	FY	555TFS	8TFW	Gordon III, Capt W. S.	Monsees, 1Lt J. H.	Ford 03	AIM-7
26/10/67	MiG-17	F-4D	66-0274	FY	555TFS	8TFW	Logeman, Capt J. D.	McCoy II, 1Lt F. E.	Ford 01	AIM-7
06/11/67	MiG-17	F-4D	66-7601		435TFS	8TFW	Simmonds, Capt D. D.	McKinney Jr, 1Lt G. H.	Sapphire 01	20mm
06/11/67	MiG-17	F-4D	66-7601		435TFS	8TFW	Simmonds, Capt D. D.	McKinney Jr, 1Lt G. H.	Sapphire 01	20mm
17/12/67	MiG-17	F-4D	66-8709	OC	13TFS	432TRW	Baker, Capt D. (USMC)	Ryan Jr, 1Lt J. D.	Gambit 03	AIM-4
19/12/67	MiG-17	F-4D	66-7601		435TFS	8TFW	Moore, Maj J. D.	McKinney Jr, Maj G. H.	Nash 01	20mm
03/01/68	MiG-21	F-4D	66-7748	FG	433TFS	8TFW	Bogoslofski, Maj B. J.	Huskey, Capt R. L.	Tampa 01	20mm
03/01/68	MiG-17	F-4D	66-7594	FO	435TFS	8TFW	Squier, Lt-Col C. D.	Muldoon, 1Lt M. D.	Olds 01	AIM-4
18/01/68	MiG-21	F-4D	66-8720	FO	435TFS	8TFW	Simonet, Maj K. A.	Smith, 1Lt W. O.	Otter 01	AIM-4
05/02/68	MiG-21	F-4D	66-8714	OC	13TFS	432TRW	Hill, Capt R. G.	Huneke, 1Lt B. V.	Gambit 03	AIM-4
06/02/68	MiG-21	F-4D	66-8688	FG	433TFS	8TFW	Boles, Capt R. H.	Battista, 1Lt R. B.	Buick 04	AIM-7
12/02/68	MiG-21	F-4D	66-8690	FO	435TFS	8TFW	Lang Jr, Lt-Col A. E.	Moss, 1Lt R. P.	Buick 01	AIM-7
14/02/68	MiG-17	F-4D	66-7661	FO	435TFS	8TFW	Williams Jr, Col D. O.	Feighny Jr, 1Lt J. P.	Killer 01	AIM-7
14/02/68	MiG-17	F-4D	66-7554		555TFS	8TFW	Howerton, Maj R. D.	Voigt II, 1Lt T. L.	Nash 03	20mm
21/02/72	MiG-21	F-4D	65-0784	OY	555TFS	432TRW	Lodge, Maj R. A.	Locher, 1Lt R. C.	Falcon 62	AIM-7
01/03/72	MiG-21	F-4D	66-7463	OY	555TFS	432TRW	Kittinger Jr, Lt-Col J. W.	Hodgson, 1Lt R. A.	Falcon 54	AIM-7
30/03/72	MiG-21	F-4D	66-0230	OC	13TFS	432TRW	Olmstead Jr, Capt F. S.	Volloy, Capt G. R.	Papa 01	AIM-7
16/04/72	MiG-21	F-4D	66-7550	PN	13TFS	432TRW	Cherry, Maj E. D.	Feinstein, Capt J. S.	Basco 03	AIM-7

Date	Enemy	Type	Serial	Code	Squadron	Wing	Pilot	Back-seater	Callsign	Weapon
16/04/72	MiG-21	F-4D	66-7463	OY	13TFS	432TRW	Olmstead Jr, Capt F. S.	Maas, Capt S.	Basco 01	AIM-7
16/04/72	MiG-21	F-4D	66-0280	PN	523TFS	432TRW	Null, Capt J. C.	Vahue, Capt M. D.	Papa 03	AIM-7
08/05/72	MiG-19	F-4D	66-7463	OY	13TFS	432TRW	Crews, Maj B. P.	Jones Jr, Capt K. W.	Galore 03	AIM-7
08/05/72	MiG-21	F-4D	65-0784	OY	555TFS	432TRW	Lodge, Maj R. A.	Locher, Capt R. C.	Oyster 01	AIM-7
10/05/72	MiG-21	F-4D	66-7463	OY	555TFS	432TRW	Ritchie, Capt R. S.	DeBellevue, Capt C. B.	Oyster 03	AIM-7
10/05/72	MiG-21	F-4D	65-0784	OY	555TFS	432TRW	Lodge, Maj R. A.	Locher, Capt R. C.	Oyster 01	AIM-7
10/05/72	MiG-21	F-4D	66-8734	OY	555TFS	432TRW	Markle, 1Lt J. D.	Eaves, Capt S. D.	Oyster 02	AIM-7
11/05/72	MiG-21	F-4D	66-7661	OY	555TFS	432TRW	Nichols, Capt S. E.	Bell, 1Lt J. R.	Gopher 02	AIM-7
12/05/72	MiG-19	F-4D	66-8756	OY	555TFS	432TRW	Frye, Lt-Col W. T.	Cooney, Lt-Col J. P.	Harlow 02	AIM-7
23/05/72	MiG-19	F-4E	67-0281		35TFS	366TFW	Beckers, Lt-Col L. L.	Huwe, Capt J. F.	Balter 01	AIM-7
23/05/72	MiG-21	F-4E	67-0333		35TFS	366TFW	Beatty Jr, Capt J. M.	Sumner, 1Lt J. M.	Balter 03	20mm
31/05/72	MiG-21	F-4E	68-0338	ED	13TFS	432TRW	Leonard, Capt B. G.	Feinstein, Capt J. S.	Gopher 03	AIM-9
31/05/72	MiG-21	F-4D	65-0801	OC	555TFS	432TRW	Ritchie, Capt R. S.	Pettit, Capt L. H.	Icebag 01	AIM-7
02/06/72	MiG-19	F-4E	67-0210	ZF	58TFS	432TRW	Handley, Maj P. W.	Smallwood, 1Lt J. J.	Brenda 01	20mm
21/06/72	MiG-21	F-4E	67-0283	JV	469TFS	388TFW	Christiansen, Lt-Col V. R.	Harden, Maj K. M.	Icwman 03	AIM-9
08/07/72	MiG-21	F-4E	67-0270	LA	4TFS	366TFW	Hardy, Capt R. F.	Lewinski, Capt P. T.	Brenda 03	AIM-7
08/07/72	MiG-21	F-4E	67-0362	ED	555TFS	432TRW	Ritchie, Capt R. S.	DeBellevue, Capt C. B.	Paula 01	AIM-7
08/07/72	MiG-21	F-4E	67-0362	ED	555TFS	432TRW	Ritchie, Capt R. S.	DeBellevue, Capt C. B.	Paula 01	AIM-7
18/07/72	MiG-21	F-4D	66-0271	OC	13TFS	432TRW	Baily, Lt-Col C. G.	Feinstein, Capt J. S.	Snug 01	AIM-9
29/07/72	MiG-21	F-4E	67-0292	LA	4TFS	366TFW	Taft, Lt-Col T. E.	Imaye, Capt S. M.	Pistol 01	AIM-7
29/07/72	MiG-21	F-4D	66-0271	OC	13TFS	432TRW	Baily, Lt-Col C. G.	Feinstein, Capt J. S.	Cadillac 01	AIM-7
12/08/72	MiG-21	F-4E	67-0239	ZF	58TFS	432TRW	Richard, Capt L. (USMC)	Ettel, Lt-Cdr M. J. (USN)	Dodge 01	AIM-7
15/08/72	MiG-21	F-4E	69-7235	SC	336TFS	8TFW	Sheffler, Capt F. W.	Massen, Capt M. A.	Date 04	AIM-7
19/08/72	MiG-21	F-4E	69-0291	LA	4TFS	366TFW	White, Capt S. E.	Bettine, Capt F. E.	Pistol 03	AIM-7
28/08/72	MiG-21	F-4D	66-7463	OY	555TFS	432TRW	Ritchie, Capt R. S.	DeBellevue, Capt C. B.	Buick 01	AIM-7
02/09/72	MiG-19	F-4E	67-0392	JV		388TFW	Lucas, Maj J. I. (34TFS)	Malloy, 1Lt D. (35TFS)	Eagle 03	AIM-7
09/09/72	MiG-21	F-4E	67-0327	ZF	555TFS	432TRW	Tibbett, Capt C. B.	Hargrove, 1Lt W. S.	Olds 03	20mm
09/09/72	MiG-19	F-4D	66-0267	OY	555TFS	432TRW	Madden Jr, Capt J. A.	DeBellevue, Capt C. B.	Olds 01	AIM-9
09/09/72	MiG-19	F-4D	66-0267	OY	555TFS	432TRW	Madden Jr, Capt J. A.	DeBellevue, Capt C. B.	Olds 01	AIM-9
12/09/72	MiG-21	F-4E	67-0275	JJ	35TFS	388TFW	Beckers, Lt-Col L. L.	Griffin, 1Lt T. M.	Finch 01	AIM-9/20mm
12/09/72	MiG-21	F-4E	67-0268		35TFS	388TFW	Retterbush, Maj G. L.	Autrey, 1Lt D. L.	Finch 03	20mm
12/09/72	MiG-21	F-4D	65-0608		469TFS	388TFW	Mahaffey, Capt M. J.	Sheilds, 1Lt G. I.	Robin 02	AIM-9
16/09/72	MiG-21	F-4E	68-0338	ED	555TFS	432TRW	Tibbett, Capt C. B.	Hargrove, 1Lt W. S.	Chevy 03	AIM-9
05/10/72	MiG-21	F-4E	68-0493	JJ	34TFS	388TFW	Coe, Capt R. E.	Webb III, 1Lt O. E.	Robin 01	AIM-7
06/10/72	MiG-19	F-4E	66-0313	JV	34TFS	388TFW	Clouser, Maj G. L.	Brunson, 1Lt C. H.	Eagle 03	Manoeuvring
06/10/72	MiG-19	F-4E	67-0392	JV	34TFS	388TFW	Barton, Capt C. D.	Watson, 1Lt G. D.	Eagle 04	Manoeuvring
08/10/72	MiG-21	F-4E	69-0276	JJ	35TFS	388TFW	Retterbush, Maj G. L.	Jasperson, Capt R. H.	Lark 01	20mm
12/10/72	MiG-21	F-4D	66-0268	OY	555TFS	432TRW	Madden Jr, Capt J. A.	Pettit, Capt L. H.	Vega 01	Manoeuvring
13/10/72	MiG-21	F-4D	66-7501	OC	13TFS	432TRW	Westphal, Lt-Col C. D.	Feinstein, Capt J. S.	Olds 01	AIM-7
15/10/72	MiG-21	F-4E	67-0301	JJ	34TFS	388TFW	Holtz, Maj R. L.	Diehl, 1Lt W. C.	Parrot 03	AIM-9
15/10/72	MiG-21	F-4E	67-0232	ZF	307TFS	432TRW	Rubus, Capt G. M.	Hendrickson, Capt J. L.	Buick 03	20mm
15/10/72	MiG-21	F-4D	66-7463	OY	523TFS	432TRW	McCoy, Maj I. J.	Brown, Maj F. W.	Chevy 01	AIM-9
21/12/72	MiG-21	F-4D	66-0240	OY	555TFS	432TRW	Sholders, Capt G. L.	Binkley, 1Lt E. D.	Bucket 01	Manoeuvring
22/12/72	MiG-21	F-4D	66-0269	OY	555TFS	432TRW	Brunson, Lt-Col J. E.	Pickett, Maj R. S.	Buick 01	AIM-7
28/12/72	MiG-21	F-4D	66-7468	OY	555TFS	432TRW	McKee, Maj H. L.	Dubler, Capt J. E.	List 01	AIM-7
07/01/73	MiG-21	F-4D	65-0796		4TFS	432TRW	Howman, Capt P. D.	Kullman, 1Lt L. W.	Crafty 01	AIM-7

US NAVY

Date	Enemy	Type	Serial	Code	Squadron	Wing	Pilot	RIO	Callsign	Weapon
09/04/65	MiG-17	F-4B	151403	NG	VF-96	CVW-9	Murphy, Lt(JG) T. M.	Fegan, Ens R. J.	Showtime 602	AIM-7
17/06/65	MiG-17	F-4B	151488	NE	VF-21	CVW-2	Page, Cdr L.	Smith, Lt J. C.	Sundown 101	AIM-7
17/06/65	MiG-17	F-4B	152219	NE	VF-21	CVW-2	Batson, Lt J. E. D.	Doremus, Lt-Cdr R. B.	Sundown 102	AIM-7
06/10/65	MiG-17	F-4B	150634	NL	VF-151	CVW-15	MacIntyre, Lt-Cdr D.	Johnson, Lt(JG) A.	Switch Box 107	AIM-7
13/07/66	MiG-17	F-4B	151500	NL	VF-161	CVW-15	McGuigan, Lt W. M.	Fowler, Lt(JG) R. M.	Rock River 216	AIM-9
20/12/66	An-2	F-4B	152022	NH	VF-114	CVW-11	Wisely, Lt H. D.	Jordan, Lt(JG) D. L.	Linfield 215	AIM-7
20/12/66	An-2	F-4B	153019	NH	VF-213	CVW-11	McCrea, Lt D.	Nichols, Ens D.	Black Lion 110	AIM-7
24/04/67	MiG-17	F-4B	153000	NH	VF-114	CVW-11	Southwick, Lt C. E.	Laing, Ens J. W.	Linfield 210	AIM-9
24/04/67	MiG-17	F-4B	153077	NH	VF-114	CVW-11	Wisely, Lt H. D.	Anderson, Lt(JG) G. L.	Linfield 00	AIM-9
10/08/67	MiG-21	F-4B	152247	NH	VF-142	CVW-14	Freeborn, Lt G. H.	Elliot, Lt(JG) R. J.	Dakota 202	AIM-9
10/08/67	MiG-21	F-4B	150431	NK	VF-142	CVW-14	Davis, Lt-Cdr R. C.	Elie, Lt-Cdr G. O.	Dakota 2??	AIM-9
26/10/67	MiG-21	F-4B	149411	NK	VF-143	CVW-14	Hickey, Lt(JG) R. P.	Morris, Lt(JG) J. G.	Tap Room 1??	AIM-7
30/10/67	MiG-17	F-4B	150629	NK	VF-142	CVW-14	Lund, Lt-Cdr E. P.	Borst, Lt(JG) J. R.	Dakota 203	AIM-7
09/05/68	MiG-21	F-4B	153036	NG	VF-96	CVW-9	Hefferman, Maj J. (USAF)	Schumacher, Lt(JG) F. A.	Showtime 1??	AIM-7
10/07/68	MiG-21	F-4J	155553	AE	VF-33	CVW-6	Cash, Lt R.	Kain, Lt J. E.	Root Beer 212	AIM-9
28/03/70	MiG-21	F-4J	155875	NK	VF-142	CVW-14	Beaulier, Lt J. E.	Barkley, Lt S. J.	Dakota 201	AIM-9
19/01/72	MiG-21	F-4J	157267	NG	VF-96	CVW-9	Cunningham, Lt R. H.	Driscoll, Lt(JG) W. P.	Showtime 112	AIM-9
06/03/72	MiG-17	F-4B	153019	NL	VF-111	CVW-15	Weigand, Lt G. L.	Freckleton, Lt(JG) W. C.	Old Nick 201	AIM-9
06/05/72	MiG-17	F-4B	150456	NL	VF-51	CVW-15	Houston, Lt-Cdr J. B.	Moore, Lt K. T.	Screaming Eagle 100	AIM-9
06/05/72	MiG-21	F-4J	157249	NH	VF-114	CVW-11	Hughes, Lt R. G.	Cruz, Lt(JG) A. J.	Linfield 206	AIM-9

06/05/72	MiG-21	F-4J	157245	NH	VF-114	CVW-11	Pettigrew, Lt-Cdr K. W.	McCabe, Lt(JG) M. J.	Linfield 201	AIM-9
08/05/72	MiG-17	F-4J	157267	NG	VF-96	CVW-9	Cunningham, Lt R. H.	Driscoll, Lt(JG) W. P.	Showtime 112	AIM-9
10/05/72	MiG-21	F-4J	157269	NG	VF-92	CVW-9	Dose, Lt C.	McDevitt, Lt-Cdr J.	Silver Kite 211	AIM-9
10/05/72	MiG-17	F-4J	155769	NG	VF-96	CVW-9	Connelly, Lt M. J.	Blonski, Lt T. J. J.	Showtime 106	AIM-9
10/05/72	MiG-17	F-4J	155769	NG	VF-96	CVW-9	Connelly, Lt M. J.	Blonski, Lt T. J. J.	Showtime 106	AIM-9
10/05/72	MiG-17	F-4B	151398	NL	VF-51	CVW-15	Cannon, Lt K. L.	Morris, Lt R. A.	Screaming Eagle 111	AIM-9
10/05/72	MiG-17	F-4J	155749	NG	VF-96	CVW-9	Shoemaker, Lt S. C.	Crenshaw, Lt(JG) K. V.	Showtime 111	AIM-9
10/05/72	MiG-17	F-4J	155800	NG	VF-96	CVW-9	Cunningham, Lt R. H.	Driscoll, Lt(JG) W. P.	Showtime 100	AIM-9
10/05/72	MiG-17	F-4J	155800	NG	VF-96	CVW-9	Cunningham, Lt R. H.	Driscoll, Lt(JG) W. P.	Showtime 100	AIM-9
10/05/72	MiG-17	F-4J	155800	NG	VF-96	CVW-9	Cunningham, Lt R. H.	Driscoll, Lt(JG) W. P.	Showtime 100	AIM-9
18/05/72	MiG-19	F-4B	153068	NF	VF-161	CVW-5	Bartholomay, Lt H. A.	Brown, Lt O. R.	Rock River 110	AIM-9
18/05/72	MiG-17	F-4B	153915	NF	VF-161	CVW-5	Arwood, Lt P. E.	Bell, Lt J. M.	Rock River 105	AIM-9
23/05/72	MiG-17	F-4B	153020	NF	VF-161	CVW-5	McKeown, Lt-Cdr R. E	Ensch, Lt J. C.	Rock River 100	AIM-9
23/05/72	MiG-17	F-4B	153020	NF	VF-161	CVW-5	McKeown, Lt-Cdr R. E.	Ensch, Lt J. C.	Rock River 100	AIM-9
11/06/72	MiG-17	F-4B	149473	NL	VF-51	CVW-15	Teague, Cdr F. S.	Howell, Lt R. M.	Screaming Eagle 114	AIM-9
11/06/72	MiG-17	F-4B	149457	NL	VF-51	CVW-15	Copeland, Lt W. W.	Bouchoux, Lt D. R.	Screaming Eagle 113	AIM-9
21/06/72	MiG-21	F-4J	157307	AC	VF-31	CVW-3	Flynn, Cdr S. C.	John, Lt W. H.	Bandwagon 101	AIM-9
10/08/72	MiG-21	F-4J	157299	AC	VF-103	CVW-3	Tucker, Lt-Cdr R. E.	Edens, Lt(JG) S. B.	Clubleaf 206	AIM-7
11/09/72	MiG-21	F-4J	155526	AJ	VMFA-333	CVW-8	Lasseter, Maj L. T.	Cummings, Capt J. D	Shamrock 201	AIM-9
28/12/72	MiG-21	F-4J	155846	NK	VF-142	CVW-14	Davis, Lt(JG) S. H.	Ulrich, Lt(JG) G. H.	Dakota 214	AIM-9
12/1/73	MiG-17	F-4B	153045	NF	VF-161	CVW-5	Kovaleski, Lt V. T.	Wise, Lt(JG) J. A.	Rock River 102	AIM-9

All kills are dated by Zulu time. Maj Moore/Maj McKinney's kill on 19 December 1967 was shared with an F-105. Maj Clouser/1Lt Brunson's kill on 6 October 1972 was shared with Capt Barton/1Lt Watson's as listed.

APPENDIX III: US NAVY/MARINE CORPS F-4 SQUADRON CONVERSION DATES

US NAVY

Unit	Details	Remarks
VF-11 *Red Rippers*	F-8E → F-4B 07/66 → F-4J late 1973 → F-14A 07/80	Atlantic Fleet. One curtailed war cruise: *Forrestal* fire.
VF-14 *Top Hatters*	F3H → F-4B 05/63 → F-14A 01/73	Atlantic Fleet. One war cruise.
VF-21 *Freelancers*	F3H → F-4B late 1962 → F-4J 06/68 → F-4S 12/79 → F-4N → F-14A 11/83	Final conversion to F-4N for operations from *Coral Sea*.
VF-31 *Tomcatters*	F3H → F-4B 10/63 → F-4J 01/68 → F-14A 01/81	Atlantic Fleet. One war cruise.
VF-32 *Swordsmen*	F-8D → F-4B late 1965 → F-14A 02/74	Atlantic Fleet. One war cruise.
VF-33 *Starfighters/Tarsiers*	F-8E → F-4B 11/64 → F-4J 10/67 → F-14A 10/81	Flew F-4J longer than any other front-line unit.
VF-41 *Black Aces*	F3H → F-4B 02/62 → F-4J 02/67 → F-4B 1973 → F-4N 1974 → F-14A 04/76	Atlantic Fleet. One war cruise.
VF-51 *Screaming Eagles*	F-8J → F-4B mid-1971 → F-4N early 1974 → F-14A 06/78	One war cruise with F-4.
VF-74 *Be-Devilers*	F4D-1 → F4H-1 07/61 → F-4J 1/71 → F-4S late 1981 → F-14A 06/73	First operational Atlantic F-4 unit. Last Atlantic deployed unit (with VF-103).
VF-84 *Jolly Rogers*	F-8C → F-4B 06/64 → F-4J 02/67 → F-4B 1973 → F-4N 1974 → F-14A 06/76	First deployed F-4J unit.
VF-92 *Silver Kings*	F3H → F-4B 11/63 → F-4J mid-1968	8 war cruises with VF-96 (record). Was to have been F-14A unit but disestablished 1975.
VF-96 *Fighting Falcons* (as VF-142)	F-8A → F-4B 07/62 → F-4J 08/68	As for VF-92 (above).
VF-101 *Grim Reapers*	F4D-1/F3H → F4H-1F (F-4A) 06/61 → F-4B (N at Key West) → F-4J 12/66 → F-14A 02/76	Continued to use F-4J until 08/77 also. First unit with F-4J. One carrier deployment with CVW-8 in 1971.
VF-102 *Diamondbacks*	F4D-1 → F4H-1 (F-4B) 09/61 → F-4J late 67 → F-14A 07/81	Second Atlantic F-4 unit.
VF-103 *Sluggers*	F-8E → F-4B 03/65 → F-4J late 1968 → F-4S 1981 → F-14A 01/83	Last operational Atlantic Fleet unit (with VF-74).
VF-111 *Sundowners*	F-8H → F-4B early 1971 → F-4N 12/74 → F-14A 02/79	Began conversion to F-4J early 1976 but deployed on *Roosevelt*, so F-4N adopted.
VF-114 *Fighting Aardvarks*	F3H → F4H-1 (F-4B) mid-1961 → F-4J 09/69 → F-14A 05/76	All ten F-4 cruises on *Kitty Hawk*. Disestablished 04/93.
VF-116 *Black Lions*	F-4B/G 09/64	Commissioned for a few days owing to administrative error. A few F-4Gs marked. Became VF-213.
VF-121 *Pacemakers*	F4H-1F (F-4A) 12/60 → F-4J 04/67 → F-4S 1980 (some)	First USN Phantom sqn. Disestablished 09/80.
VF-142 *Ghost Riders*	F-3B → F-4B late 1963 → F-4J mid-1969 → F-14A mid-1974	7 war cruises.
VF-143 *Pukin' Dogs*	F-3B → F4H-1 (F-4B) 06/62 → F-4J 02/69 → F-14A mid-1974	Originally designated VF-53. 7 war cruises.
VF-151 *Vigilantes*	F3H → F-4B early 1964 → F-4N 03/73 → F-4J 07/77 → F-4S 12/80 → F/A-18 05/86	Last deployed USN F-4 unit, with VF-161. Only ex-F-4 unit to stay with F/A-18.
VF-154 *Black Knights*	F-8D → F-4B 11/65 → F-4J 08/68 → F-4S 12/79 → F-4N mid-1980 → F-14A 01/84	Like VF-21, flew all four F-4 models.
VF-161 *Chargers*	F3H → F-4B 11/64 → F-4N 03/73 → F-4J summer 1977 → F-4S 12/80 → F/A-18 1986	Last F3H Demon unit. Last deployed F-4 unit (with VF-151). Disbanded 04/88.

Unit	Aircraft	Notes
VF-171 *Aces*	F-4B 08/77 → F-4J 11/78 → F-4S 04/81	Oceana-based VF-171 had F-4J; VF-171 (Det Key West) used F-4N. Disestablished 06/84.
VF-191 *Satan's Kittens*	F-8J → F-4J 06/76	Decommissioned 03/78. Re-established with F-14A 12/86.
VF-194 *Red Lightnings*	F-8J → F-4J 06/76	Decommissioned Mar 1978. Re-established with F-14A 12/86.
VF-201 *Hunters*	F-8H → F-4N 1974 → F-4S early 1984 → F-14A 02/87	Dallas-based Reserve unit.
VF-202 *Superheats*	F-8H → F-4N 04/76 → F-4S early 1984 → F-14A04/87	Flew last F-4S on USN inventory to AMARC, 05/87.
VF-213 *Black Lions*	F3H → F-4G/B early 1964 → F-4B 1966 → F-4J 08/69 → F-14A 09/76	Briefly VF-116. First F-4J unit with ACLS.
VF-301 *Devil's Disciples*	F-8L → F-4B 06/74 → F-4N late 1975 → F-4S 08/81 → F-14A late 1984	Took over F-4S from VF-21/VF-154 in exchange for F-4N.
VF-302 *Stallions*	F-8K → F-4B 12/74 → F-4N late 1975 → F-4S 11/80 → F-14A late 1985	First USN Reserve F-4 unit. Last F-4 sqn at Miramar.
VX-4 *Evaluators*	F4H-1 (F-4B) 1961 → F-14A mid-1975	Used F-4N/J/S also. Last F-4S was retired 1986.
VX-5 *Vampires*	F4H-1 (F-4B) 1962	Used various F-4 marks to test weapons.
VAQ-33 *Firebirds*	EA-1F → EF-4B 02/70 → F-4J by 1980	Used a pair of F-4Ss until 01/81.
Blue Angels	F11F → F-4J 01/69 → A-4F late 1973	F-4s used until August 1973.

Various marks of F-4 were in use by the Naval AirTest Center (until 1988); the Naval Test Pilot's School at Patuxent River; the Naval Air Test Facility at Lakehurst, New Jersey; the Pacific Missile Test Center at Point Mugu, California; the Naval Missile Center and Naval Air Weapons Center at China Lake, California (still using the QF-4B/J/N drones); the Naval Weapons Evaluation Center at Kirtland AFB, New Mexico; and the Naval Air Development Center. One other unit (VF-22 LI) used the F-4B briefly in 1969–70, its aircraft coded '7L'.

US MARINE CORPS

Unit	Aircraft	Notes
VMFA-112 *Wolfpack* or *Cowboys*	F-8A → F-4N 12/75 → F-4J 07/83 → F-4S 02/85 → F/A-18 09/92	Code 'MA'. Last USMC F-8 unit. Last USMC F-4 unit.
VMFA-115 *Silver Eagles*	F4D-1 → F-4B 09/63 → F-4J 08/75 → F-4S 08/82 → F/A-18 07/85	Code 'VE'. Vietnam 1965–72. Carrier deployed (CVW-17) 1980 and 1981.
VMFA-122 *Crusaders*	F-8 → F-4B 07/65 → F-4J 12/75 → F-4S 01/83 → F/A-18 02/86	Code 'DC'. First USMC FH-1 and F-8 unit. Was to have flown F-14A from 1974.
VMFA-134 *Hawks* or *Smokes*	A-4F → F-4N 03/84 → F-4S 11/85 → F/A-18 05/89	Code 'MF'. First USMC Reserve F/A-18A unit.
VMFA-212 *Lancers*	F-8E → F-4J 04/68 → F-4S 02/81 → F/A-18 04/89	Code 'WD'. First USMC F/A-18C unit.
VMFA-232 *Red Devils*	F-8E → F-4J 09/67 → F-4S 02/79 → F/A-18 03/89	Code 'WT'. Last USMC F-4 unit in SEA.
VMFA-235 *Death Angels*	F-8E → F-4J 10/68 → F-4S 01/82 → F/A-18 08/89	Code 'DB'. Last F-4S withdrawn 02–03/89. Last regular USMC F-4 unit.
VMFA-251 *Thunderbolts*	F-8 → F-4B 11/64 → F-4J 06/71 → F-4S 05/81 → F/A-18 04/86	Code 'DW'. First regular F-4S sqn. On F-4S until 11/85.
VMFA-312 *Checkerboards*	F-8E → F-4B 03/66 → F-4J 02/73 → F-4S 07/81 → F/A-18 1988	Code 'DR'. Last F-4 flight from Beaufort made 07/87.
VMFA-314 *Black Knights*	F4D-1 → F4H-1 06/62 → F-4N mid-1975 → F/A-18 08/82	Code 'VW'. First USMC F-4 unit. First F/A-18A unit.
VMFA-321 *Black Barons* or *Hell's Angels*	F-8K → F-4B 01/74 → F-4N mid-1977 → F-4S 09/84 → F/A-18 1991	Code 'MG'. Last F-4S flights made in 07/91.
VMFA-323 *Death Rattlers*	F-8E → F-4B 08/64 → F-4N 1974 → F/A-18 early 1983	Code 'WS'.
VMFA-333 *Shamrocks*	F-8E → F-4J 03/68 → F-4S 12/81 → F/A-18 12/87	Code 'DN'. Some F-4Ns in 1979. Two carrier war cruises. Two peacetime cruises. Deactivated 31/03/92.
VMFA-334 *Falcons*	F-4J 06/67	Code 'WU'. First USMC F-4J unit. First VMFA to leave SEA. Disestablished 12/71.
VMFA-351	F-4N spring 1977	Code 'MC'. Second USMC Reserve F-4 unit. Existed for one year (disestablished mid-1978).
VMFA-451 *Warlords*	F-8E → F-4J 01/68 → F-4S 1978 → F/A-18 late 1987	Code 'VM'.First F-4S unit in USN/MC. Last F-4S to AMARC during 10/86.
VMFA-513 *Flying Nightmares* (Korea)	F4D-1 → F-4B 01/63	Code 'WF'.Third USMC F-4 unit. To cadre status 30/06/70. Later re-established with AV-8A Harriers.
VMFA-531 *Gray Ghosts*	F4D-1 → F4H-1 11/62 → F-4N 08/75 → F/A-18 05/83	Code 'EC'. 'Joint first' USMC F-4 unit (with VMFA-314. Deactivated and scheduled to acquire F-14As from 06/75 but reactivated on F-4N instead. Disestablished 31/03/91.
VMFA-542 *Bengals*	F-4B 10/63	Code 'WH'. Operated from Atsugi, Japan, and Da Nang, SVN. Disestablished 06/70.
VMFAT-101 *Sharpshooters*	F-4J 01/69 → F/A-18 03/88	Code 'SH'. Also had B/N/S models at various stages. Trained USN crews after June 1974.
VMFAT-102 *Hawks*	F-4B 1967 → F-4J 1969	Code 'KB'. Disestablished 1974. Assets to VMAT-101.
VMCJ-1	RF-8A → RF-4B 10/66	Code 'RM'. Transferred assets to VMFP-3 08/75.
VMCJ-2 *Playboys*	RF-8A → RF-4B 1965	Code 'CY'. Transferred assets to VMFP-3 1975.
VMCJ-3 *Eyes & Ears*	RF-8A → RF-4B 05/65	Code 'TN'. Transferred assets to VMFP-3, 07/75. Became VMAQ-2.
VMFP-3 *Eyes of the Corps* or *Specters*	RF-4B 07/75	Code 'RF'. Established 01/07/75 with RF-4Bs from former VMCJs. Re-equipped with SURE RF-4Bs. Deactivated 09/90.

Above: *Black Barons* F-4S BuNo **153904**, marked for VMFA-231's retirement ceremony on **31 July 1991**. (Tim Laming)
Left: Phantoms have been leased to civilian operators performing contract work for the US Department of Defense. Tracor's Flight Systems Inc at Mojave, California, has flown many examples, including this F-4D, serial number **N402AV** (which replaced F-4C **63-7567**, currently preserved at Travis AFB, California). The test aircraft is seen releasing a Teledyne Ryan Aeronautical **BQM-145A** UAV, which was intended to serve as a platform for the ATARS advanced tactical reconnaissance system. ATARS was cancelled in **1993**, giving a further lease of life to the USAF RF-4C variant. Many more Phantoms will percolate into civil test duties during the next few years. (TRA)

APPENDIX IV: US MARINE CORPS F-4 UNIT DEPLOYMENTS (ACTIVE UNITS)

MAG	Dates	Station	MAW
VMF(AW)-115 (code 'VE')			
24	00/09/63 to 07/07/65	MCAS Cherry Point	2nd
13	07/07/65 to 26/07/65	NAS Atsugi	1st
13	26/06/65 to 10/10/65	MCAS Iwakuni, Japan	1st
11	10/10/65 to 31/12/65	Da Nang AB, SVN	1st
13	01/01/66 to 15/04/66	MCAS Iwakuni, Japan	1st
11	15/04/66 to 15/02/67	Da Nang AB, SVN	1st
15	15/02/67 to 14/05/67	MCAS Iwakuni, Japan	1st
13	15/05/67 to 24/08/70	Chu Lai, SVN	1st
11	24/08/70 to 01/03/71	Da Nang AB, SVN	1st
11	01/03/71 to 06/04/72	MCAS Iwakuni, Japan	1st
11	06/04/72 to 16/06/72	Da Nang AB, SVN	1st

MAG	Dates	Station	MAW
11	16/06/72 to 31/08/73	Nam Phong AB, Thailand	1st
11	31/03/73 to 17/12/74	Naha AB, Japan	1st
11	17/12/73 to 11/08/77	MCAS Iwakuni, Japan	1st
11	22/07/77 to 00/07/85	MCAS Beaufort (2 cruises on *Forrestal*, Dec 1980 and 01/03/81 to 15/09/81)	2nd
VMFA-122 (code 'DC')			
–	00/07/65 to 00/08/67	MCAS El Toro	3rd
11	00/08/67 to 01/09/68	Da Nang AB, SVN	1st
15	01/09/68 to 05/12/69	MCAS Iwakuni, Japan	1st
13	01/12/69 to 00/09/70	Chu Lai, SVN	1st
24	00/09/70 to 00/04/72	MCAS Kaneohe Bay, Hawaii	1st

15	00/04/73 to 00/09/72	MCAS Iwakuni, Japan	1st
24	00/09/72 to 00/08/74	MCAS Kaneohe Bay, Hawaii	1st
31	04/12/75 to 00/02/86	Re-established at MCAS Beaufort	2nd

VMFA-212 (code 'WD')

24	00/05/68 to 11/04/72	MCAS Kaneohe Bay, Hawaii (from 00/03/68, 6-month TDY at Iwakuni on rotation with VMFA-232 and VMFA-235)	1st
15	11/04/72 to 20/06/72	Da Nang AB, SVN (forward-deployed)	1st
24	24/06/72 to 00/00/88	MCAS Kaneohe Bay, Hawaii	1st

VMFA-232 (code 'WT')

33	19/09/67 to 27/03/69	MCAS El Toto	3rd
13	27/03/69 to 07/09/69	Chu Lai, SVN	1st
15	07/09/69 to 06/04/72	MCAS Iwakuni, Japan (9th MAB)	1st
15	06/04/72 to 20/06/72	Da Nang AB, SVN (forward-deployed)	1st
15	20/06/72 to 01/09/73	Nam Phong AB, Thailand (forward-deployed)	1st
15	01/09/73 to 14/11/73	NAS Cubi Point	1st
15	14/11/73 to 17/12/73	MCAS Iwakuni, Japan	1st
15	17/12/73 to 12/02/74	Naha AB, Japan	1st
15	12/02/74 to 07/10/77	MCAS Iwakuni, Japan	1st
24	07/10/77 to 00/10/88	MCAS Kaneohe Bay, Hawaii (rotational TDY to Iwakuni – see above)	1st

VMFA-235 (code 'DB')

24	00/10/68 to 00/03/89	MCAS Kaneohe Bay, Hawaii (rotational TDY to Iwakuni – see above)	1st

VMFA-251 (code 'DW')

32	27/11/64 to 00/03/71	MCAS Beaufort	2nd
31	31/03/71 to 00/11/85	MCAS Beaufort	2nd

VMFA-312 (code 'DR')

32	00/02/66 to 15/02/71	MCAS Beaufort	2nd
14	15/02/71 to 01/08/74	MCAS Cherry Point	2nd
31	01/08/74 to 29/07/87	MCAS Beaufort	2nd

VMFA-314 (code 'VW')

–	00/06/62 to 00/08/65	MCAS El Toro	3rd
15	03/01/65 to 03/01/66	MCAS Iwakuni, Japan (forward-deployed)	1st
11	03/01/66 to 00/04/66	Da Nang AB, SVN	1st
15	00/04/66 to 00/00/67	MCAS Iwakuni, Japan	1st
13	00/00/67 to 00/09/70	Chu Lai, SVN (dets to Da Nang and Iwakuni)	1st
11	00/09/70 to 00/01/83	MCAS El Toro	–

VMFA-323 (code 'WS')

–	00/08/64 to 00/11/65	MCAS El Toro	3rd
11	01/12/65 to 01/03/66	Da Nang AB, SVN	1st
13	00/04/66 to 05/07/66	Chu Lai AB, SVN (det)	1st
11	05/07/66 to 31/12/66	Taiwan (det) Da Nang AB	1st
13	31/12/66 to 00/05/67	Chu Lai AB, SVN	1st
13	00/05/67 to 16/08/67	MCAS Iwakuni, Japan	1st
13	16/08/67 to 00/03/69	Chu Lai AB, SVN	1st
11	00/03/69 to 14/09/82	MCAS El Toro (deployed with CVW-14 on Coral Sea 00/11/69 to 00/06/80)	3rd

VMFA-333 (code 'DN')

31	13/03/68 to 00/08/87	MCAS Beaufort (deployed with CVW-8 on America 05/06/72 to 24/03/73—WestPac war cruise;	2nd

only USMC F-4 unit to do this— and 00/07/81 to 00/12/81. With CVW-8, *Nimitz*, 00/07/76 to 00/02/77.

VMFA-334 (code 'WU')

33	06/06/67 to 00/08/68	MCAS El Toro	3rd
11	00/08/68 to 00/01/69	Da Nang AB, SVN	1st
13	00/01/69 to 00/11/69	Chu Lai AB, SVN	1st
15	00/11/69 to 00/03/71	MCAS Iwakuni, Japan	1st
11	00/03/71 to 00/07/71	MCAS El Toro	1st
13	00/07/71 to 31/12/71	MCAS El Toro	3rd

VMFA 151 (code 'VM')

31	15/01/68 to 00/03/88	MCAS Beaufort	2nd

VMFA-513 (code 'WF')

–	00/01/63 to 00/11/64	MCAS El Toro	3rd
11	11/11/64 to 00/06/65	NAS Atsugi	1st
11	15/06/65 to 10/10/65	Da Nang AB, SVN	1st
24	00/10/65 to 30/06/70	MCAS Cherry Point	2nd

VMFA-531 (code 'EC')

24	16/11/62 to 11/06/64	MCAS Cherry Point (det to Key West 00/02/63 to 00/06/63)	2nd
11	00/06/64 to 00/04/65	NAS Atsugi	1st
11	10/04/65 to 00/07/65	Da Nang AB, SVN	1st
24	00/07/65 to 00/04/68	MCAS Cherry Point	2nd
33	00/04/68 to 00/12/70	MCAS El Toro	3rd
13	00/12/70 to 00/09/71	MCAS El Toro	3rd
11	00/09/71 to 01/07/75	MCAS El Toro (F-14 transition cancelled)	
11	29/08/75 to 24/11/82	MCAS El Toro (WestPac deployment with CVW-14, *Coral Sea*, 00/11/79 to 00/06/80)	3rd

VMFA-542 (code 'WH')

–	00/10/63 to 00/04/65	MCAS El Toro	3rd
11	00/04/65 to 10/07/65	MCAS Iwakuni, Japan	1st
11	10/07/65 to 03/12/65	Da Nang AB, SVN	1st
11	03/12/65 to 01/03/66	MCAS Iwakuni, Japan	1st
11	01/03/66 to 01/08/66	Da Nang AB, SVN	1st
11	01/08/66 to 10/12/66	MCAS Iwakuni, Japan	1st
11	10/12/66 to 31/12/66	Da Nang AB, SVN	1st
11	31/12/66 to 00/05/67	MCAS Iwakuni, Japan	1st
15	00/05/67 to 10/07/68	MCAS Iwakuni, Japan (det to Chu Lai)	1st
11	10/07/68 to 31/01/70	Da Nang AB, SVN	1st
–	12/02/70 to 30/06/70	MCAS El Toro	3rd

VMFAT-101 (code 'SB' or 'SH')

MCC TRG-10	03/01/69 to 01/10/87	MCAS Yuma	3rd

VMFAT-201 (code 'KB')

MCC TRG-20	00/00/67 to 30/09/74	MCAS Cherry Point	2nd

VMCJ-1 (code 'RM')

11	00/10/66 to 01/07/70	Da Nang AB, SVN	1st
15	01/07/70 to 30/07/75	MCAS Iwakuni, Japan	1st

VMCJ-2 (code 'CY')

–	00/00/65 to 30/07/75	MCAS Cherry Point	2nd

VMCJ-3 (code 'TN')

–	00/00/65 to 00/00/75	MCAS El Toro	3rd

VMFP-3 (code 'RF')

11	00/00/75 to 30/09/90	MCAS El Toro	–

APPENDIX V: US AIR FORCE ACTIVE F-4 PHANTOM UNITS 1963–93

The following entries are divided into parent organizations in numerical sequence first, then their component squadrons at each relevant base. Since many Wings and component squadrons have followed diverging and converging histories at different bases over the last three decades, individual squadron histories must be tracked using the cross-references supplied. Squadron nicknames are contemporary versions where known, as are F-4 models, tail-codes and colours.

The two-letter Distinctive Unit Identity (DUI) code system was first introduced by PACAF F-4 Wings in November 1966 with the intention that the first letter signify the Wing and the second letter the squadron, although some duplications and anomalies inevitably occurred. TAC began using the system in July 1968, with the first letter generally denoting the base's first initial and the second (A, B, C etc) the squadrons in order of their numerical designation or reactivation. USAFE introduced codes in the spring of 1970, following the TAC system where possible but with the sequence R,S,T etc for the second letter. All Wing tail markings were standardized following Directive AFM66-1, which stipulated common Wing DUIs at each base. The process was initiated within TAC and USAFE from June 1972, though it took many months to reach PACAF owing to the large numbers of aircraft movements in that theatre and was not fully implemented until 1975. In July 1992, following the formation of Air Combat Command, the codes were revised and extended to all aircraft under any given Wing authority, even if geographically displaced. The current thinking is that the Major-Generals commanding the new 'Superwings' should be able readily to keep tabs on their own, and their colleagues', aircraft at a glance.

The squadron colours listed represent those actually applied to the tips of vertical tails or in a stripe above the rudder (which was occasionally repeated on the tips of other appendages) and are not necessarily the 'squadron colours' per se. For example, squadrons wearing yellow markings were invariably known as 'Gold Squadron' (and in those instances where 'gold' or 'silver' has been listed, then those metallic colours were applied to the Phantoms). Similarly, many dielectric fin-caps (particularly those found on LORAN- and ARN-modified machines) were left black and the individual squadron colour was not applied above the rudder either, so they have been listed as 'black'.

Regular variants of the Phantom are noted. 'Misc F-4' denotes a collection which often included YF-4s, NF-4s and so on in addition to several aircraft of regular front-line marks. 'F-4 etc' signifies that other aircraft types were operated by a squadron, such as F-105s, RF-101s or F-15s. Finally, North American readers should note that the dates provided are given in European format, i.e. day/month/year.

Squadron	Model	Code	Fin colour

1st TFW
MacDill AFB, Florida
Reactivated at MacDill AFB 01/10/70 through redesignation of the 15th TFW. Deactivated 30/06/75 when Wing became 56th TFW (1st TFW designation being reassigned to Langley AFB, Virginia, pending 'Ready Team' re-formation on F-15).

45th TFS	F-4E	FB	Red

Transferred from 15th TFW control 01/10/70. Redesignated 71st TFS 01/07/71.

46th TFS	F-4E	FD	Yellow

Transferred from 15th TFW control 01/10/70. Redesignated 27th TFS 01/07/71.

47th TFS	F-4E	FE	Green
		FE	Blue

Transferred from 15th TFW control 01/10/70. Colour to blue. Redesignated 94th TFS 01/07/71.

4530th TTS	F-4E	FF	White

Transferred from 15th TFW control 01/10/70. Redesignated 4501st TFRS 01/10/71.

27th TFS	F-4E	FD	Yellow
		FF	Yellow

Reactivated through redesignation of 46th TFS. Recoded 'FF' 06/72 Redesignated 61st TFS/56th TFW 30/07/75.

71st TFS	F-4E	FB	Red
		FF	Red

Reactivated through redesignation of 45th TFS. Recoded 'FF' 06/72. Redesignated 62nd TFS/56th TFW 30/07/75.

94th TFS *Hat in the Ring*	F-4E	FE	Blue
		FF	Blue

Reactivated through redesignation of 47th TFS 01/07/71. Recoded 'FF' 06/72. Redesignated 62nd TFS/56th TFW 30/07/75.

4501st TFRS	F-4E	FF	White

Activated through redesignation of 4530th TTS 01/10/71. Transferred to 56th TFW control 30/07/75.

3rd TFW
Kunsan AB, South Korea
Reactivated at Kunsan 15/03/71, absorbing aircraft formerly operated by the 475th TFW (at Misawa AB, Japan), under new squadron designations. On 16/09/74 Wing was replaced by 8th TFW control and the 3rd TFW designation passed to Clark AB in the Philippines, taking over the assets of the 405th FW.

35th TFS *Phantoms*	F-4D	UP	Light blue

Reactivated 15/03/71, using former 67th TFS/475th TFW aircraft. Deployed (split) to 366th TFW at DaNang AB, SVN, and the 8th TFW at Ubon RTAFB, Thailand, 01/04/72, consolidating at Ubon shortly afterwards. Force was then relocated to 388th TFW at Korat RTAFB, Thailand, 12/06/72. Returned to Kunsan AB 12/10/72. Transferred to 8th TFW control 16/09/74.

36th TFS *Flying Fiends*	F-4D	UK	Red
	F-4E	UK	Red

Reactivated 15/05/71 using former 356th TFS/475th TFW aircraft. Relocated at Osan AB, South Korea 13/11/71. Converted to F-4Es 06/74, having begun transferring F-4Ds 08/07/74. Formally passed to 8th TFW control 16/09/74 (and to 51st CW control 30/09/74).

80th TFS *Headhunters*	F-4D	UD	Yellow
		UP	Yellow

Transferred from attachment to 475th TFW Det 1 15/03/71. Recoded 'UP'. Transferred to 8th TFW control 16/09/74.

Clark AB, Philippines
Assumed control of former 405th FW assets 09/74. Introduced first 'Advanced Wild Weasel' F-4G aircraft to Pacific in summer 1979, followed by first PACAF ARN-101(V) DMAS F-4Es from 1981. Phantoms gradually phased out between 10/90 and 06/91, last three F-4Es departing 03/06/91, nine days before eruption of Mount Pinatubo and subsequent onslaught by tropical typhoon 'Yunya', which effectively pre-empted planned 09/91 inactivation date. Designation transferred to F-15-equipped Wing at Elmendorf, Alaska, 19/12/91.

1st TS	F-4C	PA	Yellow

Transferred from 405th FW control 16/09/74. Converted to F-4Es borrowed from 3rd and 90th TFSs and passed to 6200th TFTG control 01/01/80.

25th TFS	F-4E	–	–

Short-lived. Transferred from 432nd TFW 18/12/75 and designation moved without personnel and equipment to 18th TFW 19/12/75 after squadron's assets had been used to re-equip 90th TFS (see below).

3rd TFS *Peugeots*	F-4E	PN	Blue
		PN	Red/white/blue

Reactivated 15/12/75. On 17/12/75 it received crews and equipment of 421st TFS/432nd TFW, which had arrived at Clark 12–13/12/75. Upgraded to ARN-101 F-4Es from c1981 and to Pave Tack during 1984. Deployed four-aircraft detachment 16/02/91–19/03/91 to 7440th CW at Incirlik AB, Turkey, for participation in Operation 'Proven Force'/ 'Desert Storm' (see 7440th CW entry for full details) and operations at Clark ceased in 06/91. Individual aircraft names included 68-0312 *Bataan* (assigned to Cdr 3rd TFW).

90th TFS *Pair-O-Dice* or	F-4D	PN	Red
Dicemen	F-4E	PN	Red
	F-4E/G	PN	Red
		PN	(Red dice)

Transferred from 405th FW control 16/09/74. Converted to F-4Es 19–20/12/75, drawing personnel and equipment from the 25th TFS (see above). Officially received its first two (69-275 and -279) of twelve supplementary F-4Gs 30/07/79. Phase-out began during 10/90 and was completed by 05/91, F-4s going to 35th and 52nd Wings and Idaho ANG, or AMARC. 90th FS designation subsequently transferred to 21st CW control at Elmendorf, Alaska, on 17/05/91, re-equipping with F-15Es.

4th TFW ('Fourth But First')
Seymour-Johnson AFB, North Carolina

Received first F-4D 27/01/67. Entire Wing deployed to Kunsan AB, South Korea, 29/01/68 to c29/07/68 in response to *Pueblo* Crisis. Squadron deployments followed. Initially converted to F-4Es 1970–71 and was first with slatted-wing F-4Es late the following year. Elements also deployed to Thailand during 1972 as part of Operation 'Constant Guard'. Supported Operation 'Nickel Grass' (emergency resupply effort to Israel) 10/73. Performed numerous 'Crested Cap' deployments to NATO, to which it was dual-committed. Converted to F-15Es 1989–90. Individual aircraft included F-4D 66-7678 (assigned to Cdr 4th TFW Col 'Chuck' Yeager).

334th TFS *Eagles*	F-4D	SA	Blue
	F-4E	SA	Blue
		SJ	Blue

Coded 'SA' 07/68. Deployed to Kunsan 16/12/69–31/05/70. Converted to F-4Es 07/70–31/10/70. Deployed to Ubon RTAFB, Thailand, 11/04/72–08/07/72 and 25/09/72–12/03/73. Recoded 'SJ' 07/72. Last 4th TFW squadron to convert to F-15Es, ceasing F-4E operations on 28/12/90.

335th TFS *Chiefs*	F-4D	SB	Green
	F-4E	SB	Green
		SJ	Green

Coded 'SB' 07/68. Deployed to Kunsan 08/12/69–23/05/70. Converted to F-4Es 10/70–16/02/71. Deployed to Ubon RTAFB, Thailand, 08/07/72–21/12/72. Recoded 'SJ' 05/72. Second 4th TFW squadron to convert to F-15Es, beginning 01/03/90.

336th TFS *Rocketeers*	F-4D	SC	Yellow
	F-4E	SC	Yellow
		SJ	Yellow

Coded 'SC' 07/68. Converted to F-4Es 04/70–17/07/70. Deployed to Ubon RTAFB, Thailand 12/04/72–25/09/72 and 09/03/73–07/09/73. Recoded 'SJ' 07/72 at Ubon. First 4th TFW squadron to convert to F-15Es, beginning 01/10/89.

337th TFS *Falcons*	F-4E	SJ	Red

Reactivated 01/04/82 (facilitated by conversion of 21st TFW to F-15s) and deactivated 30/09/85.

8th TFW ('Attaquez et Conquerez' or 'Wolfpack')
George AFB, California

Reactivated through redesignation of 32nd TFW on 25/07/64. Moved to Ubon RTAFB, Thailand (see below). Scheduled F-4 training ceased 16/07/64.

68th TFS *Lightning Lancers*	F-4C	–	–

Transferred from 32nd TFW control 25/07/64. Deployed to Korat RTAFB, Thailand, 24/08/65–06/12/65. Transferred to 479th TFW control 06/12/65.

431st TFS	F-4C	–	–

Transferred from 32nd TFW control 25/07/64. Deployed to Ubon RTAFB, Thailand 26/09/65–c06/12/65. Transferred to 479th TFW control 06/12/65.

433rd TFS *Satan's Angels*	F-4C	–	–

Reactivated 25/07/64. Transferred with Wing to Ubon RTAFB 06–08/12/65.

497th TFS	F-4C	–	–

Transferred from 32nd TFW control 25/07/64. Attached to 479th TFW at George AFB 06–08/12/65. Transferred with Wing to Ubon RTAFB 08/12/65.

Ubon Airfield, Thailand

Moved to Ubon 06–08/12/65. Converted to F-4Ds from 28/05/67 (first F-4Ds to be deployed to combat zone) and subsequently undertook many specialist Pave tasks connected with this mark. Later moved to Kunsan (see below).

25th TFS *Assam Dragons*	F-4D	FA	Black/yellow
		WP	Black

Transferred from 33rd TFW 28/05/68. First with LORAN F-4Ds. Recoded 'WP' c01/73. Deactivated 05/07/74, designation passing to 432nd TRW. Individual aircraft names included 66-7583 *Nancy's Pants*, 66-8782 *Flave* (Sqn Cdr), 66-8777 *Miss Magic*, 66-8784 *Flipper of the Sky*, 66-8787 *Dragon Wagon*, 66-8793 *Sour Kraut*.

433rd TFS *Satan's Angels*	F-4C	FG	Green
	F-4D	FG	Green
		WP	Green

Transferred from George AFB 06–08/12/65. Coded 'FG' early 1967. Converted to F-4Ds 24/10/67. Operated Pave Knife Phantoms. Recoded 'WP' 01/73. Deactivated 23/07/74. Individual aircraft included F-4C 63-7629 *Ripchord*, F-4D 65-0725 *Inferno*, F-4D 66-7764 *Ol' Eagle Eye*.

435th TFS *Eagle Squadron*	F-4D	FO	Red
		FO	Black
		WP	Red

Replaced F-104Cs with F-4Ds from 4th TFS/33rd TFW, from Eglin AFB, Florida, 07/67, standing down from F-104 operations 19/07/67. Recoded 'WP' 01/73. Deactivated 08/08/74.

497th TFS *Night Owls*	F-4C	FP	Black
	F-4D	FP	Black
		WP	Black

Transferred from George AFB 08/12/65. Coded 'FP' early 1967. Recoded 'WP' early 1974. Deactivated 16/09/74. Individual aircraft included F-4C 63-7680 *Candy*, F-4D 66-0239 *Sweet Vicki*, F-4D 66-7668 *Georgie Girl*, F-4D 66-0279 *Terrible Tyke*.

555th TFS *Triple Nickel*	F-4C	FY	Yellow

Located at Udorn RTAFB, Thailand (having been transferred from Naha AB, Okinawa, 27/02/66). Remained attached to 12th TFW 25/02/66–24/03/66 and reassigned there 25/03/66. To Ubon RTAFB 20/07/66. Coded 'FY' early 1967. Re-equipped with F-4D aircraft from 40th TFS/33rd TFW, from Eglin AFB, Florida, 28/05/67 to become first F-4D squadron in SEA. Attached to 432nd TRW 28/05/68 and transferred to same Wing at Udorn RTAFB 01/06/68.

The following F-4 squadrons deployed to Ubon and 8th TFW control 1972–73 under Operation 'Constant Guard' (unit/code/colour/dates; refer to appropriate Wing entries for further squadron details):

35th TFS/3rd TFW	D/UP	Light blue	01/04/72–12/06/72*

334th TFS/4th TFW	E/SA	Blue	11/04/72–08/07/72	
	E/SJ	Blue	25/09/72–12/03/73	
335th TFS/4th TFW	E/SJ	Green	08/07/72–21/12/72	
336th TFS/4th TFW	E/SC, SJ	Yellow	12/04/72–15/09/72	
	E/SJ	Yellow	09/03/73–07/09/73	
308th TFS/31st TFW	E/ZF	Green	11/12/72–11/06/73	
58th TFS/33rd TFW	E/ED	Blue	08/06/73–14/09/73	

*One day only before being reunited with the other half of the squadron at Da Nang AB.

Kunsan AB, South Korea

Moved without personnel or equipment 09/74 to Kunsan, where it took over assets of 3rd TFW. Later converted to F-16s, first of which arrived 14/09/81.

35th TFS *First to Fight*	F-4D	UP	Blue	
		WP	Blue	

Transferred from 3rd TFW control 16/09/74. Recoded 'WP'. Converted to F-16s 1981.

36th TFS *Flying Fiends*	F-4E	UK	Red	

Located at Osan AB, South Korea. Transferred from 3rd TFW control 16/09/74. To 51st CW control 30/09/74.

80th TFS *Juvats* or	F-4D	UP	Yellow	
Headhunters		WP	Yellow	

Transferred from 3rd TFW control 16/09/74. Recoded 'WP'. Converted to F-16s 1981.

497th TFS *Night Owls*	F-4D	WP	Red	

Reactivated 11/78. Based at Taegu AB, South Korea. To 51st CW control 01/01/82.

10th TRW
RAF Alconbury, England

Received first 'Photo-Phantoms' to replace RB-66s 12/05/65 (first USAFE Wing to operate RF-4Cs), comprising most FY64 Block 20–24 RF-4Cs (serials 1000 to 1009 becoming known as *Triple Nuts*, *Nuts-One* etc). Two squadrons deactivated 1976, aircraft being transferred to ANG. Converted to A-10s from 1987 and redesignated 10th TFW, receiving new squadrons.

1st TRS	RF-4C	–	–	
	RF-4C	AR	Blue/white	
	RF-4C	AR	Blue	
	RF-4C	AR	Black	

Received first RF-4Cs 12/05/65. First in USAFE with Pave Tack. Deactivated 29/05/87. Aircraft names included 68-0555 *Triple Nickel*, 68-0567 *Starize*.

30th TRS	RF-4C	–	–	
	RF-4C	AS	Red/white	
		AR	Red	

Received aircraft 09/65. Recoded 'AR' 06/72. Deactivated 01/04/76. Aircraft names included 64-1000 *Triple Nuts*, 64-1009 *Nuts-Nine*.

32nd TRS	RF-4C	–	–	
	RF-4C	AT	Yellow/white	
		AR	Yellow	

Transferred from 26th TRW 15/08/66. Recommenced operations 31/10/66. Recoded 'AR' 06/72. Deactivated 01/01/76.

12th TFW

Converted from F-84s to Phantoms 12/63–07/64 (first Phantom assigned on 05/12/63) close on heels of 4453rd CCTW also located at MacDill AFB, Florida, becoming first operational Wing to receive F-4C, and declared ready 10/64. Transferred to Camn Ranh Bay AB, SVN 08/11/65. Moved without equipment or personnel to Phu Cat AB, SVN, 31/03/70, replacing 37th TFW there, and deactivated 17/11/71.

MacDill AFB, Florida

555th TFS *Triple Nickel*	F-4C	–	–	

Reactivated 08/01/64. Deployed to Naha AB, Okinawa 08/12/64–18/03/65 (first TAC Phantom squadron to deploy to Pacific region; attached to 51st FIW 11/12/64–15/03/65) and 06/11/65–25/02/66 (attached to 51st FIW 11/11/65–25/02/66). To Udorn RTAFB, Thailand, 27/02/66 (attached to 8th TFW 25/02/66–24/03/66). To 8th TFW control 25/03/66.

557th TFS	F-4C	–	–	

Converted from F-84s. Transferred to 836th AD control (detached) 08/11/65–01/12/65. See Camn Ranh Bay section below.

558th TFS *Hammers*	F-4C	–	–	

Converted from F-84s. Detached 09/03/65–16/06/65 (51st FIW at Naha AB, Okinawa 12/03/65–15/06/65). Transferred to Camn Ranh Bay, SVN, 08/11/65.

559th TFS	F-4C	–	–	

Converted from F-84s. Detached 09/07/65–07/09/65 (51st FIW at Naha, Okinawa, 09/06/65–15/11/65 [*sic*]). Transferred to 836th AD control (detached) 08/11/65–27/12/65. See Camn Ranh Bay section below.

Camn Ranh Bay

391st TFS	F-4C	XT	Yellow	

Transferred from 366th TFW at Holloman AFB, New Mexico 26/01/66. Attached from 2nd AD 26/01/66–31/03/66 and from 7th AF 01/04/66–22/06/66 and assigned from 23/06/66. Coded from 12/66. Transferred to 475th TFW 22/07/68.

557th TFS *Sharkbaits*	F-4C	XC	Red	

Transferred from 836th AD control (detached) 01/12/65. Coded 12/66. Deactivated 09/03/70. Individual aircraft names included 63-7534 *Mystic Skater*, 64-0665 *Hell's Angel*, 64-7588 *Joltin' Josie II*, 640851 *Rapid Rabbit*, 64-7675 *Tricky Vics*, 64-0817 *Miss Sel-Ala II* (marked thus for the Eglin AFB Museum).

558th TFS *Hammers*	F-4C	XD	Tan	
		XT	Yellow	

Transferred from MacDill AFB 08/11/65. Coded from 12/66. Detached to Kunsan AB, South Korea, 04/02/68–10/03/68 (under 4th TFW control 04/02/68–10/03/68 and 26/03/68–22/07/68). Recoded 'XT' (yellow) 22/07/68 (aircraft ex-391st TFS machines). Deactivated 09/03/70. Individual aircraft names included 63-7522 *Saintly Sinner*, 64-0770 *Jeannie*.

559th TFS *Billy Goats*	F-4C	XN	Blue	

Transferred from 836th AD control (detached) 27/12/65. Coded from 12/66. Deactivated 22/03/70. Individual aircraft names included 63-7413 *Blue Avenger*, 63-7708 *Half Fast*, 63-7604 *Sugar Foot II*, 64-0704 *Shehasta*.

Phu Cat, South Vietnam

389th TFS *Thunderbolts*	F-4D	HB	Red	

Transferred from 37th TFW control 31/03/70. Deactivated 15/10/71.

480th TFS *Warhawks*	F-4D	HK	–	

Transferred from 37th TFW control 31/03/70. Ceased combat operations on 20/10/71. Deactivated 17/11/71.

15th TFW
MacDill AFB, Florida

Converted from F-84s to F-4Cs 05/64–07/64. Deactivated 01/10/70 through redesignation of Wing to 1st TFW.

43rd TFS	F-4C	–	–	
	F-4E	FB	Blue	

Reactivated 08/01/64. Detached to Clark AB, Philippines, 17/08/65–

20/10/65 and Camn Ranh Bay, SVN, 21/10/65–c04/01/66. Converted to F-4Ds 1967, to F-4Es 1968. Coded 'FB' (blue) 07/68. Reassigned to Alaskan Air Command 13/03/70. Recoded 'FC' and transferred to Elmendorf AB, Alaska, 23/06/70. Transferred to 21st CW control 15/07/70.

| 45th TFS | F-4C | – | – |
| | F-4E | FC | Red |

Converted from F-84s. Detached to Ubon RTAFB, Thailand, 04/04/65–10/08/65 as the USAF Phantom squadron to fly combat missions, where it achieved first USAF Phantom MiG kills (2 MiG-17 on 10/07/65). Converted to F-4Ds 1967, to F-4Es 1968. Coded 'FC' (red) 07/68. Recoded 'FB' 07/70. Transferred to 1st TFW control 01/10/70.

| 46th TFS | F-4C | – | – |
| | F-4D | FD | Yellow |

Converted from F-84s. Detached to Clark AB, Philippines, 11/05/65–22/08/65 (405th FW 15/05/65–02/08/65). Also detached 01/11/65–10/11/65. Converted to F-4Ds 1967, to F-4Es 1968. Coded 'FD' (yellow) 07/68. Transferred to 1st TFW control 01/10/70.

| 47th TFS | F-4C | – | – |

Converted from F-84s. Detached to Ubon, Thailand, 22/07/65–27/11/65. Received first F-4D 21/01/67 and converted to F-4Es early 1968. Coded 'FE' (green) 07/68. Transferred to 1st TFW control 01/10/70.

| 4530th TTS | F-4E | FF | |

Activated 20/01/68 but probably operated no aircraft until 1970. Transferred to 1st TFW control 01/10/70.

18th TFW ('Unguibus et Rostro')
Kadena AB, Okinawa
Operated RF-4Cs alongside F-105s from 02/67. In 1971 two F-4C squadrons added, drawing aircraft from 347th TFW from Yokota AB, Japan; more formed during 1975. Converted to F-15s 1979–80.

| 12th TFS Bald Eagles | F-4D | ZZ | Yellow |

Reactivated 29/11/75. Deployed to Kunsan AB, South Korea, 08/76–09/76. Converted to F-15s 1979–80.

| 15th TRS Cotton Pickers | RF-4C | ZZ | Black/yellow |

Received first aircraft 04/02/67. Maintained detachment at Osan AB, South Korea, for much of its career. Eventually transferred to 460th TRG control 01/10/89.

| 25th TFS Assam Dragons | F-4D | ZZ | Green |

Transferred without personnel or equipment (WOPE) from 3rd TFW 19/12/75. Subsequently manned and equipped drawing aircraft and crews from 12th and 44th TFSs. Reduced to zero strength 22/08/80.

| 44th TFS Vampires | F-4C | ZL | Blue |
| | F-4D | ZZ | Blue |

Reactivated 15/05/71 with aircraft and crews from 36th/347th TFW previously stationed at Yokota. Deployed to Kunsan AB, South Korea, 03/04/72–02/06/72 and 27/07/72–08/09/72. Converted to F-4Ds, coded 'ZZ', 06/75. Converted to F-15s 1979–80.

| 67th TFS Fighting Cocks | F-4C/Cww | ZG | Red |
| | | ZZ | Red |

Reactivated 15/03/71 with aircraft and crews from 35th TFS/347th TFW previously stationed at Yokota. Received fourteen F-4Cww's from 80th TFS/347th TFW in 04/71. Deployed to Kunsan AB, South Korea, 02/06/72–28/07/72, 08/09/72–16/10/72 and 08/76–09/76. Sent detachments of 'Wild Weasels' to Korat RTAFB, Thailand, 23/09/72–18/02/73 (six aircraft) and 20/04/75–02/05/75 (ten). Recoded 'ZZ' 1975. Converted to F-15s 1979 and SEAD role taken over by 90th TFS/3rd TFW at Clark Field. Individual F-4Cww aircraft names included 63-7423 Jail Bait, 63-7470 Rub-a-Dub-Dub, Two Men in a Tub, 63-7474 Brain Damage, 64-0791 Squirrelly Bird, 64-0840 Super Cocks Swiss Samlar.

21st CW ('Fortitudo Et Preparatio')
Elmendorf AB, Alaska
Began operating F-4Es 23/06/70. Both squadrons controlled by 343rd TFG 01/10/77–01/01/80 . Redesignated 21st TFW 01/10/79.

| 18th TFS Arctic Foxes | F-4E | FC | Blue |
| | | FS | Blue |

Reactivated 01/10/77. Converted to A-10s at Eielson AFB, Alaska, 1982. Some aircraft coded 'FS' in 1977 owing to incorrect interpretation of Tec Orders by donor units.

| 43rd TFS Polar Bears | F-4E | FC | Blue |
| | | FC | Gold |

Assigned to Alaskan Air Command 13/03/70. Transferred to Elmendorf AFB 23/06/70 when 18 aircraft relocated from 15th TFW at MacDill AFB, Florida, these being assigned to 21st CW control 15/07/70. Colour to gold. Converted to F-15s 01/03/82–16/11/82.

26th TRW ('Saber Es Poder')
Toul Rosières AB, France
Reactivated at Toul-Rosières 19/04/65 and shortly afterwards underwent conversion to RF-4C. In 10/66, after 22nd TRS and 32nd TRS had moved to Mountain Home AFB, Idaho, and RAF Alconbury, England, respectively, the Wing headquarters moved to Ramstein AB, West Germany, where unit's 38th TRS had been based since 01/66. Move brought about by French decision to withdraw from NATO.

| 22nd TRS Bees | RF-4C | – | – |

From 01/12/65. Transferred to the 67th TRW 19/09/66.

| 32nd TRS | RF-4C | – | – |

Transferred from 66th TRW with RF-101s 01/10/65 and subsequently converted to RF-4Cs. Transferred to 10th TRW 15/08/66.

| 38th TRS | RF-4C | – | – |

Based at Ramstein AB. Transferred from 66th TRW with RF-101s 01/01/66 then converted to RF-4Cs.

Ramstein AB, West Germany
| 38th TRS | RF-4C | RR | Green/white |

Transferred to Zweibrücken (see below).

| 526th TFS Black Knights | F-4E | RS | Red |

Converted from F-102s 1970. To 86th TFW control 31/01/73.

Zweibrücken AB, West Germany
On 31/01/73 Wing moved to Zweibrücken AB, taking control of 17th TRS from 86th TFW, 38th TRS also moving. First with TEREC and AN/APD-10 SAR RMS. Deactivated 04/04/91.

| 17th TRS Hooters | RF-4C | ZR | Red |

Transferred from 86th TFW control 31/01/73. Deactivated 31/12/78.

| 38th TRS | RF-4C | ZR | Green/white |

Transferred from Ramstein AB 16/01/73. Detachment deployed to 7440th CW at Incirlik AB, Turkey, 03/02/91–11/03/91 for participation in Operation 'Desert Storm'. Deactivated 03/04/91.

| 417th TFS | – | – | – |

Former Ramstein (50th TFW), Mountain Home (67th TRW) and Holloman (49th TFW) F-4 squadron reactivated at Zweibrücken 01/10/78 but never formed, receiving only initial personnel and one Phantom (!) before coming under 86th TFW control at Ramstein 01/11/78 as 'paper' unit WOPE. Some sources claim that unit never existed at Zweibrücken.

31st TFW ('Return with Honor')
Homestead AFB, Florida
Reactivated through redesignation of 4531st TFW 15/10/70. Redesignated 31st TTW 30/03/81. Reverted to TFW status 01/10/84.

436th TFS — F-4E — ZD — Red
Transferred from 4531st TFW 15/10/70 and redesignated 306th TFS 30/10/70.

478th TFS — F-4E — ZE — Blue
Transferred from 4531st TFW 15/10/70 and redesignated 309th TFS 30/10/70.

560th TFS — F-4E — ZF — Green
Transferred from 4531st TFW 15/10/70 and redesignated 308th TFS 30/10/70.

306th TFS

F-4E	ZD	Red
	ZF	Yellow

Redesignated from 436th TFS 15/10/70 with code 'ZD'/red, then redesignated 307th TFS 15/07/71. 306th TFTS reactivated 01/07/78 with code 'ZF'/yellow. Converted to F-4Ds 1979 and deactivated 01/09/83.

307th TFS

F-4E	ZD	Red
	ZF	Red
F-4D	ZF	Red
	HS	Red

Redesignated from 306th TFS 15/07/71 following reassignment of unit number from 401st TFW. Recoded 'ZF' 06/72. Deployed to Udorn RTAFB, Thailand, 29/07/72–28/10/72. Converted to F-4Ds 1980. Redesignated 307th TFTS 01/07/83. Recoded 'HS' 12/86. Converted to F-16s 1988.

308th TFS *Emerald Knights*

F-4E	ZF	Green
F-4D	ZF	Green

Redesignated from 560th TFS 30/10/70. Deployed to Udorn RTAFB, Thailand, 28/04/72–29/07/72 and to Ubon RTAFB, Thailand, 11/12/72–11/06/73. Converted to F-4Ds 1980. Redesignated 308th TFS 09/10/80. Converted to F-16s 1986.

309th TFS *Wild Ducks*

F-4E	ZE	Blue
	ZF	Blue
F-4D	ZF	Blue

Redesignated from 478th TFS 30/10/70. Recoded 'ZF' 06/72. Converted to F-4Ds 1980. Redesignated 309th TFTS 01/07/82. Converted to F-16s 1986.

32nd TFG, 17th AF
Soesterburg, Holland

32nd TFS *Wolfhounds* — F-4E — CR — Orange
Converted from F-102s to F-4Es beginning 06/08/69 (first USAFE squadron to fly gun-equipped F-4E). Converted to F-15s 13/12/78, last F-4E having departed 09/78.

32nd TFW
George AFB, California
Reactivated 06/04/64. Deactivated 25/07/64 when replaced by 8th TFW which assumed control of all three squadrons on that date.

68th FIS — F-4C — – — –
Reactivated 16/06/64.

431st FIS — F-4C — – — –
Reactivated 18/05/64.

497th FIS — F-4C — – — –
Reactivated 18/06/64.

33rd TFW
Eglin AFB, Florida
Reactivated 01/04/65, taking over control of 786th, 787th, 788th and 789th TFSs from an unknown organization, and began receiving F-4Cs the following month; on 20/06/65 these squadrons were redesignated 4th, 16th, 25th and 40th TFSs. 25th TFS operated test support division for TAWC 07/65–12/67 when that unit was scheduled to go to SEA, and task was taken over by 4533rd TTS(T). In 1975 33rd TFW took over maintenance of 4485th TS aircraft which were recoded from 'EG' to 'ED' and acquired 33rd TFW decals. The Wing's early training and work-up function meant that several squadrons 'gelled' under 33rd TFW at Eglin and deployed with a new designation, leaving the residual squadron at Eglin to be stocked up with fresh aircraft and crews. Other bases and Wings performed a similar function as opposed to pure crew training, notably 363rd TRW at Shaw AFB, South Carolina. Wing received its first F-4Ds 21/06/66 and F-4E ground schools began 11/67, first examples of which arrived shortly afterwards. Last Phantom (F-4E 68-0466) departed 25/05/79, when Wing converted to F-15s.

4th TFS *Fightin' Fuujins*

F-4C	–	–
F-4D	–	–
F-4E	EB	Red/white

Converted to F-4Ds 1966. Re-equipped 435th TFS/8th TFW during 07/67. Converted to F-4Es 1968 (training having begun 11/67). Coded 'EB' (red/white) 07/68. Transferred to 366th TFW 12/04/69.

16th TFS

F-4C	–	–
F-4D	–	–
F-4E	ED	Blue/white

Converted to F-4Ds 1966. Re-equipped 13th TFS/432nd TRW 10/67 (detached 13/10/67–31/10/67). Converted to F-4Es 1968, coded 'ED' (blue/white). Re-equipped 421st TFS of 366th TFW 23/04/69. Deployed to Kunsan AB, South Korea, 26/05/70–09/09/70. Redesignated 58th TFS 01/11/70.

25th TFS *Assam Dragons*

F-4C	–	–
F-4D	–	–

Converted to F-4Ds 1966. Transferred to 8th TFW 28/05/68.

40th TFS *Satans*

F-4C	–	–
F-4D	–	–
F-4E	EE	Green/white

Converted to F-4Ds 1966 and re-equipped 555th TFS/8th TFW 05/67. Converted to F-4Es 1968, coded 'EE' (green/white) by 07/68 as first combat-ready F-4E squadron (Nellis, Nevada-based 4525th FWW test and evaluation unit was first TAC unit to receive the type, but most of their examples lacked fully operational radar systems). Squadron deployed to SEA to re-equip 469th TFS of 388th TFW 17/11/68 (see 388th TFW entry), then re-formed with more F-4Es to equip 34th TFS/388th TFW 05/69 and deactivated.

4533rd TTS (Test)

F-4D	EG	Black/white
F-4D/E	EG	Black/white

Activated 07/12/67. Later added F-4E. Deactivated 12/04/71, when replaced by 4485th TS/USAFTAWC.

4485th TS
See 4533rd TTS and Wing header, above. Squadron remains active under USAFTAWC control. See 3246th TW.

58th TFS *Gorillas*

F-4E	ED	Blue
	EG	Blue

Redesignated from 16th TFS 01/11/70. Deployed to Udorn RTAFB, Thailand, 29/04/72–14/10/72 and to Ubon RTAFB, Thailand, 08/06/73–14/09/73. Recoded 'EG' 1978. Converted to F-15s 1978–79.

59th TFS *Golden Pride*

F-4E	ED	Yellow
	EG	Yellow

Reactivated 01/07/73. Recoded 'EG' 1978. Converted to F-15s 1978–79.

35th TFW
Da Nang, South Vietnam
Wing organized at Da Nang AB 08/04/66, replacing 6252nd TFW 'holding Wing'. Replaced at Da Nang by 366th TFW 10/10/66 (35th TFW in turn replacing 366th TFW as host Wing at Phan Rang AB, SVN).

390th TFS *Wild Boars* F-4C – –
Transferred from 6252nd TFW control 08/04/66. To 366th TFW control 10/10/66.

480th TFS *Warhawks* F-4C – –
Transferred from 6252nd TFW control 08/04/66. To 366th TFW control 10/10/66.

George AFB, California
Operated F-4s again under this Wing at George AFB from 01/10/71, when 35th TFW superseded 479th TFW. Redesignated 35th TTW 01/07/84. Reverted to 35th TFW nomenclature 05/10/89 and further redesignated 35th FW by 01/10/91. Deactivated 30/06/92; George AFB closed 15/12/92.

431st TFTS F-4D GA Red
F-4E GA Red
Replaced 4435th TFRS 15/01/76. To F-4E pooled with 563rd TFS 07/78–10/78. Deactivated 01/10/78.

434th TFS F-4E GD Light blue
GA Light blue
Transferred from 479th TFW control 01/10/71. Recoded 'GA' 06/72. Crews deployed to Takhli RTAFB, Thailand, 12/08/72–06/10/72. Redesignated 434th TFTS 01/10/75. Completed last training class 10/01/76. Deactivated 01/04/76.

4435th TFRS F-4C/E GB White
F-4C/D/E GA Red
F-4D GA Red
Redesignated from 4546th TTS/479th TFW 01/10/71. Recoded 'GA' 06/72. Colour to red 12/72. To F-4C/D/E. To F-4D. Redesignated 431st TFTS 15/01/76.

4452nd CCTS F-4D GC Blue
GA Blue/white
Transferred from 479th TFW control 01/10/71. Recoded 'GA' 06/72. Redesignated 20th TFTS 01/12/72.

4535th CCTS F-4C GA Red
Transferred from 479th TFW control 01/10/71. Redesignated 21st TFTS 01/12/72.

20th TFTS *Silver Lobos* F-4D GA Blue
F-4C/D/E/F GA Blue
F-4E/F GA Blue
F-4E GA Silver/black
Reactivated through redesignation of 4452nd CCTS 01/10/71. To F-4C/D/E. Also operated WGAF F-4F 1973–77. Converted to F-4Es still as part of *Luftwaffe* training support. Colour to silver 1981. Deactivated 05/06/92 and aircraft transferred to 9th FS/49th FW at Holloman AFB, New Mexico, 07/92.

21st TFTS *Cheetahs* F-4C GA White
F-4C/D/E GA White
F-4Cww/G GA/WW White
F-4E GA Black
Reactivated through redesignation of 4535th TFTS 01/10/71. To F-4C/D/E. To F-4C/G pooled with 39th TFTS. Redesignated 21st TFS 09/10/80 with F-4Es, tail colour black. Redesignated 21st TFTS 01/07/83. Deactivated 30/06/91.

39th TFTS *Cobras* F-4C/Cww GA White
F-4Cww/G GA/WW White
F-4E GA Gold
Reactivated 01/07/77, replacing 563rd TFTS (see below), when it flew F-4C/Cww pooled with 21st TFTS. Received first production F-4G (69-239) 28/04/78, coded 'WW'. F-4G-related personnel and equipment transferred to 562nd TFTS 09/10/80. Reactivated again 12/02/82 as 39th TFS with new squadron tail colour (gold) using Pave Spike F-4Es released by 21st TFW. Deactivated again 11/05/84.

561st TFS *Black Knights* F-4E GA Red
F-4G WW Yellow
Received F-4Es from 431st TFTS/563rd TFS pool 10/78. Converted from F-105s to F-4Gs and recoded 'WW' (yellow) 1980, relinquishing F-4Es by 12/80. Transferred to 37th TFW control 30/03/81. Passed back to 35th TFW control 05/10/89 with F-4Gs. Deployed to Sheikh Isa AB, Bahrain, 15/08/90–04/91. Became 561st FS 01/10/91. Deactivated 30/06/92. Reactivated with F-4Gs 01/02/93 under 57th FWW at Nellis AFB, Nevada.

562nd TFTS *Weasels* F-4E/G GA White
F-4G WW Blue
Received personnel and equipment from 39th TFTS 09/10/80, replacing F-105s. Passed to 37th TFW control 30/03/81 with F-4Gs and code 'WW'. Passed back to 35th TFW control 05/10/89 with new colour (blue). Deactivated 30/06/92.

563rd TFS *Aces* F-4C/Cww GA White
F-4G WW Red
Reactivated 31/07/75, drawing F-4Cww aircraft from 66th FWS/57th FWW (and operated F-4C in pool with the 21st TFTS). Non-operational from 01/07/77, replaced by 39th TFTS, with whom F-4G personnel began training 24/07/78. Recommenced operations 01/10/78 as F-4G unit, coded 'WW' (red), becoming fully operational on 01/01/79. Transferred to 37th TFW control 30/03/81 (see 37th TFW). Individual aircraft included F-4G 69-7208 *City of Victorville/Sweet Sixteen*.

Sheikh Isa AB, Bahrain
Short-lived 35th TFW(P) was established 08/90 with arrival of 561st TFS during opening phase of Operation 'Desert Shield' and subsequently became host to several specialist Active and ANG Phantom units deployed from the US and Europe for combat duties during Operation 'Desert Storm'.

12th TRS *Blackbirds* RF-4C BA Orange-red
Deployed from Bergstrom AFB, Texas, 20/12/90. Returned home 16/04/91. See 12th TRS/67th TRW.

81st TFS *Panthers* F-4G SP Yellow
Deployed from Spangdahlem AB, Germany, beginning 05/09/90 with eight aircraft, subsequently reinforced. Two elements of eight aircraft returned to Spangdahlem 05/04/91 and 10/05/91, with detachment redeploying to 4404th CW(P) at Dhahran Airport, Saudi Arabia. See 81st TFS/52nd TFW and 81st FS/4404th CW(P).

106th TRS *Recce Rebels* RF-4C BH Camo
Deployed with eight aircraft 08/90–03/91 from Birmingham-based Alabama ANG. Not officially called to Active duty and thus retained ANG status (refer to ANG unit history). Individual aircraft with markings included 64-1047 *Scud Seeker* (412 sorties—unit total), 65-0833 (245 sorties), 65-0853 (106th TRS logos/90 sorties; Cdr's aircraft).

153rd TRS RF-4C – –
One 153rd TRS Mississippi ANG jet on loan to the 117th TRW deployed. Not officially called to Active duty.

192nd TRS *High Rollers* RF-4C – –
Crews (but only one aircraft, 65-0886) assigned from Reno, Nevada ANG 12/90–03/91. Retained ANG status, flying 106th TRS RF-4Cs. Refer to ANG unit history for further squadron details.

561st TFS *Black Knights* F-4G WW Yellow
Deployed from 35th TFW at George AFB, California, 15/08/90–04/91 (see George AFB, above, for further details). Individual aircraft names (chalked, or carried on nose APR-47 covers) included 69-7207 *Laura L*, 69-7263 *#1 SAM Slammer*, 69-7300 *Miss Carole*.

36th TFW ('Fightin' 36th')
Bitburg AB, West Germany
Received first operational F-4Ds in USAF 22/03/66 to replace F-105s, in time for Operation 'Gully Jump' 07/68–11/68, and received first F-4Es the

following year, with Wing an all-F-4E unit by 30/09/73. Converted to F-15s beginning with first arrivals 27/04/77 as part of Operation 'Ready Team', having ceased Phantom operations 09/03/77.

22nd TFS	F-4D	BR	Red/white
		BT	Red
	F-4E	BT	Red

Squadron reactivated with F-4Ds late 1971 and recoded 'BT'(red) 06/72. Converted to F-4Es 09/73. Ceased F-4 operations 25/10/76. Squadron is former FBS and unconnected with 22nd TRS mentioned elsewhere.

23rd TFS *Fighting Hawks*	F-4D	BS	Blue/red

Moved to Spangdahlem AB, West Germany, 05/69, and formally transferred to 52nd TFW control 31/12/71.

53rd TFS *Tigers*	F-4D	BT	Yellow
	F-4E	BT	Yellow

Converted to F-4Es 09/73. Ceased F-4 operations 01/02/77.

525th TFS *Bulldogs*	F-4E	BU	Blue
		BT	Blue

Redesignated from 525th FIS to TFS 01/10/69 and converted from F-102s to F-4Es from 12/11/69. Recoded 'BT' 06/72. Ceased F-4 operations 09/03/77.

37th TFW ('Defenders of the Crossroads')
Phu Cat AB, South Vietnam
Received two F-4D squadrons transferred from 366th TFW in 1969 to replace F-100s. Replaced through redesignation to 12th TFW 31/03/70.

480th TFS *Warhawks*	F-4D	HK	Camo green

Transferred from 366th TFW 15/04/69. Transferred to 12th TFW control 31/03/70.

389th TFS *Thunderbolts*	F-4D	HB	Red

Transferred from 366th TFW 15/06/69. Transferred to 12th TFW control 31/03/70.

George AFB, California
Reactivated 30/03/81 at George AFB, taking over 'Wild Weasel' contingent at the base. Subsequently adopted mixed 'hunter-killer' squadrons composed of F-4Gs and F-4Es. Wing authority passed back to 35th TFW 01/10/89 (37th TFW designation being transferred to 4450th TG F-117A Stealth Wing at Tonopah, Nevada).

561st TFS *Black Knights*	F-4G	WW	Yellow
	F-4E/G	WW	Yellow

Transferred from 35th TFW control 30/03/81. Operated F-4Es from 08/82. Transferred to 35th TTW control 01/10/89.

562nd TFTS *Weasels*	F-4G	WW	White
	F-4E/G	WW	Blue

Transferred from 35th TFW control 30/03/81. Operated F-4Es from 08/82; colour to blue. Transferred to 35th TTW control 01/10/89.

563rd TFS *Aces*	F-4G	WW	Red
	F-4E/G	WW	Red

Transferred from 35th TFW control 30/03/81. Operated F-4Es from 1986. Deactivated 25/09/89.

39th AD
Misawa AB, Japan
Received F-4Cs (displaced by F-4Ds in the combat zone in SEA) by 11/67. Direct control replaced by that of subordinate 475th TFW 01/68.

356th TFS *Green Demons*	F-4C	UK	Green

Converted from F-100s by 11/67. Transferred to 475th TFW control 15/01/68.

67th TFS *Fighting Cocks*	F-4C	UP	Red

Transferred WOPE from 18th TFW 15/12/67. Transferred to 475th TFW control 15/01/68.

41st AD
Yokota AB, Japan
Received F-4Cs (displaced by F-4Ds in the combat zone in SEA) by 10/67. Direct control replaced by that of subordinate 347th TFW 15/01/68.

35th TFS	F-4C	GG	Blue

Recommenced operations 03/10/67. Transferred to 347th TFW control 15/01/68.

36th TFS	F-4C	GL	Red

Received first Phantom 18/12/67. Transferred to 347th TFW control 15/01/68.

48th TFW ('Statue of Liberty Wing')
RAF Lakenheath, England
Converted from F-100s 01–04/72 though unit was not up to full strength until 08/74. Ceased F-4 operations 22/04/77 in preparation for conversion to F-111Fs.

492nd TFS *Eagles* (or	F-4D	LK	Multi
Bowlers)		LN	Multi
		LN	Blue

Recommenced operations 01/02/72. Recoded 'LN' (blue) 06/72.

493rd TFS *Bomb in the*	F-4D	LK	Multi
Ring (or *Roosters*)		LN	Multi
		LN	Yellow

Recommenced operations 04/72. Recoded 'LN' (yellow) 06/72.

494th TFS *Felix Iste Te*	F-4D	LK	Multi
Vorabit (or *Panthers*)		LN	Multi
		LN	Red

Recommenced full operations 25/07/74. Recoded 'LN' (red) 06/72.

49th TFW ('Tutor Et Ultor')
Holloman AFB, New Mexico
Converted to F-4Ds from F-105s beginning 03/67 while based at Spangdahlem AB, West Germany. Wing moved to Holloman AFB 30/06/68 and aircraft from 8th and 9th TFSs temporarily assigned to 7149th TFW 01/07/68-15/07/68 pending shift of equipment and personnel. First NATO/TAC 'dual-committed' F-4 Wing in USAF with 'global mobility'. Received Mackay Trophy in 1969 for 'most meritorious flight of the year', when Wing returned non-stop from deployment to Germany in stream of six dozen jets which performed 504 air refuellings en route with no aborts. 49th TFW also deployed *in toto* to Takhli AB, Thailand, 06/05/72–02/10/72 as part of Operation 'Constant Guard'. Converted to F-15s from 10/77.

7th TFS *Bunyabs*	F-4D	–	–
		HB	Blue
		HO	Blue

Recoded 'HO' 06/72. Converted to F-15s 1977.

8th TFS *The Black Sheep*	F-4D	–	–
		HC	Yellow
		HO	Yellow

Recoded 'HO' 06/72. Converted to F-15s 1978.

9th TFS *Iron Knights*	F-4D	–	–
		HD	Green
		HO	Green
	F-4E	HO	Silver or German flag
		GA	

Recoded 'HO' 06/72. Converted to F-15s 1978. Re-formed with ex-20th FS/35th FW F-4Es late 07/92 when *Luftwaffe*'s RTU and FWIC schools transferred to Holloman from George AFB, California, acquiring new designation 9th FS in process. Still current as last operational USAF F-4E squadron. By 08/92 had thirteen FY67/68 F-4Es and four FY75 *Luftwaffe*-owned F-4Es on strength. Individual aircraft (most currently feature armoured head insignia on noses) include 75-0632 (1st GAFTS) logos.

417th TFS *Red Rockets*	F-4D	HE	Red
		HO	Red

Transferred from 67th TRW 15/11/70. Comprised first batch deployed to Takhli, Thailand, during 05/72. Recoded 'HO' 06/72. Deactivated 30/04/77.

50th TFW
Hahn AB, West Germany
Converted to F-4Ds from F-100s from 09/66. Converted to F-16s 1982.

10th TFS	F-4D	HR	Blue
	F-4E	HR	Blue

Converted to F-4Es 07/76–09/76. Converted to F-16s 1982.

81st TFS *Panthers*	F-4D	ZS	Yellow
	F-4Cww	ZS	Yellow

Converted to F-4Cs 05/69, adding F-4Cww from 12/69, the first 'Wild Weasel' Phantom squadron in USAFE. Detached to Zweibrücken AB, West Germany 15/06/71 and transferred to 86th TFW control 15/07/71 and subsequently 52nd TFW control from 15/01/73.

313rd TFS *Bulldogs*	F-4E	HR	White

Reactivated 15/11/76. Recommenced operations 27/12/76. Converted to F-16s 1982.

417th TFS *Red Rockets*	F-4D	—	—

Based at Ramstein AB, West Germany. Transferred to 67th TRW 15/07/68.

496th TFS *World's Finest*	F-4E	HS	Black/yellow
		HR	Red

Converted from F-102s 14/02/70. Recoded 'HR' (red) 06/72. Converted to F-16s 1982.

51st Composite Wing
Osan AB, South Korea
As 51st FIW, Wing operated several F-4C squadrons at Naha AB, Okinawa, on periodic assignment from MacDill AFB, Florida-based 12th TFW 11/64–02/66 (see squadron entries under the 12th TFW). Began operating own Phantoms at Osan AB from 30/09/74 when, as 51st CW, it assumed control of 36th TFS (formerly under 3rd and 8th TFW control), adding 497th TFS eight years later. Redesignated 51st TFW 01/07/82. Relinquished last Phantoms in favour of F-16s by 01/89.

36th TFS *Flying Fiends*	F-4E	UK	Red
		OS	Red

Transferred from 8th TFW control 30/09/74. Recoded 'OS' (red) 11/74. Conversion to F-16s completed 06/01/89.

Taegu AB, South Korea
Operated concurrently with 36th TFS at Osan, which served as headquarters.

497th TFS *Night Owls*	F-4D	OS	Black
	F-4E	OS	Black
		GU	Black

Transferred from 8th TFW control 01/01/82. Converted to F-4E 04/82. Recoded 'GU' 1985. Deactivated 24/01/89.

52nd TFW ('Master of the Sky' or 'The Fighting 52nd')
Spangdahlem AB, Germany
Reactivated 31/12/71, taking control of F-4D-equipped 23rd TFS from 36th TFW. Later specialized in ARN-101 digital F-4E and 'Wild Weasel' F-4G. Received first F-16s 04/07/87, rapidly supplanting F-4Es. Redesignated 52nd FW 09/91.

23rd TFS *Fighting Hawks*	F-4D	BS	Blue
		SP	Blue
	F-4E	SP	Blue
	F-4E/G	SP	Blue
	F-4G/F-16	SP	Blue

Refer to 36th TFW. Recoded 'SP' 07/72. Operated ARN-92 LORAN F-4Ds from 02/75. Converted to F-4Es 09/81–04/82. Also operated F-4Gs from 12/83. F-4Es replaced by F-16s 1987. Deployed mixed contingent of 25 aircraft (including twelve F-4Gs) to 7440th CW at Incirlik AB, Turkey, 12/90, in support of Operation 'Proven Force', returning on 15/03/91. All-F-16 complement 09/91.

81st TFS *Panthers*	F-4Cww	SP	Yellow
	F-4G	SP	Yellow
	F-4E/G	SP	Yellow
	F-4G/F-16	SP	Yellow
	F-4G	SP	Yellow

Transferred from 86th TFW 15/01/73. Received first F-4G (69-273) 28/03/79. Last F-4Cww departed 26/07/79. Batch of F-4Es assigned to squadron for training purposes from 09/78 but all transferred to 480th TFS by c04/80. Operated F-4E/G mix from 12/83. F-4Es replaced by F-16s 1987. Reverted to all F-4G complement 12/90 during Operation 'Desert Shield'/'Desert Storm' when unit deployed to Sheikh Isa AB, Bahrain, 05/09/90–10/05/91, coming under 35th TFW(P) control. Subsequently maintained detachment at Dhahran, Saudi Arabia (4404 CW[P]), with other elements at Incirlik AB, Turkey (7440th CW). Redesignated 81st FS 01/10/91 as F-4G squadron again with 25 aircraft and began to fragment F-4G assets during 1993 (many aircraft returning to US for assignment to 561st FS/57th FWW from 21/01/93). Last six F-4Gs expected to remain under 81st TFS control until at least 01/94 (exact status of these remains in flux).

480th TFS *Warhawks*	F-4D	SP	Red
	F-4E	SP	Red
	F-4E/G	SP	Red
	F-4G/F-16	SP	Red

Reactivated 15/11/76. Converted to F-4Es beginning 09/78. Also operated F-4Gs from 12/83. F-4Es replaced by F-16s 1987. Provided some aircraft to bolster 23rd TFS and 81st TFS numbers forward-deployed to SW Asia in support of Operation 'Desert Storm' 12/90–04/91. All-F-16 complement effective as of 01/01/91.

56th TFW
MacDill AFB, Florida
Reactivated 30/07/75 through redesignation of 1st TFW. Redesignated 56th TTW 01/10/81. Last F-4E departed 29/09/78. First F-4D received 05/10/77. Converted to F-16s, first of which arrived 22/10/79.

4501st TFRS	F-4E	MC	White

Transferred from 1st TFW control 30/07/75. Redesignated 13th TFTS 15/01/76.

13th TFTS	F-4E	MC	White
	F-4D	MC	Black

Redesignated from 4501st TFRS 15/01/76. Completed conversion to F-4Ds 25/08/78. Squadron colour to black. Deactivated 30/06/82, replaced by F-16-equipped 72nd TFTS.

61st TFS	F-4E	MC	Yellow
	F-4D	MC	Yellow

Reactivated through redesignation of 27th TFS/1st TFW 30/09/75. Completed conversion to F-4Ds 30/04/78. Converted to F-16s shortly afterwards, last F-4D flight taking place 19/11/79.

62nd TFS	F-4E	MC	Blue
	F-4D	MC	Blue

Reactivated through redesignation of 94th TFS/1st TFW 30/09/75. Completed conversion to F-4D 04/02/78. Converted to F-16s shortly afterwards, last F-4D flight taking place on 14/11/80.

63rd TFS	F-4E	MC	Red
	F-4D	MC	Red

Reactivated through redesignation of 71st TFS/1st TFW 30/09/75. Completed conversion to F-4Ds 26/05/78. Converted to F-16s 01/10/81.

57th FIS, ADC
NAS Keflavik, Iceland

Converted from F-102s to F-4Cs 04/73 and introduced gloss FS 16473 Aircraft Gray scheme to operational Phantoms (previously employed on AFSC and AFSWC F-4s only). Upgraded to F-4Es (first arrival 21/03/78), only active USAF F-4Es to feature FS 16473 on operations, most F-4Cs being transferred to ADWC at Tyndall AFB, Florida. Reassigned from ADC to ADTAC 01/10/79. Converted to F-15s 11/85. Represented last Active F-4E interceptor unit, unit's final F-4E departing 25/11/85.

57th FIS Black Knights	F-4C	–	Black/white
	F-4E	–	Black/white

Aircraft included F-4C 63-7436 Wind It Timex, F-4E 66-0382 (Cdr's aircraft), F-4C 63-7576 (Bicentennial and colour markings).

57th FWW
Nellis AFB, Nevada

Reactivated 15/10/69, replacing 4525th FWW, subordinate to Nellis's TFWC. Redesignated 57th TTW 01/04/77. Reverted to 57th FWW 01/03/80. Last F-4E transferred 17/06/85.

66th FWS Weasels	F-4Cww etc	WD	Black/yellow
		WA	Black/yellow

Operated F-4Cww aircraft and academics from 09/71 in concert with F-105G and T-39 'Weasels', drawing Phantoms from 414th FWS. Recoded 'WA' 06/72. Ceased operations 25/07/75, when function assumed by 563rd TFTS/35th TFW at George AFB, California.

414th FWS	F-4C/Cww/D/E	WD	Black/yellow
	F-4E	WA	Black/yellow

Redesignated from 4538th CCTS/4525th FWW 15/10/69. Recoded 'WA' 06/72. Special weapons detachments deployed to 432nd TRW control at Udorn RTAFB, Thailand, on two occasions during 1972. Performed F-4 Fighter Weapons School duty until deactivated 30/12/81, when replaced by F-4-FWIC (which reported directly to TFWC HQ). Transferred last F-4E 17/06/85, when F-4 FWIC duty passed to 127th TFS/184th TFG, Kansas ANG, at McConnell AFB.

Det 1, 414th FWS	F-4D	WZ	Black/yellow

Activated 15/10/69. Deployed two aircraft to Udorn RTAFB, Thailand, for special trials in spring 1971 and deactivated 30/06/71 when replaced by 422nd FWS.

422nd FWS Vampires	F-4D/E	WD	Black/yellow
	F-4E etc	WA	Black/yellow

Replaced Det 1, 414th FWS, and absorbed new F-4Es for FOT&E duties. Recoded 'WA' 06/72 and F-4Ds phased out by 02/73. Redesignated 422nd TES 01/06/81. Ceased F-4E operations 1985. Reactivated with F-4Gs 01/02/93 using former Det 6/79th TEG assets. Parent Wing now known as the 57th Test Group.

561st FS Black Knights	F-4G	WA	Black/yellow

Reactivated 01/09/93. Deactivated 26/03/95. Last operational flight flown from Dhahran 09/01/96 and last of the unit's eight F-4Gs flown to AMARC 26/03/95.

58th TFTW ('Phantom College')
Luke AFB, Arizona

Received first Phantom 05/71 as F-4C training began to be transferred from 4453rd CCTW at Davis-Monthan AFB, Arizona (35th TFW at George AFB in California subsequently becoming major F-4E RTU and 'Wild Weasel' school from 1975, specializing in this model from 1979, and Florida Wings F-4D RTUs from 1977, although assignees would not necessarily fly those specific marks operationally and latter units frequently concentrated on 'short' or 'transition' conversion training. See 4453rd CCTW for aircraft squadron handovers to Luke). Luke's aircraft noted for distinctive high-visibility wing and fuselage stripes and one-off 'Ferris' splintered grey F-4C (63-7598). Redesignated 58th TTW 01/04/77. Made last F-4C training flight 17/09/82, first F-16s arriving 06/12/82. Aircraft of note included 63-7584 (Cdr's multi-striped aircraft; two MiG kills marked), 63-7676 (Bicentennial markings).

310th TFTS Tophats	F-4C	LA	Green

Converted from A-7Ds 1971. Converted to F-16s 1982.

311th TFTS Sidewinders	F-4C	LA	Yellow

Recommenced operations c31/10/71. Converted to F-16s 1982.

426th TFTS Killer Claws	F-4C	LA	Blue

Recommenced operations c02/10/71. To 405th TTW control and to F-15s 01/01/81.

550th TFTS Silver Eagles	F-4C	LA	Red

Recommenced operations 01/07/71. Converted to F-15s 1978 and transferred to 405th TTW control.

66th TRW ('Omnia Conspicimus')
RAF Upper Heyford, England

Transferred from Laon AB, France, with two squadrons of RF-101s and received first RF-4Cs 27/03/69, these going to 17th TRS. Wing deactivated 01/70, new RF-4C squadron being transferred to Zweibrücken AB, West Germany (freeing base for F-111 operations under 20th TFW, which was in process of concluding F-100 operations).

17th TRS Hooters	RF-4C	–	–

Converted from RF-101s from 03/69 and transferred to 86th TFW 02/01/70.

67th TRW ('Lux Ex Tenebris')
Mountain Home AFB, Idaho

Re-formed 01/01/66 at Mountain Home AFB with RF-4Cs. Aircraft redistributed between Bergstrom AFB, Texas, and Shaw AFB, South Carolina, 07/71.

7th TRS	RF-4C	–	–
	RF-4C	KT	Green

Reactivated 1965 under unidentified organization as initial RTU school and assigned to 67th TRW control 01/01/66. Acquired code 'KT' (green) 1967. Deactivated 15/07/71.

10th TRS	RF-4C	–	Yellow
	RF-4C	KR	Yellow

Reactivated 08/01/66. Served as RTU for crews bound for combat in SEA. Acquired code 'KR' (yellow) 1967. Deactivated 10/71.

11th TRS	RF-4C	–	–

Short-lived at Mountain Home. Reactivated 11/65 and passed to 67th TRW control 08/04/66 as 11th TRS Photographic (Jet). Deployed and integrated with 6461st TRS/432nd TRW at Udorn RTAFB, Thailand, 25/10/66, which adopted 11th TRS designation on that date.

12th TRS *Blackbirds*   RF-4C   –   –
Short-lived at Mountain Home. Reactivated as 12th TRS Photographic (Jet) 01/07/66 and deployed to Tan Son Nhut, SVN, on 02/09/66 (see 460th TRW entry). Later reactivated under 67th TRW control at Bergstrom (see below).

22nd TRS *Bees*   RF-4C   KS   Blue
Reassigned from Toul-Rosières AB, France, 20/09/66. Served as RTU and transferred to 363rd TRW at Shaw on 15/07/71.

417th TFS *Red Rockets* or   F-4D   KB   Red
Bandits
Transferred from Ramstein AB, West Germany (while under 50th TFW control), 01/07/68. Physically transferred again to 49th TFW at Holloman AFB, New Mexico 15/11/70.

Bergstrom AFB, Texas
Transferred from Mountain Home AFB, Idaho, 15/07/71 with three squadrons of RF-4Cs. Became major RF-4C RTU during changeover that took place between 03/82-09/82, when Phantom Recce school moved from 363rd TRW at Shaw AFB, South Carolina, permitting transfer or reactivation of two training squadrons (until task passed to ANG in 1990). Retitled 67th RW 10/91 and finally deactivated 08/92.

4th TRS   RF-4C   BB   Light blue
Transferred from 75th TRW control 15/07/71 and redesignated 45th TRS 15/10/75.

9th TRS   RF-4C   BC   Yellow
Transferred from 75th TRW control 15/07/71 and redesignated 12th TRS 31/08/71.

12th TRS *Blackbirds*   RF-4C   BC   Orange
    BA   Orange
Reactivated using former 9th TRS assets 31/08/71. Codes to 'BA' 06/72. Deployed to Sheikh Isa AB, Bahrain, during Operation 'Desert Shield'/'Desert Storm'. Redesignated 12th RS 10/91. Was last Active RF-4C squadron at time of disbandment 28/08/92.

45th TRS *Polka Dots*   RF-4C   BB   Blue
    BA   Blue
Reactivated using former 4th TRS assets 15/10/71. Codes to 'BA' 06/72. Deactivated 10/75 and reactivated 1982 as 45th TRTS. Deactivated again 09/89.

62nd TRTS   RF-4C   BA   Yellow
Transferred from 363rd TRW control 07/82. Deactivated 1991.

91st TRS   RF-4C   BA   White
    BA   Red
Transferred from 75th TRW control 15/07/71. Colour later changed to red. Deactivated 1991.

75th TRW
Bergstrom AFB, Texas
Reactivated 17/05/66; organized 01/07/66. Deactivated 15/07/71; assets taken over by 67th TRW (see above).

4th TRS   RF-4C   BB   Light blue
Reactivated 18/11/66. Coded 07/68. Transferred to 67th TRW 15/07/71.

9th TRS   RF-4C   BC   Yellow
Reactivated 01/09/69. Transferred to 67th TRW control 15/07/71.

14th TRS   RF-4C   –   –
Reactivated 03/04/67. Transferred to 432nd TRW 06/11/67 (attached to that Wing 28/10/6/–05/11/67).

91st TRS   RF-4C   BA   White
Recommenced operations c15/09/67. Coded 7/68. Transferred to 67th TRW control 15/07/71.

79th TEG, USAFTAWC
Eglin AFB, Florida
See 4485th TS, USAFTAWC, for details.

81st TFW ('Blue Dragons')
RAF Bentwaters, England
First F-4C arrived 10/65, to replace F-101s. Conversion complete by 04/66. Upgraded to F-4Ds in stages, many of Wing's F-4Cs being transferred to *Ejercito del Aire Español* as C-12s. Converted to A-10s from 1979.

78th TFS *Bushmasters*   F-4C   –   –
    F-4D   WR   Red
Based at nearby RAF Woodbridge, England. Converted to F-4Ds 05/69. Coded 'WR' (red) 1970. Converted to A-10s 1979.

91st TFS   F-4C   WS   Blue
    F-4D   WR   Blue
Coded 1970. Recoded 'WR' 06/72. Converted to F-4Ds 09/73. Converted to A-10s 1979.

92nd TFS   F-4C   WT   Yellow
    F-4D   WR   Yellow
Coded 1970. Recoded 'WR' 06/72. Converted to F-4Ds 09/73. Converted to A-10s 1979.

86th TFW ('Virtus Perdurat')
Zweibrücken AB, West Germany
Reactivated at Zweibrücken 01/11/69 and transferred to Ramstein 31/01/73 (see below).

17th TRS *Hooters*   RF-4C   –
    RF-4C   ZR   Red
Transferred from 66th TRW 12/01/70. Coded 'ZR' (red) 1970. Transferred to 26th TRW control 31/01/73.

81st TFS *Panthers*   F-4C   ZS   Yellow
Attached from 50th TFW 15/06/71, assigned 15/07/71. Transferred to 52nd TFW 15/01/73.

Ramstein AB, West Germany
Transferred from Zweibrücken 31/01/73 and undertook F-4E operations with two distinct taskings. Ground-attack F-4Es were on strength until 30/06/86, conversion to F-16s having begun during 12/85. During this transition ANG FIS Phantoms deployed on rotation to fulfil 526th TFS's 'Zulu Alert' air-defence commitments, code-named Project 'Creek Klaxon'.

512th TFS *Vigilare Pro Pace*   F-4E   RS   Black/yellow
Reactivated 15/11/76 with nuclear and daylight precision-attack role. Converted to F-16s beginning 21/12/85. Individual aircraft names included 68-0480 *Knight Stalker* (with giant 'sabre-tooth mouth').

526th TFS *Black Knights*   F-4E   RS   Red/black
Transferred from 26th TRW control 31/03/73. Only dedicated Active Phantom air superiority squadron. Converted to F-16s 1986.

347th TFW ('Our Might Always')
Yokota AB, Japan
Activated 15/01/68, taking over from 41st AD while squadrons listed below were in the process of converting from F-105s to F-4Cs displaced from combat assignments by introduction of F-4D to 8th and 366th TFWs in the combat zone. Deactivated 15/05/71 (squadron designations passing to 3rd TFW at Kunsan AB, South Korea, and aircraft to 18th TFW at Kadena AB,

Okinawa). Wing designation then passed to two different F-111 units before being reactivated at Moody AFB, Georgia (see below).

35th TFS *First to Fight*   F-4C   GG   Blue
Transferred from 41st AD control 15/01/68. Deactivated 15/03/71; aircraft to 67th TFS/18th TFW.

36th TFS *Flying Fiends*   F-4C   GL   Red
Transferred from 41st AD control 15/01/68. Deactivated 15/05/71; aircraft to 44th TFS/18th TFW.

80th TFS *Headhunters*   F-4C/Cww   GR   Yellow
Converted from F-105s 03/68. To 475th Det 1 control at Kunsan AB, South Korea, 15/02/71. Was PACAF F-4Cww squadron prior to transferring its fourteen aircraft to 67th TFS 04/71. Until late 1969/early 1970 'Weasel' aircraft were distributed among all six F-4C squadrons in Japan (each squadron having at least one aircraft), although these were not operated in 'Wild Weasel' role until consolidation with *Headhunters* in early 1970.

Moody AFB, Georgia
Reactivated at Moody 30/09/75 and subsequently assigned to Rapid Deployment Joint Task Force. Deployed to Cairo West, Egypt, 06/80–10/80 in support of Operation 'Proud Phantom'. Converted to F-16s from 1987.

68th TFS *Lightning Lancers*   F-4E   MY   Red
Reactivated at Moody 30/09/75 and equipped with F-4Es. Began conversion to F-16s from 01/04/87

69th TFS *Fighting 69th*   F-4E   MY   Green
   or *Dragons*
Took over aircraft and crews from 339th TFS 01/07/83 and began conversion to F-16s 01/01/88.

70th TFS *White Knights*   F-4E   MY   Blue
   F-4E   MY   Blue/white
Reactivated 08/09/75 and assigned to Moody 30/09/75. Began conversion to F-16s 01/10/87.

339th TFS *Dragons*   F-4E   MY   Green
Reactivated 22/03/76 and commenced operations 05/05/76. Redesignated 69th TFS 01/07/83.

363rd TRW ('Voir C'est Savoir')
Shaw AFB, South Carolina
The 363rd TRW was an element of Shaw's TARC (Tactical Air Reconnaissance Center) when it received its first RF-4C during 08/64 (assigned to subordinate 4415th CCTS/4411st CCTG). Wing remained major RTU and FOT&E centre for 'Photo-Phantom' until duty finally passed to 67th TRW at Bergstrom AFB, Texas, 03–09/82. Fresh aircraft and crews often formed at Shaw for combat reassignment to Udorn RTAFB, Thailand (432nd TRW), or Tan Son Nhut, SVN (460th TRW), *en bloc*. Following cessation of hostilities in SEA, Wing maintained RTU function for USAF and several overseas RF-4 operators while elements fulfilled TAC/ NATO recce tasking by deploying on numerous 'Salty Bee' manoeuvres to Europe. Redesignated 363rd TFW 01/10/82, when it began to convert to F-16s, and relinquished last RF-4Cs when 16th TRS was deactivated 09/89, twenty-five years after Wing began operations on type.

4415th CCTS   RF-4C   –   –
   RF-4C   JL   White
First unit to conduct RF-4C operations, formally receiving first aircraft 24/09/64. Initially came under 4411st CCTG control until it passed to 4402nd CCTG control 01/07/66 (4402nd CCTG being similarly subordinate to TARC). Reported directly to 363rd TRW from 01/02/67. Coded 07/68. Deactivated, aircraft transferred to 33rd TRTS 15/10/69.

4416th TS   RF-4C etc   –   –
   RF-4C etc   JM   Grey

Received RF-4Cs 1964 for operational evaluation work, test trials and fine-tuning devices ready for combat operations (squadron also operating RF-101s and EB/RB-66s which reported to TARC until 01/07/66, then directly to the 363rd TRW, then again to TARC from 01/07/67). Coded 07/68. Performed 'Peace Eagle' trials of G-139 HIAC-1 (on RF-4C 66-0419) 1970. Deactivated 11/70.

9th TRS   RF-4C   –   –
Formed at Shaw 1965. Det 1 organized 09/05/66 and departed for 432nd TRW at Udorn RTAFB, Thailand, 26/07/66, being redesignated 6461st TRS on arrival on 29/07/66 (see 432nd TRW). Remaining equipment and personnel at Shaw transferred to other units by 15/08/66.

16th TRS   RF-4C   –   Yellow
   JM   Yellow
   JO   Yellow
   SW   Multi
Converted to RF-4Cs 06/65 and declared combat-ready 08/65 Nine aircraft deployed to 2nd AD at Tan Son Nhut 27/10/65, arriving in place by 30/10/65, to become first RF-4C combat unit assigned to combat in SEA (see 460th TRW entry; was transferred from 2nd AD to 460th TRW control and subsequently to 475th TFW at Misawa, Japan). Designation transferred back to Shaw from Misawa 15/02/71 and squadron redesignated 16th TRTS 06/71. Recoded 'JO' 07/72. Became 16th TRS and recoded 'SW' (multi-coloured) 01/10/82. Last active recce squadron at Shaw, deactivated 15/09/89.

18th TRS   RF-4C   JP   Light blue
   JO   Light blue
Converted from RF-101s 10/70–11/70 after squadron had been reassigned to 363rd TRW 30/01/70. Recoded 'JO' 07/72. Deactivated 30/09/79.

22nd TRS *Bees*   RF-4C   JO   Red
Reassigned from Mountain Home AFB, Idaho, 15/07/71. Deactivated 15/10/71 when aircraft transferred to 62nd TRS.

33rd TRTS *Falcons*   RF-4C   JL   White
   RF-4C   JO   White
Reactivated and took over assets of 4415th CCTS 15/10/69. Recoded 'JO' 07/72. Deactivated 01/10/82.

62nd TRS   RF-4C   JO   Red
Reactivated 15/10/71, taking over assets of the 22nd TRS. Aircraft and support equipment transferred to 67th TRW at Bergstrom AFB, Texas, 07/82 as 62nd TRTS.

366th TFW ('Audentes Fortuna Juvat' or 'Gunfighters')
Holloman AFB, New Mexico
Converted from F-84s to F-4Cs at Holloman AFB 1965. Wing transferred to Phan Rang, SVN, 20/03/66 alongside 389th TFS (remaining squadrons deploying elsewhere, as noted below).

389th TFS   F-4C   –   –
Detached to unknown unit/location 15/09/65–16/12/65. Moved to Phan Rang AB 11/03/66–20/03/66.

390th TFS   F-4C   –   –
Reassigned to 6252nd TFW at DaNang AB, SVN, 29/10/65 (and attached to 405th FW c04/11/65–18/11/65).

391st TFS   F-4C   –   –
Transferred to 12th TFW at Camn Ranh Bay, SVN, 26/01/66.

480th TFS   F-4C   –   –
Received first F-4C 02/65, completing conversion from F-84s by 07/07/65. Transferred to 6252nd TFW at DaNang AB, SVN, 01/02/66.

Phan Rang AB, SVN
389th TFS   F-4C   –   –

Transferred from Holloman AFB, New Mexico, 11/03/66–20/03/66. Designation transferred to Da Nang AB, SVN, 10/10/66.

Da Nang AB, South Vietnam
Reassigned to Da Nang WOPE 10/10/66, taking over the Phantoms on station (previously operated by provisional 6252nd TFW and, from 08/04/66, by 35th TFW; the former Wing designation disappeared from the Phantom world altogether while the latter moved to Phan Rang, SVN, to assume control of the F-100s assigned there—see 35th TFW entry). 366th TFW acquired nickname 'Gunfighters' after introducing SUU-16/A 20mm gun pod to combat service, this accounting for five of Wing's eighteen MiG kills in SEA. Converted to F-4Ds by 01/68, then new F-4Es during 04/69. Transferred to Takhli RTAFB, Thailand, 27/06/72.

389th TFS *Thunderbolts*	F-4C	–	Red
	F-4C/D	AA–AZ	Red

Transferred from Phan Rang AB, SVN, 10/10/66 taking over miscellaneous F-4Cs left by 35th TFW. By 01/67 squadron had adopted individual aircraft codes in 'AA'–'AZ' range. Upgraded to F-4Ds by 01/68. Transferred to 37th TFW control 15/06/69. Individual aircraft included F-4D 66-7646/'AH' *The Toot* (389th TFS Cdr's mount).

390th TFS *Wild Boars*	F-4C	–	Blue
	F-4C/D	BA–BZ	Blue
	F-4D	LF	Blue

Transferred from Holloman AFB, New Mexico, 29/10/65, squadron coming under 6252nd and then 35th TFW control before being reassigned to 366th TFW at Da Nang on 10/10/66. By 01/67 codes in 'BA'–'BZ' range had been adopted. Upgraded to F-4Ds by 01/68 and codes subsequently standardized as 'LF'. Deactivated 14/06/72, aircraft distributed between 8th TFW and 432nd TRW. Individual aircraft included F-4D 66-8800/'BX' *Roadrunner*, F-4D 66-8805/'BT' *William Lee*.

480th TFS *Warhawks*	F-4C	–	Green
	F-4C/D	CA–CZ	Green

Transferred from Holloman AFB, New Mexico, 01/02/66, squadron coming under 6252nd and then 35th TFW control before being reassigned to 366th at DaNang 10/10/66. By 01/67 codes in 'CA'–'CZ' range had been adopted. Converted to F-4Ds by 03/68; transferred to 37th TFW at Phu Cat, SVN, 15/04/69. Individual aircraft included F-4D 66-8775/'CO' *The Saint*.

4th TFS *Fightin' Fuujins*	F-4E	LA	Yellow

Established with F-4Es 12/04/69 after transfer from 33rd TFW at Eglin AFB, Florida. Moved to Takhli RTAFB, Thailand, 27/06/72 and to 432nd TRW control at Udorn RTAFB, Thailand, 10/72 (see 432nd TRW for further details).

421st TFS *Black Widows* or	F-4E	LC	Red
Kiss of Death			

Established with F-4Es 26/04/69 based on *matériel* supplied by 16th TFS/33rd TFW from Eglin AFB, Florida. Deployed to Kunsan AB, South Korea, 23/04/69–26/06/69 en route to Da Nang. Undertook field trials of TISEO. Moved to Takhli RTAFB, Thailand, 27/06/72 and thence to 432nd TRW control at Udorn RTAFB, Thailand, 10/72 (see 432nd TRW for further details). Individual aircraft included 67-0316 ('happy shark's-mouth' markings), 68-0317 *Hey Jude* (TISEO aircraft belonging to 57th FWW).

366th TFW at DaNang hosted nine-aircraft detachment which deployed from 35th TFS/3rd TFW, from Kunsan AB, South Korea, 01/04/72. This was reconsolidated with remainder of its squadron under 8th TFW control at Ubon, Thailand, twenty-four hours later (before the entire detachment was relocated under 388th TFW control at Korat RTAFB, Thailand, 12/06/72).

Takhli RTAFB, Thailand
366th TFW HQ moved to Takhli RTAFB, Thailand, 27/06/72 and was deactivated there 31/10/72; see 4th and 421st TFSs above, which moved to Takhli in 06/1972 alongside parent Wing to fly operations there until 10/72, when 4th and 421st TFSs moved to 432nd TRW control at Udorn RTAFB,

Thailand. On 01/11/72 parent 366th TFW designation transferred to new F-111 Wing at Mountain Home AFB, Idaho. During this time base (and not 366th TFW, which had not yet moved to Takhli) played host to entire 49th TFW on 'Constant Guard' deployment from Holloman AFB, New Mexico, 06/05/72–02/10/72 (see 49th TFW entry for squadron details).

388th TFW ('Libertas Vel Mors')
Korat RTAFB, Thailand
Converted from F-105s to F-4Es between 11/68 and 05/69. Moved WOPE to Hill AFB, Utah, 23/12/75 (see below).

34th TFS *Rams*	F-4E	JJ	Camo
	F-4D	JJ	Camo

F-4Es replaced F-105s 05/69 (last F-105 mission flown 09/05/69), having been re-equipped and manned by 40th TFS/33rd TFW c10/05/69. Re-equipped with F-4Ds 06/74–07/74. Deactivated 23/12/75. Individual aircraft included F-4Es 67-0208 *Here Come Da Judge*, -0306 *War Lover*, -0261 *Okie*, -0313 *Spunky VI*, -0279 *Wreckin' Crew*, -0320 *Can-Do*, -0288 *Arkansas Traveler*, -0342 *Li'l Buddha*.

469th TFS *Fighting Bulls*	F-4E	JV	Green

First F-4Es assigned to combat zone in SEA, initial sixteen aircraft deploying 17/11/68 under 'Operation 47 Buck 9', replacing F-105s, using *matériel* and crews supplied by 40th TFS/33rd TFW. Deactivated 31/10/72. Individual aircraft names included 67-0287 *Positive Thinker*, 68-0322 *Little Chris*, 68-0308 *Betty Lou*.

388th TFW also hosted combat deployment of eighteen F-4Ds of 35th TFS/3rd TFW from Kunsan AB, South Korea, from 01/04/72. These were transferred to 388th TFW control on 12/06/72 before returning to Kunsan 12/10/72 (see 35th TFS/3rd TFW for further squadron details). It also hosted six F-4Cww's of 67th TFS deployed 23/09/72–18/02/73 and ten F-4Cww's 20/04/75–02/05/75.

Hill AFB, Utah
Wing designation moved WOPE to Hill AFB 23/12/75 (a 58th TFTW F-4C freshly re-worked at the co-located Ogden Depot Center serving as showpiece during ceremony that day) and began receiving F-4Ds 01/76. Converted to F-16s from 06/01/79.

4th TFS *Devils*	F-4D	HL	Yellow

Ex-Da Nang (366th TFW) and Udorn (432nd TRW) Phantom squadron. Commenced operations 10/03/76. Converted to F-16s 1979.

34th TFS *Rams*	F-4D	HL	Red

Ex-Korat Phantom squadron (388th TFW). Commenced operations 01/04/76. Converted to F-16s 1979.

421st TFS *Black Widows*	F-4D	HL	Red

Ex-Da Nang (366th TFW) and Udorn (432nd TRW) Phantom squadron. Commenced operations 03/08/76. Converted to F-16s 1979.

401st TFW ('Caelum Arena Nostra')
Torrejon AB, Spain
Assigned to Torrejon 27/04/66 and established as first all-F-4E Phantom Wing in USAFE 07/70, undergoing a longer-lasting re-formation on 15/07/71. Converted to F-4Cs 09/73 following major reshuffle of Phantoms within TAC and USAFE ('Creek Align') and assisted Spanish transition to C-12 (F-4C) co-located at Torrejon under *Ala da Caza 12*. Also flew joint manoeuvres with Persian 'Peace Roll' Phantoms on CENTO exercises such as 'Shabaz' prior to Iranian Revolution. Converted to F-4Ds from 25/08/78 as part of Operation 'Creek Realign II' and ceremoniously converted to first F-16s 05/02/83, making last F-4D training flight 30/06/83.

307th TFS	F-4E	TL	–

Converted from F-100s to F-4Es, receiving its first aircraft 09/01/70. Designation relinquished to F-4F-equipped 31st TFW at Homestead AFB, Florida, 13/07/71, when aircraft and crews in Spain adopted new designation 612th TFS.

353rd TFS *Black Panthers*   F-4E   TK   –
Converted from F-100s to F-4Es 1970. Designation relinquished to A-7-equipped 354th TFW at Myrtle Beach AFB, South Carolina, 13/07/71, when aircraft and crews in Spain adopted new designation 614th TFS.

612th TFS *Screaming Eagles*   F-4E   TJ   Black/white
                                    F-4C   TJ   Black/white
                                    F-4D   TJ   Black/white
Reactivated at Torrejon 15/07/71 with F-4Es using former 307th TFS assets. Re-equipped with F-4Cs 1973 and with F-4Ds 1978–79. First to convert to F-16s 1983.

613th TFS *Squids*   F-4E   TL   Yellow
                          F-4C   TJ   Yellow
                          F-4D   TJ   Yellow
Transferred from England AFB, Louisiana, 28/04/66 and received first F-4Es 1970. Converted to F-4Cs 1973. Code to 'TJ' 06/72. Upgraded to F-4Ds 1978–79. Third squadron to convert to F-16s 1983.

614th TFS *Lucky Devils*   F-4E   TK   Red
                                F-4C   TJ   Red
                                F-4D   TJ   Red
Reactivated at Torrejon 15/07/71 with F-4Es through redesignation of 353rd TFS. Converted to F-4Cs 1973. Code to 'TJ' 06/72. Upgraded to F-4Ds 1978–79. Second squadron to convert to F-16s 1983.

405th FW
Clark Field, Philippines
Replaced 6200th ABW 09/05/59 in pre-Phantom era, without 'Tactical' prefix and acquired Phantoms from 11/67. Deactivated 09/74 when 3rd TFW took over force (and designation passed to F-15 training Wing at Luke AFB, Arizona).

1st TS   F-4C   PA   Yellow
Activated 15/10/70 through redesignation of 6400th TS. Passed from direct 13th AF to 405th TFW control 30/04/70. Duties passed to operational squadrons not long afterwards.

90th TFS *Pair-O-Dice*   F-4D   PN   Red
Reactivated 15/12/72 as 'paper' squadron and operational on 31/08/73 when it replaced 523rd TFS. Transferred to 3rd TFW control *in situ* 16/09/74.

523rd TFS *Crusaders*   F-4D   PN   Red
Converted from F-100s to F-4Ds 11/67–01/68. Maintained 'Formosa Detachment' at Tainan, Taiwan. Deployed to 432nd TRW at Udorn RTAFB, Thailand, 09/04/72–25/10/72 as part of Operation 'Constant Guard'. Designation transferred to F-111-equipped 27th TFW 31/08/73, assets passing to 90th TFS.

432nd TRW ('Bring Back The Pictures . . . And Kill MiGs')
Udorn RTAFB, Thailand
Organized 18/09/66 to assume command of mix of fighter and reconnaissance Phantoms. Later allocated aircraft from other Wings from PACAF and on TDY from CONUS (see below). Redesignated 432nd TFW 15/11/74. Relieved of all tactical duties 30/11/75; deactivated 18/12/75.

6461st TRS   RF-4C   –   –
Deployed as Det 1 of 9th TRS 26/07/66 from 363rd TRW, Shaw AFB, South Carolina, arriving with new designation 6461st TRS 29/07/66. Originally reported to 460th TRW control until establishment of 432nd TRW parent Wing 18/09/66. Redesignated 11th TRS 25/10/66 when 11th TRS deployed from 67th TRW and the two units were integrated.

11th TRS *Inferne Ibimus*   RF-4C   OO   Black
Designation transferred from 67th TRW at Mountain Home AFB, Idaho 25/10/66, unit taking over assets of 6461st TRS. Deactivated 10/11/70. Individual aircraft names included 65-0849 *Hey Bud*, -0905 *Tumbleweed*.

13th TFS *Black Panthers*   F-4D   OC   Blue
                                          UD   Blue
Attached 21/10/67, assigned 15/11/67. Performed trials with Pave Fire II. Code to 'UD' 1974. Deactivated 30/06/75. Individual aircraft included 66-7755/'OC' (shark's-mouth markings), -8273/'OC' *Ripley's Believe It or Not*, -8702/'OC' *Mr Snoopy*, -8707/'OC' *Ro Ho*.

14th TRS   RF-4C   OZ   Red
                         UD   Red
Attached from 75th TRW control 28/10/67 and assigned 06/11/67 (having deployed for work in high-threat areas when RF-101-equipped 20th TRS stood down at Tan Son Nhut, SVN, 31/10/67). First and only RF-4C combat squadron equipped with LORAN RF-4Cs. Code to 'UD' 1974. Deactivated 30/06/75.

25th TFS *Assam Dragons*   F-4E   UD   Black/yellow
Designation transferred from 8th TFW at Ubon RTAFB, Thailand, 05/07/74, taking over several aircraft of th 555th TFS (see below). Cadre of personnel and aircraft transferred to 3rd TFW at Clark Field, Philippines, 19–20/12/75 (where it relinquished equipment to 90th TFS before designation passed next day to new squadron created under 18th TFW at Kadena AB, Okinawa).

555th TFS *Triple Nickel*   F-4D   OY   Green
                                 F-4E   –   Orange
Assigned from 8th TFW control 28/05/68 and transferred 01/06/68. Converted to 'Rivet Haste' F-4Es 11/72–01/73. 'Phamous Phantom' MiG-killing squadron's designation transferred as a number only to 58th TFTW at Luke AFB, Arizona, as 555th TFS on 05/07/74 (which ceremonially adopted it on receipt of first F-15 to enter operational inventory 14/11/74), equipment at Udorn passing to 25th TFS. Individual aircraft included F-4Ds 66-7463/'OY' (six MiG kill stars marked), -7554/'OY' *Trapper John*, -8806/'OY' *Sex Machine*.

4th TFS *Fightin' Fuujins*   F-4E   LA   Yellow
                                  F-4D   UD   Yellow
Attached from 366th TFW control 29/10/72 and assigned 31/10/72. To F-4Ds by 31/01/73 and recoded 'UD' 1974. Transferred to 388th TFW 12/75.

421st TFS Black Widows   F-4E   LC   Red
                             F-4E   UD   White
Attached from 366th TFW control 31/10/72. Recoded 'UD' (white) by 1974. Detached to Clark AB, Philippines, 13–14/12/75, transferring personnel and equipment to 90th TFS 15/12/75. Deactivated 23/12/75.

'UD' tail-codes were not fully implemented and several aircraft flew without them, or with the codes from their previous assignment, until 12/75. The following F-4 squadrons deployed to Udorn 1972 under Operation 'Constant Guard' (refer to appropriate Wing entries for further details, noting that most of these dates reflect base departures as opposed to arrivals):

58th TFS/33rd TFW	E/ED	Blue	29/04/72–14/10/72
308th TFS/31st TFW	E/ZF	Green	28/04/72–29/07/72
307th TFS/31st TFW	(308th a/c)		29/07/72–28/10/72
523rd TFS/405th TFW	D/PN	Red	09/04/72–24/10/72

460th TRW
Tan Son Nhut AB, South Vietnam
Reorganized 18/02/66 to assume responsibility of tac-photo RF-101 and RF-4C assets (jet) stationed in Republic of SVN, formerly under 2nd AD control.

12th TRS *Blackbirds*   RF-4C   –   –
                                     AC   Orange
Reactivated as 12th TRS Photo (Jet) 01/07/66 at Mountain Home AFB, Idaho, and assigned to Tan Son Nhut 02/09/66. Coded 'AC' (orange) 1967. Designation later replaced 4th TRS at Bergstrom AFB, Texas, 31/08/71 and aircraft were redistributed.

16th TRS	RF-4C	–	–
		AE	Yellow

Declared combat-ready 08/65 at Shaw AFB, South Carolina and nine aircraft deployed to 2nd AD control at Tan Son Nhut 27/10/65, arriving 30/10/65 to become first RF-4C combat unit assigned to war zone in SEA (see 363rd TRW entry). Flew first missions 31/10/65. Formally passed to 460th TRW control 02/02/66. Coded 'AE' (yellow) 1967. Transferred to 475th TFW at Misawa AB, Japan, 15/03/70.

Taegu AB, South Korea

460th TRG reactivated 01/10/89 to assume control of 15th TRS/18th TFW RF-4Cs stationed there. Deactivated c1991, when most aircraft transferred to ROKAF.

15th TRS *Cotton Pickers*	RF-4C	GU	– –

474th TFW
Nellis AFB, Nevada

As part of Operation 'Ready Switch', Wing converted from F-111s to F-4Ds following preparatory work-up using small number of aircraft pooled at Nellis under 4474th TFW(P). Wing formally converted 06/08/77, when last F-111 departed to 366th TFW at Mountain Home AFB, Idaho. Converted to F-16s, receiving first new aircraft 11/80 and conducting last Phantom sortie 12/06/81.

428th TFS *Buccaneers*	F-4D	NA	Blue

First to convert to F-16s, from 14/11/80.

429th TFS *Black Falcons*	F-4D	NA	Yellow

Second to convert to F-16s, 1981.

430th TFS *Tigers* or *The Beachball Squadron*	F-4D	NA	Red

Third to convert to F-16s, 1981. Flew final F-4 operational sortie 12/06/81.

475th TFW
Misawa AB, Japan

Reactivated 21/12/67 and assigned to Misawa 15/01/68, replacing 39th AD which was operating F-4Cs transferred from SEA. Provided special-operations reconnaissance detachments to combat zone. Deactivated 15/05/71, passing aircraft and resources to 3rd TFW at Kunsan AB, South Korea (see 3rd TFW).

16th TRS	RF-4C	UE	Blue

Transferred from 460th TRW at Tan Son Nhut AB, SVN, 16/03/70 (detachments of four aircraft reportedly remained at 7th AF HQ at Tan Son Nhut and at Nakhon Phanom, Thailand, for real-time weather reconnaissance and Fast-FAC 'Cricket' recce command and control missions over Laos in support of 'Commando Hunt'). Transferred back to 363rd TRW at Shaw AFB, South Carolina, 15/02/71, though remained attached to 475th TFW 16–22/02/71.

391st TFS *Bold Tigers*	F-4C		
	F-4D	UD	Yellow

Transferred from 12th TFW 22/07/68. Converted to F-4Ds 12/69–04/70. Maintained detachment at Kunsan AB, South Korea (which was redesignated 80th TFS 15/03/71) and formally transferred to 8th TFW control at Kunsan 16/09/74 (see 3rd TFW; 301st TFS designation was reactivated as new F-111 squadron at Mountain Home AFB, Idaho, 05/71).

67th TFS *Fighting Cocks*	F-4C	UP	Red

Transferred from 39th AD 15/01/68. Converted to F-4D 12/69. Deactivated at Misawa 15/03/71, when equipment passed to 35th TFS/3rd TFW and squadron designation was transferred to 18th TFW at Kadena AB, Okinawa (to assume control of F-4C aircraft being transferred from 347th TFW).

356th TFS *Green Demons*	F-4C	UK	Green

Transferred from 39th AD control 15/01/68. Converted to F-4Ds 12/69. Deactivated 15/05/71, when equipment passed to 36th TFS/3rd TFW at Kunsan AB, South Korea (squadron designation passing to new A-7 unit under 354th TFW at Myrtle Beach, South Carolina.).

479th TFW ('Protesctores Libertatis')
George AFB, California

Base received first Phantoms in spring 1964 following reactivation of 32nd TFW—comprising 68th, 431st and 497th FISs—on 06/04/64 which passed to 8th TFW control on 25/07/64 and thence (two of them) back to 479th TFW 06/12/65. (See below, and see 8th and 32nd TFW entries for further details.) Became all-Phantom Wing 06/67 when last F-104s departed. Deactivated as host unit 01/10/71 when 35th TFW took over at George AFB.

68th TFS	F-4C	–	–
	F-4D	GA	?

Transferred from 8th TFW to 831st AD control at George 06/12/65 as TFS and upgraded to F-4Ds 1966, being assigned to Wing 15/05/68. Coded 07/68. Deactivated at George 25/09/68, when unit was replaced by 4535th CCTS.

431st TFS *Red Devils*	F-4C	–	–
	F-4D		Red/white
	F-4E	GB	Red/white

Transferred from 8th TFW to 831st AD control 06/12/65 and converted to F-4Ds 1966. Assigned to Wing 15/06/68 and became second 479th TFW squadron to convert to F-4Es. Coded 'GB' (red) 07/68. Not operational 01/01/69–01/03/69 (see 4546th TTS). Ceased operations 31/05/70. Designation reassigned to George 15/01/76–01/01/78—see 35th TFW.

434th TFS	F-4D	GC	Light blue
	F-4D	GD	Light blue
	F-4E	GD	Light blue

Recommenced operations c01/11/66, having stood down on F-104s earlier. Converted to F-4Es, first in 479th TFW to do so, and coded 'GC' (light blue) 07/68 and 'GD' (light blue) 09/68. Passed to 35th TFW control 01/10/71.

476th TFS	F-4D	GD	Blue/white

Recommenced operations 29/07/66 after converting from F-104s. Third 479th TFW squadron to convert to F-4Es. Coded 'GD' (blue) 07/68 and deactivated 25/09/68 when replaced by 4452nd CCTS.

497th TFS	–	–	–

Short-lived. Attached in designation only as TFS to 479th TFW from 8th TFW for two days while latter Wing was established at Ubon RTAFB, Thailand. No aircraft or crews at George.

4535th CCTS	F-4D	GA	Red/white/blue
	F-4E	GA	Red/white/blue
	F-4C	GA	Red/white/blue
	F-4C	GA	Red

Assigned 25/09/68, taking over from 68th TFS. Flew F-4Ds until 08/69, F-4Es 07/69–12/69 (last 479th TFW squadron to convert to these). Flew F-4Cs from 02/70. Redesignated 4435th TFRS 1971 and transferred to 35th TFW control 01/10/71 (redesignated 21st TFTS 01/12/72).

4546th TTS	F-4E	GB	Red/white
	F-4C/E	GB	Red/white

Activated WOPE at George 01/07/68. Operational 01/01/69–01/03/69 (see 431st TFS). Reactivated again 01/06/70, replacing 431st TFS. Redesignated 4535th TTS. Flew F-4C/E combination from early 1971 and passed to 35th TFW control 01/10/71 (when redesignated 4435th TFRS).

4452nd CCTS	F-4C/D	GC	Blue/white
	F-4E	GC	Blue/white
	F-4C/E	GC	Blue/white

Activated 16/01/67 but not genuinely 'active' until 25/09/68 when it took over from 476th TFS. Flew F-4Es 05/69–08/70 and F-4Cs 02/70–10/70. Converted to F-4Ds 1971 and passed to 35th TFW control 01/10/71 (being replaced by 20th TFTS 01/12/72).

2849th ABG, OOALC
Ogden Logistics Center, Hill AFB, Utah
As subordinate unit of OOALC/AFLC, 2849th ABG flew all operational USAF models at one time or another, with long-term establishment of gloss white F-4C/D and RF-4C models engaged in TCTO verification tasks (placement of 'black boxes' and antennae etc), plus extra F-4D/Es on occasion for one-off duties over nearby Wendover-Dugway proving range. OOALC (formerly Ogden AMA) reponsible for logistical support of USAF and many FMS Phantoms around world and handled considerable proportion of Programmed Depot Maintenance 'tear-downs', aircraft being transferred on the following cyclical basis (figures in months):

Model	To FY71	FY72–75	FY76	FY77–78	FY79 and on
F-4C	24	24	30	36	36
RF-4C	24	48	48	54	54
F-4D	24	36	36	48	48
F-4E	24	48	48	54	54
F-4G	–	–	–	–	54

Programmed Depot Maintenance task was assigned to Ogden Air Matériel Area during 1962. In 06/64 it received its first F-4C when crash-damaged Phantom shipped there for initial familiarization. Re-work line established later that year and by early 1970s OOALC was refurbishing 300 Phantoms annually.

3246th TW
Eglin AFB, Florida
Formed 01/07/70 to perform weapons and countermeasures test duties for APGC (Air Proving Ground Center), later known as ADTC (Armament Development Test Center), redesignated HQ Armament Division in 1980.

3247th TS	Misc F-4 etc –		White with red diamonds
	AD		
	ET		

Activated 01/07/70 to assume control of, *inter alia*, F-4C/D/E and RF-4C aircraft formerly assigned to Center's 4533rd TW. Operated last USAF F-4D (68-8800), relegated 07/92 to the Eglin target range. Carried logo 'Phantoms Phorever 1963–1992'.

4404th CW(P)
Dhahran Airport, Saudi Arabia
Formed 1990 as host Wing to numerous units deployed during Operations 'Desert Shield'/'Desert Storm'. Continues to support several units through Operations 'Provide Comfort' and 'Southern Watch' at time of writing, including detachment of F-4G 'Wild Weasels'.

81st FS *Panthers*	F-4G	SP	Yellow

Detachment (size subsequently varying between six and a dozen aircraft) deployed 06/91 after end of Gulf War in support of continuing operations in theatre, with crews and aircraft rotating in and out on almost monthly basis, providing on-station 'Southern Watch', and 'Provide Comfort' support for Incirlik. All F-4Gs scheduled to be off-base at Spangdahlem by 30/04/93, 81st FS having received first F-16C 18/02/93. Last six aircraft (69-0263, -7267, -7286, -7291, -7558 and -7587) returned to Spangdahlem 30/03/93. However, 81st FS operations extended until 07/93 and subsequently until end of year, pending take-over of Gulf Det by 561st FS from Nellis (81st furnishing crews and support).

190th FS	F-4G	–	Idaho

Six aircraft (69-0272, -0298, -0305, -0306, -7207 and -7572) from Boise-based Idaho ANG took over from 81st FS det aircraft (call-sign 'Slip') 28/03/93, having staged through Seymour-Johnson AFB, North Carolina, and Spangdahlem AB, Germany, en route to Dhahran. Aircraft being flown and maintained by mix of 81st and 190th FS crews at time of writing.

4149th TFW(P)
Holloman AFB, New Mexico
Temporary unit 01/07/68–15/07/68 responsible for 'bedding down' Wing of F-4Ds in process of being transferred from Spangdahlem AB, West Germany (see 49th TFW entry).

4474th TFW(P)
Nellis AFB, Nevada
Established as provisional Wing 01/03/77 with F-4Ds in preparation for Operation 'Ready Switch', when intended operator the 474th TFW completed conversion from F-111As to F-4Ds. Component squadrons inlcuded 4428th, 4429th and 4430th TFS(P)s. Provisional unit deactivated 06/08/77 (see 474th TFW entry).

4453rd CCTW
MacDill AFB, Florida
Operated first Phantoms in USAF. Organized 1962 as 4453rd CCTS to operate 27 transitional F-4Bs loaned by US Navy (including twelve aircraft from Block 14n, some after initial evaluation at Edwards AFB, California, and balance from subsequent Blocks), first of which arrived 04/02/63. Received first F-4Cs to enter operational inventory 20/11/63 during formal ceremony to mark type's service introduction and undertook Combat Crew Training to fill ranks of 12th and 15th TFWs (see revelant Wing entries) which formed at MacDill soon afterwards. Redesignated HQ 4453rd CCTG 01/01/64 with three *de facto* (four AUE *de jure*) squadrons. Redesignated 4453rd CCTW 01/04/64. Wing and component squadrons transferred to Davis-Monthan AFB 01/07/64 (see below).

4454th CCTS	F-4C	–	–

Activated 01/01/64. To Davis-Monthan.

4455th CCTS	F-4C	–	–

As 4454th CCTS.

4456th CCTS	F-4C	–	–

As 4454th CCTS.

Davis-Monthan AFB, Arizona
Re-formed 07/64 as th new F-4 RTU centre. 4453rd's task and aircraft passed to 58th TFTW at Luke AFB, Arizona, 07/71, 4453rd CCTW being deactivated 30/09/71. Wing operated small number of F-4Ds from mid-1969 to early 1970.

4454th CCTS	F-4C	–	–
	F-4C	DM	Red

Coded 'DM' (red) 07/68. Deactivated 30/08/71, aircraft passing to 550th TFTS/58th TFTW.

4455th CCTS	F-4C	–	–
	F-4C	DM	Blue

Coded 'DM' (blue) 07/68. Designation passed to new A-7 unit at Davis-Monthan 08/10/71 and Phantoms to 426th TFTS/58th TFTW.

4456th CCTS	F-4C	–	–
	F-4C/D	DM	Green

Coded 'DM' (green) 07/68. Received F-4Ds mid-1969 to early 1970. Deactivated 30/07/71, aircraft passing to 310th TFTS/58th TFTW.

4485th TS, USAFTAWC
Eglin AFB, Florida
TAWC organized 11/63 to conduct trials of operational systems based on subtle updates and technical problems encountered at operational level (anything from LORAN to Sidewinder missile). Known generically as WSEP (Weapon System Evaluation Program) and also as 'Combat Echo'.

4533rd TTS(T)	Misc F-4 etc	–	White
		EG	White

Assigned F-4s during 1960s, when it reported to 33rd TFW. Aircraft and mission passed to 4485th TS 12/04/71, reporting directly to TAWC.

4485th TS	Misc F-4	EG	White
		ED	Black/white
	Misc F-4 etc	OT	Black/white

Activated 12/04/71, when it replaced 4533rd TTS, flying RF-4Cs and F-4D/Es. Recoded 'ED' c1975. F-4Gs flown by Det 5/USAF-TAWC at George AFB, California, using three aircraft pooled with 562nd TFTS (initially 35th, then 37th TFW-owned) until 07/87, when Det became autonomous and was recoded 'OT'. F-4G test force redesignated Det 6, 79th TEG, USAFTAWC, 08/92 and relocated at Nellis AFB, Nevada. Det 6/79th TEG replaced by 422nd TES, 57th TEG, at Nellis 02/93 with two aircraft (69-0277 and -7235). USAFTAWC F-4 operations have now ceased.

Thunderbirds
Nellis AFB, Nevada
Given formal designation 3600th ADT in 05/53 when Aerial Demonstration Team formed with F-84s. Team became known as *Thunderbirds* later that season and moved on to F-100s and to Nellis AFB during 1956, redesignated 4520th ADS. Term 'USAF ADS' replaced numerical designation 25/02/67. Began conversion to eight modified F-4Es (with receipt of 'T-Birds' Nos 1 and 2) 19/04/69, flying first display 01/06/69 and 518th and last Phantom show 10/11/73. During 1970–71 team deployed to Canada, the Caribbean, Europe, South America, Pacific (Hawaii) and Europe. Unit converted to more economical T-38s 1974.

Thunderbirds	F-4E	–	–

4520 CCTW
Nellis AFB, Nevada
Operated some F-4s prior to activation of 4525FWW (probably assigned to 4523rd CCTS).

4525th FWW
Nellis AFB, Nevada
Activated 01/09/66 at Nellis under base's simultaneously established TFWC (Tactical Fighter Weapons Center) status with several units flying diverse collection of tac-air types, Phantoms coming under jurisdiction of 4538th CCTS described below or *Thunderbirds* ADS. Redesignated 57th FWW 15/10/69.

4538th CCTS	Misc F-4	–	Black/yellow
	Misc F-4	WD	Black/yellow

Formed 01/09/66 and received first F-4Es to enter USAF service, beginning 03/10/67 (tail 66-286). Redesignated 414th FWS 11/10/69.

414th FWS	Misc F-4	WD	Black/yellow

Took over assets of 4538th CCTS and transferred to 57th FWW control four days later on 15/10/69.

4531st TFW
Homestead AFB, Florida
Activated 01/11/66. Elements deployed to Kunsan AB, South Korea, 07/69–09/70, to maintain presence there following *Pueblo* Crisis, in rotation with squadrons from 4th TFW. Replaced as parent Wing at Homestead AFB by 31st TFW 15/10/70.

68th TFS	F-4D	ZG	Yellow

Designation transferred from 479th TFW WOPE 01/10/68. Deployed to Kunsan AB, South Korea, 20/07/69–09/12/69 (68th TFS and 560th TFS returned to Homestead without aircraft having transferred their F-4Ds to 475th TFW; 560th TFS subsequently re-equipped with F-4Es). Reduced to zero strength 01/04/70, personnel absorbed by other three squadrons. (USAF records indicate that 68th TFS transferred aircraft to 49th TFW at Holloman AFB; presumably these were F-4Ds which were not taken on deployments to Kunsan.)

436th TFS	F-4E	ZD	Red

Recommenced operations 15/09/68. Transferred to 31st TFW control 15/10/70 (becoming 306th TFS on 30/10/70). Aircraft names included 67-0320 *City of Homestead*.

478th TFS	F-4D	–	–
	F-4D	ZE	Blue
	F-4E	ZE	Blue

Reactivated 01/11/66, receiving first F-4D 02/67. Coded 'ZE' (blue) 07/68. Upgraded to F-4Es and deployed to Kunsan AB, South Korea, 21/05/70–02/09/70. Transferred to 31st TFW control 15/10/70 (becoming 309th TFS 30/10/70).

560th TFS	F-4D	ZF	Green

Recommenced operations 01/04/69. Deployed to Kunsan AB, South Korea, 23/07/69–17/12/69. Converted to F-4Es 1970. Transferred to 31st TFW control 15/10/70 (becoming 309th TFS 30/10/70).

4756th ADW/ADWC
Tyndall AFB, Florida
Activated at Tyndall as part of ADC 07/57 and disbanded 01/68, having been replaced by parent Air Defense Weapons Center which formed 31/10/67, 4756th being deactivated 01/01/68. ADWC transferred to ADTAC control 01/10/79 and 325th FWW formed as subordinate Wing 07/81. During this time F-4s have come and gone on numerous WSEPs, mostly from operational units; however, ADWC also operated some eight ex-57th FIS F-4Cs during 1978 (most of these being passed on to 171st FIS, Michigan ANG, at Selfridge ANGB) for live weapons-firing practice to assist with ANG transition from Falcon- and Genie-equipped F-101 and F-106 to Sidewinder- and Sparrow-equipped Phantom. ADWC also hosted many F-4s between WT-76 and WT-88 for Biennial 'William Tell' air-to-air 'shooting matches' over Gulf of Mexico, where live missiles were employed.

6200th TFTG
Clark AB, Philippines

1st TS	F-4C	PA	Yellow
	F-4E	PN	Blue or red

Replaced 6400th TS (see below) 15/10/69. Assigned to 6th AD 15/10/69–15/12/69, 13th AF 15/12/69–30/04/70, 405th FW 30/04/70–16/09/74 and 3rd TFW 16/09/74–01/01/80 before finally passing to 6200th TFTG 01/01/80. Operated F-4Cs in conjunction with BQM-34A RPVs to conduct 'Combat Sage' WSEP and later drew F-4Es as required from co-located 3rd and 90th TFSs/3rd TFW.

6400th TS	F-4C	DS	–

Existed prior to formation of 6200th TFTG. Activated 01/04/67 with F-4Cs. Assigned directly to 13th AF. Transferred to 6th AD control 01/08/68. Redesignated 1st Test Squadron (see above) 15/10/69.

6252nd TFW
Da Nang AB, South Vietnam
Organized at Da Nang 08/07/65 and subsequently assumed control of, *inter alia*, the fledgeling Phantom force assigned to Da Nang for combat operations. Replaced by 35th TFW 08/04/66.

390th TFS	F-4C	–	–

Transferred from attachment from 405th FIW 18/11/65. Transferred to 35th TFW control 08/04/66.

480th TFS	F-4C	–	–

Transferred from 366th TFW 26/01/66. Transferred to 35th TFW control 08/04/66.

6510th TW/AFFTC
Edwards AFB, California

Reorganized 01/03/78 to perform aerodynamic, propulsion and avionics trials on behalf of AFFTC (Air Force Flight Test Center), which has witnessed comings and goings of Phantoms since 1960, including every USAF prototype and production variant to see service and most US Navy variants.

| 6512th TS | Misc F-4 | | Black/white crosses |
| | Misc F-4 | ED | Black/white crosses |

Active at Edwards until 07/62, then again 10/69–01/73 and 1976 to date. RF-4Cs were most numerous, several aircraft being operated for chase and test pilot school work under 6512th or direct AFFTC control. Two NRF-4Cs are retained at time of writing for various duties.

AFSWC
Kirtland AFB, New Mexico

Headquartered at Kirtland AFB, New Mexico, the Air Force Special Weapons Center operated numerous aircraft under 4900th TG, which was activated 01/08/70 and continued until 01/10/75. Aircraft also operated prior to and after this period on secondment from ADTC, AFFTC and McAir, flying over White Sands weapons range to evaluate nuclear weapons separation/ballistics, e.g. F-4G 69-7254 with rocket-powered B/Mk 61 'Tiger' thermonuclear device.

| 4900th TG | Misc F-4 etc | – | Red/white zig-zag stripe |

Above: Range instrumentation pods were standard items for fighters entering the mêlée of a 'Copper Flag' USAFIWS interceptor war game at Tyndall ADWC, Florida, and for machines embroiled in swirling manoeuvres at other ACMI ranges. The pod relayed aircraft flight data back to the ground terminals so that the events could be monitored, processed and later replayed on the 'big screen'. (Cubic Corporation)

Holloman AFB, New Mexico

6585th TG activated 01/08/70 as USAF MDTC (Missile Development Test Center) and assigned five F-4Ds plus one RF-4C to help calibrate accuracy of Army surface-to-air and USAF air-to-surface missiles. Phantom operations phased out by 10/75, duty passing to 3246th TW/ADTC at Eglin AFB, Florida.

| 6585th TG | F-4D/ | – | White with orange |
| | RF-4C | | triangles |

7440th CW
Incirlik AB, Turkey

Established 12/90 during opening build-up of forces in SW Asia under Operation 'Proven Force', designed to test new 'Superwing' concept of establishing 'Strike Package'—fighters, tankers, reconnaissance and SEAD aircraft—at one base, in this instance able to conduct operations over northern sectors of Iraq during Operation 'Desert Storm' 01/91–03/91. Wing continued to support Operations 'Provide Comfort'/'Southern Watch' at Incirlik through 1993, though with only a small detachment of F-4Gs provided by the 81st FS/4404th CW(P) from Dhahran, Saudi Arabia.

| 3rd TFS *Peugeots* | F-4E | PN | Red/white/black |

Four aircraft and seven crews deployed from 3rd TFW based at Clark AB, Philippines, for participation in Operation 'Proven Force' 16/02/91–

03/03/91 (ten aircraft departing Clark Field, of which six deployed to Europe via McGuire AFB, New Jersey, two aircraft being retained under 52nd TFW control at Spangdahlem AB, Germany). Detachment left Turkey 19/03/91, arriving at AMARC 25/03/91. F-4Es comprised 71-1086, 72-1407, 72-1199 (13th AF logos) and 73-1198.

23rd TFS *Fighting Hawks*　F-4G/F-16　SP　　–
Deployed as mixed hunter-killer unit (including twelve F-4Gs) 12/90–15/

03/91 from 52nd TFW based at Spangdahlem, Germany. Aircraft included 69-0244 *Night Stalker* (black winged rhino), 69-7582 (42 black 'Spook' mission marks—highest tally).

38th TRS　　　　　RF-4C　　　ZR　　　　Green/white
Eight aircraft deployed from 26th TRW based at Zweibrücken AB, Germany, 03/02/91–11/03/91 and flew 103 sorties. Deactivated upon return 03/04/91.

APPENDIX VI: US AIR FORCE SECOND-LINE F-4 PHANTOM UNITS 1963–93

ANG STRIKE UNITS

108th TFW ('Si Dies Venit'), New Jersey
141st TFS *Tigers*, McGuire AFB
Code 'NJ'. Converted from F-105Bs to F-4Ds from 05/81 and upgraded to F-4Es 07/85, flying F-4Ds until 02/86. Converted to KC-135Es and refuelling mission in autumn 1991, flying F-4Es until c10/91.

113th TFW, DC
121st TFS, Andrews AFB, Maryland
Code 'DC'. Converted from F-105D/Fs to F-4Ds during 06/81 and went on to become first ANG unit to train with Pave Spike and LGBs. Deployed to UK under 'Coronet Shield' during 06/83 and to Iceland as 'Coronet Kiowa' in spring 1986. Converted to F-16s 01/90.

116th TFW ('Vincet Amor Patriae'), Georgia
128th TFS, Dobbins ANGB
No code. Converted from F-105F/Gs to F-4Ds 01/83 and operated these until 03/87, deploying to Europe under 'Coronet Meteor' during 08/85. Received F-15s in spring 1986 and completed conversion 03/87.

122nd TFW, Indiana
163rd TFS *Marksmen*, Baer Field, Fort Wayne MAP
Code 'FW'; blue. Converted from F-100s to F-4Cs (mostly ex-'Wild Weasel IVs') between 11/78 and 04/79 and upgraded to F-4Es c05/86, operating these until 01/92 as last ANG F-4E unit. Converted to F-16s 1991, concurrent with State's 113th TFS/181st TFG based at Hulman Field. Individual aircraft included F-4C 63-7565 *City of Fort Wayne*.

124th RG, Idaho
190th FS, Boise
Currently operating F-4Gs and RF-4Cs. Refer to ANG recon unit histories.

131st TFW, Missouri
110th TFS *Lindbergh's Own*, Lambert Field, St Louis
Code 'SL'; red. Converted from F-100s to F-4Cs from 10/78, operating these until 01/86. Deployed to the UK under 'Coronet Cactus' in summer 1982. Upgraded to F-4Es from 02/85, being first to introduce 'Hill Gray I' and standard 'Hill Gray II' camouflage to this model. First to test one-piece windshield. Converted to F-15s from 05/91. Individual aircraft included F-4E 68-0338 (two authentic MiG kill markings).

149th TFG, Texas
182nd TFS, Kelly AFB, San Antonio
Code 'SA'; red and white Texas logo. Converted from F-100s to F-4Cs 03/79–04/79, retiring last 'Hun' 05/79. Made unit's first deployment outside CONUS to NAS Keflavik, Iceland, 20/08–04/09/81 as 'Coronet Cruise'. Operated F-4Cs until 05/86, converting to F-16s 1986. Individual aircraft included 64-0829 (two authentic MiG kills; also served with 482nd TFW).

152nd FG/RG, Nevada
192nd RS *High Rollers*, Cannon IAP, Reno
Currently operating RF-4Cs but did operate at least one F-4G decorated in

full unit regalia until conversion plans suspended. Refer to ANG reconnaissance unit histories.

158th TFG ('Green Mountain Boys'), Vermont
134th TFS, Burlington
Code 'VT'. Converted from EB-57s and DSES role to F-4Ds and strike mission beginning 01/82, flying Phantoms until 02/86 when unit converted to F-16s.

159th TFG, Louisiana
122nd TFS *Coonass Militia*, NAS New Orleans
Converted from F-100s to F-4Cs from 04/79 as TFS/TFG but with extensive air defence responsibilities. Deployed to Iceland under 'Coronet Rodeo' in summer 1982. Refer to ANG interceptor unit histories for further details.

163rd TFG, California
196th TFS, March AFB
No code; blue and white star flash. Converted from O-2s as 196th TASS to F-4Cs as 196th TFS from 01/10/82. Operated these until 06/87, having upgraded to F-4Es from 01/87. Flew these until 08/90, by which time unit had converted to RF-4Cs as 196th TRS (see ANG reconnaissance unit histories). Deployed to Spain under 'Coronet Laguna' 05–06/86. Scheduled to convert to KC-135R 1994.

181st TFG, Indiana
113th TFS, Hulman Field, Terra Haute
Code 'HF'; red, white and blue flash. Converted from F-100s to F-4Cs (mostly ex-'Wild Weasel IVs') 07–09/79, operating these until 10/87 when unit began upgrading to F-4Es. Converted to F-16s during autumn 1991. Individual aircraft included F-4Cs 63-7437 *5000 Hours/Lt. Col Wayne Yarolem/181 Tac Ftr Gp/July 1967 – April 1985* (one of first F-4Cs in 'European 1' paint scheme), 63-7568 (overall Aircraft Gray with full 'HF' code).

183rd TFG, Illinois
170th TFS, Capital Airport, Springfield
Code 'SI'. First ANG squadron to convert to F-4Cs, relinquishing F-84s and receiving first Phantom 31/01/72, followed by four more 04/72 and others trickling in subsequently. RF-4C proficiency trainers operated 10/73–07/75. Combat-ready at full strength by 1976 following lengthy work-up period. First ANG unit to deploy to Ghedi AB, Italy, being assigned there for 22 days 05/78 under 'Coronet Quail'. Received Outstanding Unit Award for two years of flawless Phantom operations up to 30/04/79. Upgraded to F-4Ds effective 01/01/81 and in 06/82 deployed to RAF Finningley, Yorkshire, under 'Coronet Bravo'. Code 'SP' applied to 66-7725 but this clashed with USAFE's 52nd TFW and 'SI' subsequently adopted. During 1984 became first unit to receive Project 'Seek Smoke' J79-GE-15E low-smoke-engine F-4Ds. Deployed to Bardufoss, Norway, and Keflavik, Iceland, autumn 1988. Completed conversion to F-16s by 01/10/89, flying F-4Ds until previous month. Individual aircraft included F-4Cs 63-7699 *Red Baron* (one authentic MiG kill marking), 64-0776 (Bicentennial logos), 64-0822 (composite aircraft rebuilt in SEA from two write-offs).

184th TFTG, Kansas
127th TFS *Jayhawks* and 177th TFTS *Jayhawkers*, McConnell AFB
No code; red 'Jayhawks' flash. 127th TFS converted from F-105s to F-4Ds winter 1979, receiving first Phantom (65-0590) 07/08/79. Group redesignated 184th TFG 08/10/79. Concurrent with the gradual phasing-out of last 'hard-wing' Phantoms from Active Air Force duty (under 31st TFW control at Homestead AFB, Florida), 184th TFG reassumed major RTU function for Reserves—including air defence, until this was transferred to 114th TFTS/142nd FIG, Oregon ANG. To fulfil these needs, 127th TFS expanded into unique 40-plus aircraft establishment—largest single USAF Phantom squadron ever to see service—until second squadron, 177th TFTS, was formed 01/02/84. These two units shared some 57 aircraft at Group's zenith, also absorbing USAF F-4 FWIC course during 1985 following its effective transfer from Nellis TFWC, Nevada. Unofficially rated as best RTU in TAC during ORI in 1986. Began flying F-16s from 03/87 with establishment of 161st TFTS, 127th TFS converting from 09/87 and 177th TFTS being deactivated 1988, Group relinquishing its eight remaining airworthy Phantoms at ceremony on 31/03/90 as last ANG strike unit to operate F-4Ds. Individual aircraft included 65-0798 *Kansas Crop Duster – KANG Pest Control*, 66-0271 (two authentic MiG kill markings; now on display), 66-7553 *Lips III*, 66-7772 *Naughty Lady*.

187th TFG, Alabama
160th TFS *Snakes*, Dannelly Field, Montgomery
Code 'AL'; red. Converted from RF-4Cs to F-4Ds and strike mission 07/83, becoming 160th TFS/187th TFG in process. Deployed to Germany under 'Coronet Meteor' in summer 1985. Converted to F-16s from 10/88.

188th TFG, Arkansas
184th TFS *Flying Razorbacks*, Fort Smith MAP
Some aircraft coded 'FS' (e.g. F-4C 64-0748); red Arkansas flash. Converted from F-100s to F-4Cs 09/79, subsequently making deployments to Panama 02/81 and Turkey under 'Coronet Crown' in autumn 1983 and 'Coronet Cherokee' in autumn 1986. Converted to F-16s 1988, relinquishing last Phantoms during 07/88 as last ANG strike unit to operate F-4Cs.

AFRes STRIKE UNITS

301st TFW
457th TFS *Spads*, Carswell AFB, Texas
Code 'TH' ('Texas Humpbacks'); Stars and Stripes flash. Converted from 'Humpback' T-Stick II F-105s to LORAN F-4Ds from 12/81, flying these until 1988. Upgraded to F-4Es from 08/87 (first AFRes unit to operate F-4Es), flying these until 05/91. Conversion to F-16s (with new 'Texas Falcons' 'TF' codes) began 12/90. Individual aircraft included F-4Ds 66-7747 *Jumbo Jet*, -8709 *Willie's Warwagon*, -8711 *The Gambler*, -8714 *Raider of the 301st* (MiG killer), -8719 *Cats Trash*; F-4Es 68-0398 *Fort Worth Phantom Pharewell*, -0450 *Swapfox*, -0461 *Christine*.

482nd TFW
93rd TFS *Makos*, Homestead AFB, Florida
Code 'FM' ('Florida Makos'); black and white chequered flash. Converting from EC-121s, 93rd TFS operated F-4C from 01/10/78 until 11/83 as first and only AFRes unit to fly F-4Cs, passing from 915th TFG to 482nd TFW control at Homestead AFB 04/81. Upgraded to F-4Ds from 09/83. Converted to F-16s from 11/89. Individual aircraft included F-4C 64-0829 *The Humping Boys from Homestead* (482nd TFW logos, two authentic MiG kill markings—ex-Robin Olds aircraft).

507th TFG
465th TFS *Sierra Hotels*, Tinker AFB, Oklahoma
Code 'SH'; blue flash. Converted from F-105s to F-4Ds from 10/80 (first AFRes unit to operate F-4Ds), flying these until 06/89 when it converted to F-16s.

906th TFG
89th TFS *Buckeye Phantoms*, Wright-Patterson AFB, Ohio
Code 'DO' ('Dayton, Ohio'); red and black chequered flash. Reorganized at Wright-Patterson AFB 07/82 and equipped with F-4Ds by 11/82, operating

these until 10/89. First operational USAF Phantom unit to use 30mm GPU-5 'Pave Claw' 'Gatling' gun pod. Converted to F-16s 1989.

924th TFG
704th TFS, Bergstrom AFB, Texas
Code 'TX' ('Texas'); Stars and Stripes flash. Converted from C-130Bs to LORAN F-4Ds from 01/07/81, flying these until 01/89, by which time unit had upgraded to ARN-101 DMAS-mod F-4Es. Converted to F-16s during 1991.

ANG INTERCEPTOR SQUADRONS

144th FIW, California
194th FIS *Bald Eagles*, Fresno Air Terminal
Converted from F-106s to F-4Ds from 11/83, also maintaining alert Det at George AFB, California. Deployed to Ramstein AB, West Germany under Project 'Creek Klaxon' 04/86–04/87 to provide air defence cover while resident 86th TFW converted from F-4Es to F-16s. Converted direct to F-16ADFs from 10/89.

154th TFG, Hawaii
199th TFS, *HANGmen*, Hickam AFB, Oahu
Converted from F-102s to F-4Cs during overlap cycle beginning 31/10/75 when it became first ANG unit to receive F-4Cs for air defence duties. Designation changed to 154th CG 11/78. Made two deployments to Philippines for 'Cope Thunder' exercises (1981, 1985) and one to Japan for 'Cope North' (1980). Converted to F-15s from 03/87 following deployment of Eagle detachment from Georgia ANG. Individual F-4Cs and names (painted yellow on camouflaged aircraft and red on grey aircraft, and mostly based on native Hawaiian birds) included 63-7415 *Koloa* (native duck: *Anas wyvilliana*), 63-7454 *'U'au* (darked-rumped petrel: *Pterodroma phaeopygia*), 63-7491 *'U'au Kani* (the 'U'au's song), 63-7505 *Moli* ('sacrifice to the gods' or 'blessed'?), 63-7511 *Hunakai* ('sea spray'), 63-7540 *Mamo* (black honeycreeper: *Drepanis pacifica*), 63-7562 *'A'o* ('to teach' or 'to instruct'), *Olili* ('joyful shiver'?!), 63-7575 *'Auku'u* (night heron: *Nycticorax nycticorax hoactli*), 63-7578 *Kolea* (Pacific golden plover: *Pluvialis dominica*), 63-7592 *'Io* (Hawaiian hawk: *Buteo solitarius*), 63-7625 *Manau O'o* ('supernatural spear'?), 63-7628 *'Ele Paio* ('black quarreller'?), 63-7632 *Ae'O* (Hawaiian stilt bird), 63-7647 *Alae'Ula* (mud hen: *Gallinula chloropus*; two MiG kills marked), 63-7649 *Nene* (native goose: *Branta sandvicensis*), 63 -7676 *Noio* (tern: *Anous tenuirostris*; two MiG kills marked), 63-7705 *'Ou* ('to project' or 'to protrude'), 64-0711 *Manu O Ku* (dove), 64-0715 *Pakalakala*, 64-0785 *'Iwa* (frigate bird: *Fregata minor palmerstoni*), 64-0792 *Pueo* (native owl: *Asio flammeus sanvichensis*), 64-0793 *Koa'e Kea* (white tropicbird: *Phaethon lepturus dorotheae*), 64-0806 *I'iwi* (scarlet honeycreeper: *Vestiaria coccinea*; four MiG kills marked), 64-0831 *'Omao'o* (native thrush: *Phaeornis obscurus*), 64-0851 *Koa'e Ula* (scarlet tropicbird), 64-0913 *'Ewa'Ewa* ('crooked and out of shape'?!), 64-0914 *Palila* (honeycreeper: *Psittirostra bailleui*).

159th TFG, Louisiana
122nd TFS *Coonass Militia*, NAS New Orleans
Converted from F-100s to F-4Cs from 04/79 as TFS/TFG but with extensive air defence responsibilities which soon dominated its tasking, giving rise to a number of *ad hoc* grey-on-grey low-visibility colour schemes. Deployed to Iceland under 'Coronet Rodeo' in summer 1982. First ANG unit to convert to F-15s, from 06/85. F-4Cs included 63-7704 (one authentic MiG kill).

191st FIG, Michigan
171st FIS *Michigan Wolves*, Selfridge ANGB
Converted from F-106s to F-4Cs during 05/78 to become first CONUS ANG F-4C interceptor unit, flying this type until 08/86. Upgraded to F-4Ds beginning 02/86 then converted to F-16s from 08/90. F-4Cs and nose art (all in full colour on grey aircraft) included 63-7412 *We Bad!*, -7442 *Shadow Demon* (two versions)/*Baby!*, -7460 *Puff the Magic Dragon*, -7475 *Defender of Freedom/Swine Trek*, -7482 *Patience My Ass*, -7529 *Trussst Me!*, -7534 *Defiance II* (two versions), -7536 *Cyrano the Fearless*, -7576 *Never Give a Sucker an Even Break*, -7583 *Never Trust a Smiling Cat* (Garfield), -7595 *Make My Day*, -7618 *Double Trouble*, -7626 *No More Mr Nice Guy*, -7666 *I Don't Get Mad, I Get Even/This One's For You Baby*; 64-0707 *Don't Mess With The Kid/I Don't Take Defeat Lightly*.

107th FIG, New York
136th FIS, Niagara Falls
Converted from F-101s to F-4Cs 08/82, which were flown until 02/87. Maintained an alert det at Charleston AFB, South Carolina. Upgraded to F-4Ds beginning 08/86. Converted to F-16s from 10/90.

119th FIG, North Dakota
178th FIS *Happy Hooligans*, **Hector Field, Fargo**
Converted from F-101s to F-4Ds over six-month cycle, receiving first aircraft 15/03/77—first ANG unit to fly F-4Ds. Tested IRSTS. Contributed aircraft and crews for 'Creek Klaxon' (see 144th FIW for further details). Converted to F-16ADFs from 09/90.

142nd FIG, Oregon
123rd FIS *Eager Beavers*, **Portland IAP**
Converted from F-101s to F-4Cs beginning 09/80 and continued to operate these until 12/89 — last ANG unit to operate F-4Cs. Converted to F-15s from 01/10/89. F-4Cs included 63-7699 (one authentic MiG kill), 64-0776 *Miss Piggy* (three authentic MiG kills).

114th TFTS *Black Hawks*, **Kingsley Field**
Grew out of a 123rd FIS F-4C det to become ANG's interceptor RTU—the 123rd FITS—at Kingsley Field, Klamath Falls, 01/04/83. Designation changed to 142 FITS 01/10/83 and to 114th TFTS 08/02/84. Converted to F-16s early 1989, relinquishing last Phantoms 12/89.

147th FIG, Texas
111th FIS *Ace In The Hole* or *Guardians of the Gulf Coast*, **Ellington ANGB, Houston**
Converted from F-101s to F-4Cs beginning 03/82, last Voodoo sortie having been flown 08/08/83. Flew F-4Cs until 01/87, having begun to upgrade to F-4Ds from 11/86. Maintained alert det at Holloman AFB, New Mexico. Converted to F-16s from 12/89, relinquishing last Phantoms 03/90.

148th FIG, Minnesota
179th FIS, Duluth IAP
Converted from F-101s to RF-4Cs and designations to TRS/TRG 01/01/76, retaining spangled North Star logos. Designation changed back to FIS/FIG 01/10/83 with acquisition of F-4Ds (last RF-4Cs departing 13/10/83). Contributed aircraft and crews for 'Creek Klaxon' (see 144th FIW for further details) and also flew dets from Loring AFB, Maine, and Tucson, Arizona. Converted directly to F-16ADFs from 07/90.

ANG RECONNAISSANCE SQUADRONS

117th TRW ('Summo Est Opportunitas'), Alabama
106th TRS *Recce Rebels*, **Birmingham MAP (Smith ANGB), and**
160th TRS, Dannelly Field, Montgomery
Code 'BH'. Received first 'Photo-Phantoms' 25/02/71 (first ANG RF-4C unit). Two squadrons eventually equipped, 106th TRS coming under 117th TRG control at Birmingham and 160th TRS under 187th TRG control. Units fully operational 1973. 117th TRG elevated to Wing status 12/74 and both squadrons reported to Birmingham (along with Minnesota and Mississippi reconnaissance Groups). 160th TRS deployed to Germany summer 1980 for participation in 'Best Focus' and converted to F-4Ds as TFS from 07/83 (later converting to F-16s—see ANG strike unit histories). 106th continued to operate RF-4Cs and conducted numerous NATO deployments, including Ramstein AB, West Germany, 03/76, UK summer 1983 under 'Coronet Joust' and again RAF Coltishall 13–26/09/86 as 'Coronet Mobile'. Parent 117th TRW later absorbed Nebraska and Idaho recce Groups when 123rd TRW ceased RF-4C operations (see below). Deployed to Sheikh Isa AB, Bahrain, 08/90–03/91 (see 35th TFW[P] in Active unit histories). Still operational, with 24 aircraft, as 106th RS/117th RW. Individual aircraft have included 64-1047 *Scud Seeker*, 65-0843 (106th TRS logos), 65-0854 (117th TRW logos/'Twenty Years of Phantoms 1971–1991').

123rd TRW, Kentucky
165th TRS, Standiford Field, Louisville
Code 'KY'. 165th TRS converted from RF-101s to RF-4Cs 1976 and parent 123rd TRG raised to TRW status (with authority over RF-4C squadrons of

Nebraska, Idaho and Nevada reconnaissance Groups, in addition to 165th TRS). Deployed to Norway under 'Coronet Snipe' in winter 1978. Won first place at 'Photo Finish 81', Gulfport, Mississippi, and in 09/82 received third Spaatz Outstanding Unit Trophy following faultless deployment to Karup, Denmark, for NATO-sponsored 'Best Focus 82' competition. Also given overall 'Outstanding' from 12th AF following ORI 13–17/05/83. Converted to C-130s and airlift mission 01/89, and control of subordinate recce Groups passed to 117th TRW.

124th TRG, Idaho
189th TRTF and 190th TRS, Boise MAP
No code. 124th FIG converted from F-102s to RF-4Cs from 10/75, becoming 124th TRG. Deployed to Norway 09/79–10/79 under 'Coronet Shetland', won 'Photo Derby' meets in 10/80 and 10/82 together with three 'Photo Finish' competitions 1983, 1984 and 1985. Second squadron, 189th TRT Flight, formed 01/09/84 as 'Photo-Phantom' RTU. Reconnaissance Weapons School deactivated 31/12/91 when Group began to absorb F-4Gs and new SEAD tasking, subsequently to be replaced by 189th TF on 16/03/92 with responsibilities for both RF-4C and F-4G training, as last Phantom RTU in ANG. 190th RS became 190th FS at this time and is currently operational on F-4G. Group due to dispose of nine remaining RF-4Cs from c11/93 and concentrate on F-4G SEAD mission.

148th TRG, Minnesota
179th TRS, Duluth IAP
No code. 148th FIG formally converted from F-101s to RF-4Cs 01/01/76 to become 148th TRG (no code). Deployed to Germany 08/79 under 'Coronet Bridle'. Subsequently converted to F-4Ds and Strategic Air Defense mission again: was redesignated 148th FIG 01/10/83 and last RF-4C departed Duluth 13/10/83 (see ANG Interceptor unit histories for details of F-4D operations).

152nd TRG, Nevada
192nd TRS *High Rollers*, **Cannon IAP, Reno**
No code. Converted from RF-101Bs to RF-4Cs from 07/75. At least one deployment to Panama Canal Zone. First place at 'Photo Finish 79' held at Boise, Idaho, 10/79; also won RAM-86 and RAM-90 hosted by the Active 67th TRW at Bergstrom AFB, Texas. Crews and one aircraft deployed to 35th TFW(P) control at Sheikh Isa AB, Bahrain, 03/12/90–20/04/91 in support of Operations 'Desert Shield'/'Desert Storm', where unit flew 412 combat sorties, returning to Reno 09/04/91. Received first F-4G 08/91 for familiarization training (69-7580 being marked up with white rudder and full *High Rollers* regalia), but plans to convert to F-4G dropped following reactivation of active 561st TFS at Nellis AFB, Nevada (see 57th FWW entry in the Active Wing histories). Expected to continue flying RF-4C until FY94, having become 192nd RS/152nd RG 16/03/92.

155th TRG ('Parati Atque Potentes'), Nebraska
173rd TRS *Flaming Arrows*, **Lincoln MAP**
No code. Converted from RF-84s to RF-4Cs from 02/72 and still active on 'Photo-Phantoms' at time of writing with 21 aircraft as 173rd RS/155th RG. Deployed to Turkey 05/80 under 'Coronet Cannon'. Plans exist for Group to convert to KC-135Rs during 1994–95. Individual RF-4Cs have included 65-0824 *Hawg Wild*, -0828 *Elmer*, -0838 *Di Joe*, -0859 *Betty Boop*, -0907 *Scrappy Do*, -0917 *Wally Gator*, -0939 *Lady Di*; 66-0417 *Cihanda Sulh*, -0418 *Girls Just Wanna Have Fun*, -0428 *Rambo II – The Sequel*.

163rd RG, California
196th RS, March AFB
No code. Shortest-lived ANG RF-4C recce unit. Converted from F-4Es (see ANG/AFRes Strike unit histories) to RF-4Cs and became 196th TRS/163rd TRG 01/07/90, redesignated RS/RG in 03/92. Destined to convert to KC-135R in FY94.

186th TRG ('Il Nous Faut Savoir'), Mississippi
153rd TRS, Key Field, Meridian
Code 'KE'. Officially converted from RF-101Cs to RF-4Cs 01/01/79, having received first RF-4Cs 09/78 and relinquishing last four Voodoos in New Year. Deployed to UK in autumn 1980 under 'Coronet Cyro', to SW Asia in 03/84 under 'Sentry Tornado' and to Italy 07/86–08/86 under 'Coronet Lake'. Became 186th ARG with KC-135Rs 01/04/92.

APPENDIX VII: OPERATION 'DA YU' (HEAVY RAIN)

RAE Farnborough physicist Andrew Fyall was charged with certifying the Concorde airliner as being safe to fly in rain—an aviation 'first'. In January and February 1974 YF-4M XT853 was despatched to SAF Tengah, Singapore, at the height of the monsoon season, after preparation at Hawker Siddeley Dynamics, Holme-on-Spalding Moor, to test various alloys. It was flown by Project Pilot Flt Lt John Fawcett AFC and Flt Lt Chris Williams as navigator (with Cdr Jeff Higgs RN in place as second pilot), with the call-sign 'Da Yu'.

For rain-erosion tests a nickel-coated radome was initially fitted to the Phantom (alongside wing leading-edge elastomers), but this precluded the use of the radar for detecting heavy rain masses; furthermore, it delaminated in the trials. A polyurethane-coated, radar-transparent version was fitted instead. The crew detected large rain clouds from 30,000ft on radar, bunted over in reheat and plunged into the monsoon at speeds of up to Mach 1.2 (850kts true airspeed) to simulate Concorde flight conditions. Samples of various Concorde structural materials were attached to modified wing tanks, at different angles to the airflow to study erosion effects. On one trial the crew felt that one of the samples was not being subjected to a sufficiently direct airflow, so it was attached to the radome instead. It fragmented in flight, damaging the windshield. In all, some thirty test sorties were flown.

The return journey proved interesting. On approach to Masireh, one of the Phantom's engines overheated and failed. John Fawcett had to recover the aircraft on one engine, in reheat. Staging through Teheran, he was unable to make radio contact with the ground, made a couple of overshoots in hazy conditions and landed. He was surrounded by a crowd of anxious Iranian officials who were obviously relieved to discover that he was an RAF officer. Unwittingly, he had overflown the Shah's palace at a time when fears of subversive behaviour by the Phantom-flying Iranian Air Force were strong. Very soon afterwards the Shah was overthrown.

Concorde's rain-erosion certification for the *Grand Livre* was duly completed in September 1975.

Below left: 'Da Yu' Project Pilot Flt Lt John Fawcett AFC and navigator Flt Lt Chris Williams by their YF-4M Phantom XT853, drawn from the RAE test fleet for the trials. (Via John Fawcett and Andrew Fyall)
Below right: The 'Da Yu' Phantom proffered the Concorde test specimen materials to the elements via the tips of both drop tanks. The starboard specimen array is shown here. (Via Andrew Fyall)
Bottom: YF-4M XT853 cruises, displaying not only the test article but also its black, elastomer-coated fin, wing and inlet lips. (Via John Fawcett)

INDEX

Page references in **bold type** refer to illustrations.